C-1

# JERUSALEM
## A Family Portrait

*Boaz Yakin* and *Nick Bertozzi*

Based on a story by Boaz Yakin and Moni Yakin
Chris Sinderson, Art Director

:01
First Second
NEW YORK

# Contents

This story is a portrait of a family and of the city they both inhabit and encompass within their waking dream of life. A single portrait added to the immense gallery of portraits of a tiny, strategically and economically insignificant desert hamlet that has for two thousand years proven unparalleled in inspiring passions and dreams. The music of its name has been a beacon to pilgrimage and crusade, an evocation of some inner world so many strive for yet inevitably fail to reach, its truth slipping through the futile grasp of an endless procession of warriors, kings, prophets, and savants. It is a stubborn little slab of reality that nevertheless shimmers like a mirage before the eyes of both the mad and the sane, uniting them into a single brotherhood of dreamers, murderers, and poets. A landscape that gazed upon at sunset turns a shepherd, mason, seamstress, or cobbler into a gatekeeper of eternity.

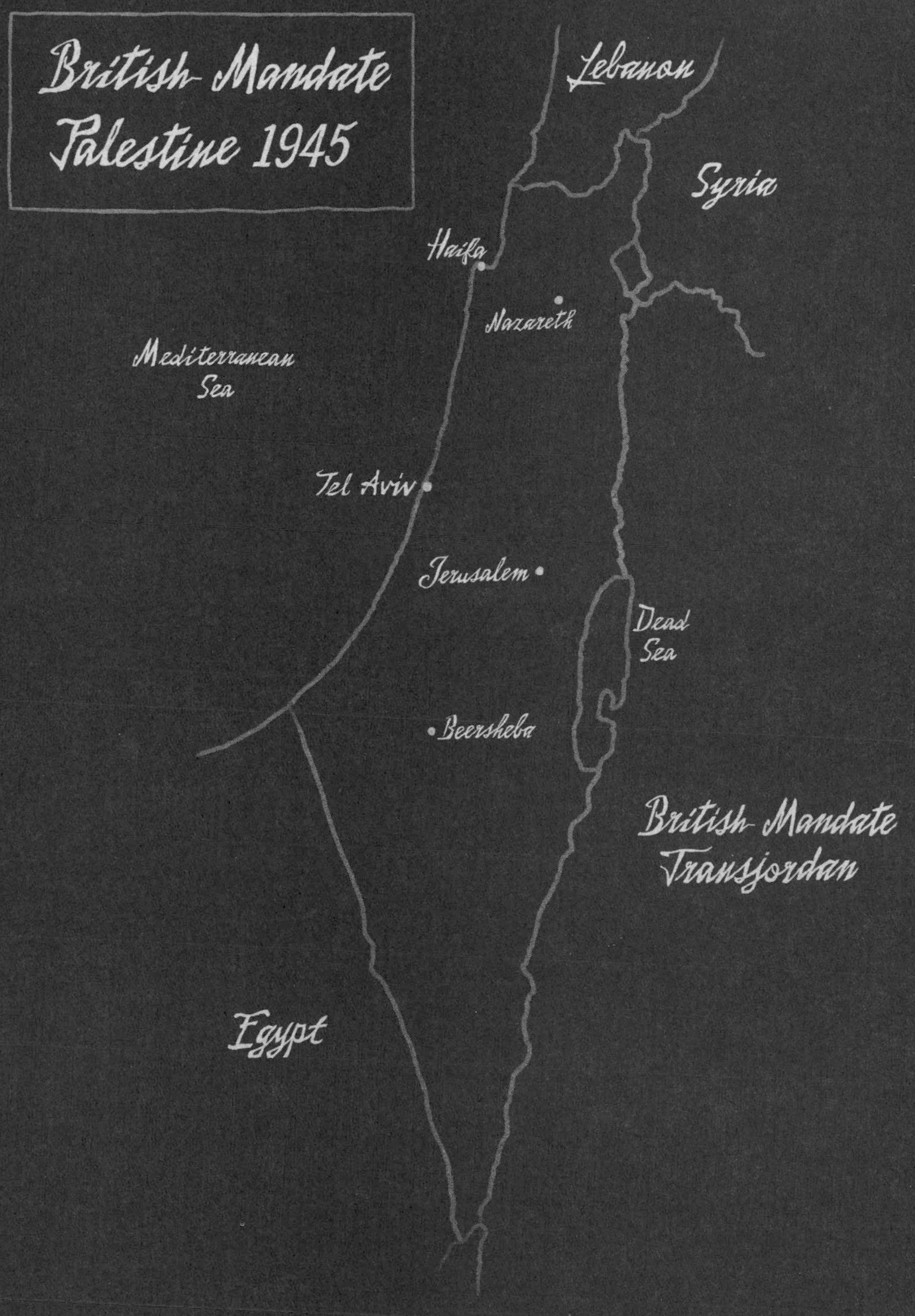
British Mandate
Palestine 1945
Lebanon
Syria
Haifa
Nazareth
Mediterranean
Sea
Tel Aviv
Jerusalem
Dead
Sea
Beersheba
British Mandate
Transjordan
Egypt

# THE CITY

**Jerusalem** was carved into the hills of a land given many names by many people; a land that since **1517** had been ruled by the Ottoman Turks for a period lasting four hundred years, during which it was most commonly referred to as Palestine. And so it was called when, after the defeat of the Ottoman Empire in the First World War, the territory fell under the control of a new power—the British Empire—in the year **1917**, when General Edmund Allenby and his troops marched through the gates of the Old City, and soon began creating new neighborhoods that stretched into precincts far from its ancient walls.

Under a mandate granted in **1920** by the newly formed League of Nations, England and France were charged with governing the formerly Ottoman territories until it was determined that they could govern themselves. France in Syria and Lebanon; Britain in Iraq, Trans-Jordan, and Palestine. But there were no fixed dates or criteria or clear paths laid out toward self-determination, the choice having been left solely to the discretion of the European powers in charge. Palestine in particular presented the British with a complex set of challenges, as it included both a native Arab population and a burgeoning Jewish community that was growing in fits and starts through several waves of immigration; at first almost innocuously, but eventually culminating in the 1930s and 40s with numbers that changed the balance in the territory in momentous ways. Adding to the small Jewish communities that had remained in Jerusalem and farther north in the city of Safed since ancient Roman rule, the new arrivals were motivated by the emergence of the Zionist movement that was born in the end of the nineteenth century. Inspired by a Viennese journalist and playwright named Theodore Herzl, who founded the World Zionist Congress in **1897**, the drive to reestablish a Jewish home in Palestine rested on a growing conviction that Jews would never be safe in Europe, as evidenced by ongoing persecutions and pogroms; and notably by what was then known as the Dreyfus Affair, a legal scandal that revealed a deep wellspring of anti-Semitism latent even in the modern and democratic nation of France. Support for Zionism made inroads among the world's Jews, but it was still more of a whisper than a shout...and many Jews, not only in Russia but all around the globe, embraced Socialism and Communism as means toward universal equality and human dignity.

Britain's position in relation to a Jewish homeland in Palestine was maddeningly ambiguous. On the one hand, in the **Balfour Declaration of 1917** it had announced that it viewed the enterprise with favor. But, in its efforts to gain allies in order to overthrow the Ottomans, Britain had also strongly supported the rise of Arab nationalism; so Britain found itself caught between incompatible aspirations. Arab opposition to Jewish immigration in Palestine hardened, and frustration with British ambivalence turned increasingly violent—erupting in a full-fledged **Arab Revolt in 1936**. This rebellion united Palestinian Arabs from all walks of life in a common cause against the British and the growing Jewish population, and from it the first vestiges of a national and political movement were born. The increasingly violent attacks on the Jewish population created a counterreaction as well, and the Zionists began to form their own military organizations, with some twenty thousand Jews bearing arms by the time the British had brutally and effectively squashed the revolt, three years after it had begun.

Despite its defeat, the Arab Revolt succeeded in encouraging the British to impose limits on and attempt to block Jewish immigration, culminating in what was known as **the White Paper of 1939**. These restrictions, adopted just as the Nazi persecutions of European Jews intensified to a fever pitch, remained in effect throughout the Holocaust and its aftermath, leading many Palestinian Jews to regard Britain as a hostile occupying power. Despite this, during the war, more than 30,000 Jews from Palestine joined the British Army to fight Nazi forces in the Middle East and in Italy. At the same time illegal immigration operations were organized, and Jewish fighting forces were expanded and equipped. They were formed into the *Haganah* and its commando unit, the *Palmach*; as well as two militant groups—the *Irgun*, and its even more radical offshoot called the *Lehi*, or Stern Gang, named after its founder Avraham Stern, a charismatic young Polish Jew who saw the expulsion of the British from the Zionist homeland as a holy cause more urgent even than the defeat of Nazi Germany across the ocean. These latter groups began an underground war of their own against the British forces in Palestine, carrying out a string of bombings and assassinations against both British and Arab targets with increasing ferocity. Having just finished putting down an Arab rebellion, the British Empire, enervated to its breaking point by the Second World War, now found itself facing a Jewish one.

# CAST OF CHARACTERS

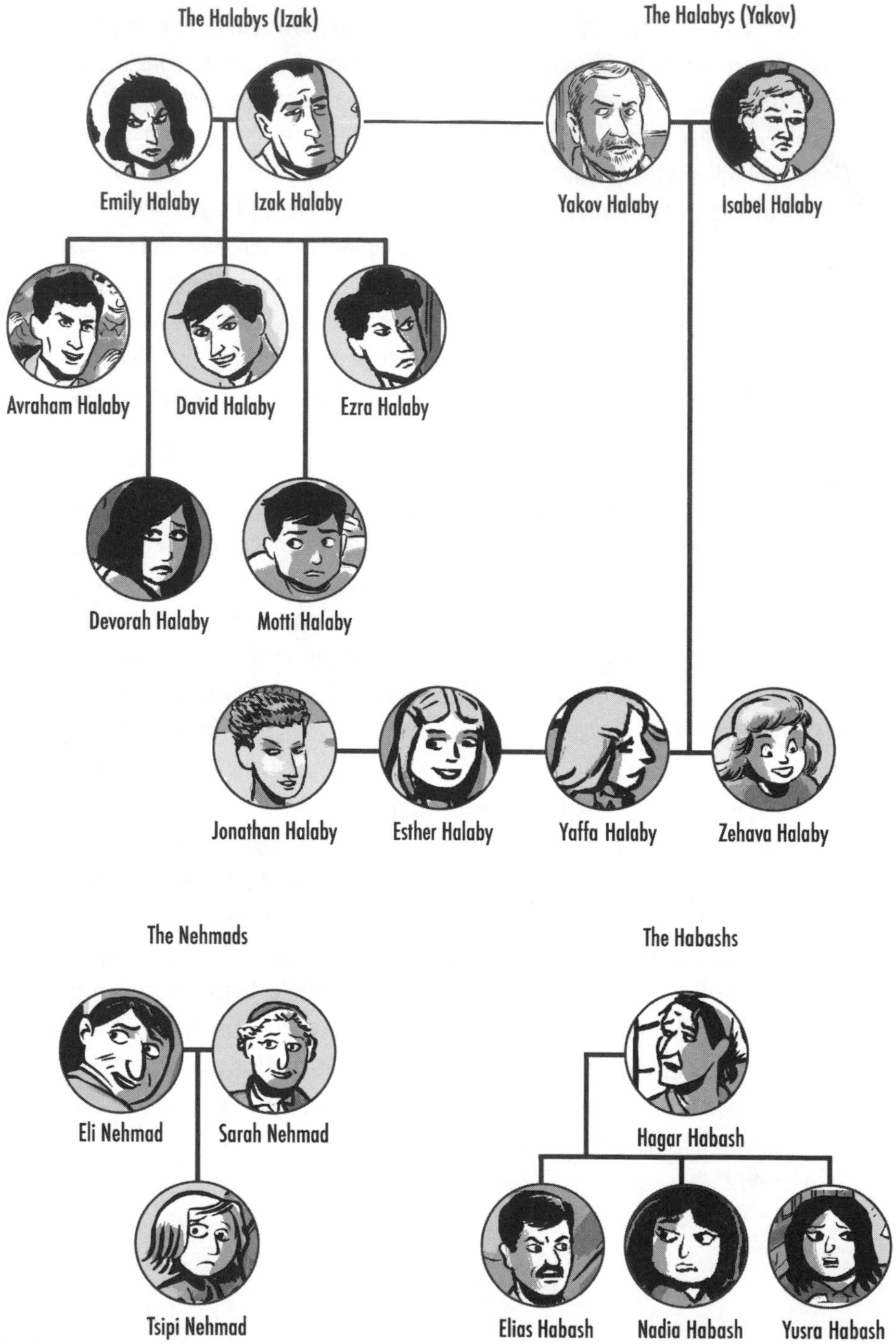
The Halabys (Izak)
Emily Halaby
Izak Halaby
Avraham Halaby
David Halaby
Ezra Halaby
Devorah Halaby
Motti Halaby
The Halabys (Yakov)
Yakov Halaby
Isabel Halaby
Jonathan Halaby
Esther Halaby
Yaffa Halaby
Zehava Halaby
The Nehmads
Eli Nehmad
Sarah Nehmad
Tsipi Nehmad
The Habashs
Hagar Habash
Elias Habash
Nadia Habash
Yusra Habash

# THE FAMILY

In the summer of **1887**, Rabbi Ismael Halaby of Aleppo, Syria, and his wife, Hagar, were blessed with their first son, **Yakov**. After the birth of four daughters Rabbi Halaby's congregants began to whisper the insult "Abu Banat"—father of daughters—behind his back. So the rabbi made a compact with his God: Should he be blessed with another son, he would gather his family and make the pilgrimage to the holy city of **Jerusalem**, where they would lay down new roots.

In the winter of **1893**, Hagar gave birth to another son, Izak. Rabbi Halaby made good on his promise and within the year he moved his family to the foothills of Jerusalem, to the tiny Jewish enclave known as **Yemin Moshe**, just outside the walls of the **Old City**.

Yakov, overcome by jealousy at the attention lavished on his brother, vowed never to allow Izak a moment's peace. Made miserable by Yakov's constant provocations, Izak learned a trade at an early age and left the family home as soon as he was able to strike out on his own. During his travels Izak met and married **Emily Betito**, of Alexandria, Egypt, and eventually he brought her back to Jerusalem where they started their family in a tiny apartment once owned by his father, now deceased, in Yemin Moshe.

In **1929** a dispute over prayer rights to the wailing wall led to a series of bloody riots; hundreds of Jews were killed by infuriated Arabs, and hundreds of Arabs slain by British Security forces. The Halaby family fled their home and relocated farther up in the precincts of British Jerusalem, to **Machane Yehuda**. This poverty stricken neighborhood was populated by a motley mixture of Jews from all across the Middle East: Iraq, Syria, Egypt, and Kurdistan; as well as a contingent of Ashkenazi Jews from Eastern European countries, although these numbered few—their brethren preferring the more urbane precincts of the newly burgeoning seaside city of Tel Aviv to the harsh, existential melancholy of Jerusalem.

# JERUSALEM

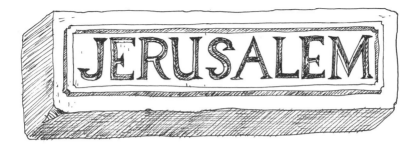

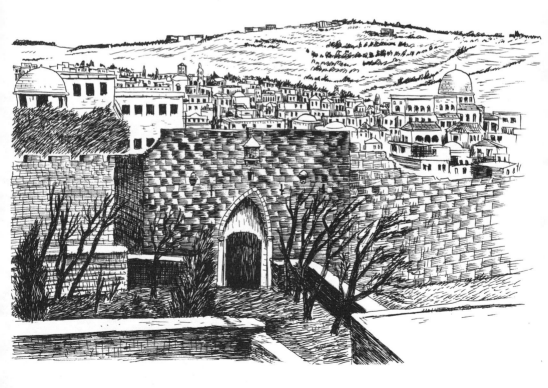

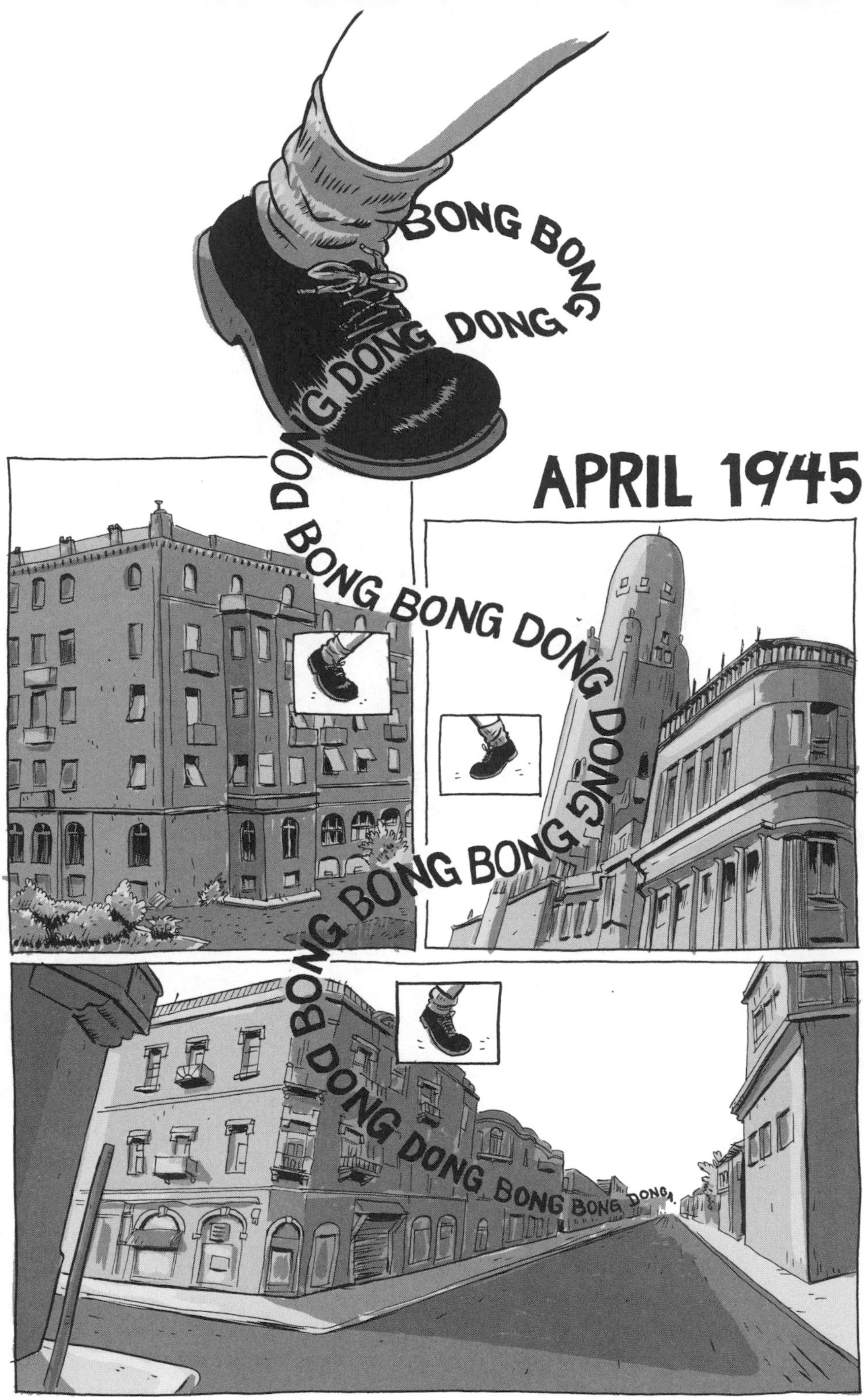
BONG BONG DONG DONG DONG
APRIL 1945
BONG BONG DONG DONG
BONG BONG BONG
DONG DONG BONG BONG DONG

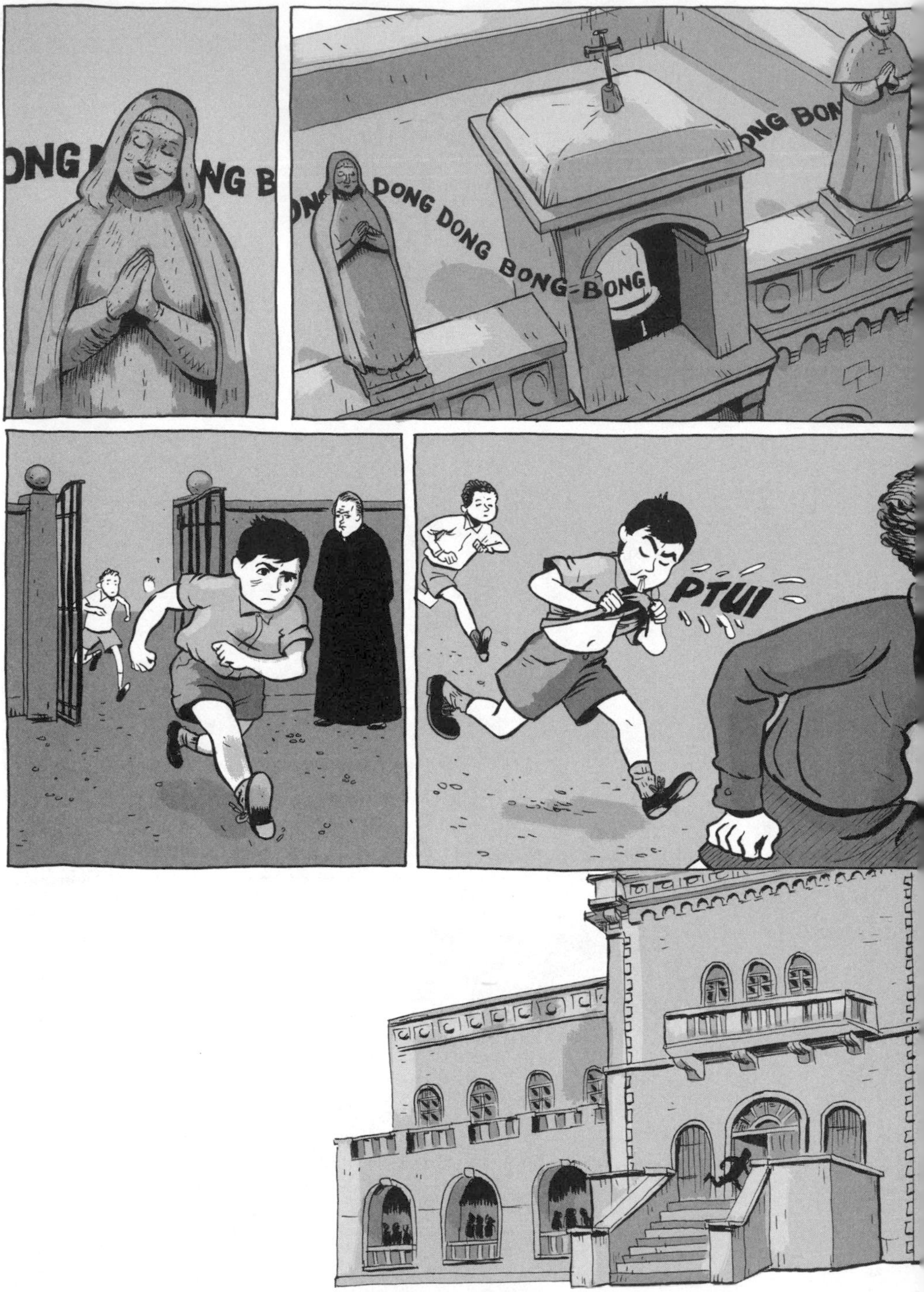
DONG DONG BONG-BONG
PTUI

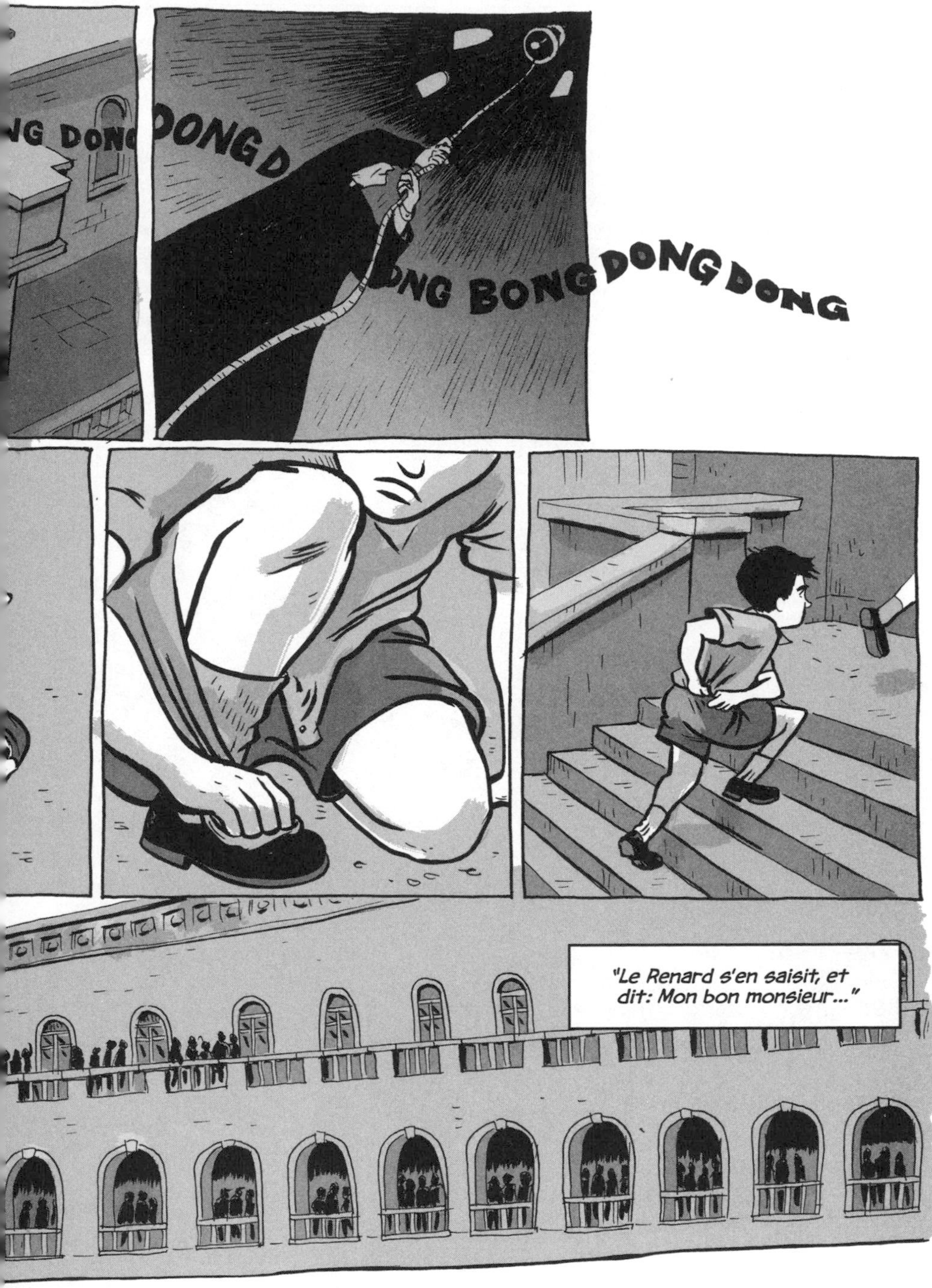
NG DONG DONG D
DNG BONG DONG DONG
"Le Renard s'en saisit, et dit: Mon bon monsieur..."

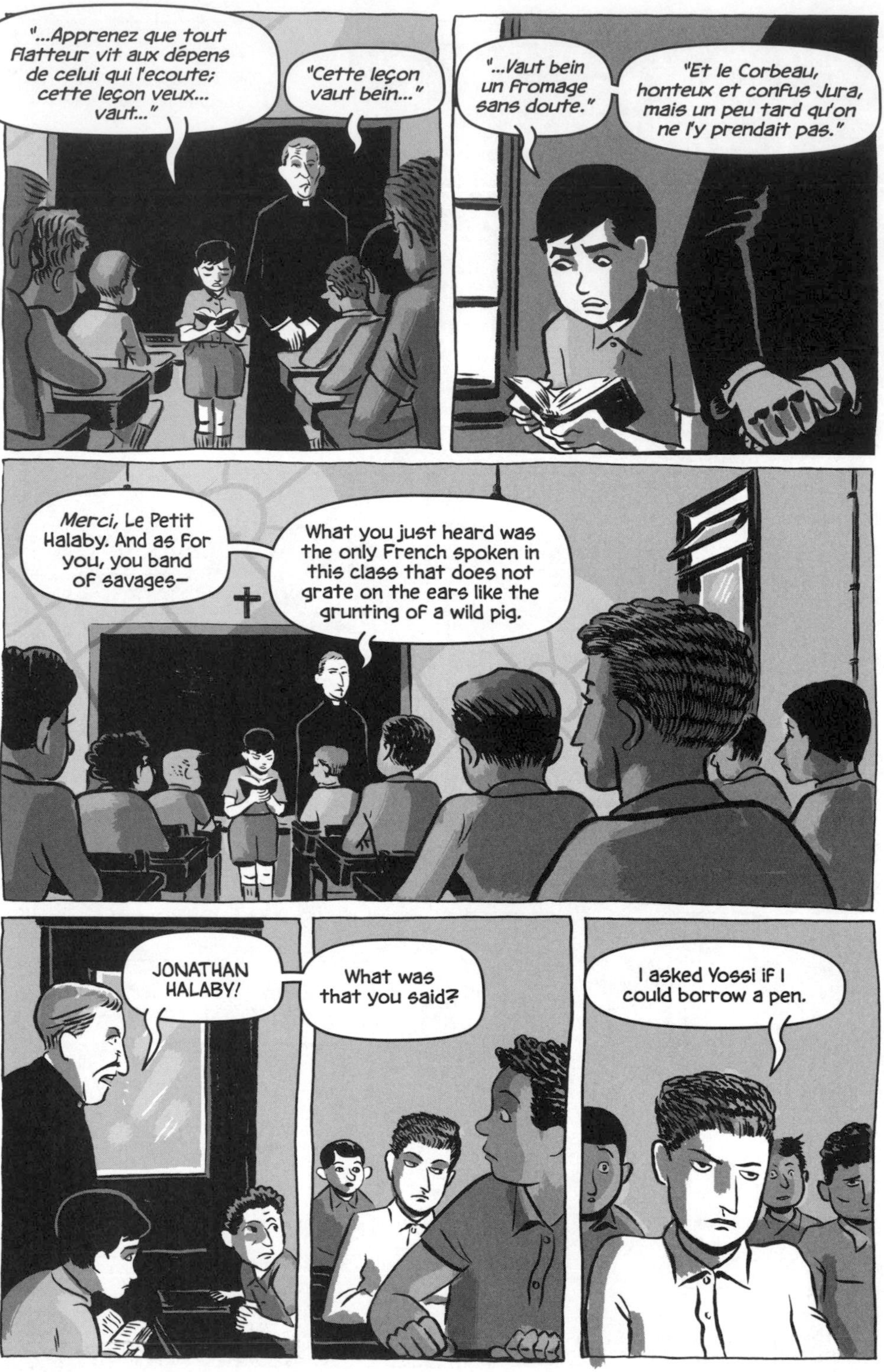
"...Apprenez que tout flatteur vit aux dépens de celui qui l'ecoute; cette leçon veux... vaut..."
"Cette leçon vaut bein..."
"...Vaut bein un fromage sans doute."
"Et le Corbeau, honteux et confus Jura, mais un peu tard qu'on ne l'y prendait pas."
Merci, Le Petit Halaby. And as for you, you band of savages—
What you just heard was the only French spoken in this class that does not grate on the ears like the grunting of a wild pig.
JONATHAN HALABY!
What was that you said?
I asked Yossi if I could borrow a pen.

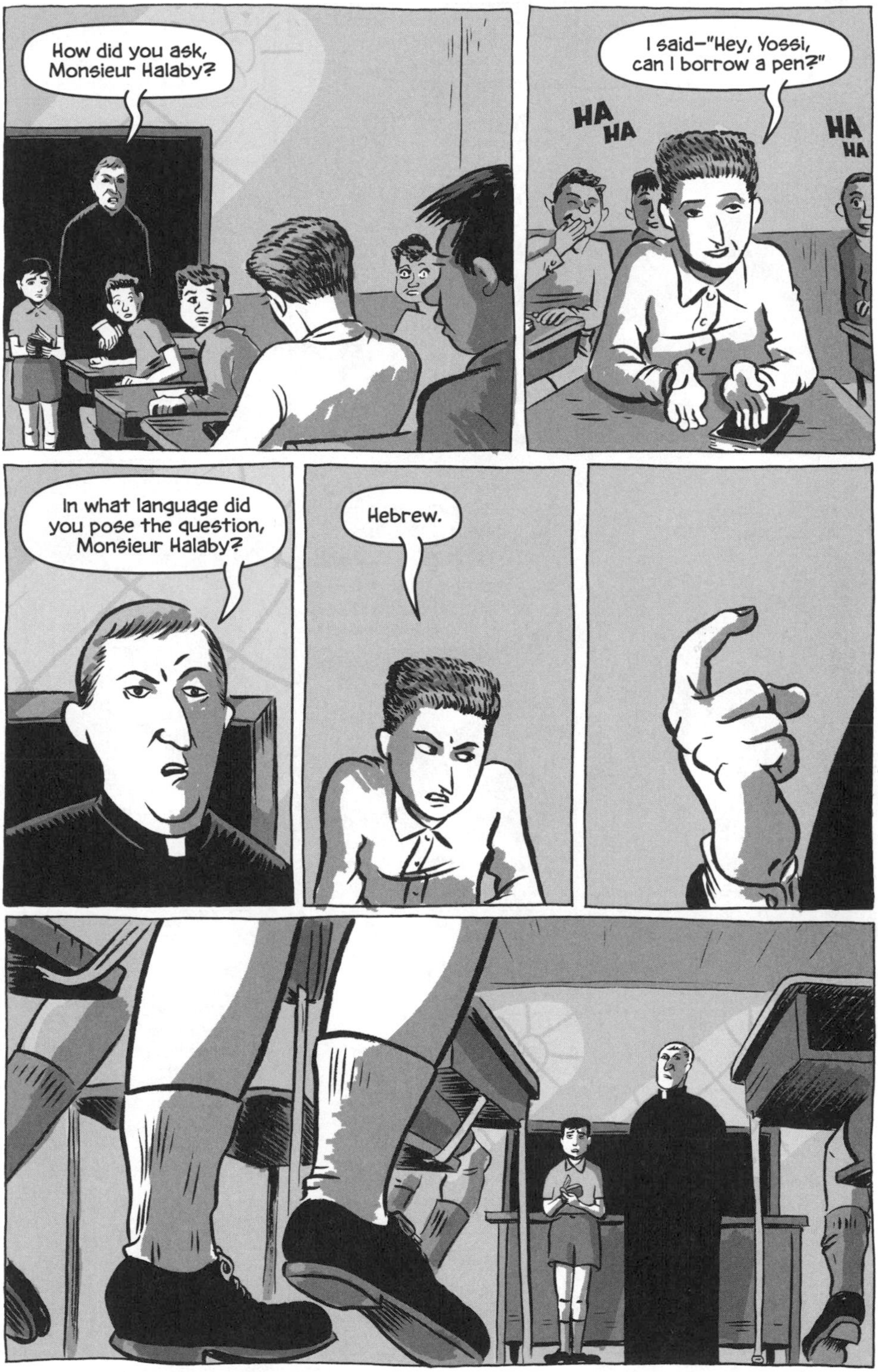
How did you ask, Monsieur Halaby?
I said–"Hey, Yossi, can I borrow a pen?"
HA HA
HA HA
In what language did you pose the question, Monsieur Halaby?
Hebrew.

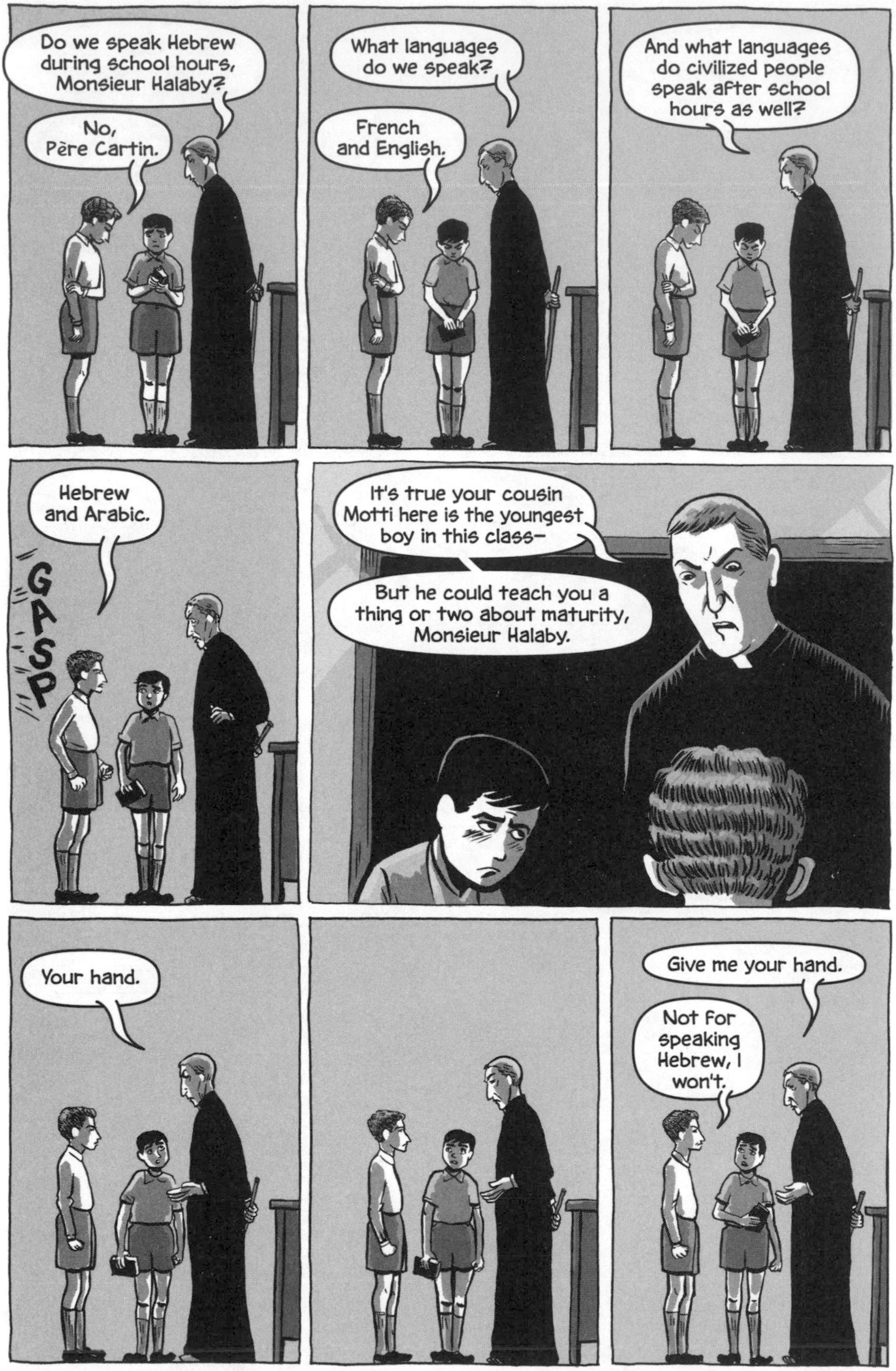
Do we speak Hebrew during school hours, Monsieur Halaby?
No, Père Cartin.
What languages do we speak?
French and English.
And what languages do civilized people speak after school hours as well?
Hebrew and Arabic.
GASP
It's true your cousin Motti here is the youngest boy in this class–
But he could teach you a thing or two about maturity, Monsieur Halaby.
Your hand.
Give me your hand.
Not for speaking Hebrew, I won't.

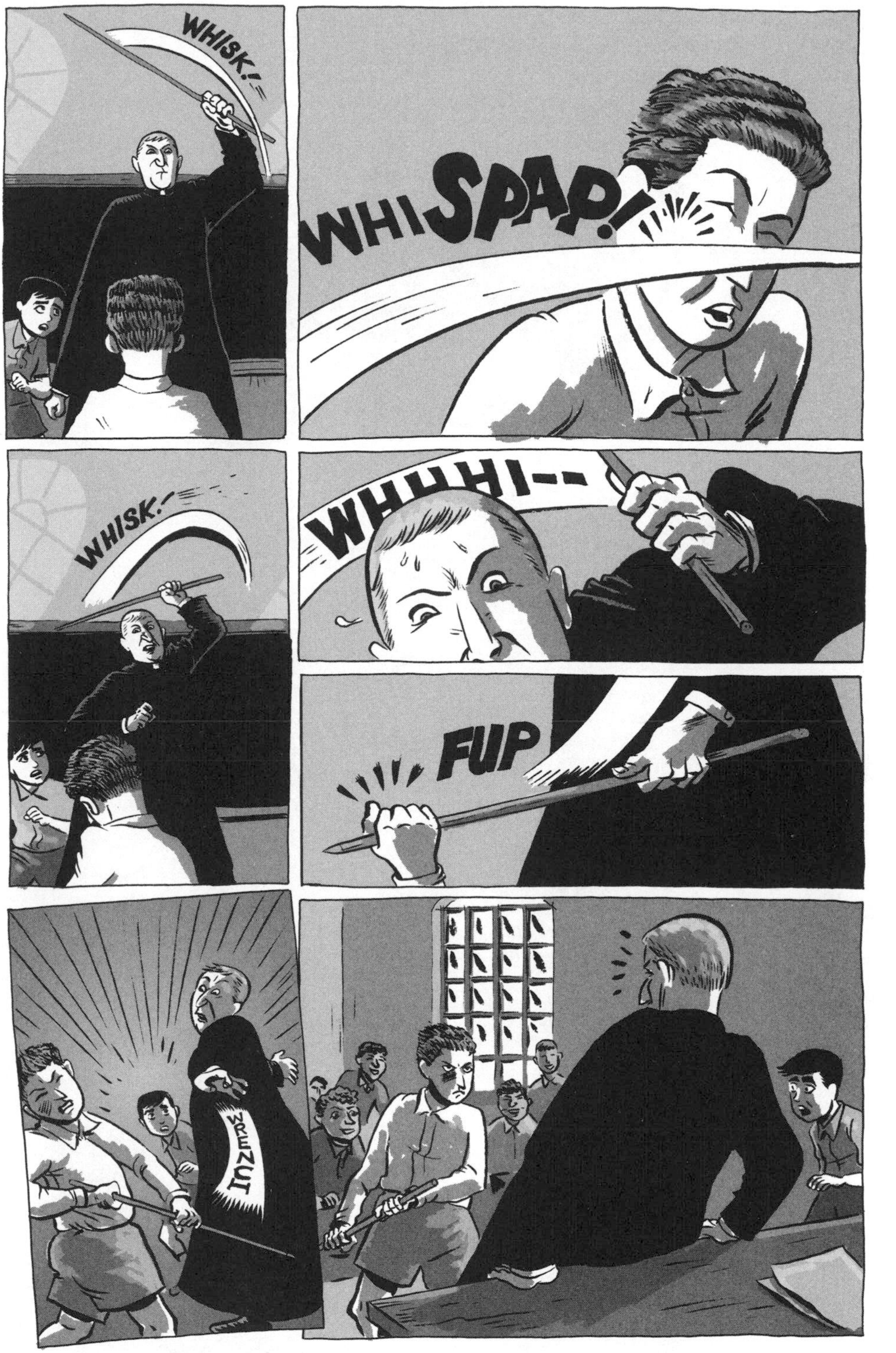
WHISK!
WHISPAP!
WHISK!
WHHHI--
FUP
WRENCH

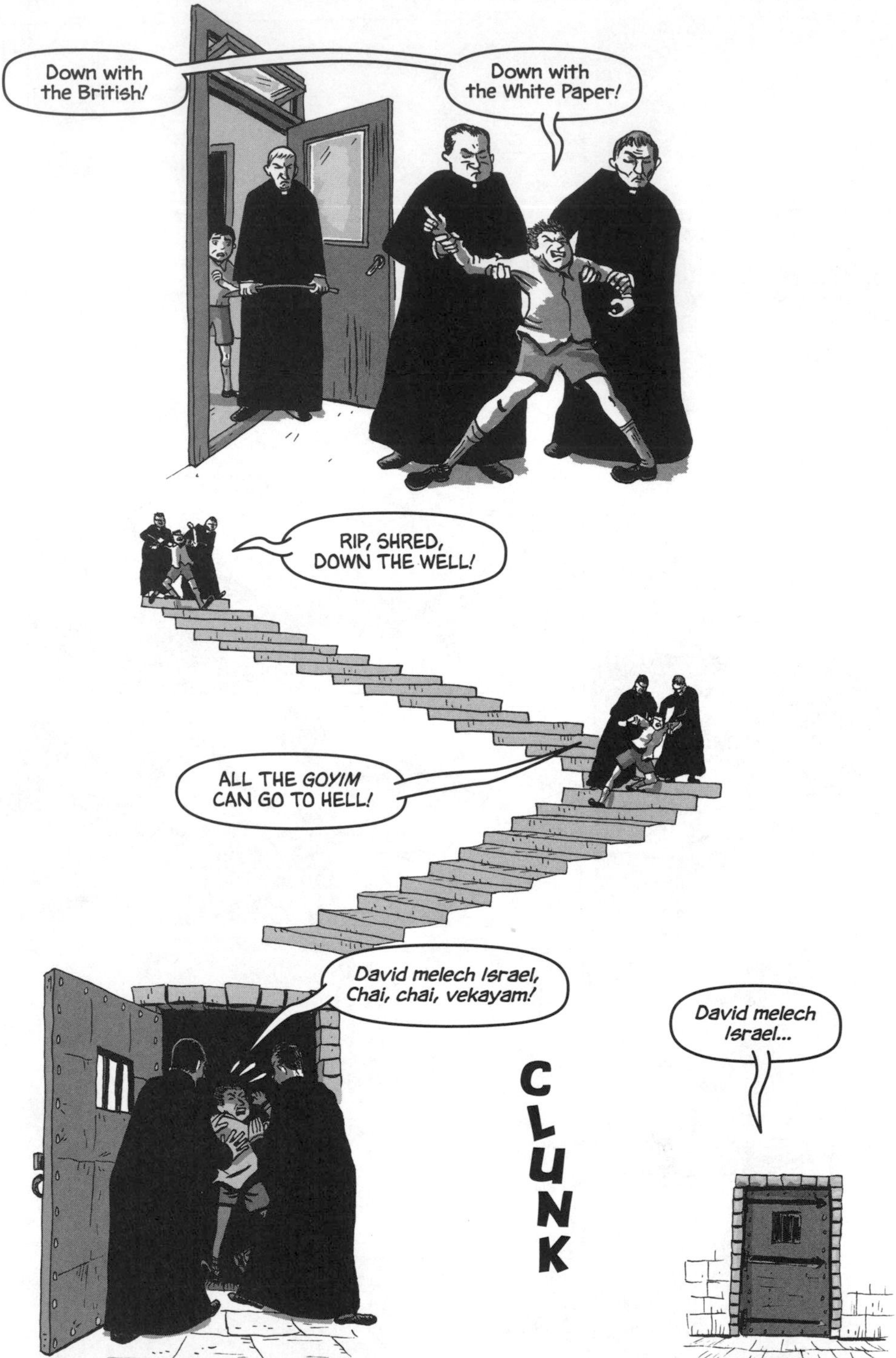
Down with the British!
Down with the White Paper!
RIP, SHRED, DOWN THE WELL!
ALL THE GOYIM CAN GO TO HELL!
David melech Israel, Chai, chai, vekayam!
CLUNK
David melech Israel...

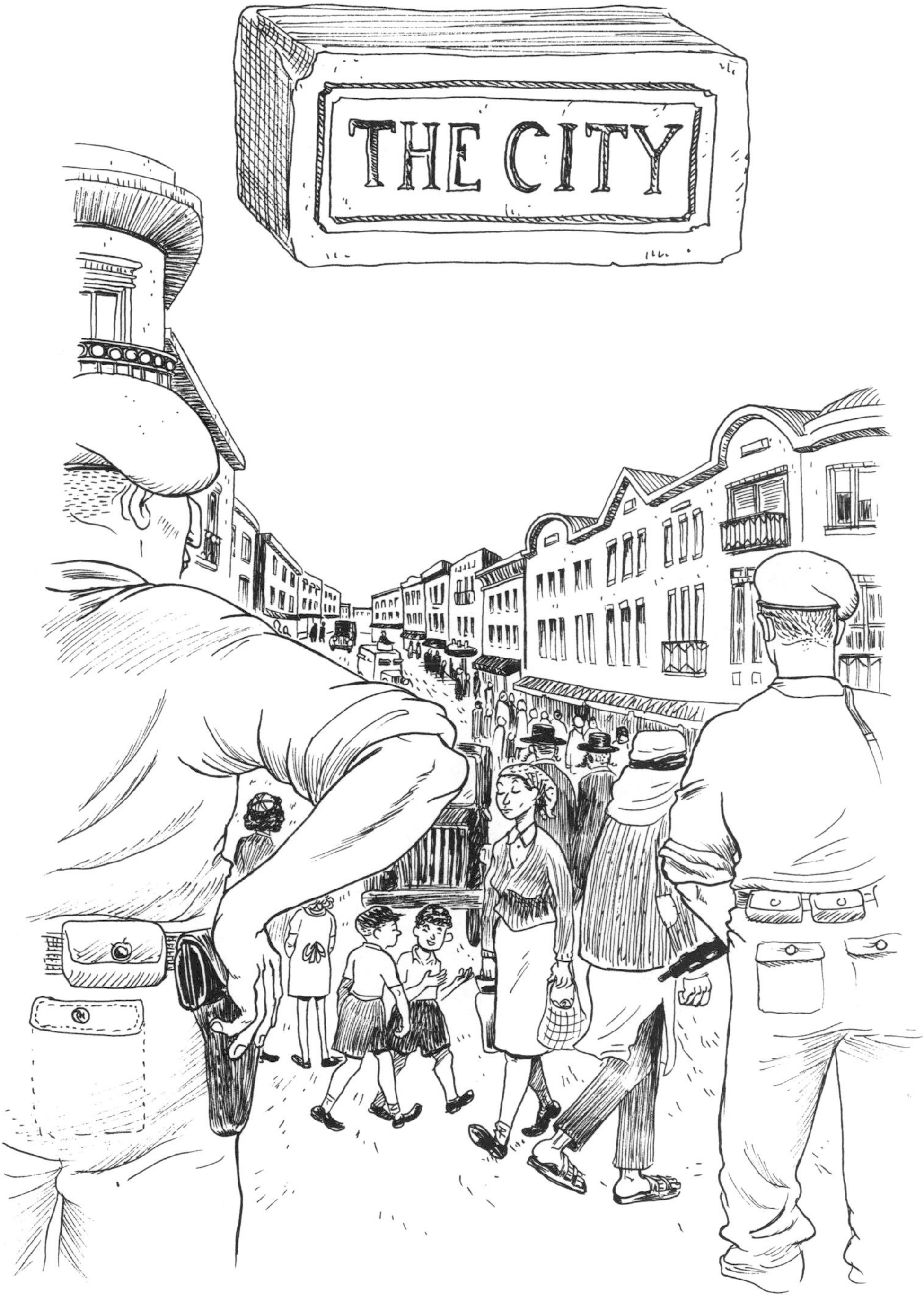
THE CITY

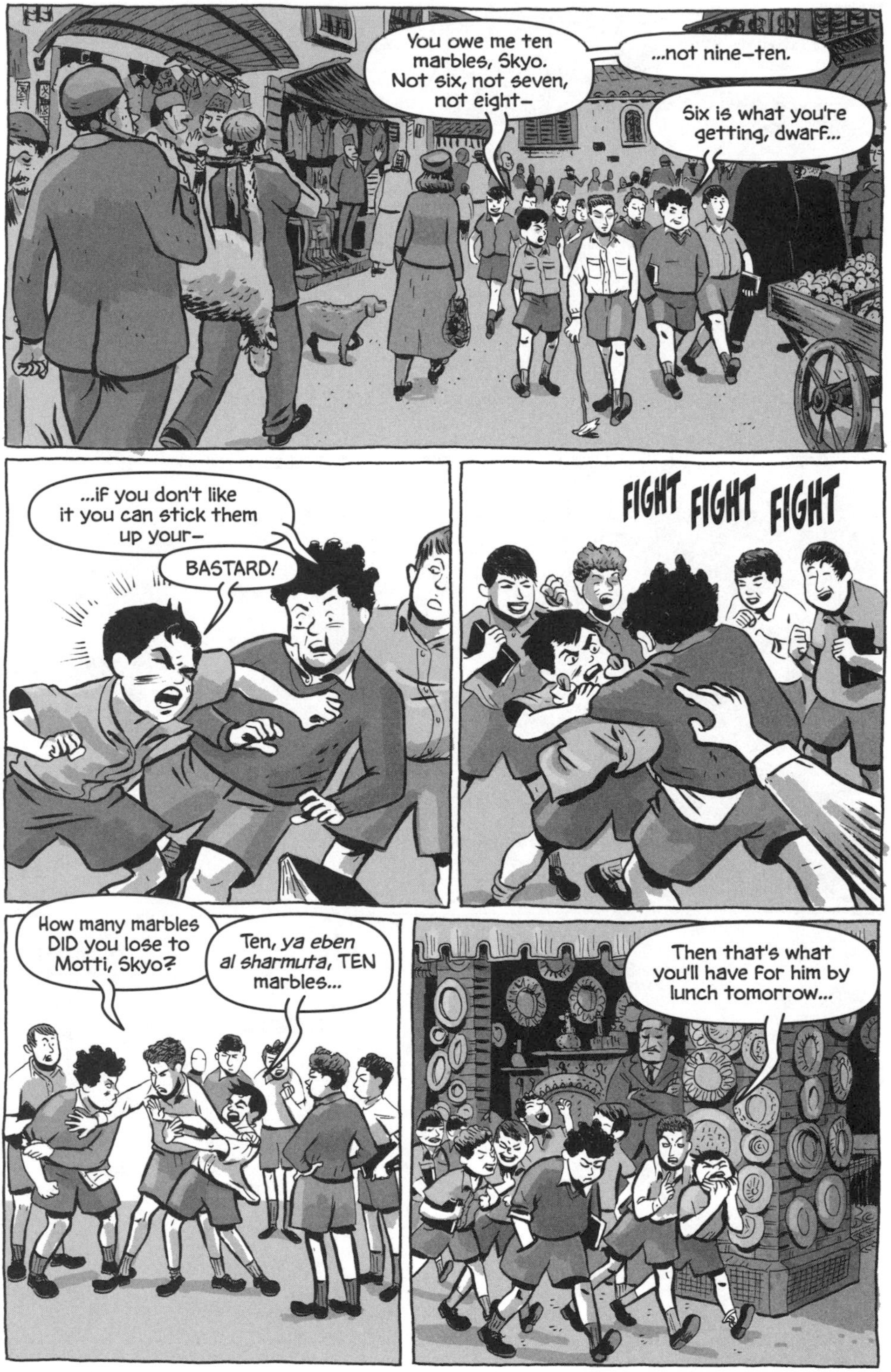
You owe me ten marbles, Skyo. Not six, not seven, not eight–
...not nine–ten.
Six is what you're getting, dwarf...
...if you don't like it you can stick them up your–
BASTARD!
FIGHT FIGHT FIGHT
How many marbles DID you lose to Motti, Skyo?
Ten, *ya eben al sharmuta*, TEN marbles...
Then that's what you'll have for him by lunch tomorrow...

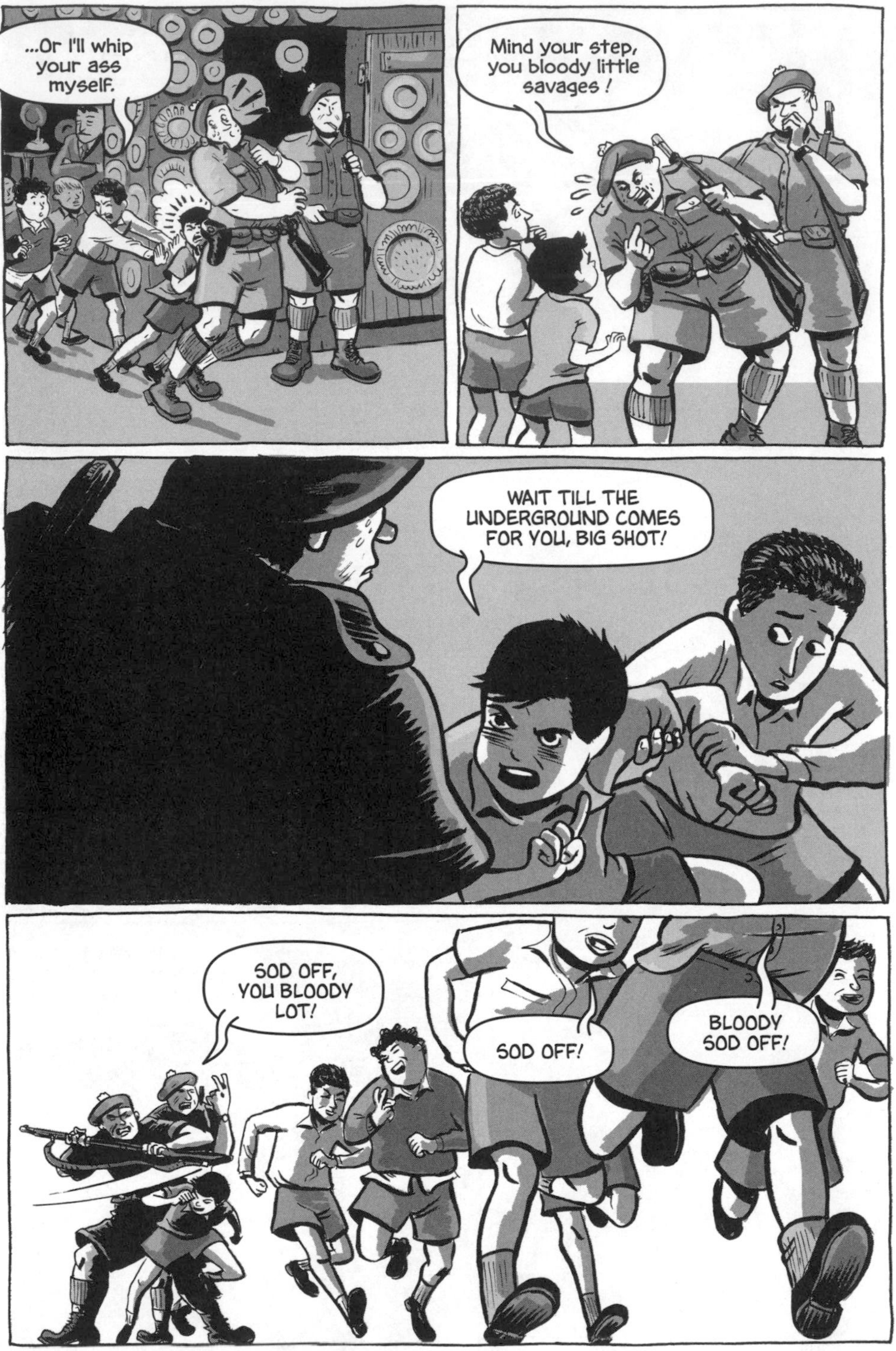
...Or I'll whip your ass myself.
Mind your step, you bloody little savages!
WAIT TILL THE UNDERGROUND COMES FOR YOU, BIG SHOT!
SOD OFF, YOU BLOODY LOT!
SOD OFF!
BLOODY SOD OFF!

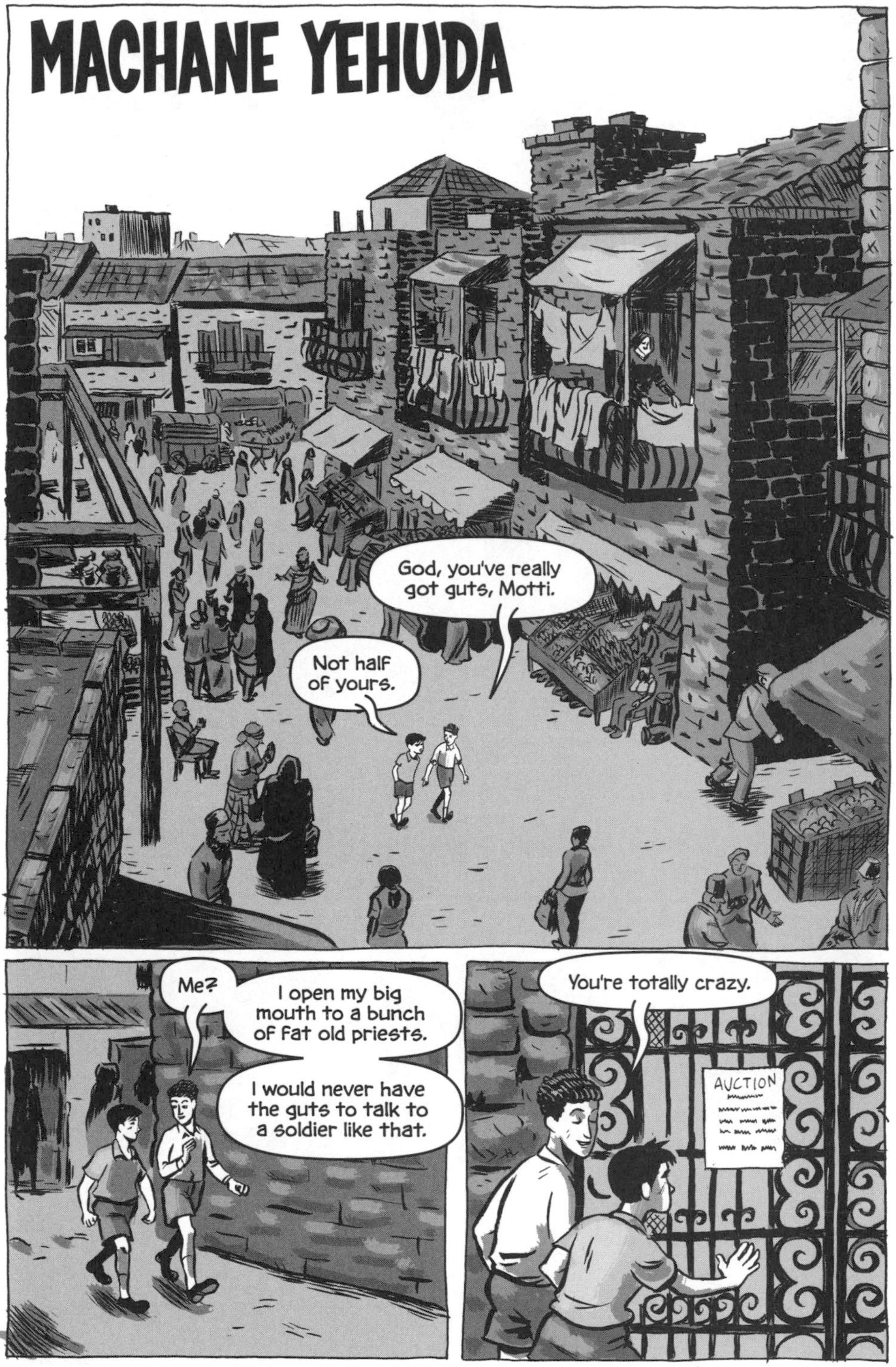
MACHANE YEHUDA
God, you've really got guts, Motti.
Not half of yours.
Me?
I open my big mouth to a bunch of fat old priests.
I would never have the guts to talk to a soldier like that.
You're totally crazy.
AUCTION

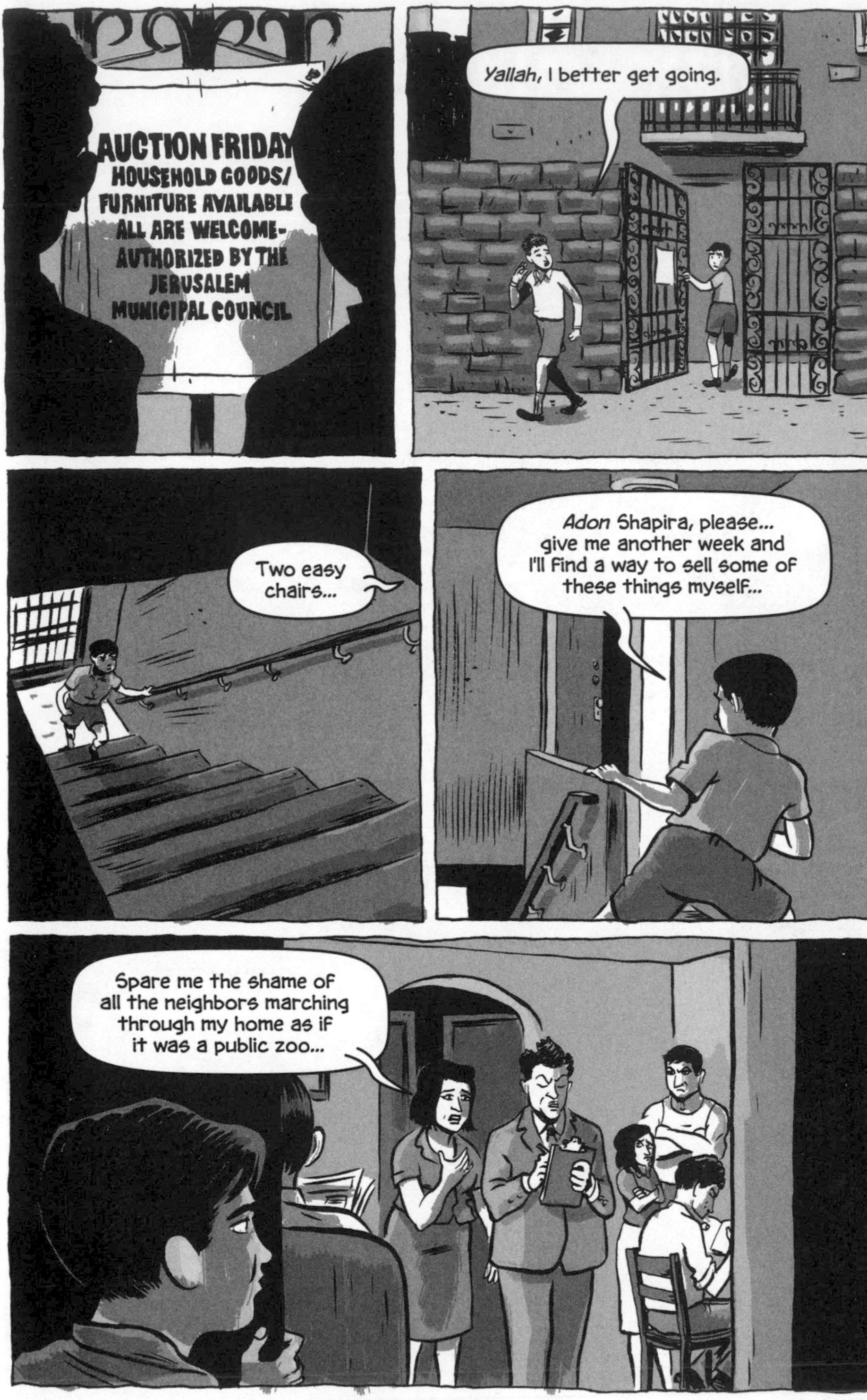
AUCTION FRIDAY
HOUSEHOLD GOODS/
FURNITURE AVAILABLE
ALL ARE WELCOME-
AUTHORIZED BY THE
JERUSALEM
MUNICIPAL COUNCIL
*Yallah*, I better get going.
Two easy chairs...
*Adon* Shapira, please... give me another week and I'll find a way to sell some of these things myself...
Spare me the shame of all the neighbors marching through my home as if it was a public zoo...

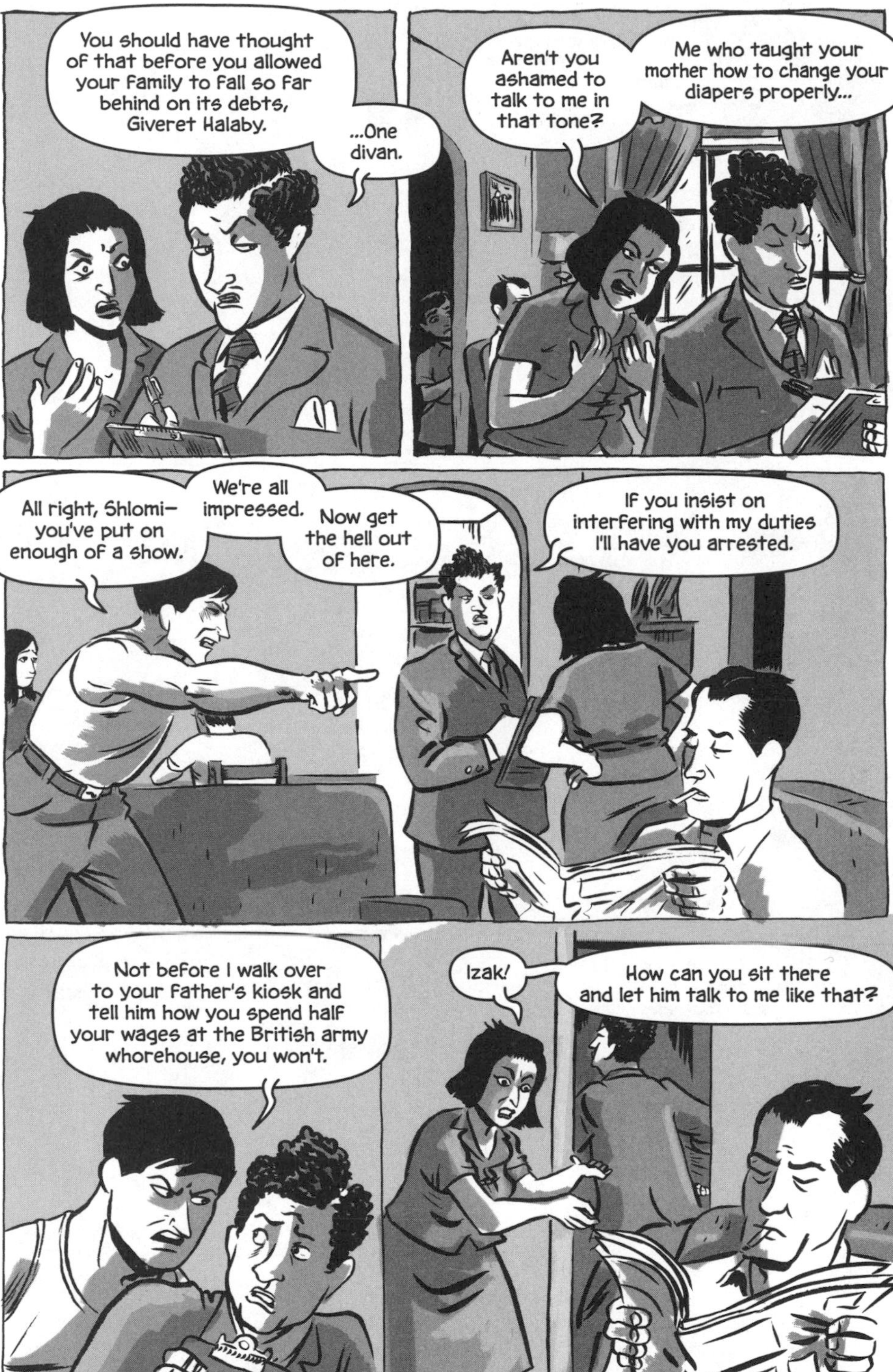
You should have thought of that before you allowed your family to fall so far behind on its debts, Giveret Halaby.
...One divan.
Aren't you ashamed to talk to me in that tone?
Me who taught your mother how to change your diapers properly...
All right, Shlomi— you've put on enough of a show.
We're all impressed.
Now get the hell out of here.
If you insist on interfering with my duties I'll have you arrested.
Not before I walk over to your father's kiosk and tell him how you spend half your wages at the British army whorehouse, you won't.
Izak!
How can you sit there and let him talk to me like that?

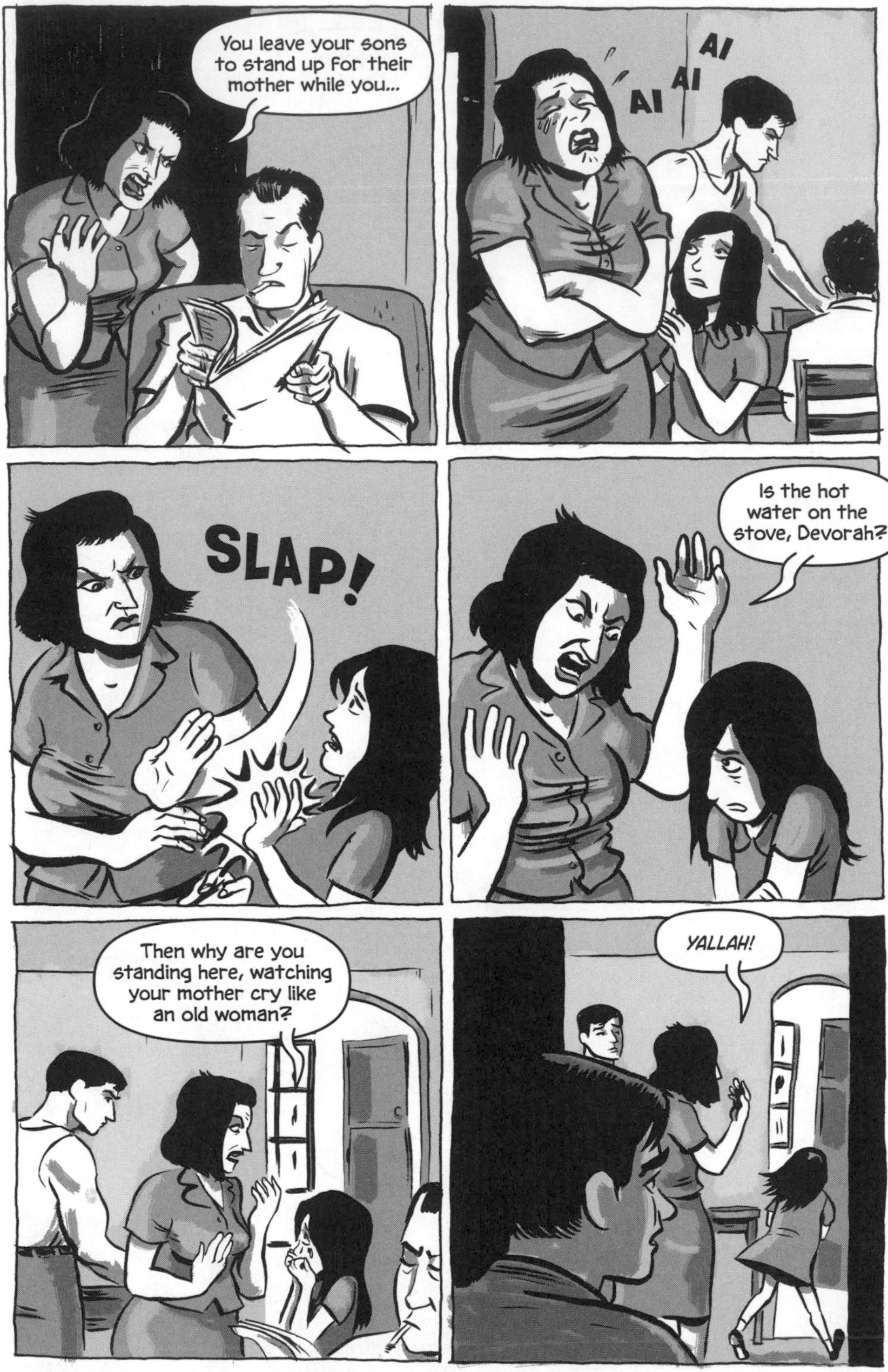
You leave your sons to stand up for their mother while you...
AI
AI
AI
SLAP!
Is the hot water on the stove, Devorah?
Then why are you standing here, watching your mother cry like an old woman?
YALLAH!

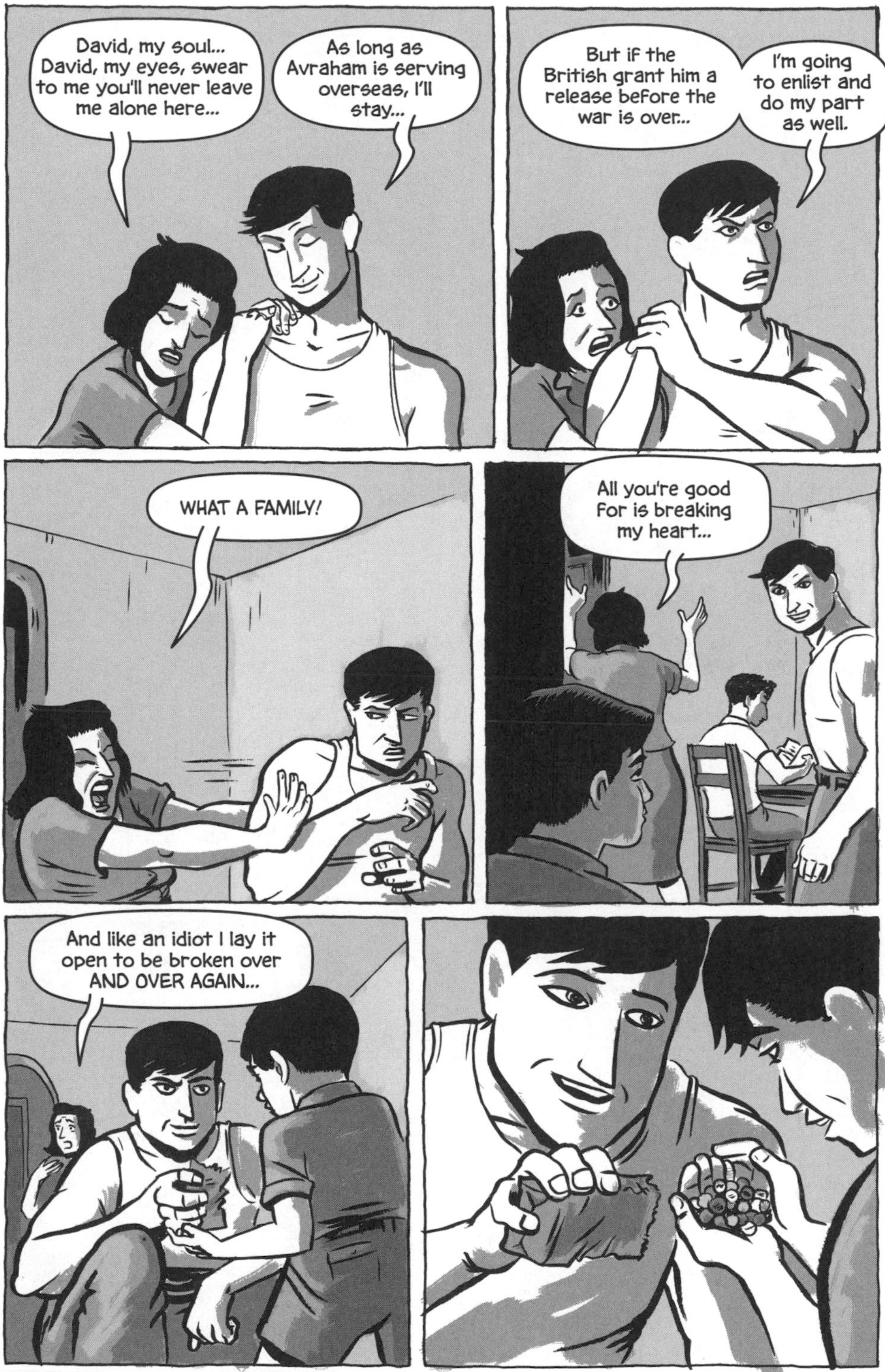
David, my soul... David, my eyes, swear to me you'll never leave me alone here...
As long as Avraham is serving overseas, I'll stay...
But if the British grant him a release before the war is over...
I'm going to enlist and do my part as well.
WHAT A FAMILY!
All you're good for is breaking my heart...
And like an idiot I lay it open to be broken over AND OVER AGAIN...

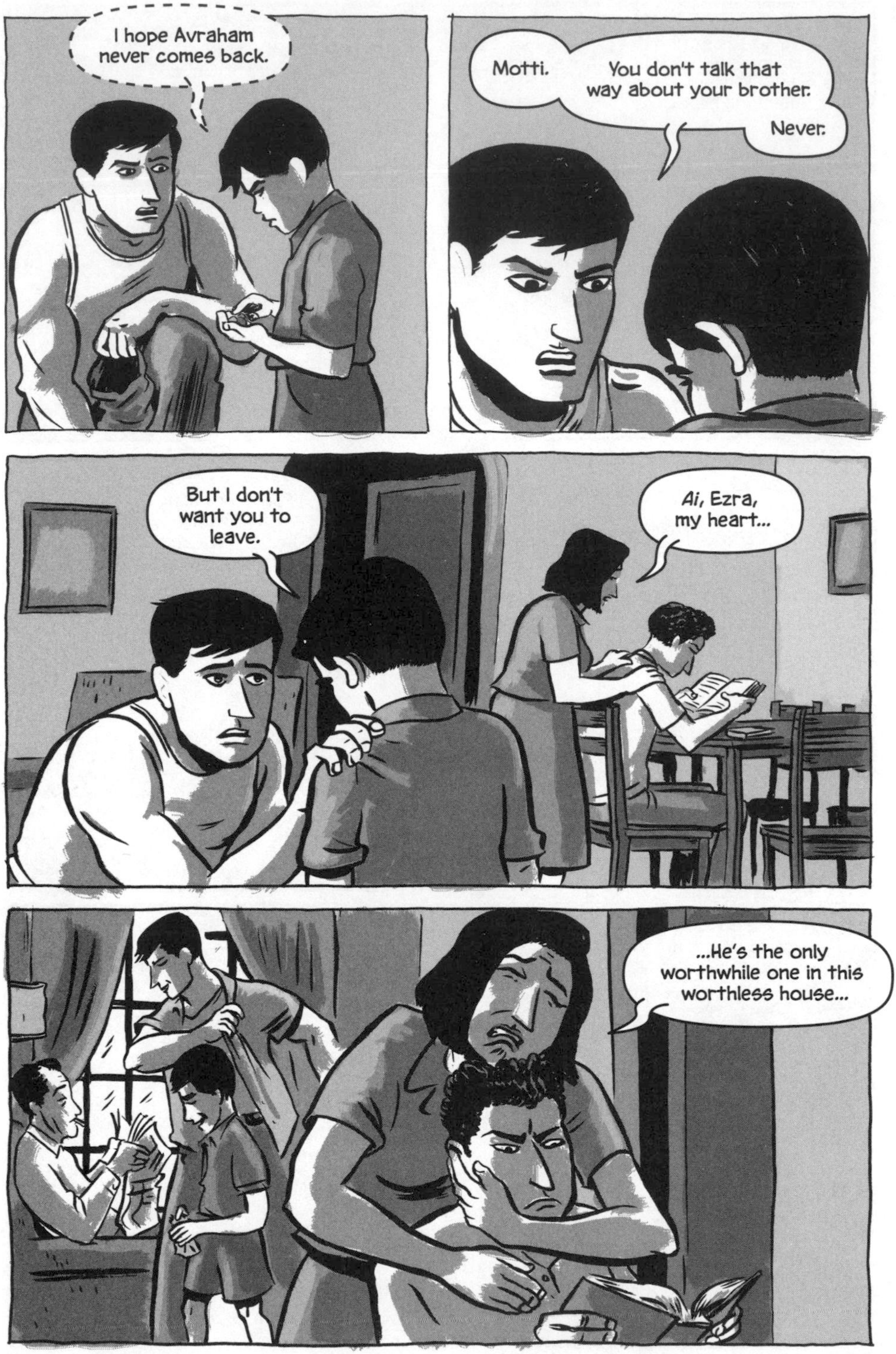
I hope Avraham never comes back.
Motti.
You don't talk that way about your brother.
Never.
But I don't want you to leave.
Ai, Ezra, my heart...
...He's the only worthwhile one in this worthless house...

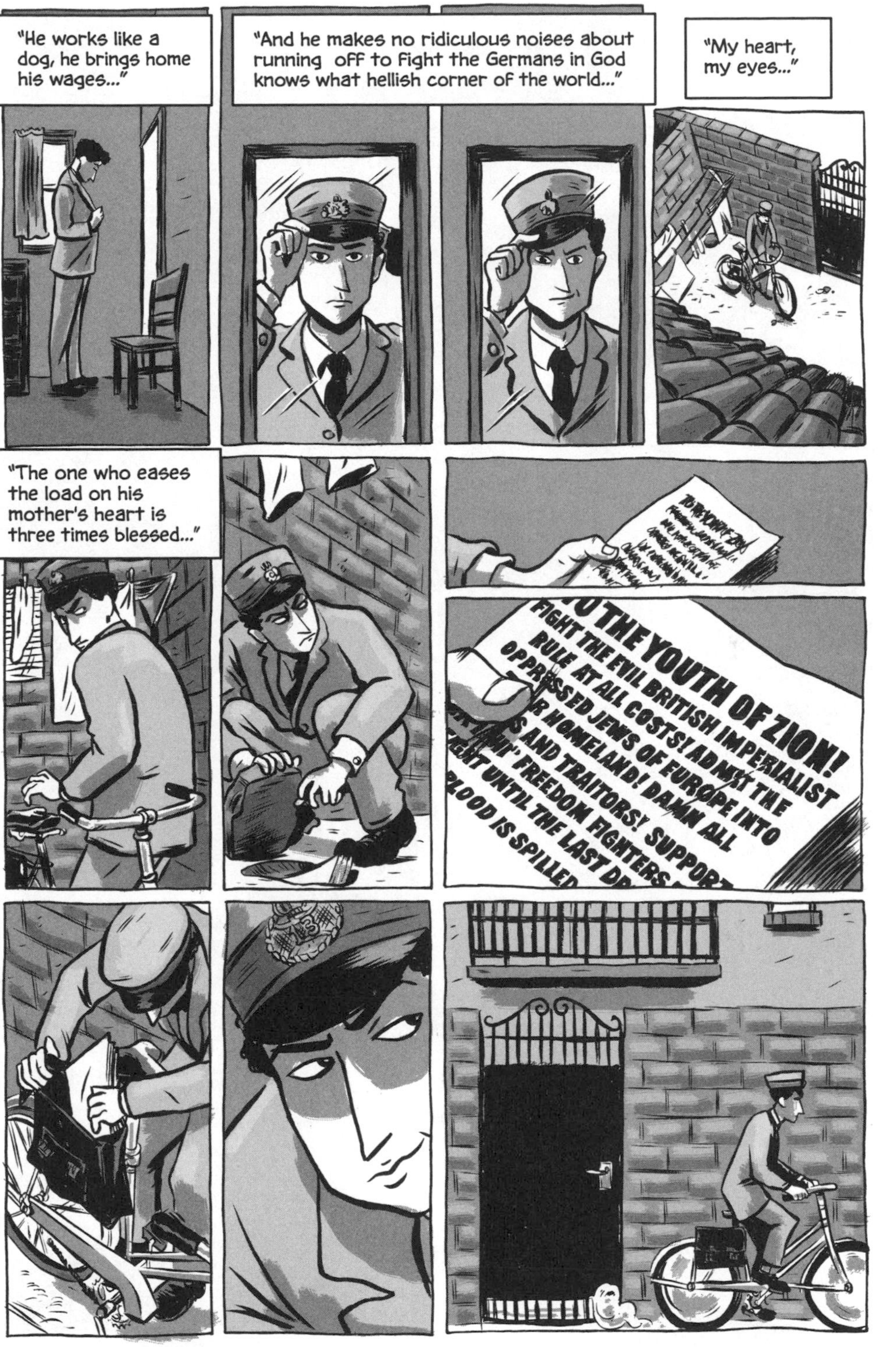
"He works like a dog, he brings home his wages..."
"And he makes no ridiculous noises about running off to fight the Germans in God knows what hellish corner of the world..."
"My heart, my eyes..."
"The one who eases the load on his mother's heart is three times blessed..."
THE YOUTH OF ZION!
FIGHT THE EVIL BRITISH IMPERIALIST
RULE AT ALL COSTS! ADMIT THE
OPPRESSED JEWS OF EUROPE INTO
HOMELAND! DAMN ALL
AND TRAITORS! SUPPORT
FREEDOM FIGHTERS
FIGHT UNTIL THE LAST
BLOOD IS SPILLED

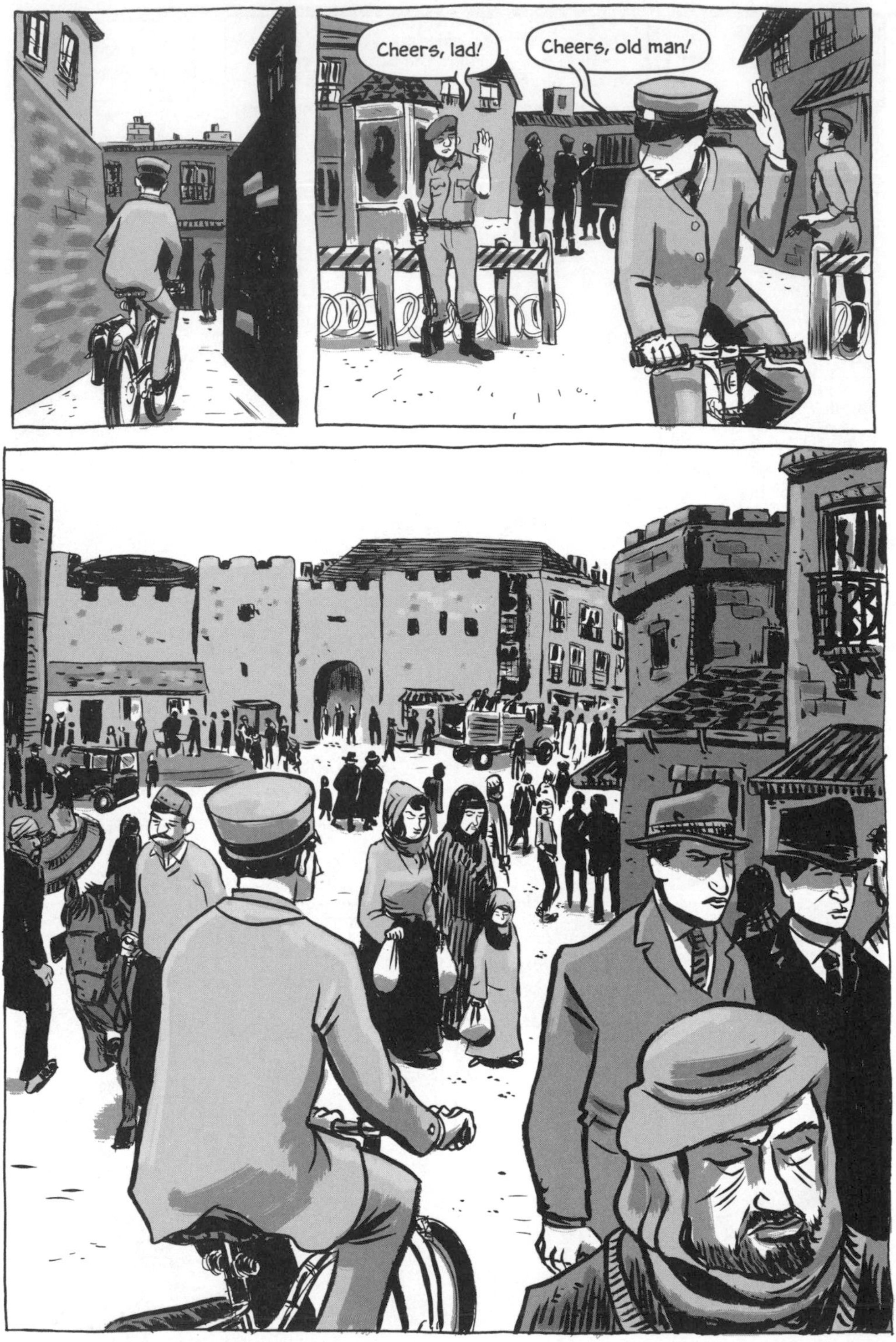
Cheers, lad!
Cheers, old man!

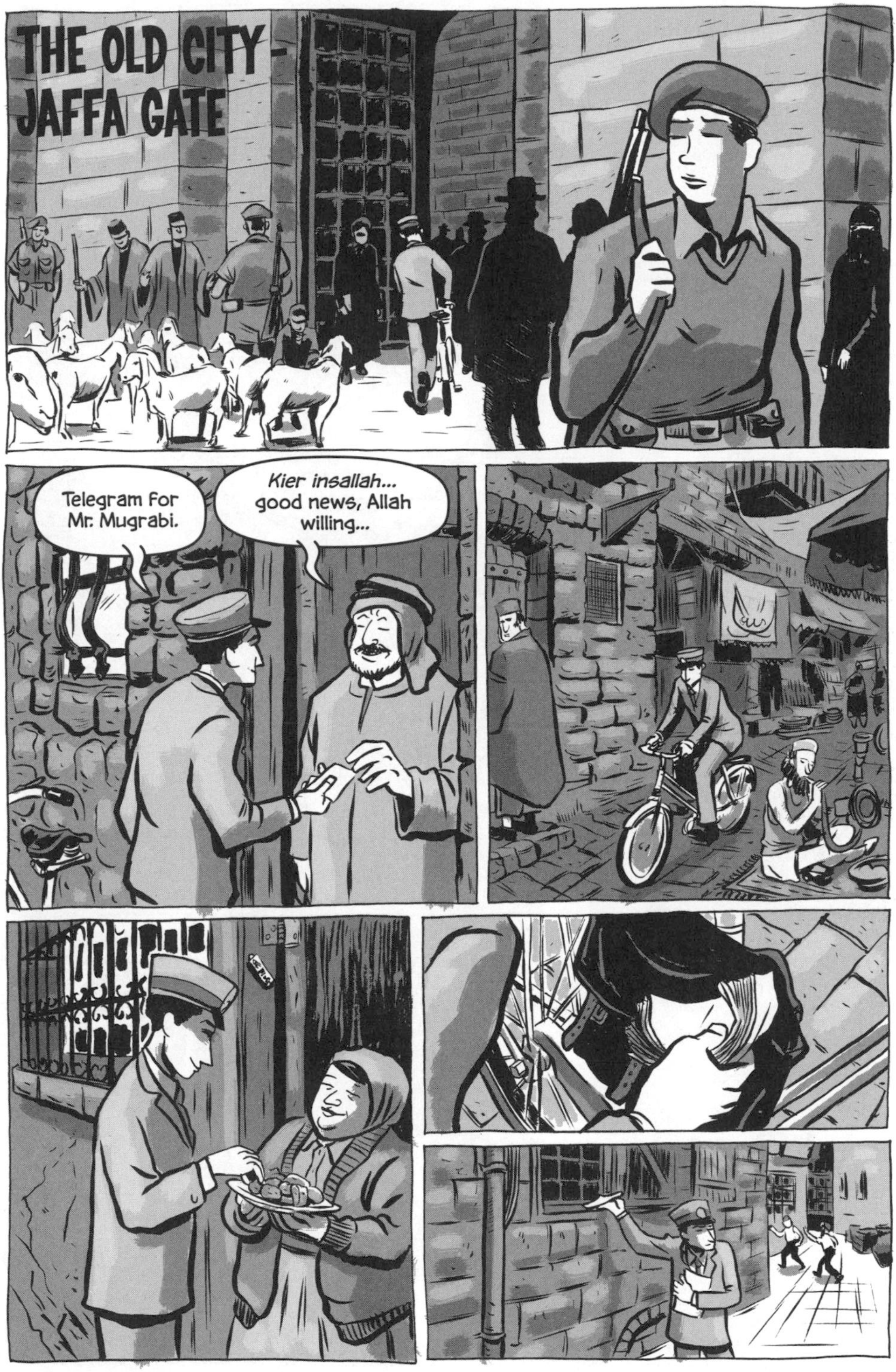
THE OLD CITY - JAFFA GATE
Telegram for Mr. Mugrabi.
Kier insallah... good news, Allah willing...

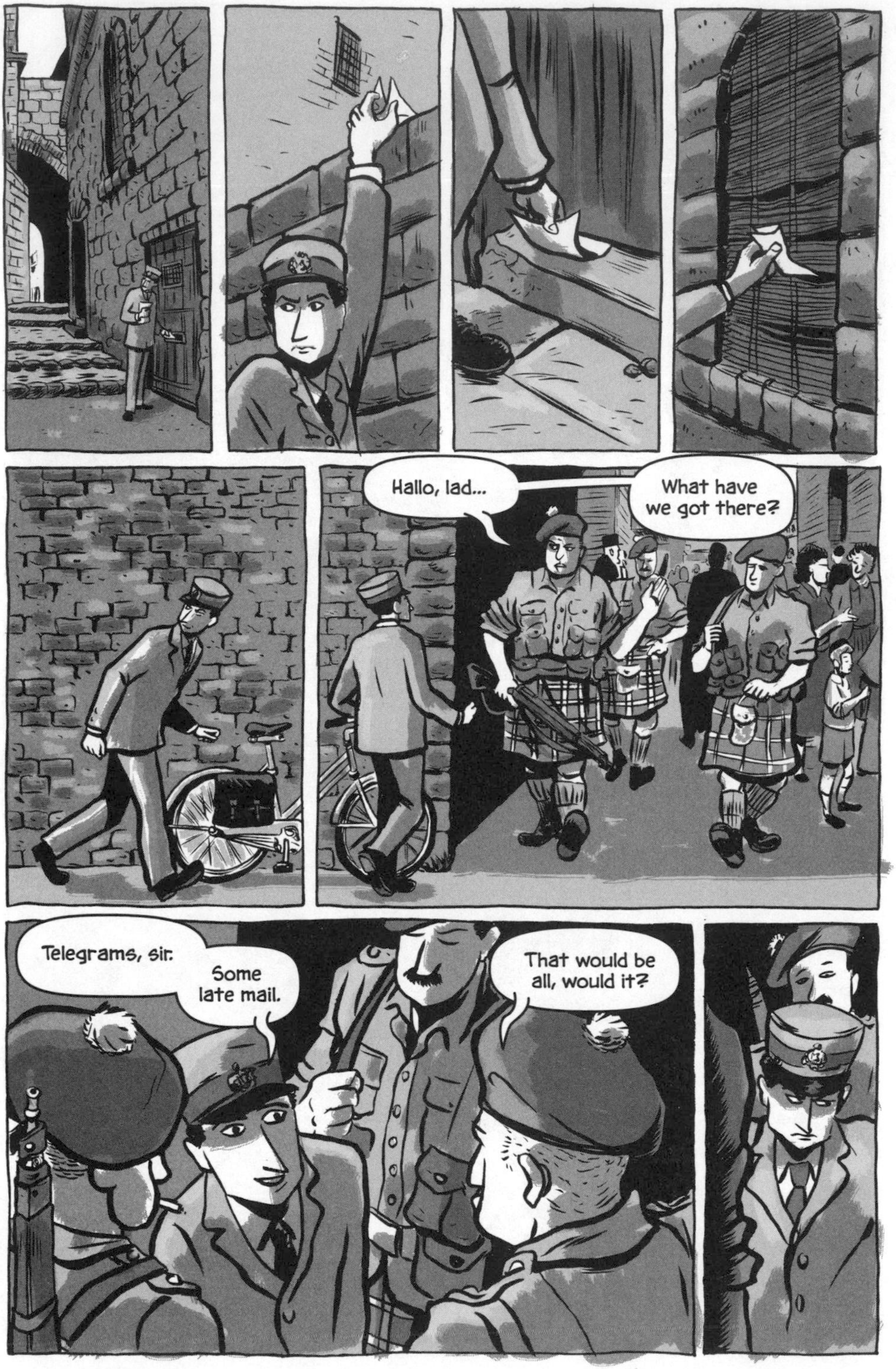

Hallo, lad...
What have we got there?
Telegrams, sir.
Some late mail.
That would be all, would it?

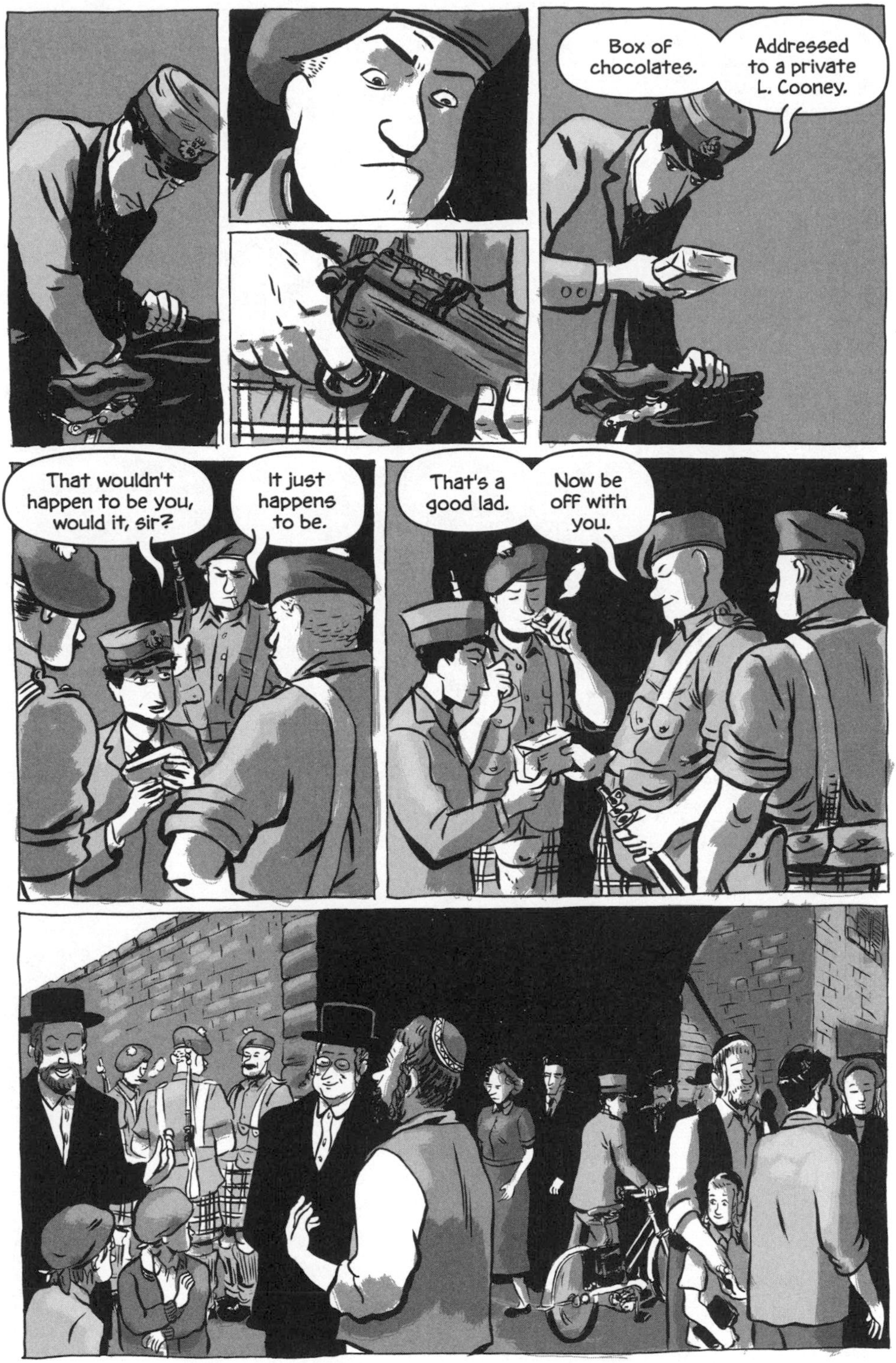
Box of chocolates.
Addressed to a private L. Cooney.
That wouldn't happen to be you, would it, sir?
It just happens to be.
That's a good lad.
Now be off with you.

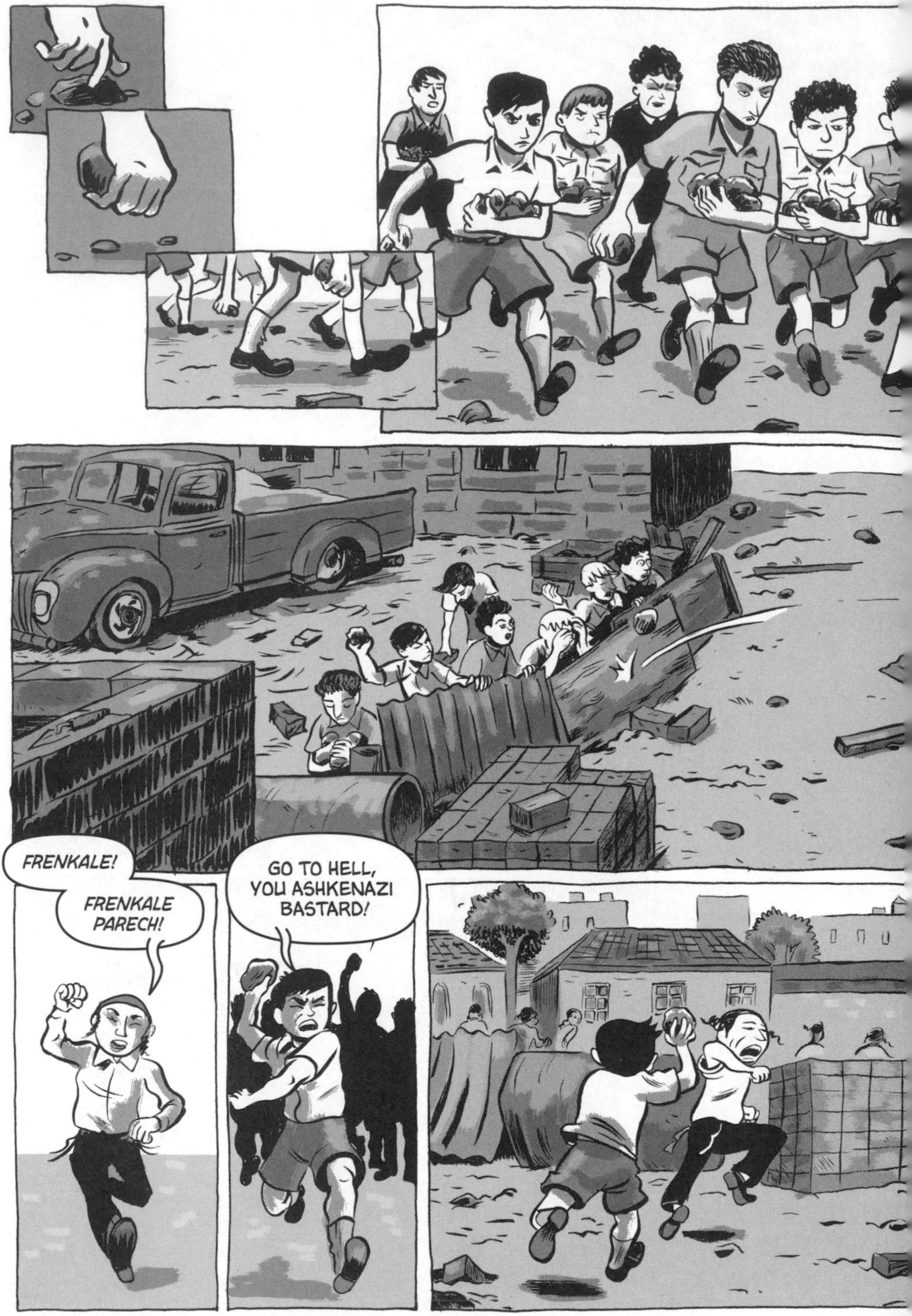
FRENKALE!
FRENKALE PARECH!
GO TO HELL, YOU ASHKENAZI BASTARD!

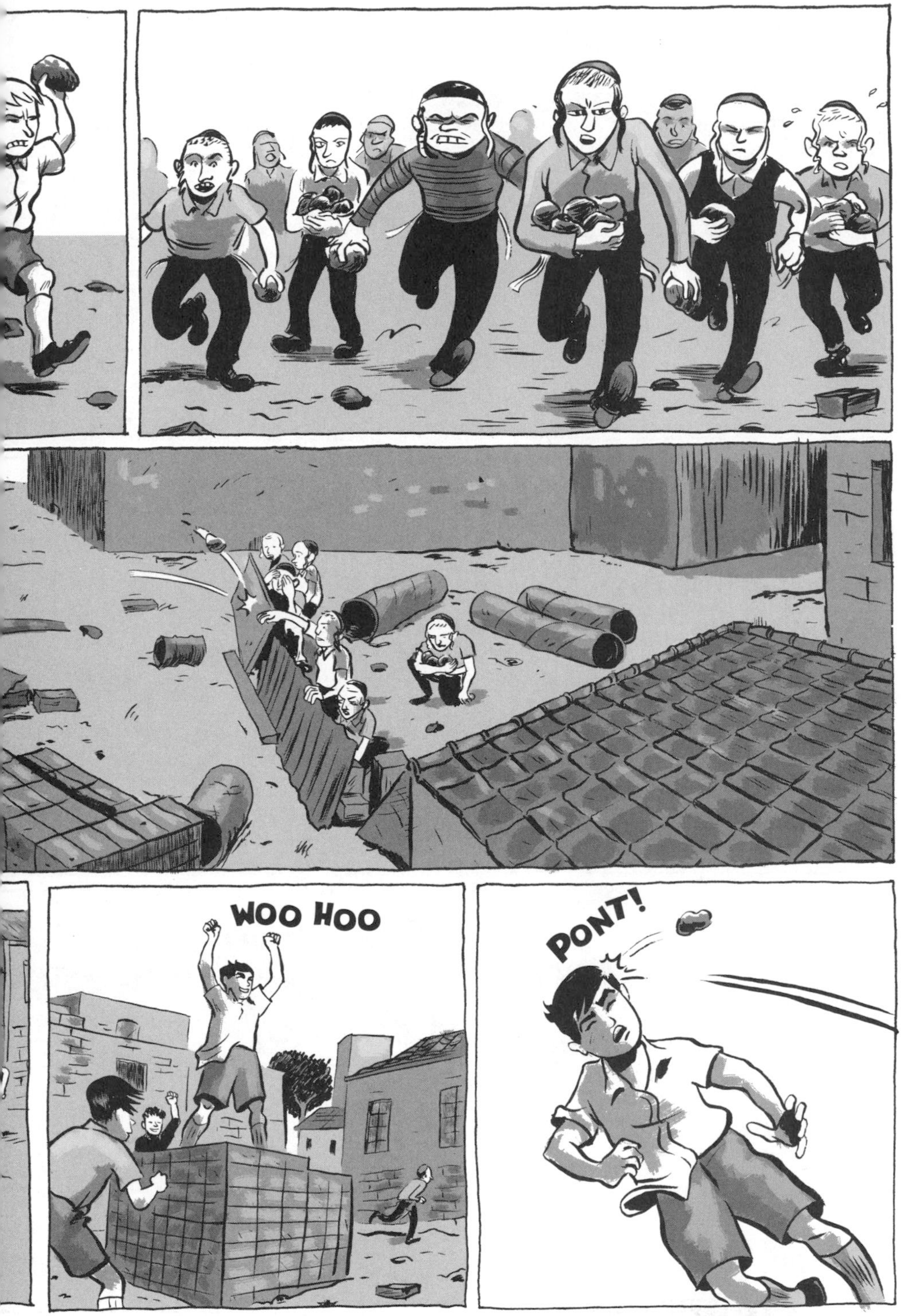
WOO HOO
PONT!

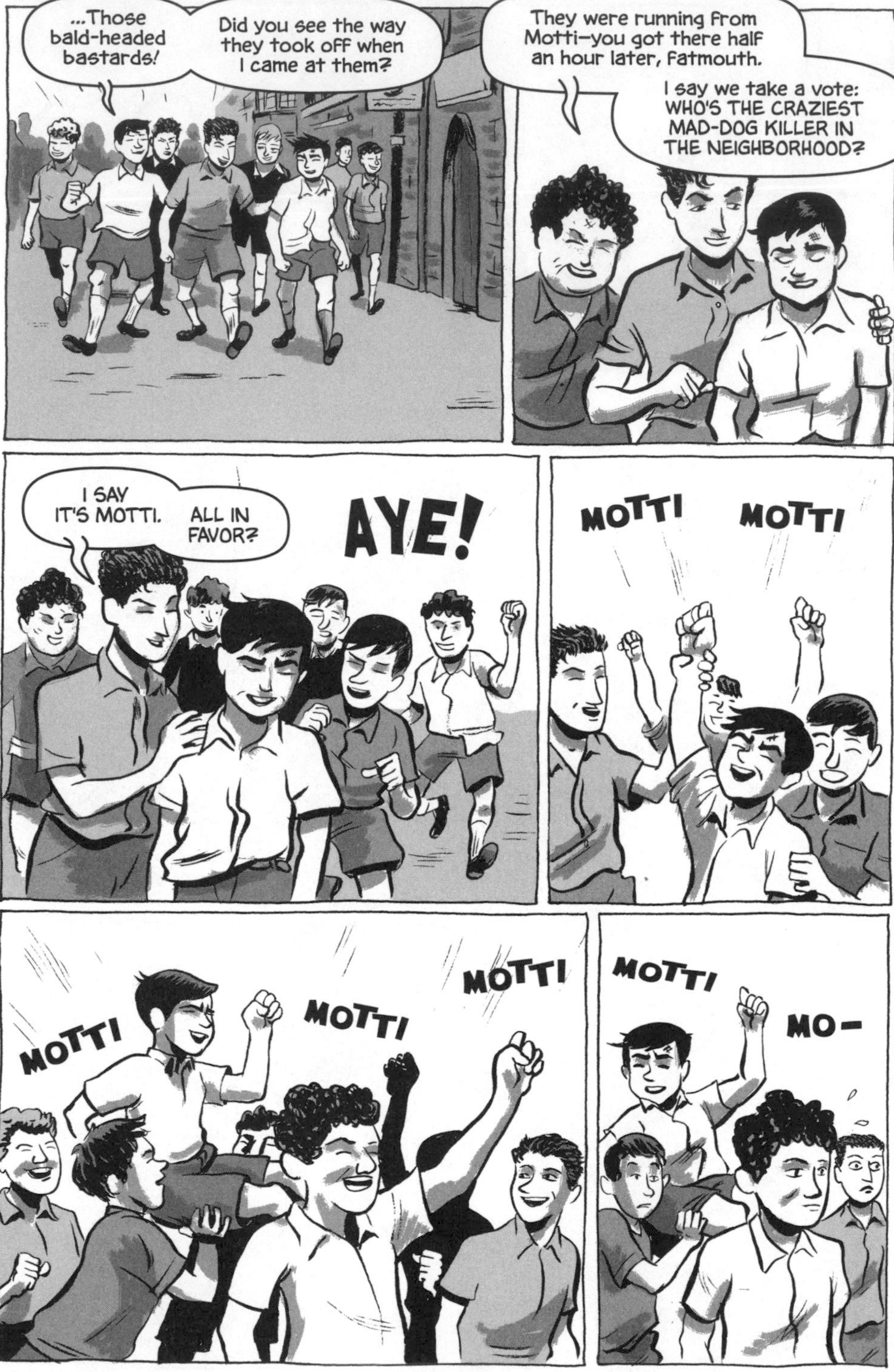
...Those bald-headed bastards!
Did you see the way they took off when I came at them?
They were running from Motti—you got there half an hour later, Fatmouth.
I say we take a vote: WHO'S THE CRAZIEST MAD-DOG KILLER IN THE NEIGHBORHOOD?
I SAY IT'S MOTTI.
ALL IN FAVOR?
AYE!
MOTTI
MOTTI
MOTTI
MOTTI
MOTTI
MOTTI
MO—

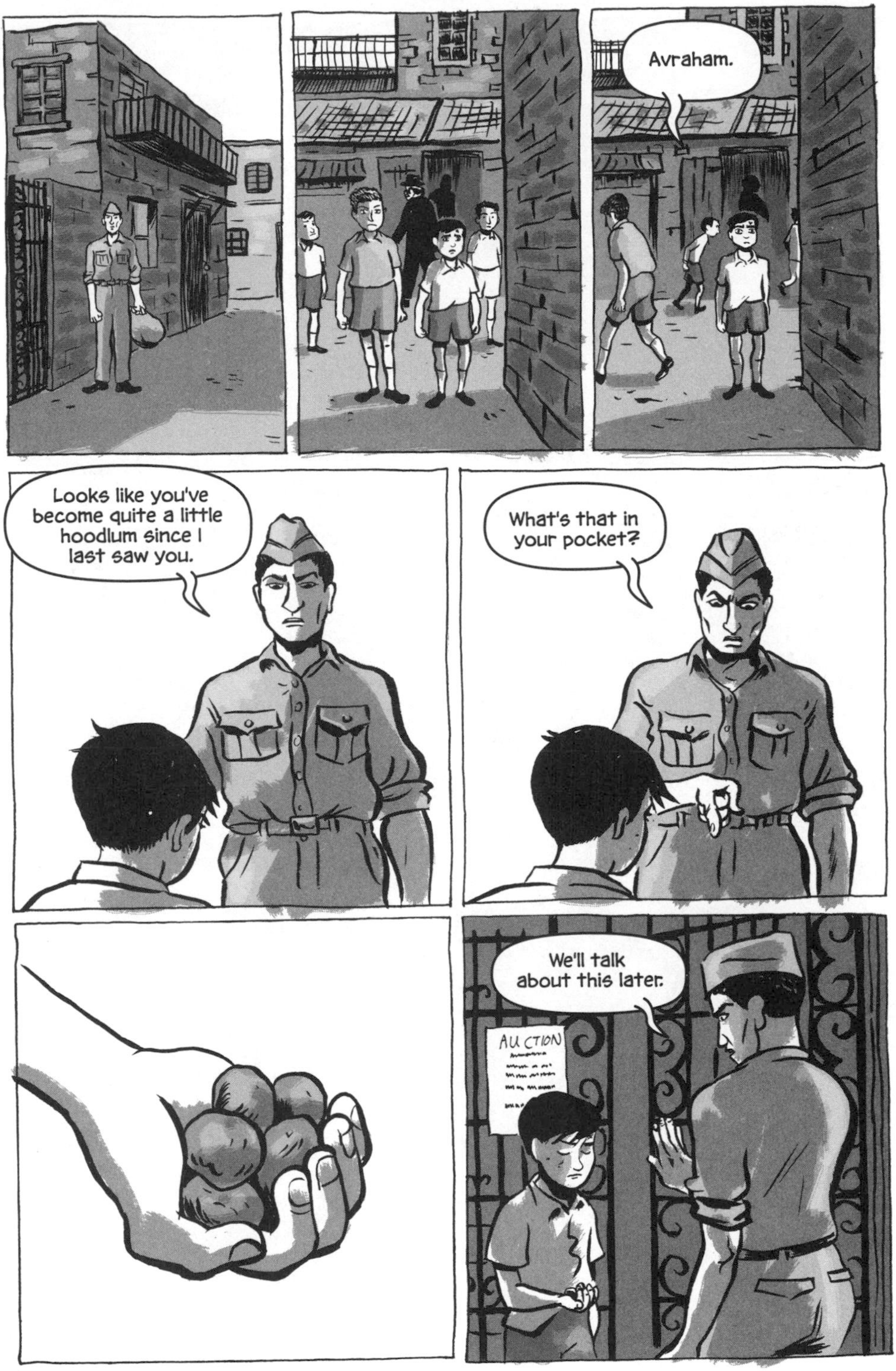

Avraham.
Looks like you've become quite a little hoodlum since I last saw you.
What's that in your pocket?
We'll talk about this later.
AUCTION

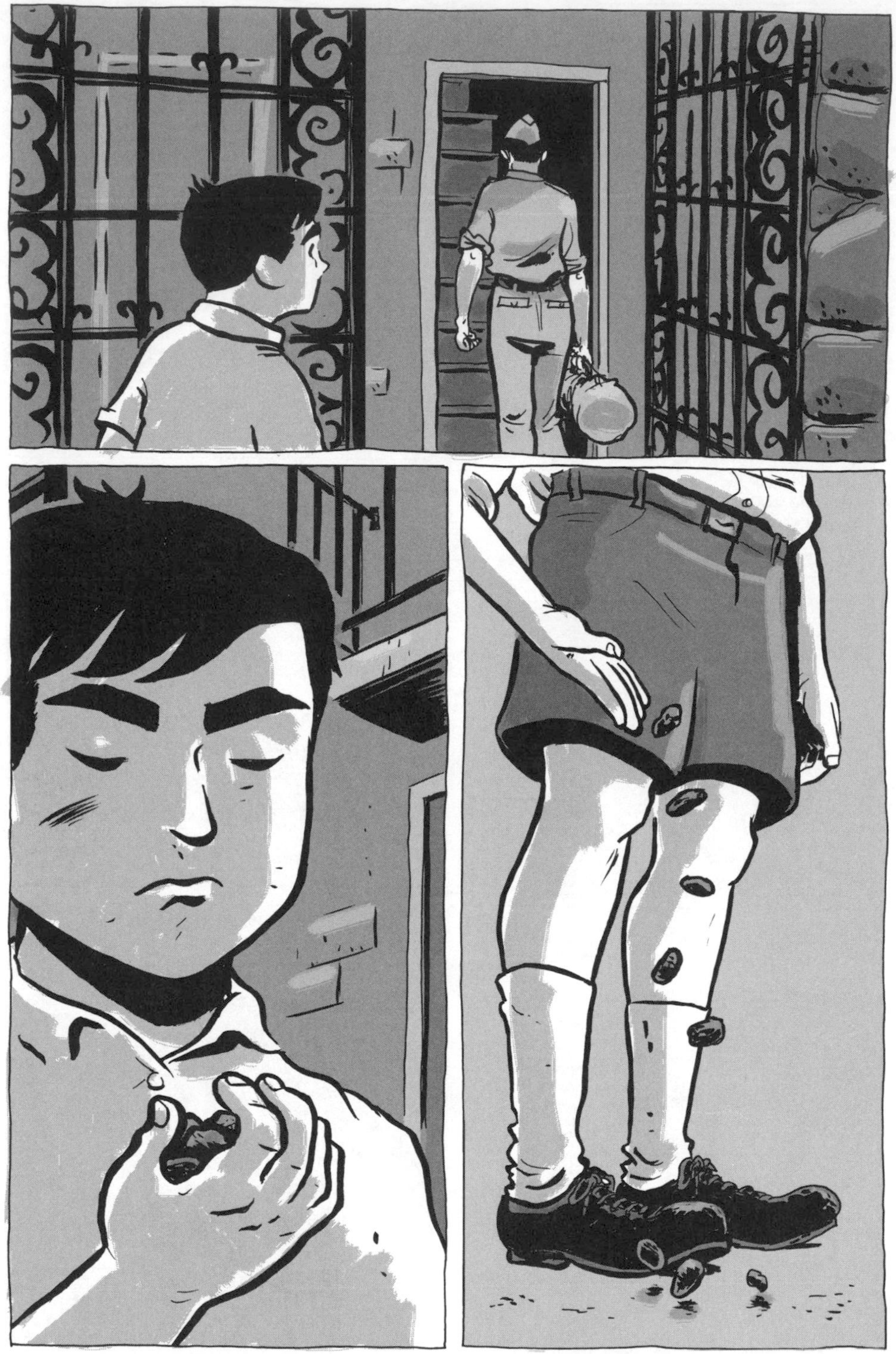

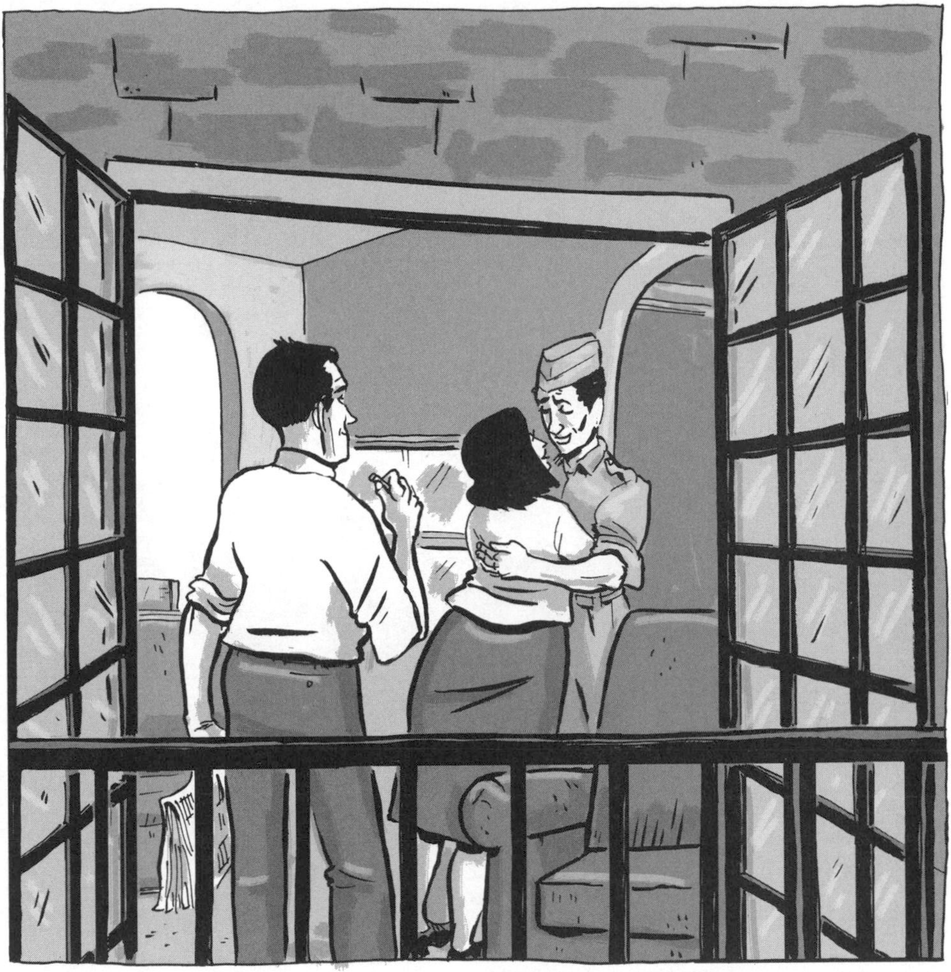

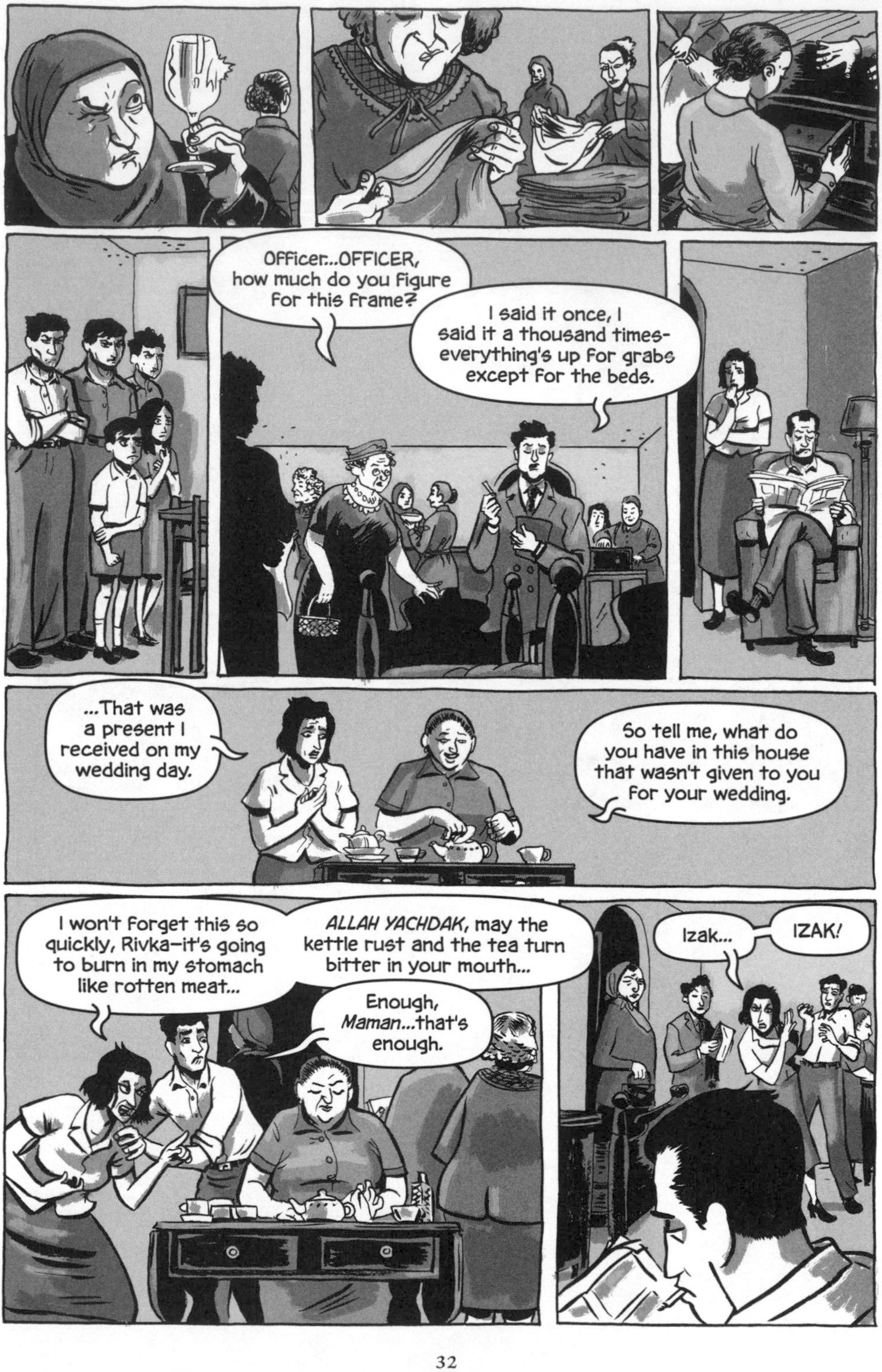
Officer...OFFICER, how much do you figure for this frame?
I said it once, I said it a thousand times-everything's up for grabs except for the beds.
...That was a present I received on my wedding day.
So tell me, what do you have in this house that wasn't given to you for your wedding.
I won't forget this so quickly, Rivka—it's going to burn in my stomach like rotten meat...
*ALLAH YACHDAK*, may the kettle rust and the tea turn bitter in your mouth...
Enough, *Maman*...that's enough.
Izak...
IZAK!

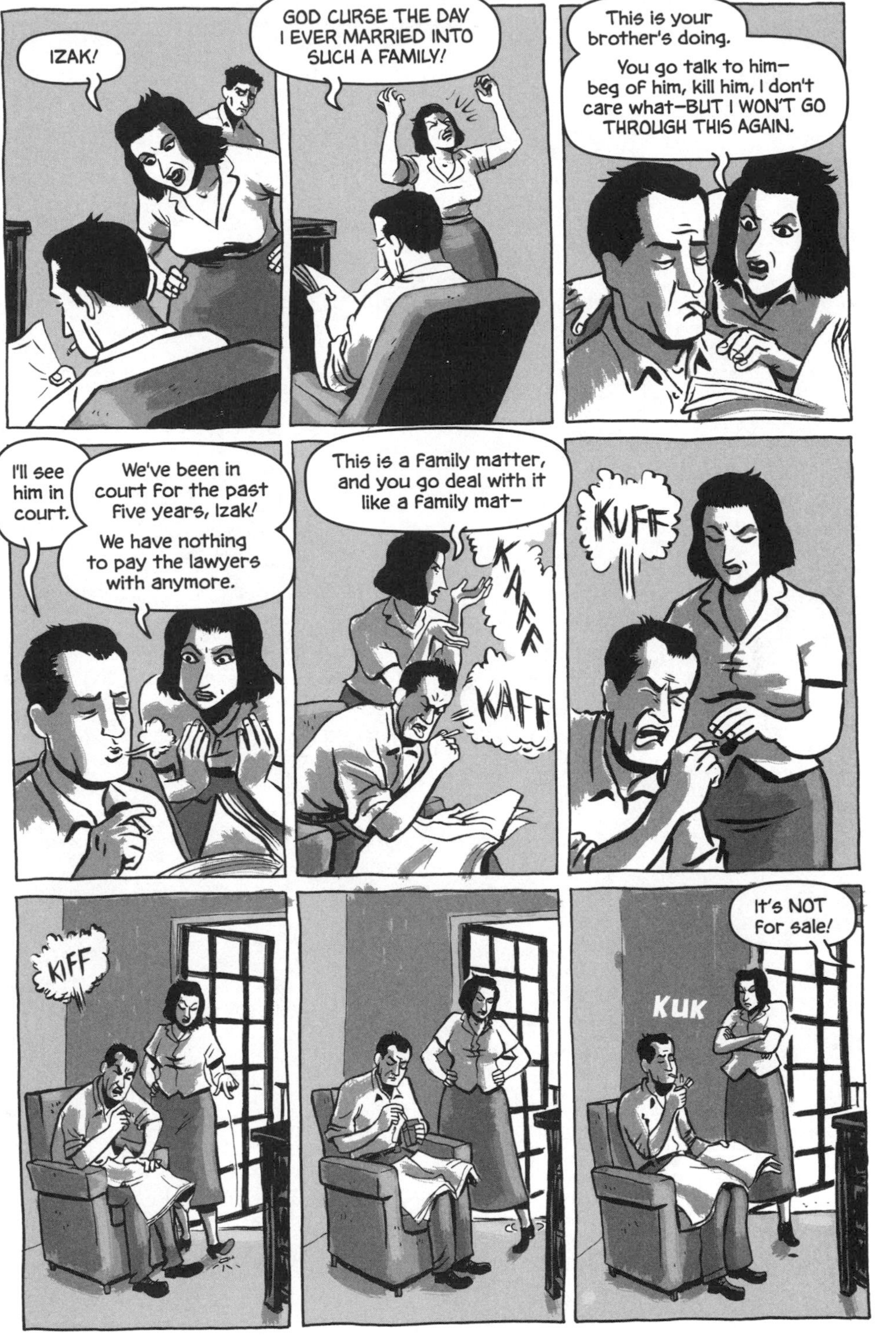
IZAK!
GOD CURSE THE DAY I EVER MARRIED INTO SUCH A FAMILY!
This is your brother's doing.
You go talk to him— beg of him, kill him, I don't care what—BUT I WON'T GO THROUGH THIS AGAIN.
I'll see him in court.
We've been in court for the past five years, Izak!
We have nothing to pay the lawyers with anymore.
This is a family matter, and you go deal with it like a family mat—
KAFF
KAFF
KUFF
KIFF
KUK
It's NOT for sale!

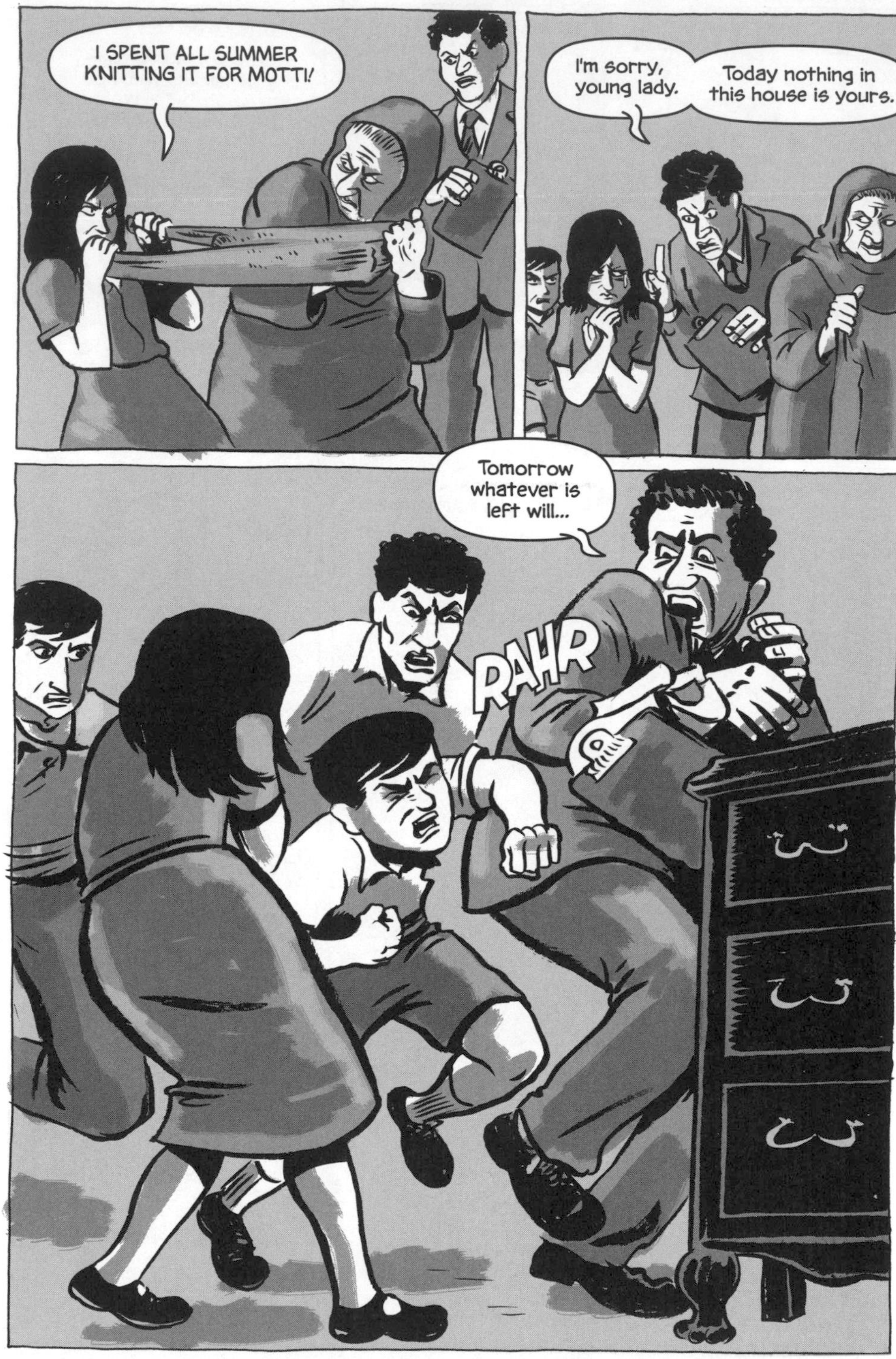
I SPENT ALL SUMMER KNITTING IT FOR MOTTI!
I'm sorry, young lady.
Today nothing in this house is yours.
Tomorrow whatever is left will...
RAHR

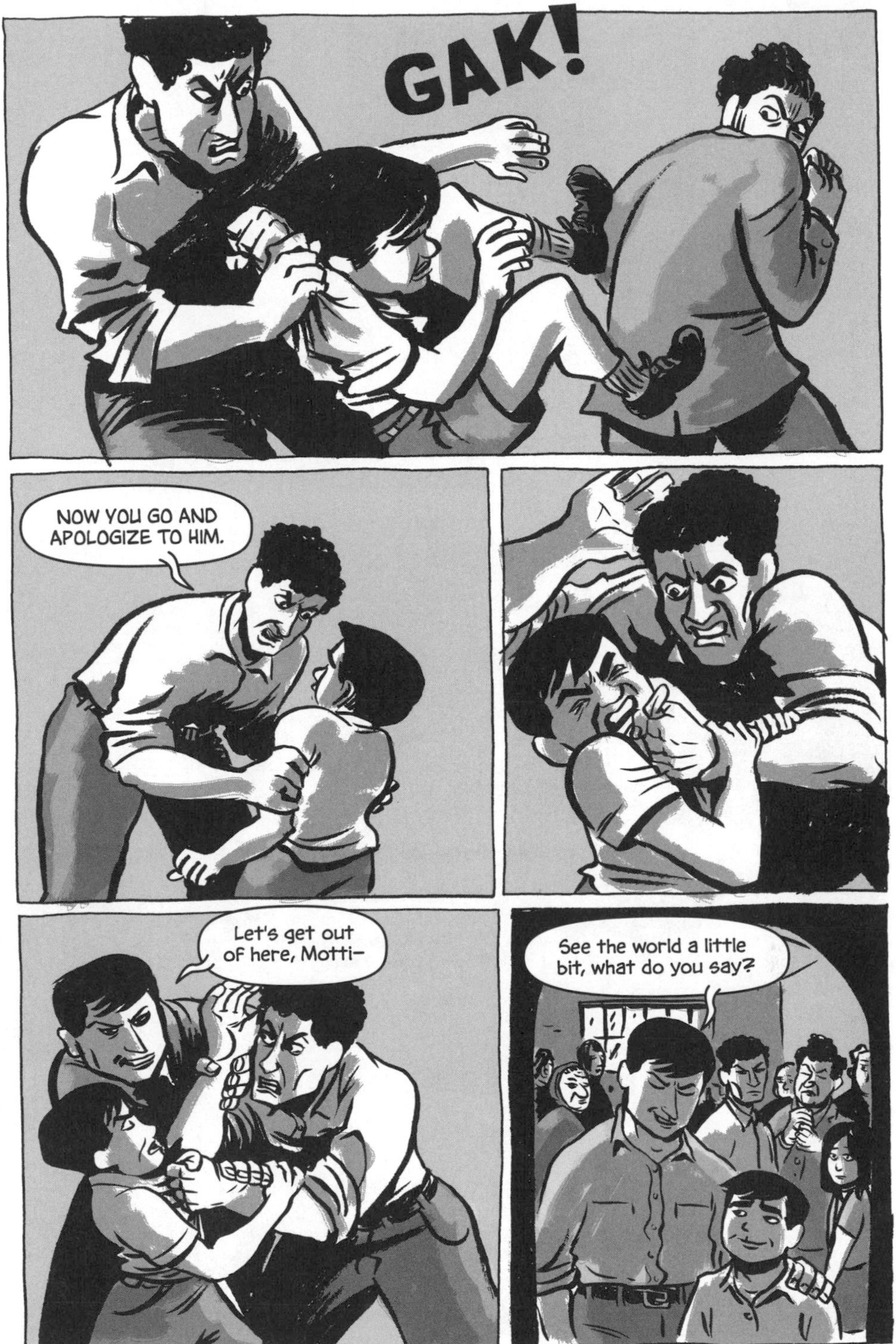
GAK!
NOW YOU GO AND APOLOGIZE TO HIM.
Let's get out of here, Motti–
See the world a little bit, what do you say?

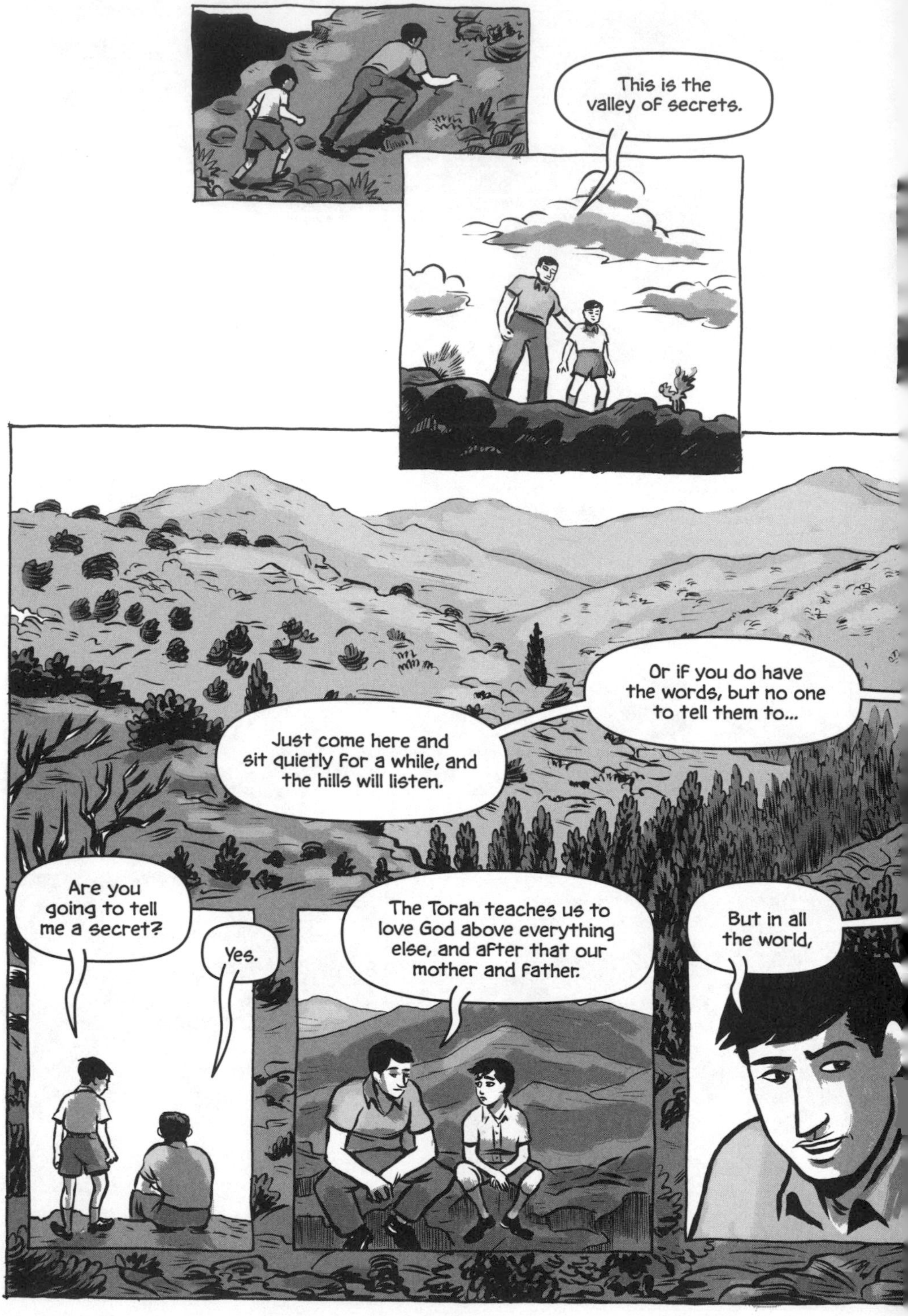
This is the valley of secrets.
Just come here and sit quietly for a while, and the hills will listen.
Or if you do have the words, but no one to tell them to...
Are you going to tell me a secret?
Yes.
The Torah teaches us to love God above everything else, and after that our mother and father.
But in all the world,

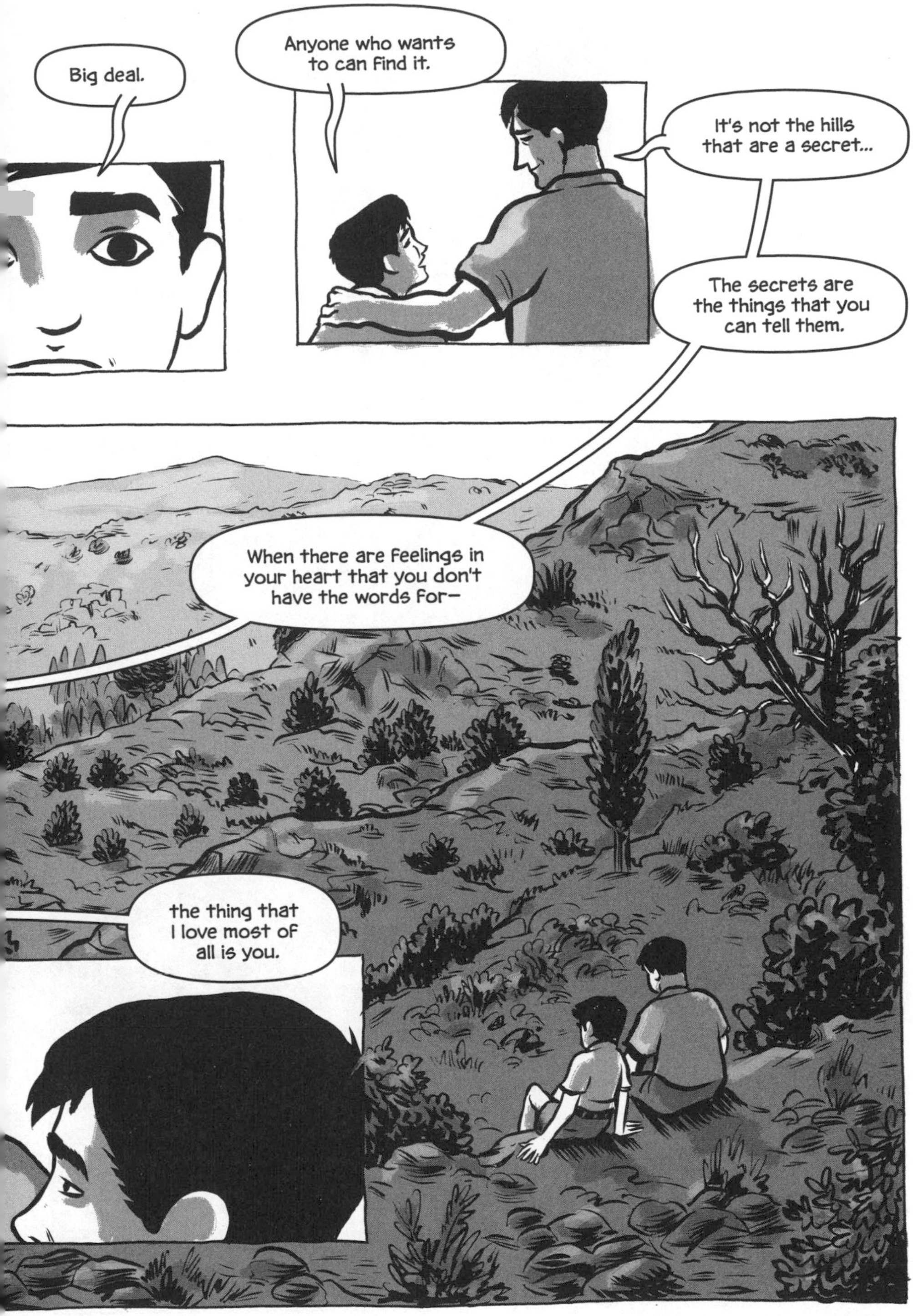
Big deal.
Anyone who wants to can find it.
It's not the hills that are a secret...
The secrets are the things that you can tell them.
When there are feelings in your heart that you don't have the words for—
the thing that I love most of all is you.

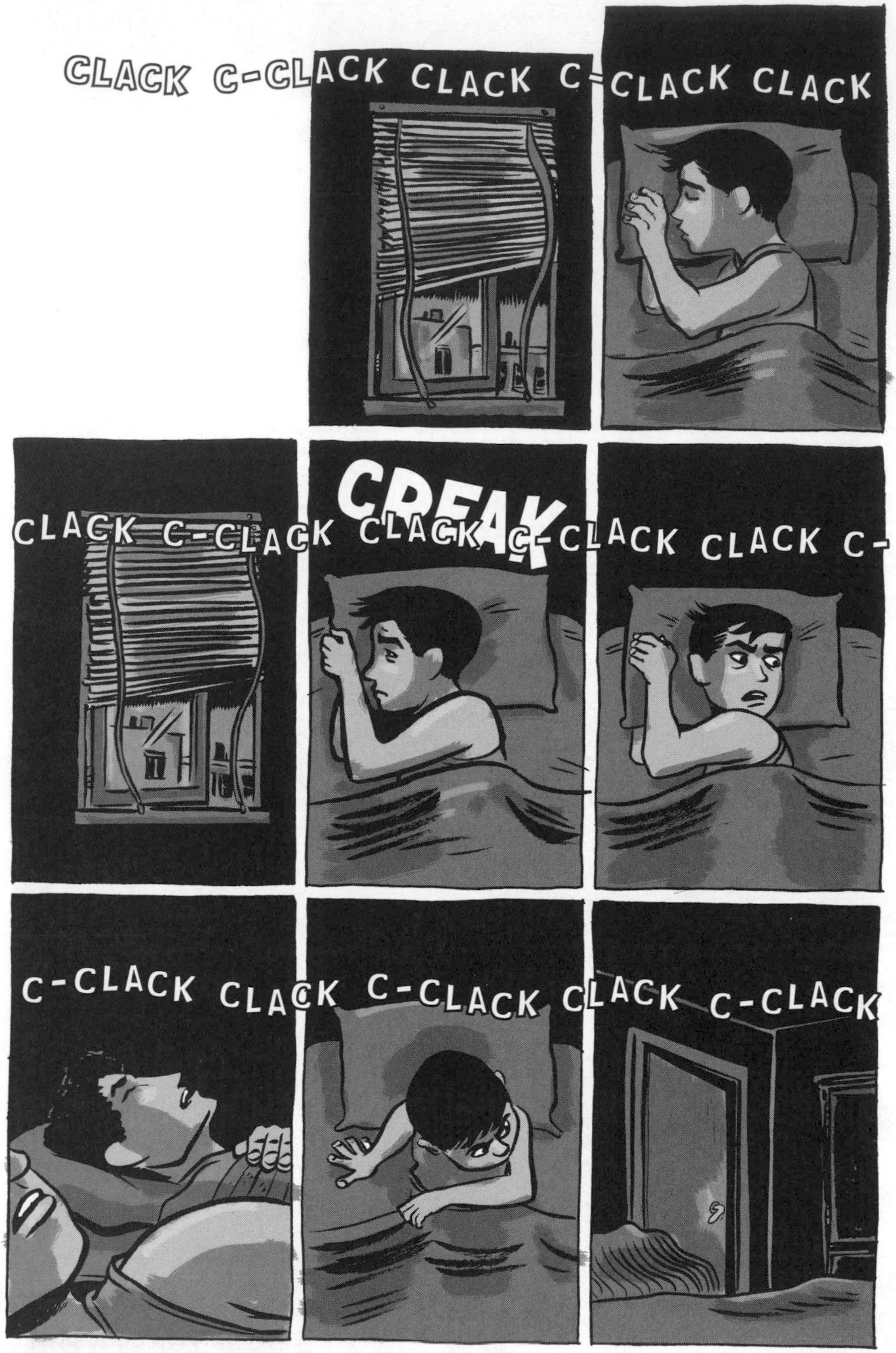
CLACK C-CLACK CLACK C-CLACK CLACK
CLACK C-CLACK CLACK C-CLACK CLACK C-
CREAK
C-CLACK CLACK C-CLACK CLACK C-CLACK

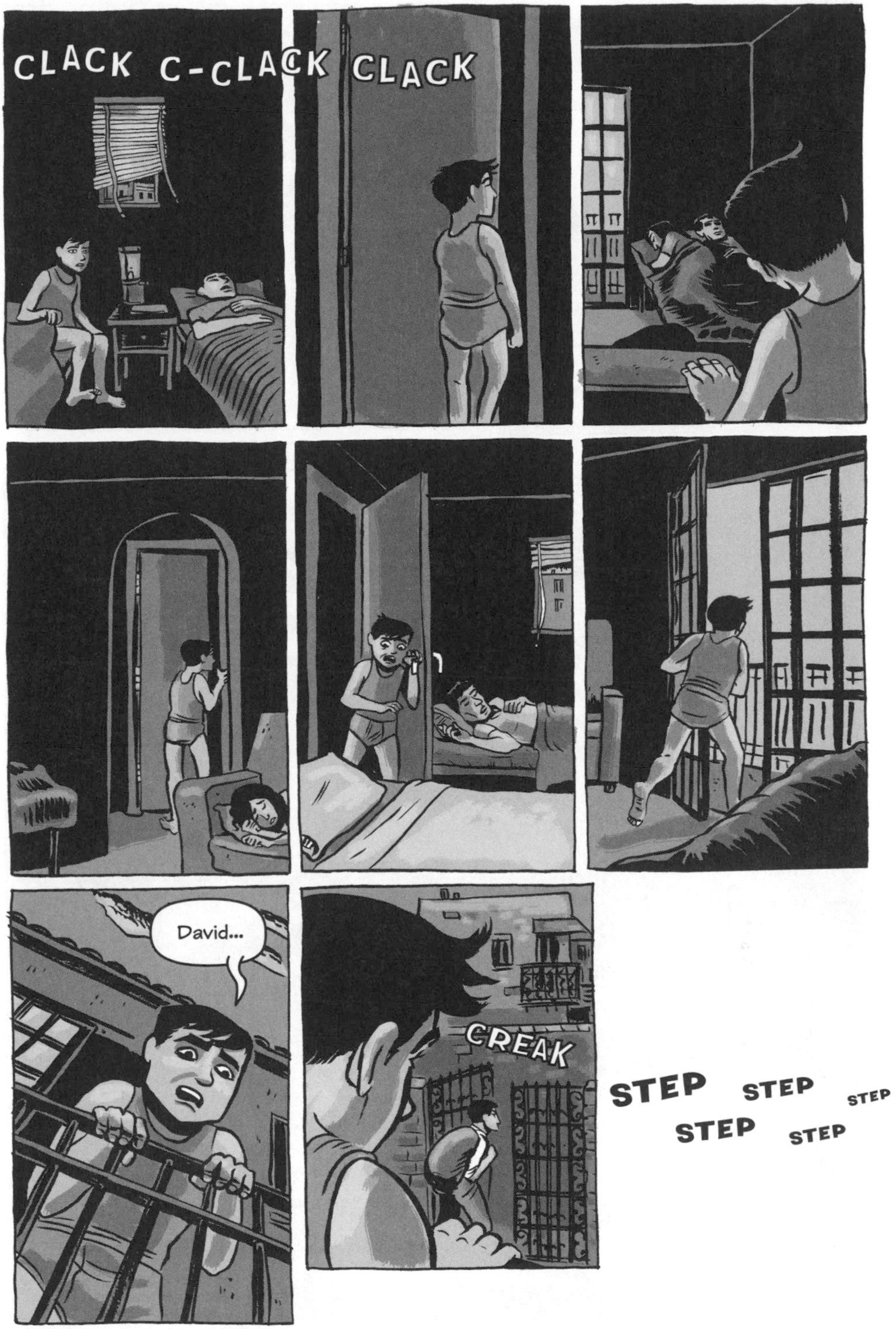
CLACK C-CLACK CLACK
David...
CREAK
STEP STEP STEP
STEP STEP

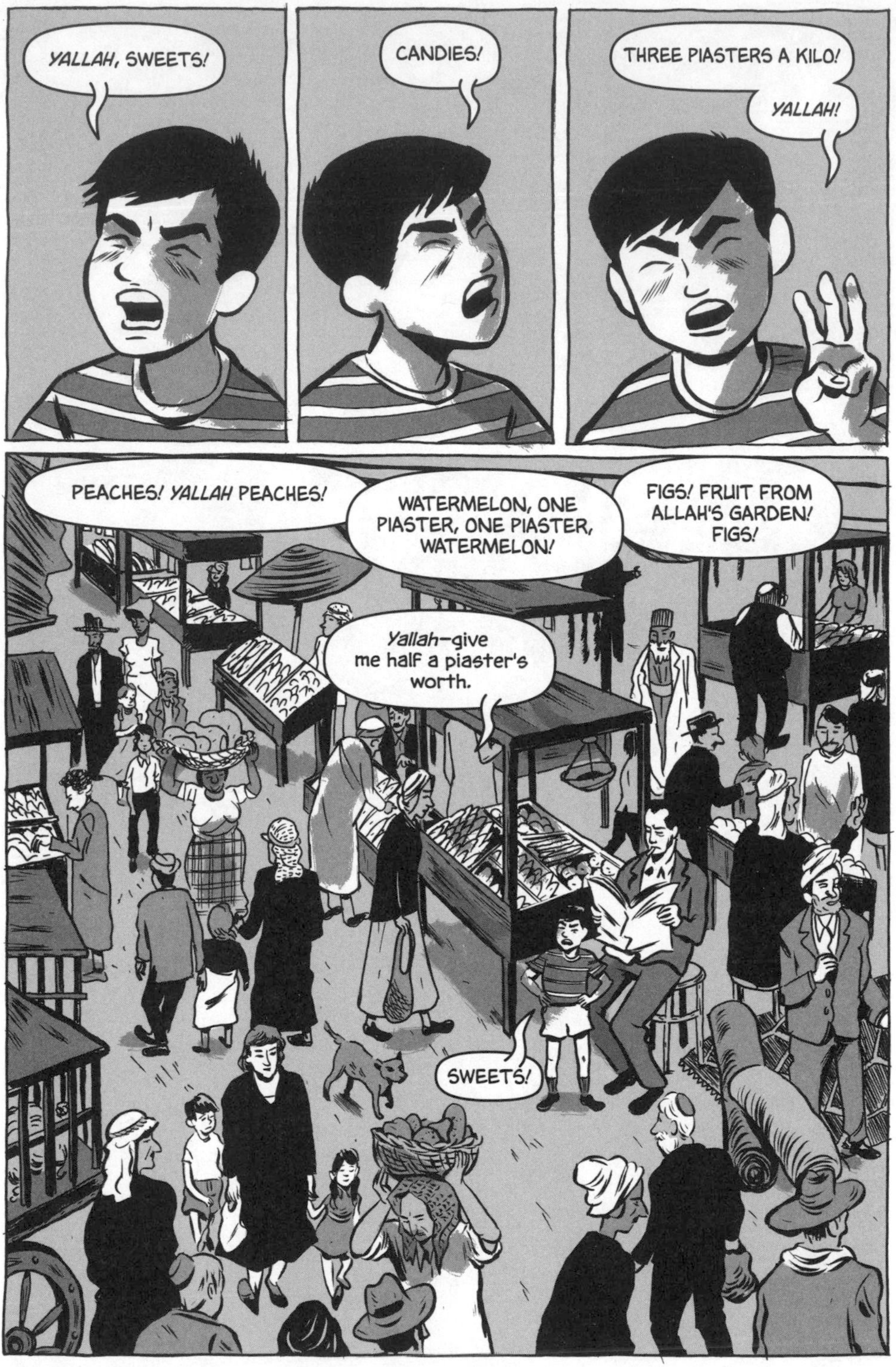
YALLAH, SWEETS!
CANDIES!
THREE PIASTERS A KILO!
YALLAH!
PEACHES! YALLAH PEACHES!
WATERMELON, ONE PIASTER, ONE PIASTER, WATERMELON!
FIGS! FRUIT FROM ALLAH'S GARDEN! FIGS!
Yallah—give me half a piaster's worth.
SWEETS!

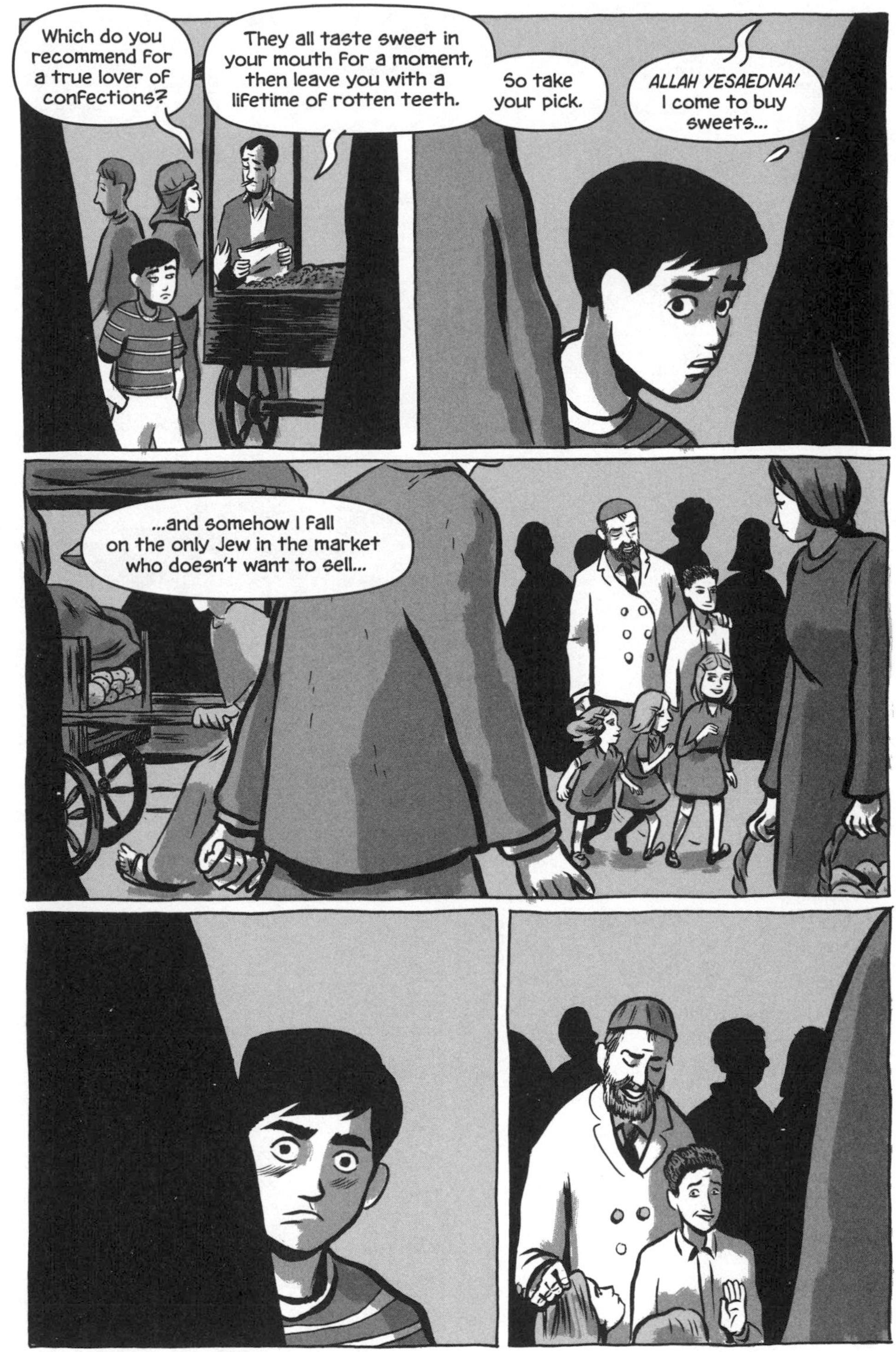
Which do you recommend for a true lover of confections?
They all taste sweet in your mouth for a moment, then leave you with a lifetime of rotten teeth.
So take your pick.
ALLAH YESAEDNA! I come to buy sweets...
...and somehow I fall on the only Jew in the market who doesn't want to sell...

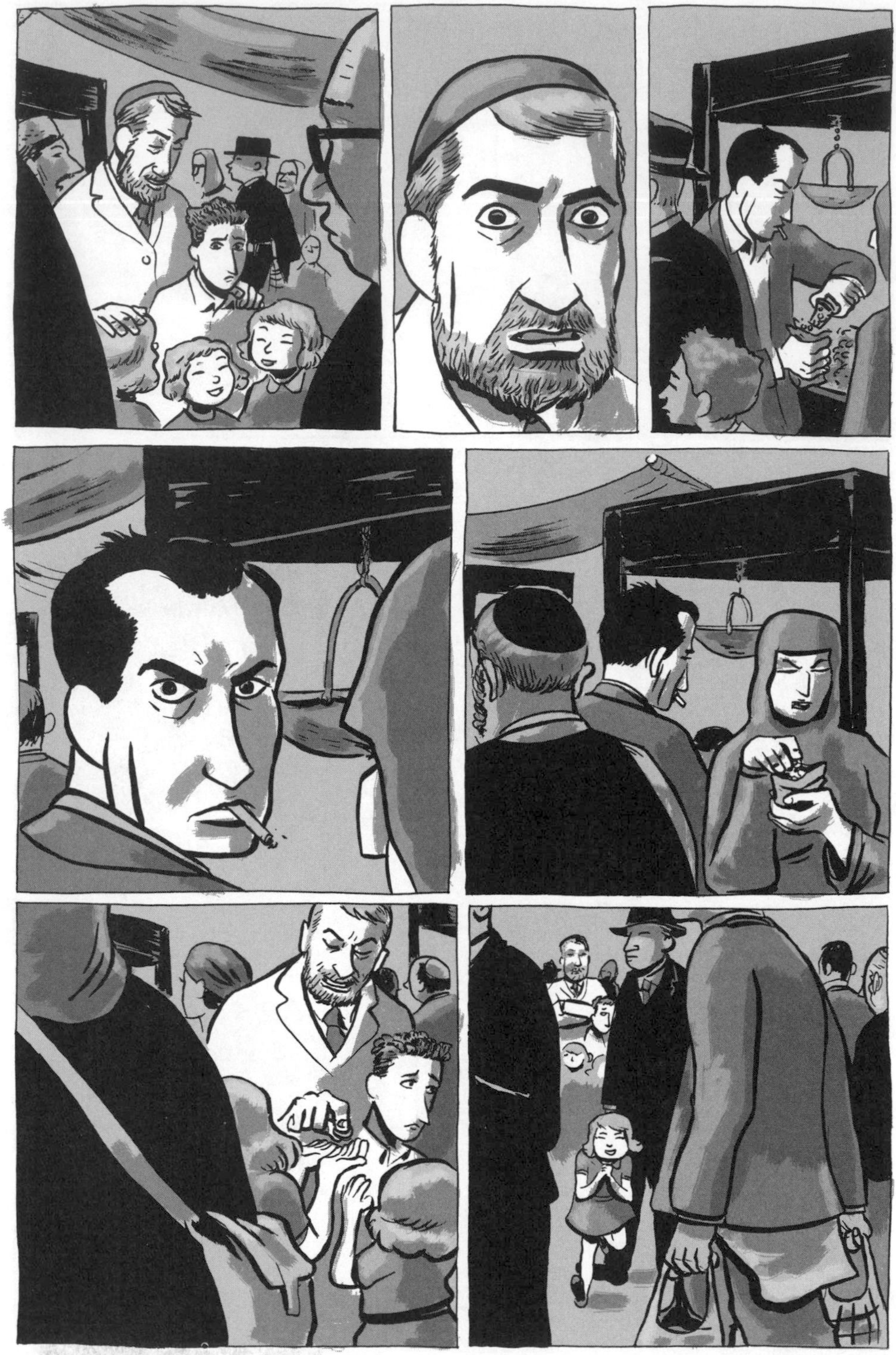

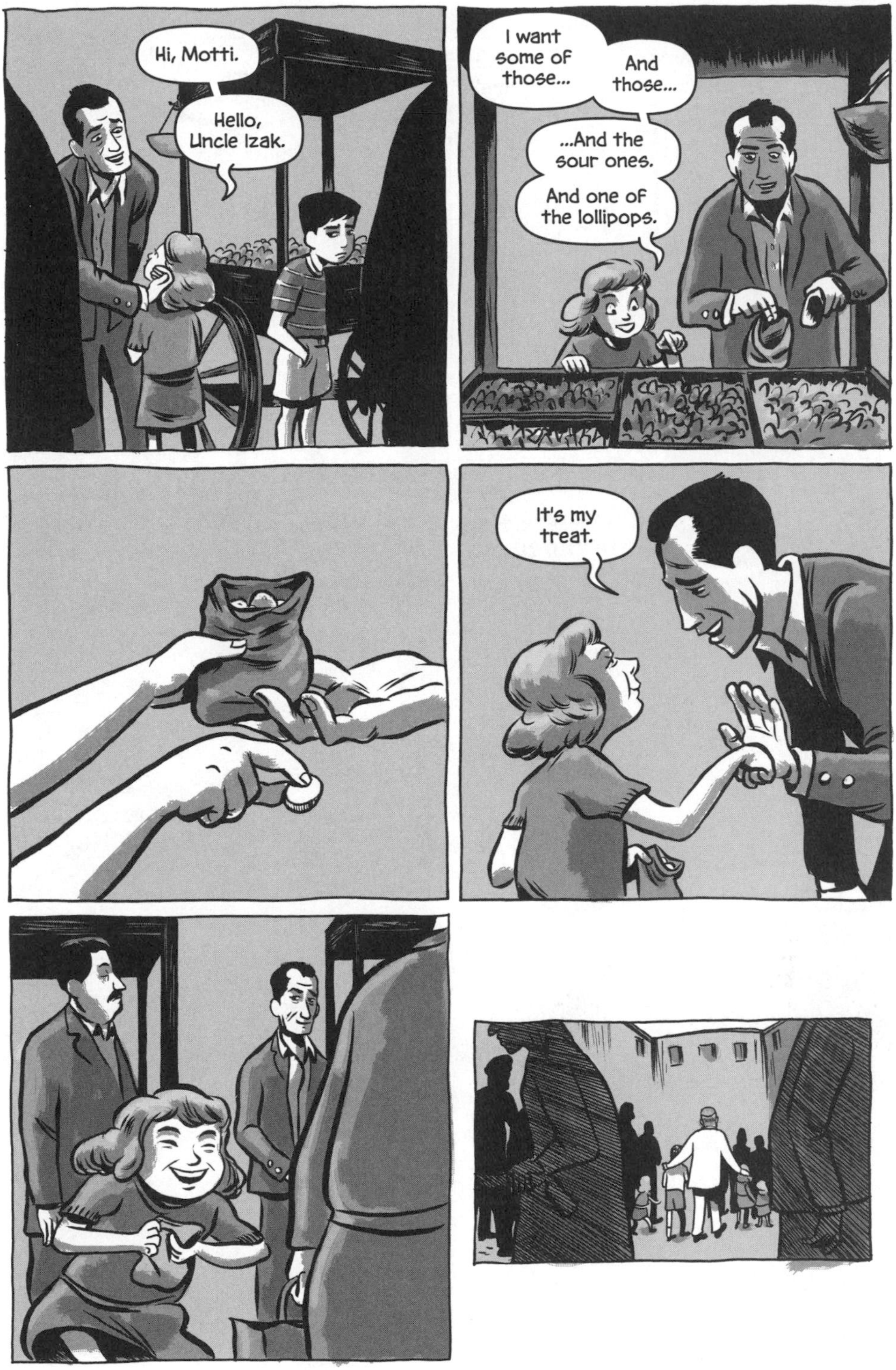
Hi, Motti.
Hello, Uncle Izak.
I want some of those...
And those...
...And the sour ones.
And one of the lollipops.
It's my treat.

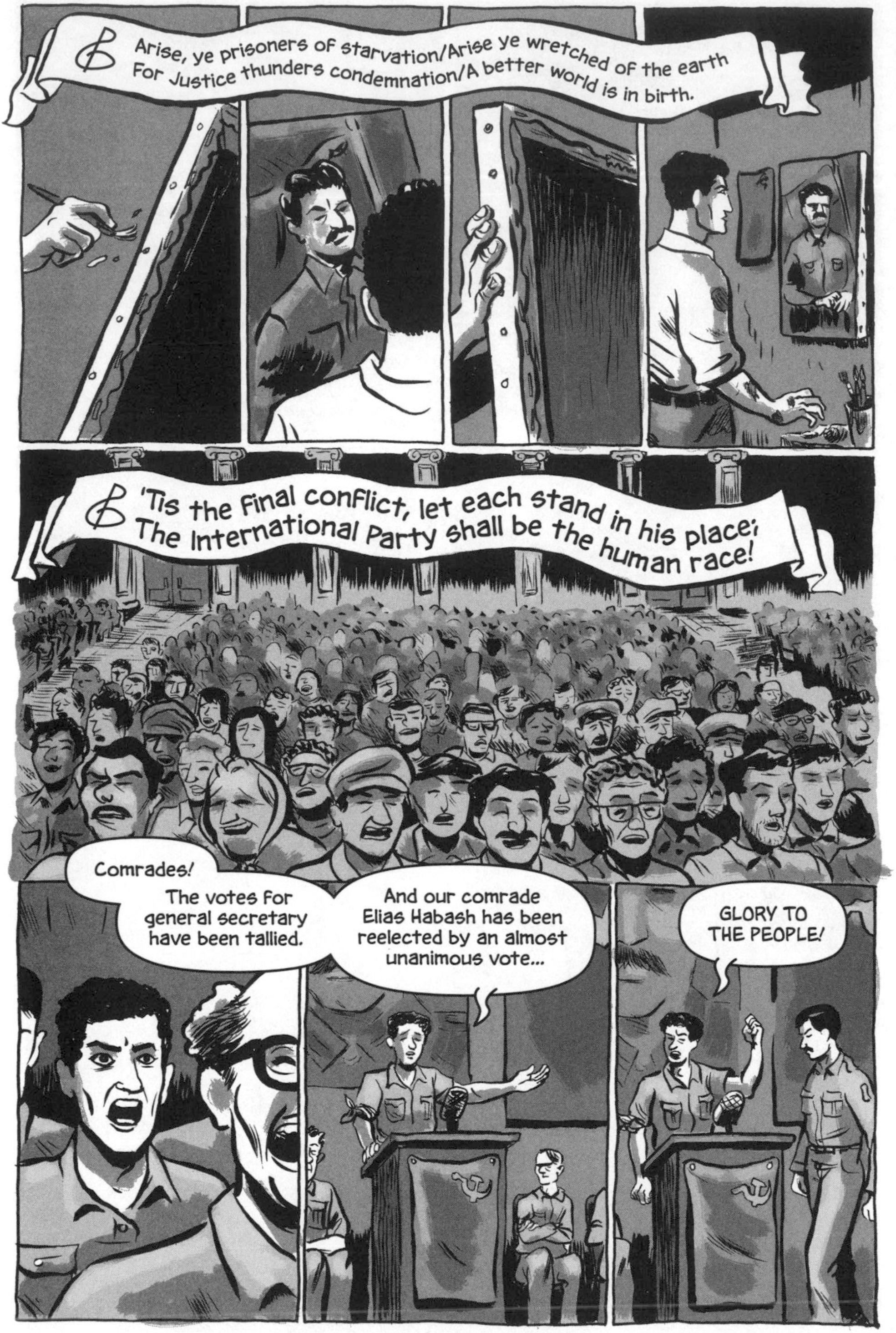
Arise, ye prisoners of starvation/Arise ye wretched of the earth
For Justice thunders condemnation/A better world is in birth.
'Tis the final conflict, let each stand in his place;
The International Party shall be the human race!
Comrades!
The votes for general secretary have been tallied.
And our comrade Elias Habash has been reelected by an almost unanimous vote...
GLORY TO THE PEOPLE!

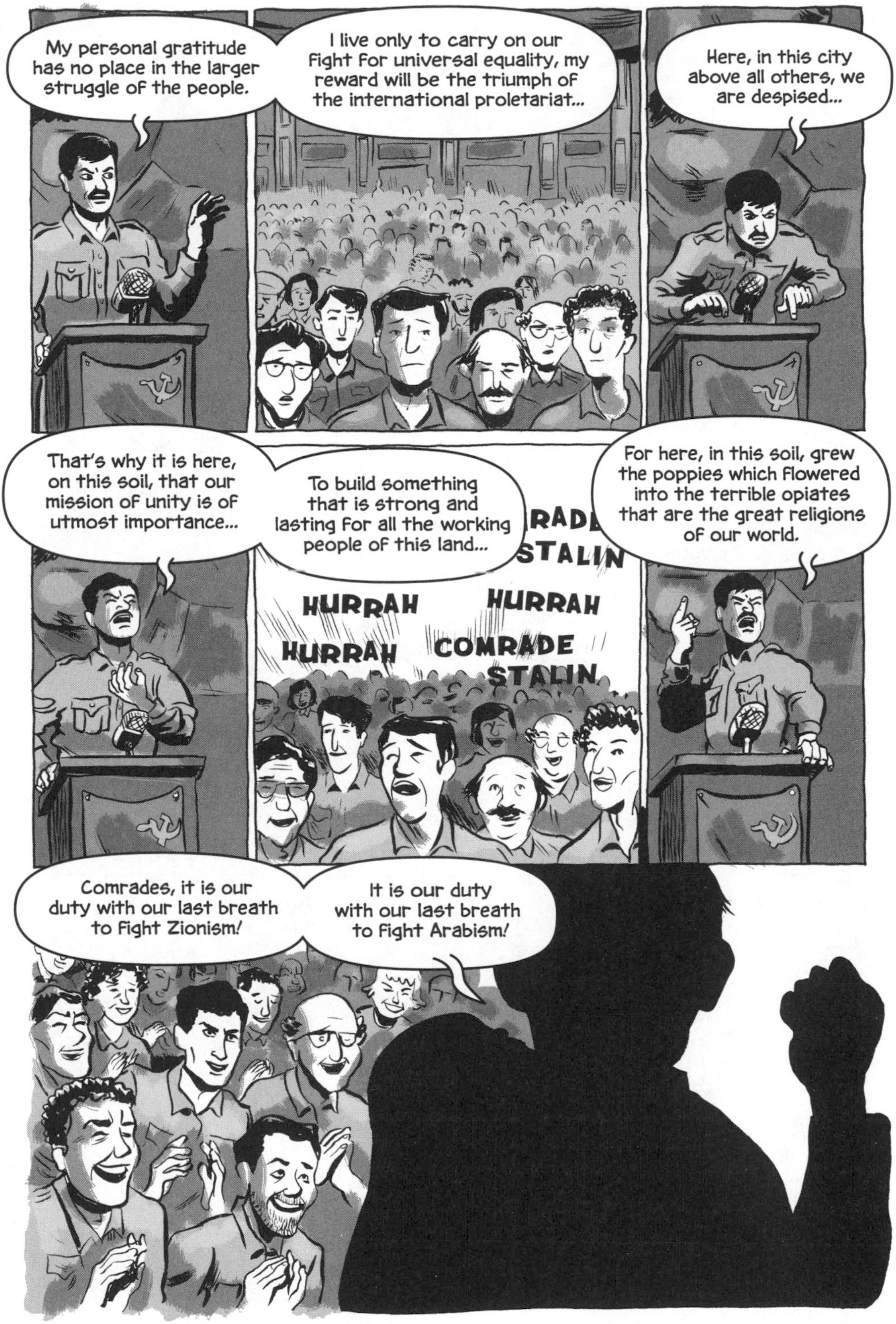
My personal gratitude has no place in the larger struggle of the people.
I live only to carry on our fight for universal equality, my reward will be the triumph of the international proletariat...
Here, in this city above all others, we are despised...
That's why it is here, on this soil, that our mission of unity is of utmost importance...
To build something that is strong and lasting for all the working people of this land...
RADE STALIN
HURRAH
HURRAH
HURRAH
COMRADE STALIN
For here, in this soil, grew the poppies which flowered into the terrible opiates that are the great religions of our world.
Comrades, it is our duty with our last breath to fight Zionism!
It is our duty with our last breath to fight Arabism!

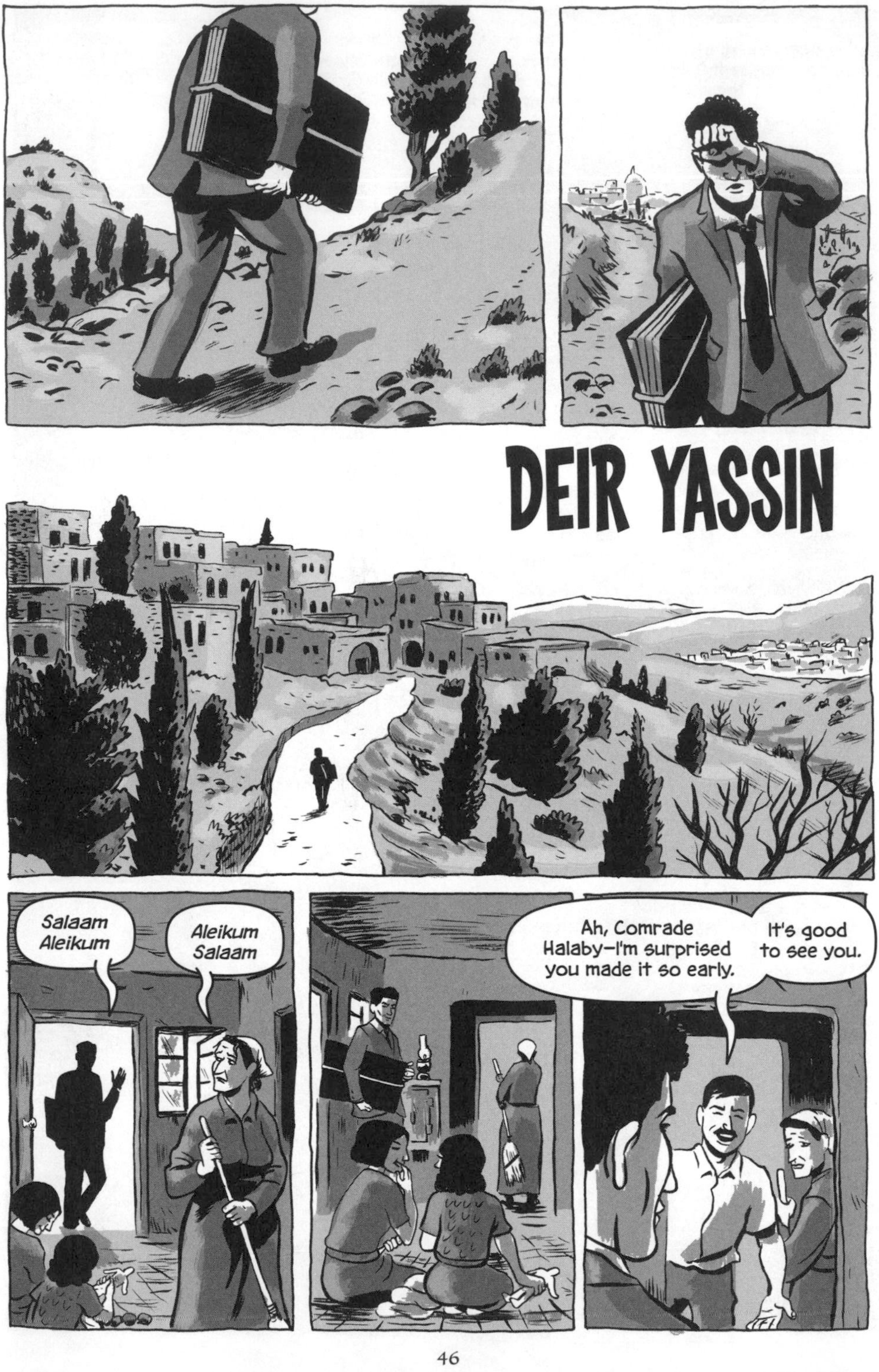
DEIR YASSIN
Salaam Aleikum
Aleikum Salaam
Ah, Comrade Halaby—I'm surprised you made it so early.
It's good to see you.

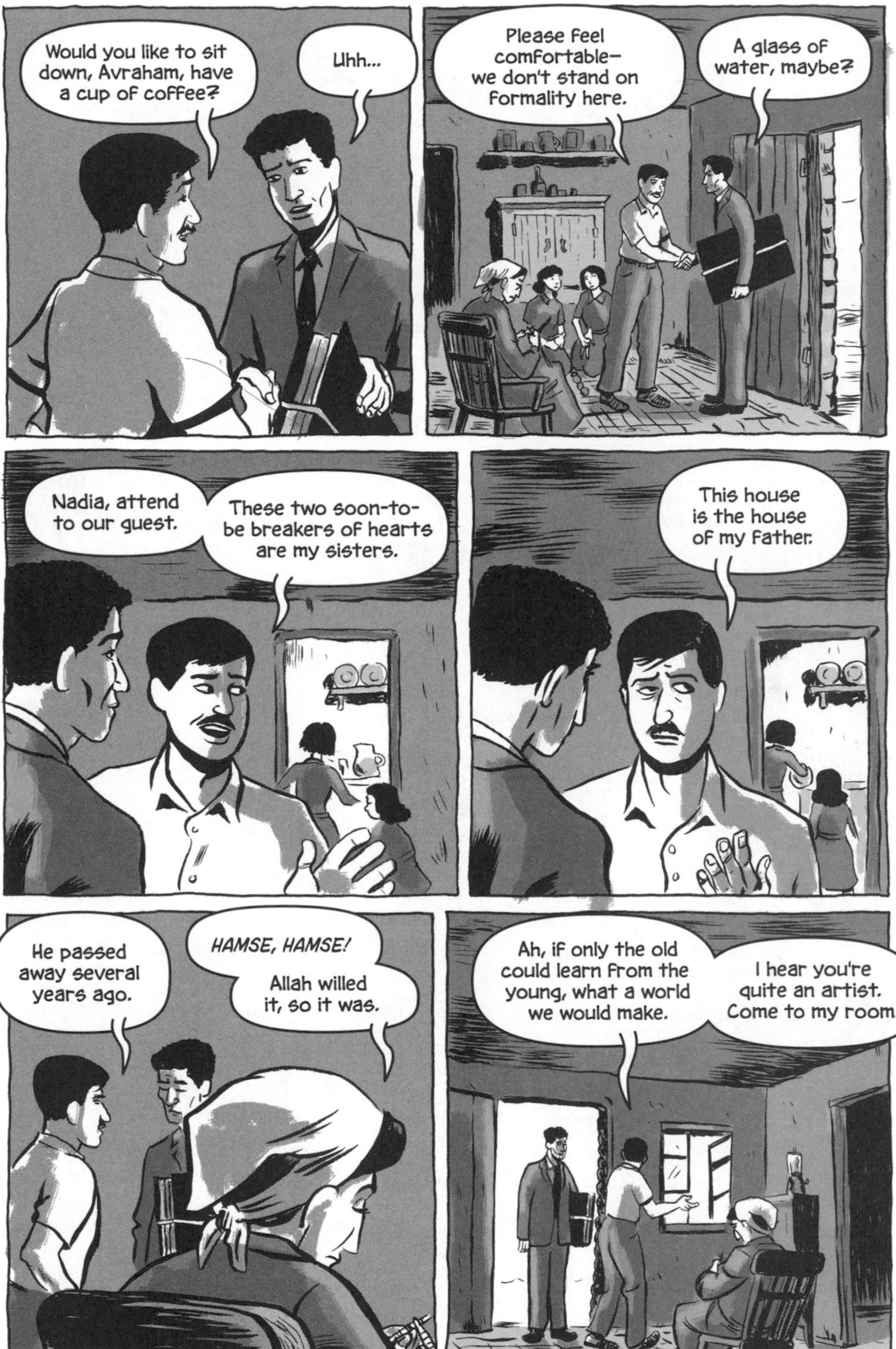
Would you like to sit down, Avraham, have a cup of coffee?
Uhh...
Please feel comfortable— we don't stand on formality here.
A glass of water, maybe?
Nadia, attend to our guest.
These two soon-to-be breakers of hearts are my sisters.
This house is the house of my father.
He passed away several years ago.
HAMSE, HAMSE!
Allah willed it, so it was.
Ah, if only the old could learn from the young, what a world we would make.
I hear you're quite an artist. Come to my room.

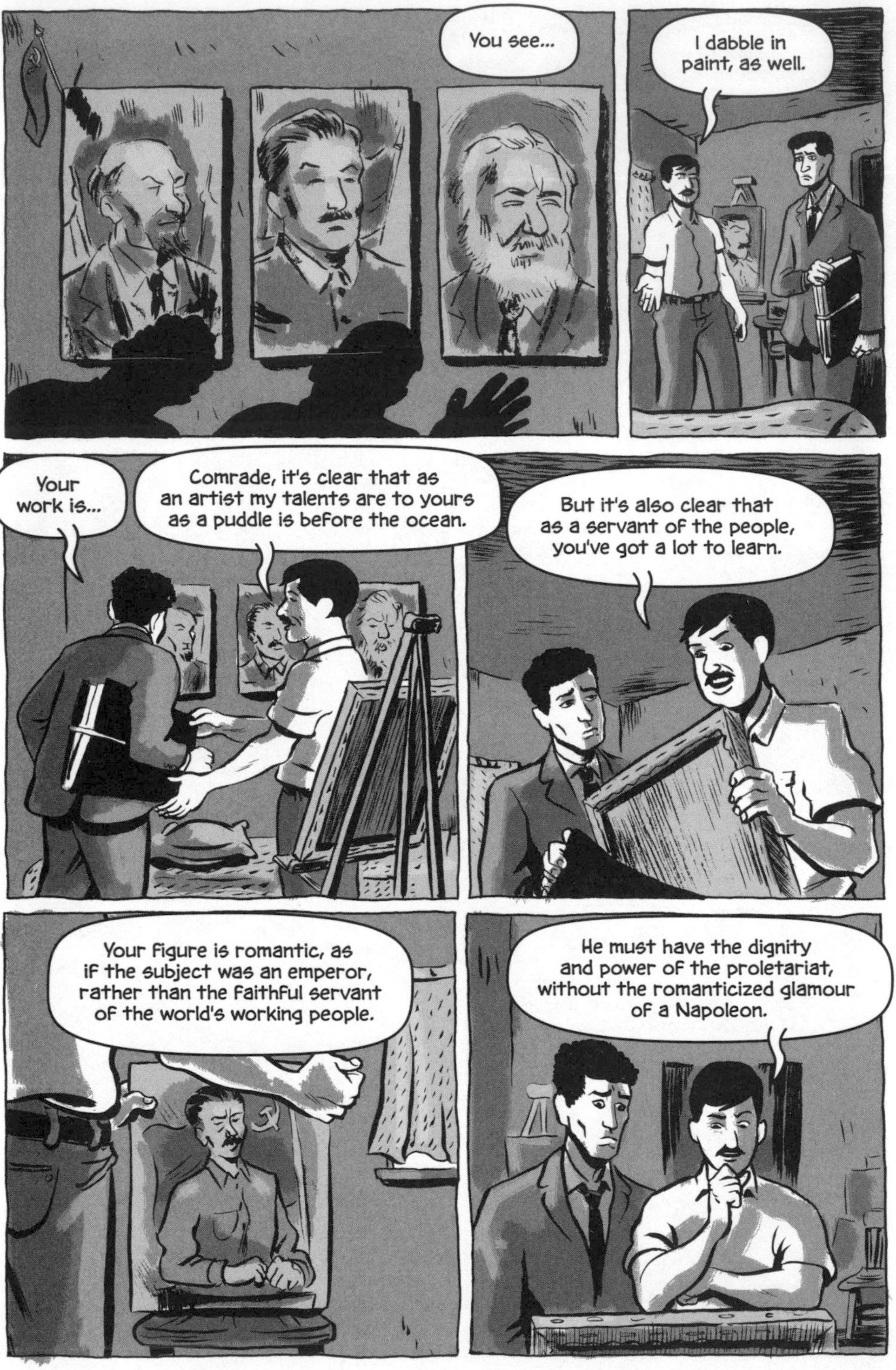
You see...
I dabble in paint, as well.
Your work is...
Comrade, it's clear that as an artist my talents are to yours as a puddle is before the ocean.
But it's also clear that as a servant of the people, you've got a lot to learn.
Your figure is romantic, as if the subject was an emperor, rather than the faithful servant of the world's working people.
He must have the dignity and power of the proletariat, without the romanticized glamour of a Napoleon.

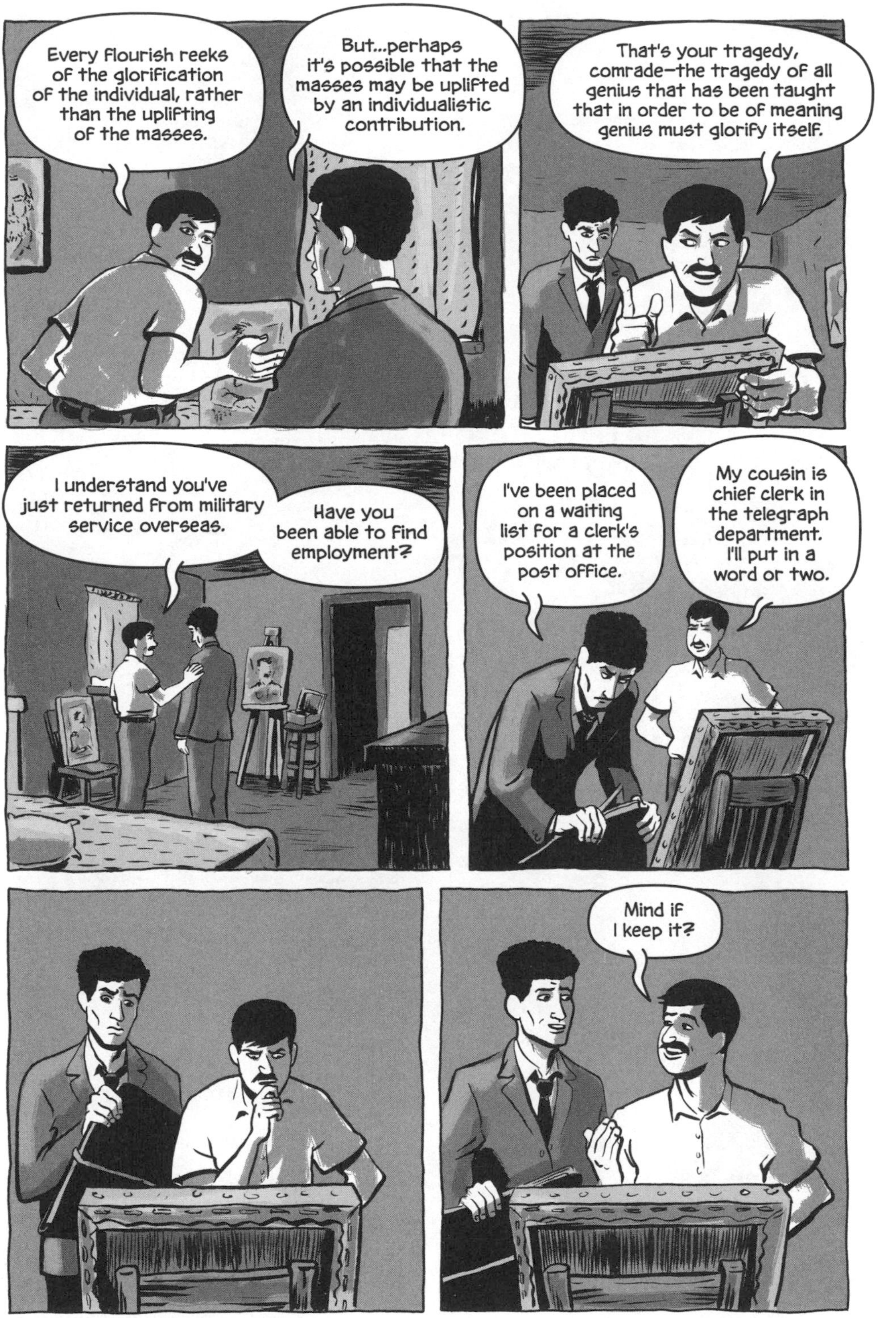
Every flourish reeks of the glorification of the individual, rather than the uplifting of the masses.
But...perhaps it's possible that the masses may be uplifted by an individualistic contribution.
That's your tragedy, comrade—the tragedy of all genius that has been taught that in order to be of meaning genius must glorify itself.
I understand you've just returned from military service overseas.
Have you been able to find employment?
I've been placed on a waiting list for a clerk's position at the post office.
My cousin is chief clerk in the telegraph department. I'll put in a word or two.
Mind if I keep it?

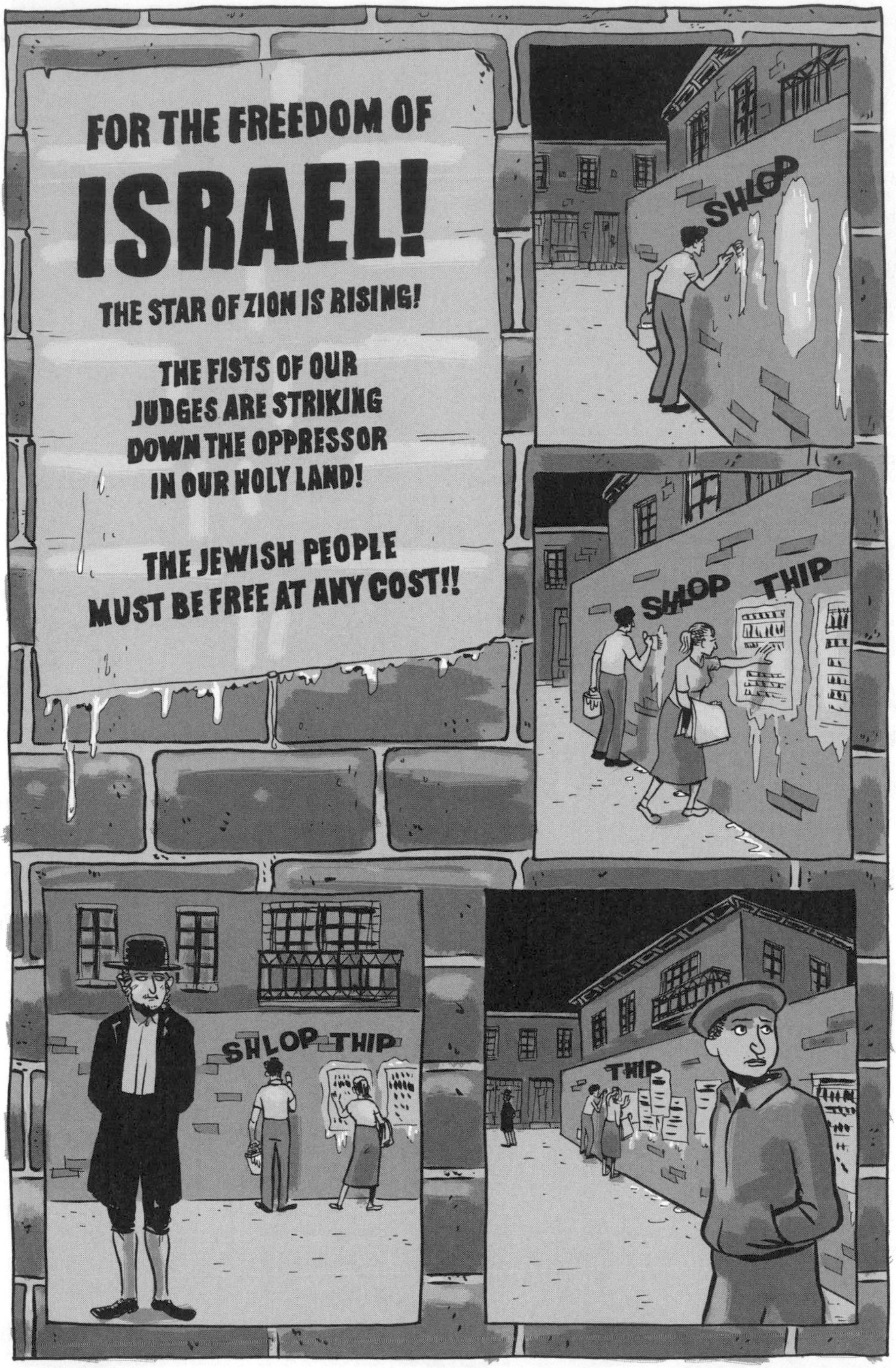
FOR THE FREEDOM OF
ISRAEL!
THE STAR OF ZION IS RISING!
THE FISTS OF OUR JUDGES ARE STRIKING DOWN THE OPPRESSOR IN OUR HOLY LAND!
THE JEWISH PEOPLE MUST BE FREE AT ANY COST!!
SHLOP
SHLOP
THIP
SHLOP
THIP
THIP

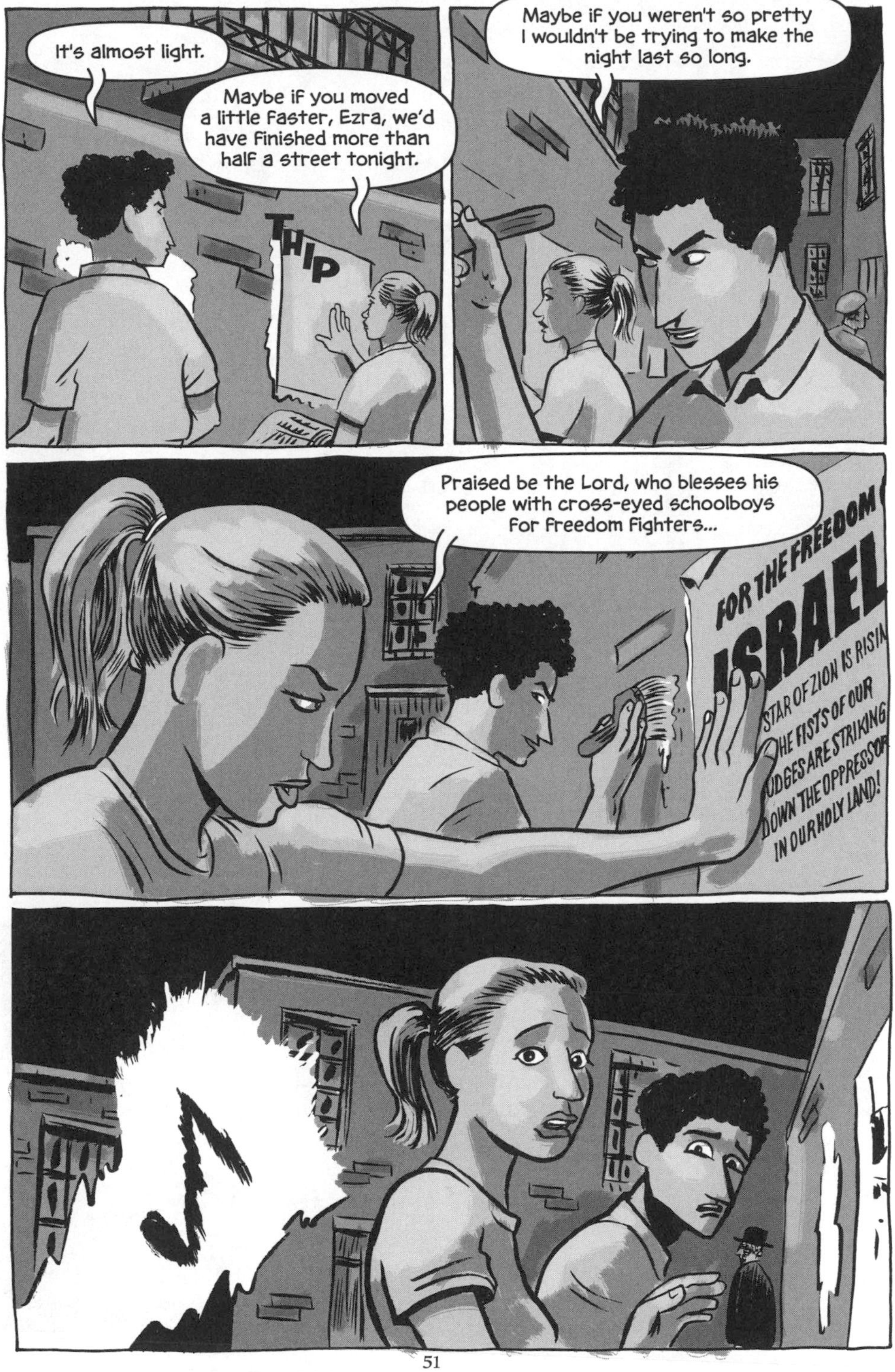
It's almost light.
Maybe if you moved a little faster, Ezra, we'd have finished more than half a street tonight.
THIP
Maybe if you weren't so pretty I wouldn't be trying to make the night last so long.
Praised be the Lord, who blesses his people with cross-eyed schoolboys for freedom fighters...
FOR THE FREEDOM
ISRAEL
STAR OF ZION IS RISIN
HE FISTS OF OUR
UDGES ARE STRIKING
DOWN THE OPPRESSOR
IN OUR HOLY LAND!

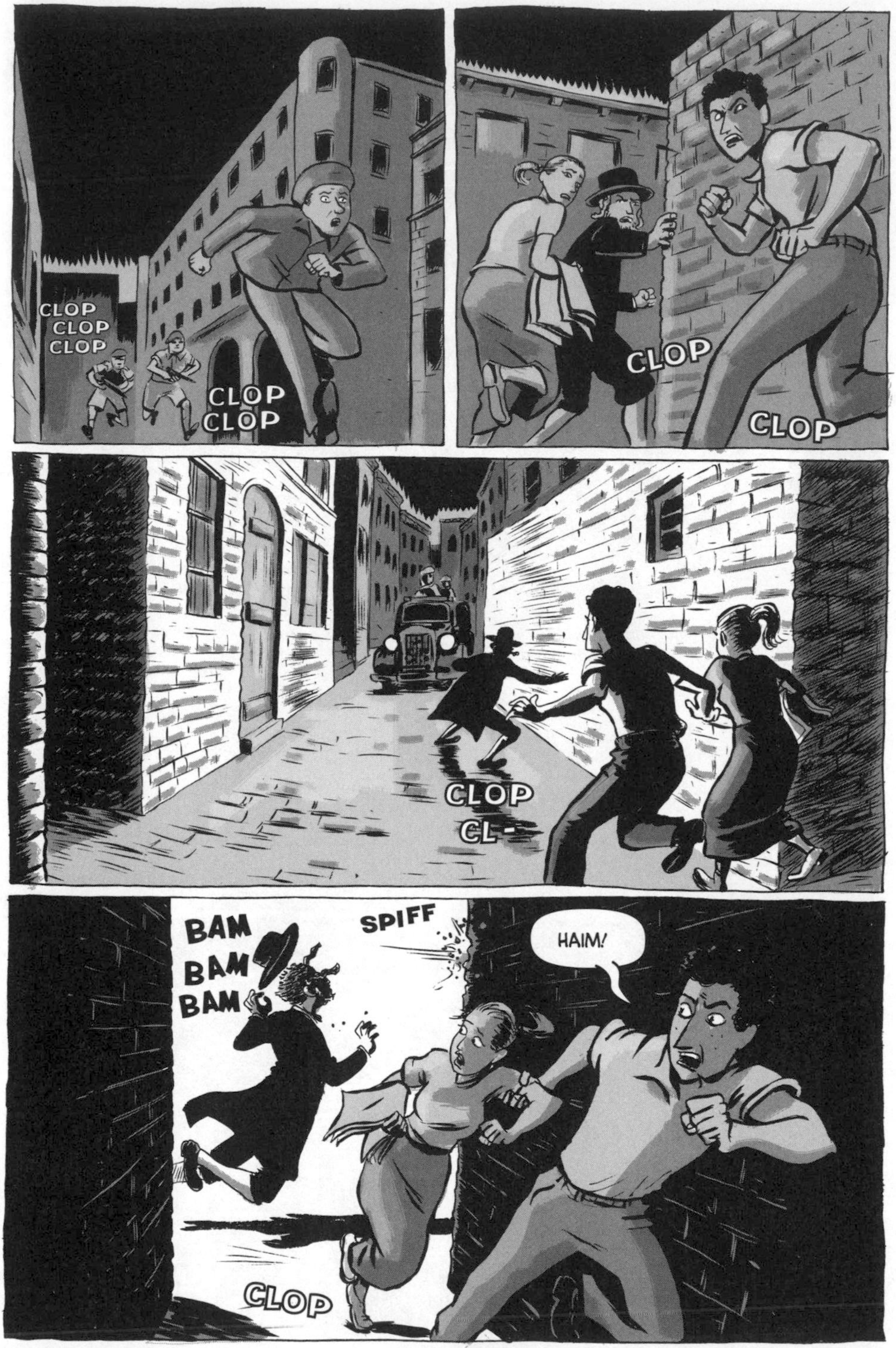
CLOP
CLOP
CLOP
CLOP
CLOP
CLOP
CLOP
CLOP
CL -
BAM
BAM
BAM
SPIFF
HAIM!
CLOP

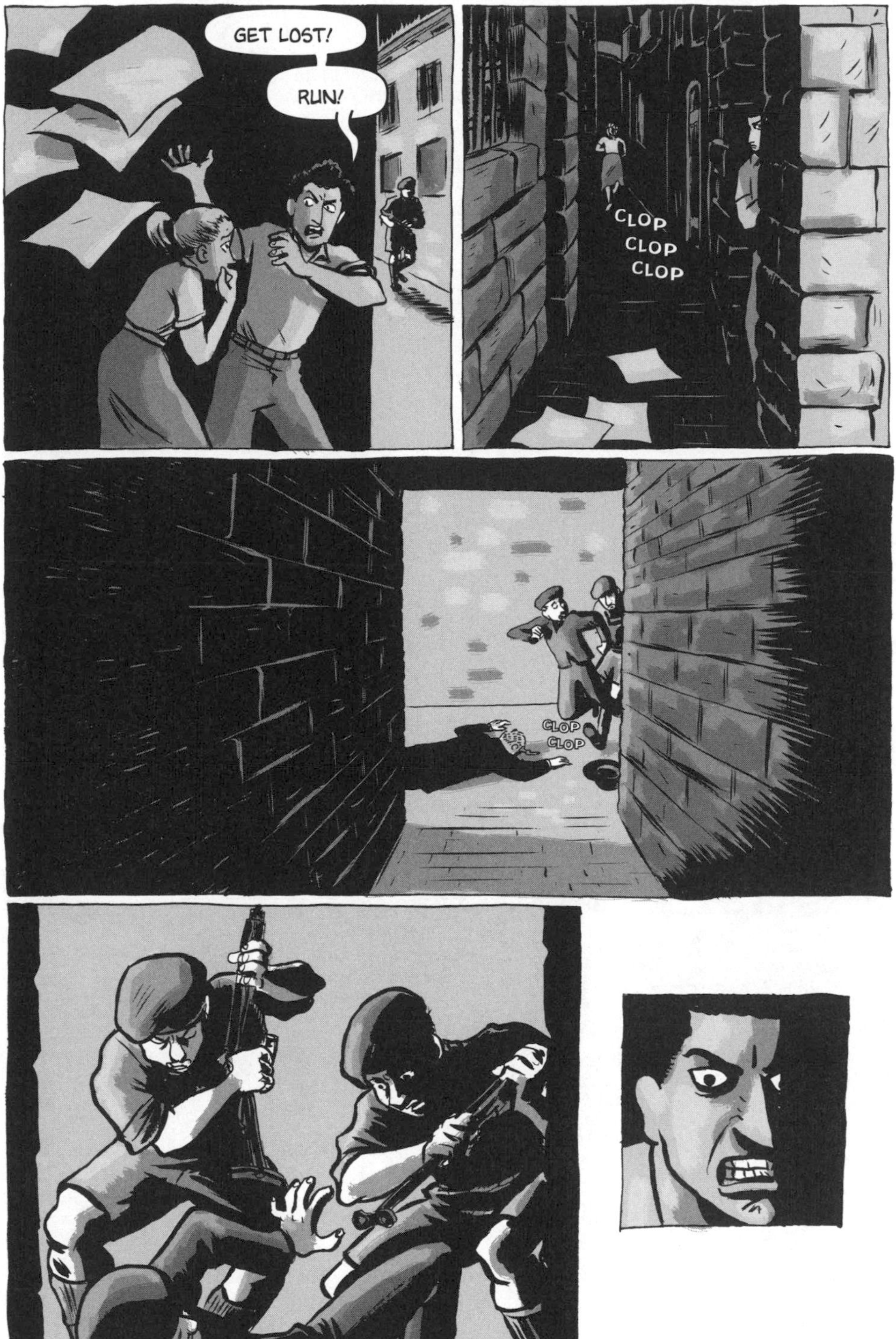
GET LOST!
RUN!
CLOP
CLOP
CLOP
CLOP
CLOP

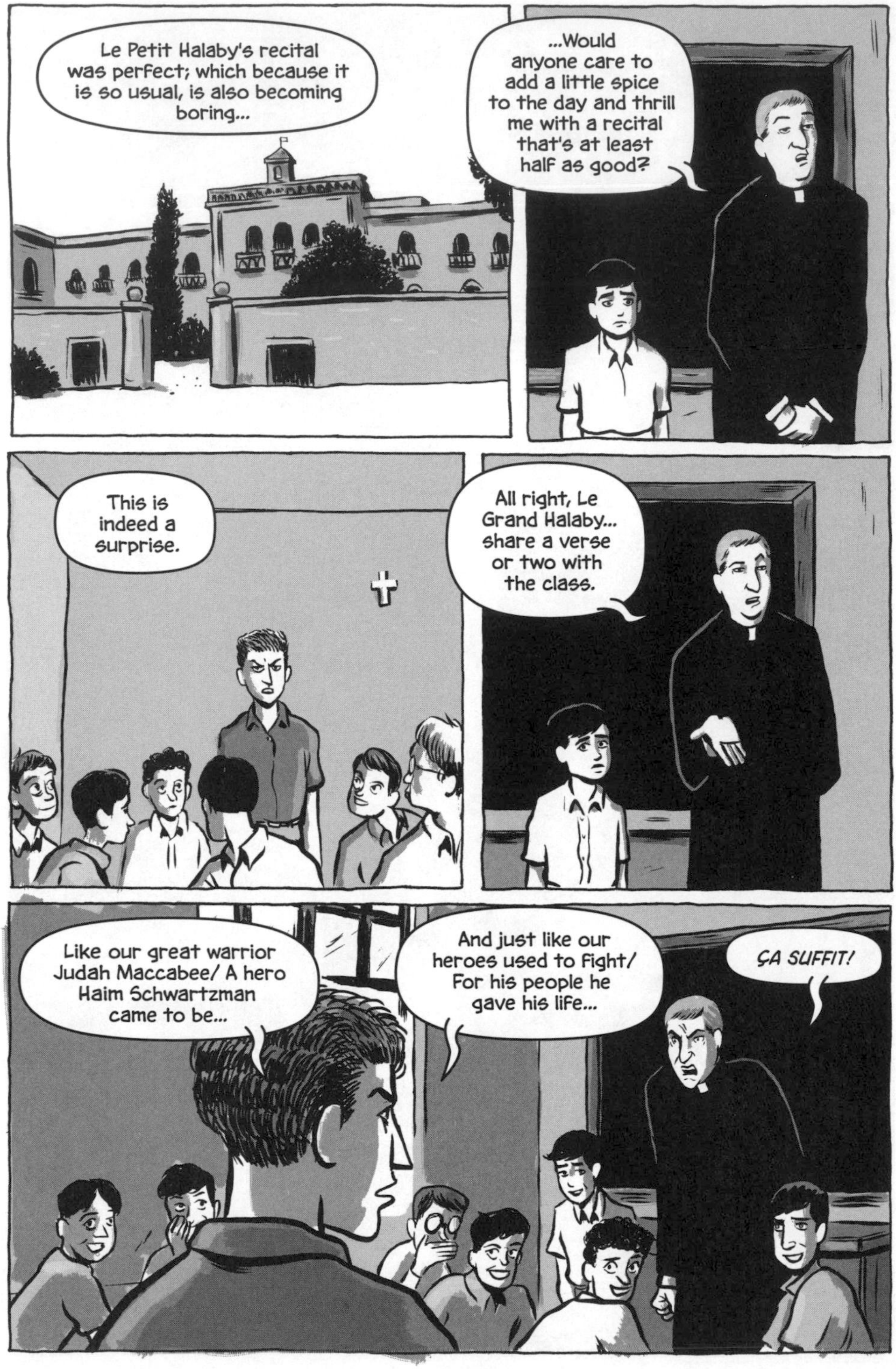
Le Petit Halaby's recital was perfect; which because it is so usual, is also becoming boring...
...Would anyone care to add a little spice to the day and thrill me with a recital that's at least half as good?
This is indeed a surprise.
All right, Le Grand Halaby... share a verse or two with the class.
Like our great warrior Judah Maccabee/ A hero Haim Schwartzman came to be...
And just like our heroes used to fight/ For his people he gave his life...
ÇA SUFFIT!

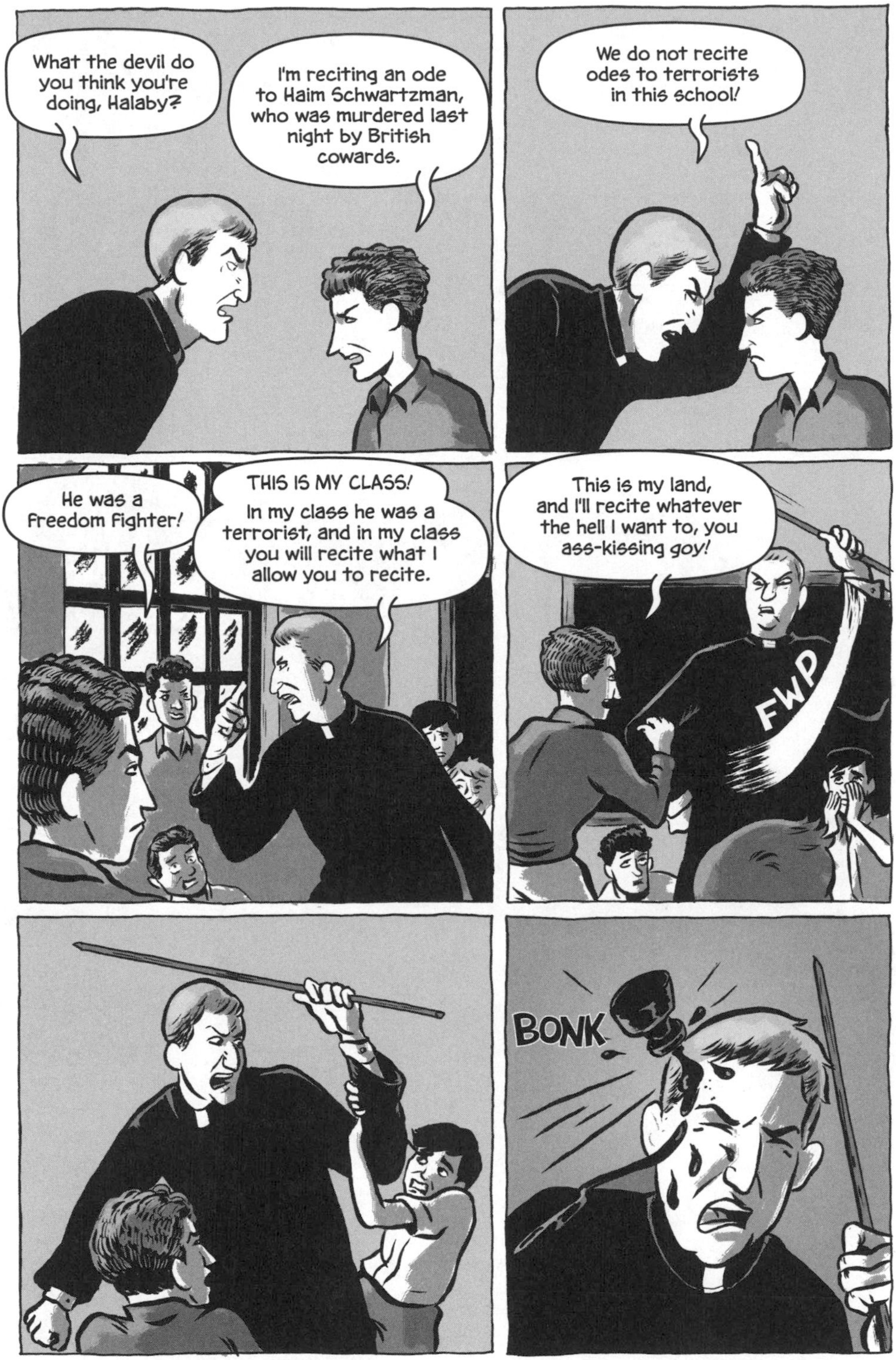
What the devil do you think you're doing, Halaby?
I'm reciting an ode to Haim Schwartzman, who was murdered last night by British cowards.
We do not recite odes to terrorists in this school!
He was a freedom fighter!
THIS IS MY CLASS!
In my class he was a terrorist, and in my class you will recite what I allow you to recite.
This is my land, and I'll recite whatever the hell I want to, you ass-kissing goy!
FWP
BONK

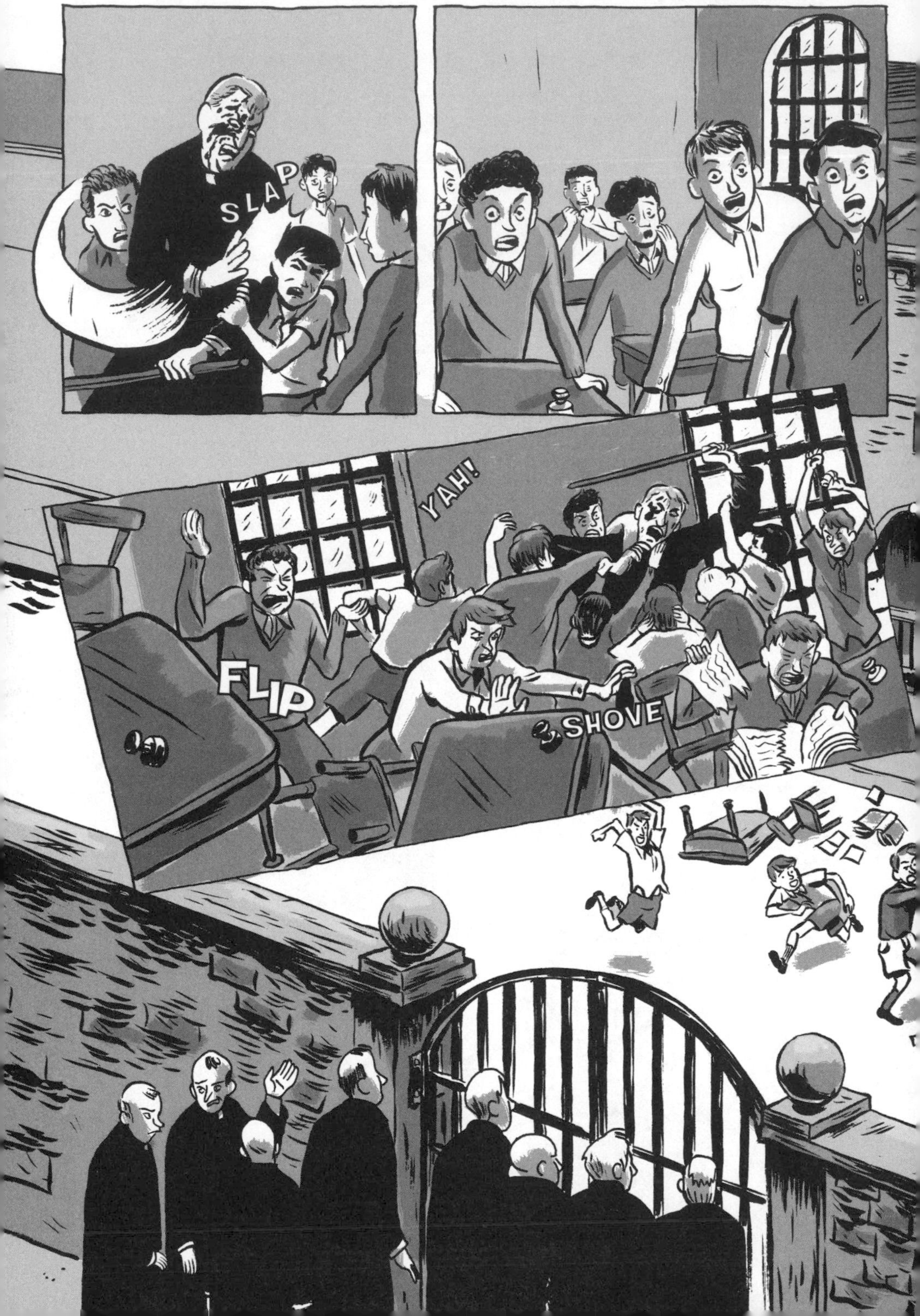
SLAP
YAH!
FLIP
SHOVE

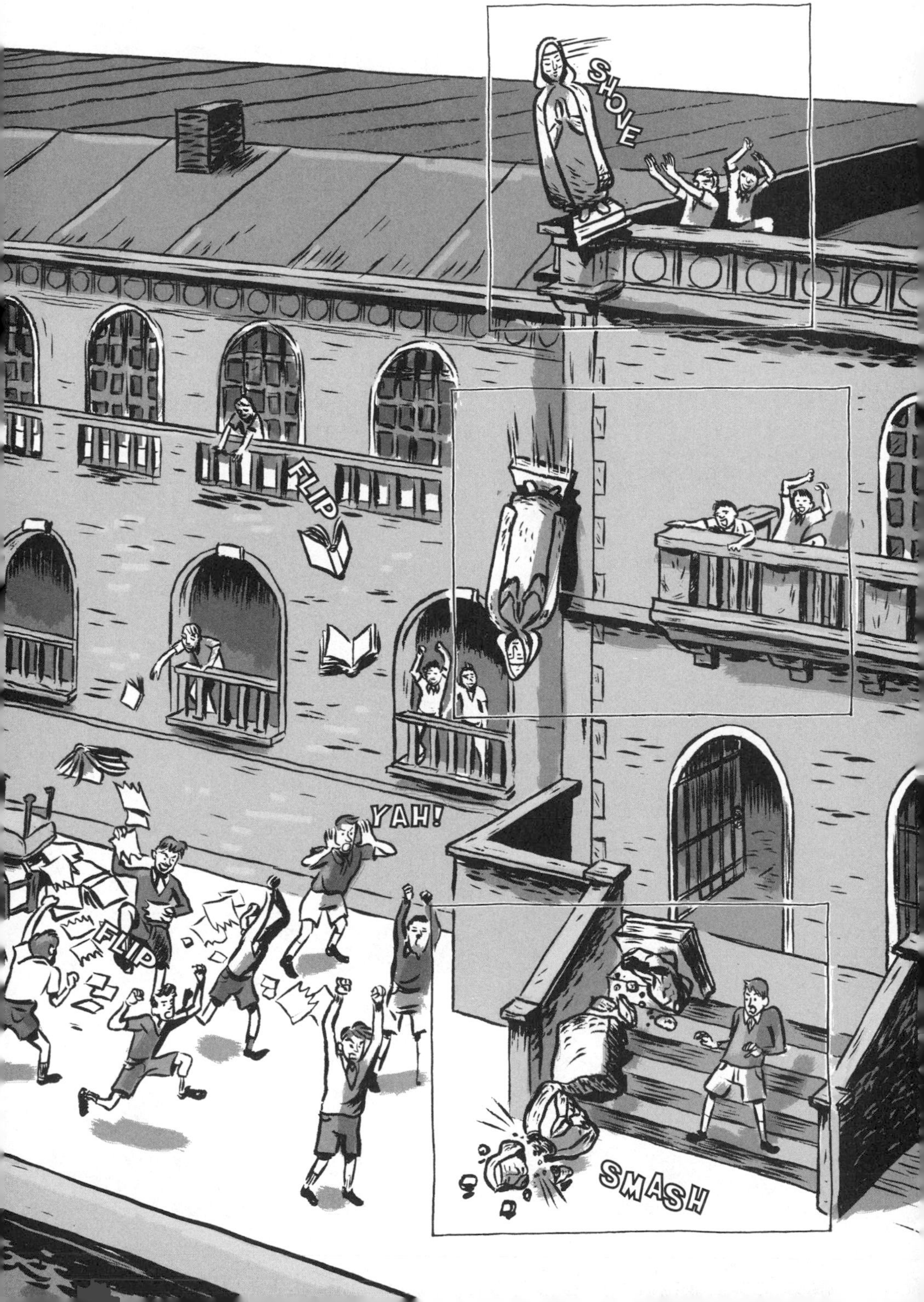
SHOVE
FLIP
YAH!
FLIP
SMASH

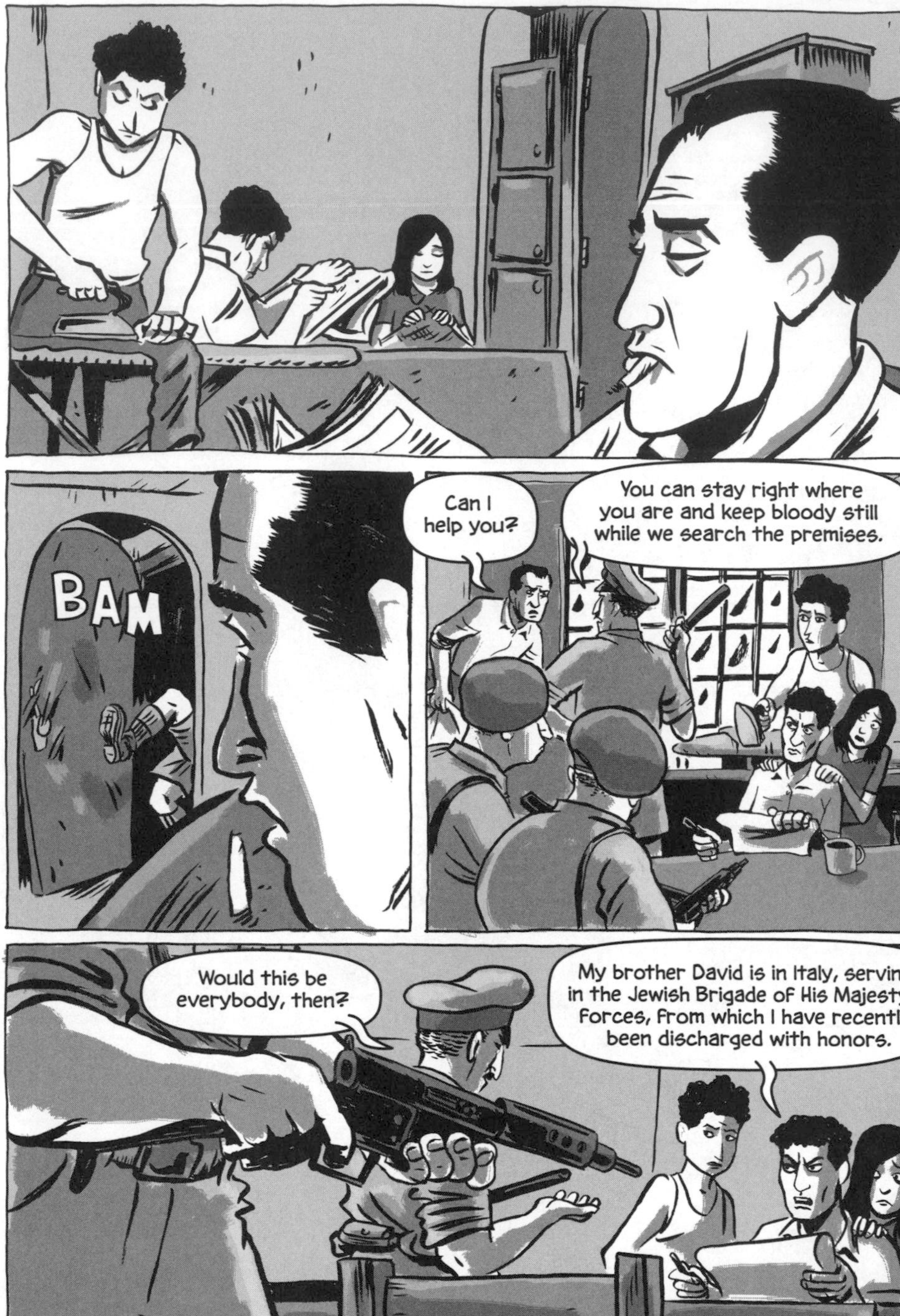
BAM
Can I help you?
You can stay right where you are and keep bloody still while we search the premises.
Would this be everybody, then?
My brother David is in Italy, serving in the Jewish Brigade of His Majesty's forces, from which I have recently been discharged with honors.

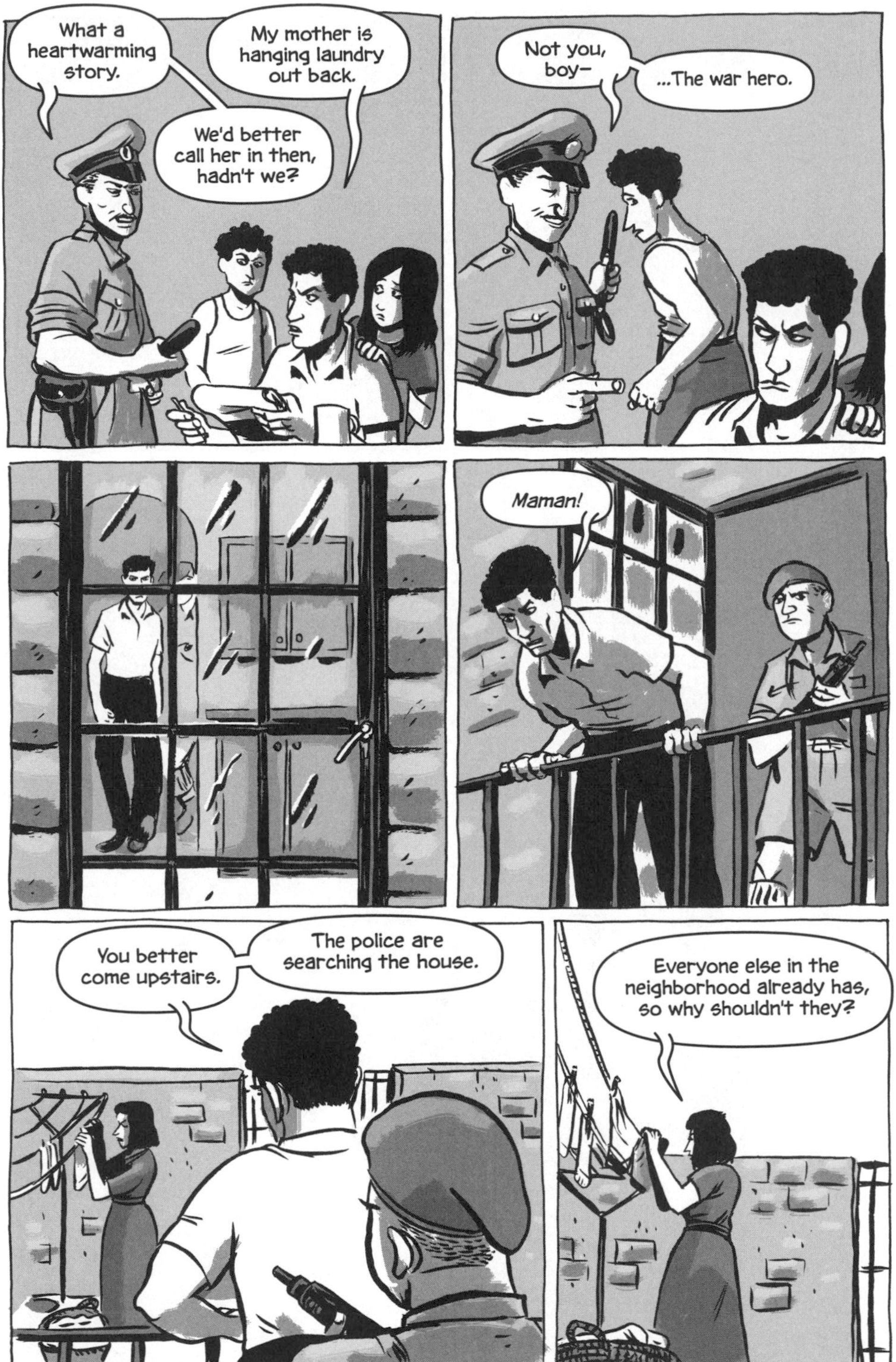
What a heartwarming story.
My mother is hanging laundry out back.
We'd better call her in then, hadn't we?
Not you, boy–
...The war hero.
Maman!
You better come upstairs.
The police are searching the house.
Everyone else in the neighborhood already has, so why shouldn't they?

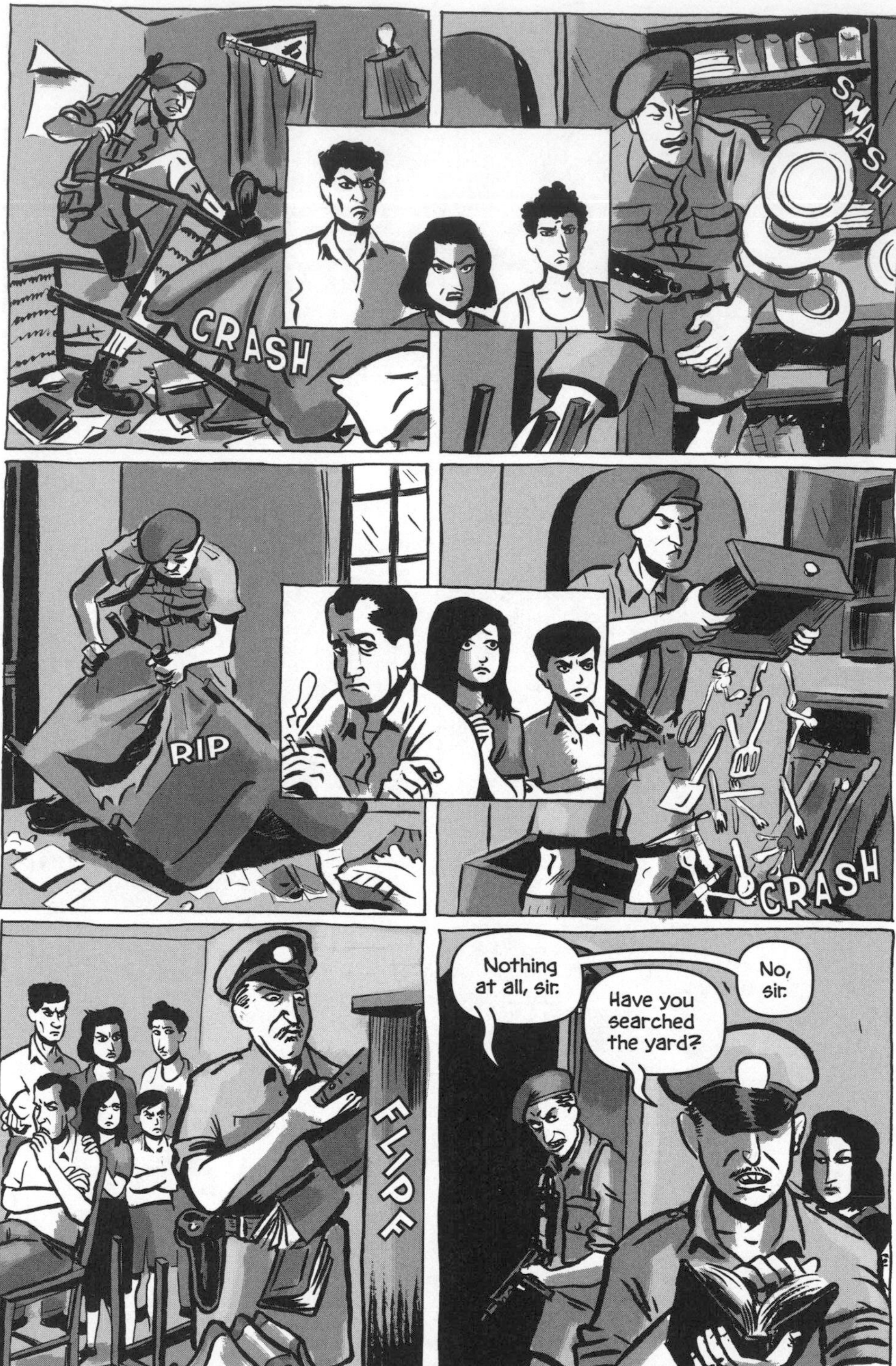
CRASH
SMASH
RIP
CRASH
FLIPF
Nothing at all, sir.
No, sir.
Have you searched the yard?

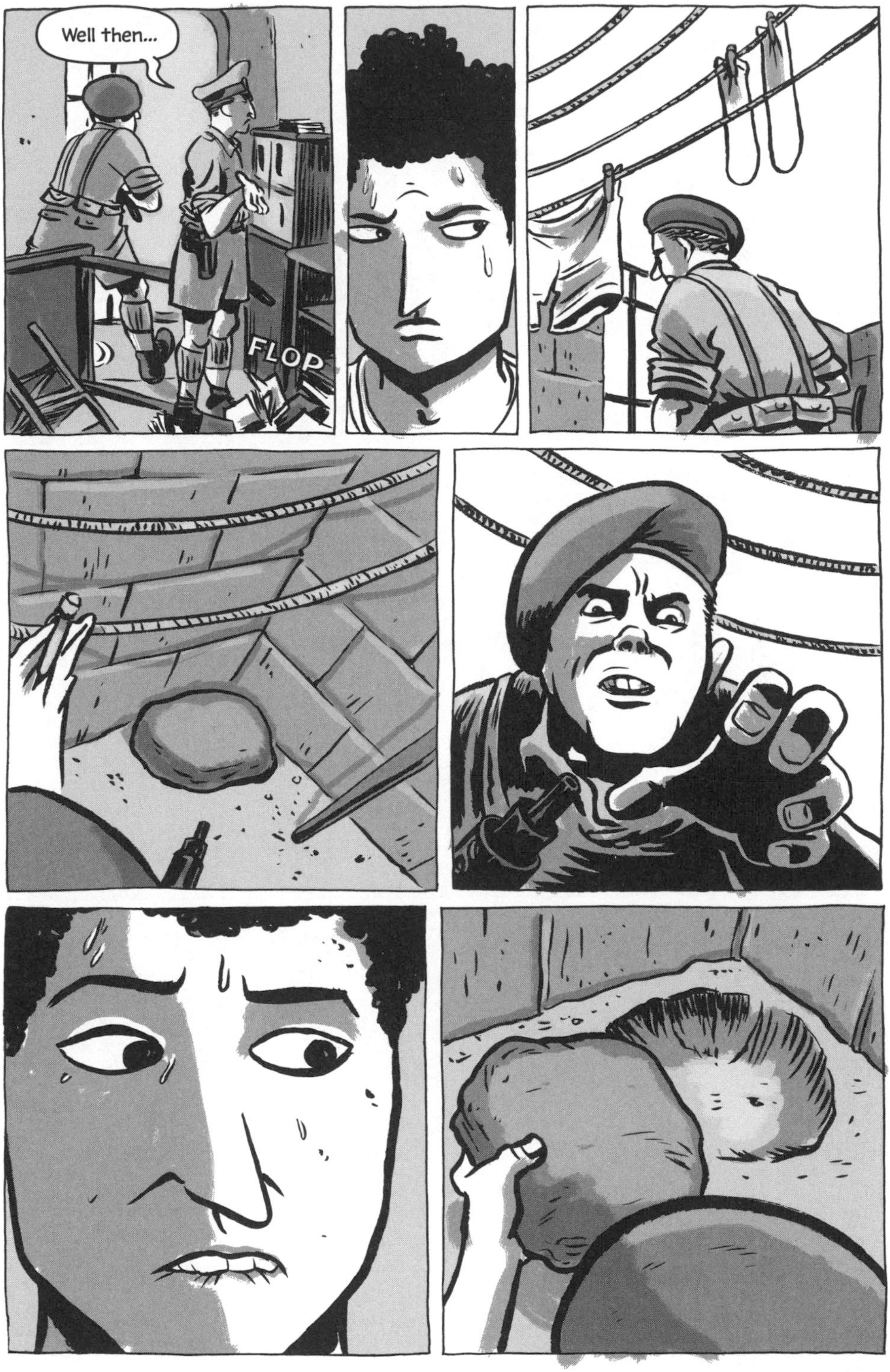
Well then...
FLOP

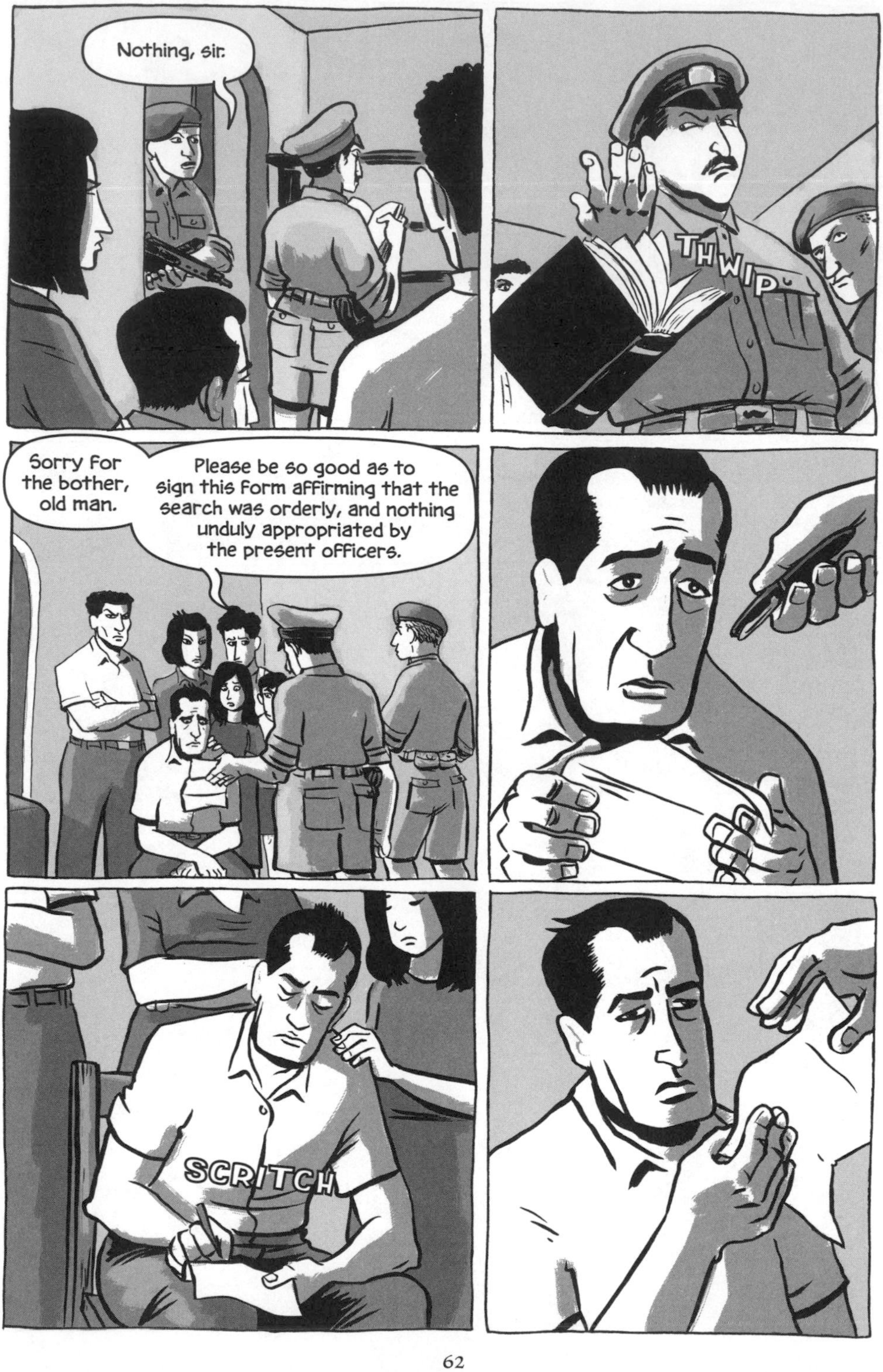
Nothing, sir.
THWIP
Sorry for the bother, old man.
Please be so good as to sign this form affirming that the search was orderly, and nothing unduly appropriated by the present officers.
SCRITCH

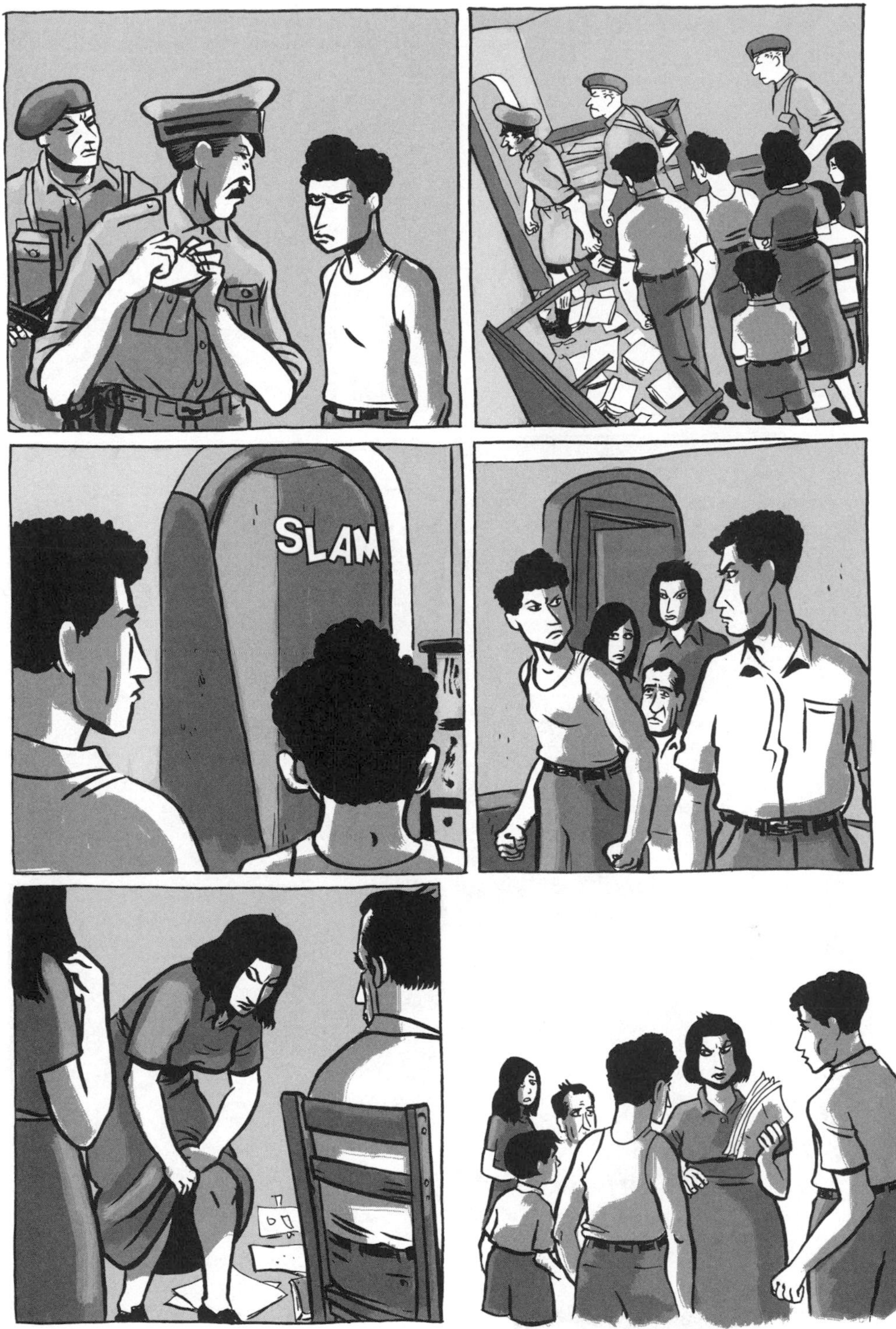
SLAM

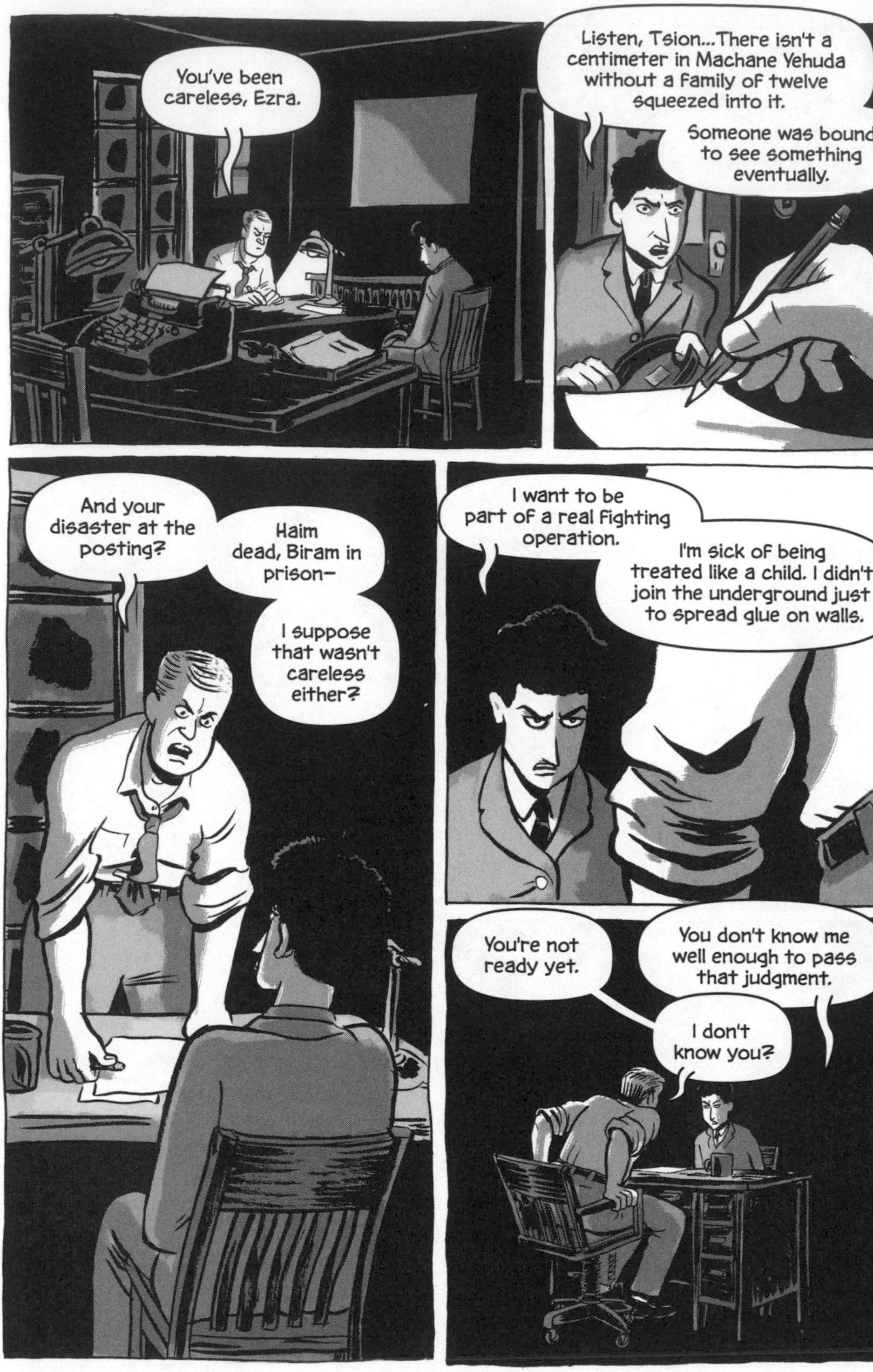

You've been careless, Ezra.
Listen, Tsion...There isn't a centimeter in Machane Yehuda without a family of twelve squeezed into it.
Someone was bound to see something eventually.
And your disaster at the posting?
Haim dead, Biram in prison—
I suppose that wasn't careless either?
I want to be part of a real fighting operation.
I'm sick of being treated like a child. I didn't join the underground just to spread glue on walls.
You're not ready yet.
You don't know me well enough to pass that judgment.
I don't know you?

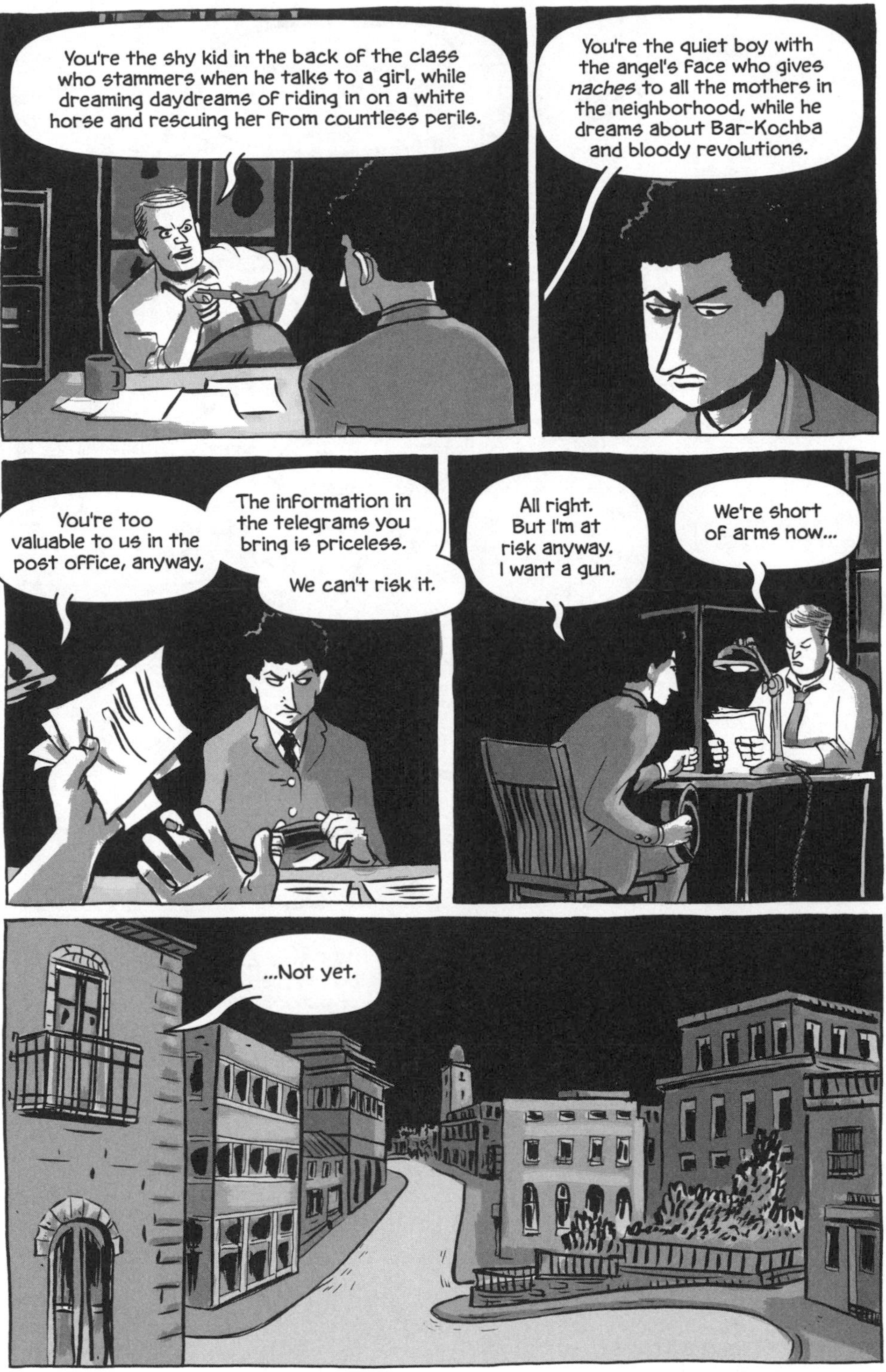
You're the shy kid in the back of the class who stammers when he talks to a girl, while dreaming daydreams of riding in on a white horse and rescuing her from countless perils.
You're the quiet boy with the angel's face who gives *naches* to all the mothers in the neighborhood, while he dreams about Bar-Kochba and bloody revolutions.
You're too valuable to us in the post office, anyway.
The information in the telegrams you bring is priceless.
We can't risk it.
All right. But I'm at risk anyway. I want a gun.
We're short of arms now...
...Not yet.

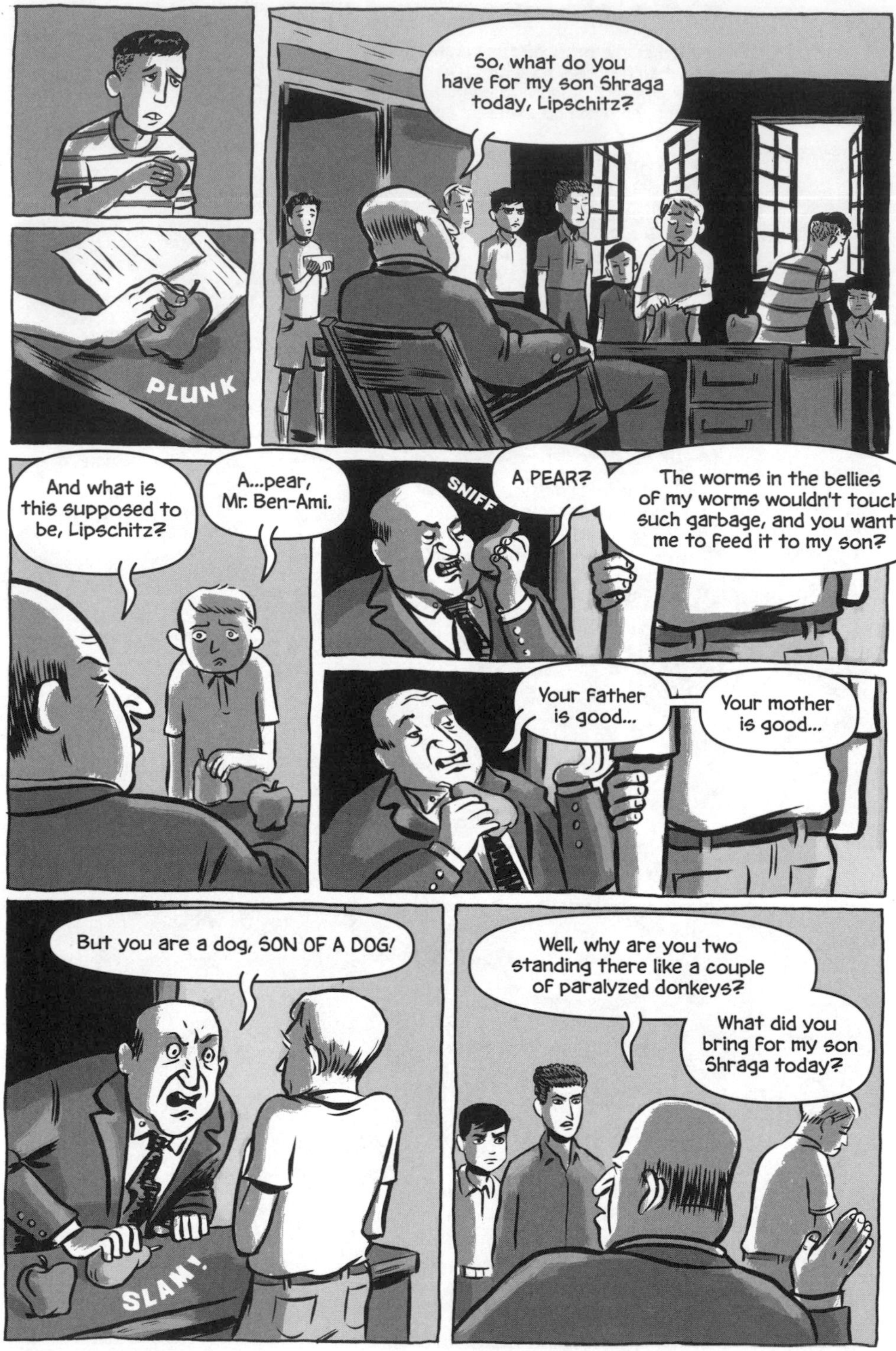
So, what do you have for my son Shraga today, Lipschitz?
PLUNK
And what is this supposed to be, Lipschitz?
A...pear, Mr. Ben-Ami.
SNIFF
A PEAR?
The worms in the bellies of my worms wouldn't touch such garbage, and you want me to feed it to my son?
Your father is good...
Your mother is good...
But you are a dog, SON OF A DOG!
SLAM!
Well, why are you two standing there like a couple of paralyzed donkeys?
What did you bring for my son Shraga today?

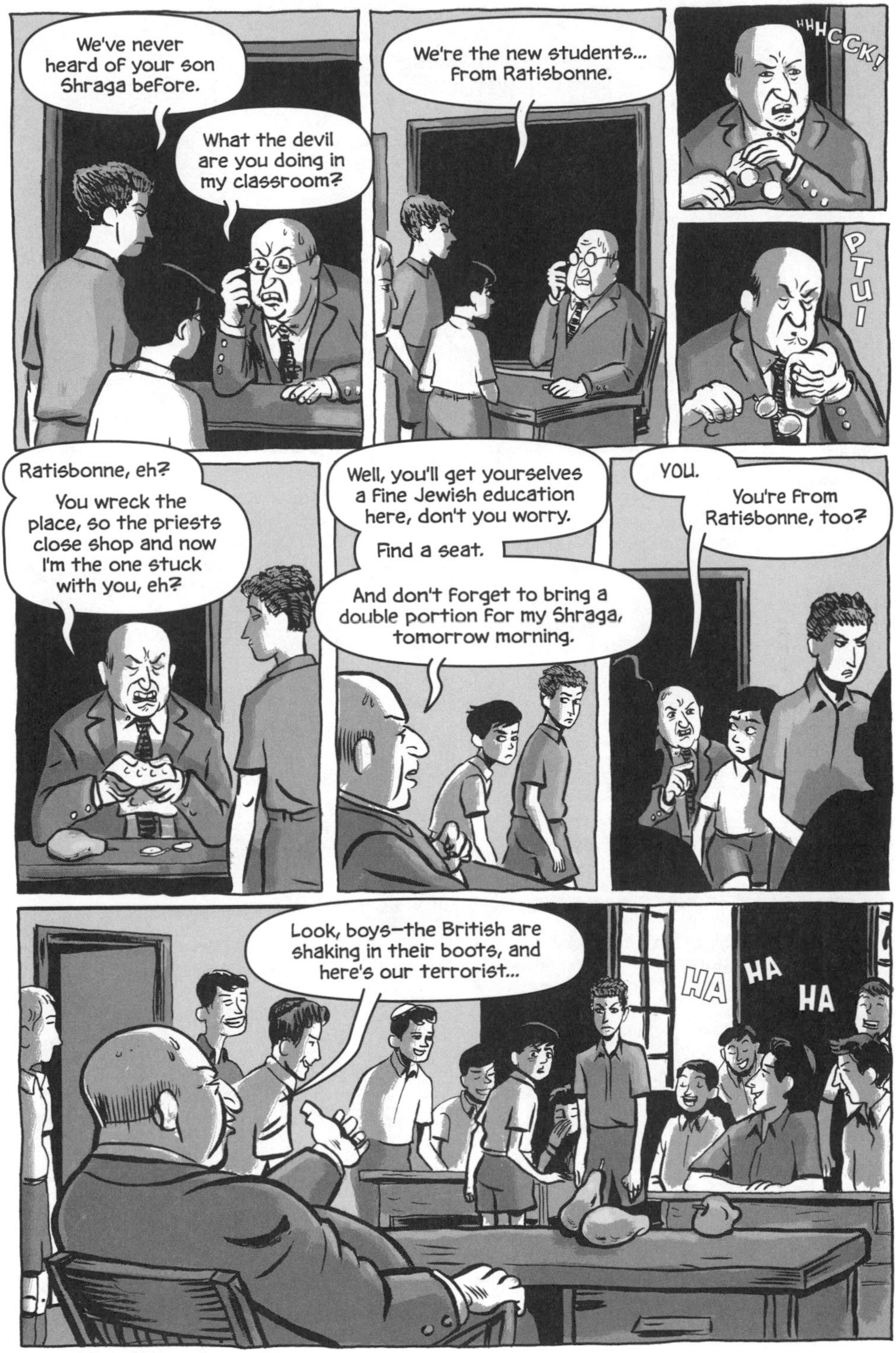
We've never heard of your son Shraga before.
What the devil are you doing in my classroom?
We're the new students... from Ratisbonne.
HHHCCK!
PTUI
Ratisbonne, eh?
You wreck the place, so the priests close shop and now I'm the one stuck with you, eh?
Well, you'll get yourselves a fine Jewish education here, don't you worry.
Find a seat.
And don't forget to bring a double portion for my Shraga, tomorrow morning.
YOU.
You're from Ratisbonne, too?
Look, boys—the British are shaking in their boots, and here's our terrorist...
HA
HA
HA

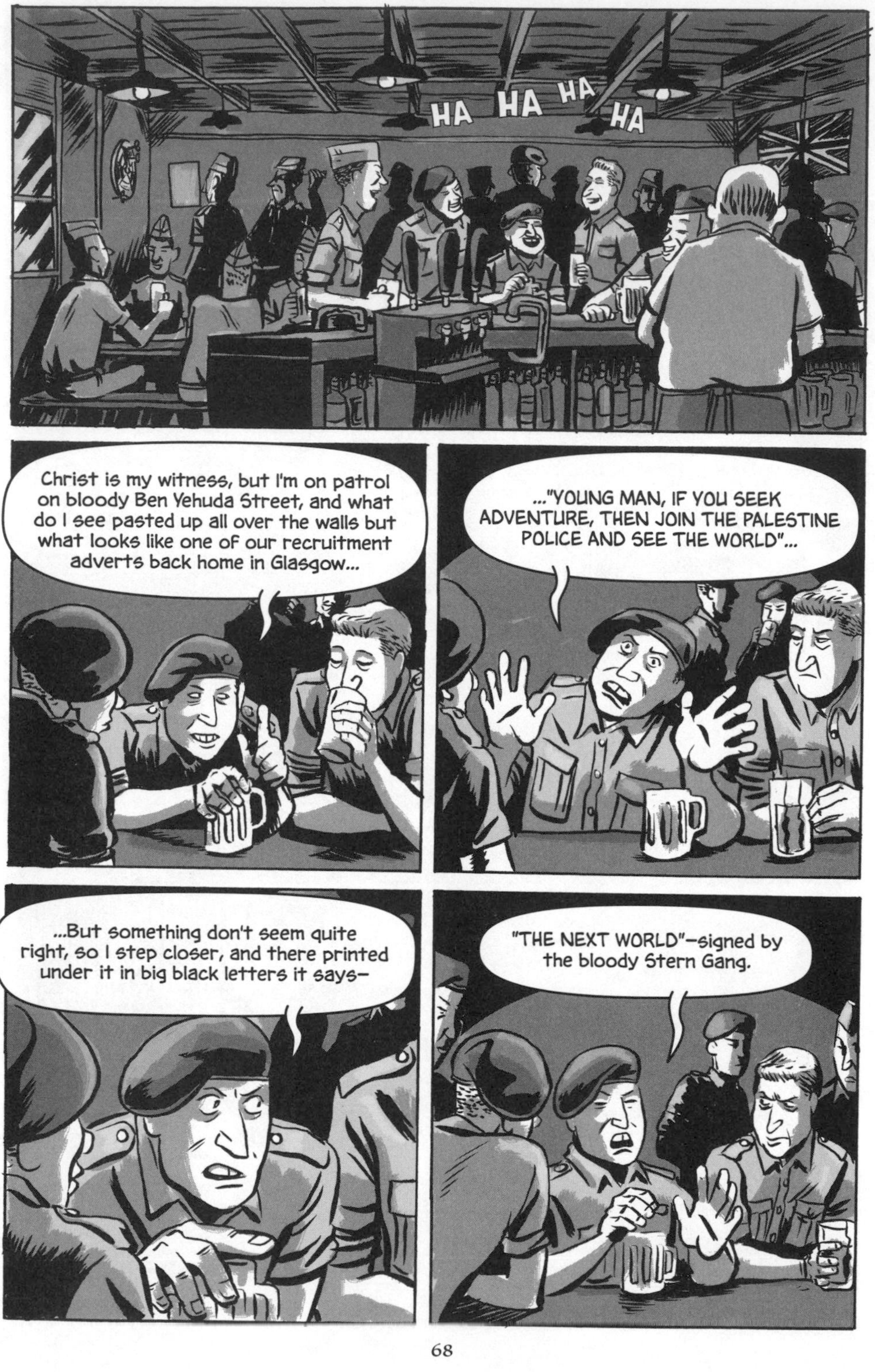
HA HA HA HA
Christ is my witness, but I'm on patrol on bloody Ben Yehuda Street, and what do I see pasted up all over the walls but what looks like one of our recruitment adverts back home in Glasgow...
..."YOUNG MAN, IF YOU SEEK ADVENTURE, THEN JOIN THE PALESTINE POLICE AND SEE THE WORLD"...
...But something don't seem quite right, so I step closer, and there printed under it in big black letters it says—
"THE NEXT WORLD"—signed by the bloody Stern Gang.

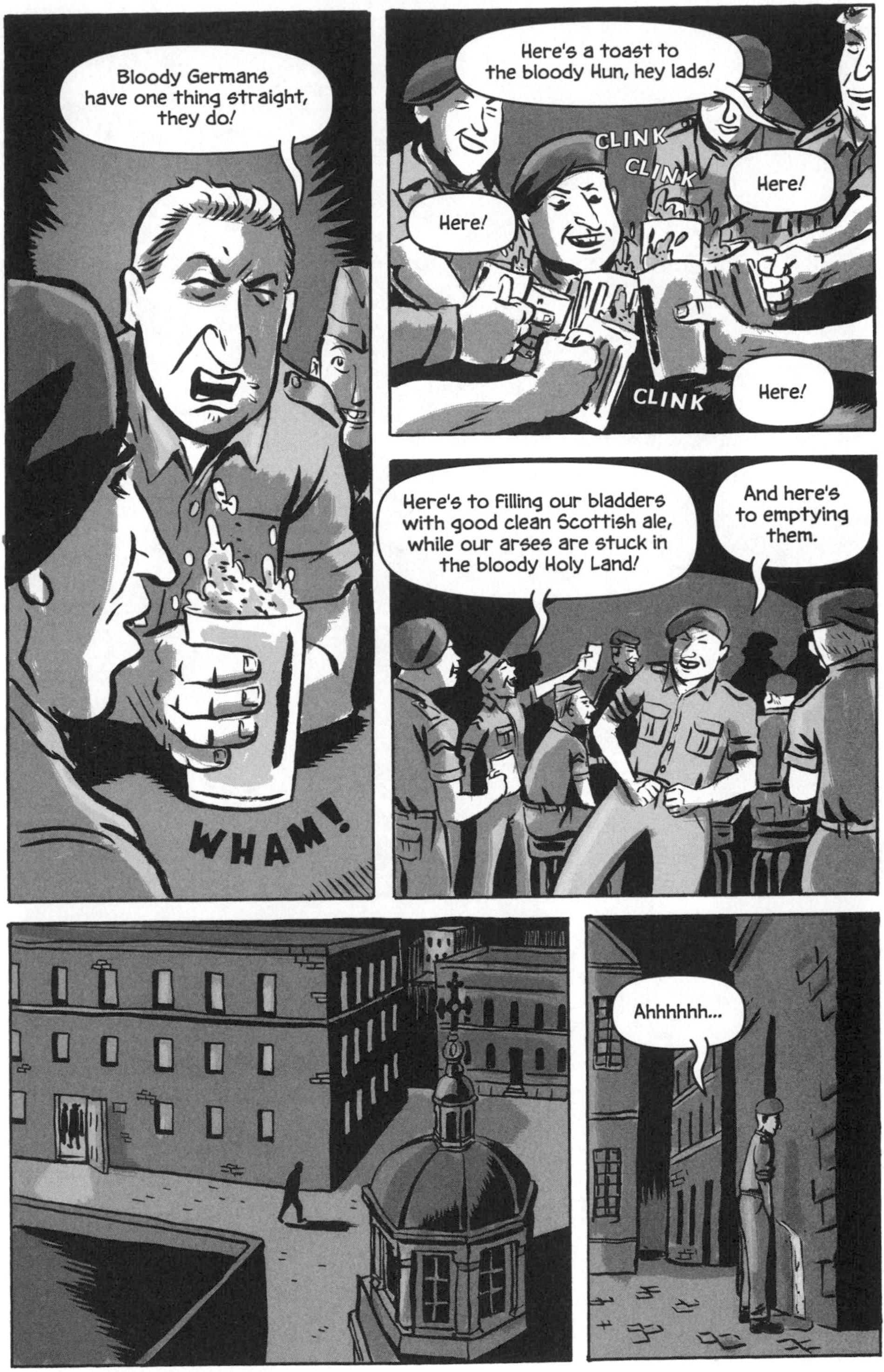

Bloody Germans have one thing straight, they do!
WHAM!
Here's a toast to the bloody Hun, hey lads!
CLINK
CLINK
Here!
Here!
CLINK
Here!
Here's to filling our bladders with good clean Scottish ale, while our arses are stuck in the bloody Holy Land!
And here's to emptying them.
Ahhhhhh...

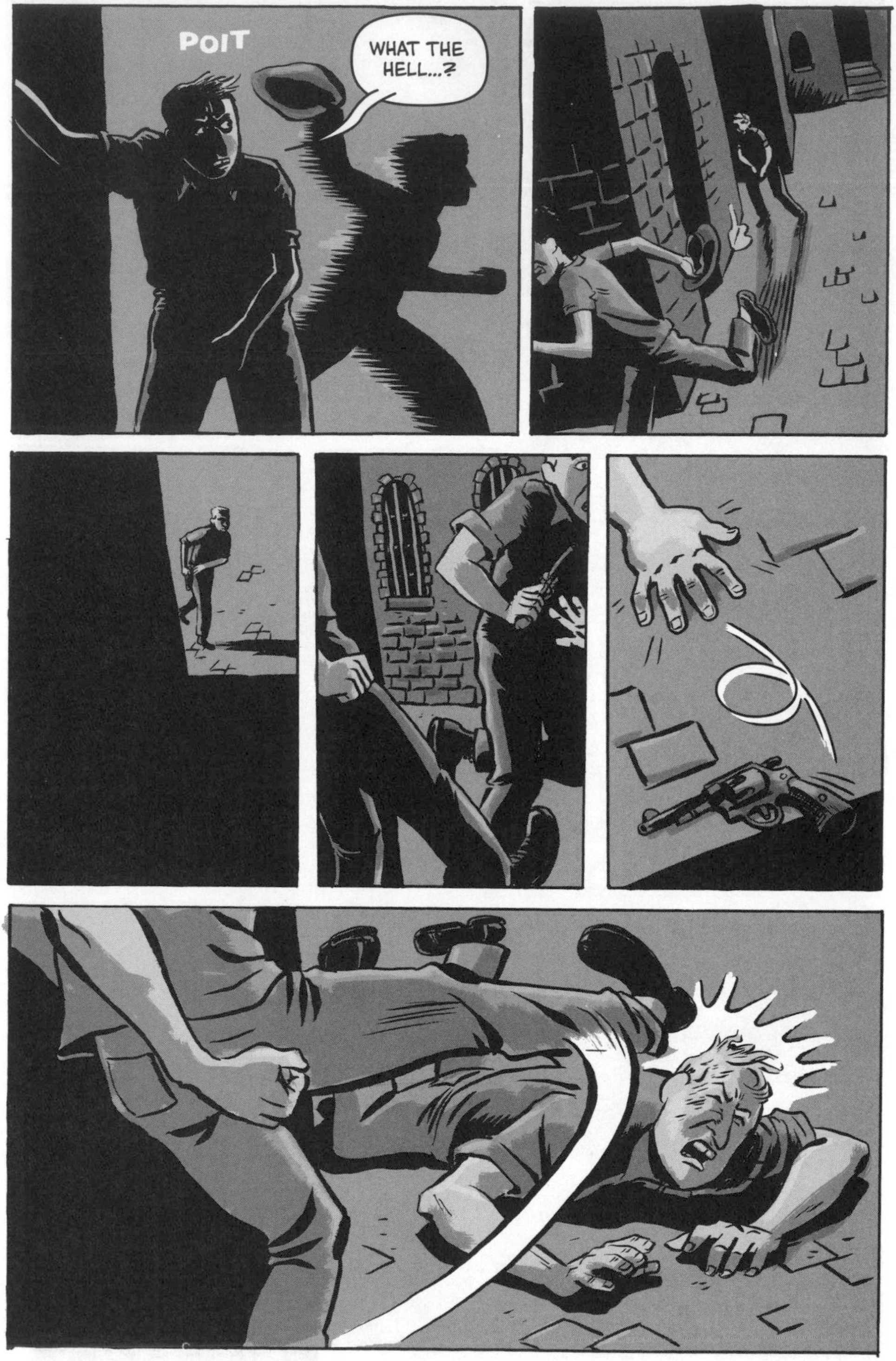
POIT
WHAT THE HELL...?

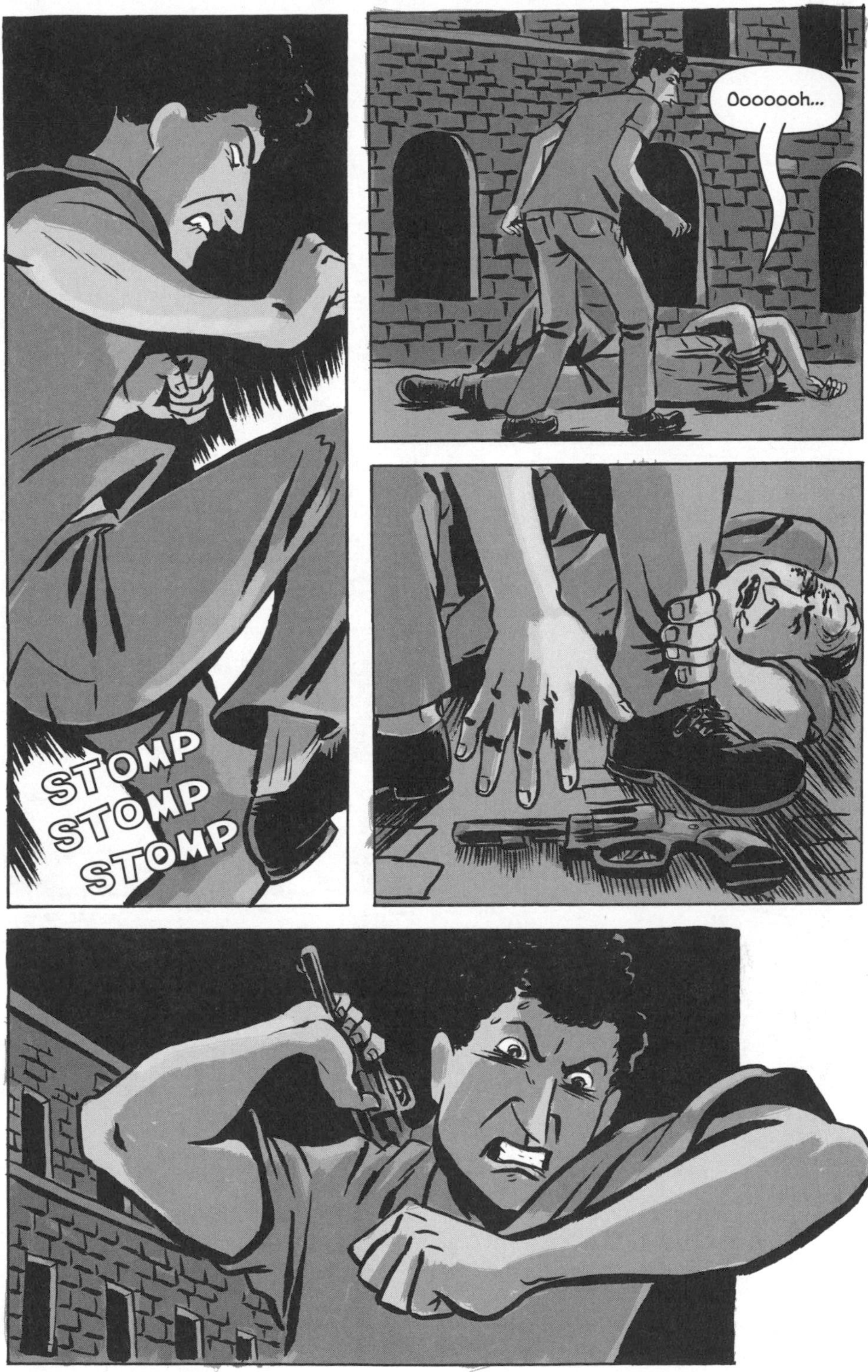
STOMP
STOMP
STOMP
Ooooooh...

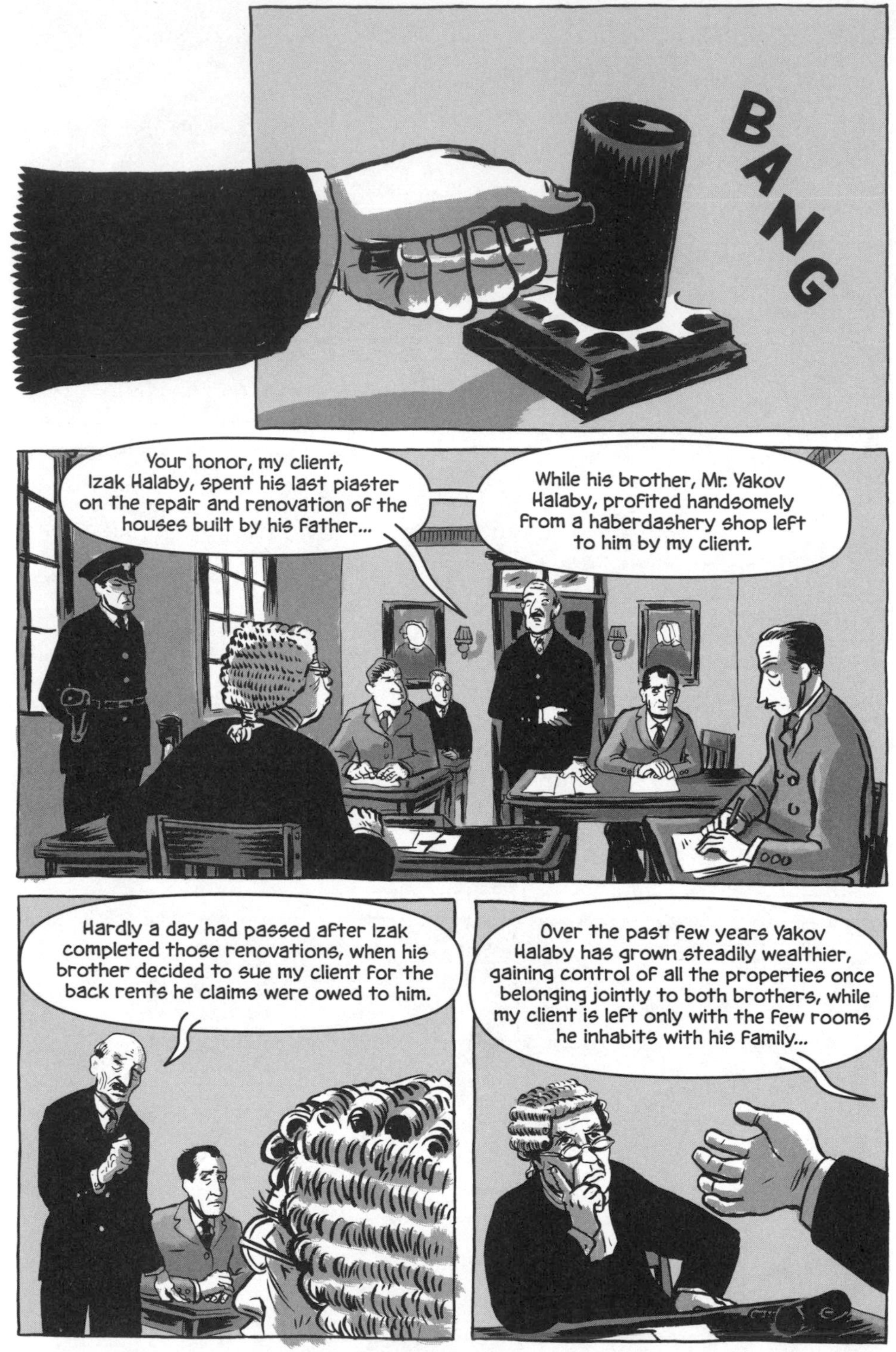
BANG
Your honor, my client, Izak Halaby, spent his last piaster on the repair and renovation of the houses built by his father...
While his brother, Mr. Yakov Halaby, profited handsomely from a haberdashery shop left to him by my client.
Hardly a day had passed after Izak completed those renovations, when his brother decided to sue my client for the back rents he claims were owed to him.
Over the past few years Yakov Halaby has grown steadily wealthier, gaining control of all the properties once belonging jointly to both brothers, while my client is left only with the few rooms he inhabits with his family...

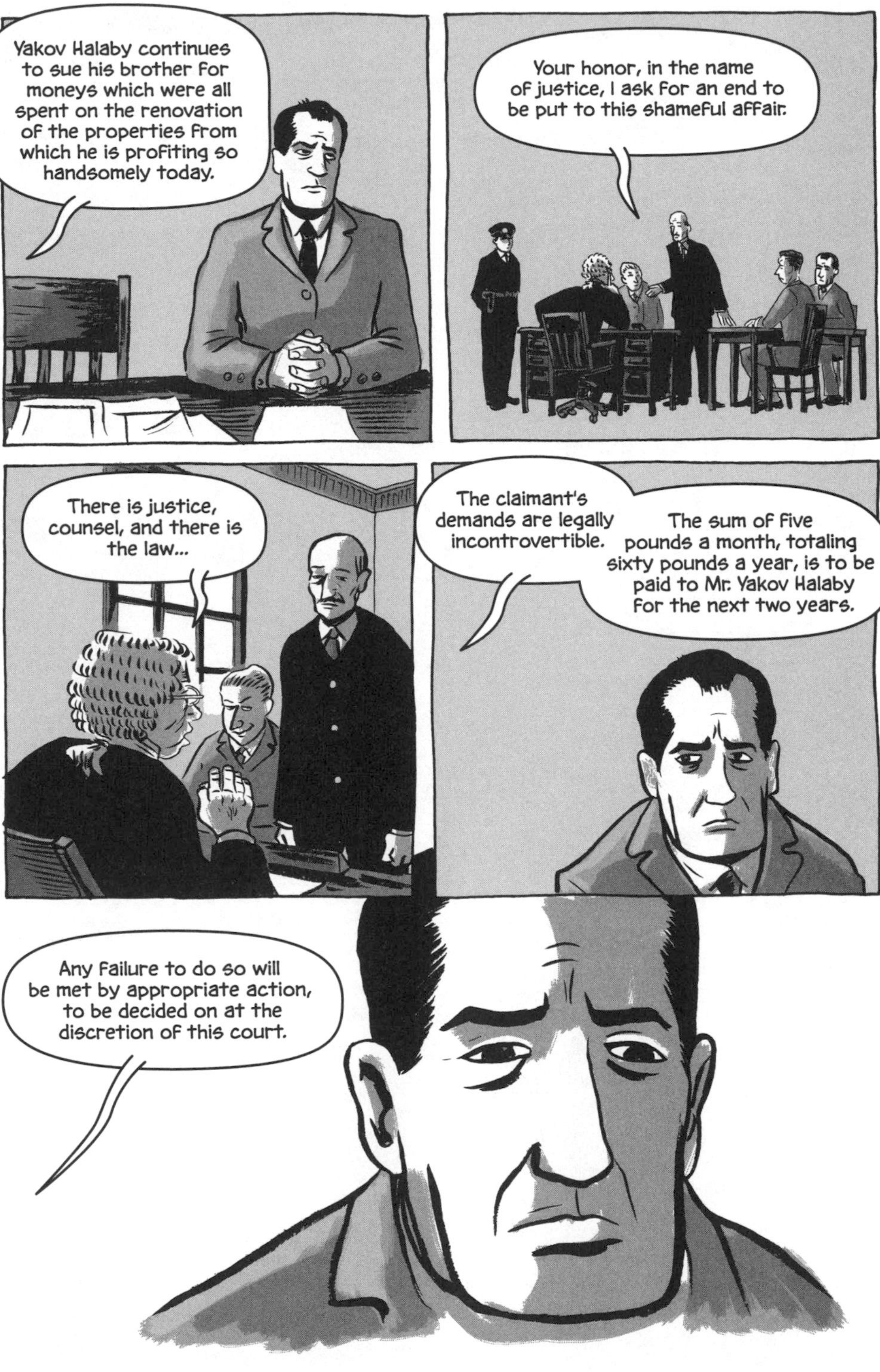
Yakov Halaby continues to sue his brother for moneys which were all spent on the renovation of the properties from which he is profiting so handsomely today.
Your honor, in the name of justice, I ask for an end to be put to this shameful affair.
There is justice, counsel, and there is the law...
The claimant's demands are legally incontrovertible.
The sum of five pounds a month, totaling sixty pounds a year, is to be paid to Mr. Yakov Halaby for the next two years.
Any failure to do so will be met by appropriate action, to be decided on at the discretion of this court.

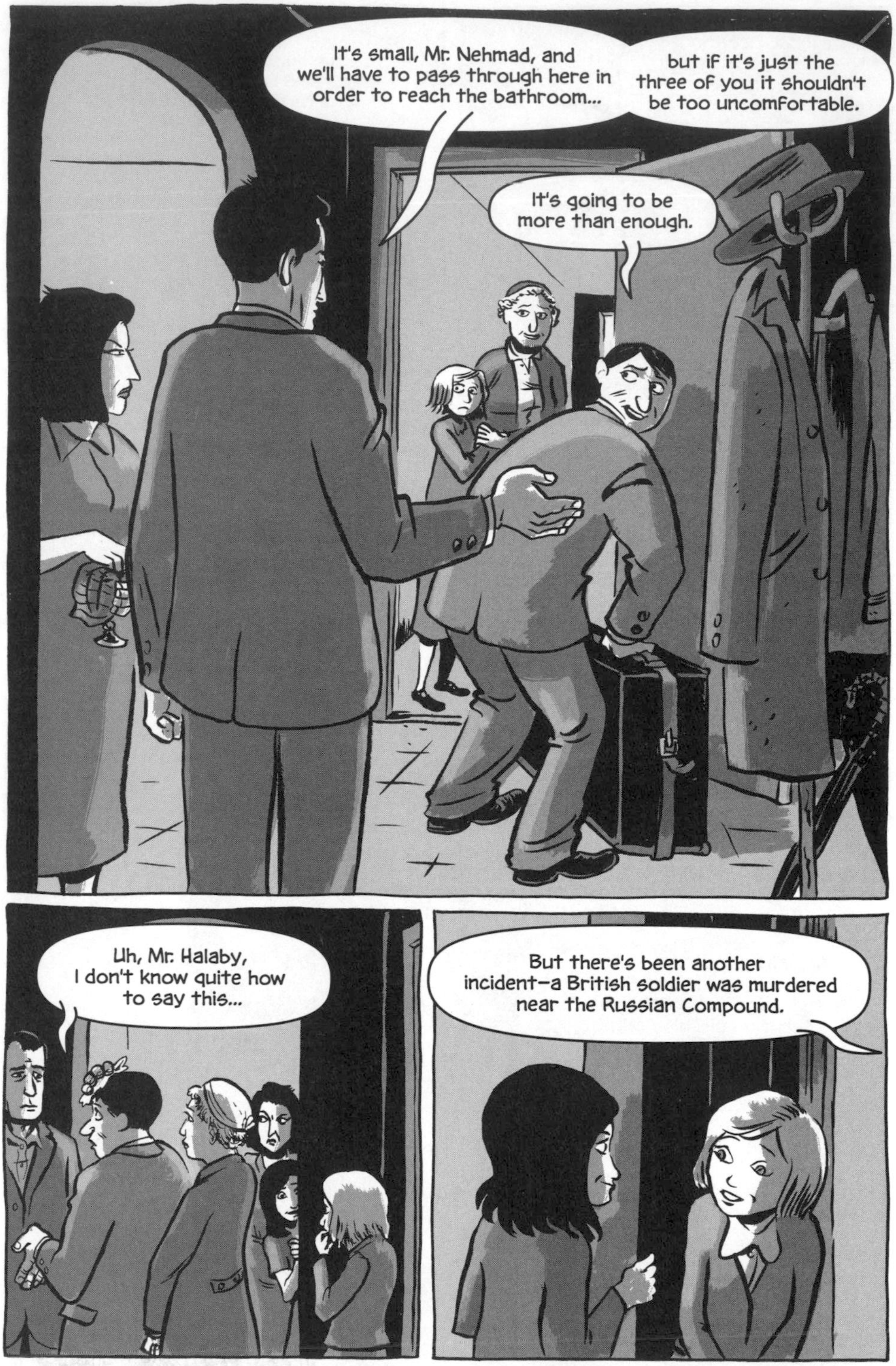
It's small, Mr. Nehmad, and we'll have to pass through here in order to reach the bathroom...
but if it's just the three of you it shouldn't be too uncomfortable.
It's going to be more than enough.
Uh, Mr. Halaby, I don't know quite how to say this...
But there's been another incident—a British soldier was murdered near the Russian Compound.

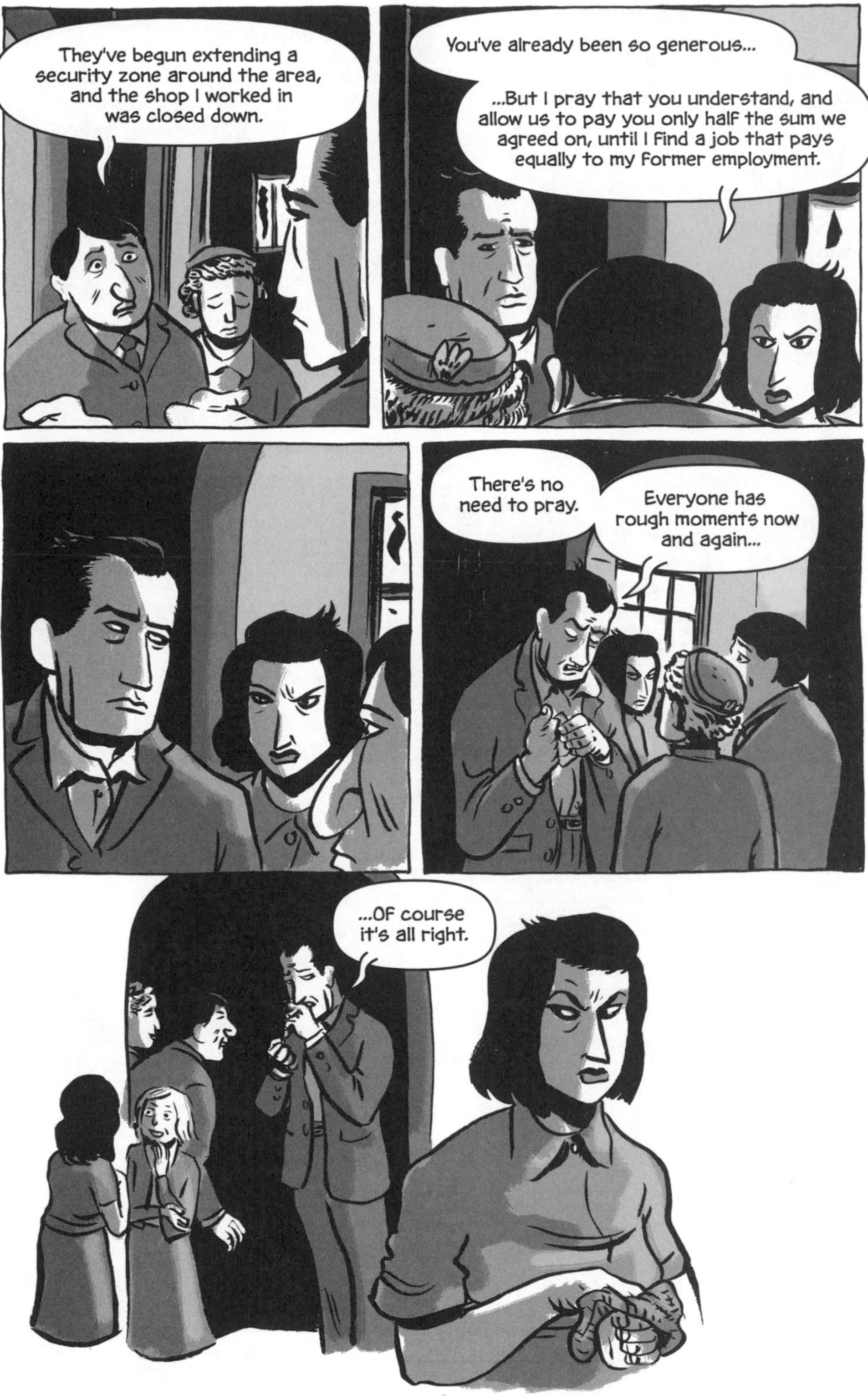
They've begun extending a security zone around the area, and the shop I worked in was closed down.
You've already been so generous...
...But I pray that you understand, and allow us to pay you only half the sum we agreed on, until I find a job that pays equally to my former employment.
There's no need to pray.
Everyone has rough moments now and again...
...Of course it's all right.

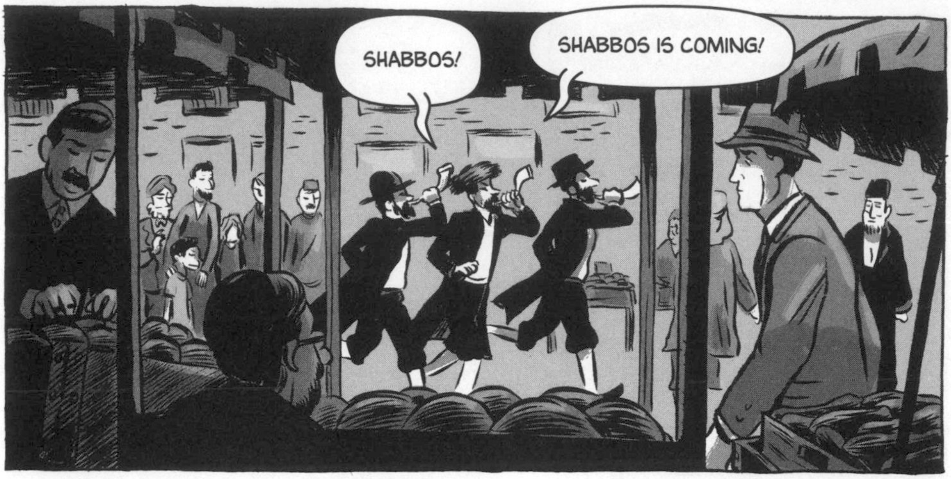
SHABBOS!
SHABBOS IS COMING!

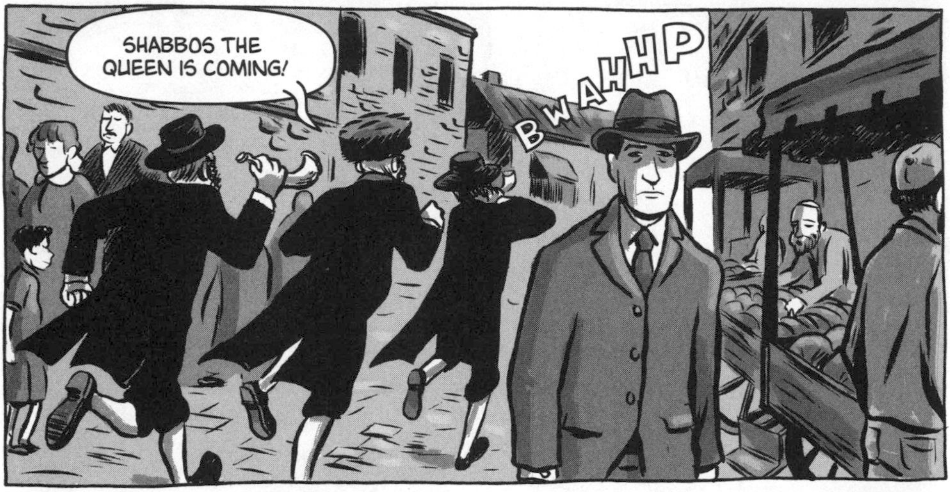
SHABBOS THE QUEEN IS COMING!
BWAHHHP

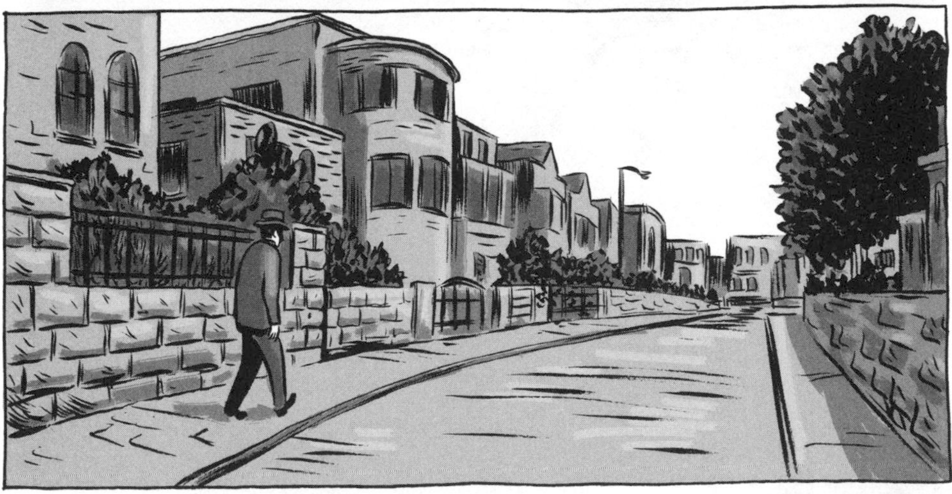

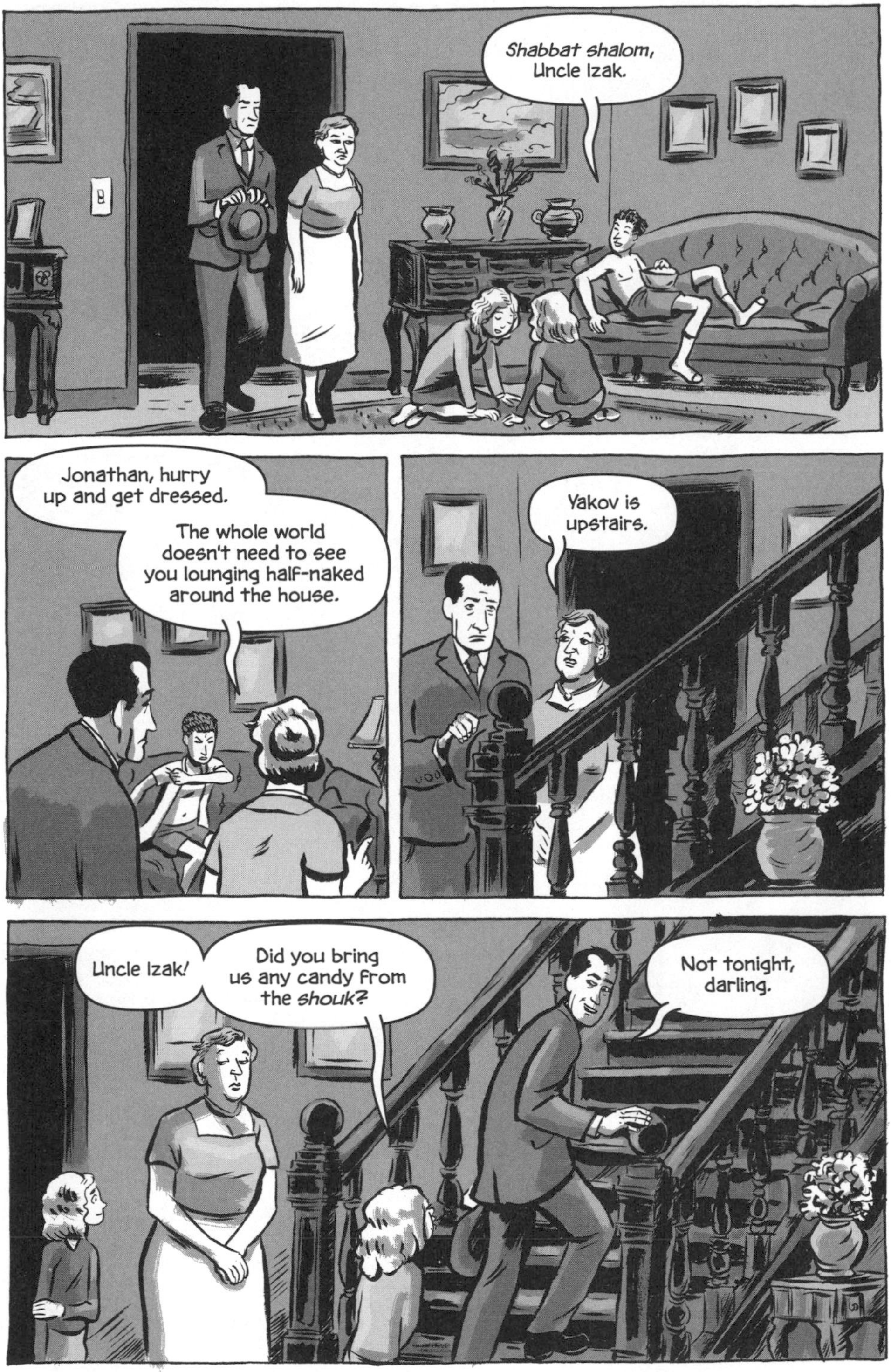
*Shabbat shalom,* Uncle Izak.
Jonathan, hurry up and get dressed.
The whole world doesn't need to see you lounging half-naked around the house.
Yakov is upstairs.
Uncle Izak!
Did you bring us any candy from the *shouk?*
Not tonight, darling.

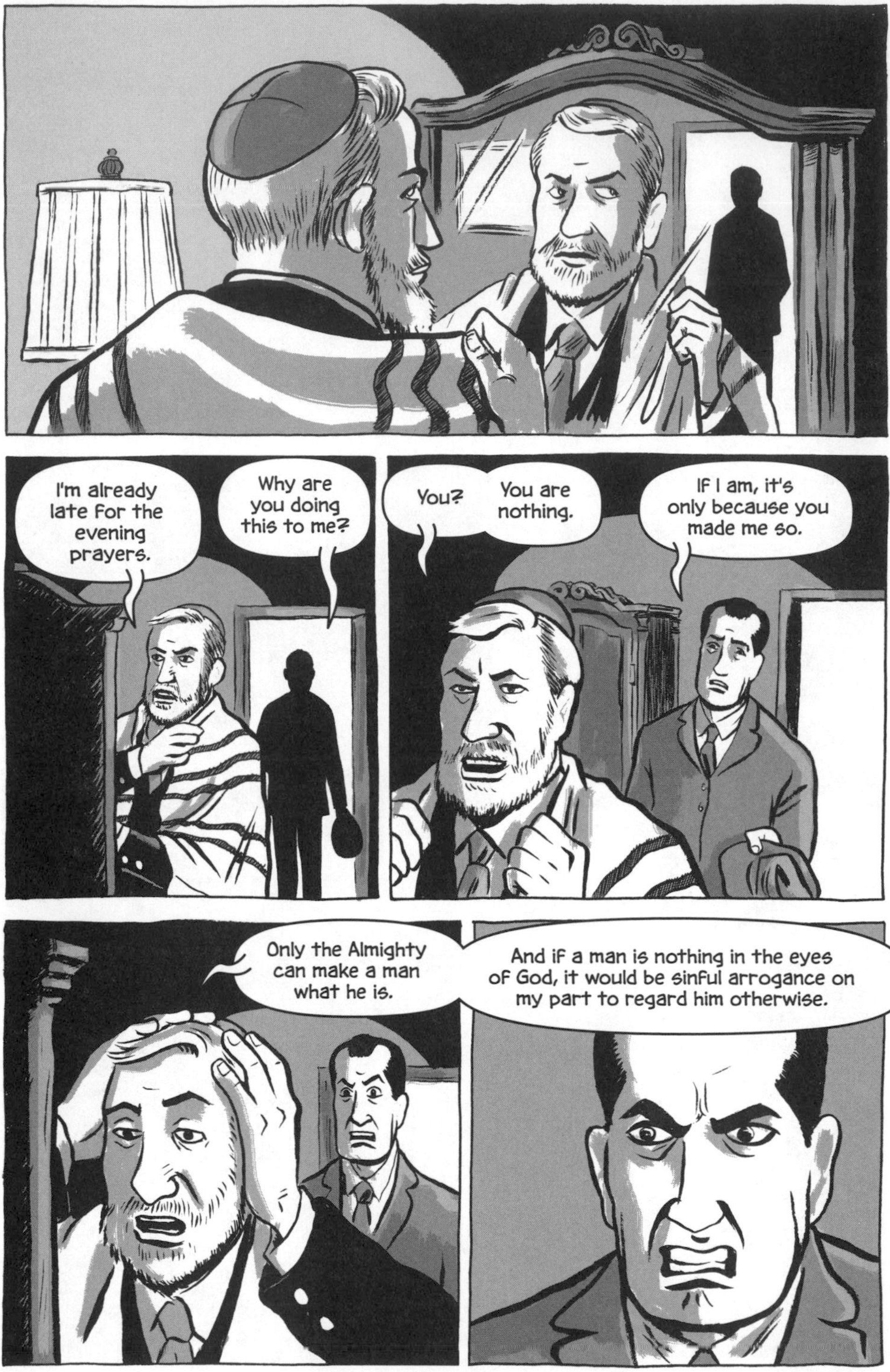
I'm already late for the evening prayers.
Why are you doing this to me?
You?
You are nothing.
If I am, it's only because you made me so.
Only the Almighty can make a man what he is.
And if a man is nothing in the eyes of God, it would be sinful arrogance on my part to regard him otherwise.

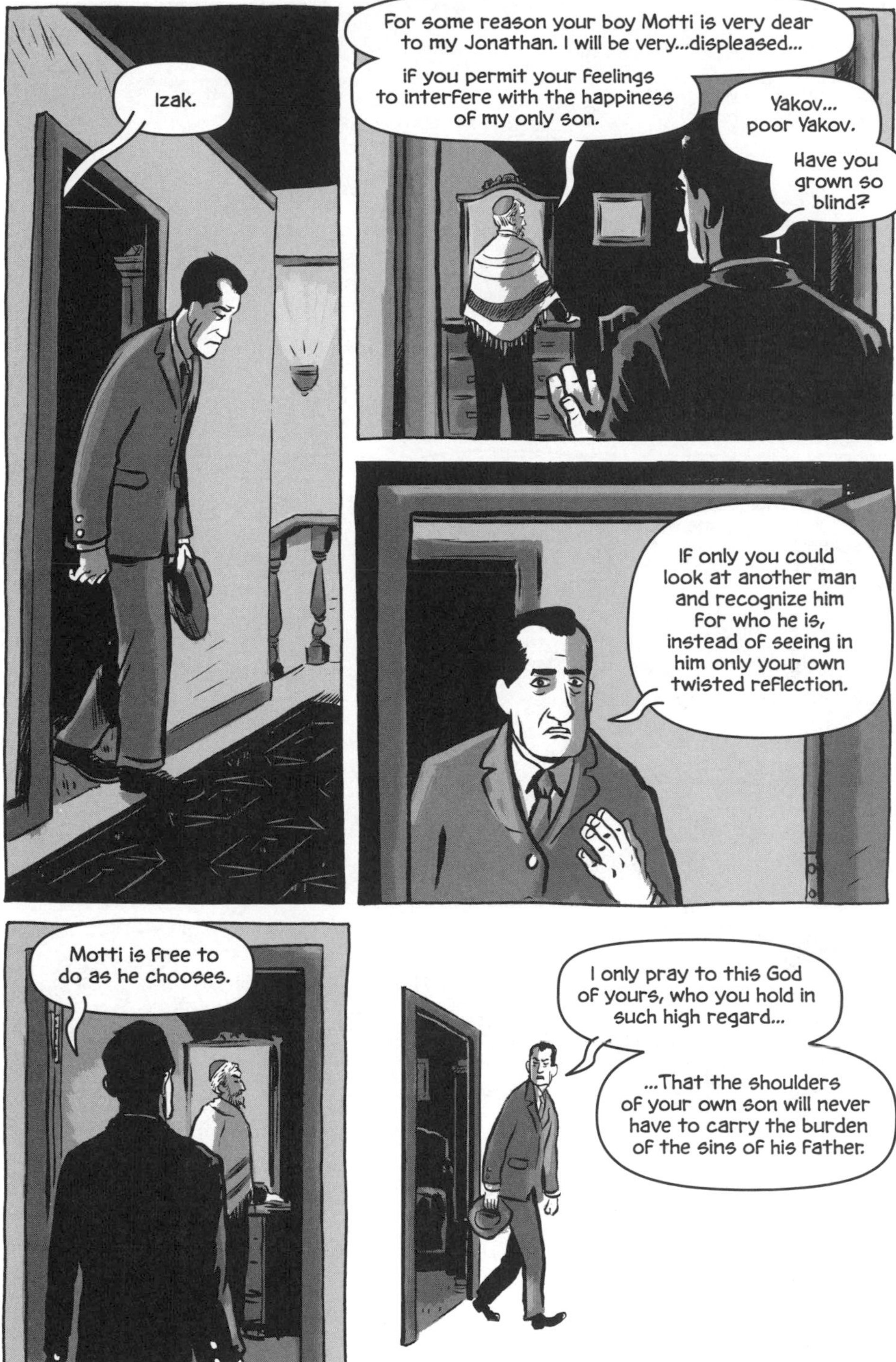
Izak.
For some reason your boy Motti is very dear to my Jonathan. I will be very...displeased...
if you permit your feelings to interfere with the happiness of my only son.
Yakov... poor Yakov.
Have you grown so blind?
If only you could look at another man and recognize him for who he is, instead of seeing in him only your own twisted reflection.
Motti is free to do as he chooses.
I only pray to this God of yours, who you hold in such high regard...
...That the shoulders of your own son will never have to carry the burden of the sins of his father.

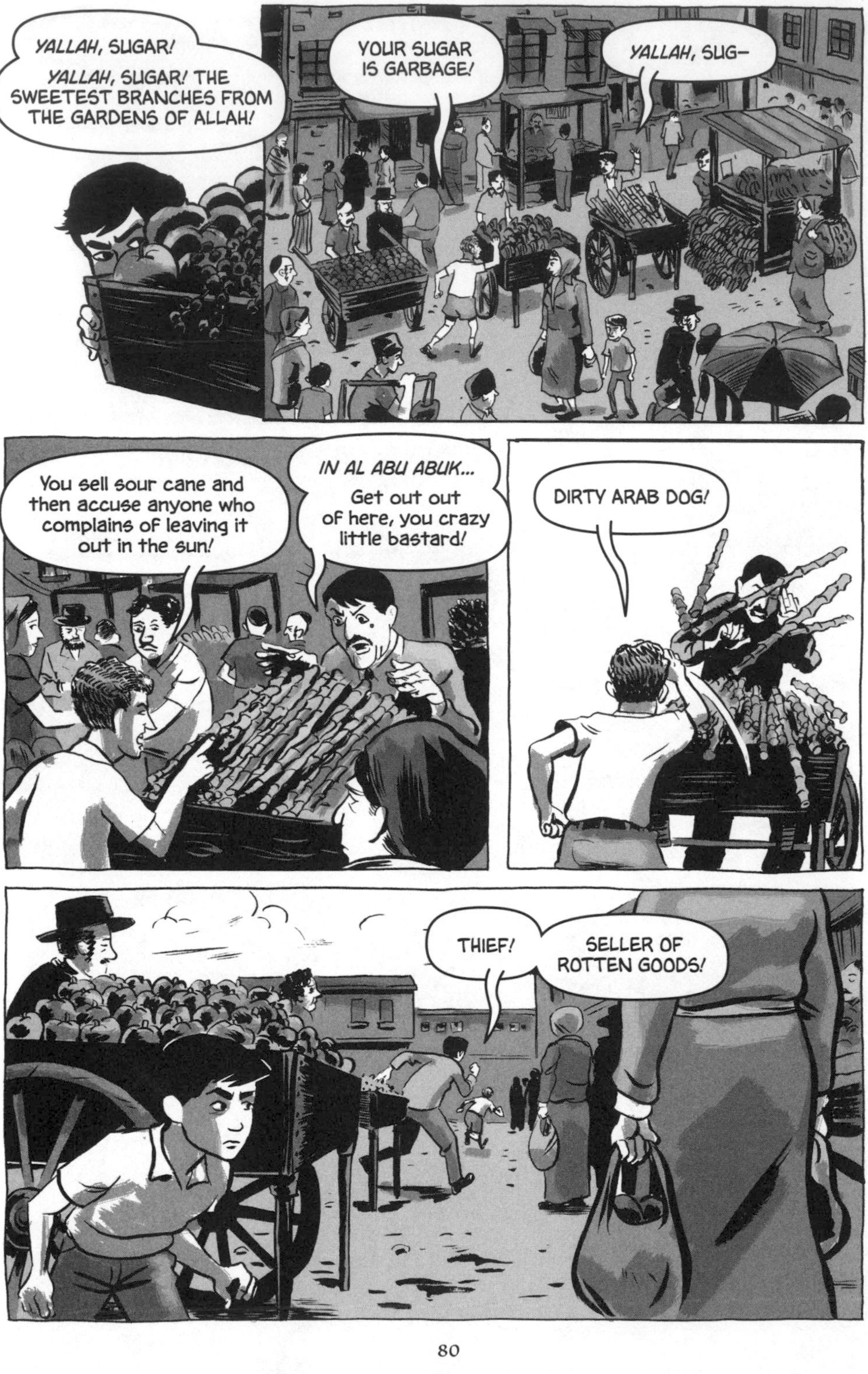
YALLAH, SUGAR!
YALLAH, SUGAR! THE SWEETEST BRANCHES FROM THE GARDENS OF ALLAH!
YOUR SUGAR IS GARBAGE!
YALLAH, SUG—
You sell sour cane and then accuse anyone who complains of leaving it out in the sun!
IN AL ABU ABUK...
Get out out of here, you crazy little bastard!
DIRTY ARAB DOG!
THIEF!
SELLER OF ROTTEN GOODS!

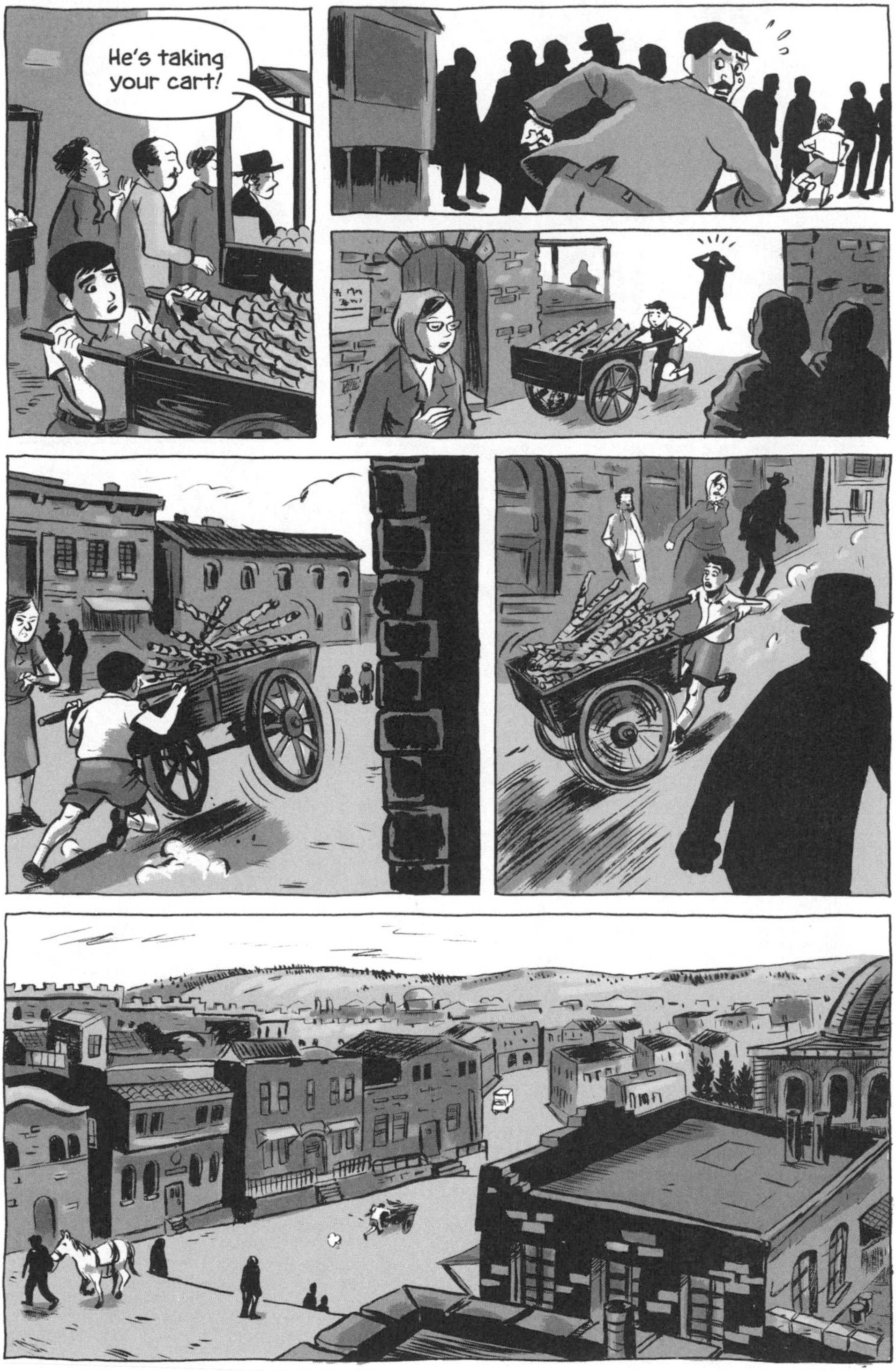
He's taking your cart!

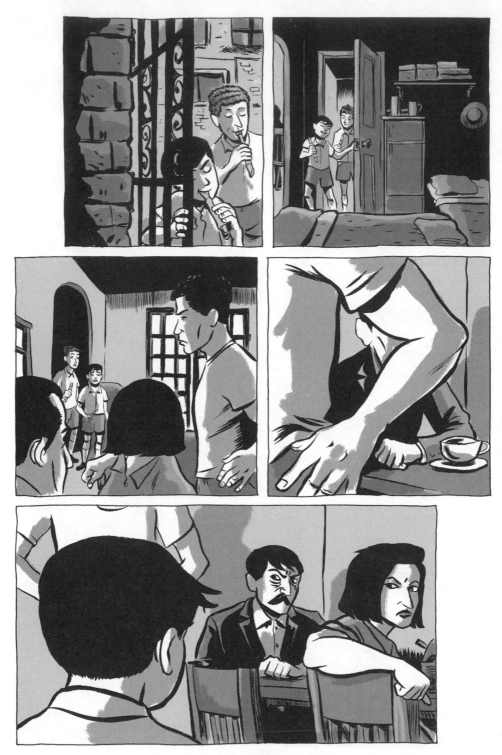

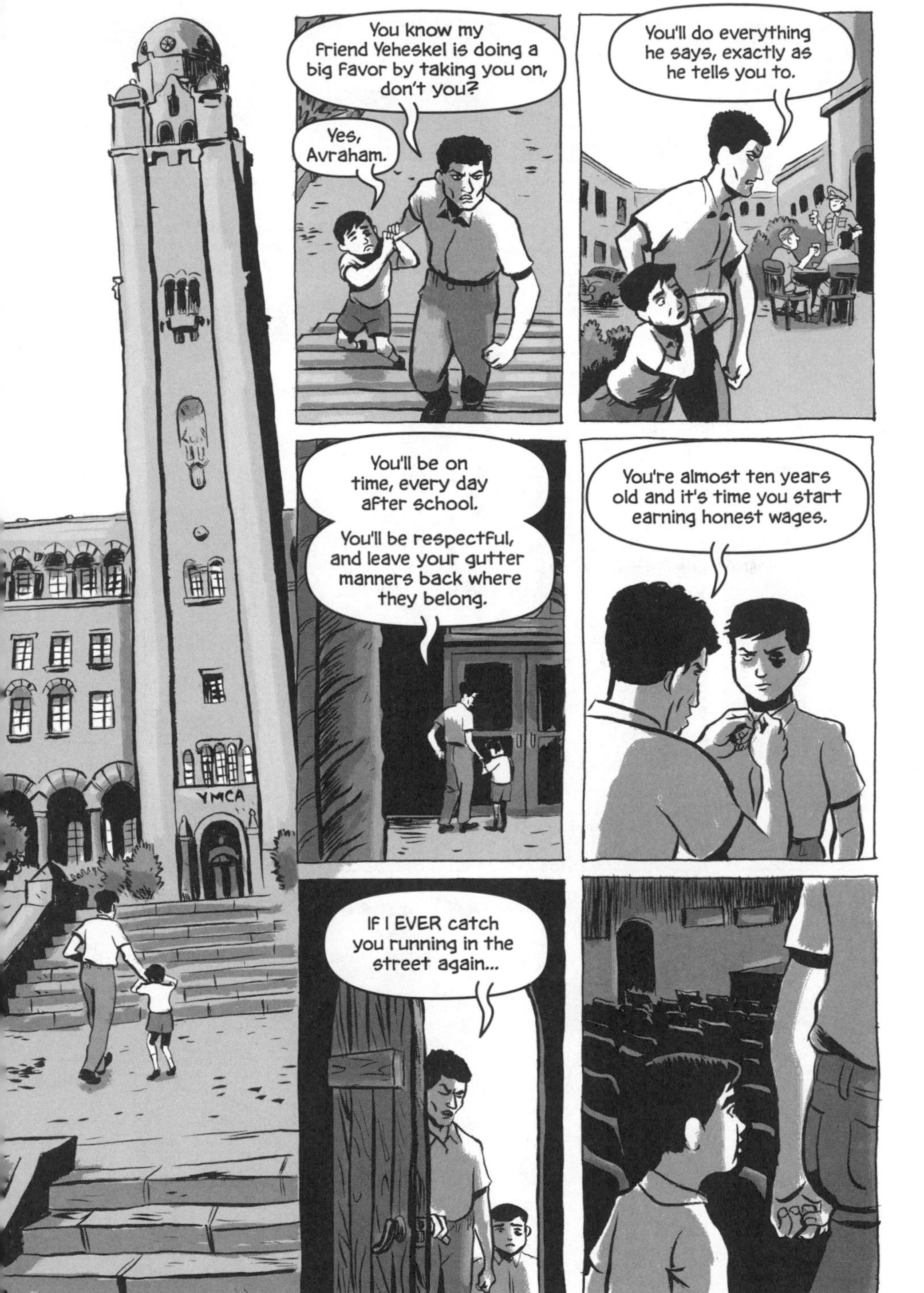
YMCA
You know my friend Yeheskel is doing a big favor by taking you on, don't you?
Yes, Avraham.
You'll do everything he says, exactly as he tells you to.
You'll be on time, every day after school.
You'll be respectful, and leave your gutter manners back where they belong.
You're almost ten years old and it's time you start earning honest wages.
IF I EVER catch you running in the street again...

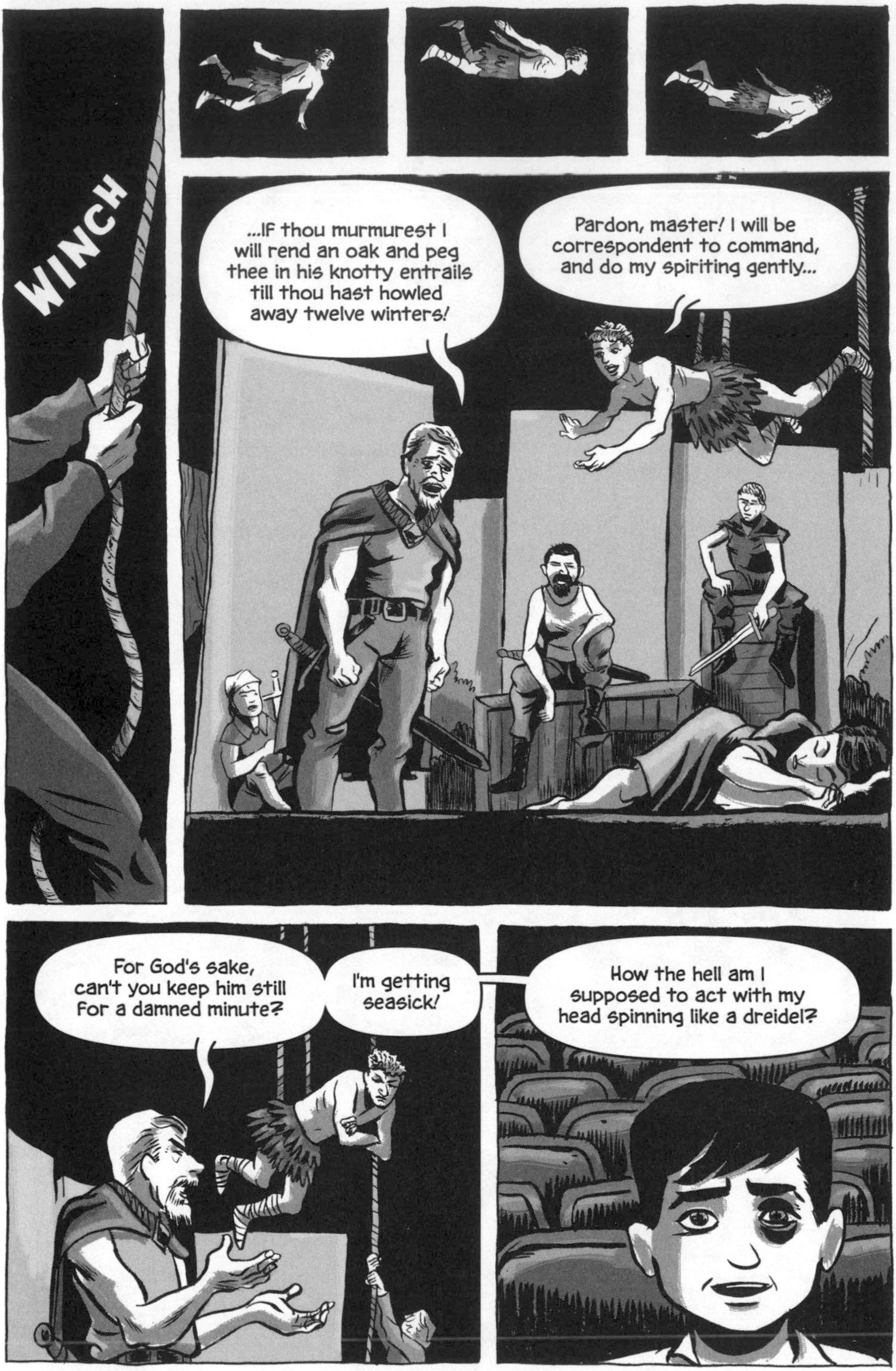
WINCH
...If thou murmurest I will rend an oak and peg thee in his knotty entrails till thou hast howled away twelve winters!
Pardon, master! I will be correspondent to command, and do my spiriting gently...
For God's sake, can't you keep him still for a damned minute?
I'm getting seasick!
How the hell am I supposed to act with my head spinning like a dreidel?

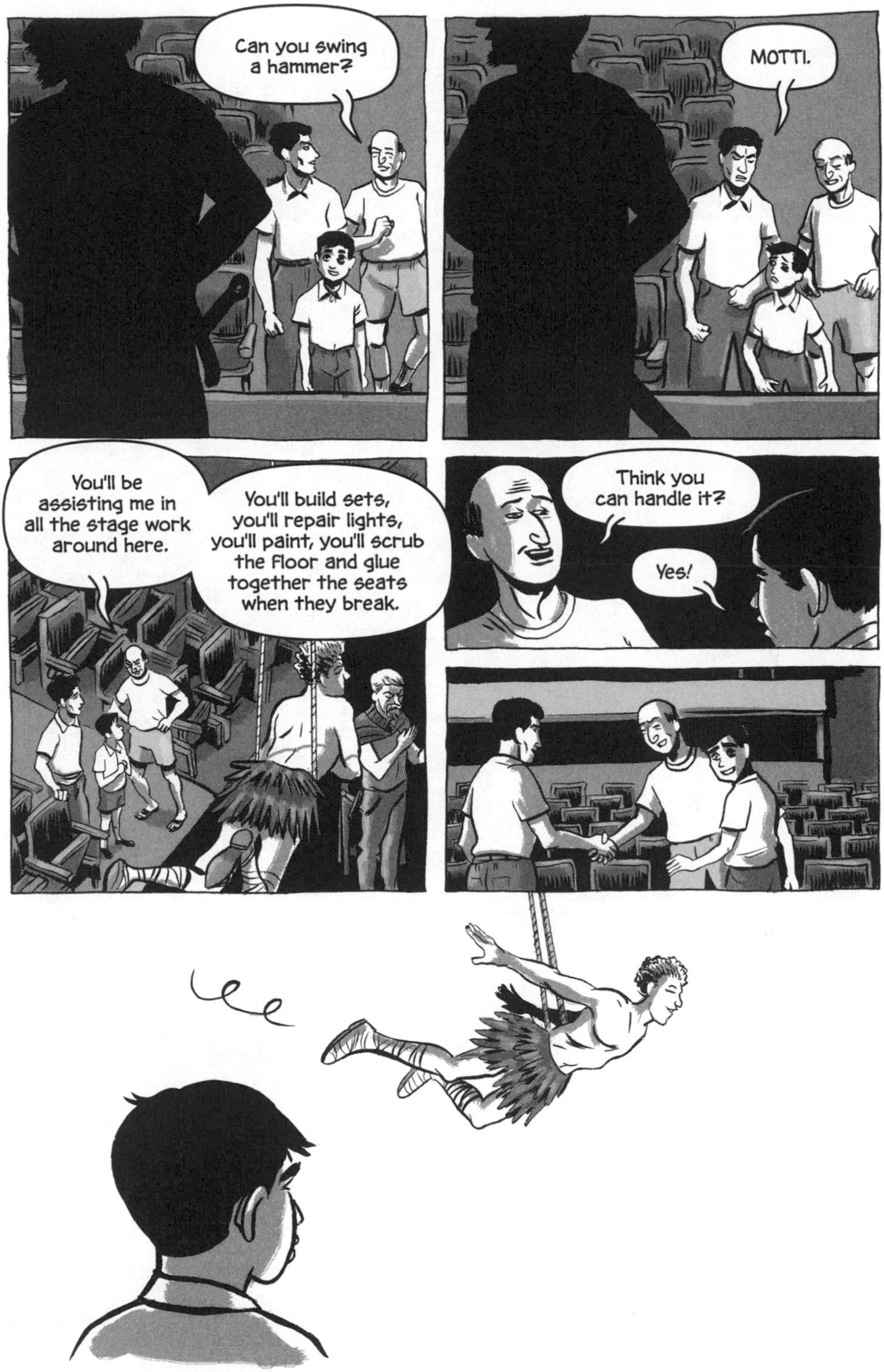
Can you swing a hammer?
MOTTI.
You'll be assisting me in all the stage work around here.
You'll build sets, you'll repair lights, you'll paint, you'll scrub the floor and glue together the seats when they break.
Think you can handle it?
Yes!

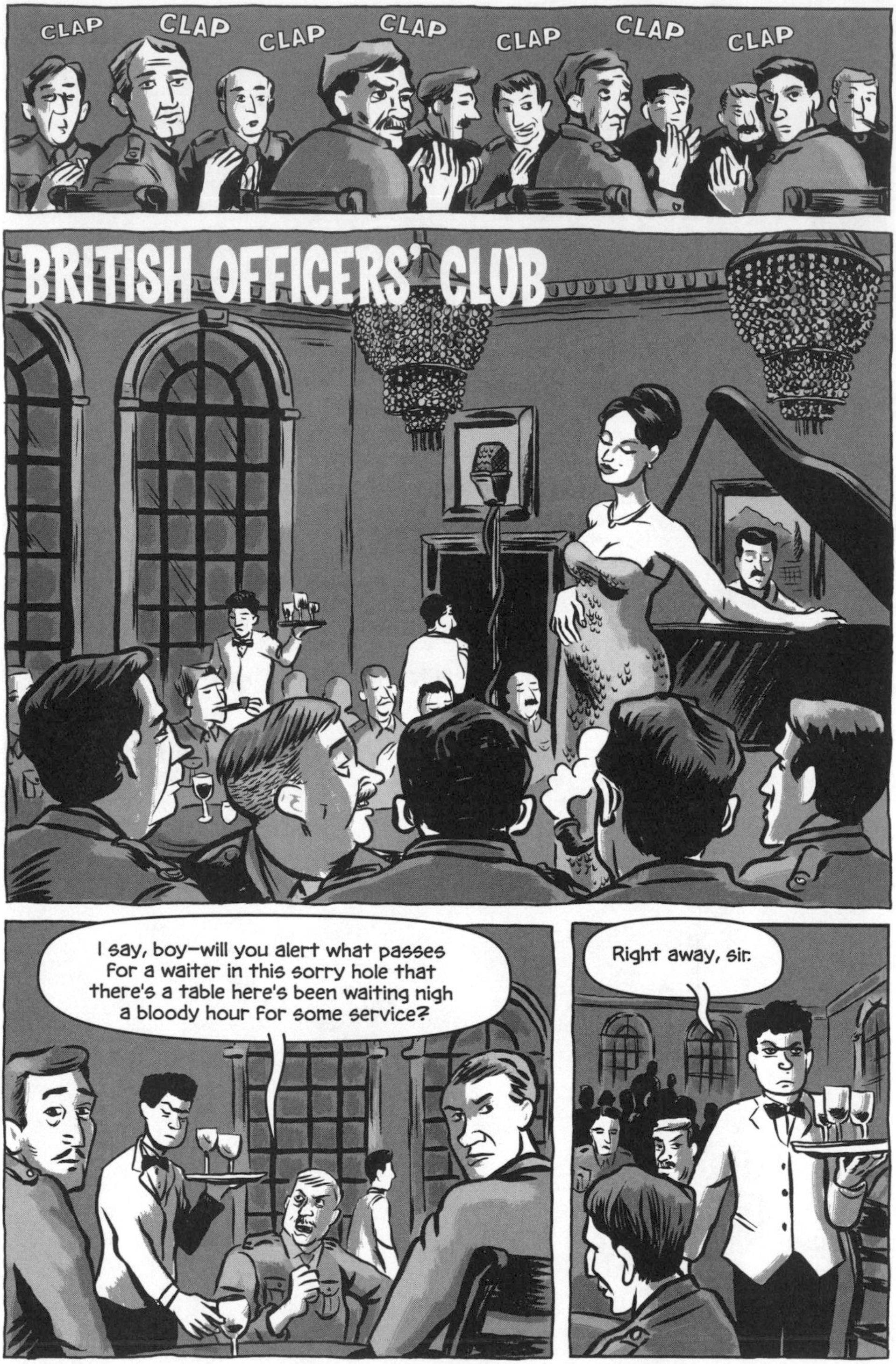
CLAP
CLAP
CLAP
CLAP
CLAP
CLAP
CLAP
BRITISH OFFICERS' CLUB
I say, boy—will you alert what passes for a waiter in this sorry hole that there's a table here's been waiting nigh a bloody hour for some service?
Right away, sir.

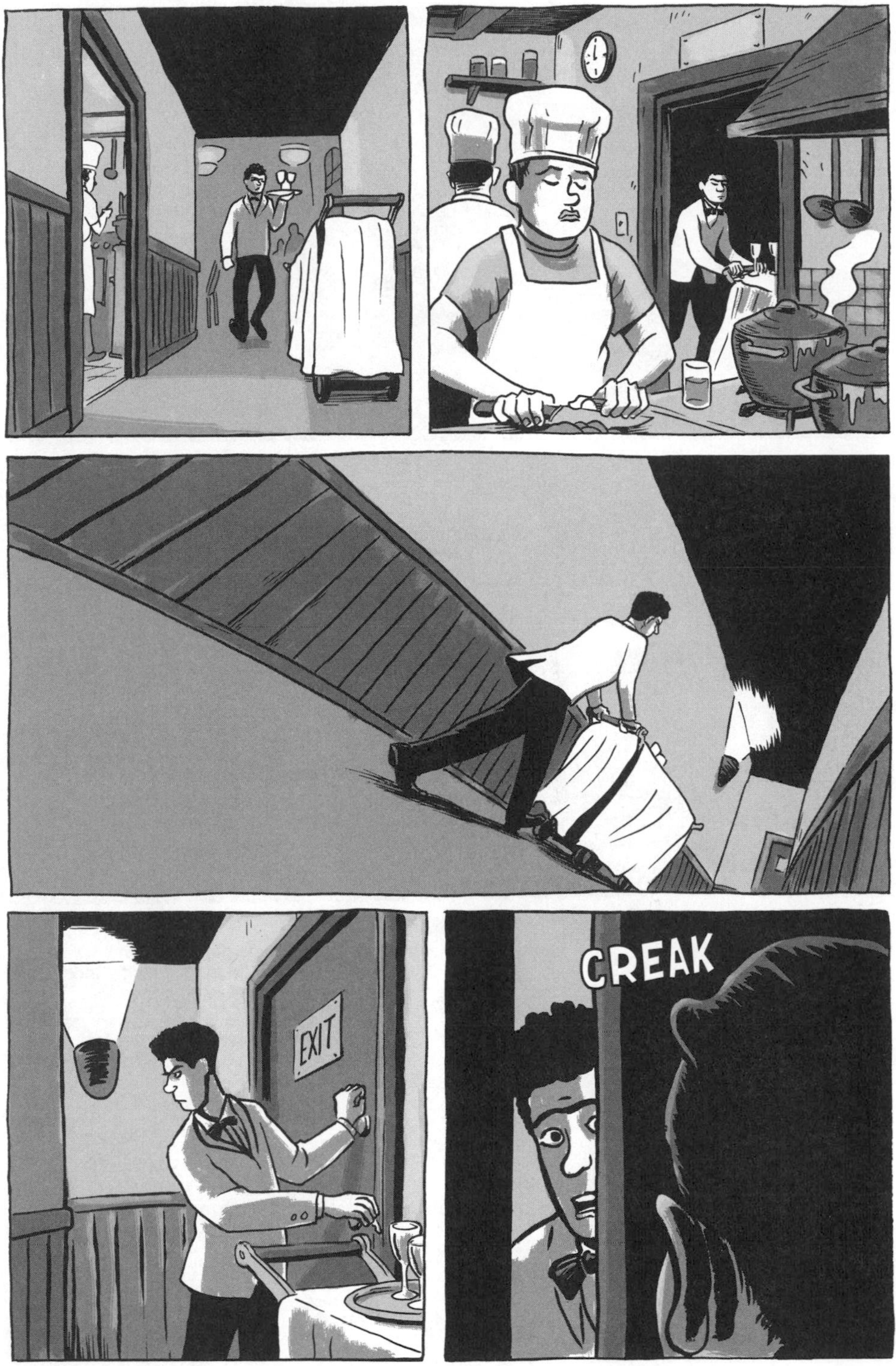
EXIT
CREAK

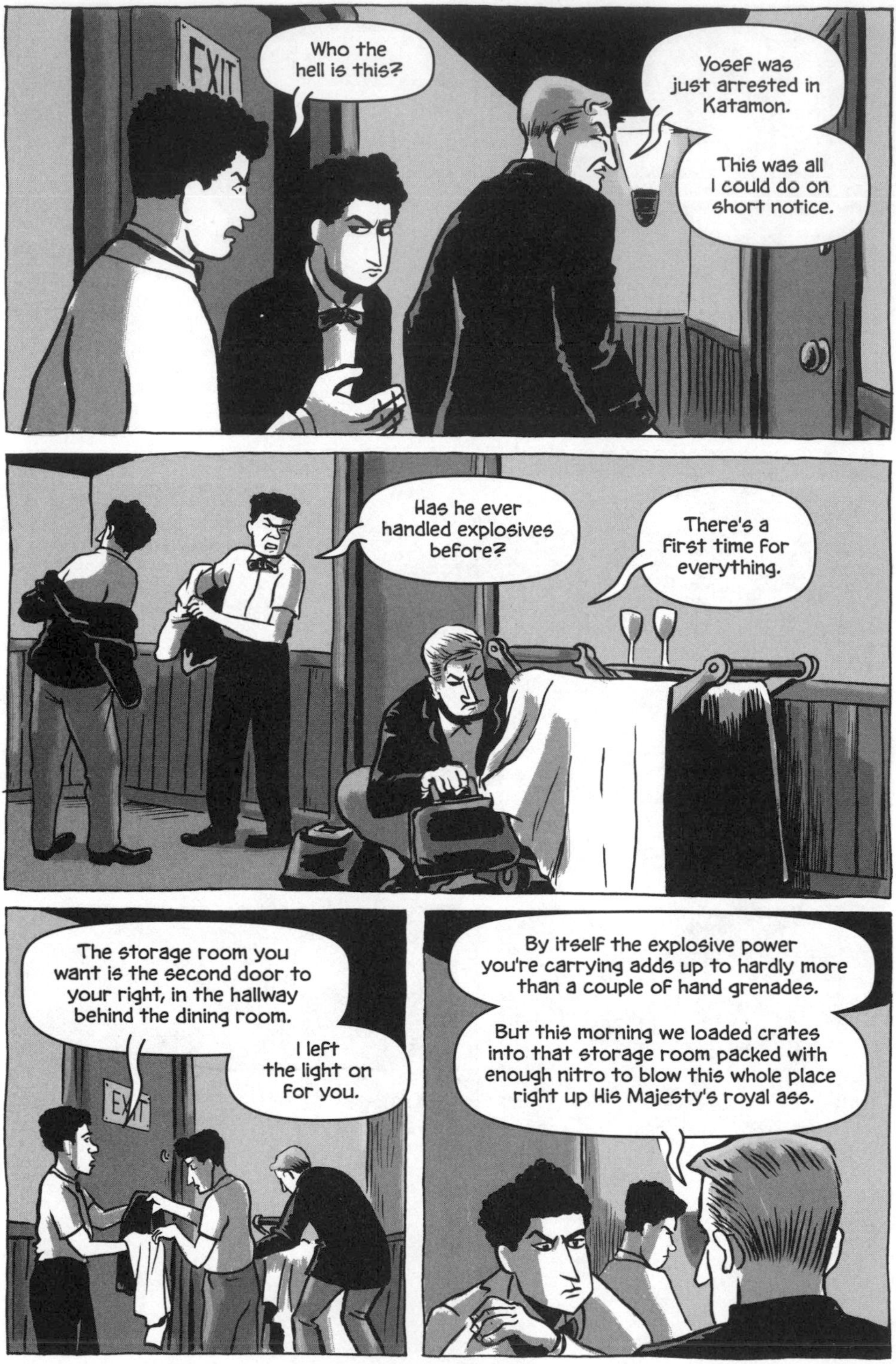
EXIT
Who the hell is this?
Yosef was just arrested in Katamon.
This was all I could do on short notice.
Has he ever handled explosives before?
There's a first time for everything.
The storage room you want is the second door to your right, in the hallway behind the dining room.
I left the light on for you.
By itself the explosive power you're carrying adds up to hardly more than a couple of hand grenades.
But this morning we loaded crates into that storage room packed with enough nitro to blow this whole place right up His Majesty's royal ass.

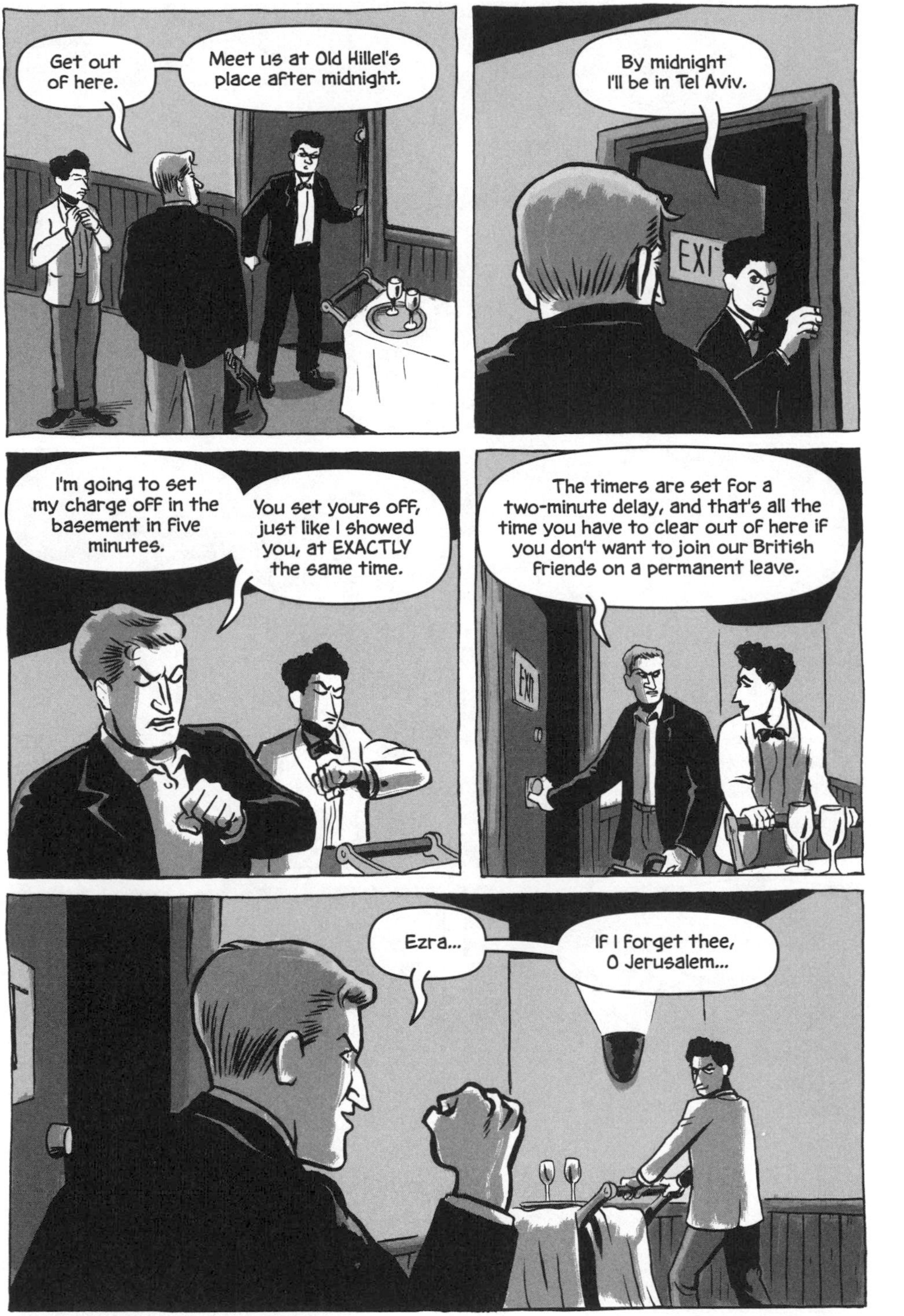
Get out of here.
Meet us at Old Hillel's place after midnight.
By midnight I'll be in Tel Aviv.
EXIT
I'm going to set my charge off in the basement in five minutes.
You set yours off, just like I showed you, at EXACTLY the same time.
The timers are set for a two-minute delay, and that's all the time you have to clear out of here if you don't want to join our British friends on a permanent leave.
EXIT
Ezra...
If I forget thee, O Jerusalem...

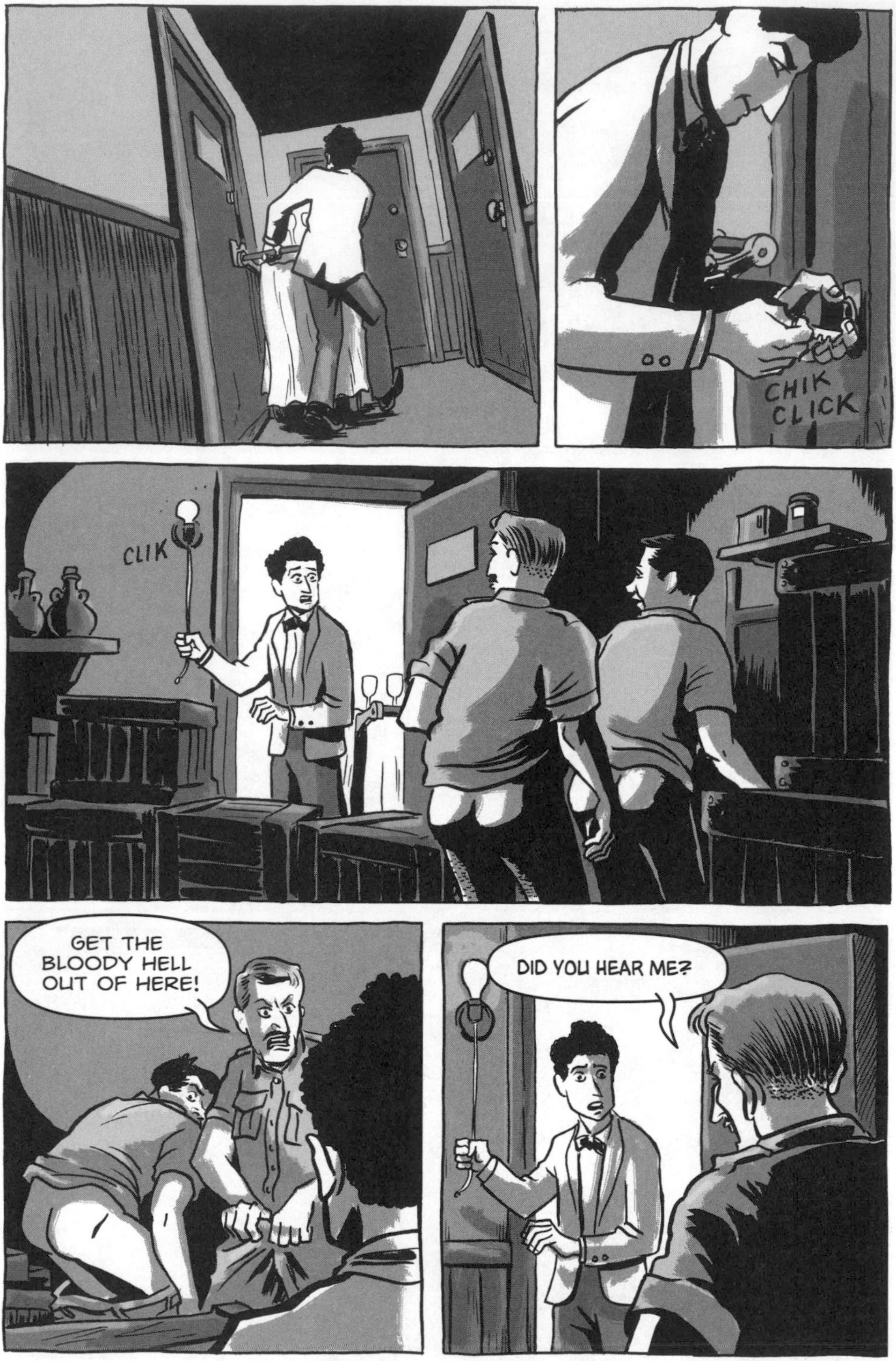
CHIK
CLICK
CLIK
GET THE BLOODY HELL OUT OF HERE!
DID YOU HEAR ME?

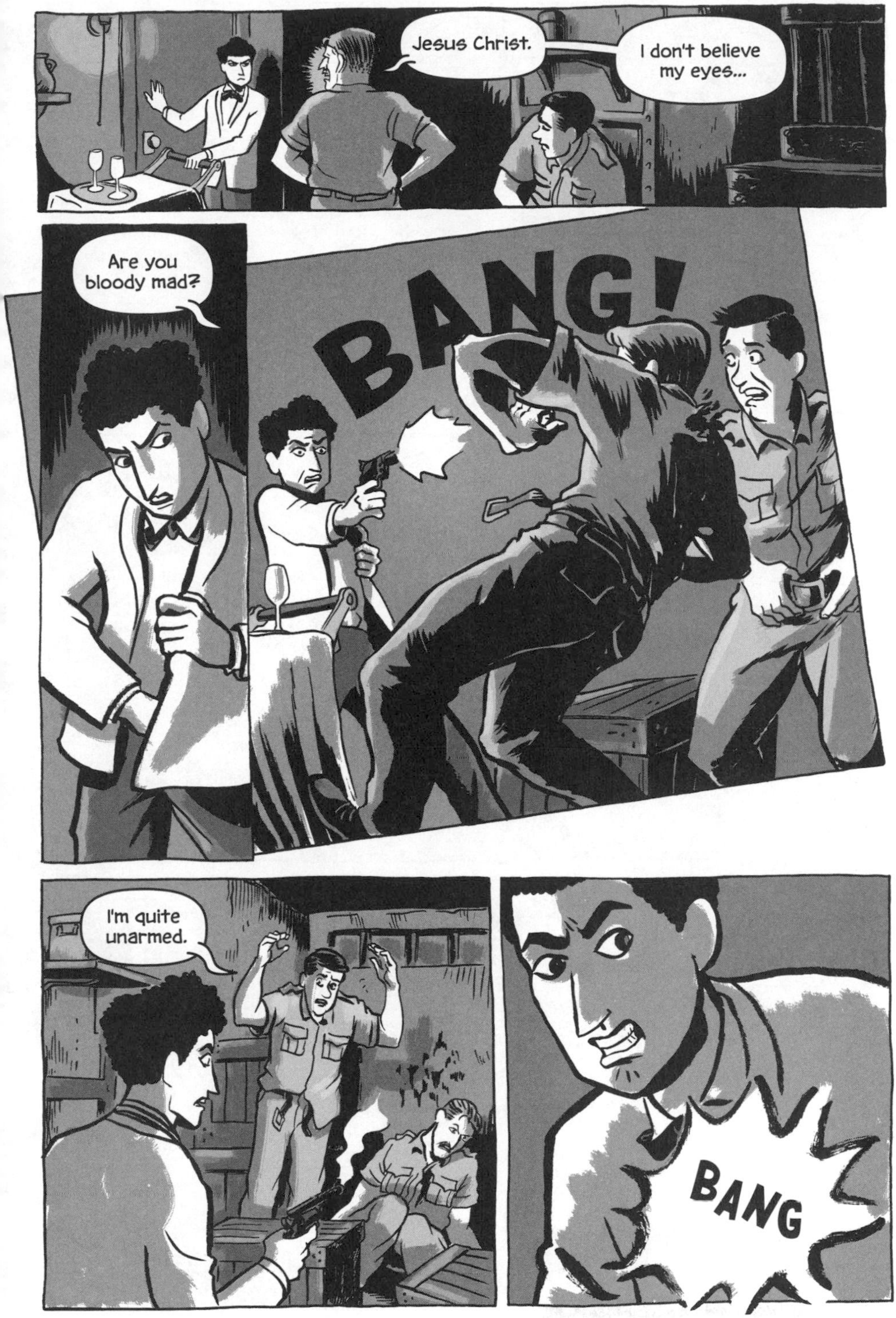
Jesus Christ.
I don't believe my eyes...
Are you bloody mad?
BANG!
I'm quite unarmed.
BANG

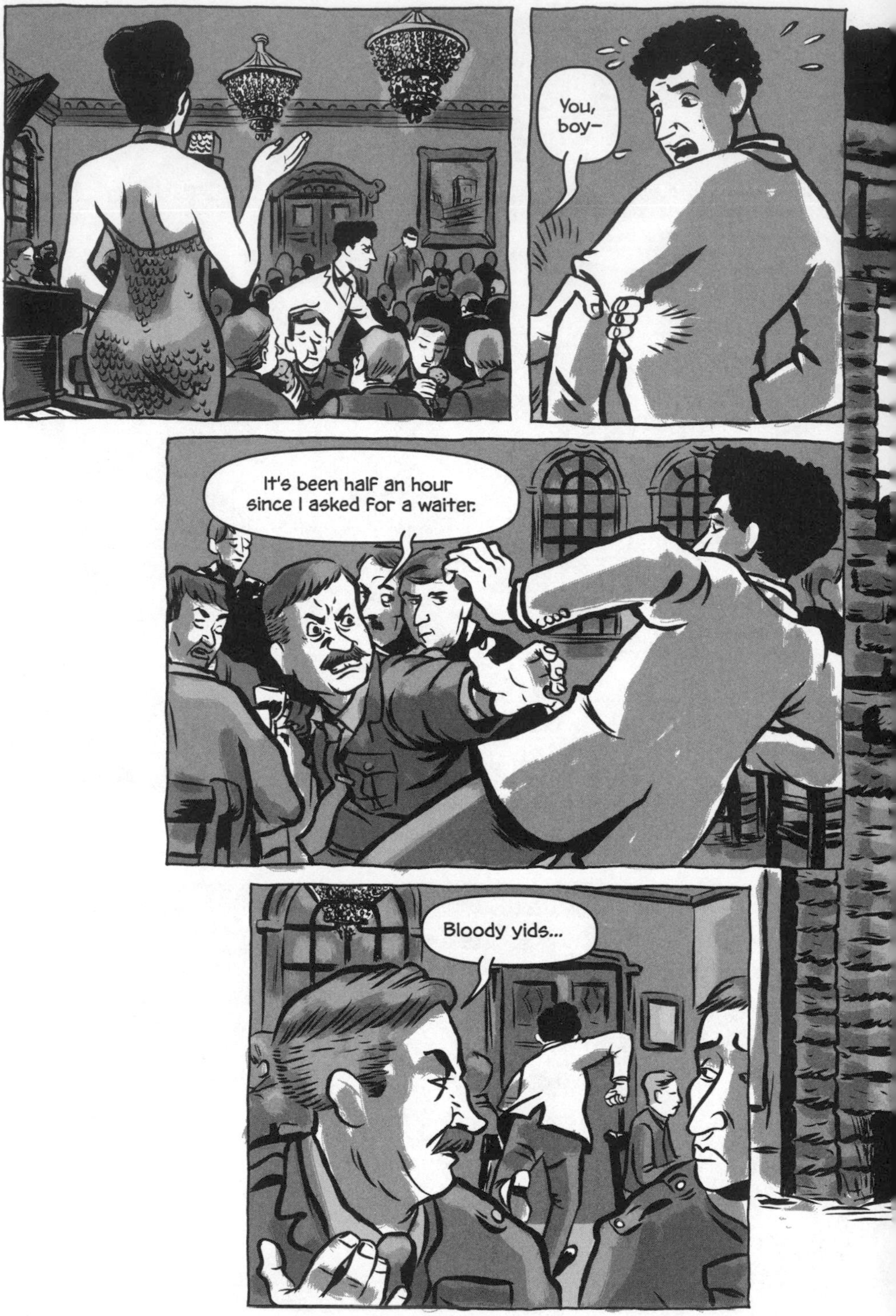
You, boy–
It's been half an hour since I asked for a waiter.
Bloody yids...

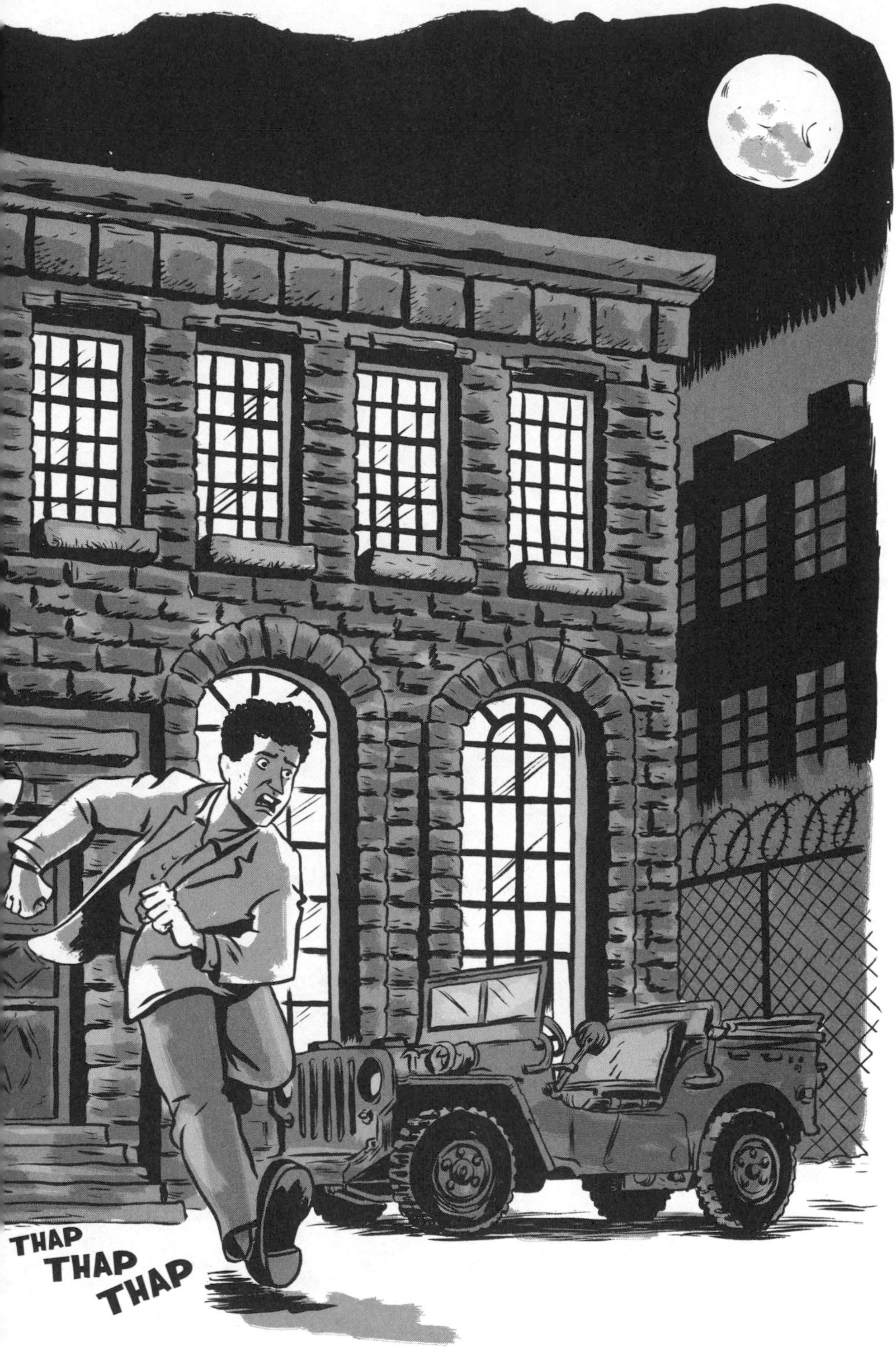
THAP
THAP
THAP

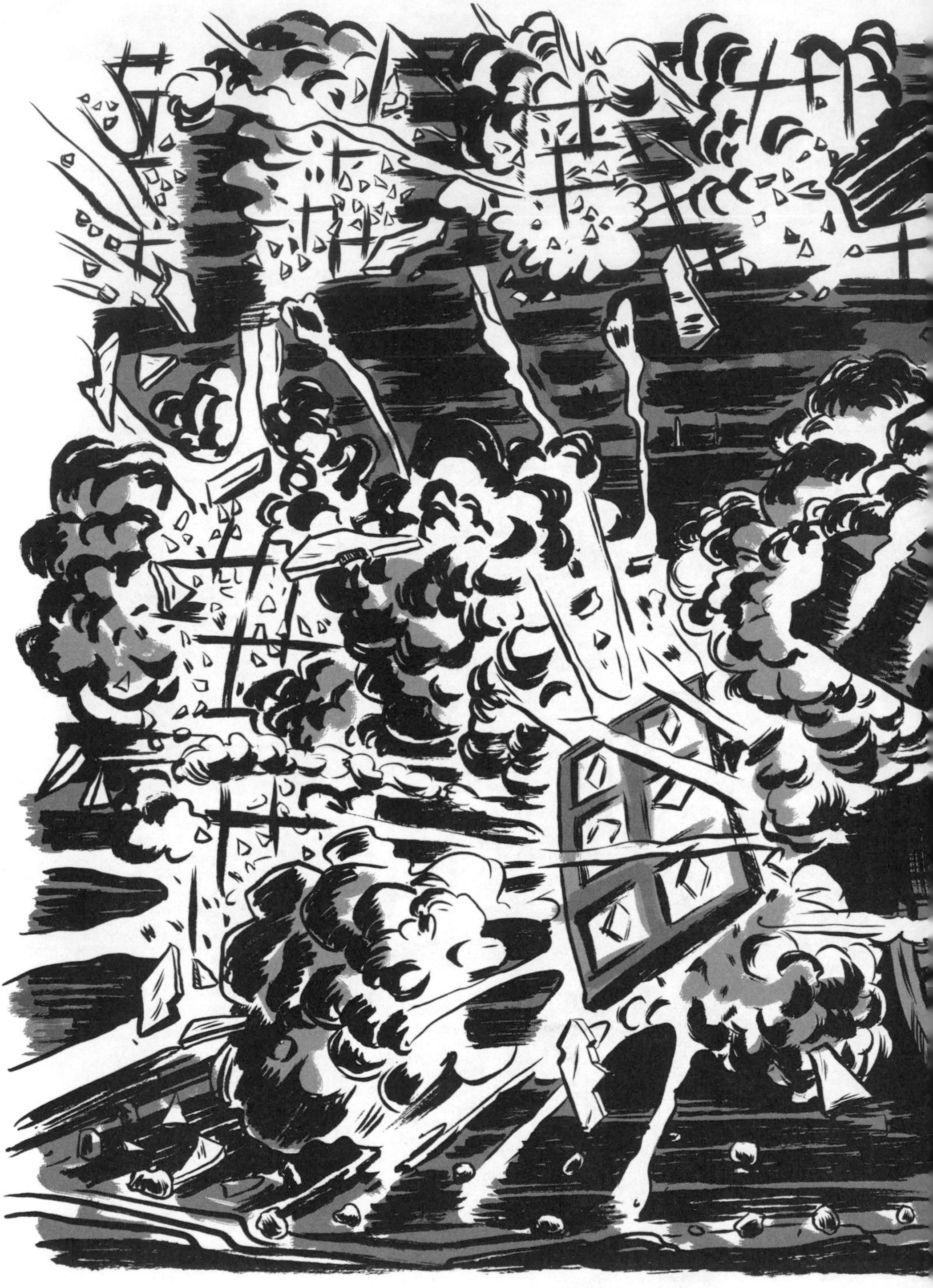

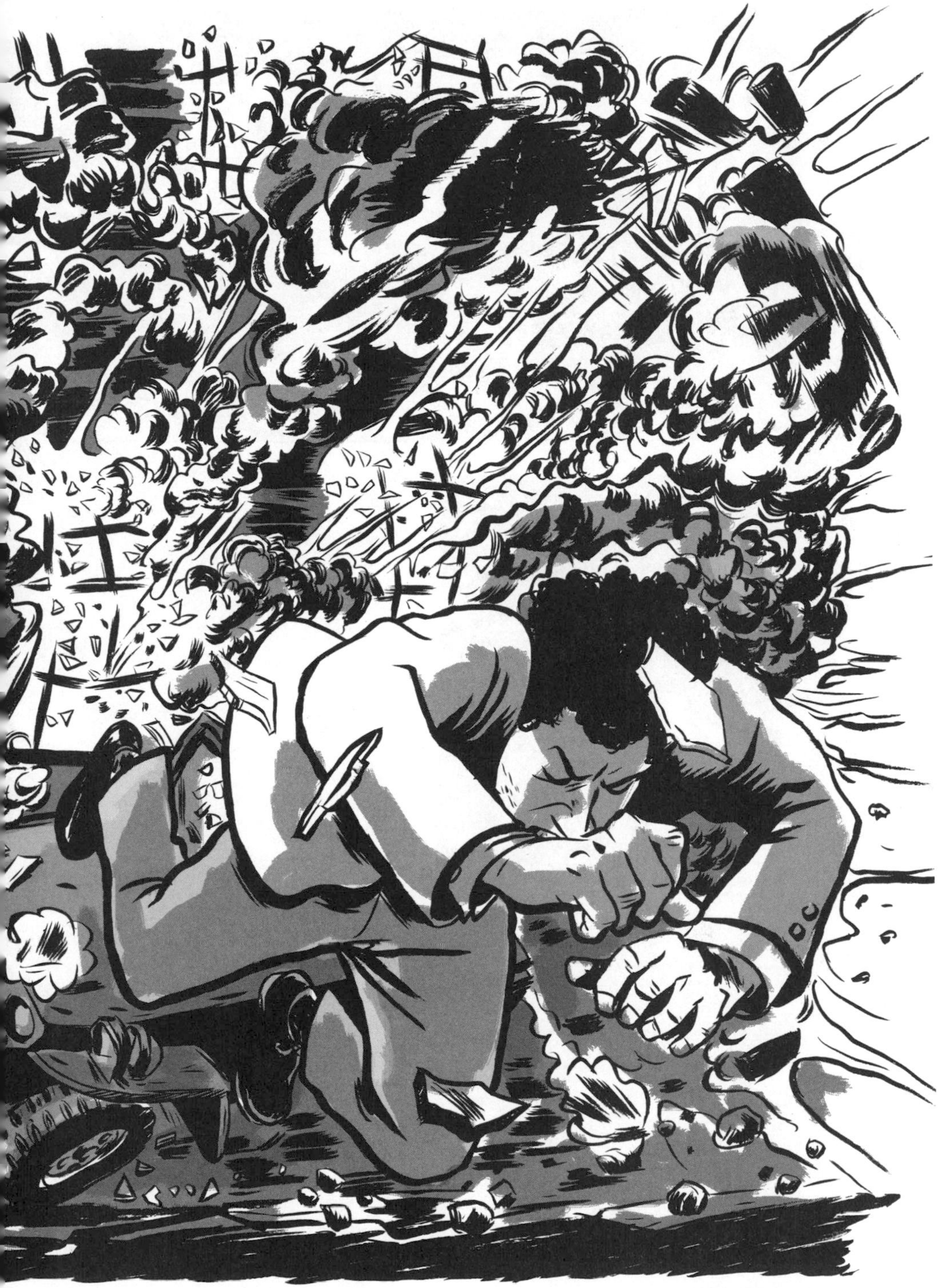

# AUGUST 1946

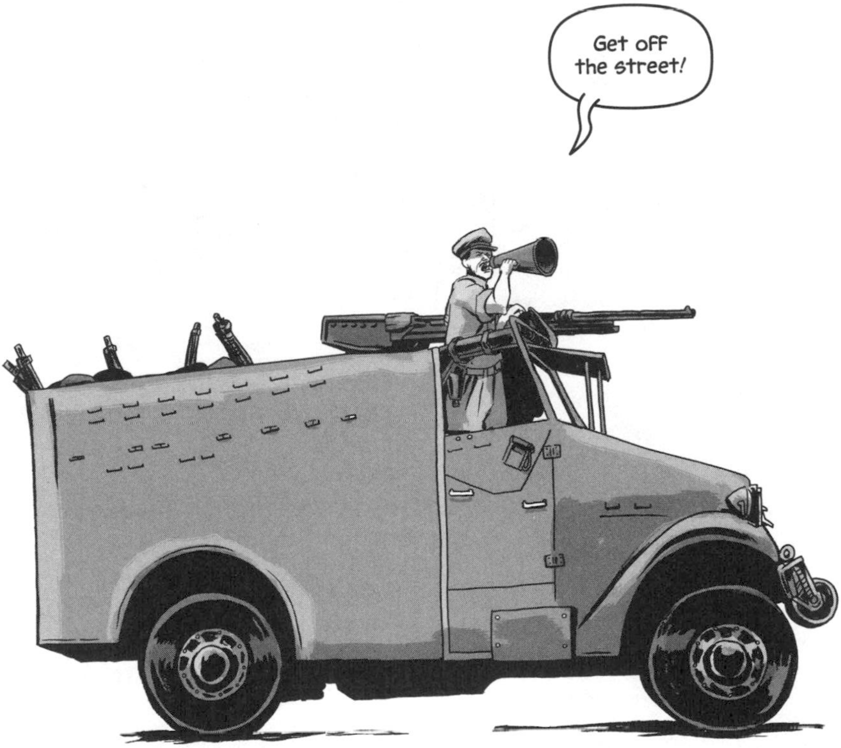
Get off the street!

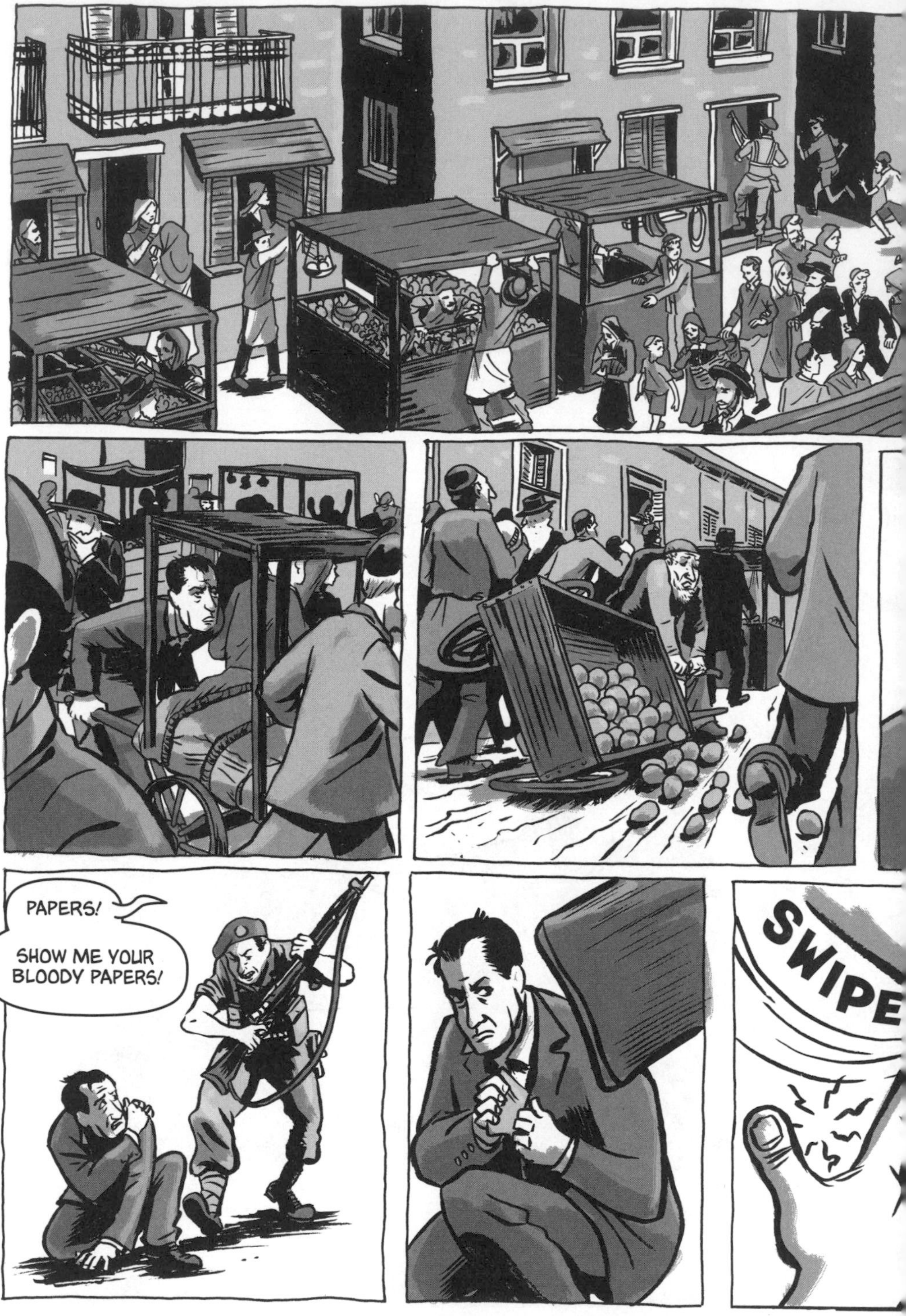
PAPERS!
SHOW ME YOUR BLOODY PAPERS!
SWIPE

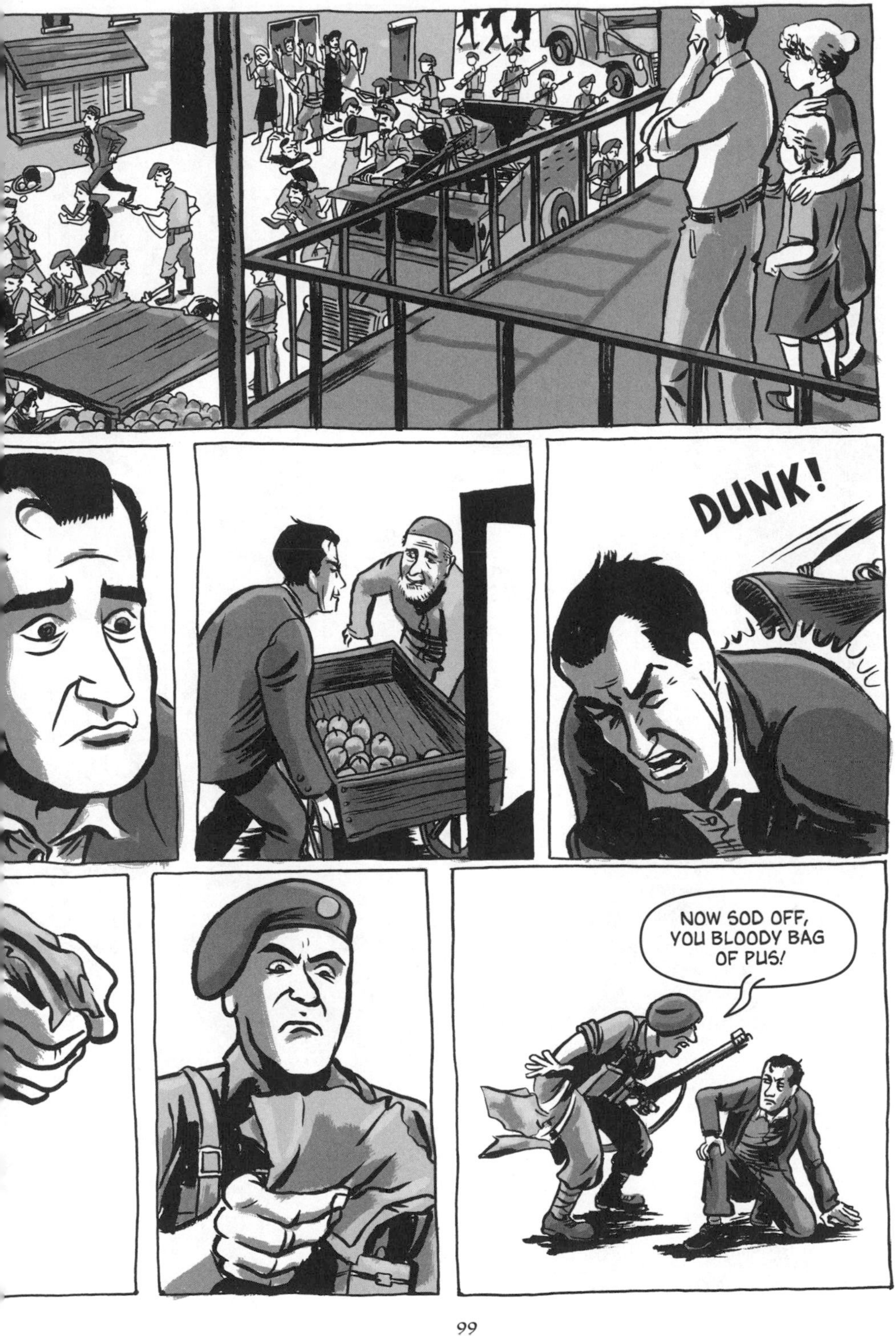
DUNK!
NOW SOD OFF, YOU BLOODY BAG OF PUS!

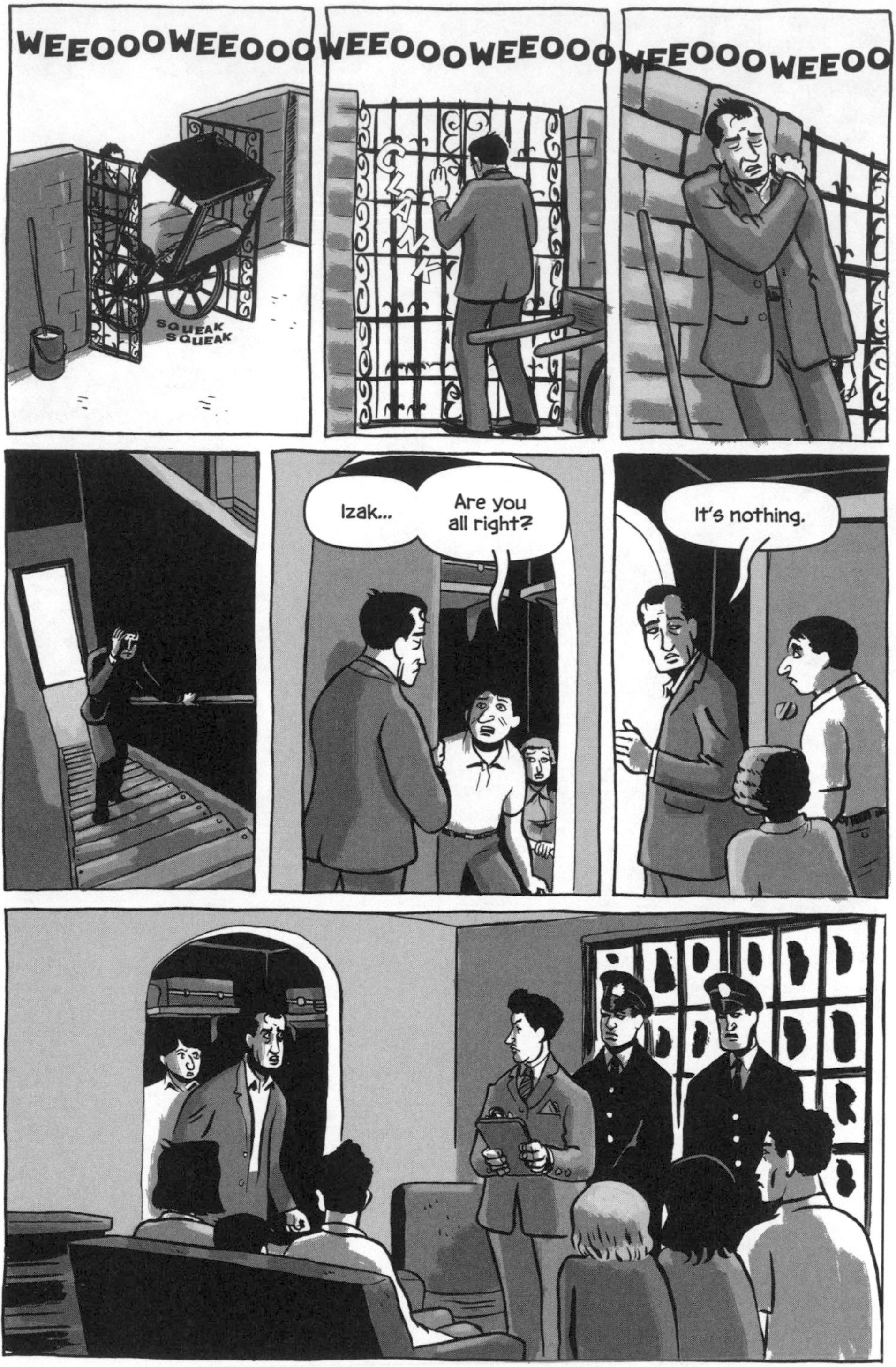
WEEOOOWEEOOO
SQUEAK SQUEAK
WEEOOOWEEOOO
CLANK
WEEOOOWEEOO
Izak...
Are you all right?
It's nothing.

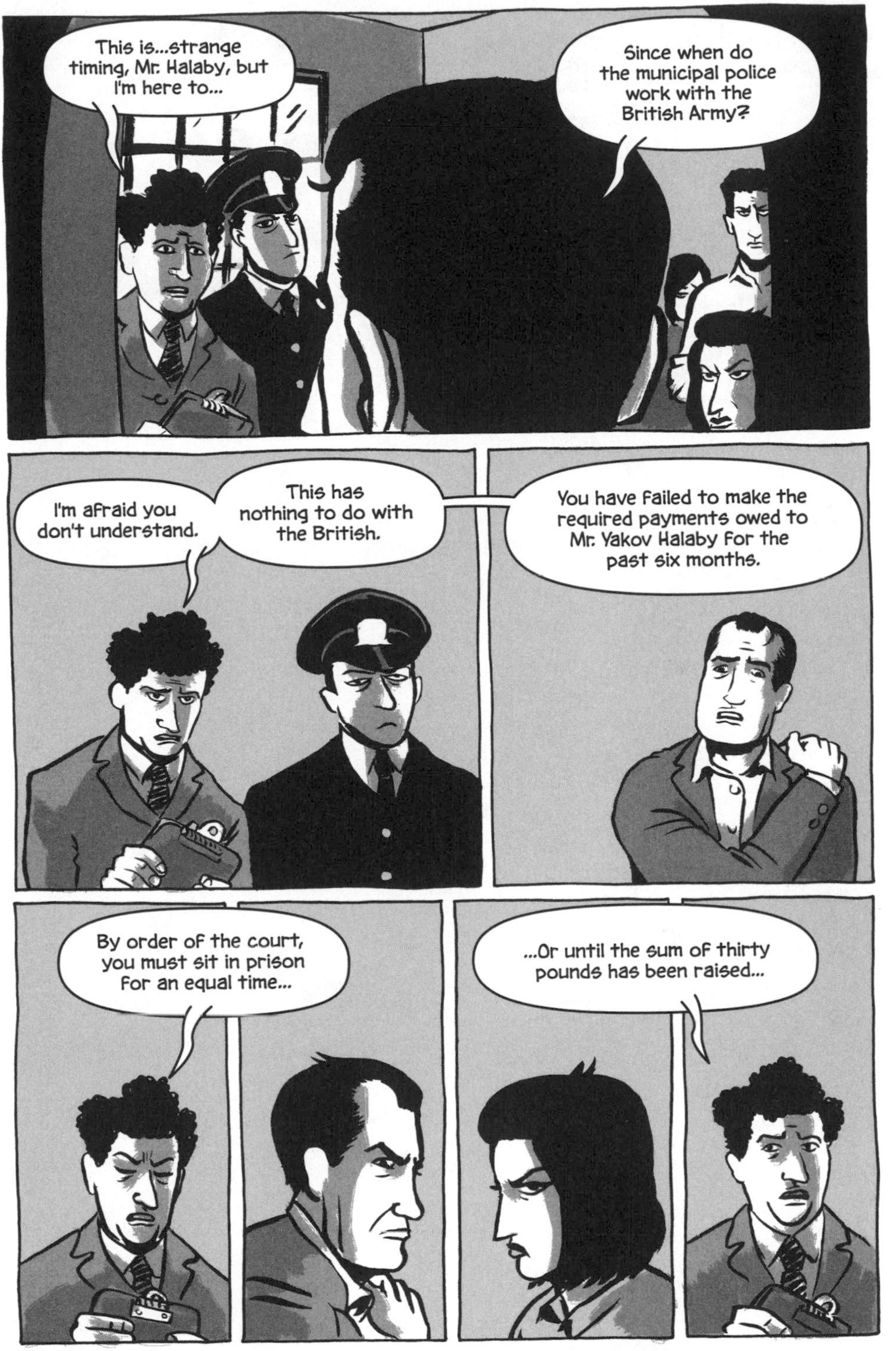
This is...strange timing, Mr. Halaby, but I'm here to...
Since when do the municipal police work with the British Army?
I'm afraid you don't understand.
This has nothing to do with the British.
You have failed to make the required payments owed to Mr. Yakov Halaby for the past six months.
By order of the court, you must sit in prison for an equal time...
...Or until the sum of thirty pounds has been raised...

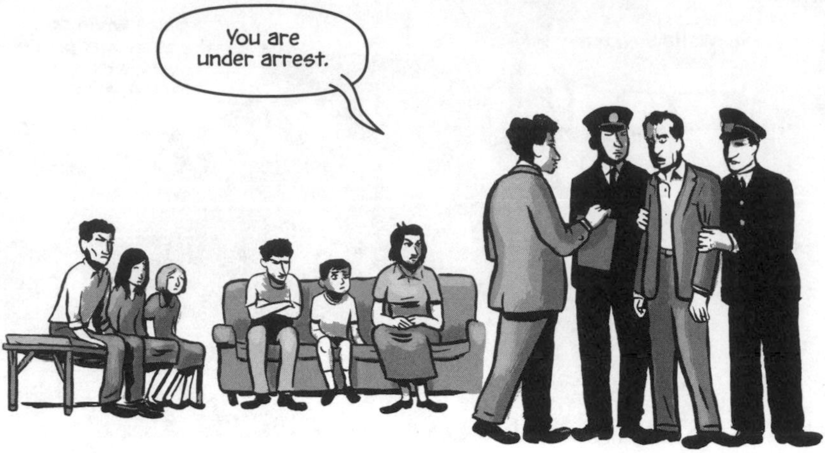
You are under arrest.

# THE LAW

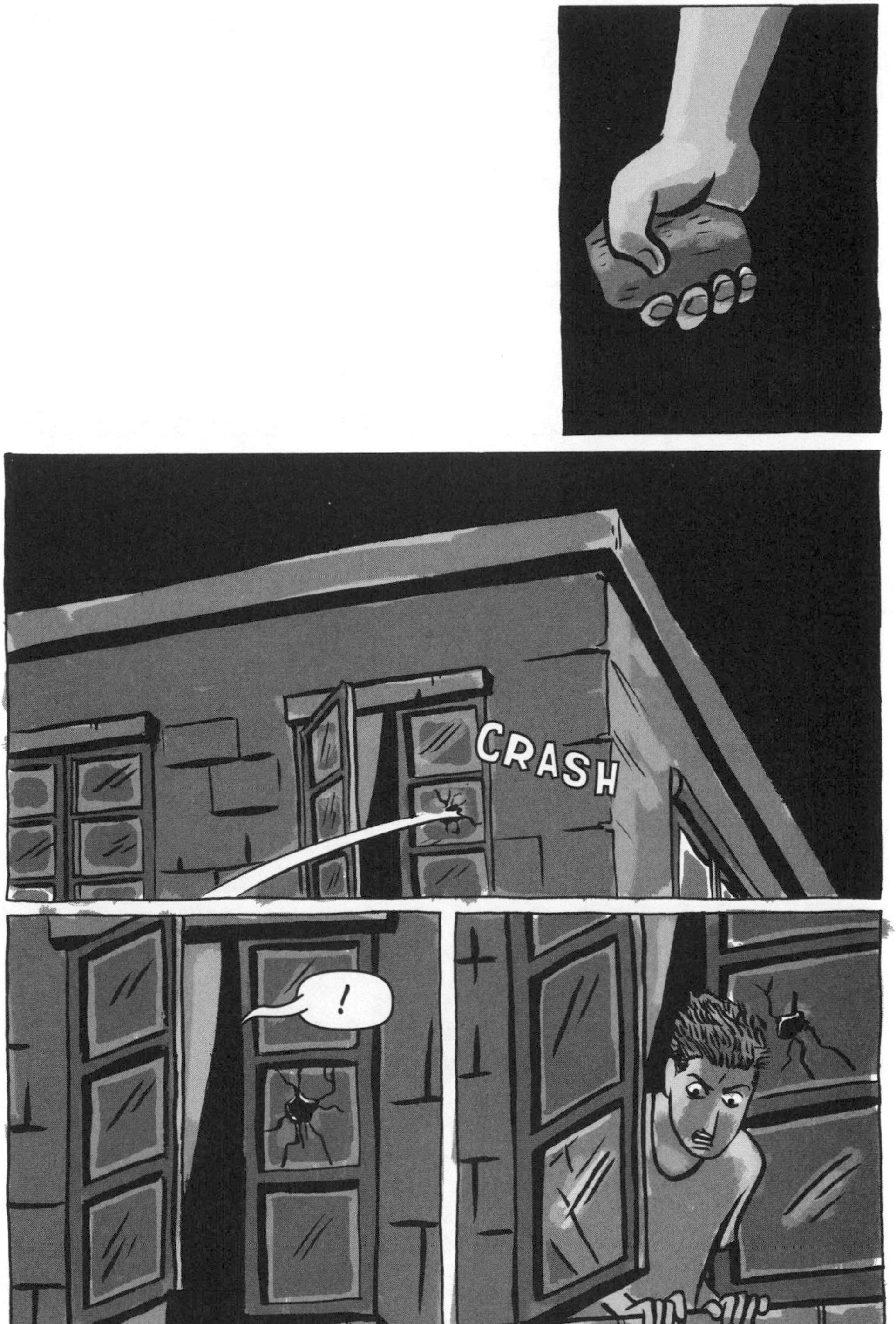
CRASH
!

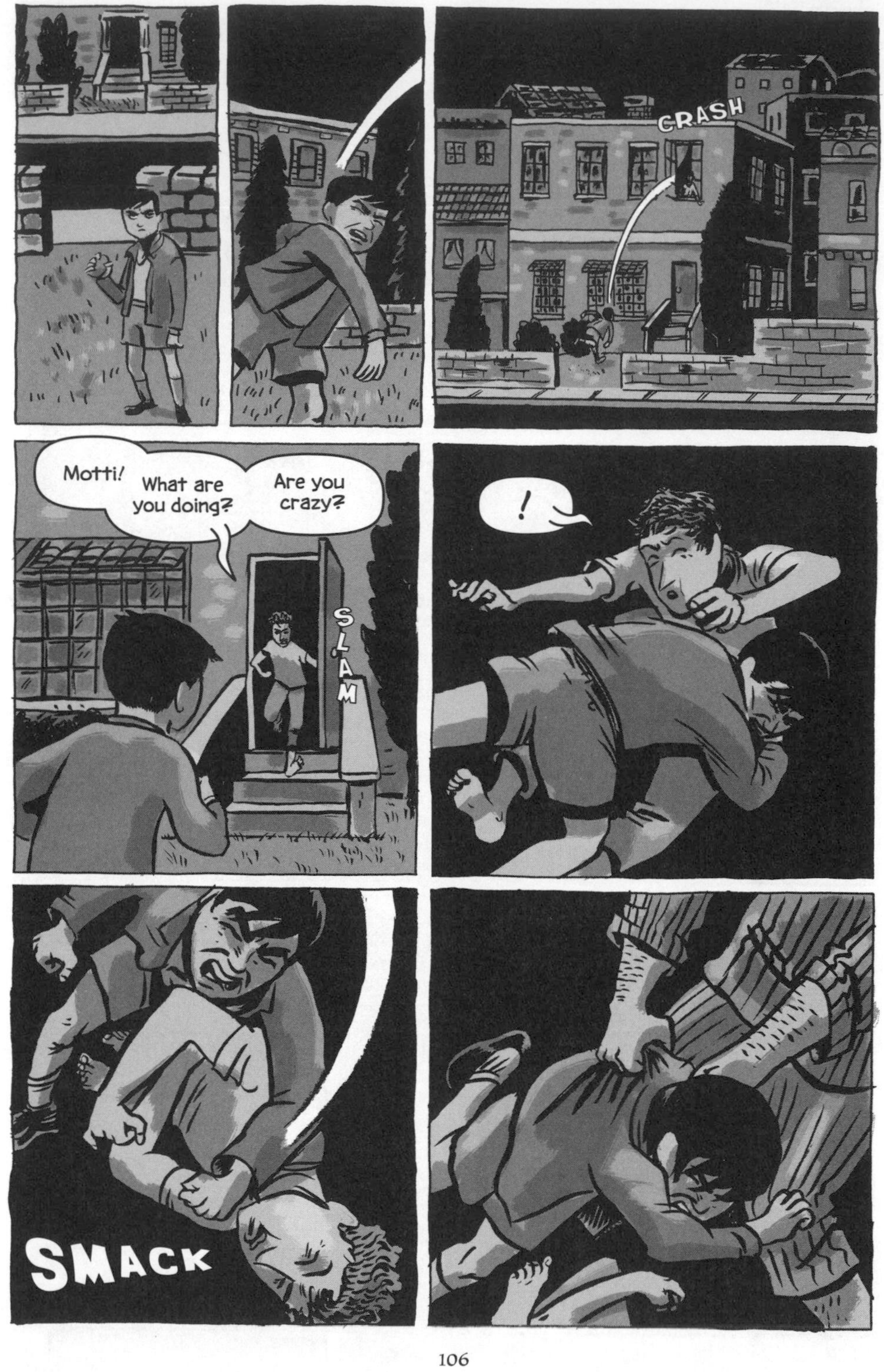
CRASH
Motti!
What are you doing?
Are you crazy?
SLAM
!
SMACK

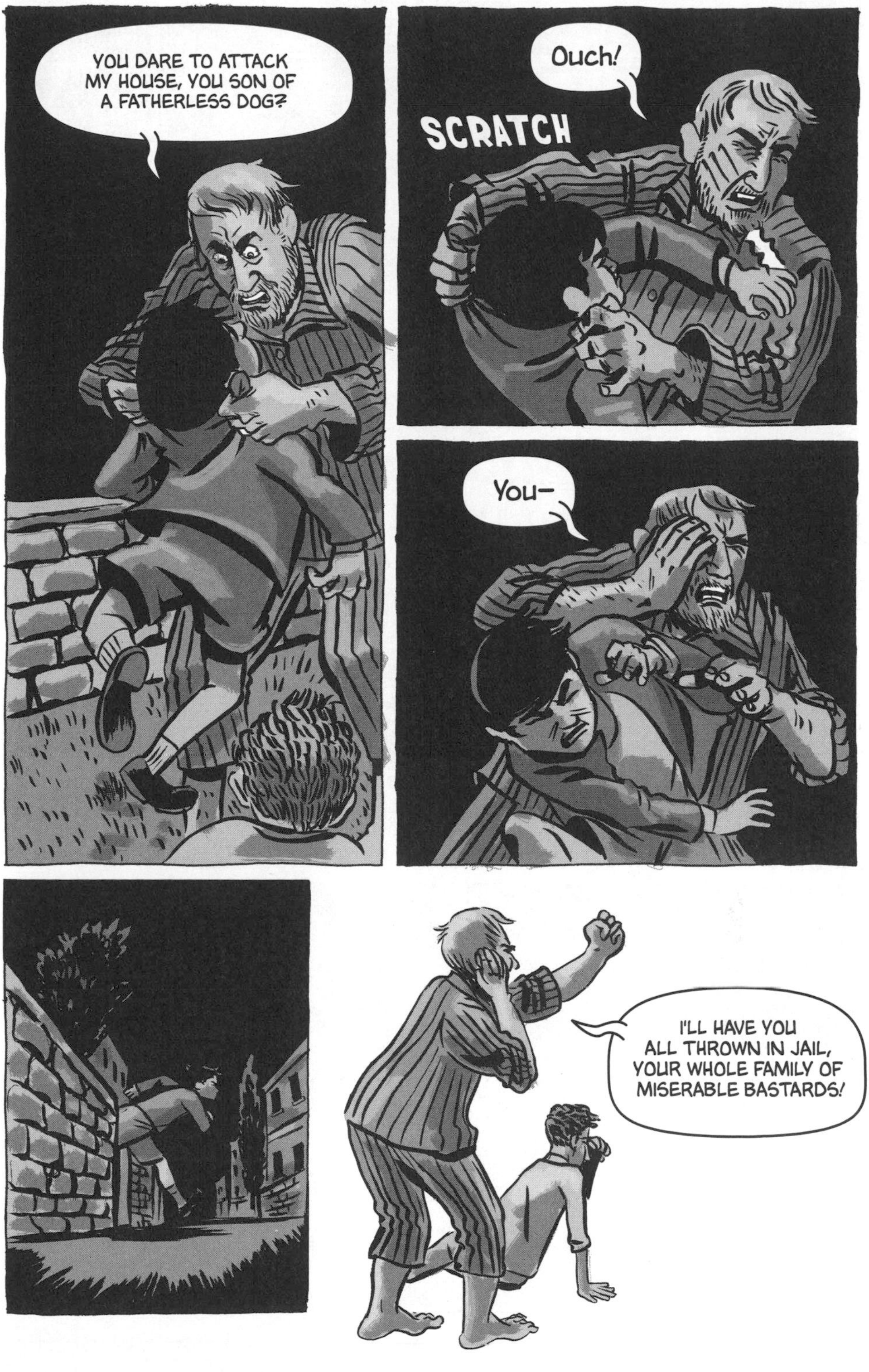
YOU DARE TO ATTACK MY HOUSE, YOU SON OF A FATHERLESS DOG?
Ouch!
SCRATCH
You-
I'LL HAVE YOU ALL THROWN IN JAIL, YOUR WHOLE FAMILY OF MISERABLE BASTARDS!

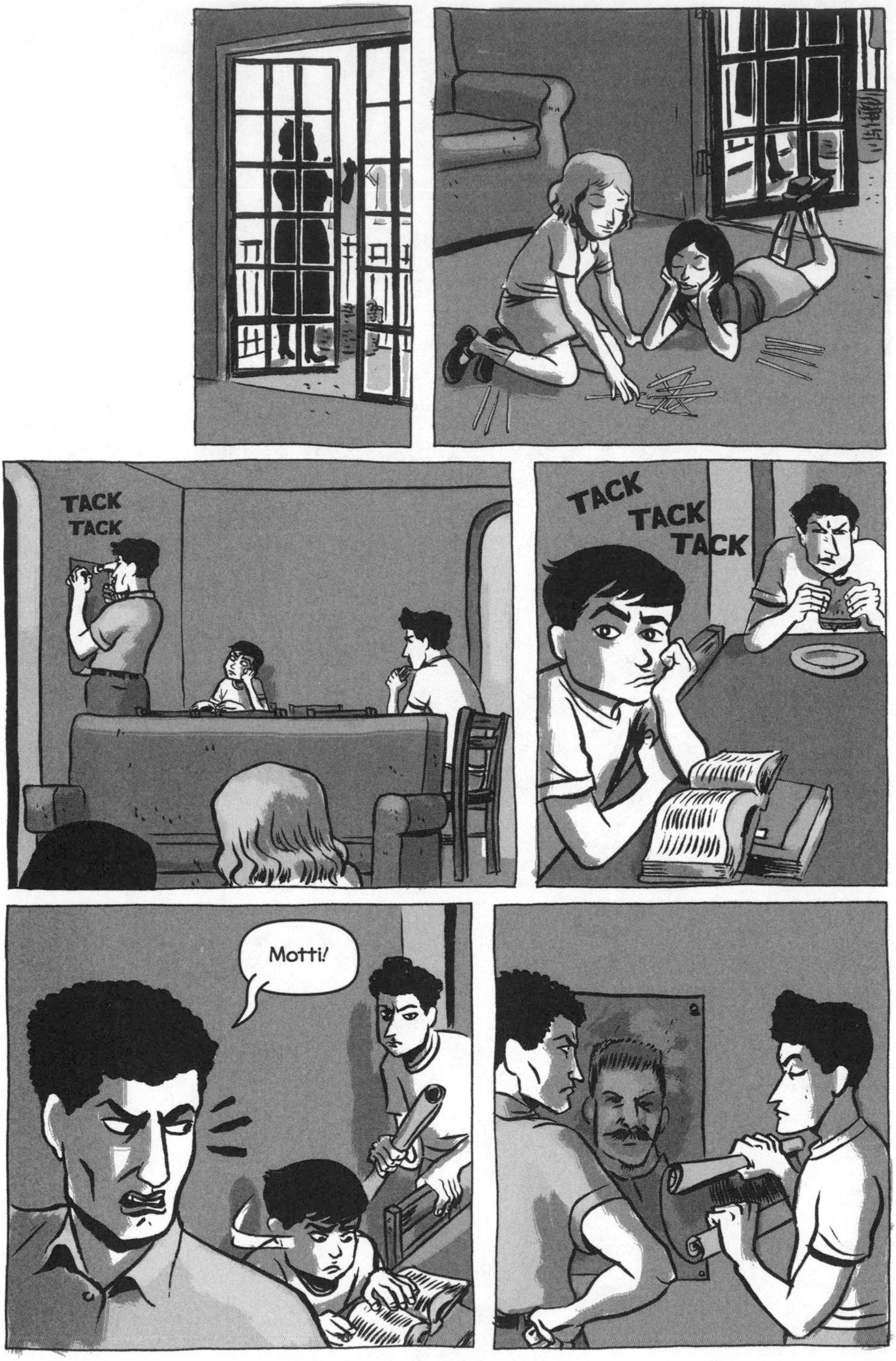
TACK
TACK
TACK
TACK
TACK
Motti!

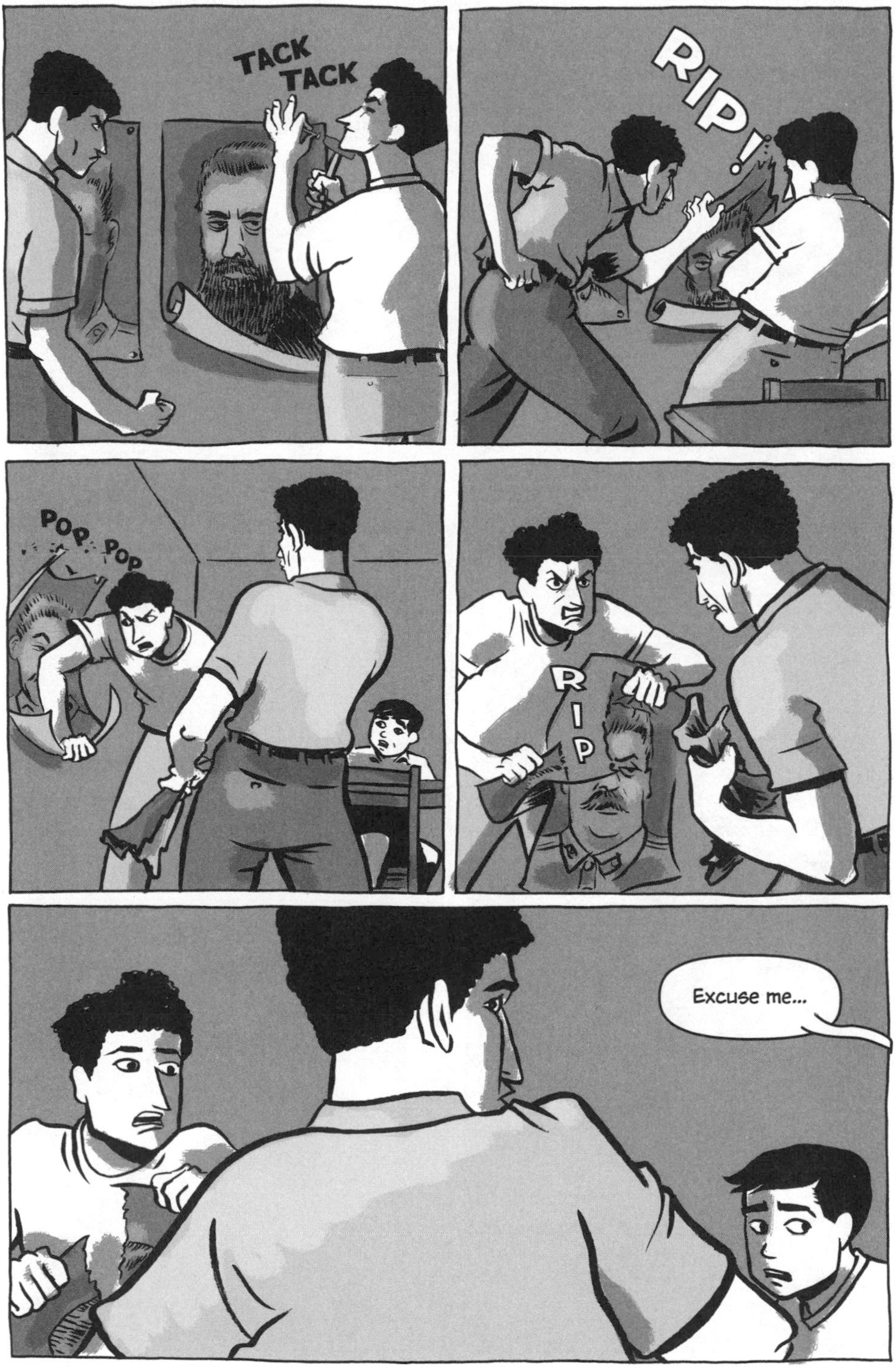
TACK
TACK
RIP!
POP
POP
R I P
Excuse me...

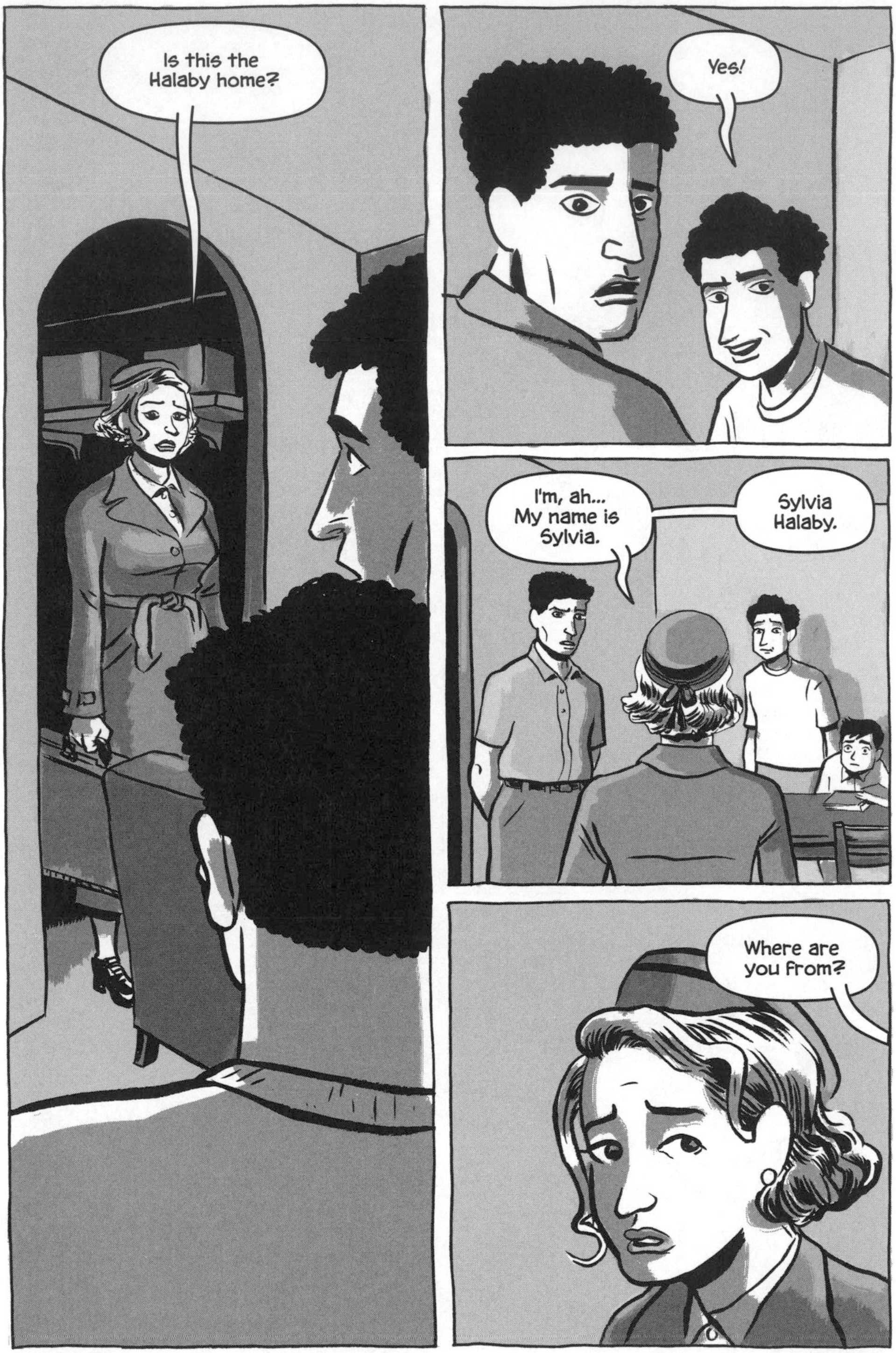
Is this the Halaby home?
Yes!
I'm, ah... My name is Sylvia.
Sylvia Halaby.
Where are you from?

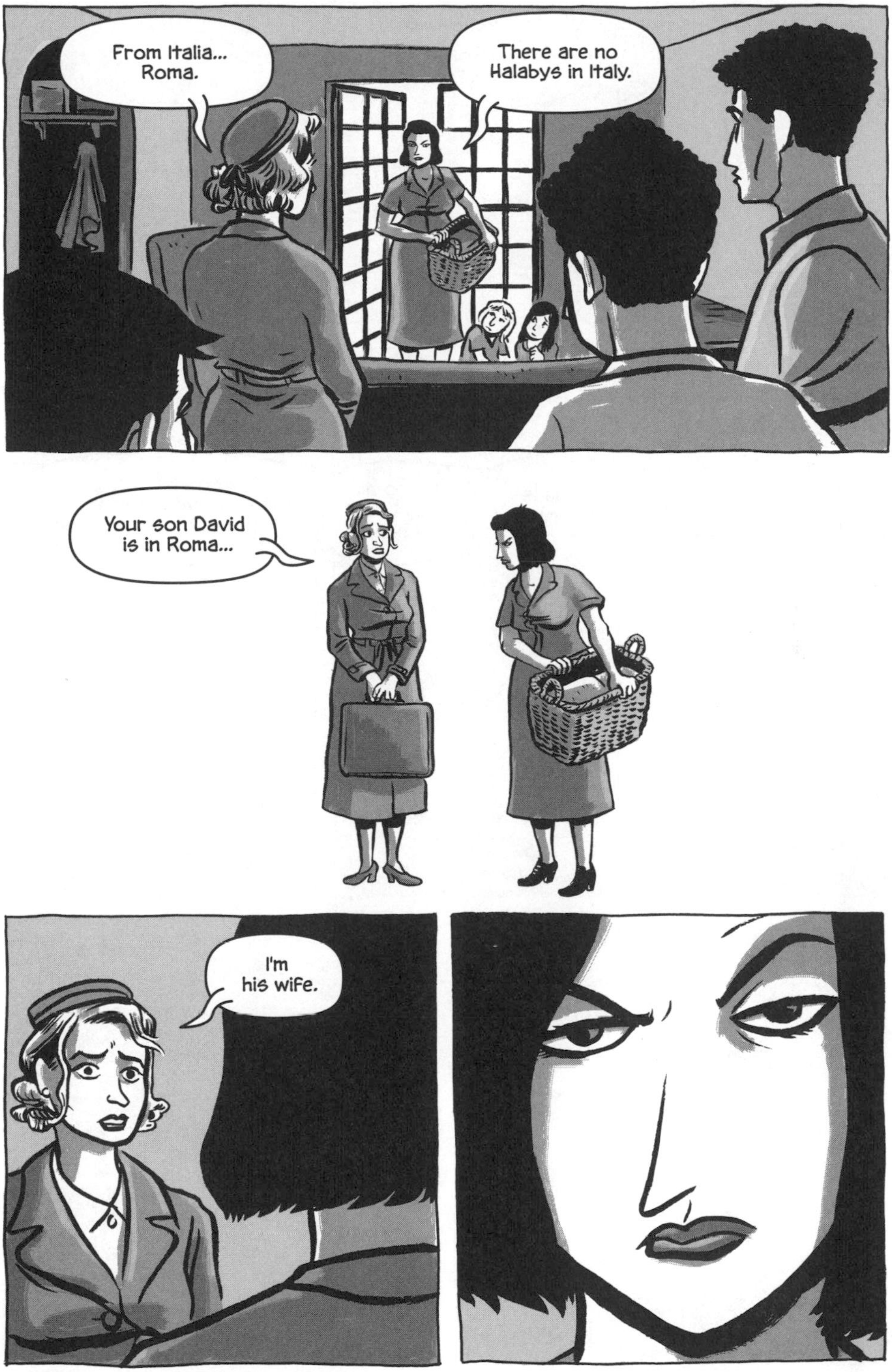
From Italia... Roma.
There are no Halabys in Italy.
Your son David is in Roma...
I'm his wife.

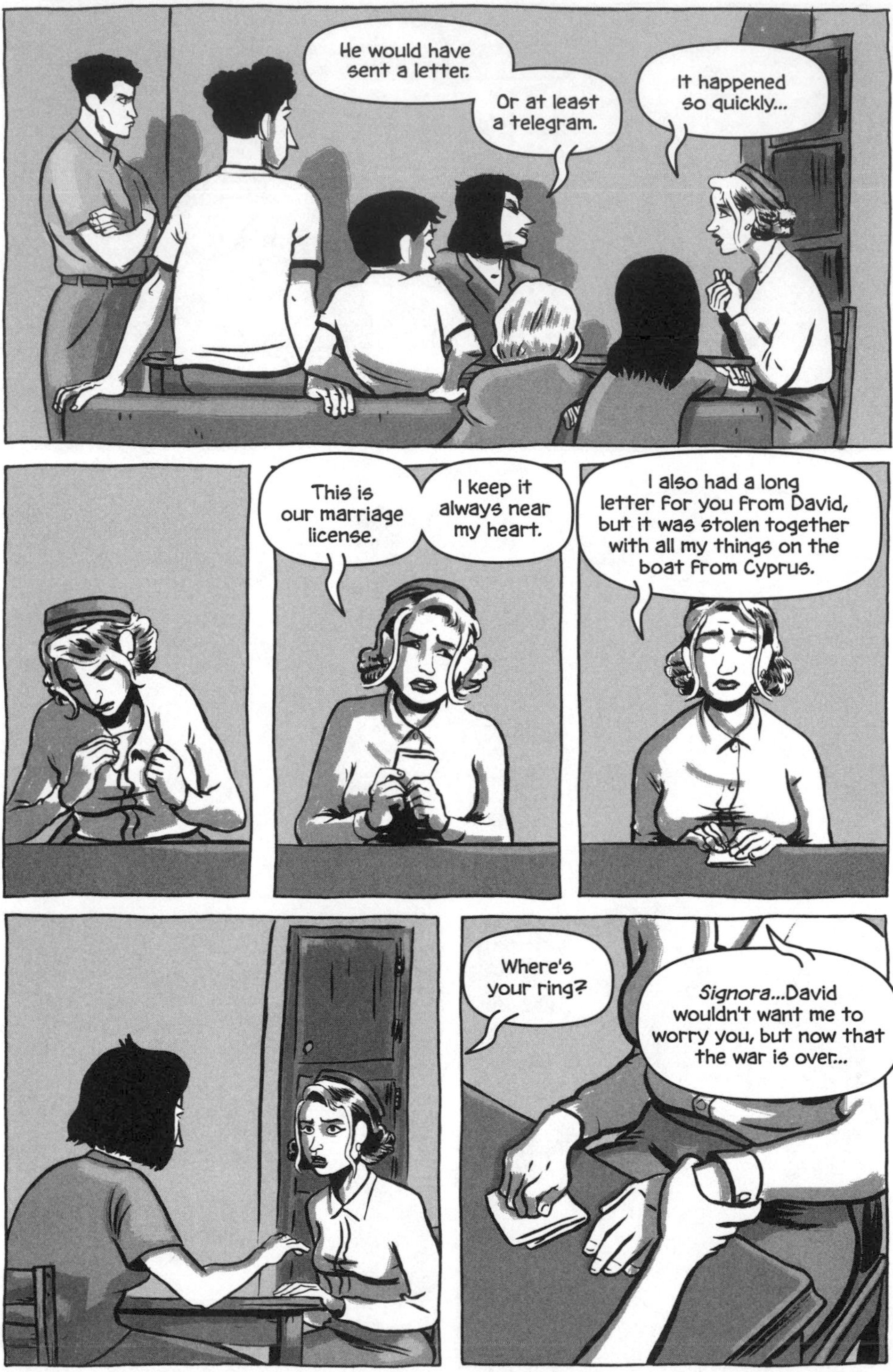
He would have sent a letter.
Or at least a telegram.
It happened so quickly...
This is our marriage license.
I keep it always near my heart.
I also had a long letter for you from David, but it was stolen together with all my things on the boat from Cyprus.
Where's your ring?
*Signora*...David wouldn't want me to worry you, but now that the war is over...

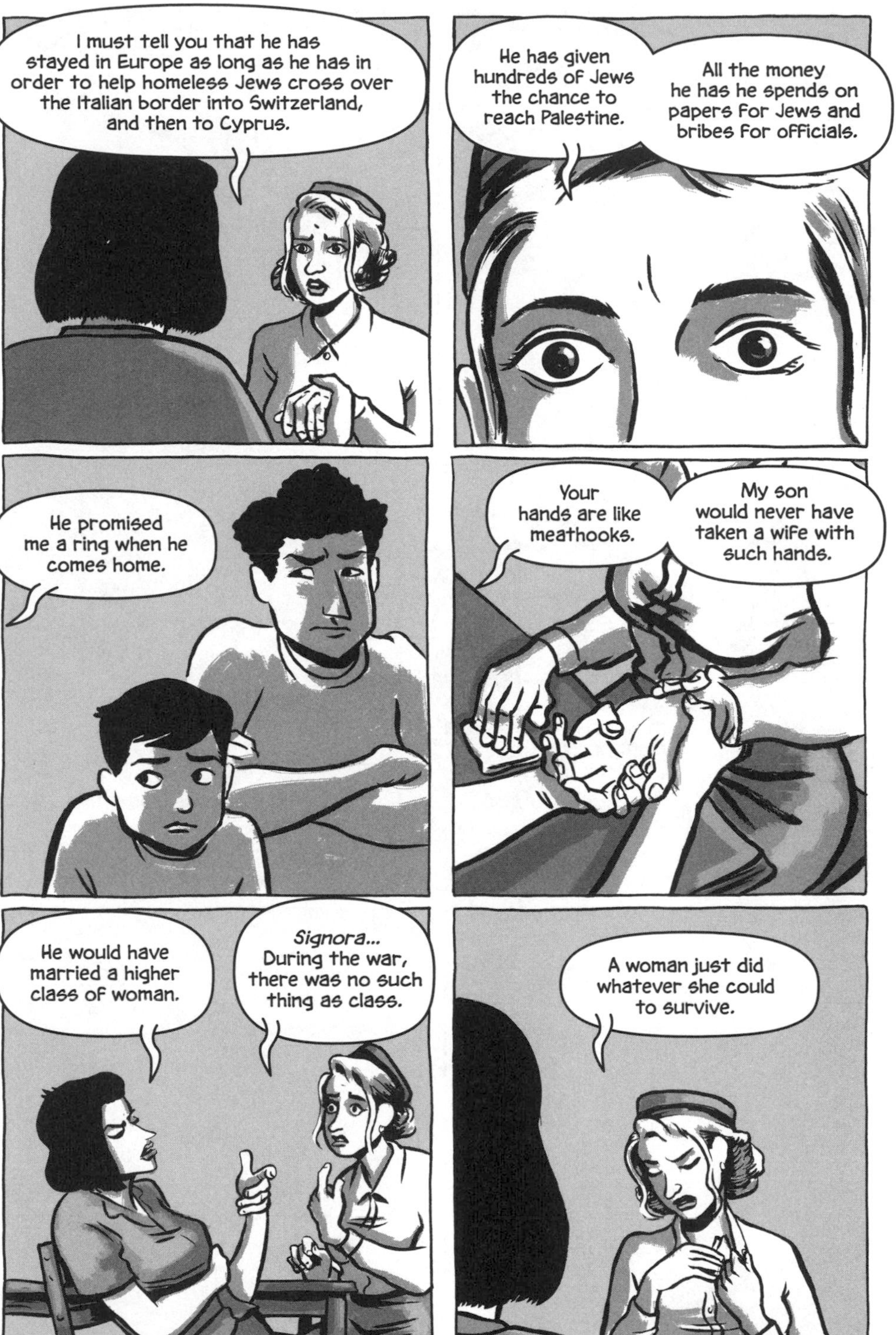
I must tell you that he has stayed in Europe as long as he has in order to help homeless Jews cross over the Italian border into Switzerland, and then to Cyprus.
He has given hundreds of Jews the chance to reach Palestine.
All the money he has he spends on papers for Jews and bribes for officials.
He promised me a ring when he comes home.
Your hands are like meathooks.
My son would never have taken a wife with such hands.
He would have married a higher class of woman.
*Signora...* During the war, there was no such thing as class.
A woman just did whatever she could to survive.

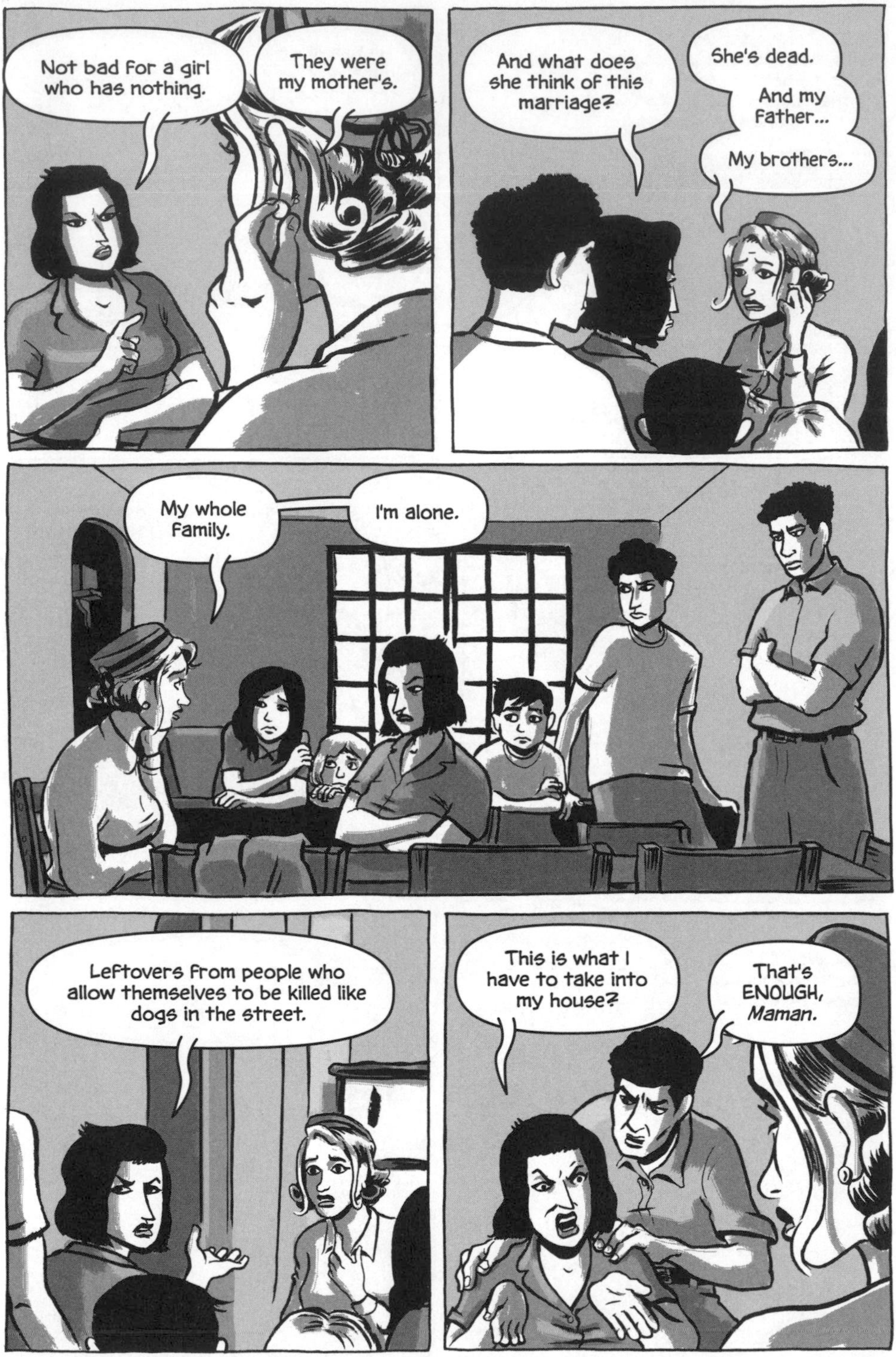
Not bad for a girl who has nothing.
They were my mother's.
And what does she think of this marriage?
She's dead.
And my father...
My brothers...
My whole family.
I'm alone.
Leftovers from people who allow themselves to be killed like dogs in the street.
This is what I have to take into my house?
That's ENOUGH, *Maman.*

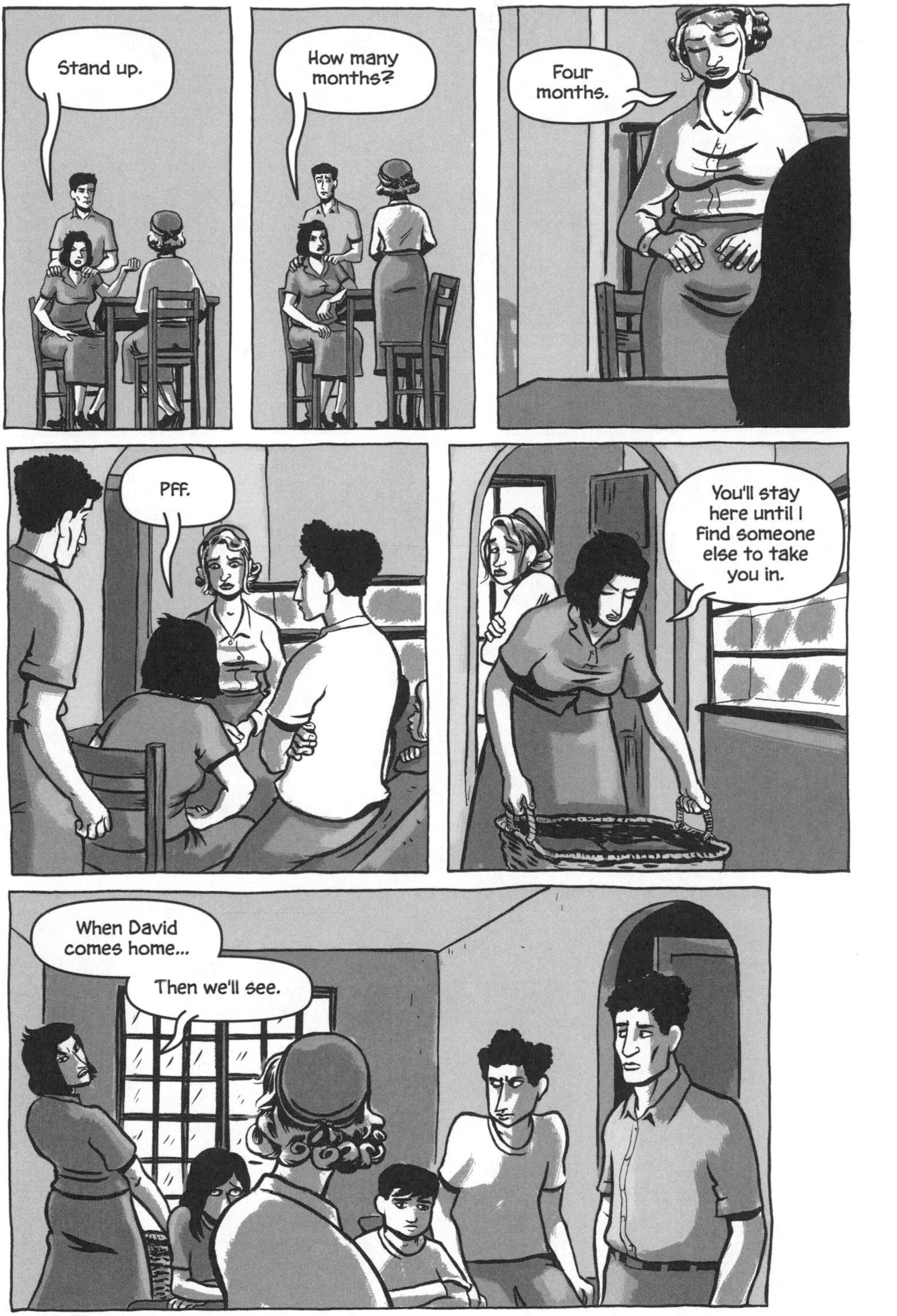
Stand up.
How many months?
Four months.
PFF.
You'll stay here until I find someone else to take you in.
When David comes home...
Then we'll see.

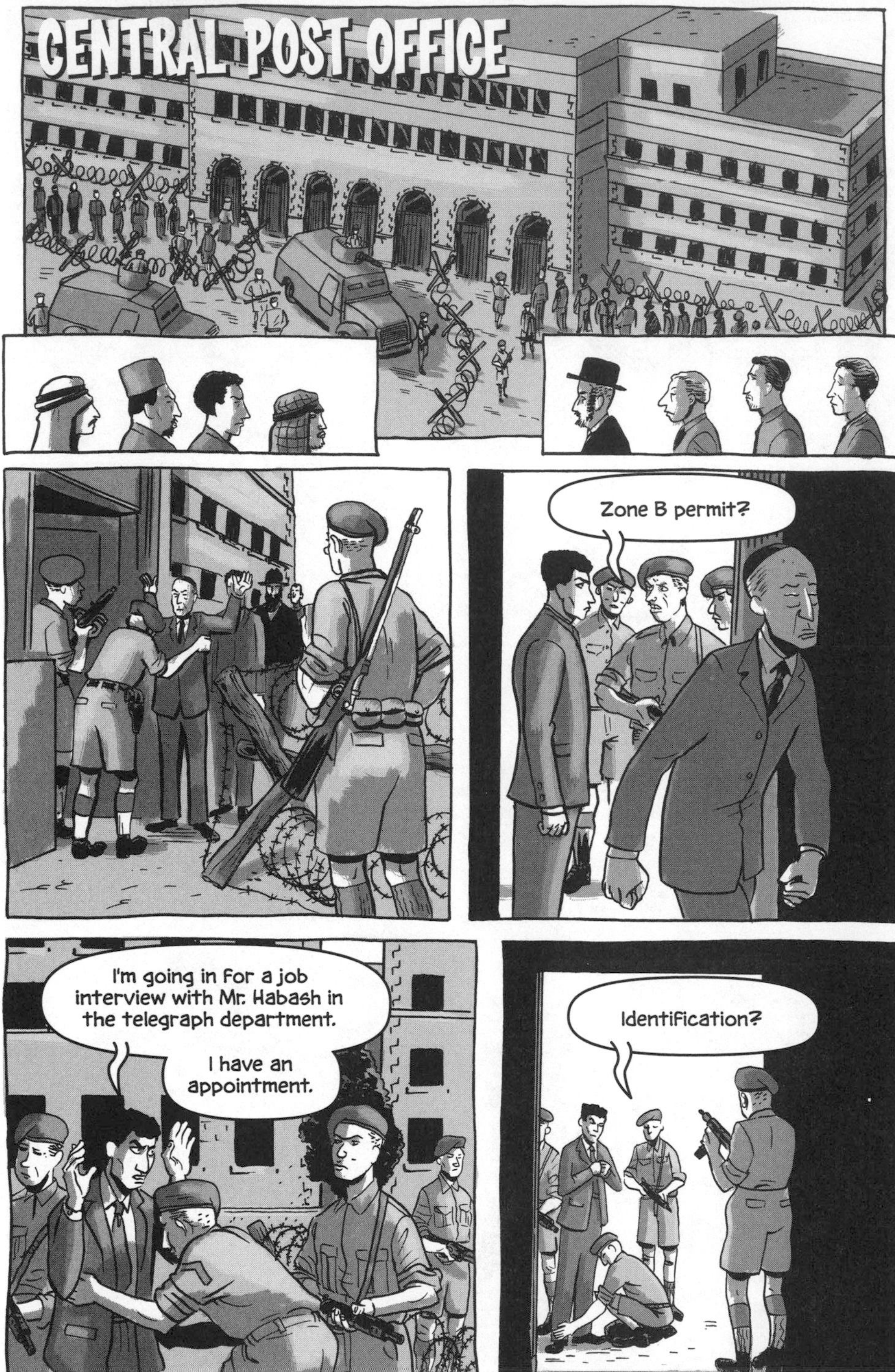
CENTRAL POST OFFICE
Zone B permit?
I'm going in for a job interview with Mr. Habash in the telegraph department.
I have an appointment.
Identification?

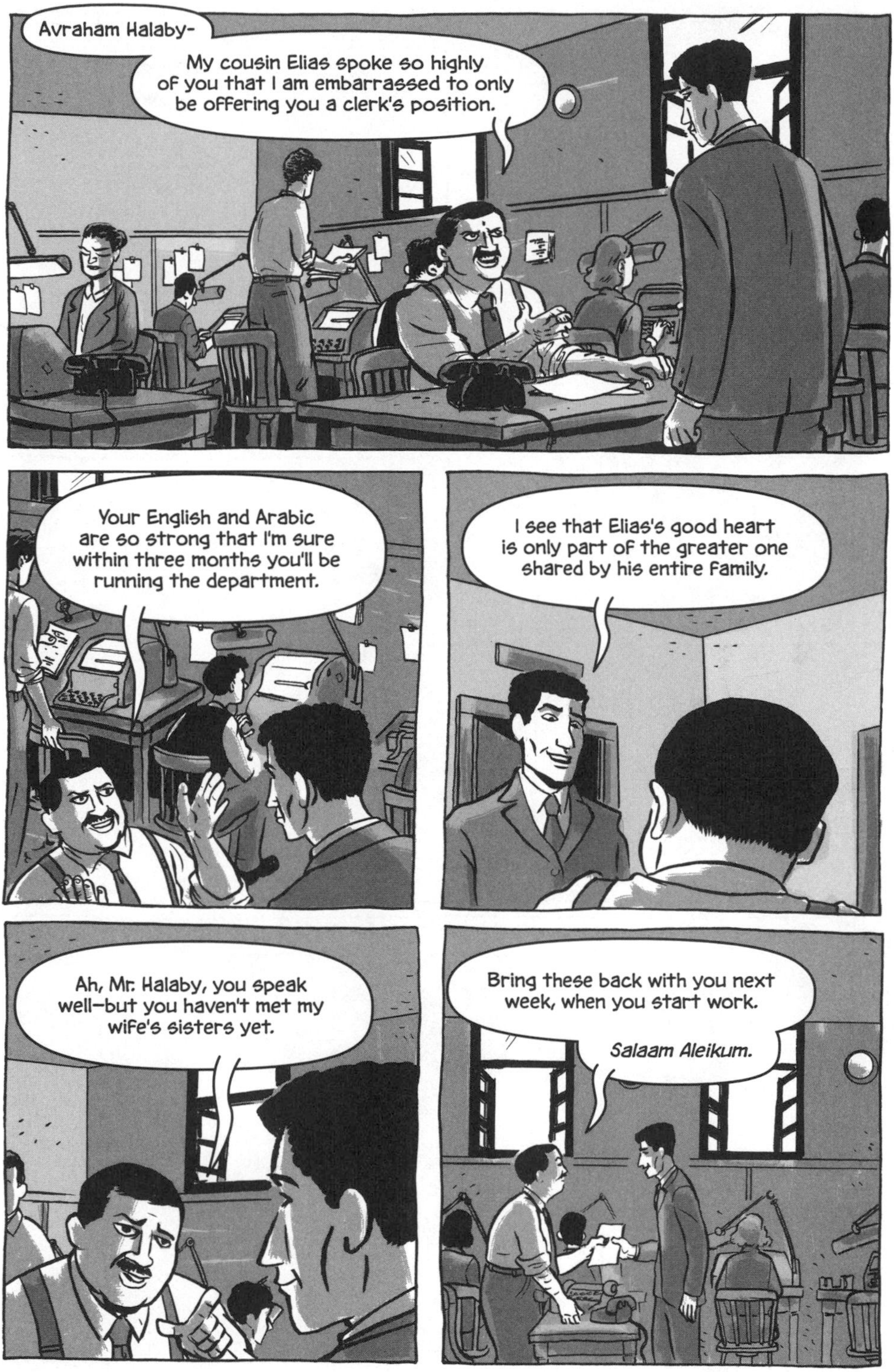
Avraham Halaby-
My cousin Elias spoke so highly of you that I am embarrassed to only be offering you a clerk's position.
Your English and Arabic are so strong that I'm sure within three months you'll be running the department.
I see that Elias's good heart is only part of the greater one shared by his entire family.
Ah, Mr. Halaby, you speak well—but you haven't met my wife's sisters yet.
Bring these back with you next week, when you start work.
Salaam Aleikum.

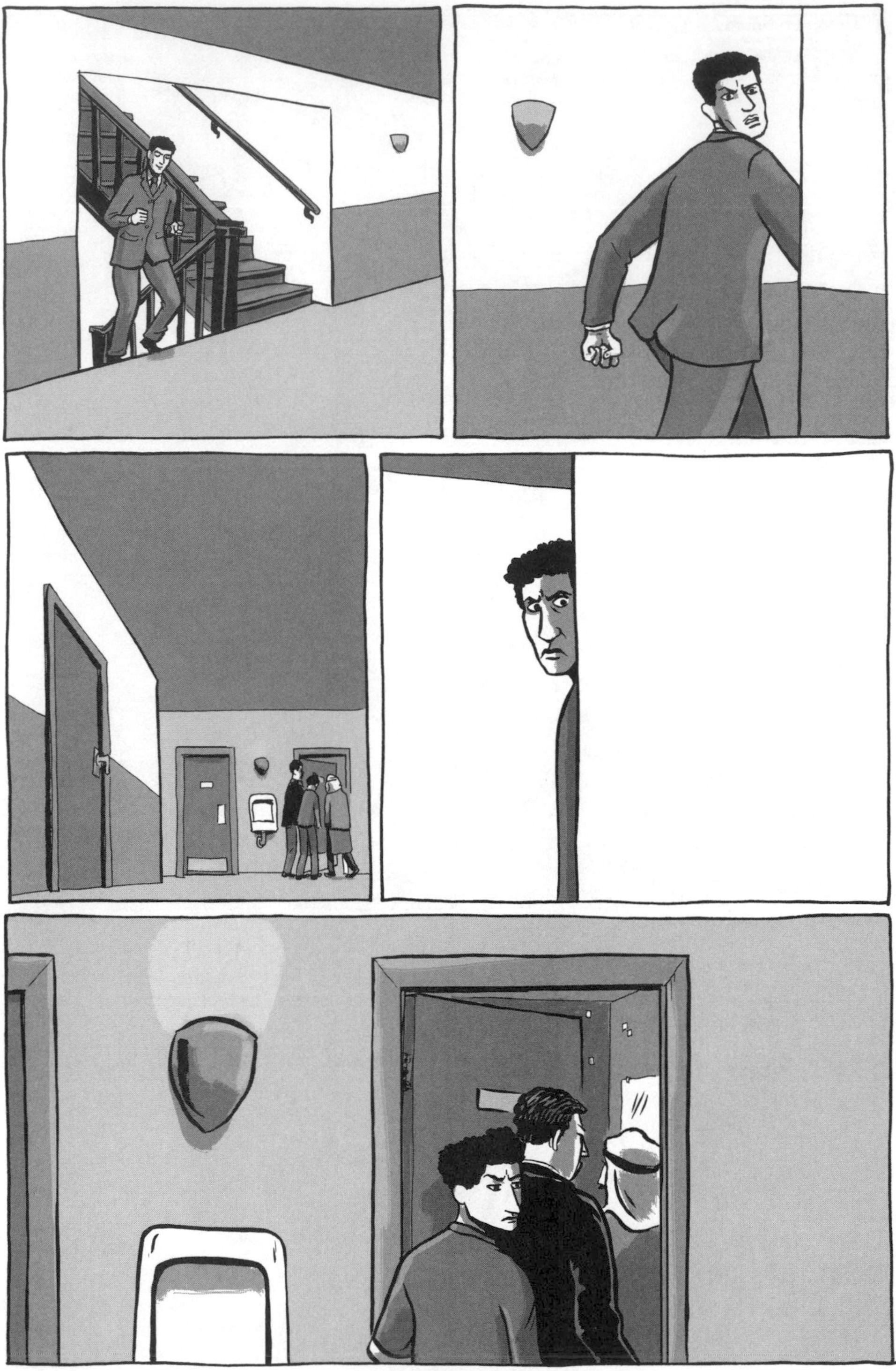

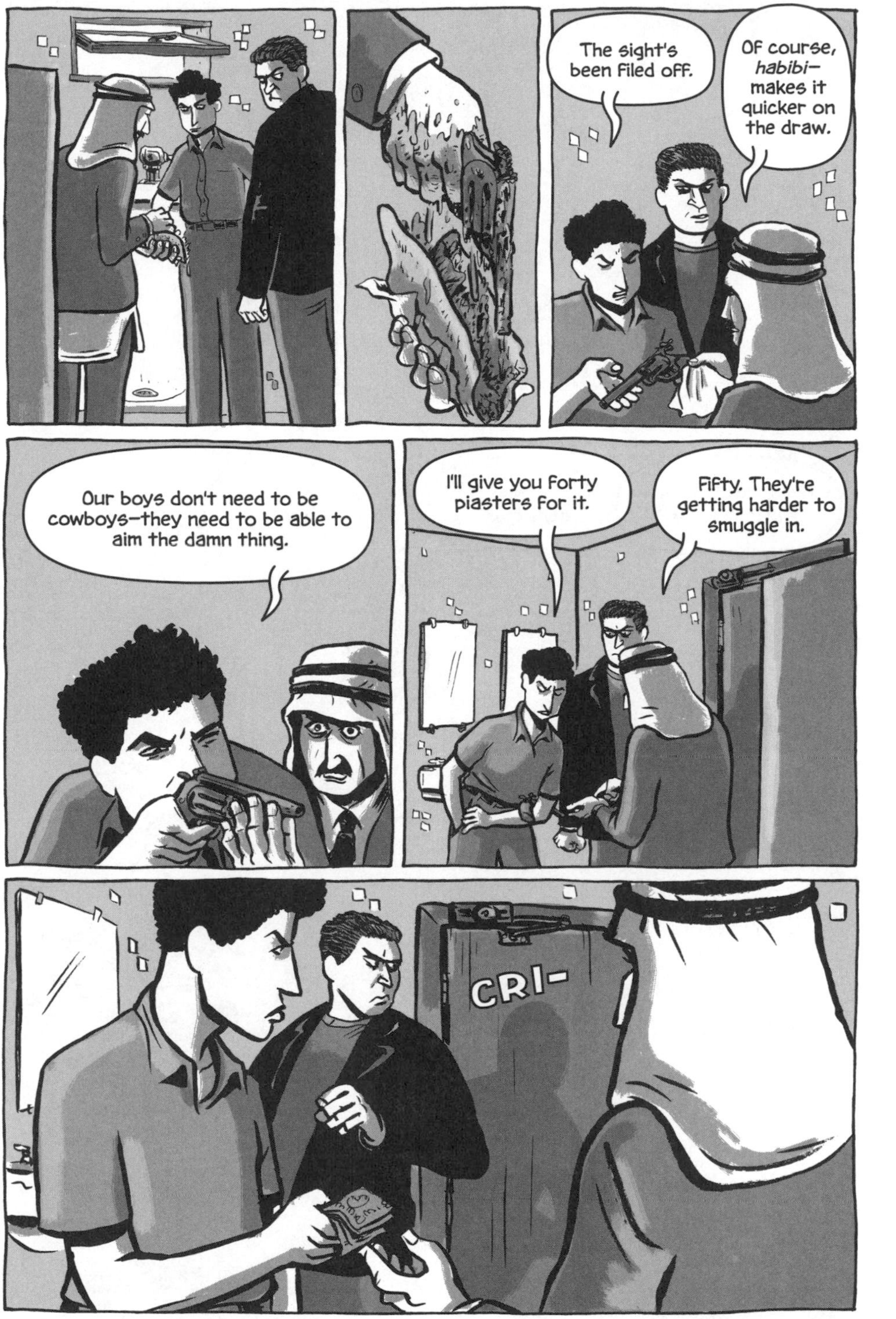
The sight's been filed off.
Of course, *habibi*—makes it quicker on the draw.
Our boys don't need to be cowboys—they need to be able to aim the damn thing.
I'll give you forty piasters for it.
Fifty. They're getting harder to smuggle in.
CRI-

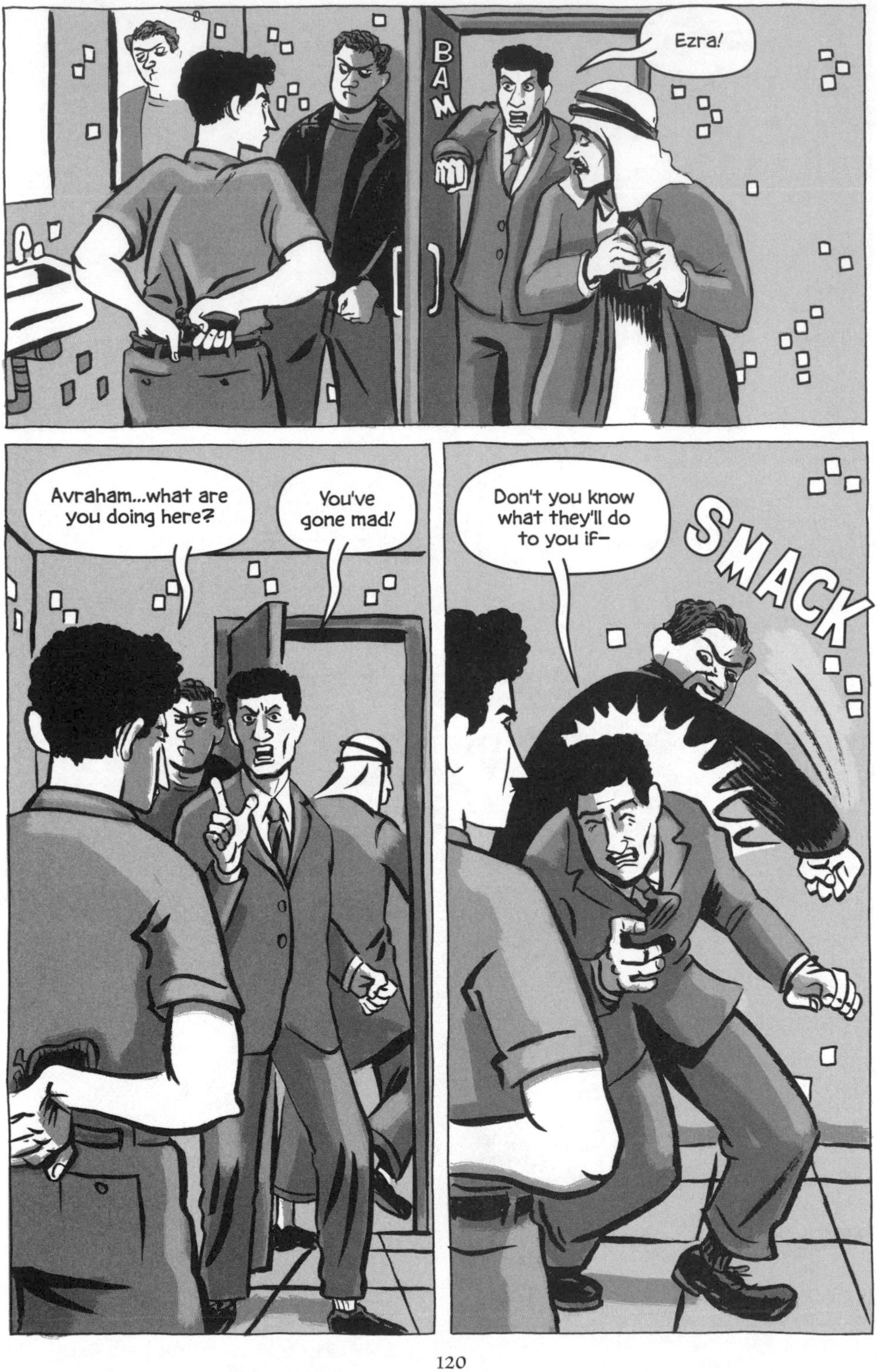

BAM
Ezra!
Avraham...what are you doing here?
You've gone mad!
Don't you know what they'll do to you if–
SMACK

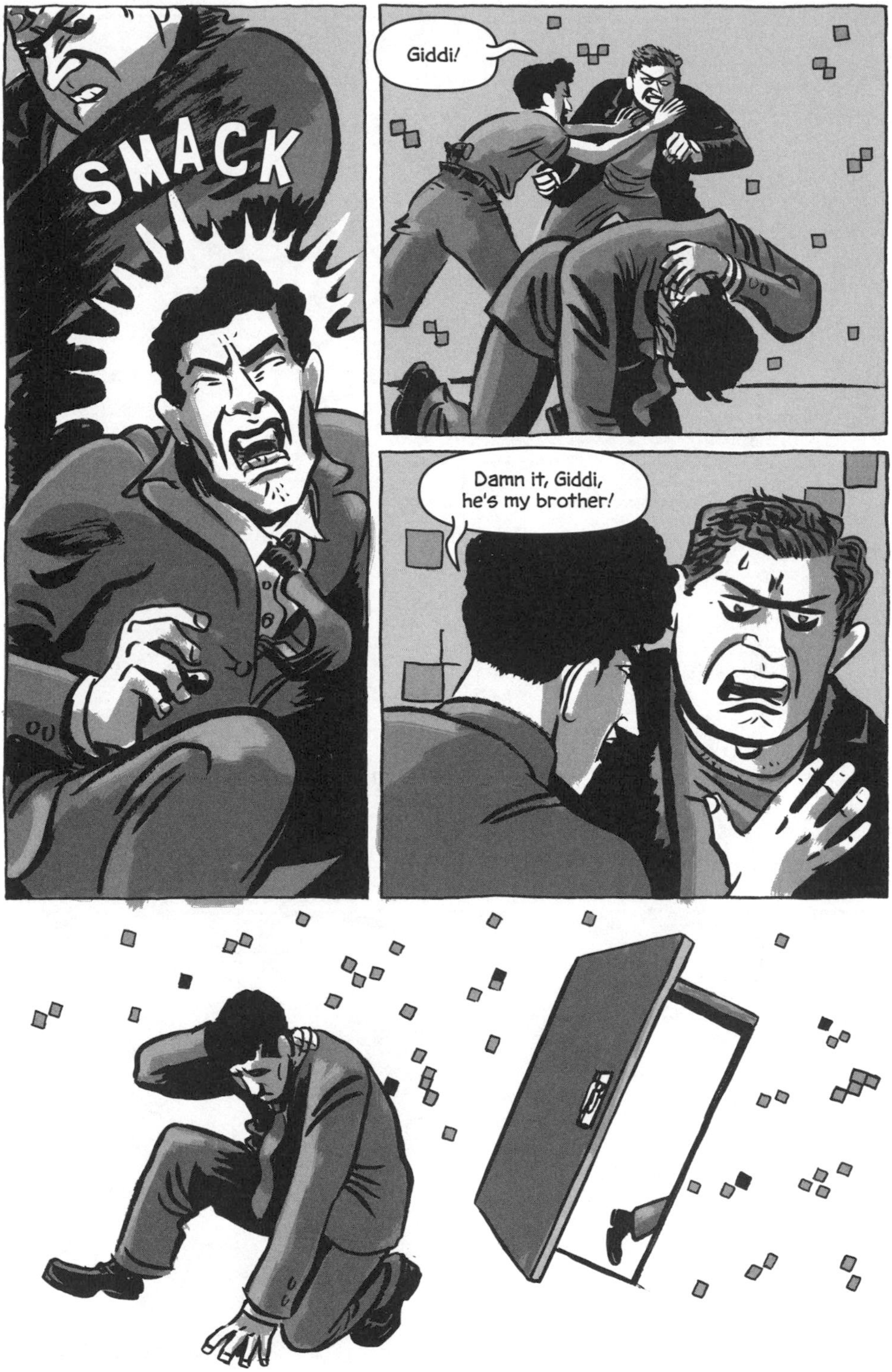
SMACK
Giddi!
Damn it, Giddi, he's my brother!

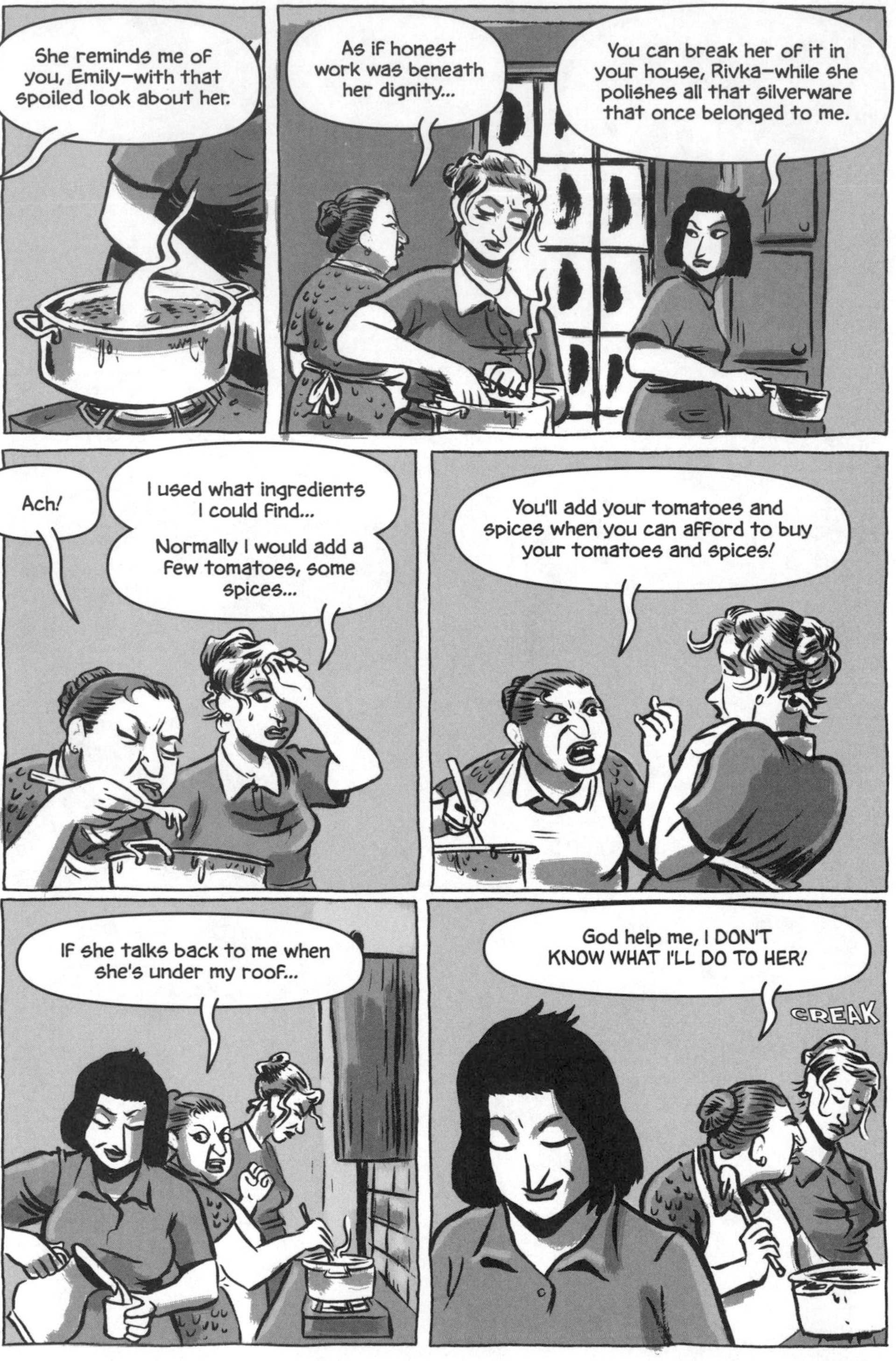
She reminds me of you, Emily—with that spoiled look about her.
As if honest work was beneath her dignity...
You can break her of it in your house, Rivka—while she polishes all that silverware that once belonged to me.
Ach!
I used what ingredients I could find...
Normally I would add a few tomatoes, some spices...
You'll add your tomatoes and spices when you can afford to buy your tomatoes and spices!
If she talks back to me when she's under my roof...
God help me, I DON'T KNOW WHAT I'LL DO TO HER!
CREAK

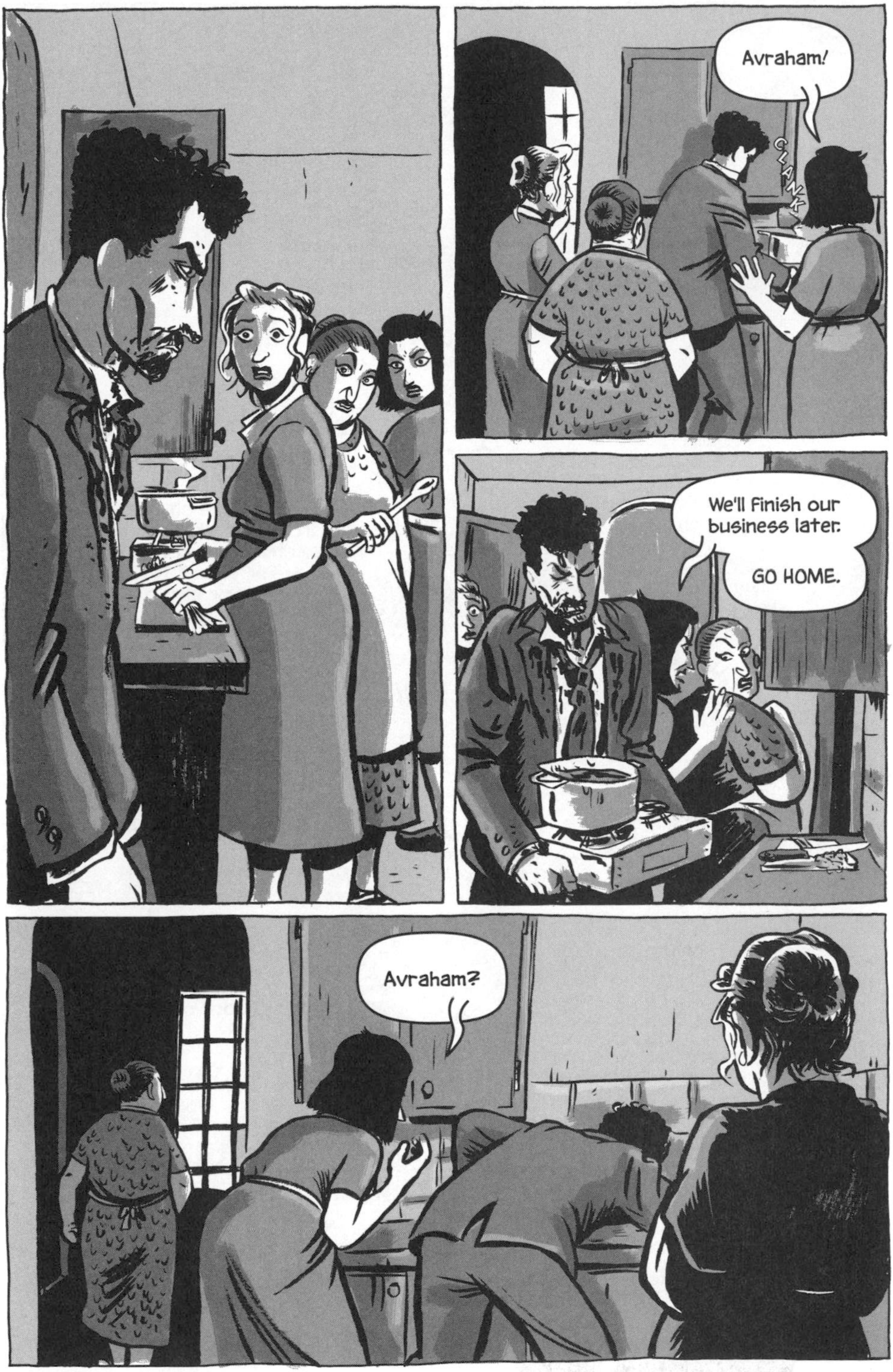
Avraham!
CLANK
We'll finish our business later.
GO HOME.
Avraham?

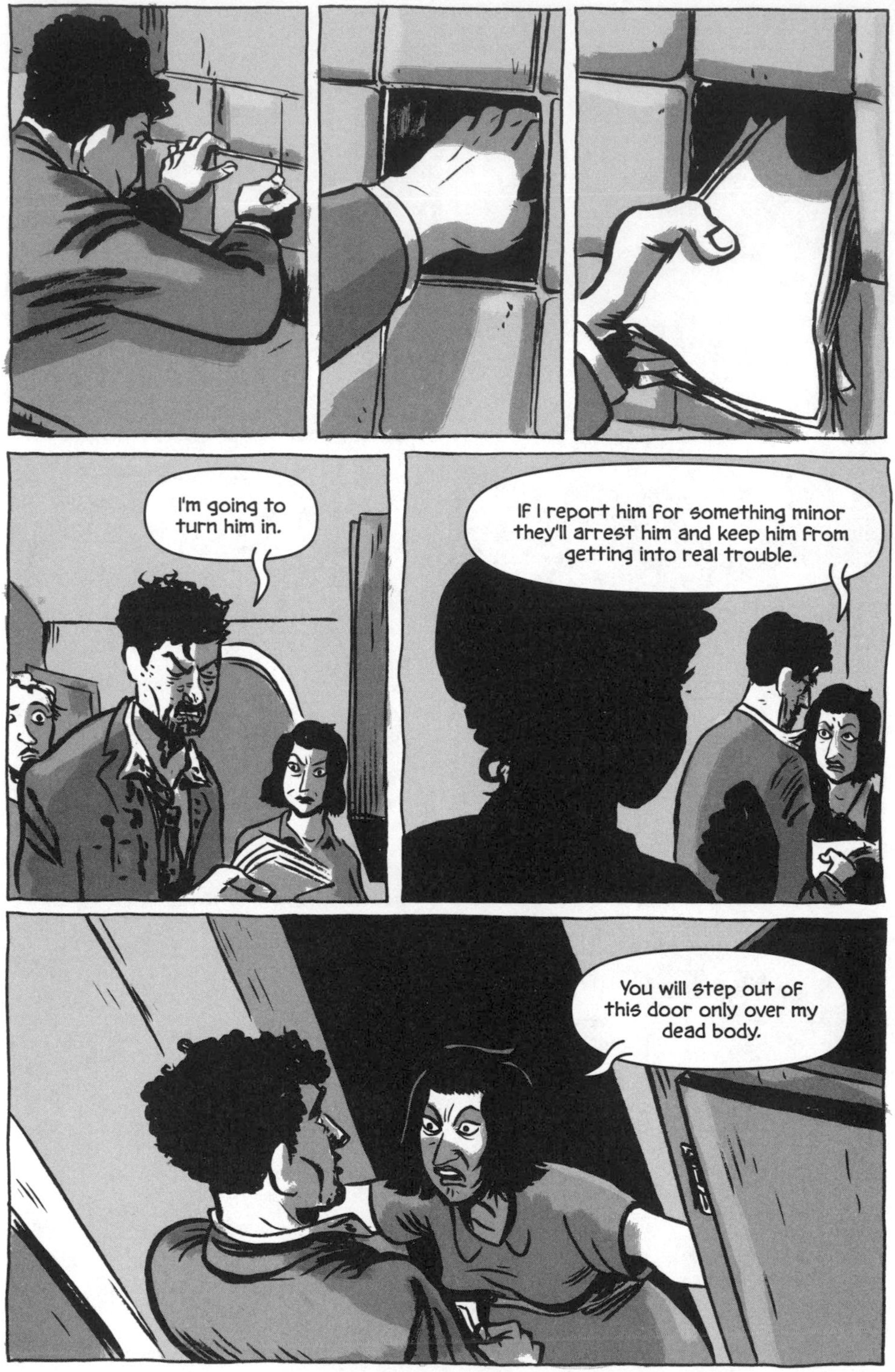
I'm going to turn him in.
If I report him for something minor they'll arrest him and keep him from getting into real trouble.
You will step out of this door only over my dead body.

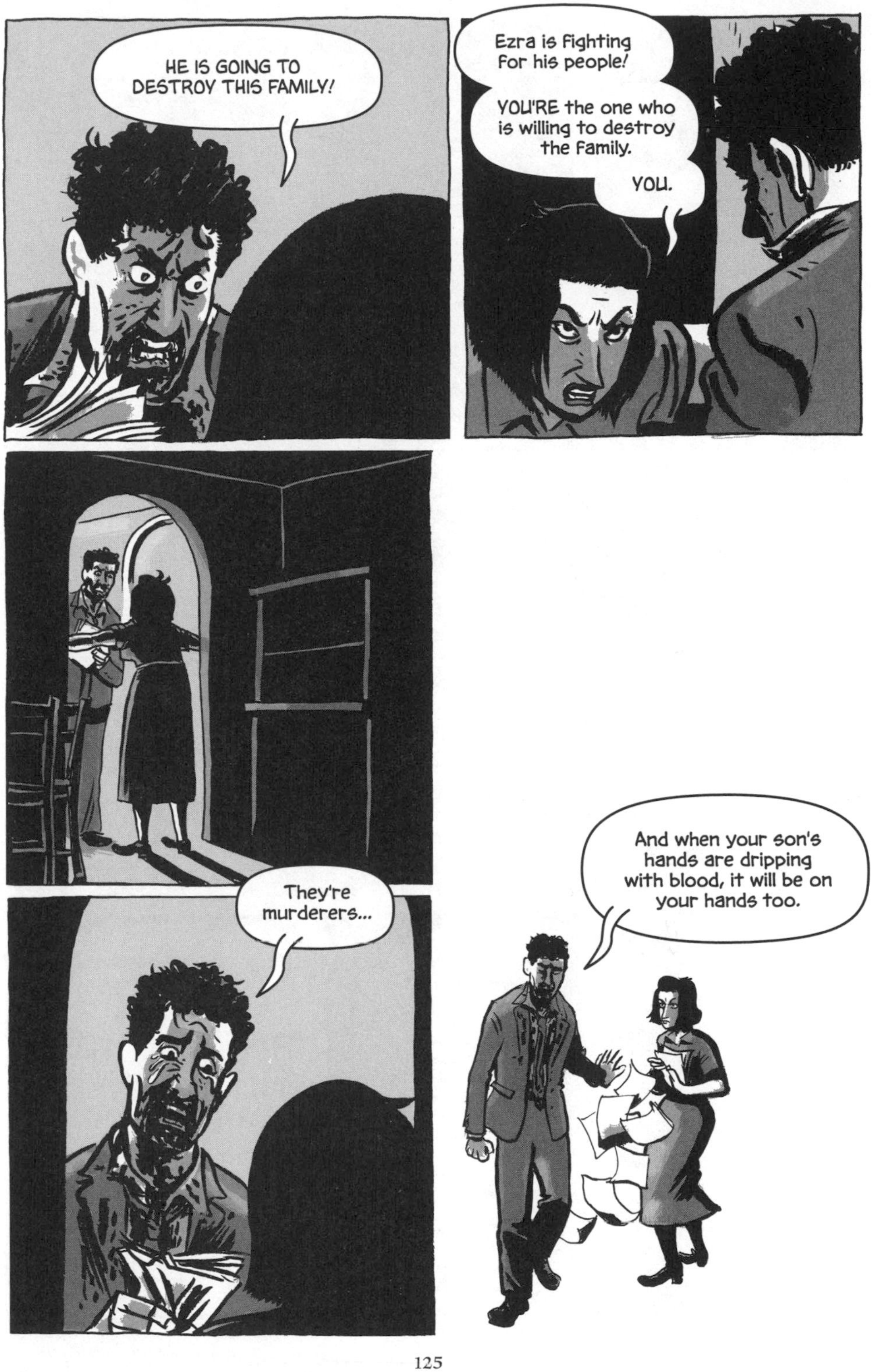
HE IS GOING TO DESTROY THIS FAMILY!
Ezra is fighting for his people!
YOU'RE the one who is willing to destroy the family.
YOU.
They're murderers...
And when your son's hands are dripping with blood, it will be on your hands too.

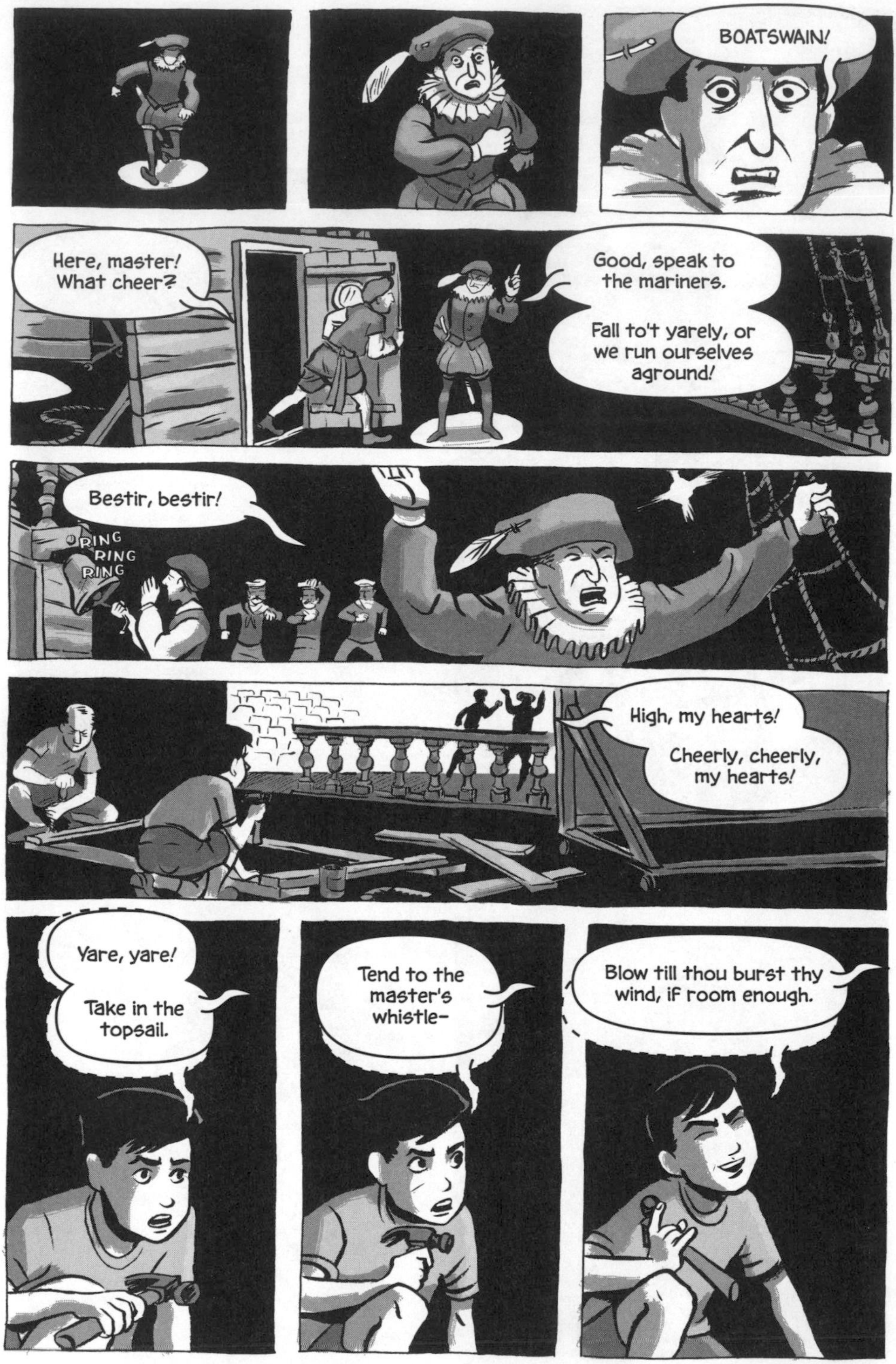
BOATSWAIN!
Here, master! What cheer?
Good, speak to the mariners.
Fall to't yarely, or we run ourselves aground!
Bestir, bestir!
RING RING RING
High, my hearts!
Cheerly, cheerly, my hearts!
Yare, yare!
Take in the topsail.
Tend to the master's whistle-
Blow till thou burst thy wind, if room enough.

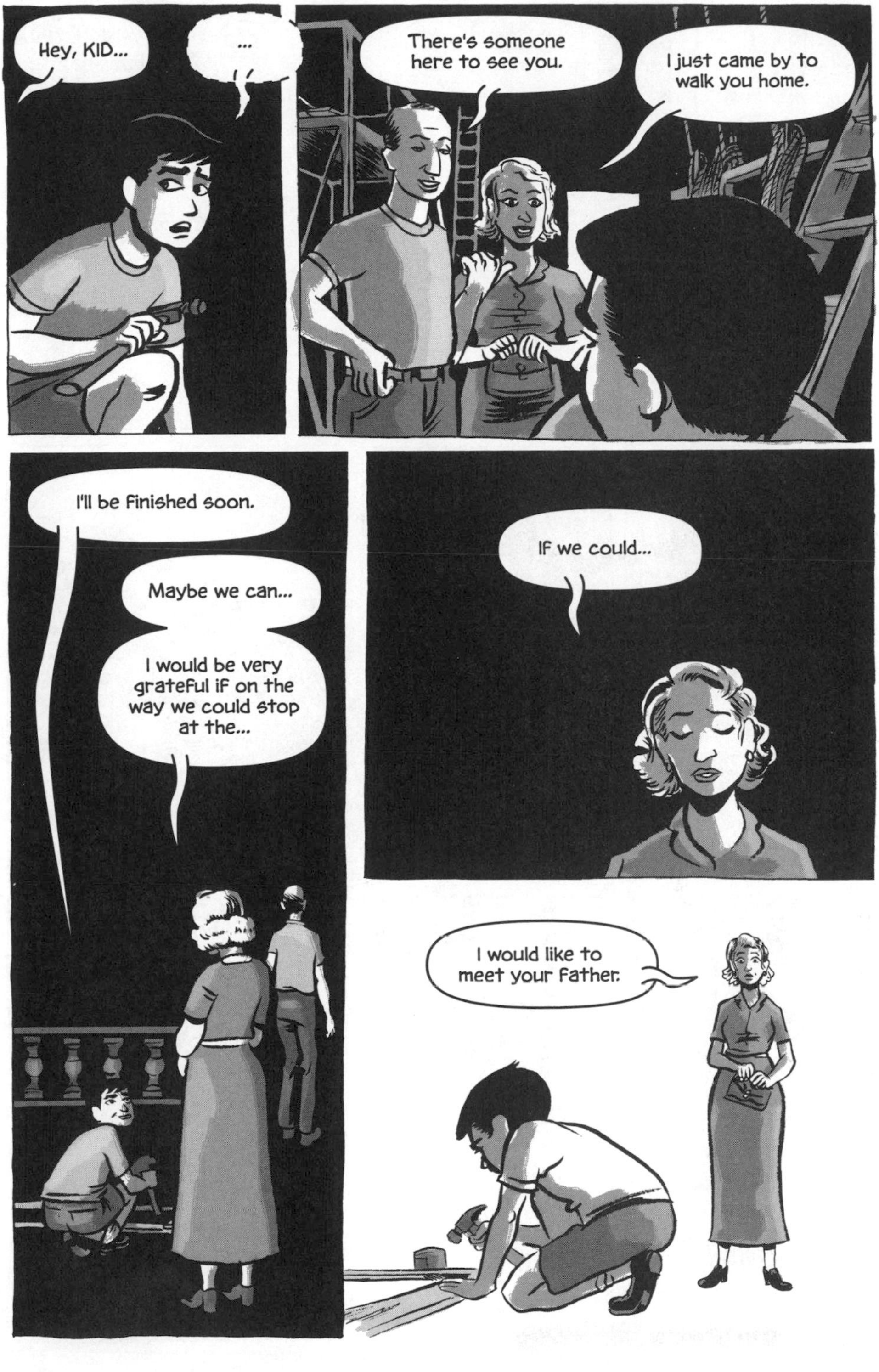
Hey, KID...
...
There's someone here to see you.
I just came by to walk you home.
I'll be finished soon.
Maybe we can...
I would be very grateful if on the way we could stop at the...
If we could...
I would like to meet your father.

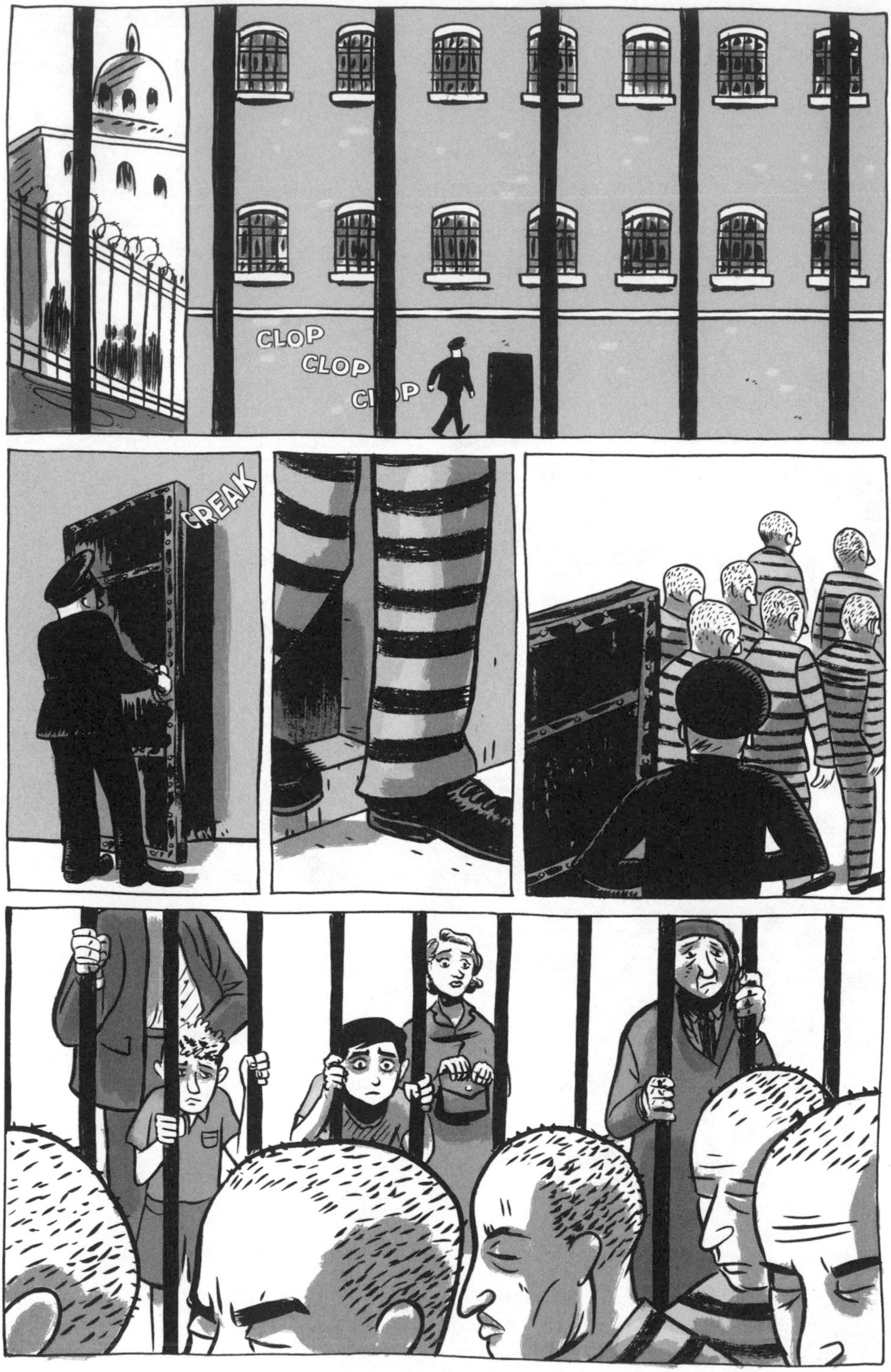
CLOP
CLOP
CLOP
CREAK

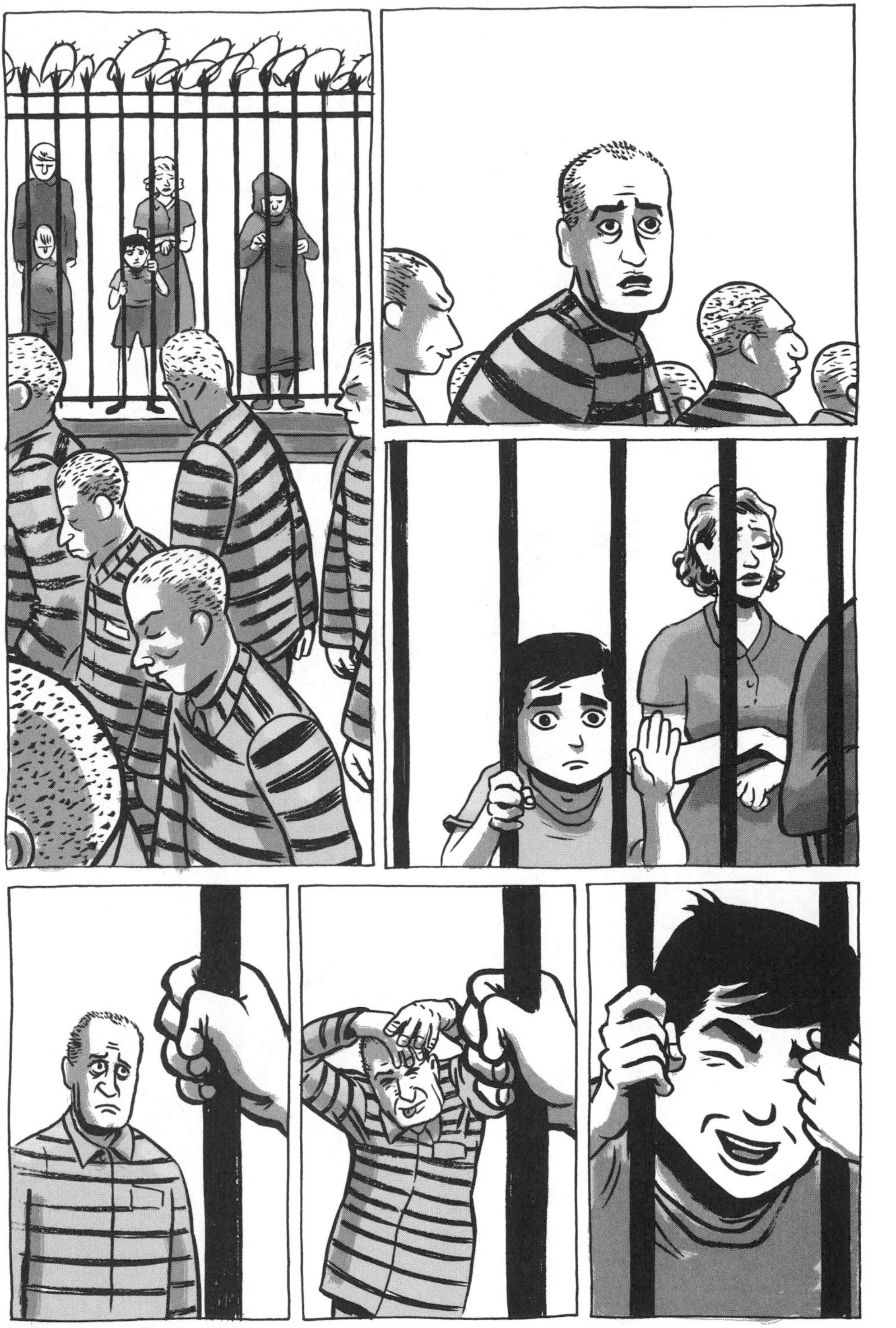

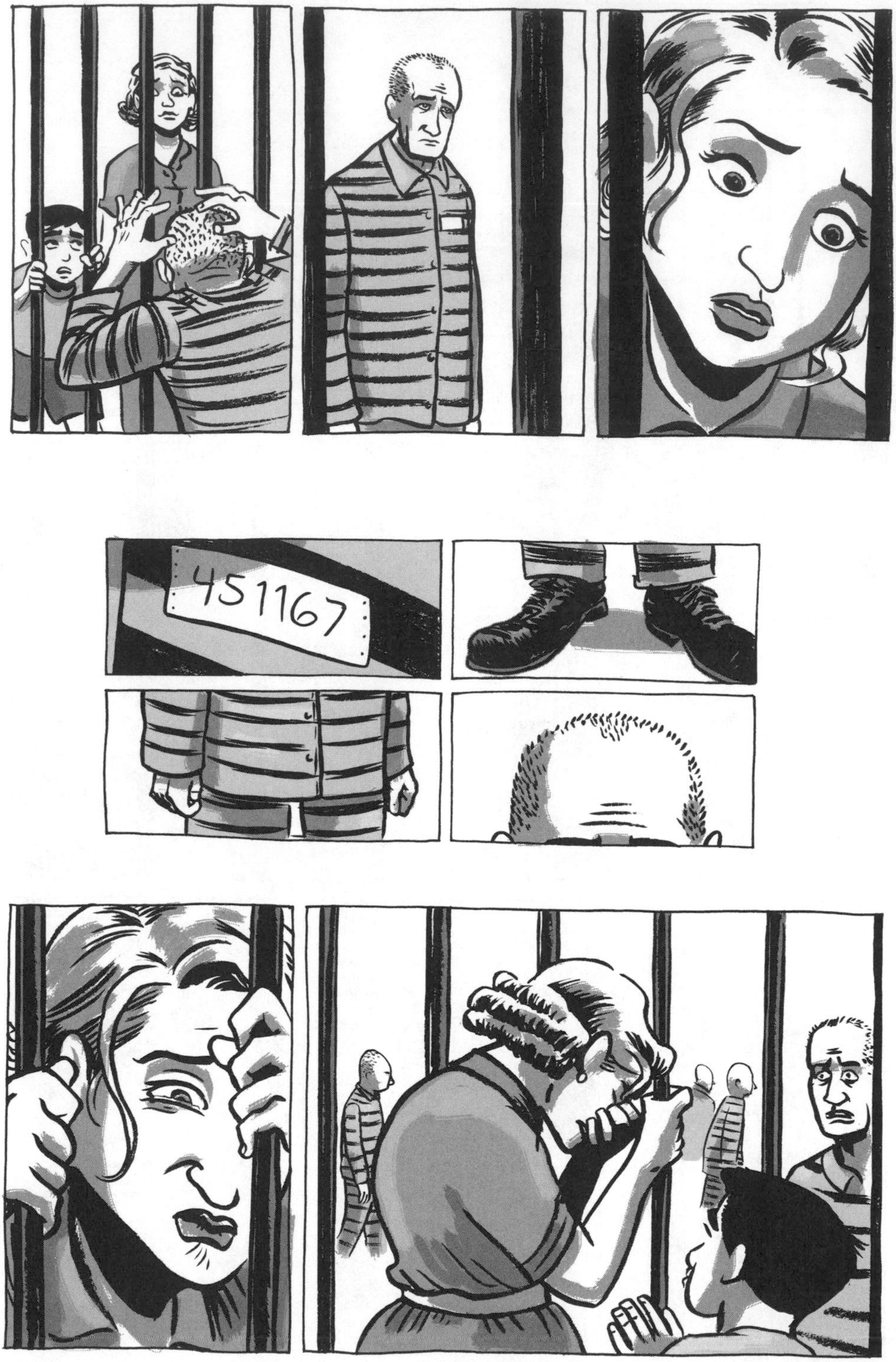
451167

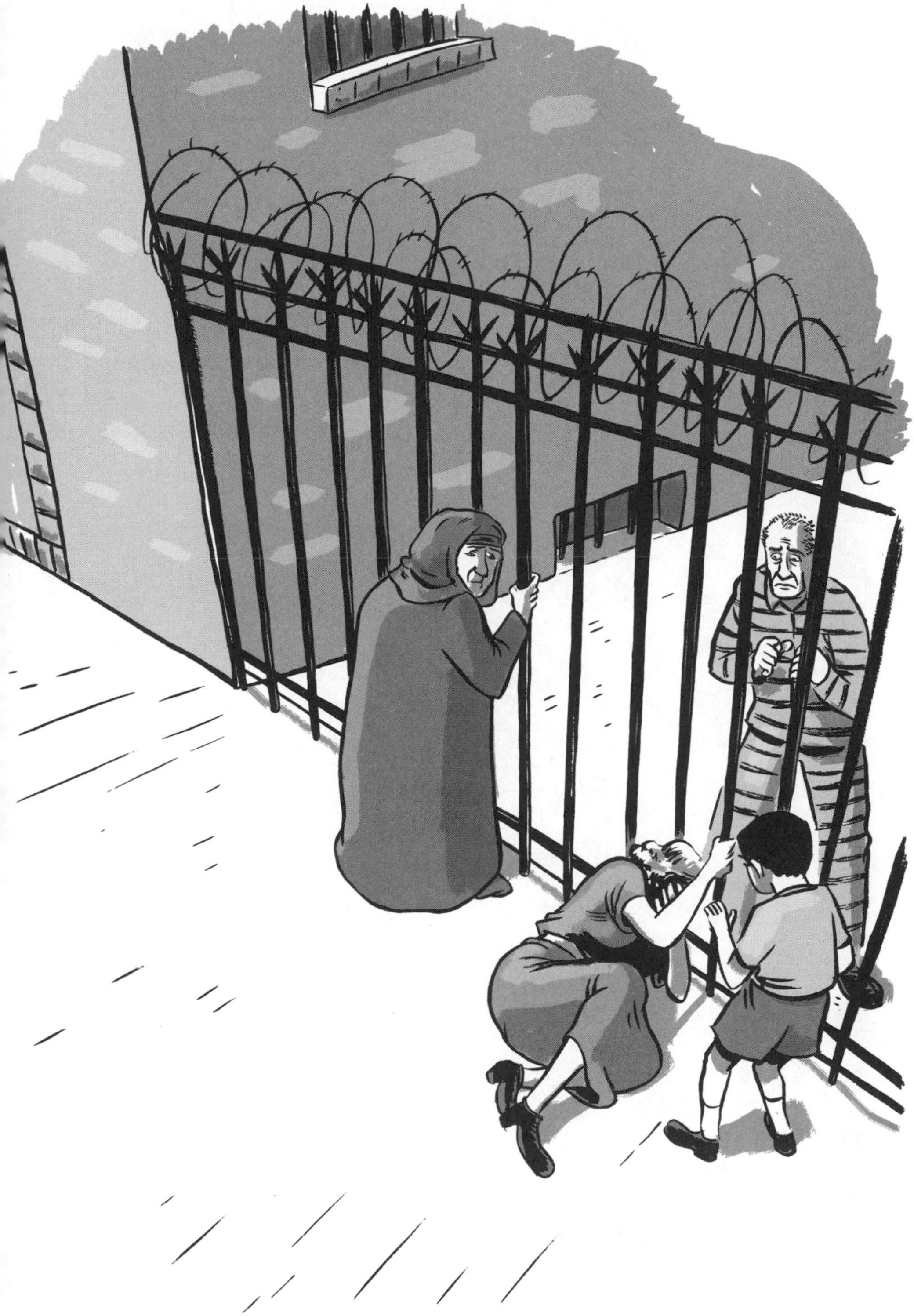

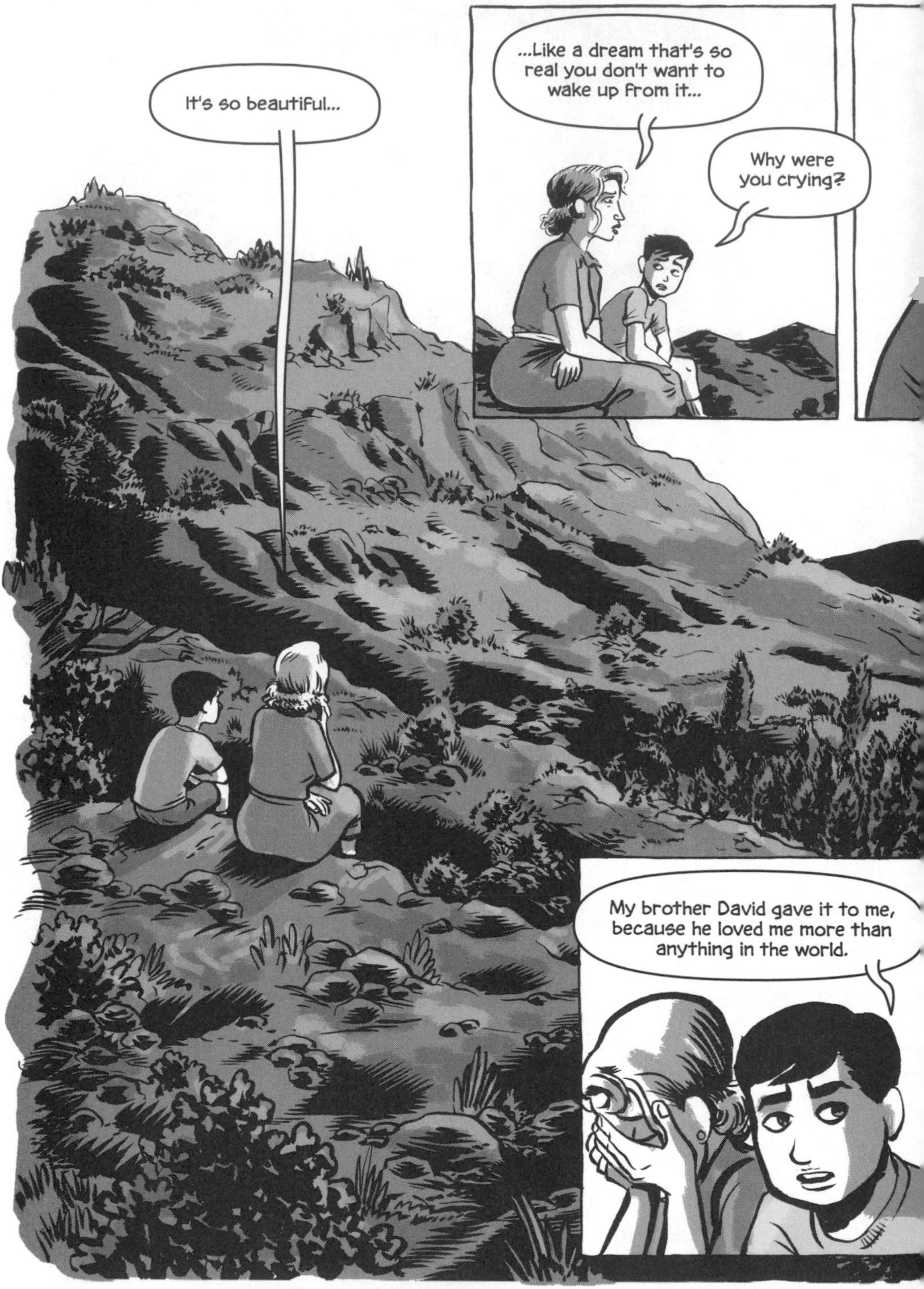
It's so beautiful...
...Like a dream that's so real you don't want to wake up from it...
Why were you crying?
My brother David gave it to me, because he loved me more than anything in the world.

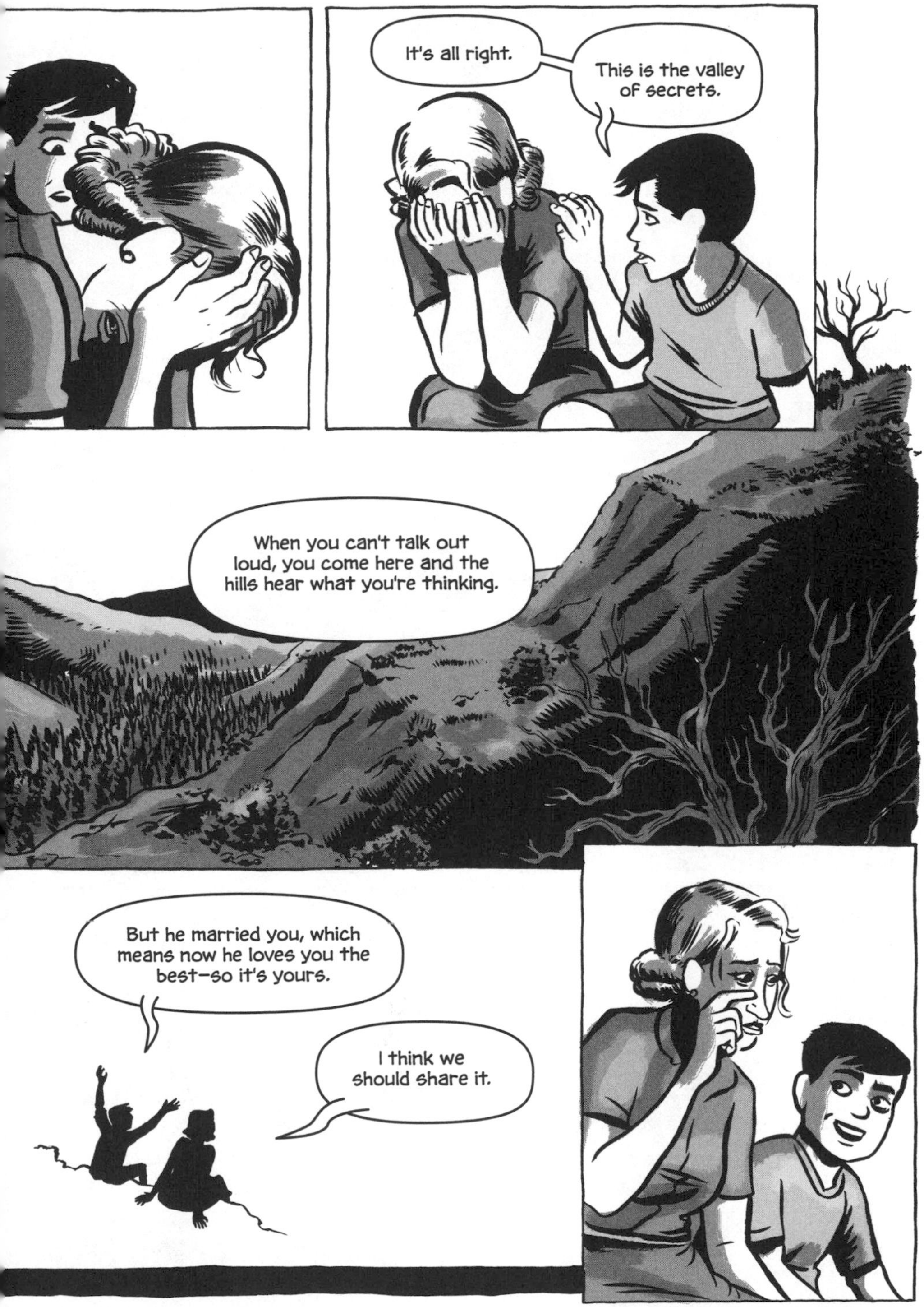
It's all right.
This is the valley of secrets.
When you can't talk out loud, you come here and the hills hear what you're thinking.
But he married you, which means now he loves you the best—so it's yours.
I think we should share it.

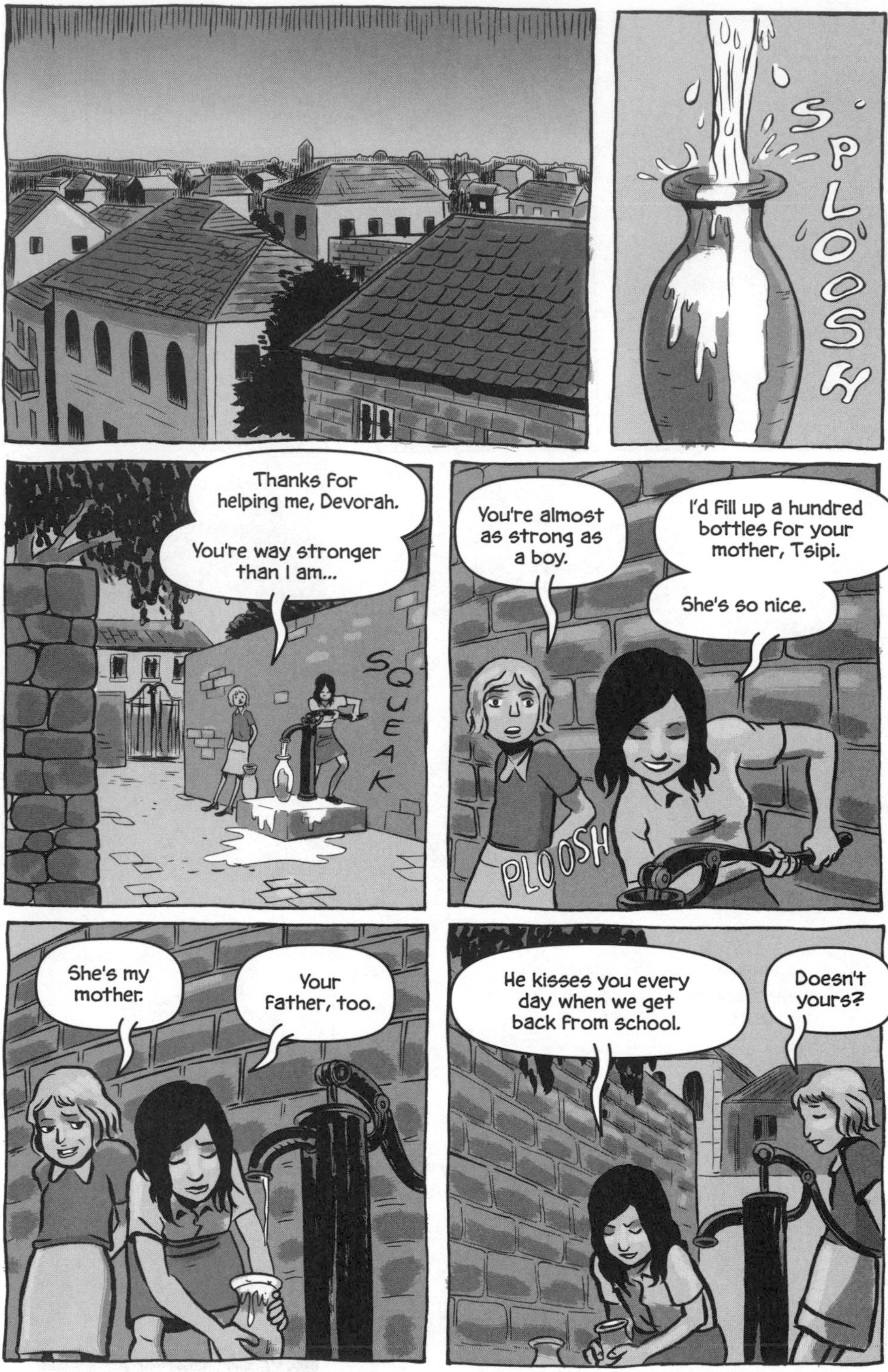
SPLOOSH
Thanks for helping me, Devorah.
You're way stronger than I am...
SQUEAK
You're almost as strong as a boy.
I'd fill up a hundred bottles for your mother, Tsipi.
She's so nice.
PLOOSH
She's my mother.
Your father, too.
He kisses you every day when we get back from school.
Doesn't yours?

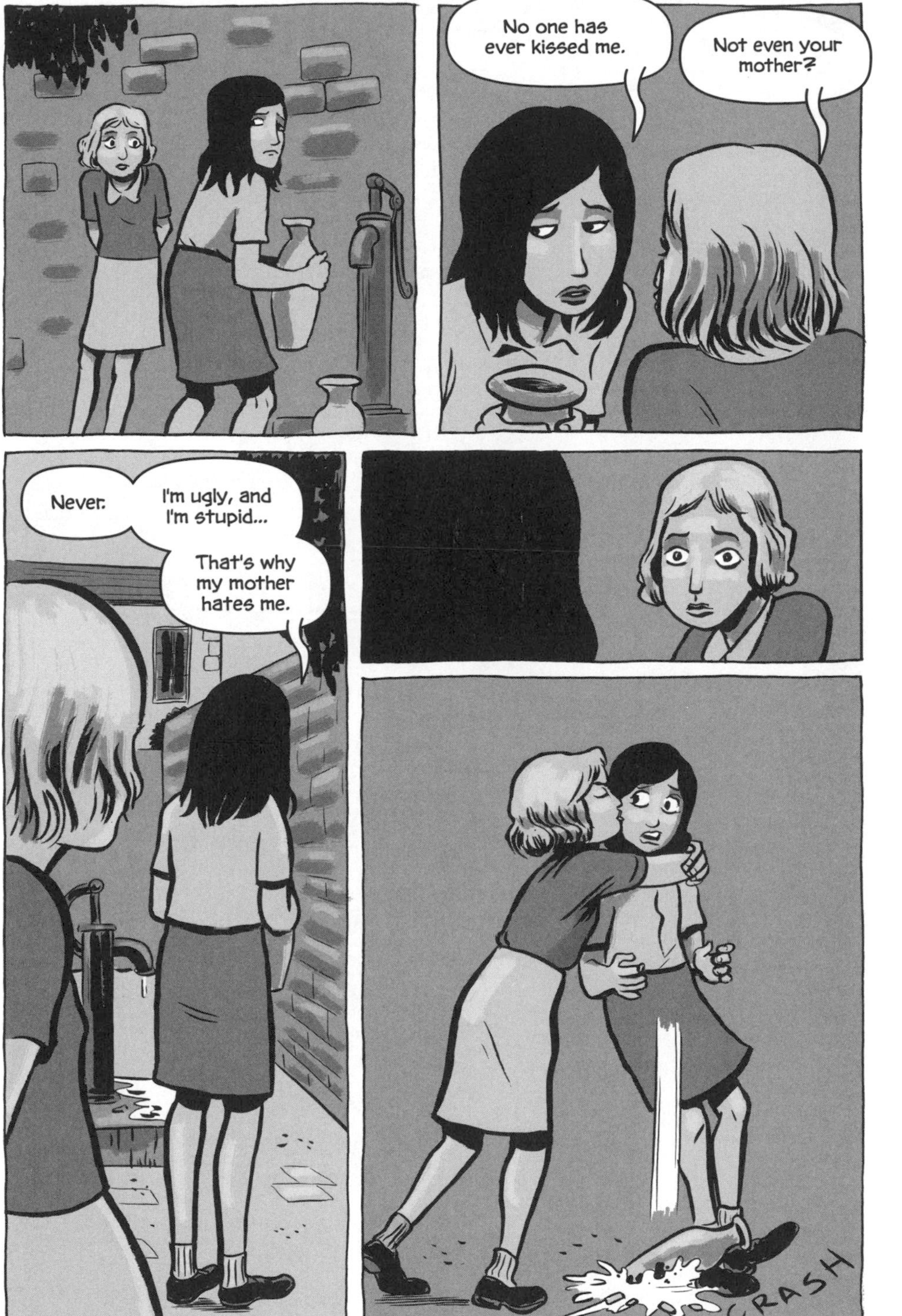
No one has ever kissed me.
Not even your mother?
Never.
I'm ugly, and I'm stupid...
That's why my mother hates me.
CRASH

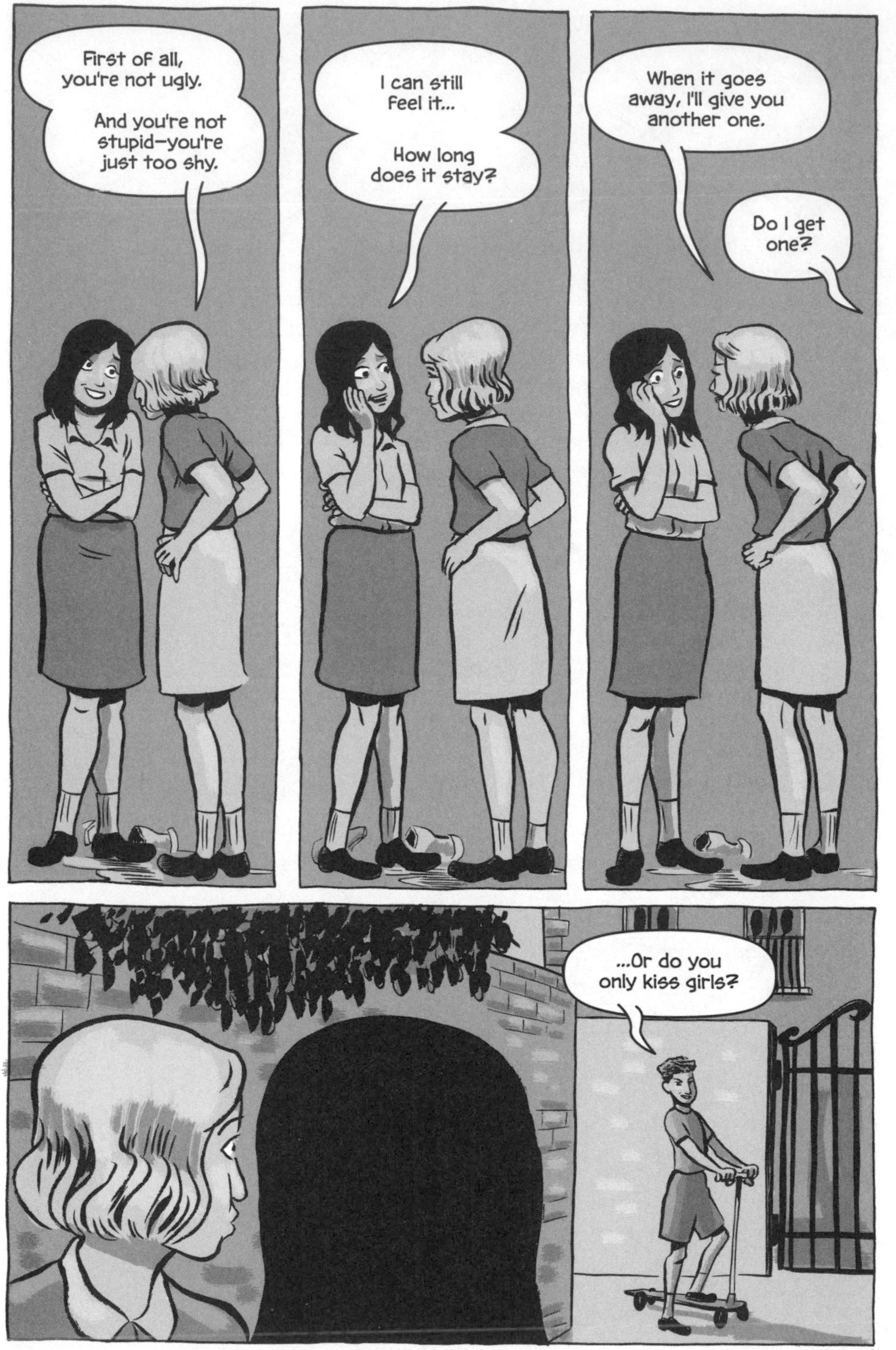
First of all, you're not ugly.
And you're not stupid—you're just too shy.
I can still feel it...
How long does it stay?
When it goes away, I'll give you another one.
Do I get one?
...Or do you only kiss girls?

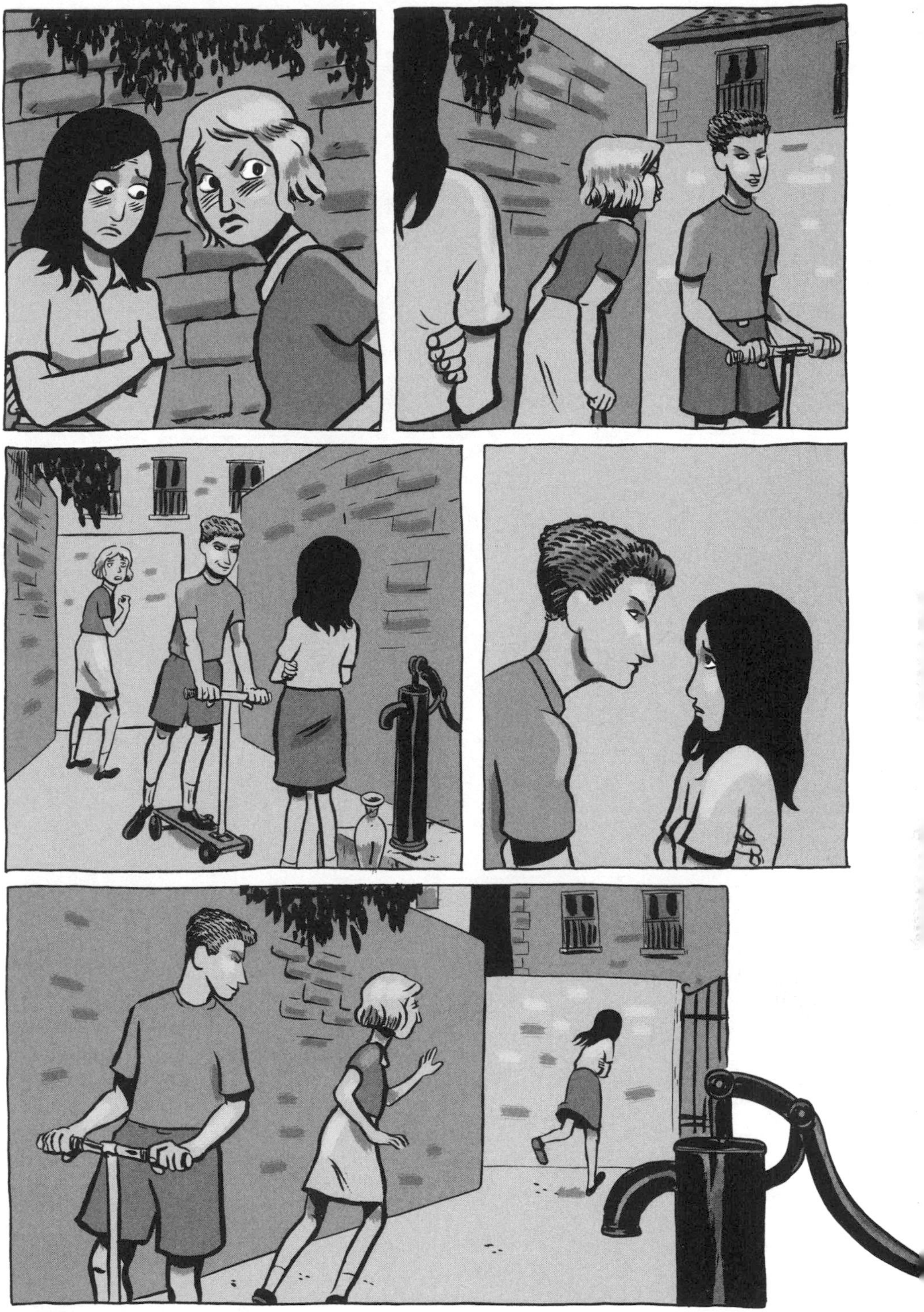

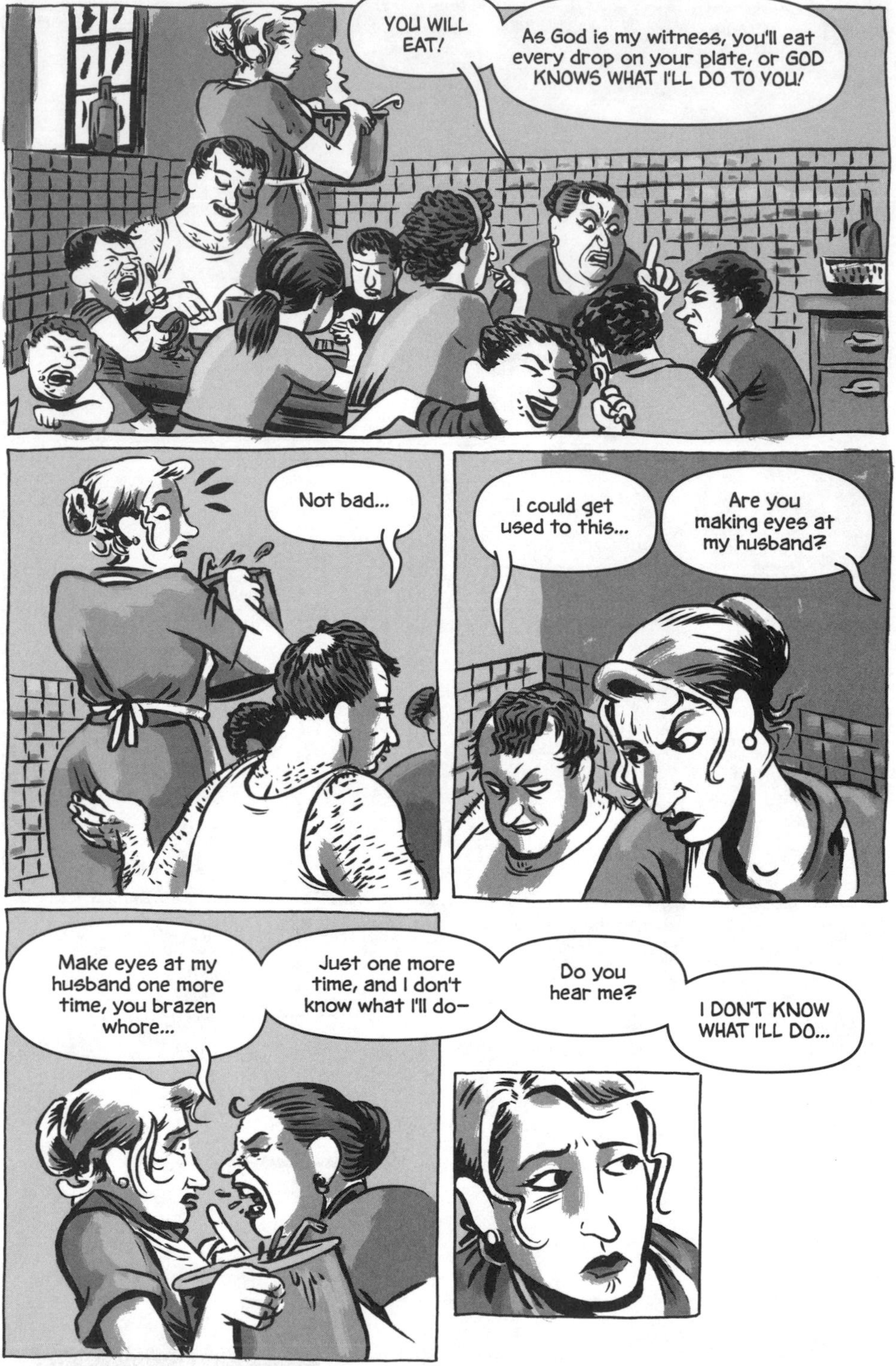
YOU WILL EAT!
As God is my witness, you'll eat every drop on your plate, or GOD KNOWS WHAT I'LL DO TO YOU!
Not bad...
I could get used to this...
Are you making eyes at my husband?
Make eyes at my husband one more time, you brazen whore...
Just one more time, and I don't know what I'll do–
Do you hear me?
I DON'T KNOW WHAT I'LL DO...

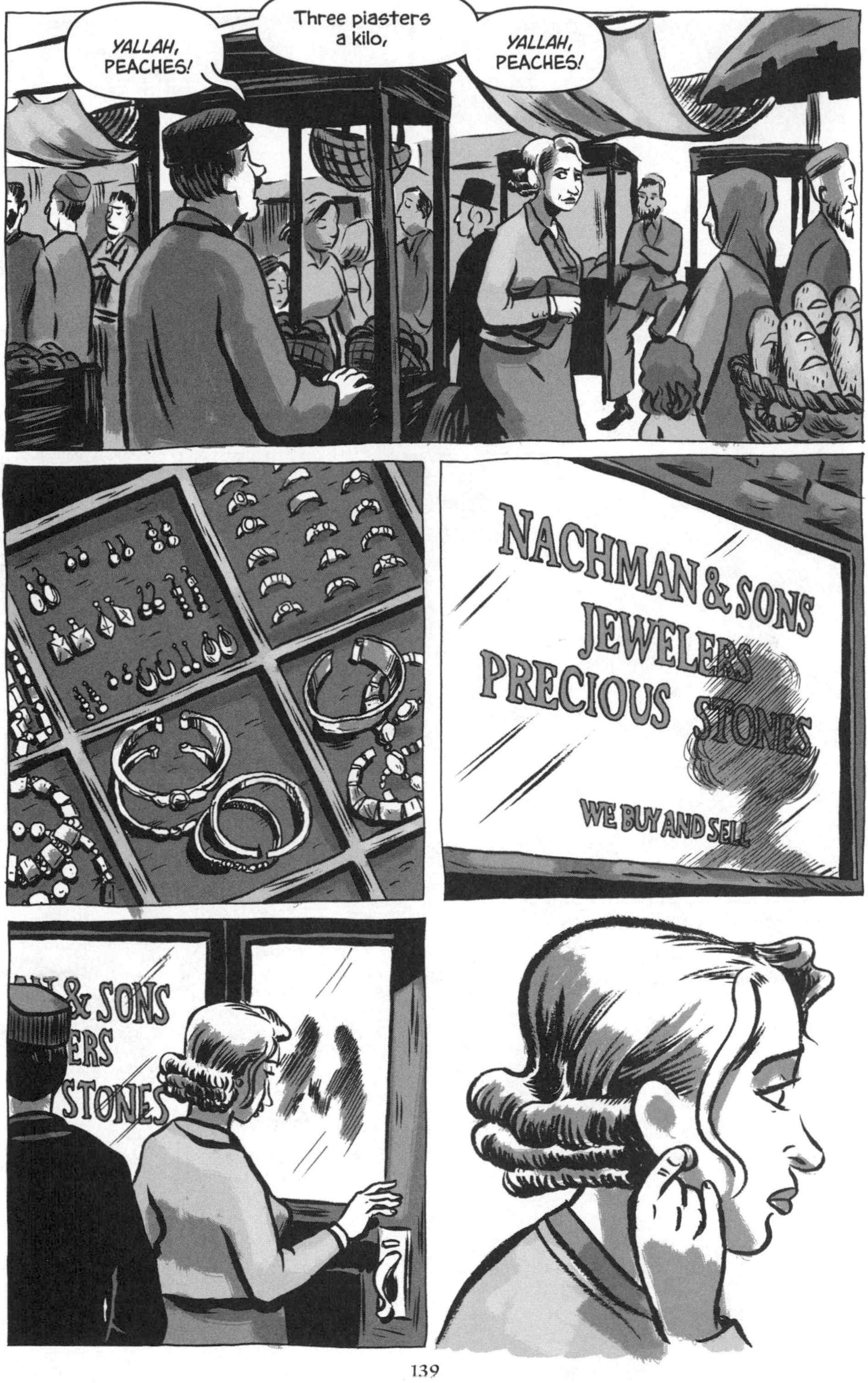
YALLAH, PEACHES!
Three piasters a kilo,
YALLAH, PEACHES!
NACHMAN & SONS
JEWELERS
PRECIOUS STONES
WE BUY AND SELL
& SONS
STONES

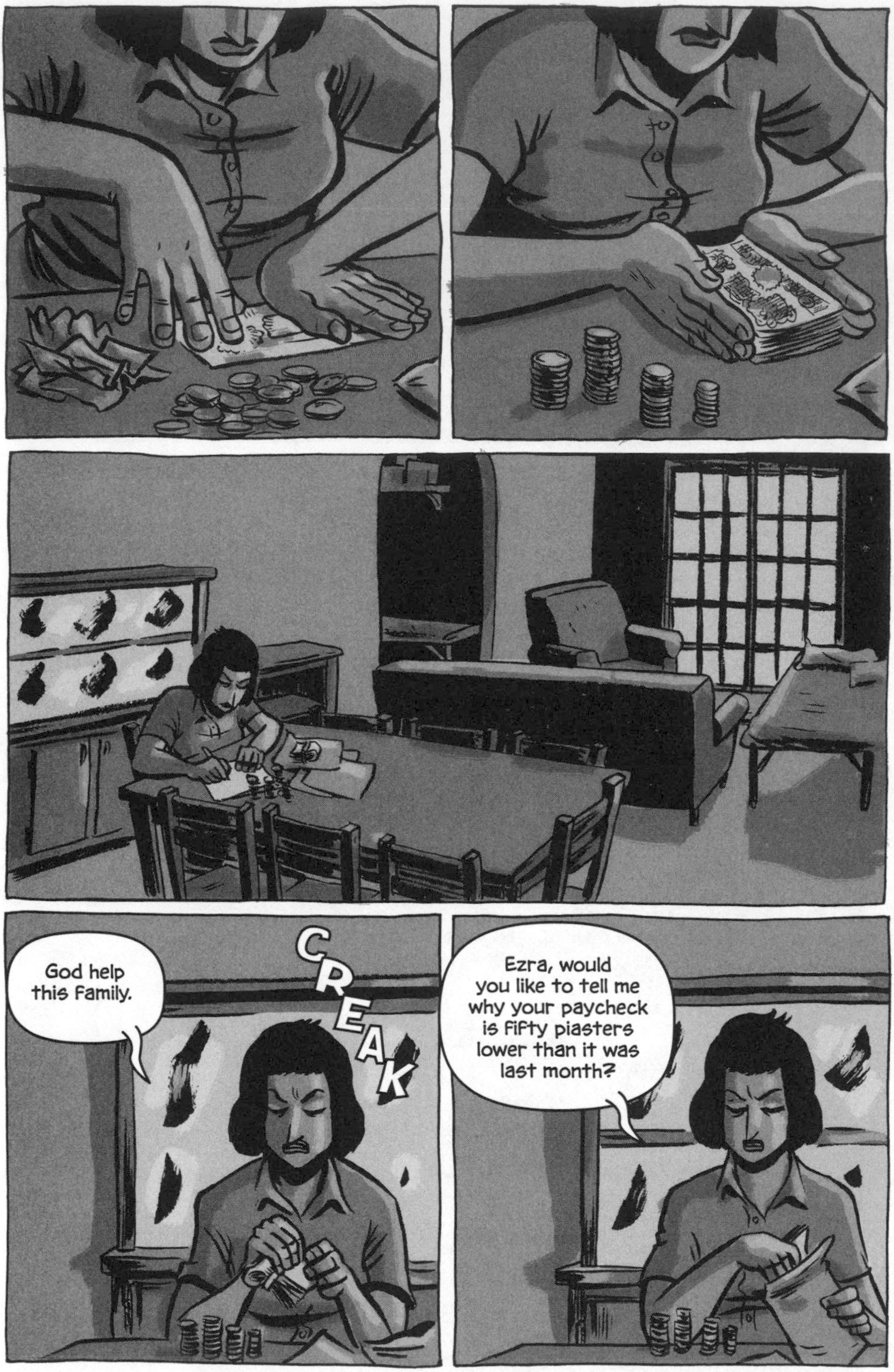
God help this family.
CREAK
Ezra, would you like to tell me why your paycheck is fifty piasters lower than it was last month?

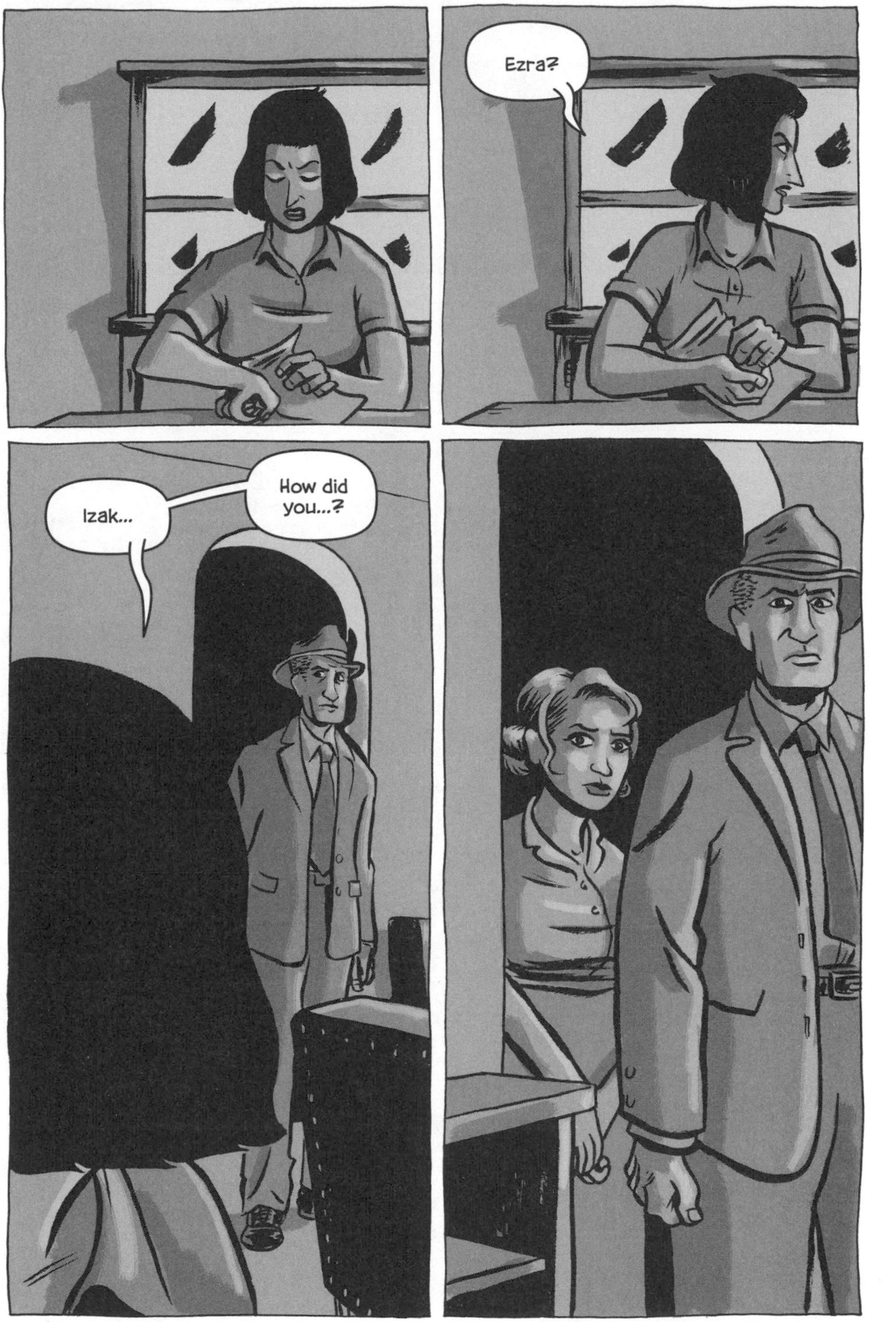
Ezra?
Izak...
How did you...?

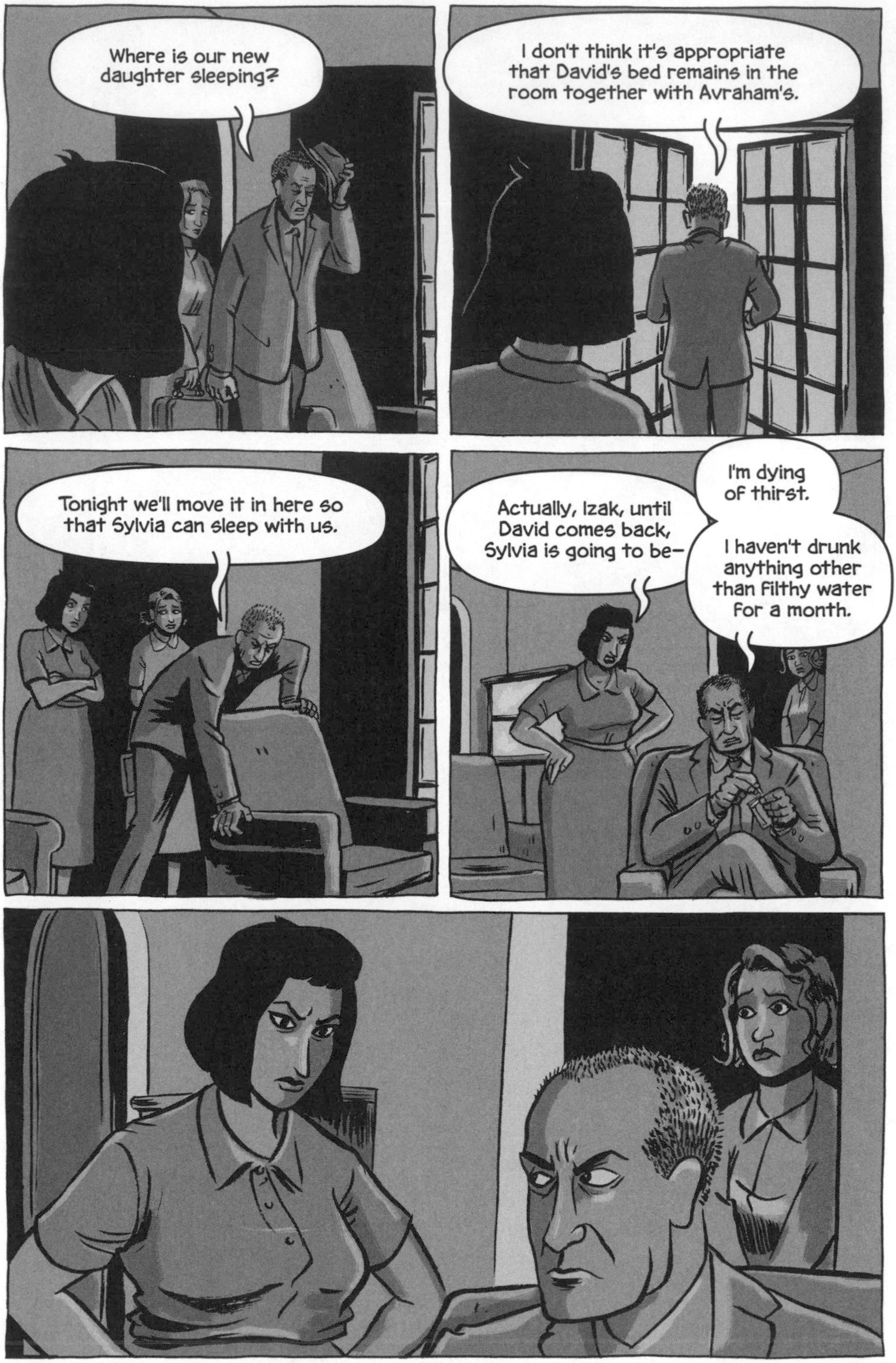
Where is our new daughter sleeping?
I don't think it's appropriate that David's bed remains in the room together with Avraham's.
Tonight we'll move it in here so that Sylvia can sleep with us.
Actually, Izak, until David comes back, Sylvia is going to be—
I'm dying of thirst.
I haven't drunk anything other than filthy water for a month.

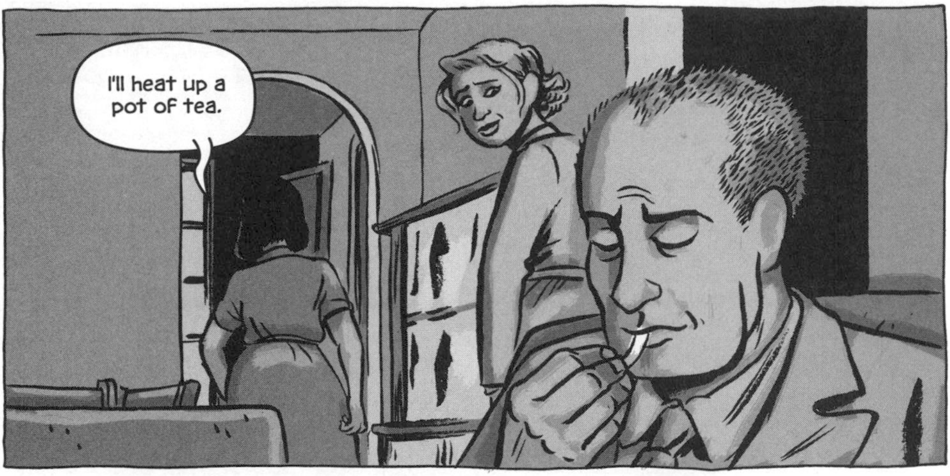
I'll heat up a pot of tea.

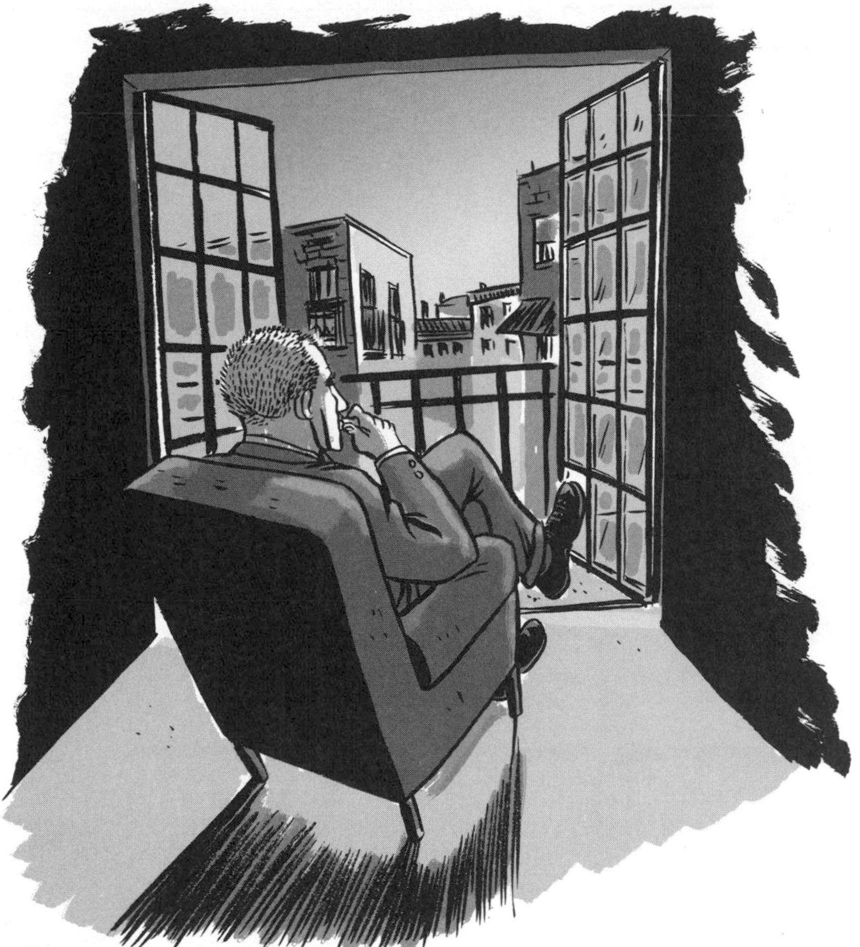

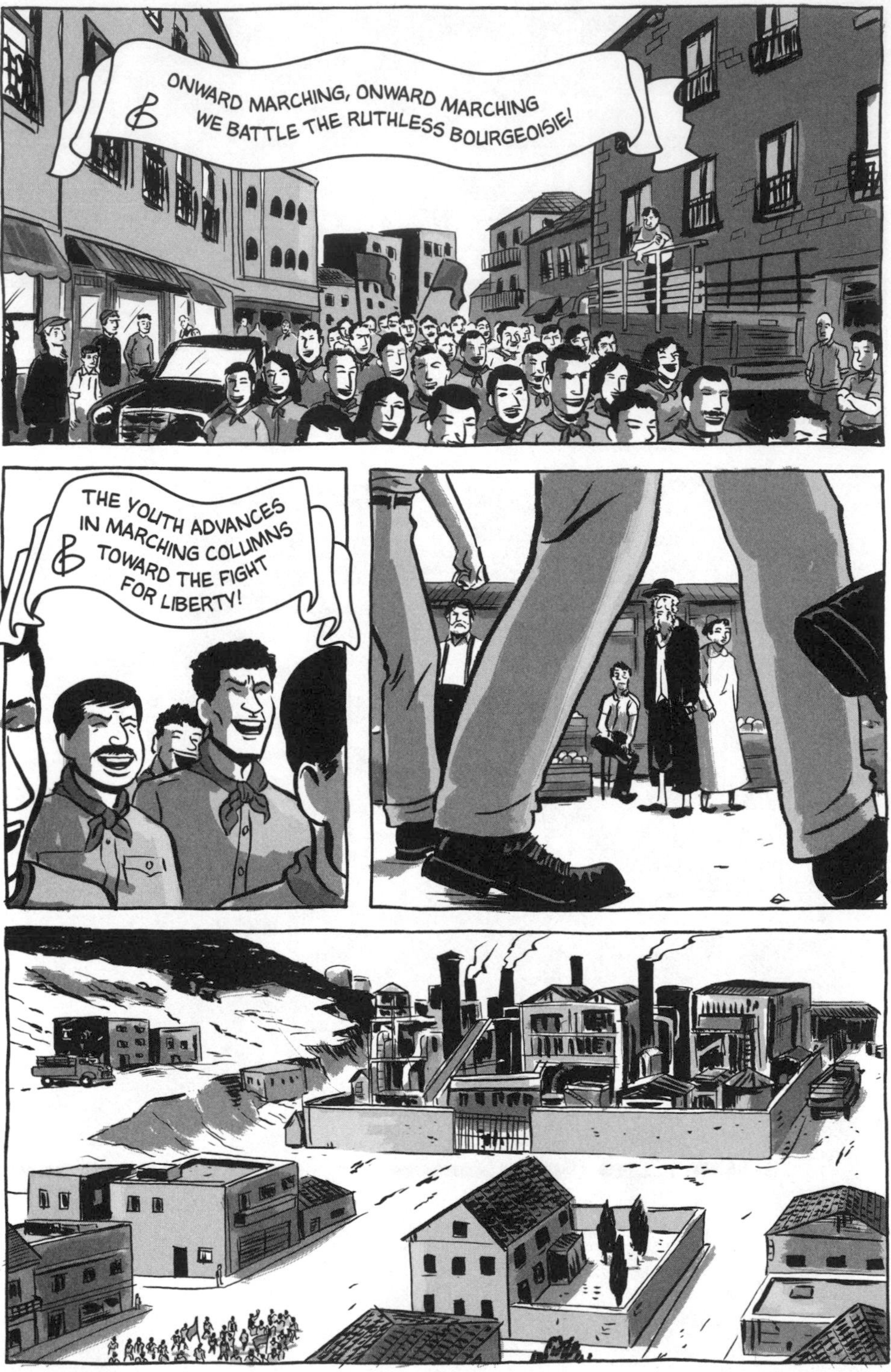
ONWARD MARCHING, ONWARD MARCHING WE BATTLE THE RUTHLESS BOURGEOISIE!
THE YOUTH ADVANCES IN MARCHING COLUMNS TOWARD THE FIGHT FOR LIBERTY!

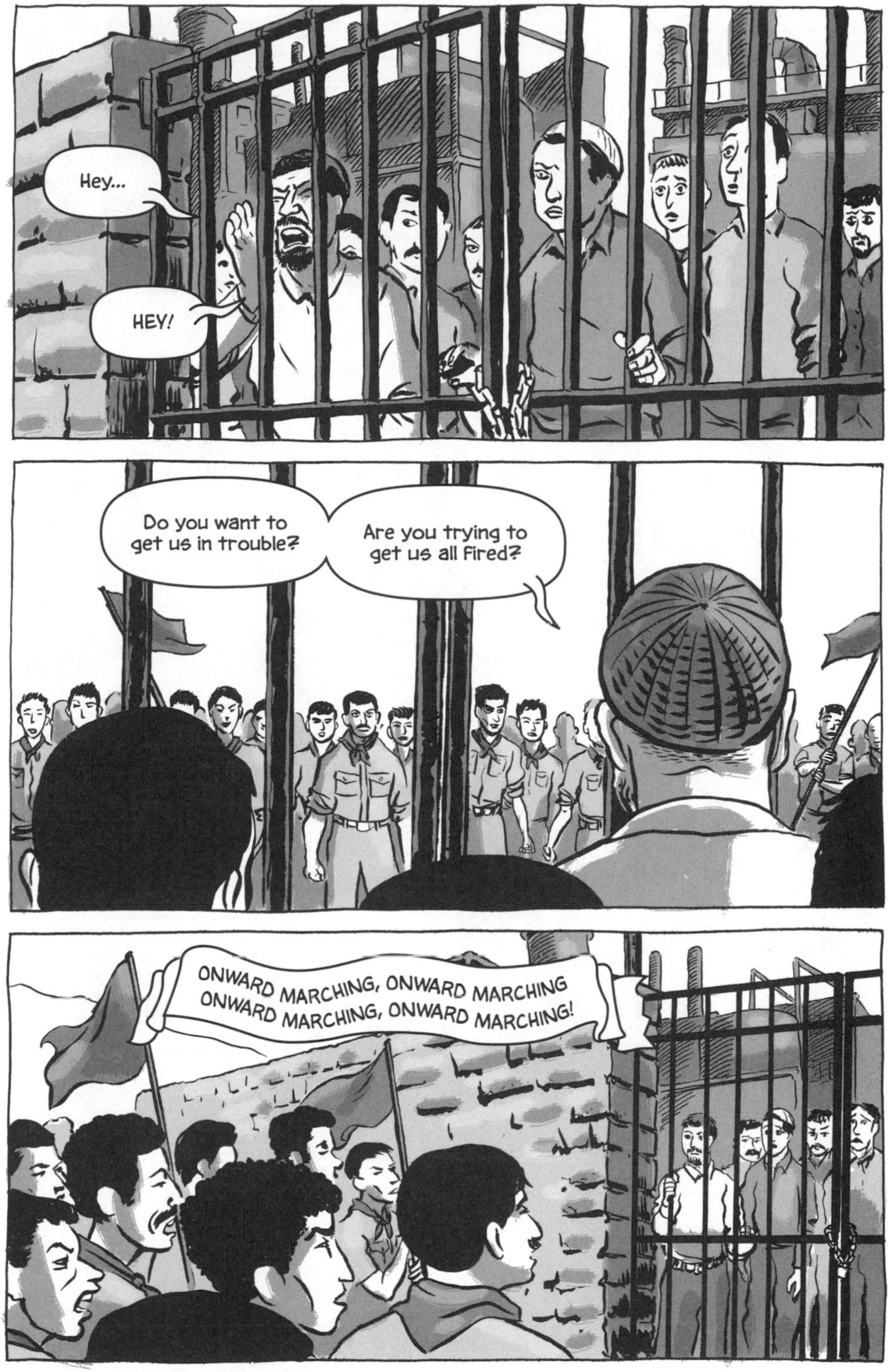
Hey...
HEY!
Do you want to get us in trouble?
Are you trying to get us all fired?
ONWARD MARCHING, ONWARD MARCHING
ONWARD MARCHING, ONWARD MARCHING!

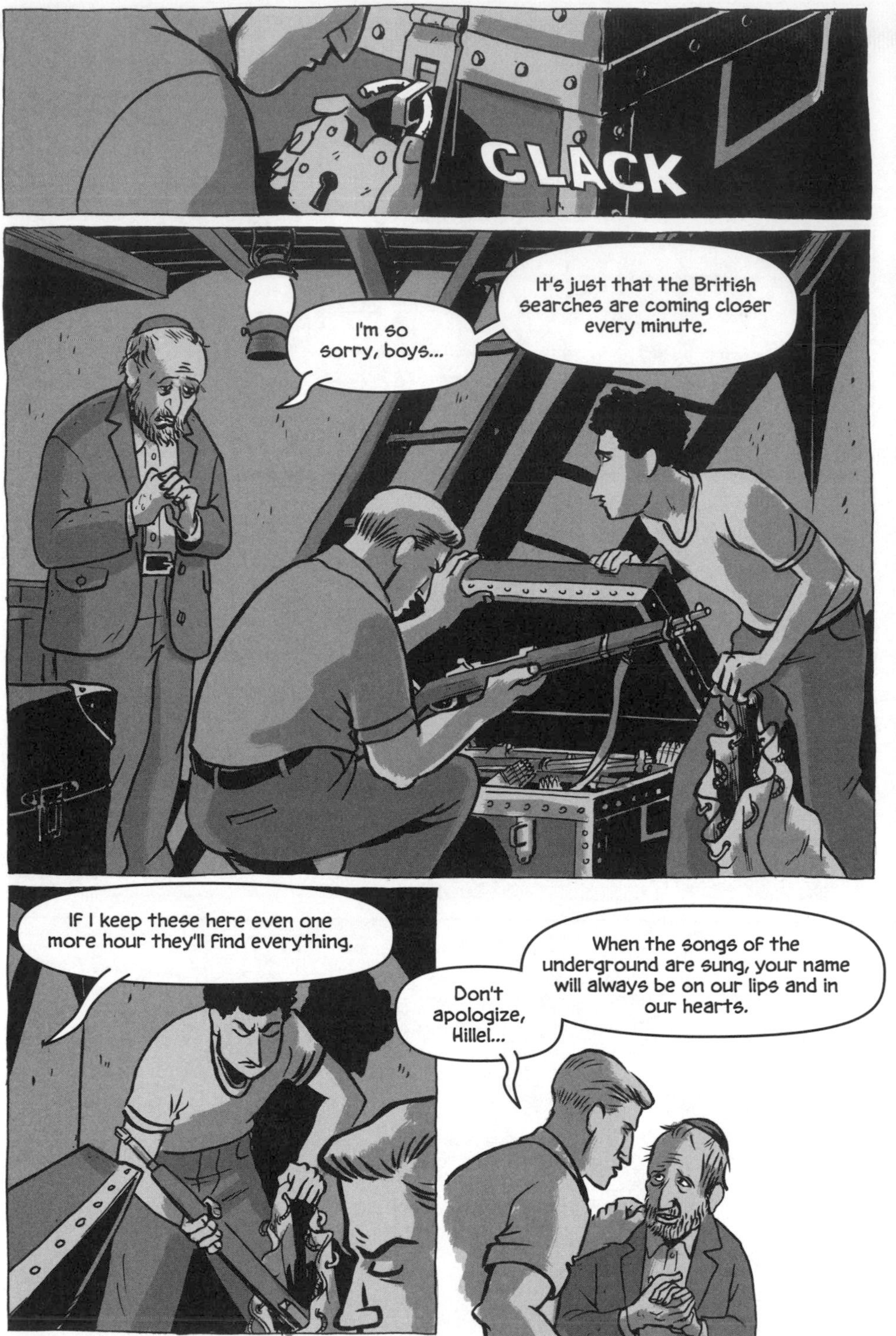
CLACK
I'm so sorry, boys...
It's just that the British searches are coming closer every minute.
If I keep these here even one more hour they'll find everything.
Don't apologize, Hillel...
When the songs of the underground are sung, your name will always be on our lips and in our hearts.

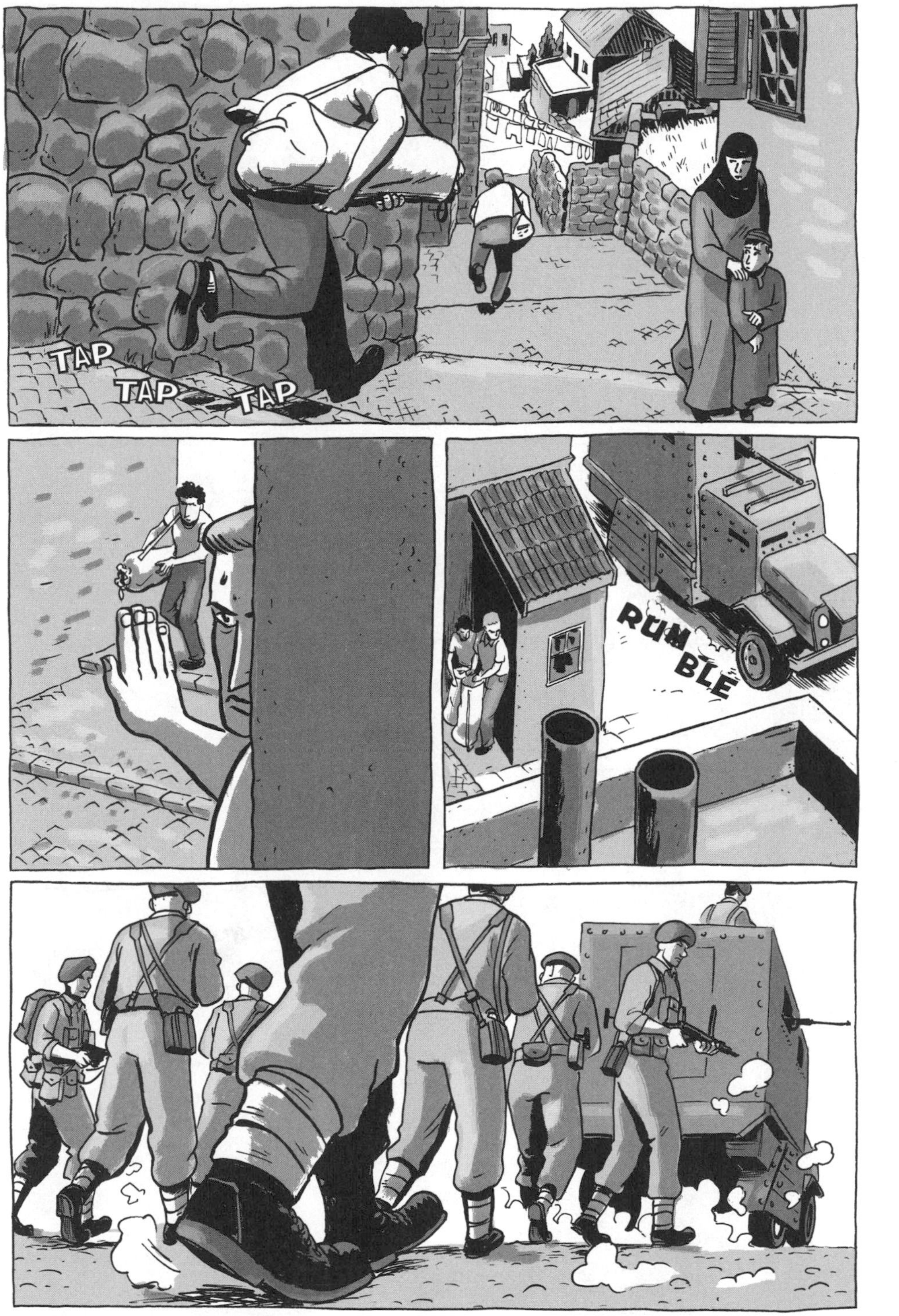
TAP
TAP
TAP
RUMBLE

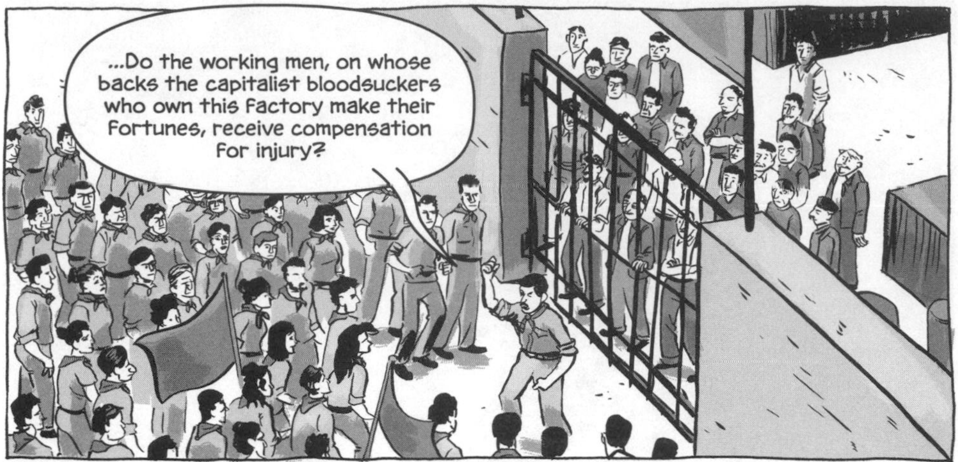
...Do the working men, on whose backs the capitalist bloodsuckers who own this factory make their fortunes, receive compensation for injury?

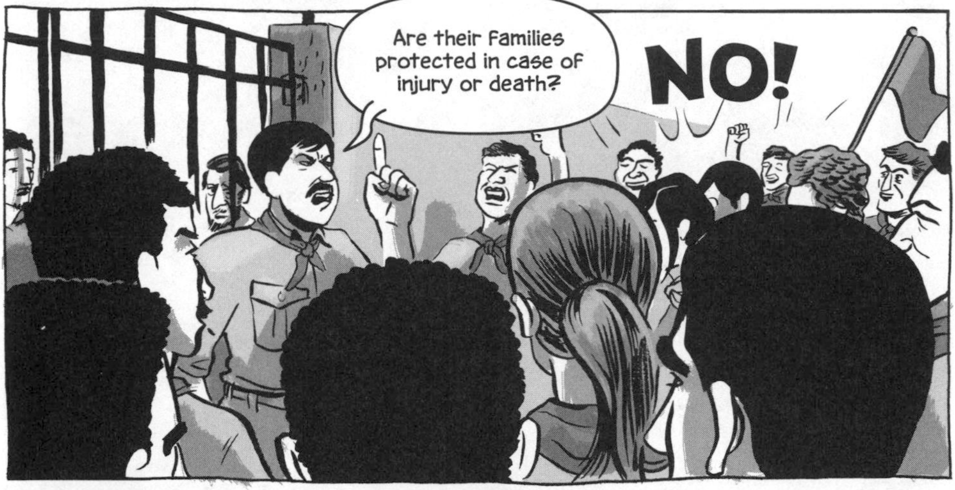
Are their families protected in case of injury or death?
NO!

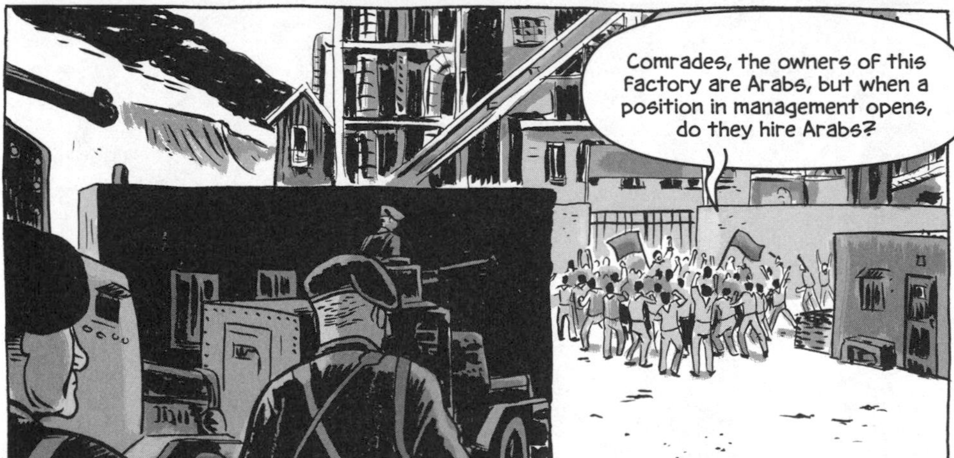
Comrades, the owners of this factory are Arabs, but when a position in management opens, do they hire Arabs?

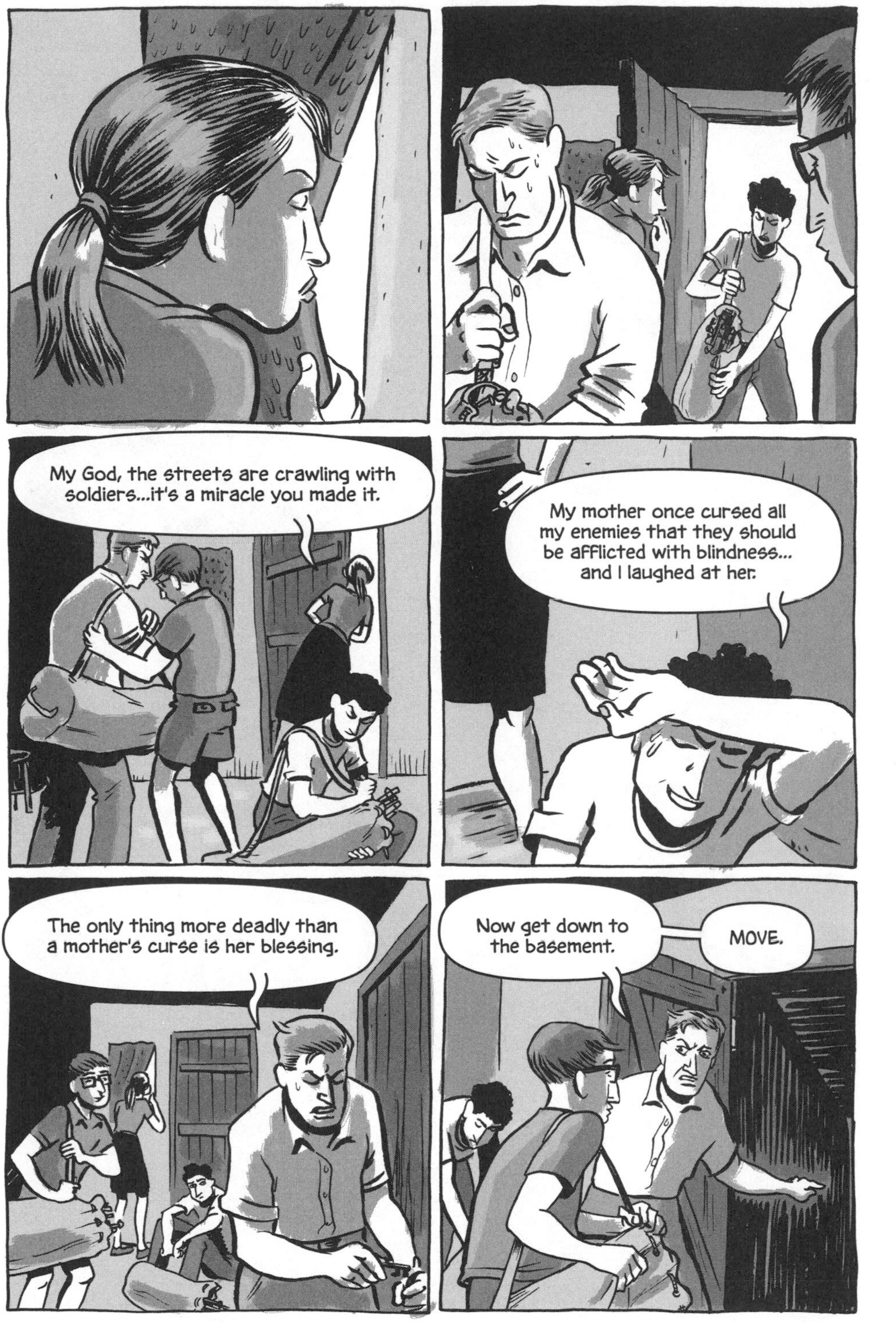
My God, the streets are crawling with soldiers...it's a miracle you made it.
My mother once cursed all my enemies that they should be afflicted with blindness... and I laughed at her.
The only thing more deadly than a mother's curse is her blessing.
Now get down to the basement.
MOVE.

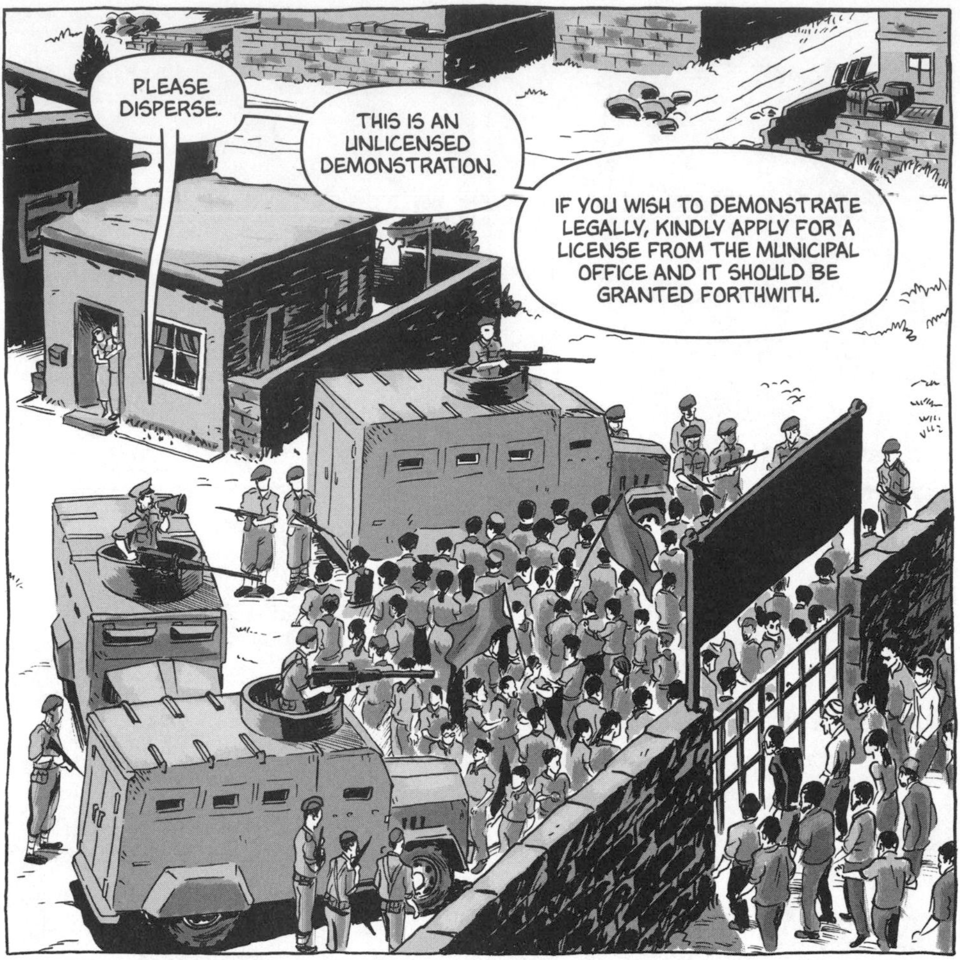
PLEASE DISPERSE.
THIS IS AN UNLICENSED DEMONSTRATION.
IF YOU WISH TO DEMONSTRATE LEGALLY, KINDLY APPLY FOR A LICENSE FROM THE MUNICIPAL OFFICE AND IT SHOULD BE GRANTED FORTHWITH.

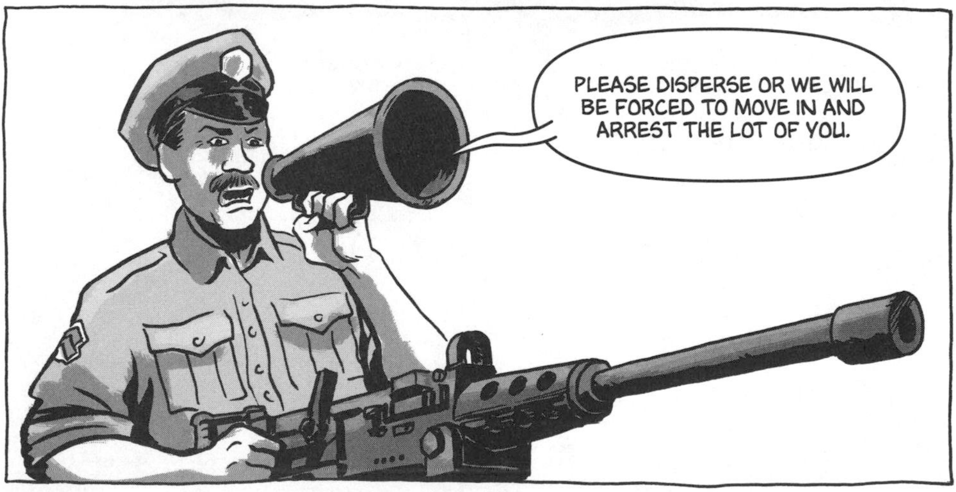
PLEASE DISPERSE OR WE WILL BE FORCED TO MOVE IN AND ARREST THE LOT OF YOU.

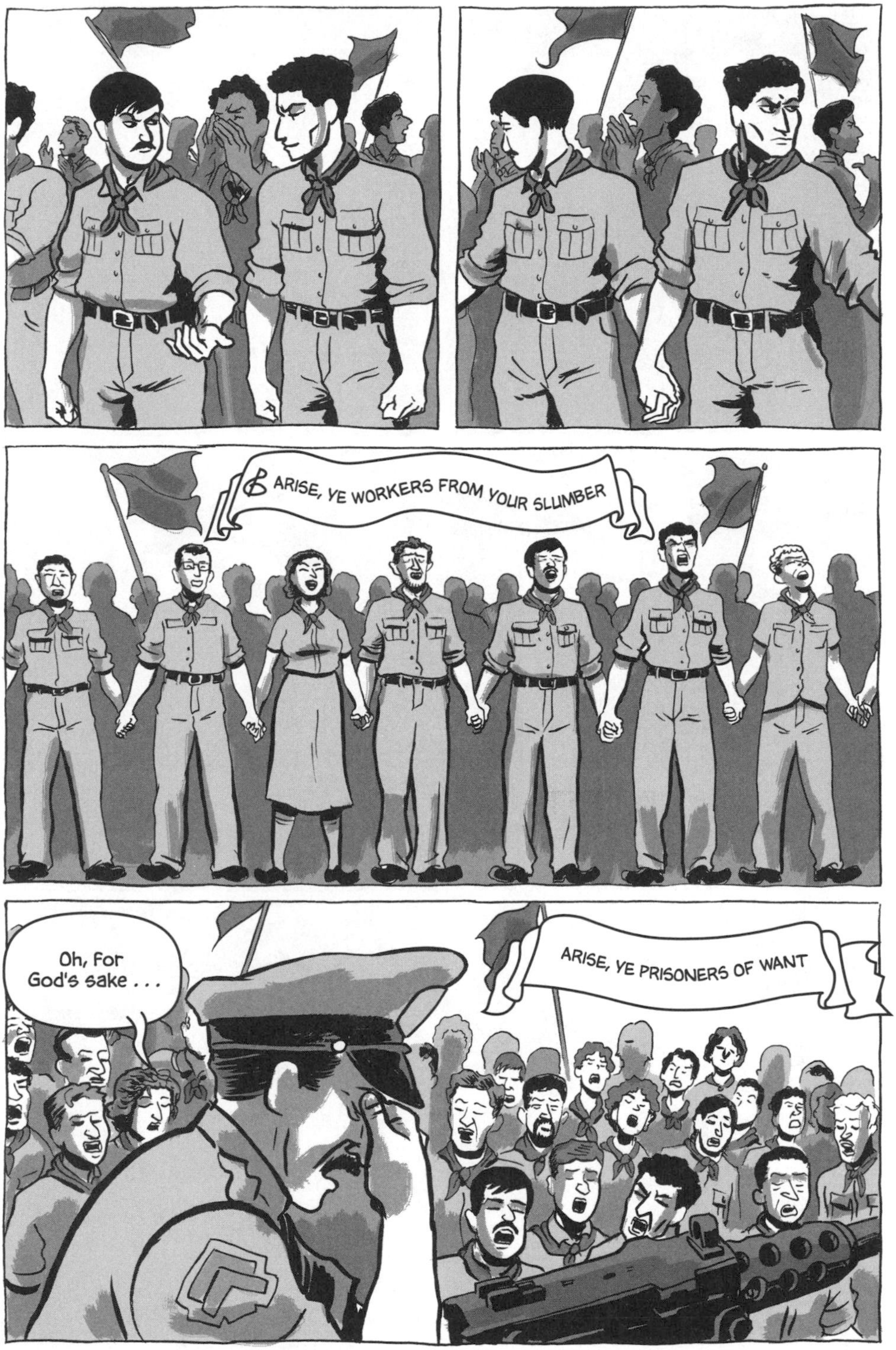

ARISE, YE WORKERS FROM YOUR SLUMBER
Oh, For God's sake . . .
ARISE, YE PRISONERS OF WANT

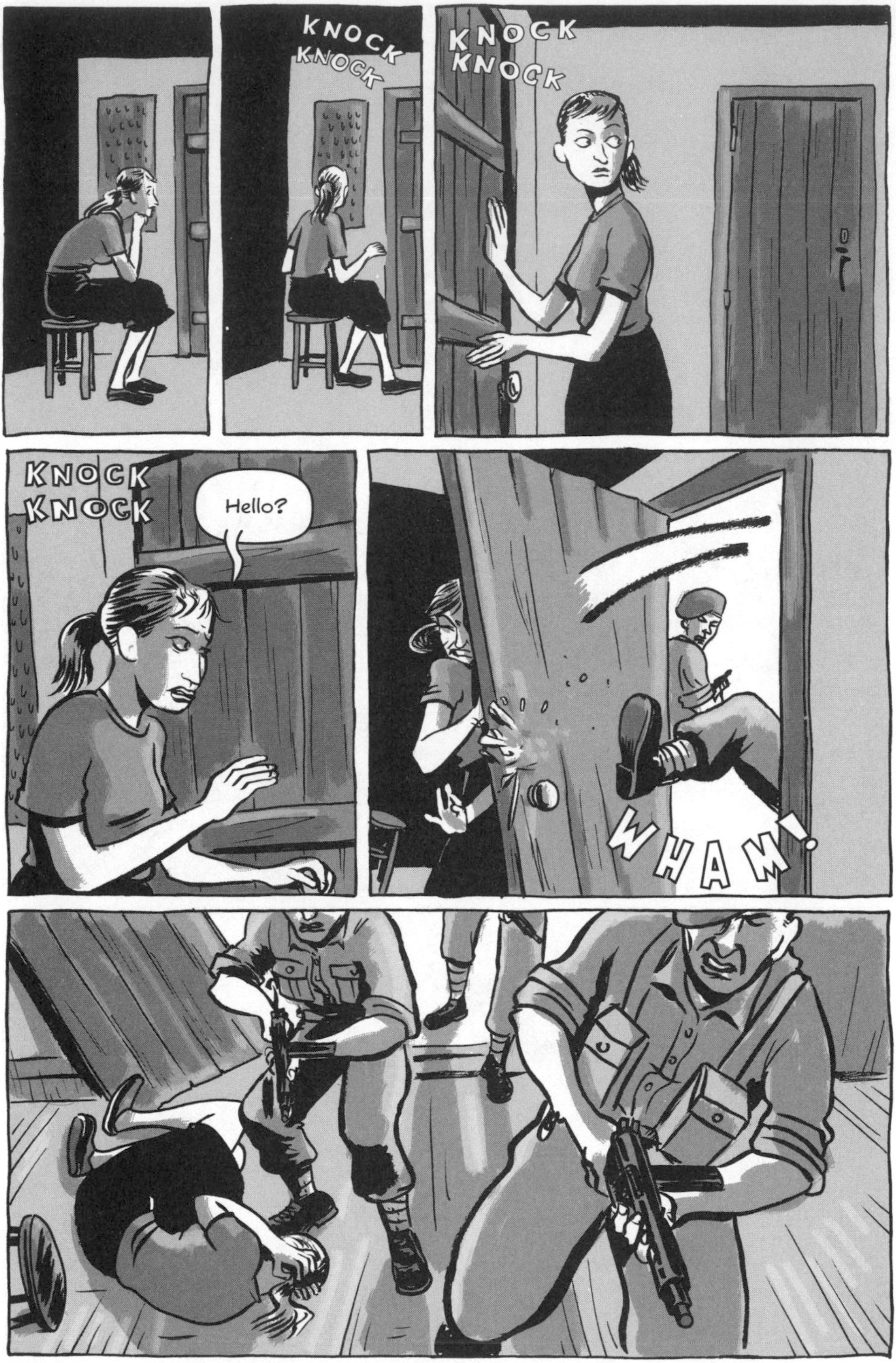
KNOCK
KNOCK
KNOCK
KNOCK
KNOCK
KNOCK
Hello?
WHAM!

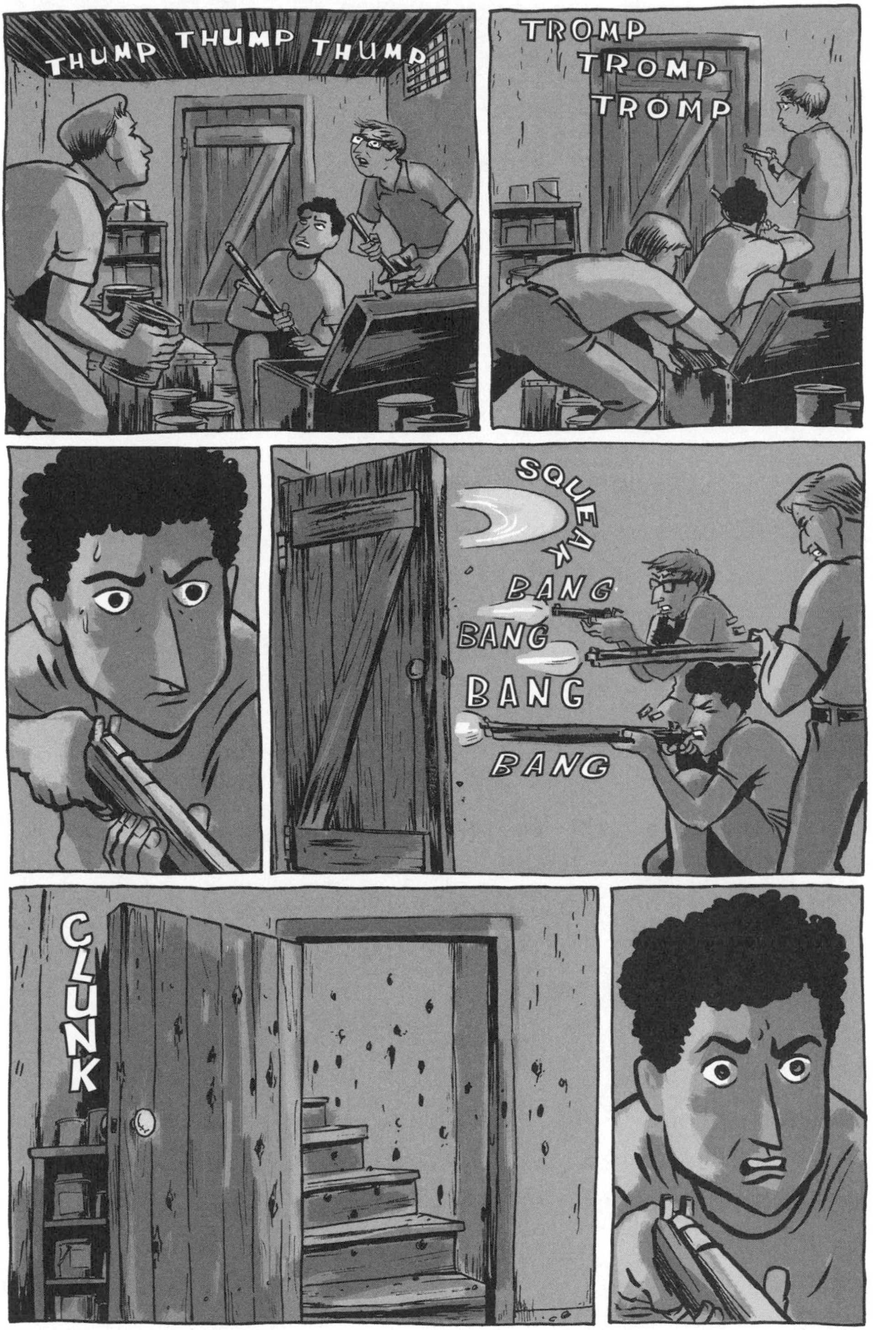
THUMP THUMP THUMP
TROMP
TROMP
TROMP
SQUEAK
BANG
BANG
BANG
BANG
CLUNK

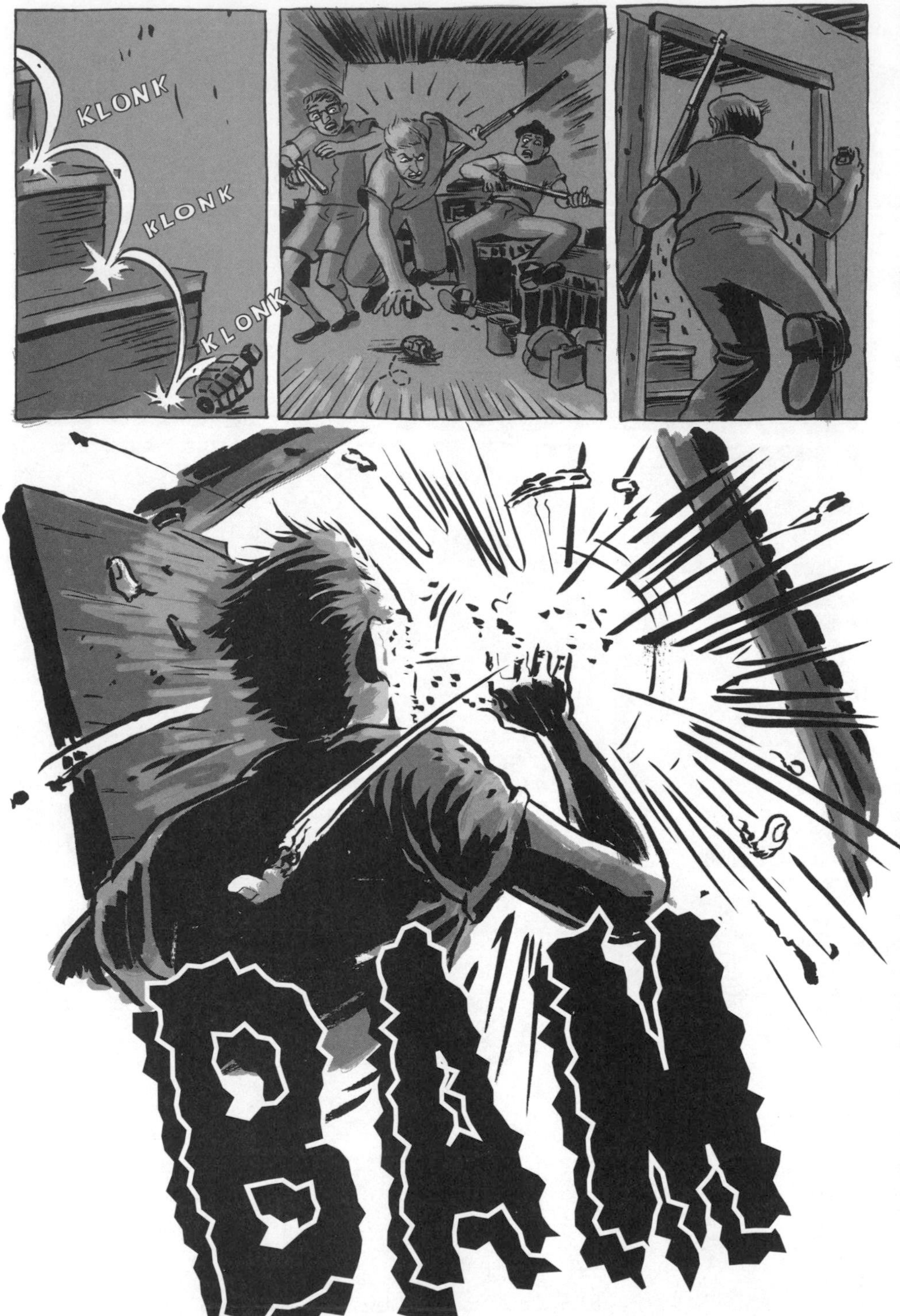
KLONK
KLONK
KLONK
BAM

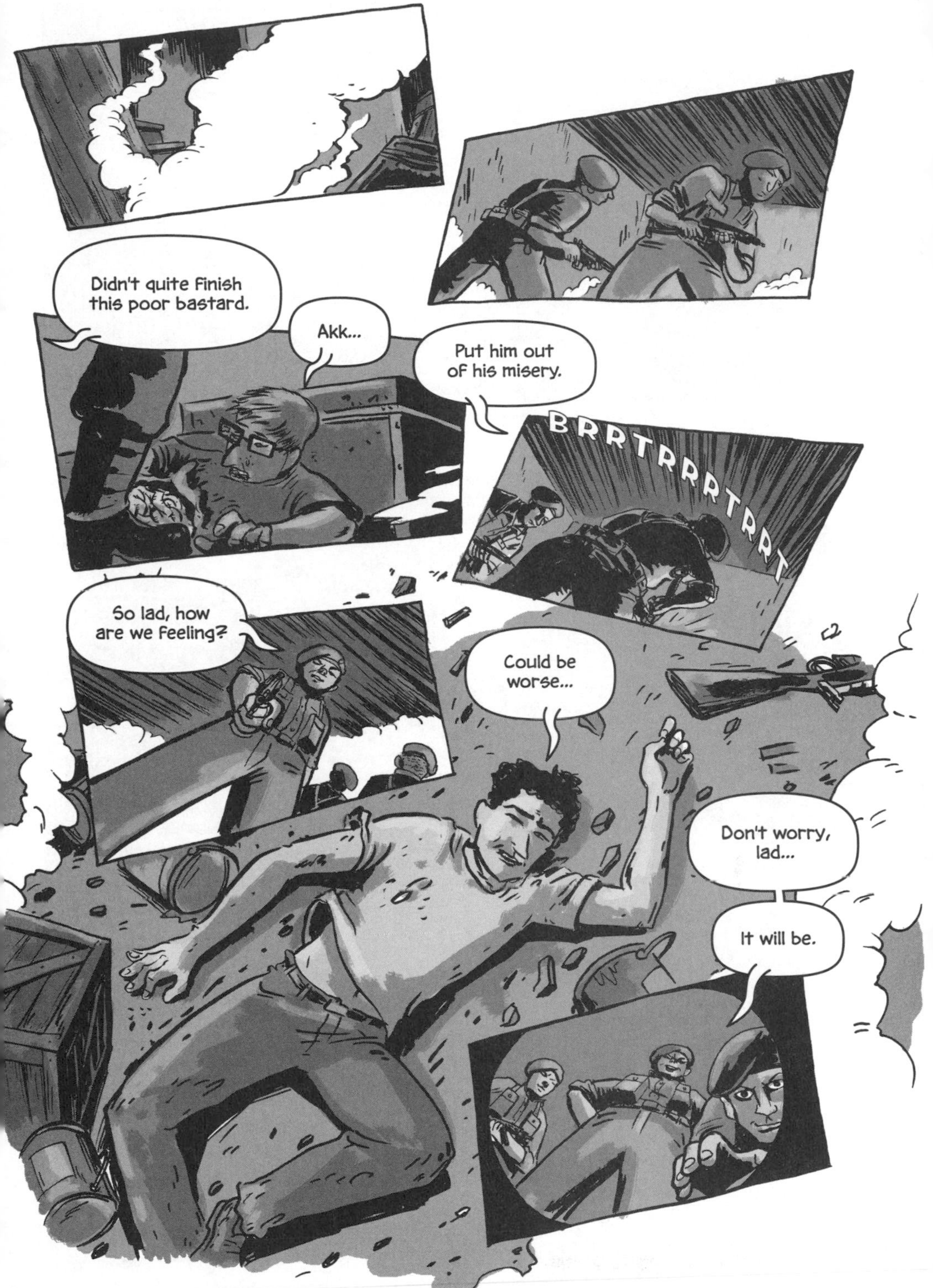
Didn't quite finish this poor bastard.
Akk...
Put him out of his misery.
BRRRTRRRRTRRRT
So lad, how are we feeling?
Could be worse...
Don't worry, lad...
It will be.

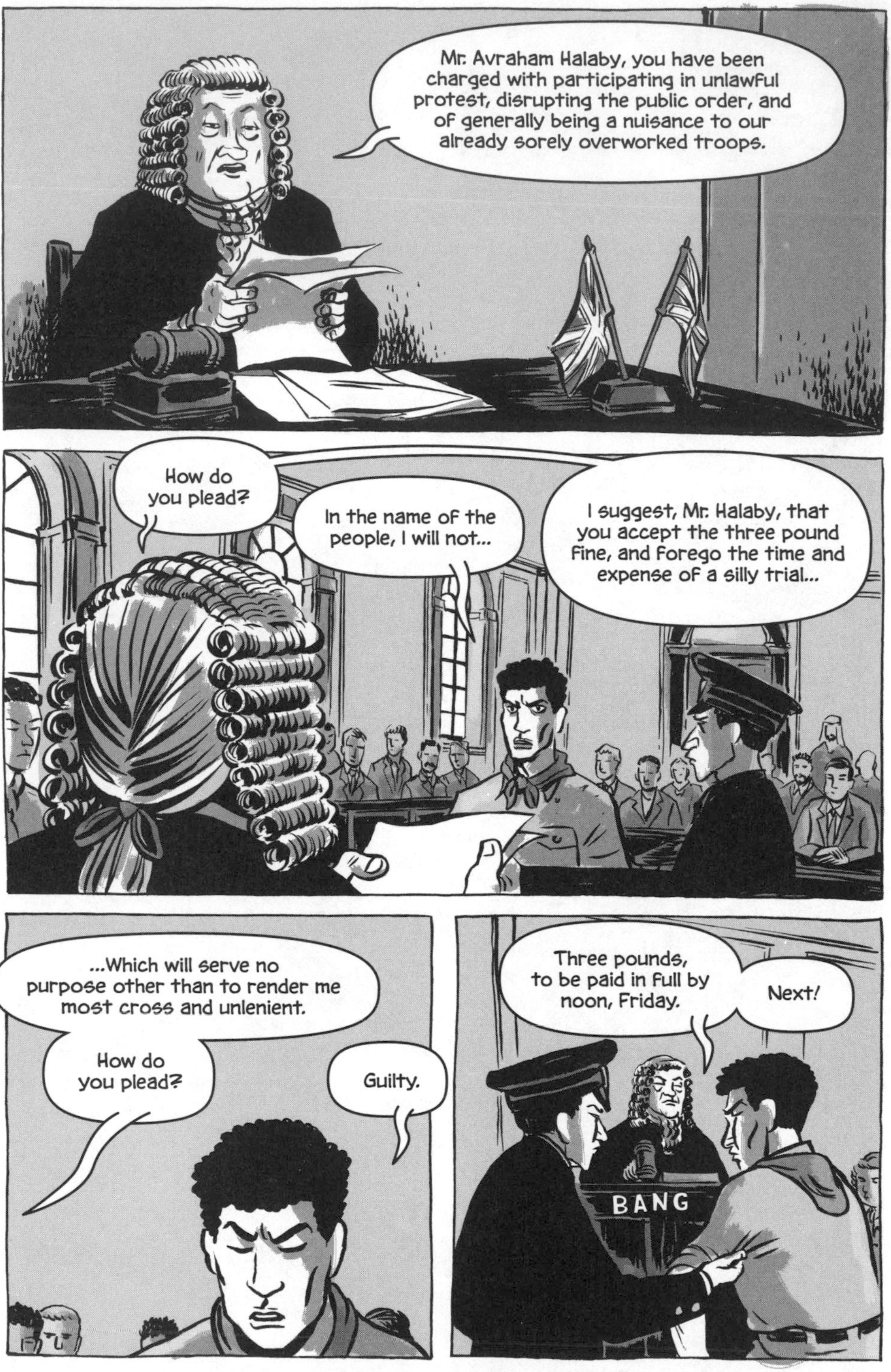
Mr. Avraham Halaby, you have been charged with participating in unlawful protest, disrupting the public order, and of generally being a nuisance to our already sorely overworked troops.
How do you plead?
In the name of the people, I will not...
I suggest, Mr. Halaby, that you accept the three pound fine, and forego the time and expense of a silly trial...
...Which will serve no purpose other than to render me most cross and unlenient.
How do you plead?
Guilty.
Three pounds, to be paid in full by noon, Friday.
Next!
BANG

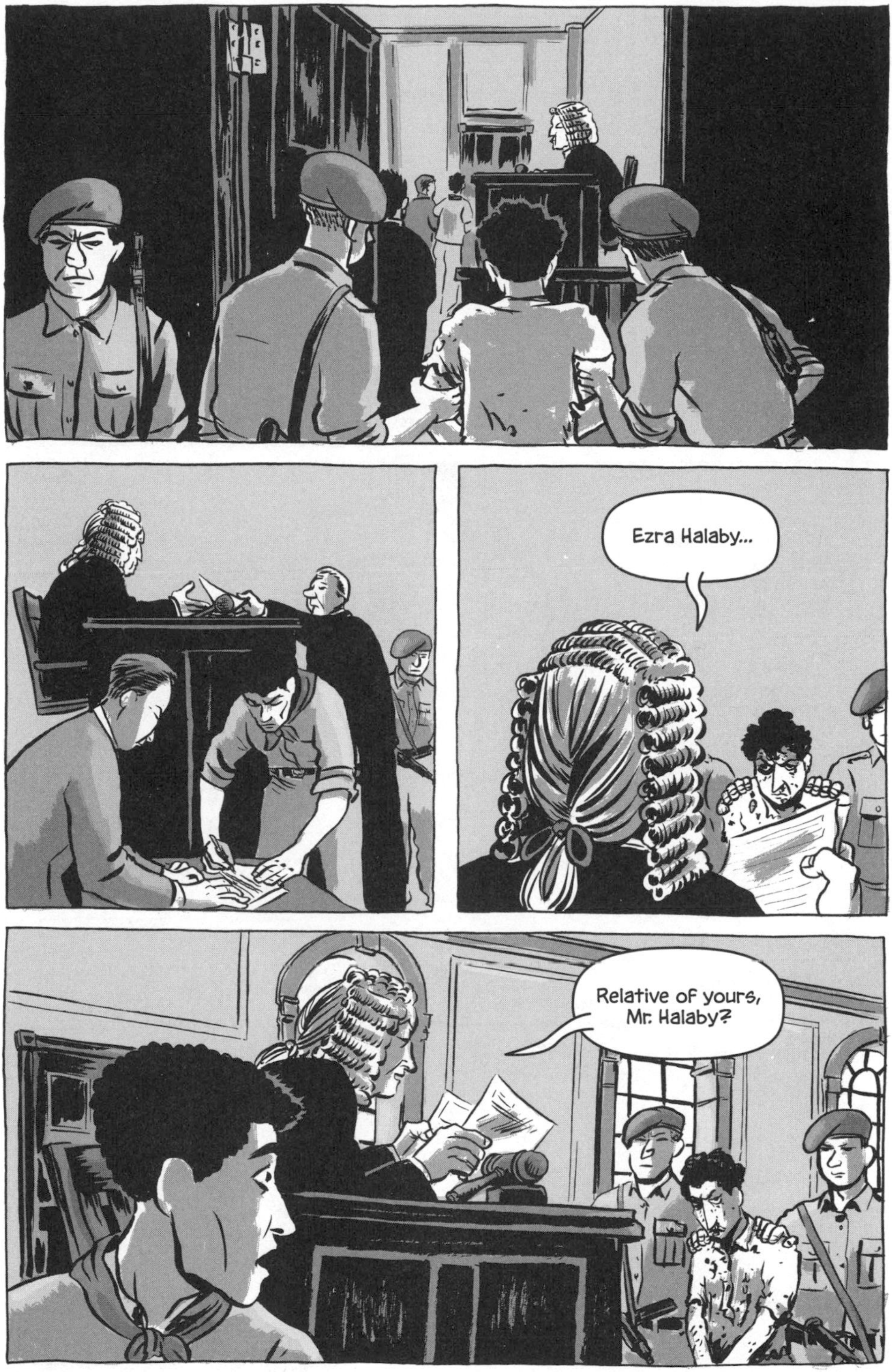
Ezra Halaby...
Relative of yours,
Mr. Halaby?

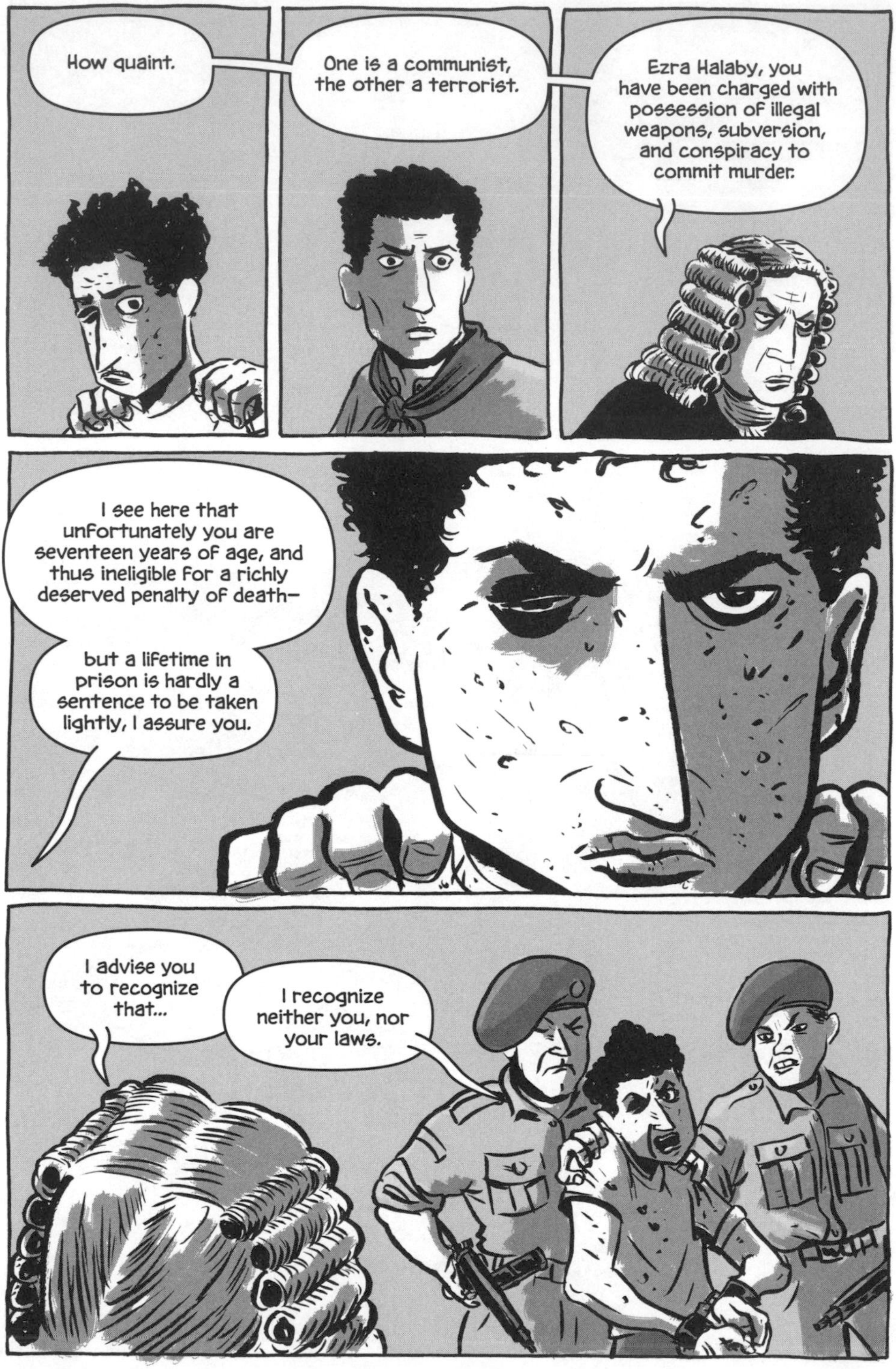
How quaint.
One is a communist, the other a terrorist.
Ezra Halaby, you have been charged with possession of illegal weapons, subversion, and conspiracy to commit murder.
I see here that unfortunately you are seventeen years of age, and thus ineligible for a richly deserved penalty of death—
but a lifetime in prison is hardly a sentence to be taken lightly, I assure you.
I advise you to recognize that...
I recognize neither you, nor your laws.

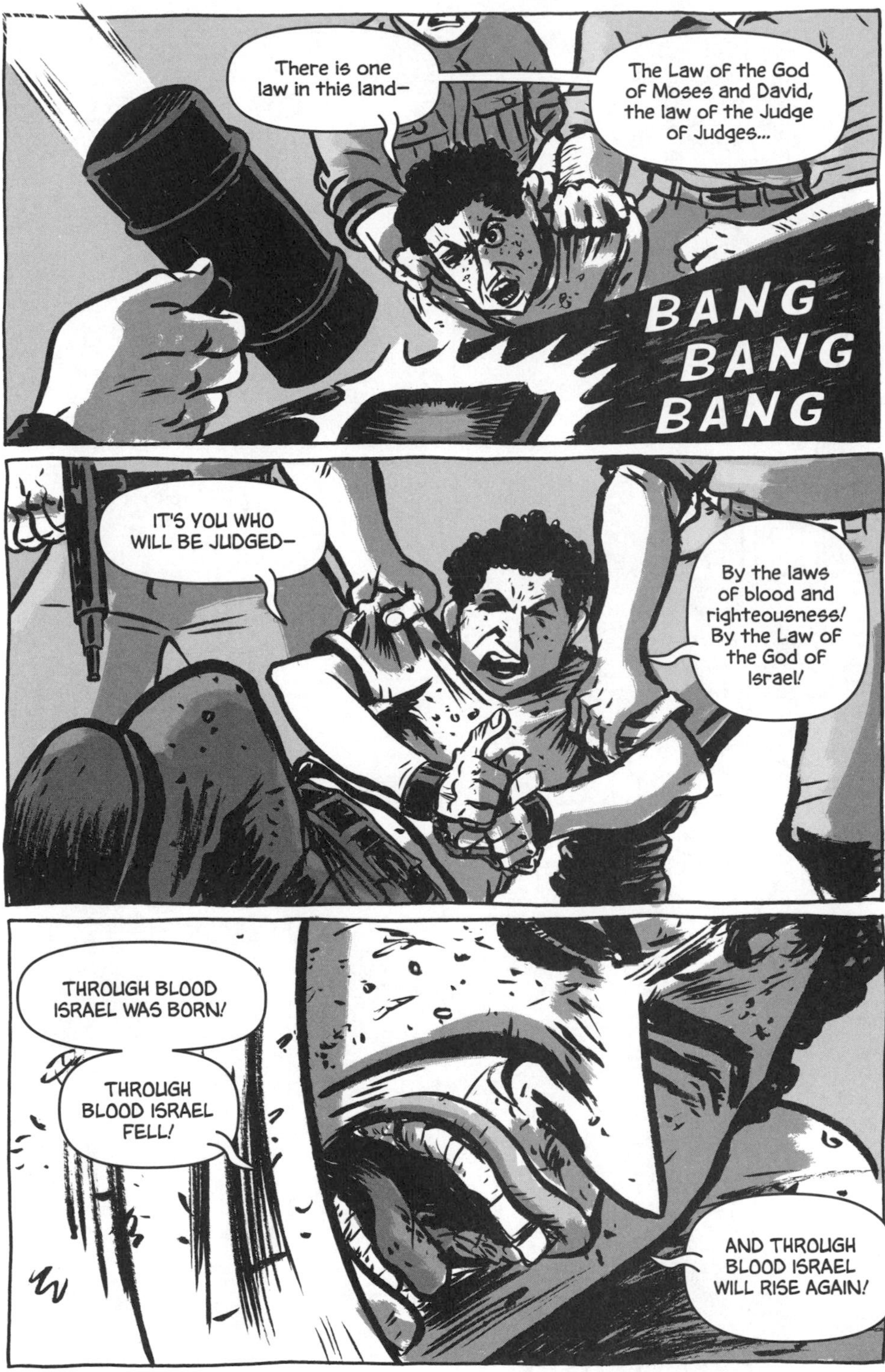
There is one law in this land—
The Law of the God of Moses and David, the law of the Judge of Judges...
BANG BANG BANG
IT'S YOU WHO WILL BE JUDGED—
By the laws of blood and righteousness! By the Law of the God of Israel!
THROUGH BLOOD ISRAEL WAS BORN!
THROUGH BLOOD ISRAEL FELL!
AND THROUGH BLOOD ISRAEL WILL RISE AGAIN!

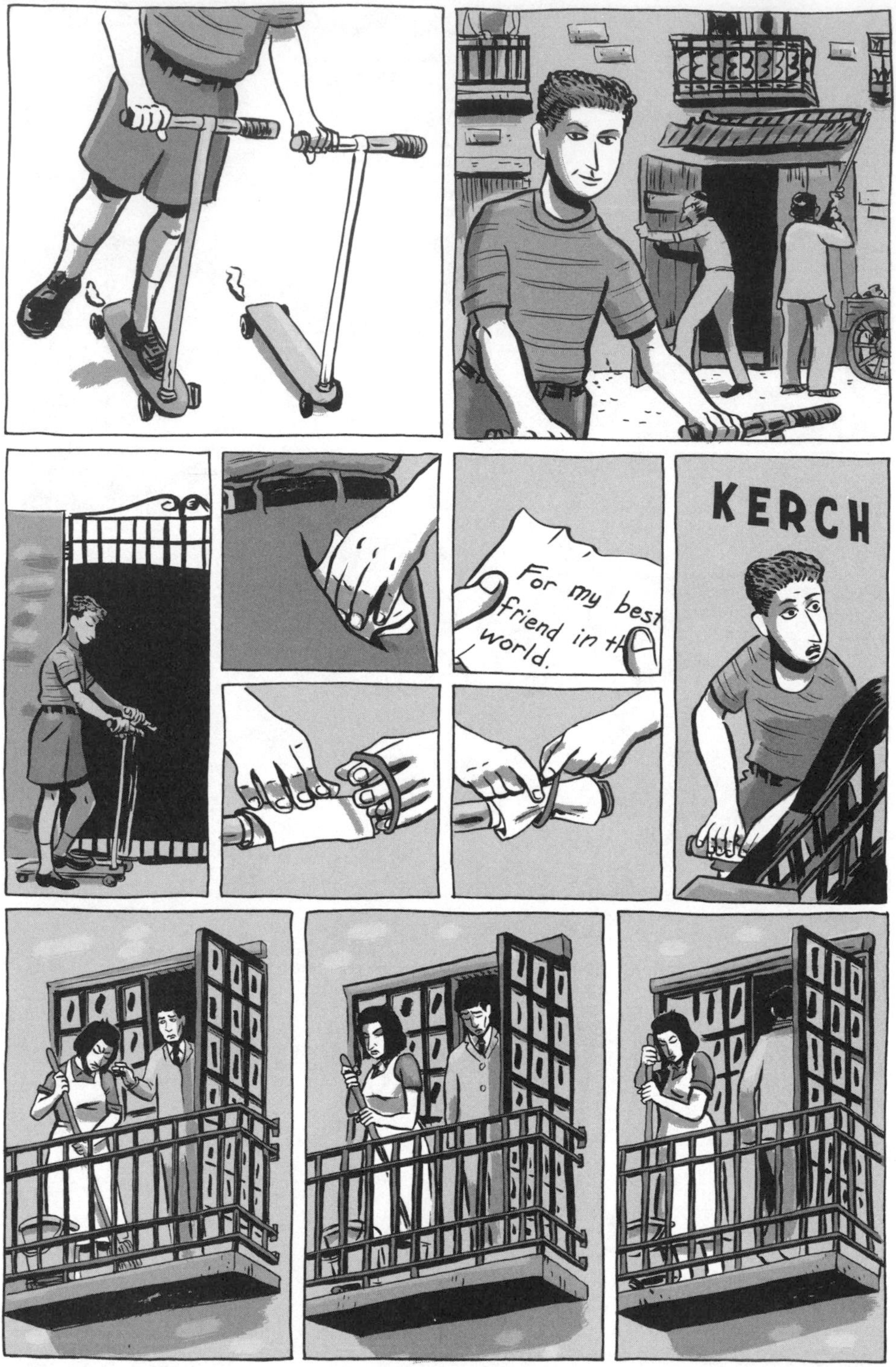
For my best friend in th world.
KERCH

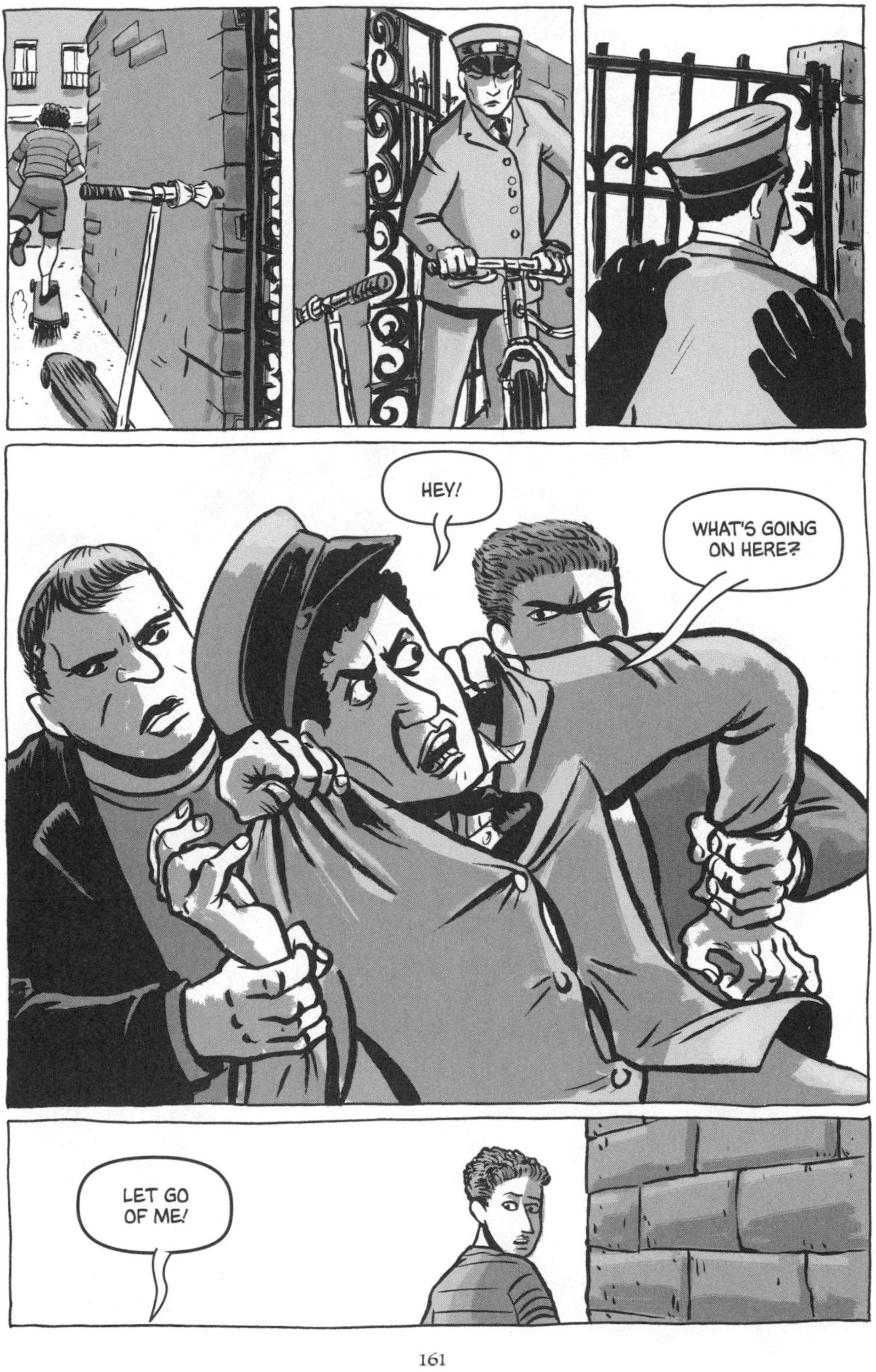
HEY!
WHAT'S GOING ON HERE?
LET GO OF ME!

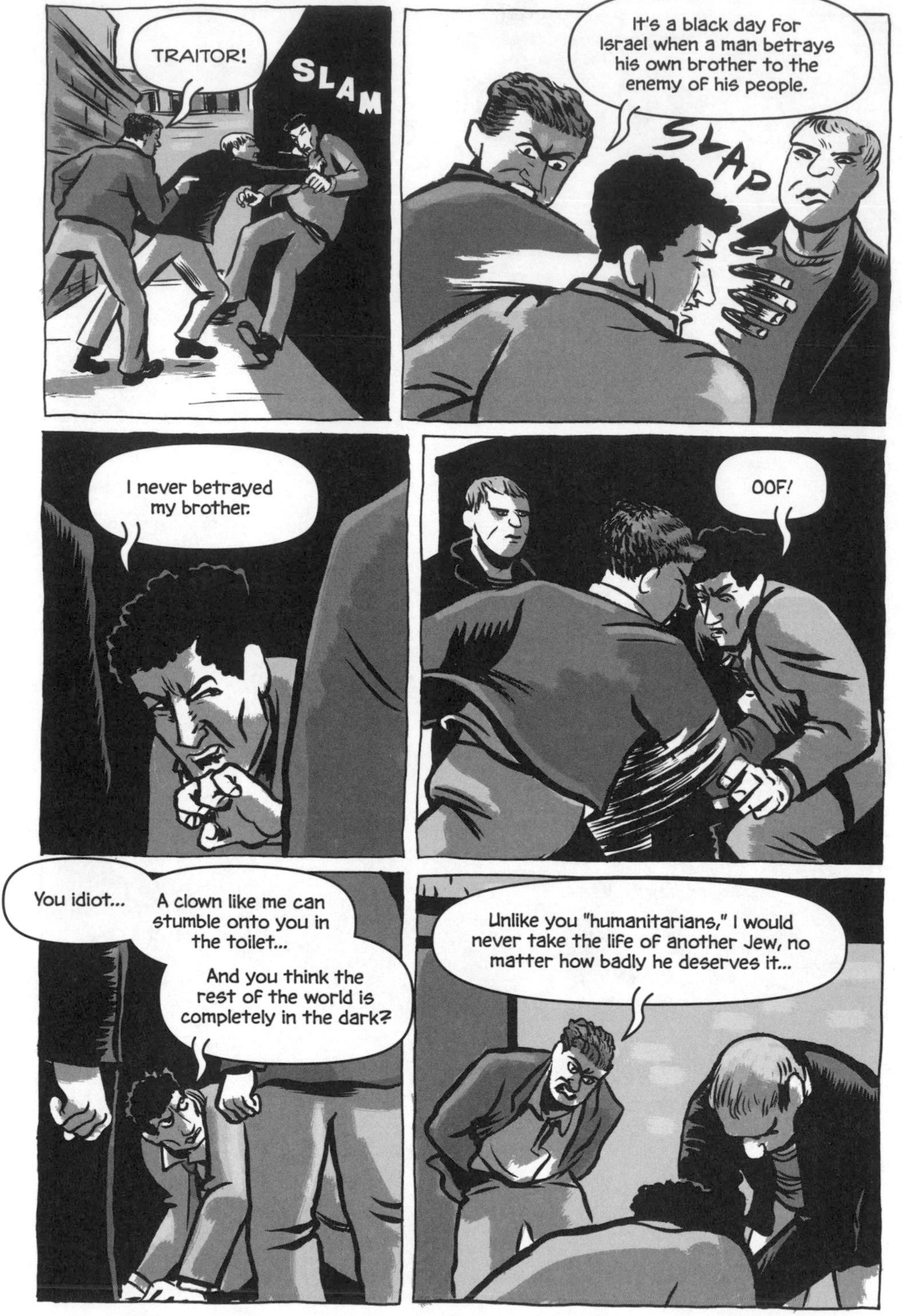
TRAITOR!
SLAM
It's a black day for Israel when a man betrays his own brother to the enemy of his people.
SLAP
I never betrayed my brother.
OOF!
You idiot...
A clown like me can stumble onto you in the toilet...
And you think the rest of the world is completely in the dark?
Unlike you "humanitarians," I would never take the life of another Jew, no matter how badly he deserves it...

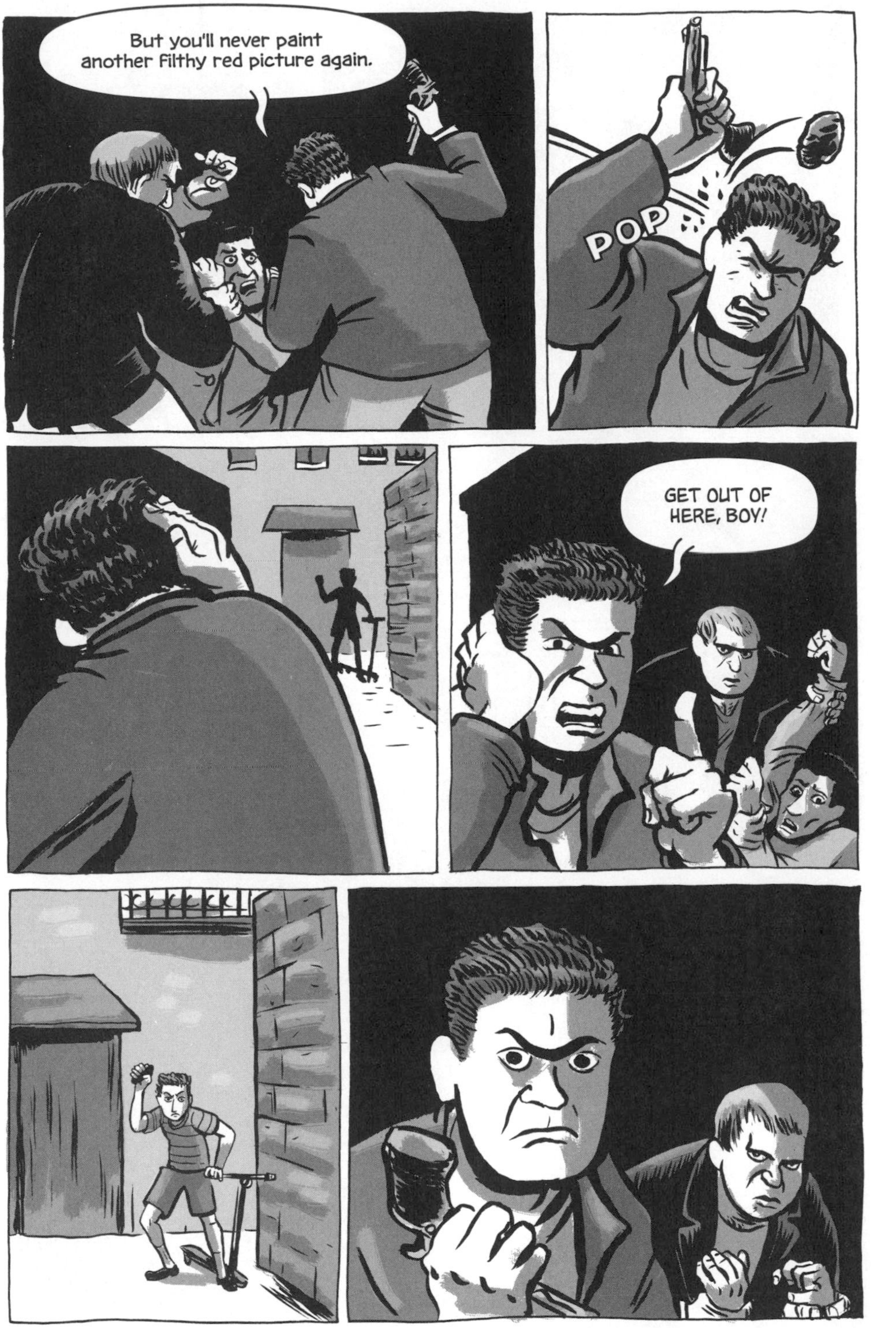

But you'll never paint another filthy red picture again.
POP
GET OUT OF HERE, BOY!

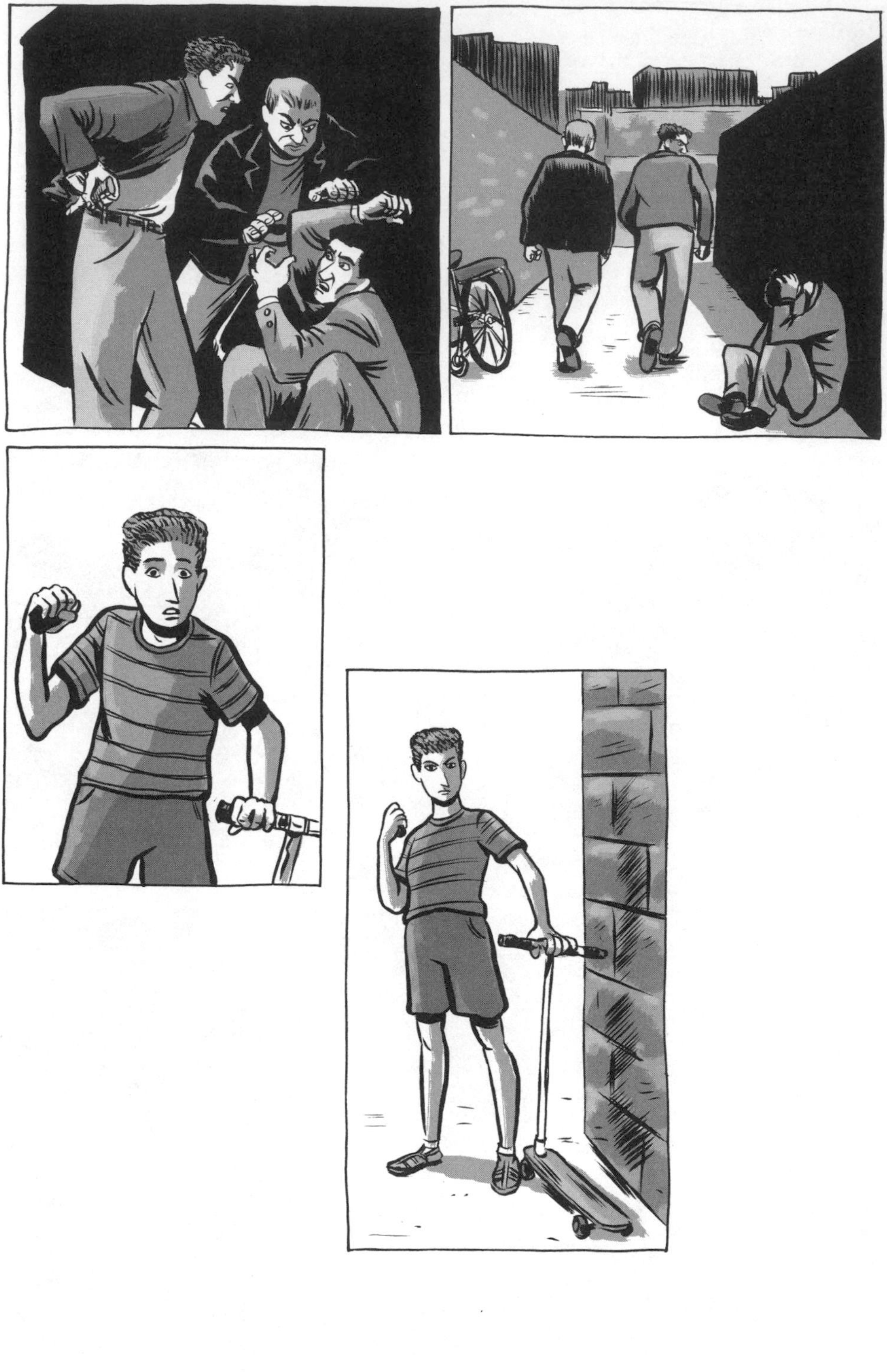

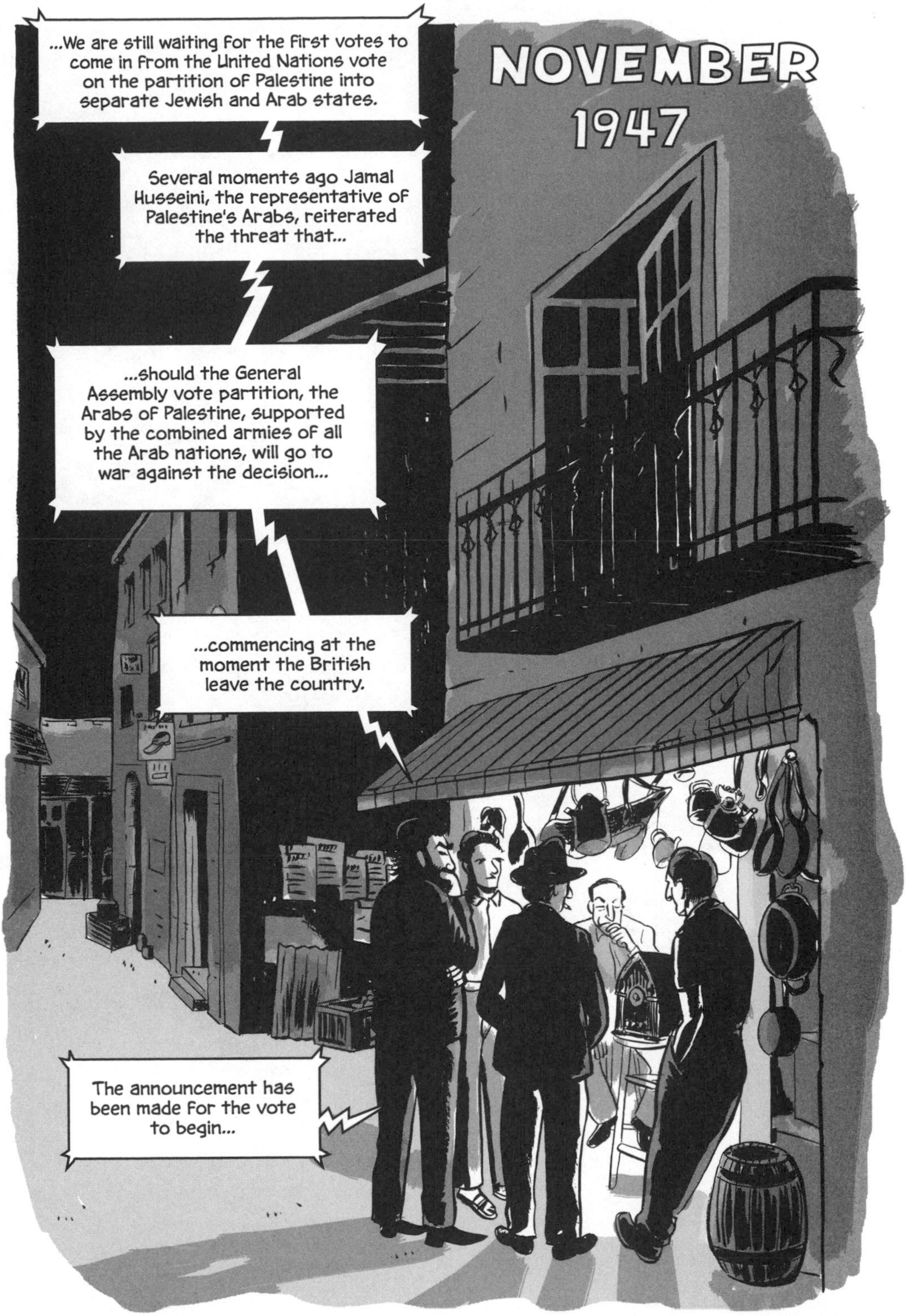
...We are still waiting for the first votes to come in from the United Nations vote on the partition of Palestine into separate Jewish and Arab states.
NOVEMBER 1947
Several moments ago Jamal Husseini, the representative of Palestine's Arabs, reiterated the threat that...
...should the General Assembly vote partition, the Arabs of Palestine, supported by the combined armies of all the Arab nations, will go to war against the decision...
...commencing at the moment the British leave the country.
The announcement has been made for the vote to begin...

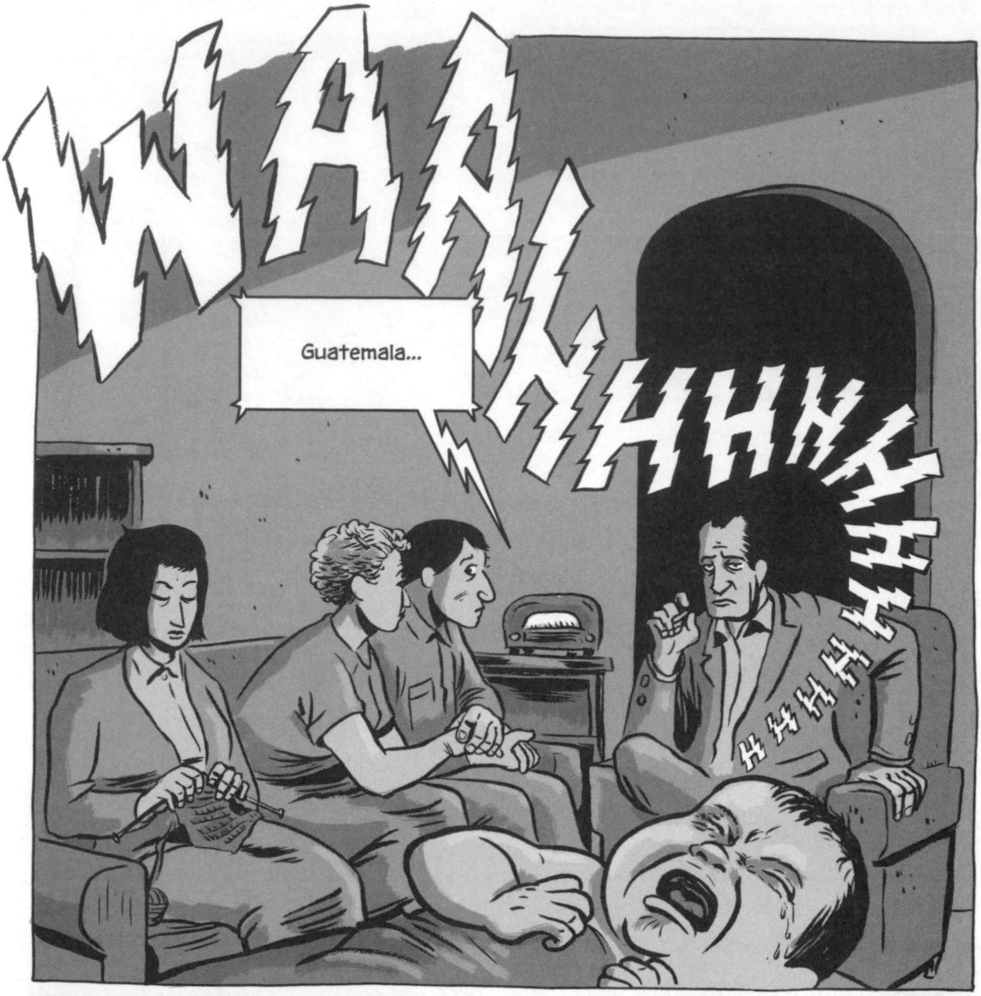
WAAHHHHHHHHHHHH
Guatemala...

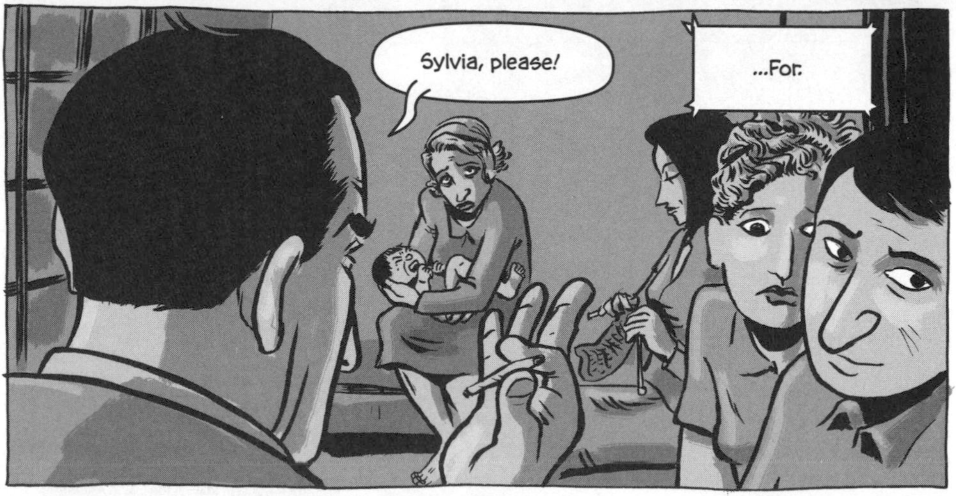
Sylvia, please!
...For.

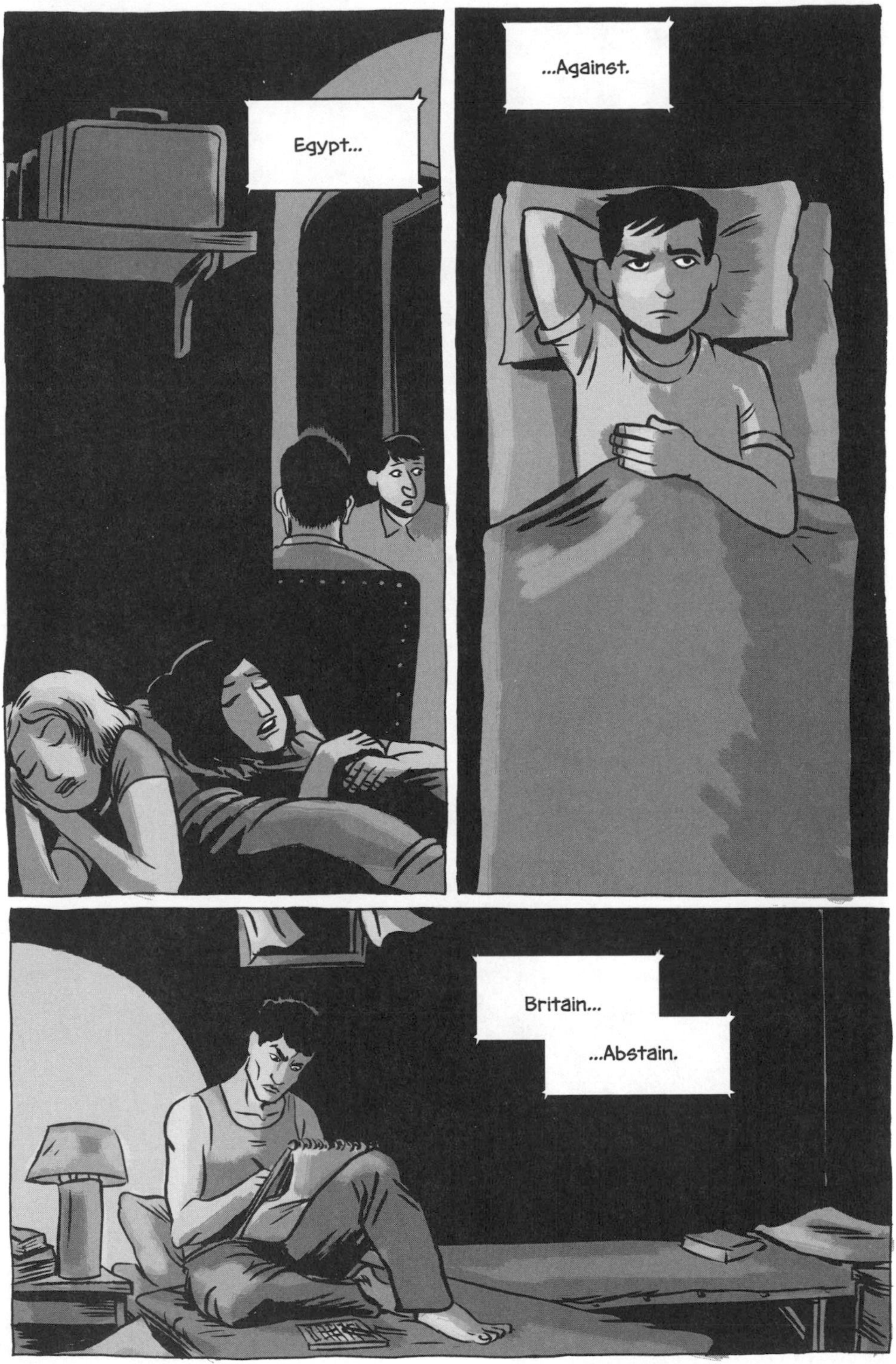
Egypt...
...Against.
Britain...
...Abstain.

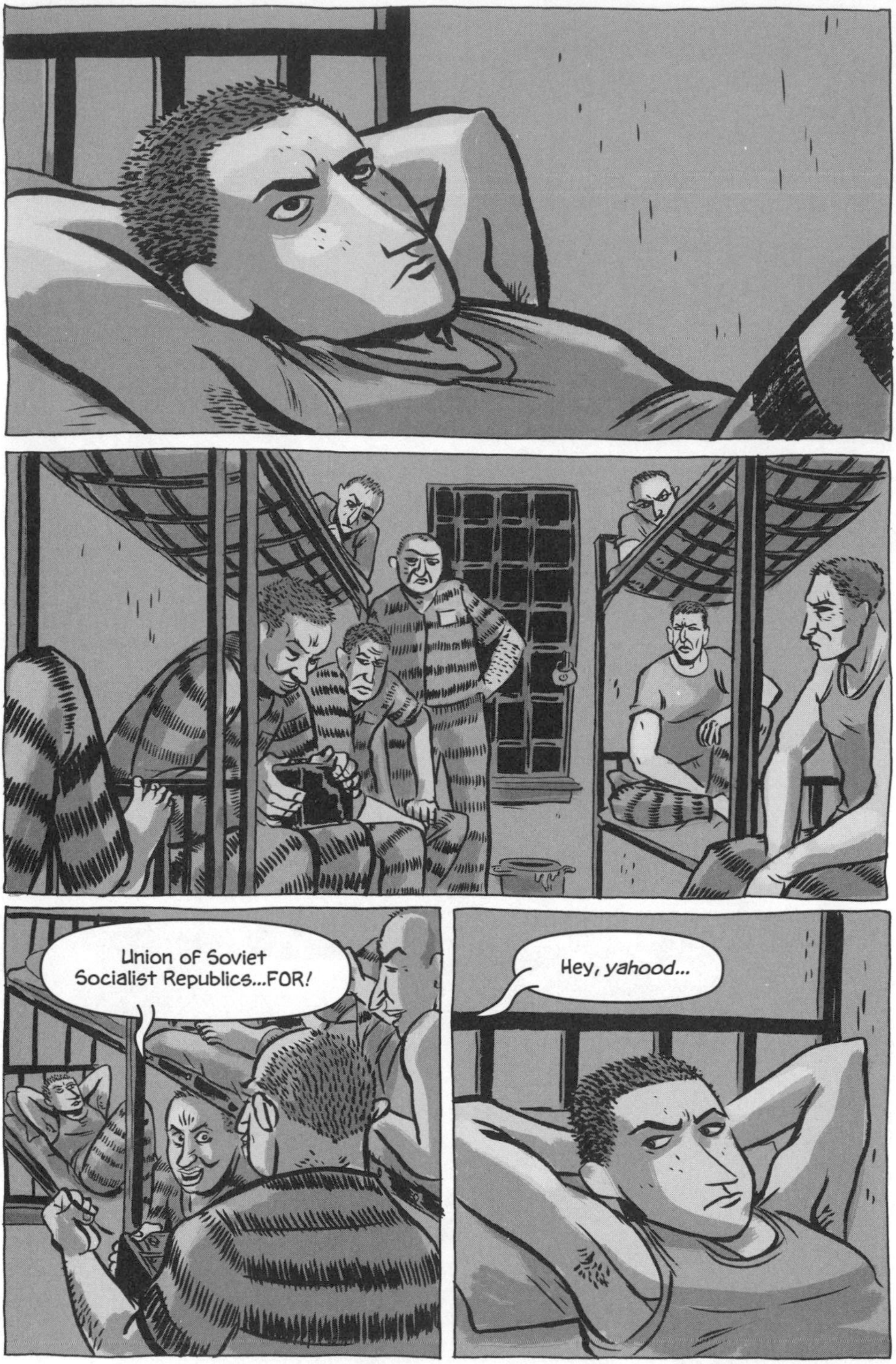
Union of Soviet
Socialist Republics...FOR!
Hey, *yahood*...

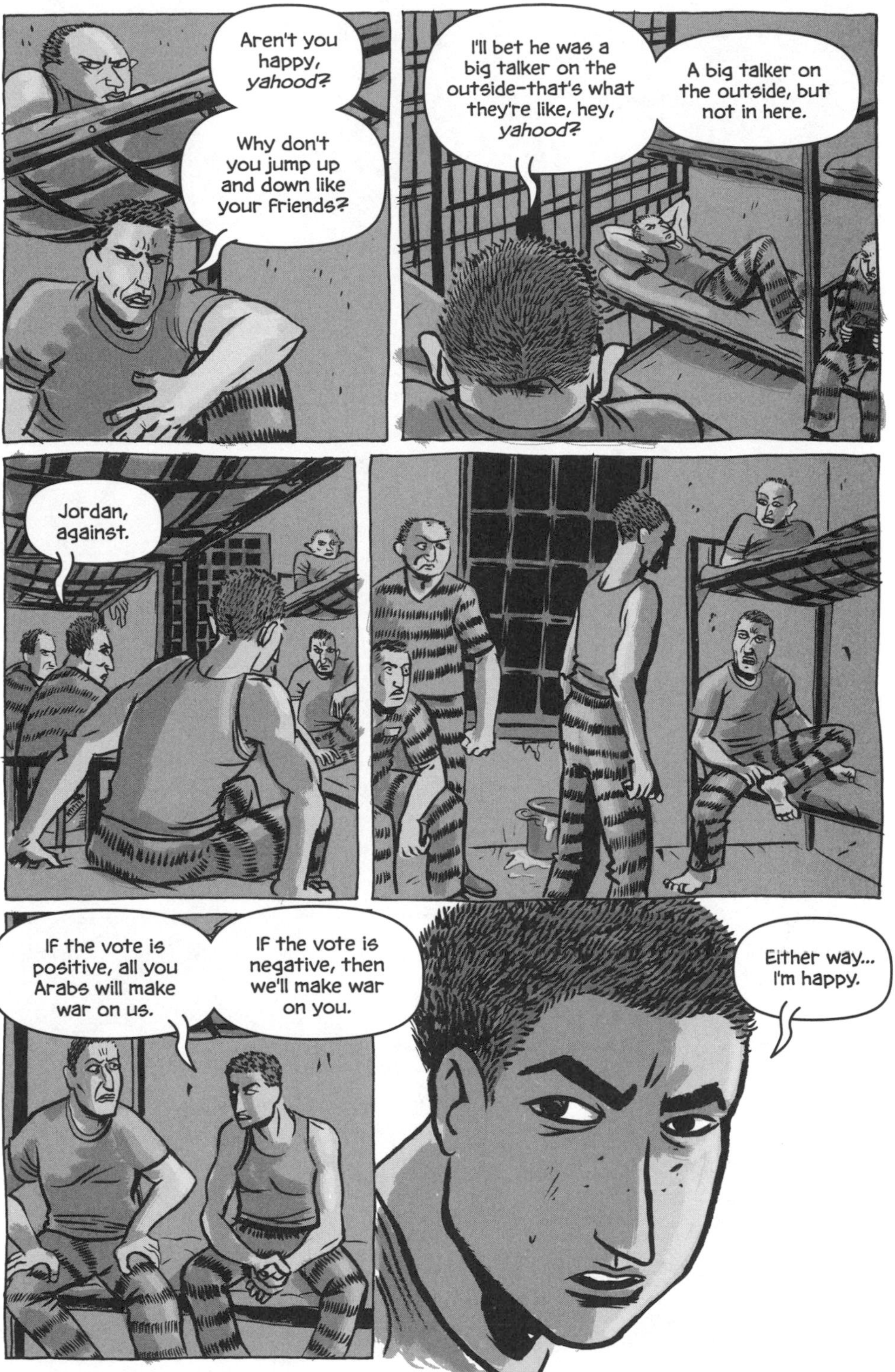
Aren't you happy, *yahood*?
Why don't you jump up and down like your friends?
I'll bet he was a big talker on the outside–that's what they're like, hey, *yahood*?
A big talker on the outside, but not in here.
Jordan, against.
If the vote is positive, all you Arabs will make war on us.
If the vote is negative, then we'll make war on you.
Either way... I'm happy.

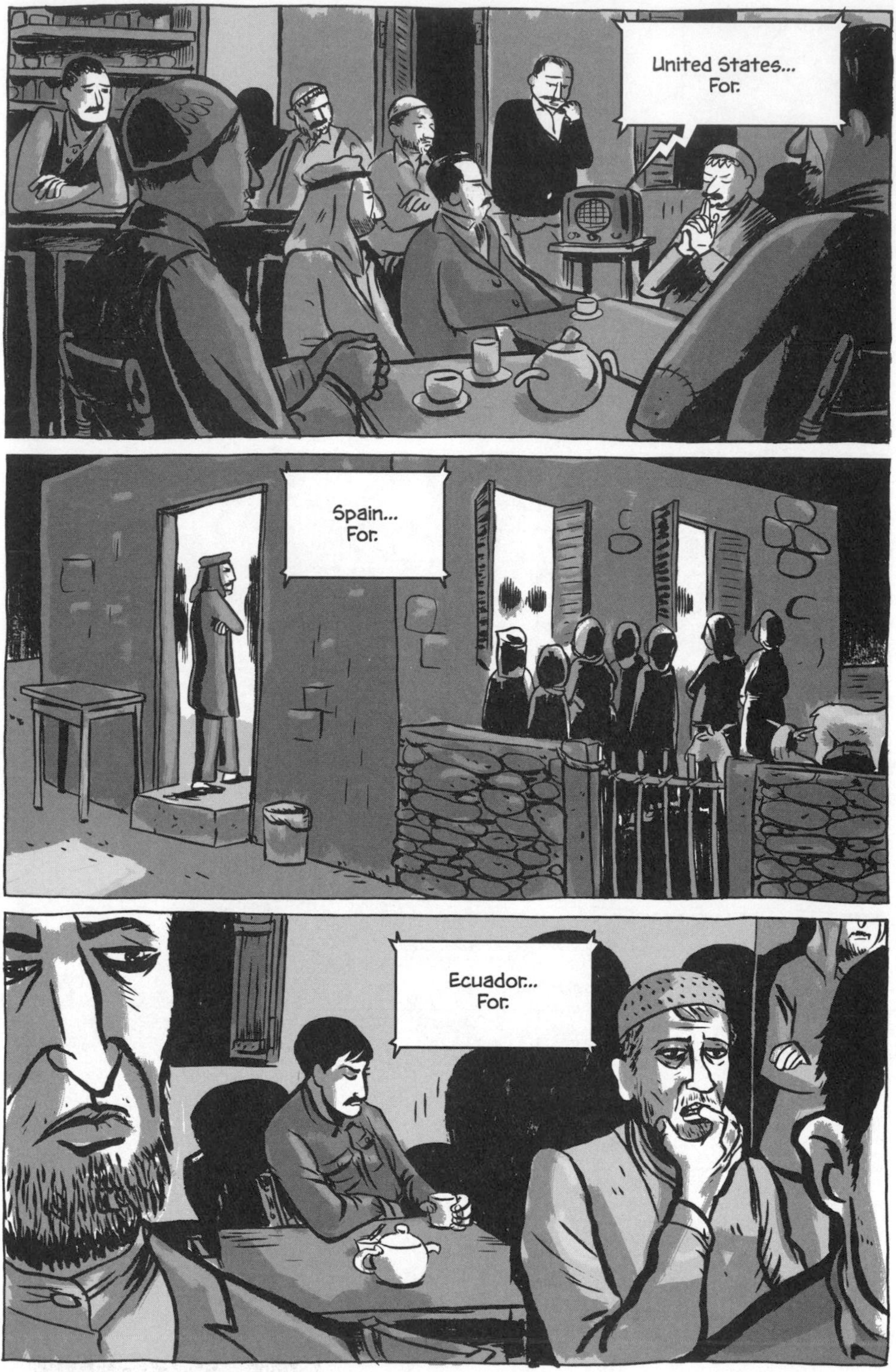
United States...
For.
Spain...
For.
Ecuador...
For.

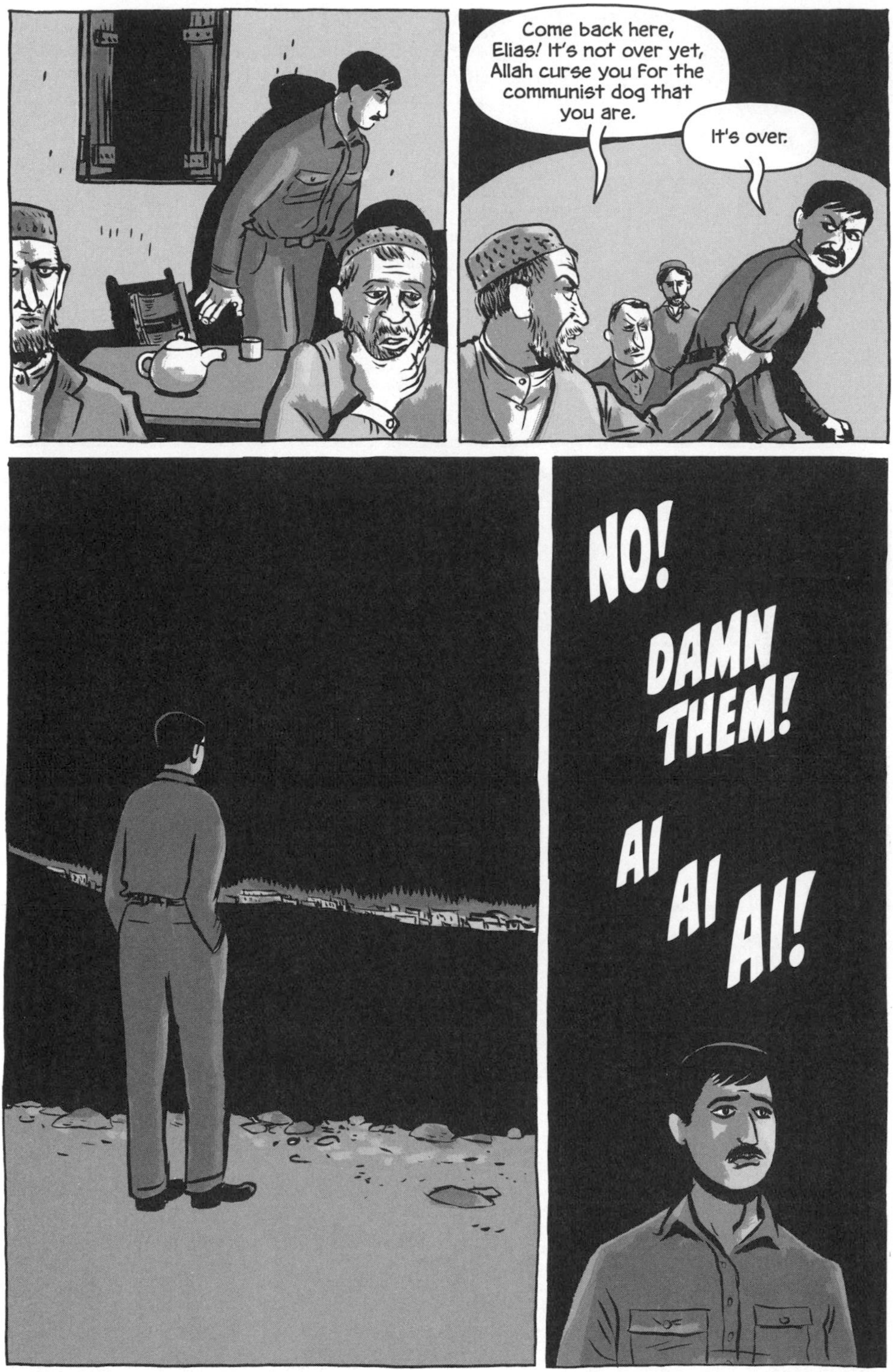
Come back here, Elias! It's not over yet, Allah curse you for the communist dog that you are.
It's over.
NO!
DAMN THEM!
AI AI AI!

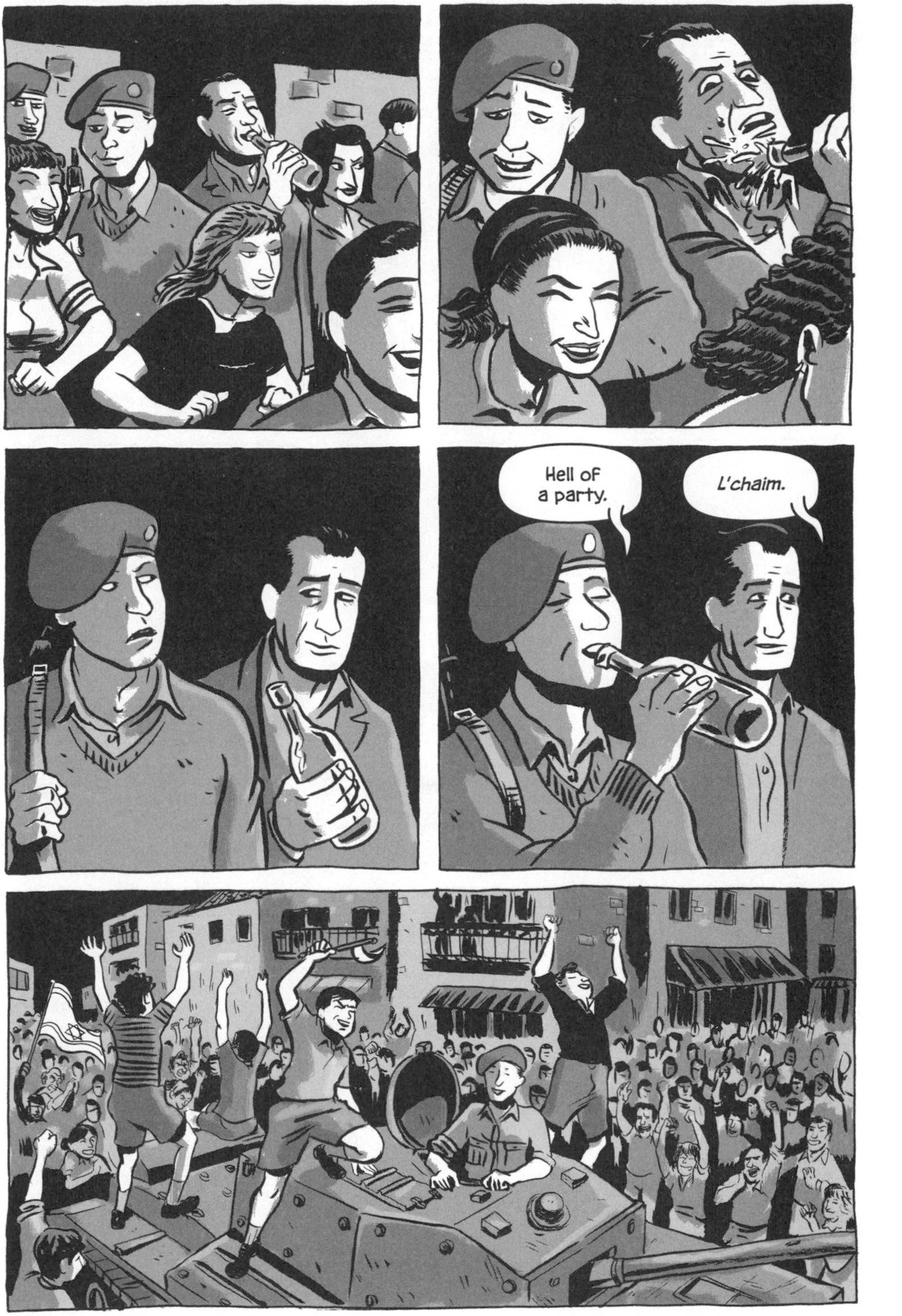
Hell of a party.
L'chaim.

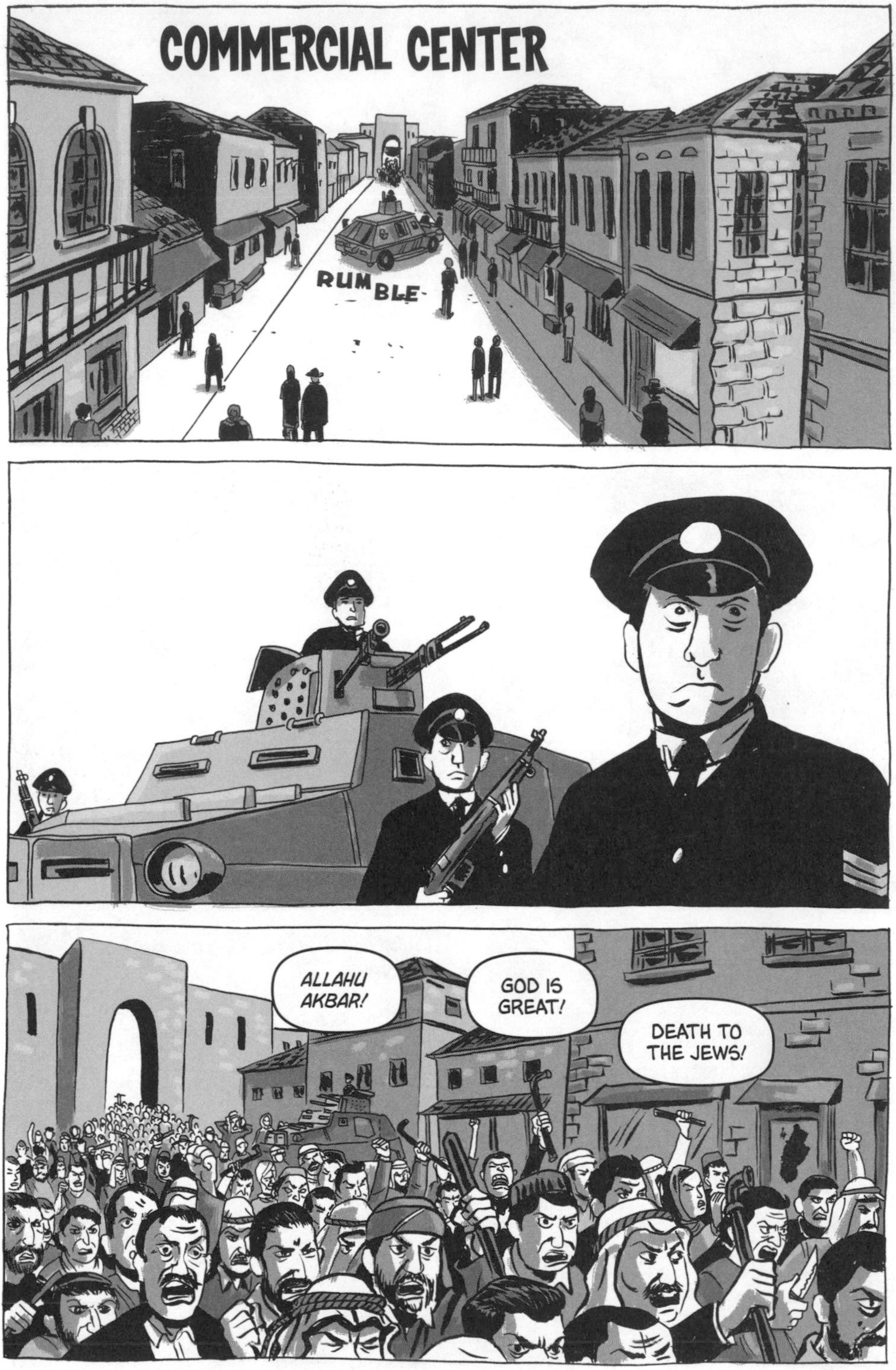
COMMERCIAL CENTER
RUMBLE
ALLAHU AKBAR!
GOD IS GREAT!
DEATH TO THE JEWS!

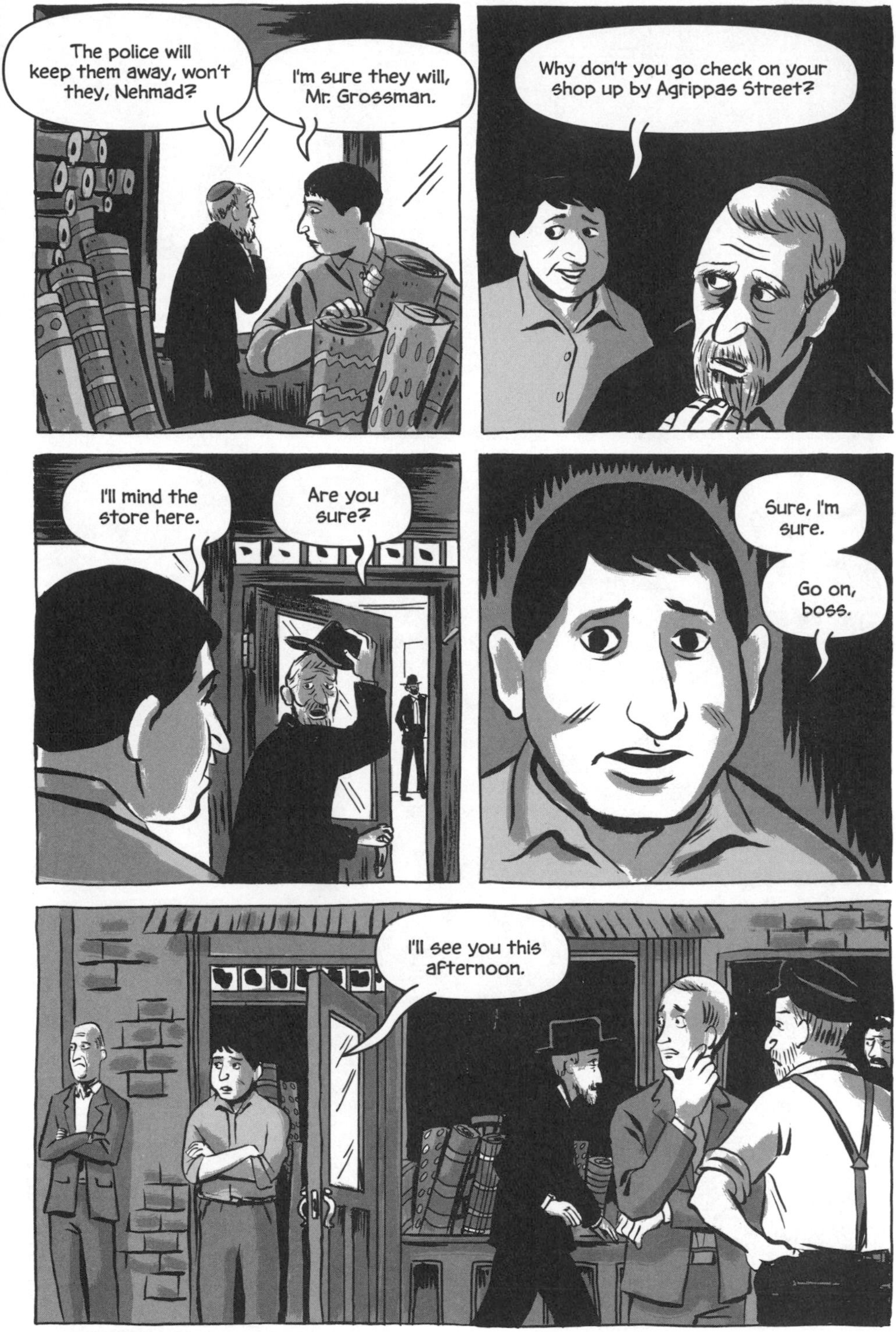
The police will keep them away, won't they, Nehmad?
I'm sure they will, Mr. Grossman.
Why don't you go check on your shop up by Agrippas Street?
I'll mind the store here.
Are you sure?
Sure, I'm sure.
Go on, boss.
I'll see you this afternoon.

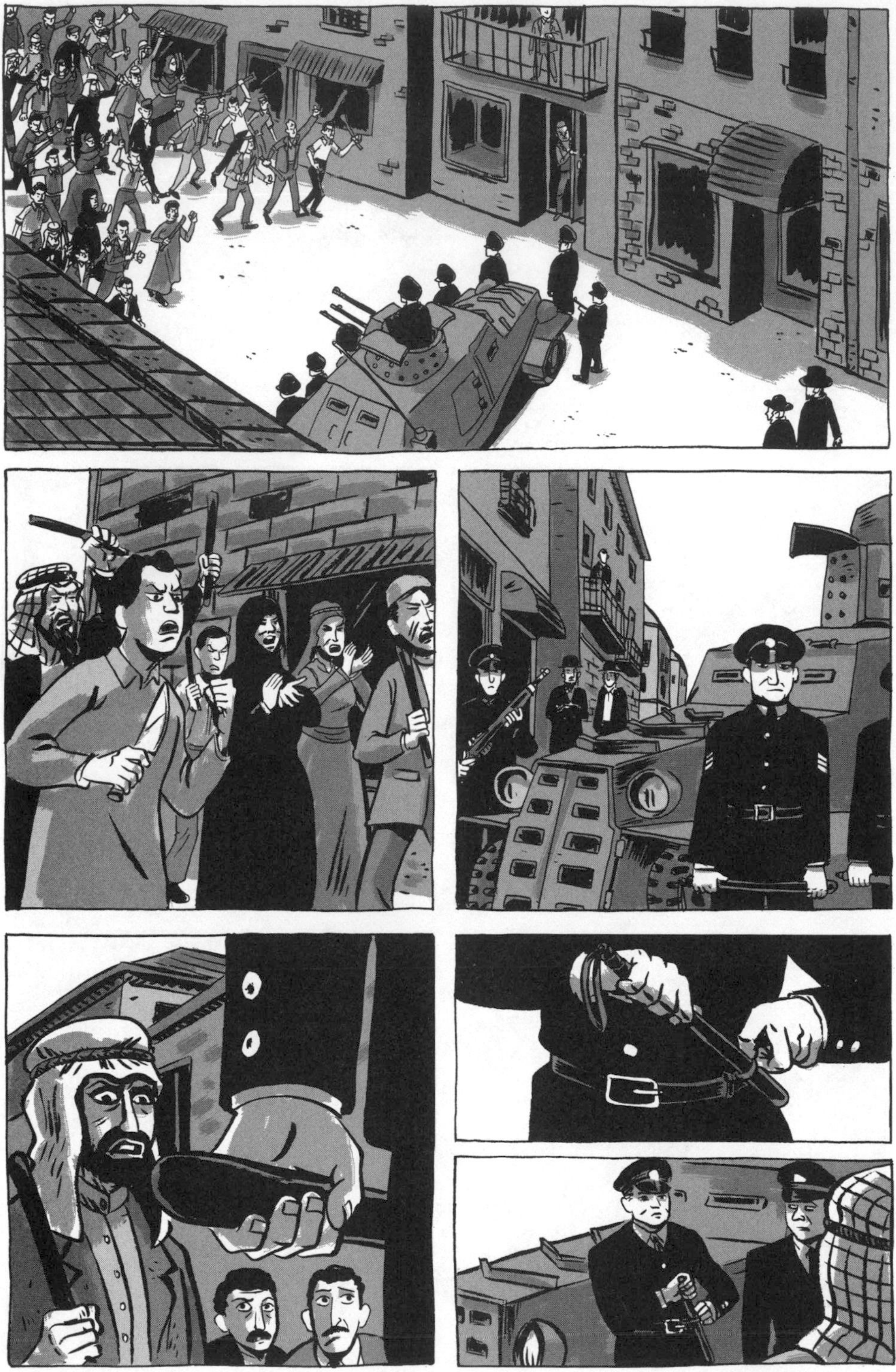

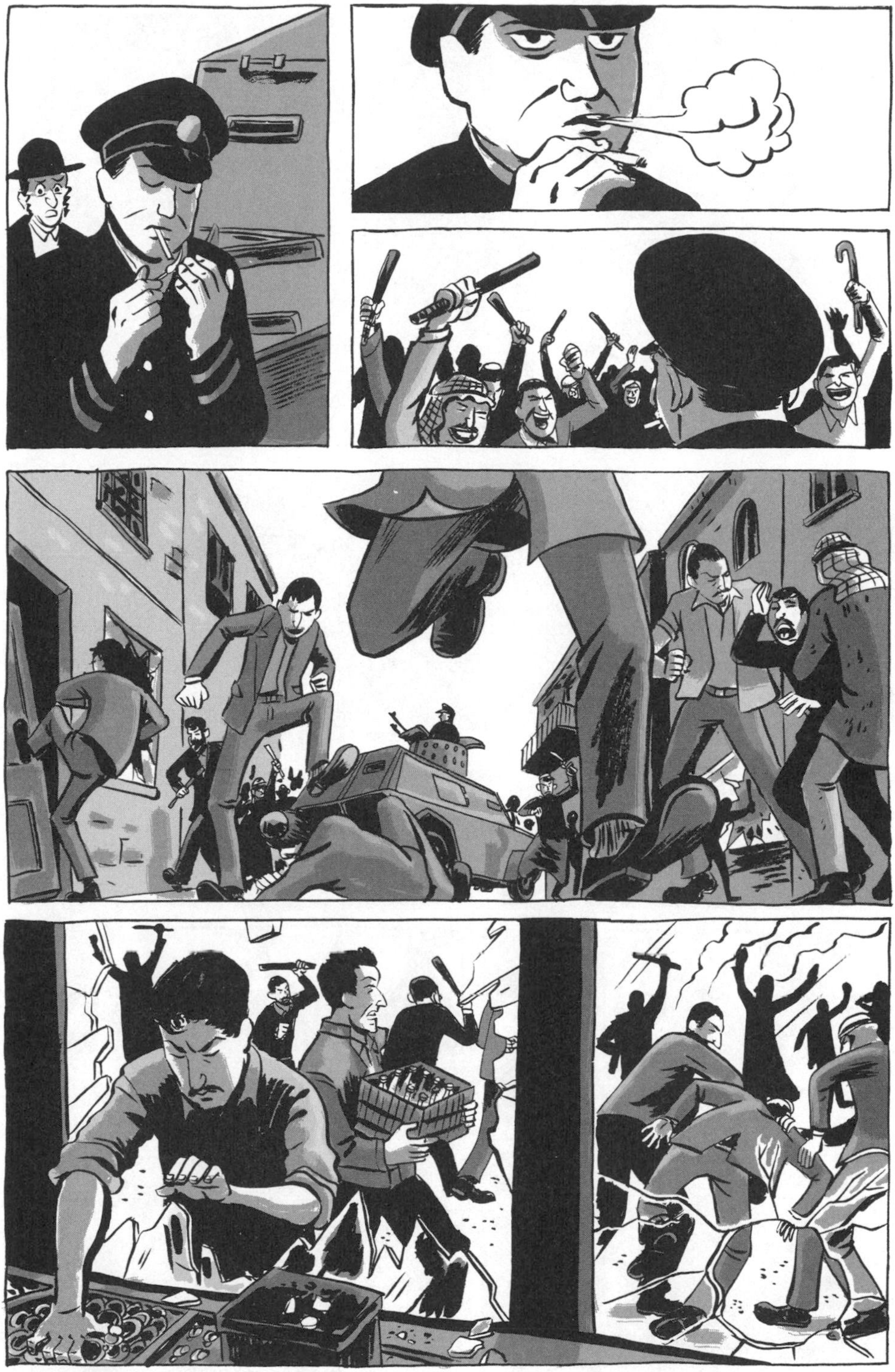

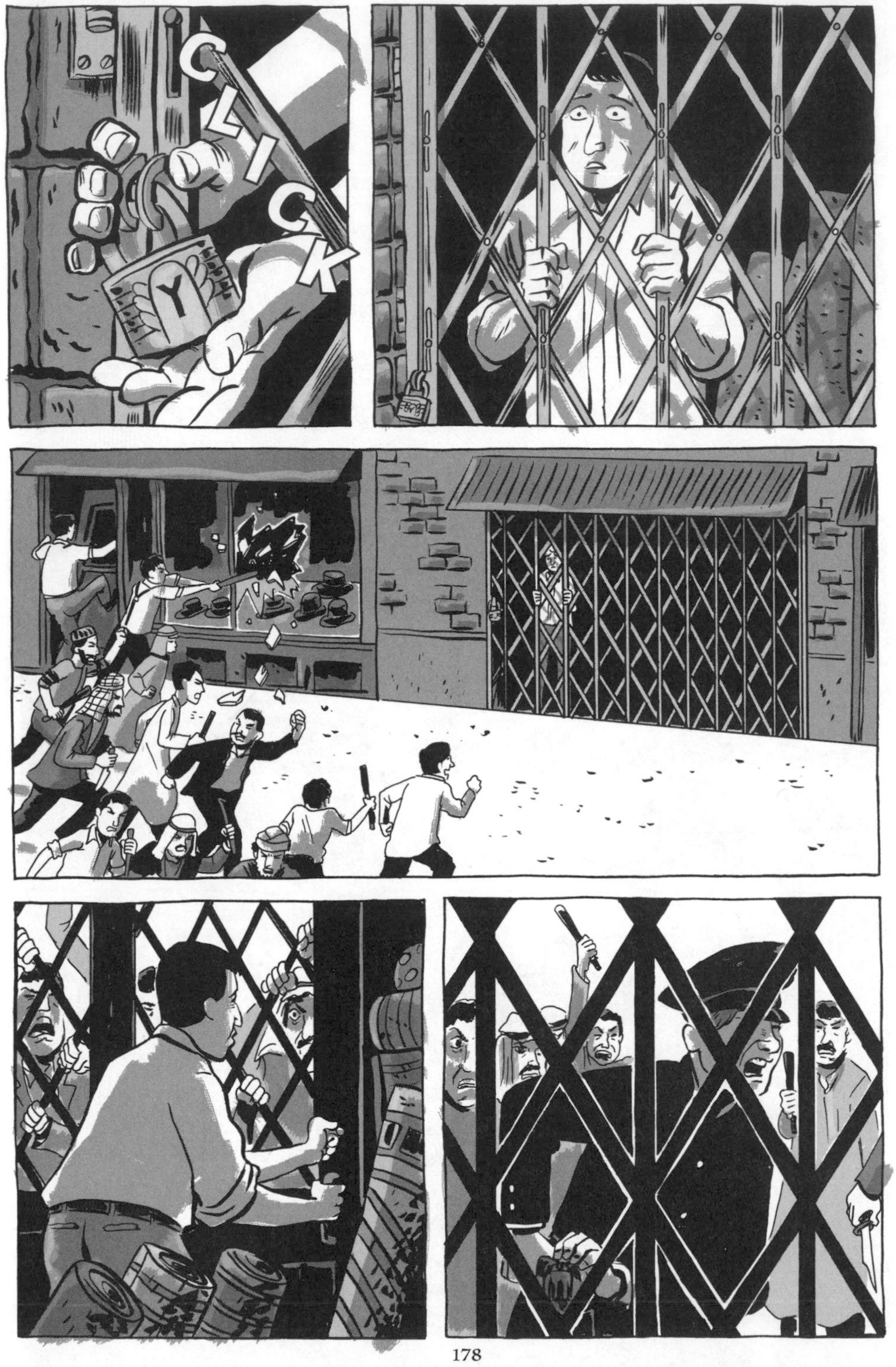
CLICK

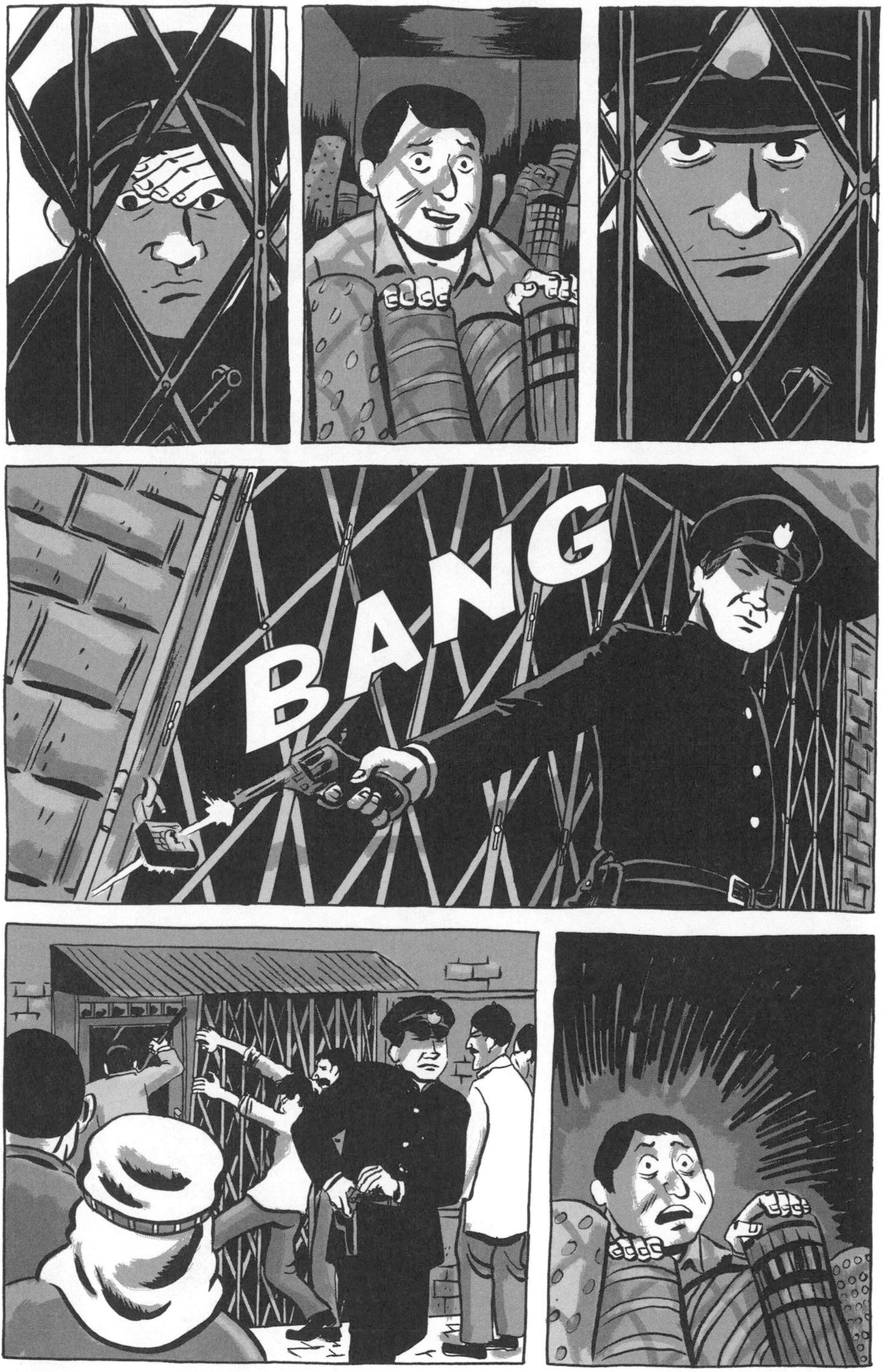
BANG

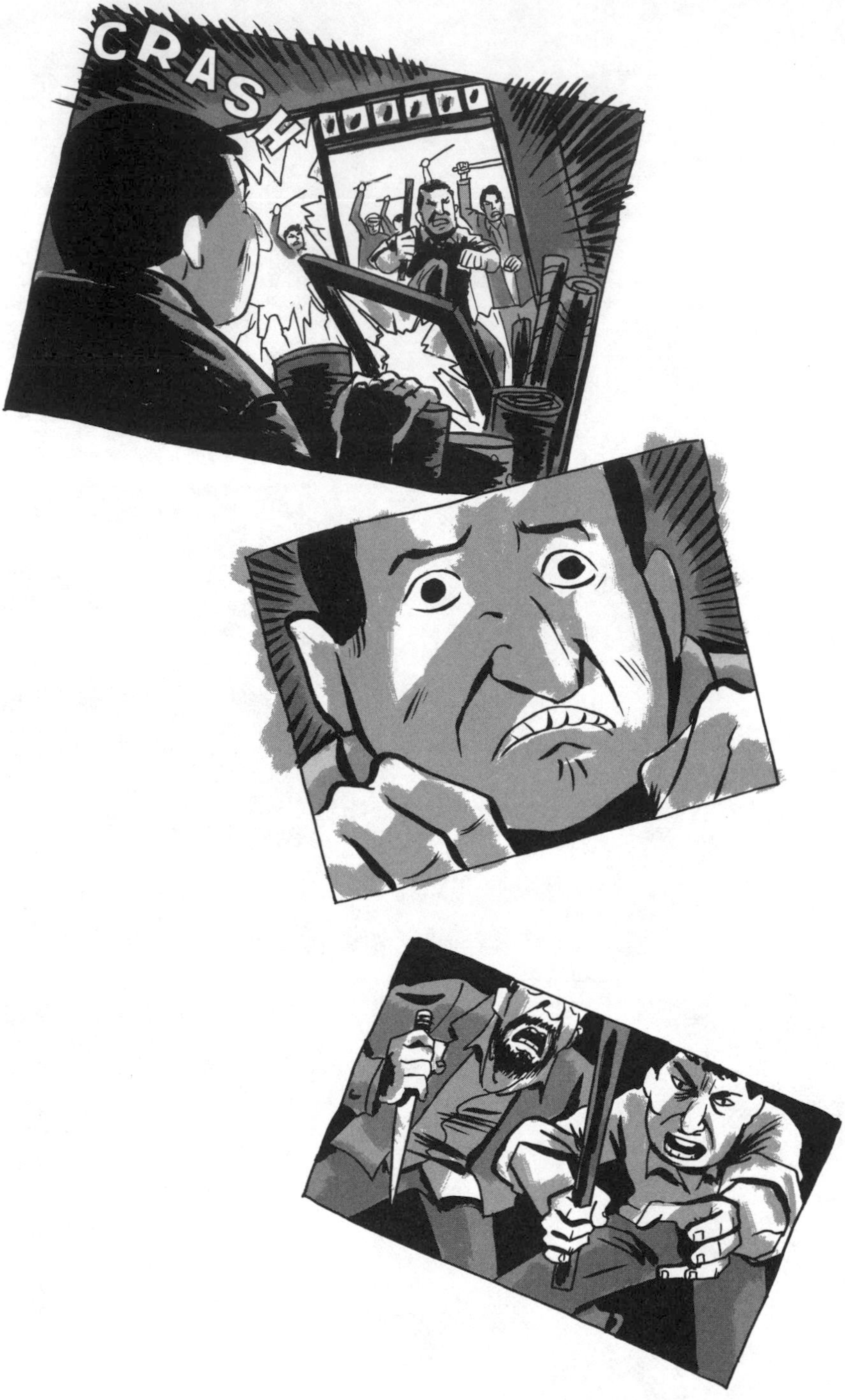
CRASH

# THE SIEGE

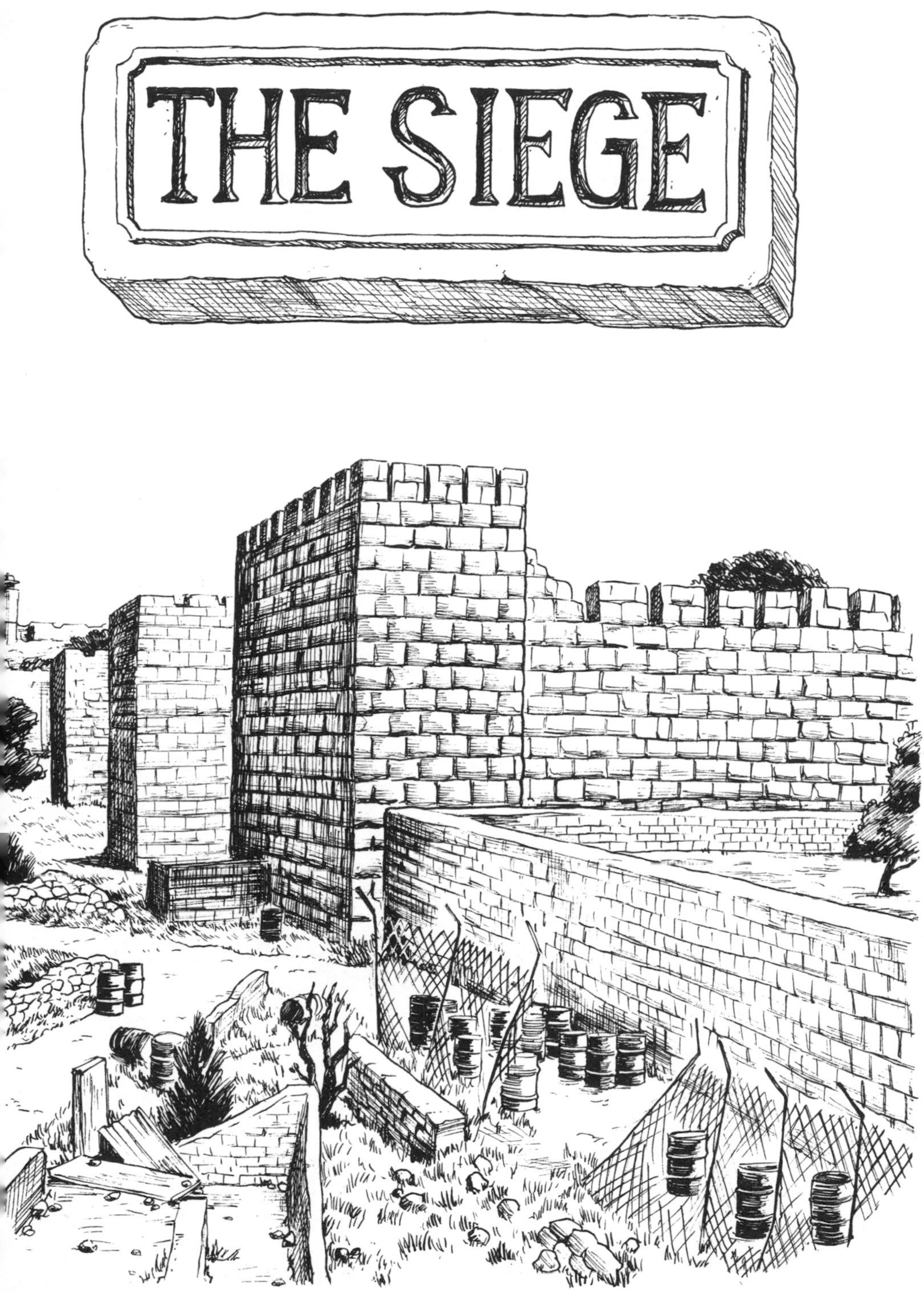

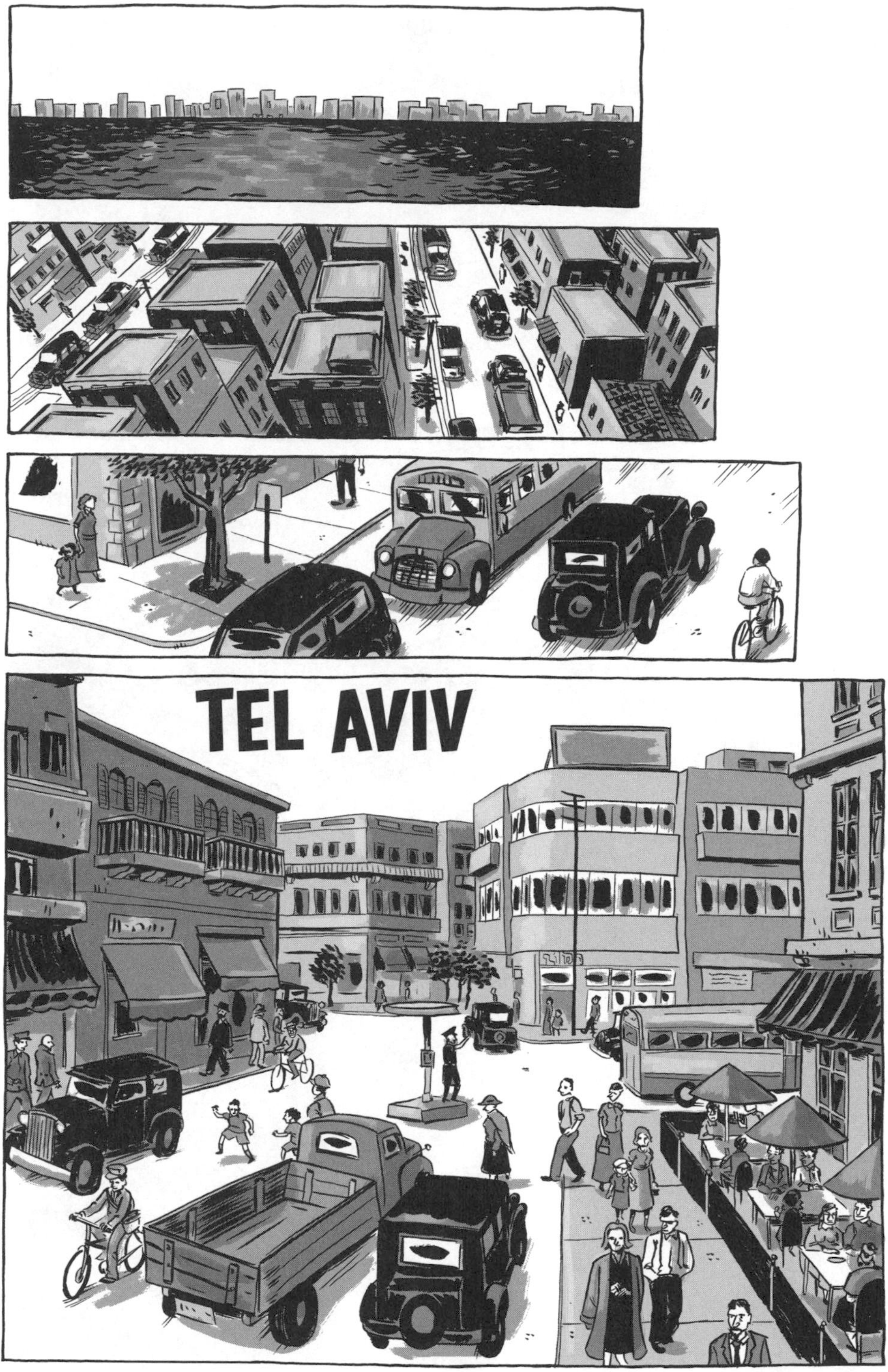
TEL AVIV

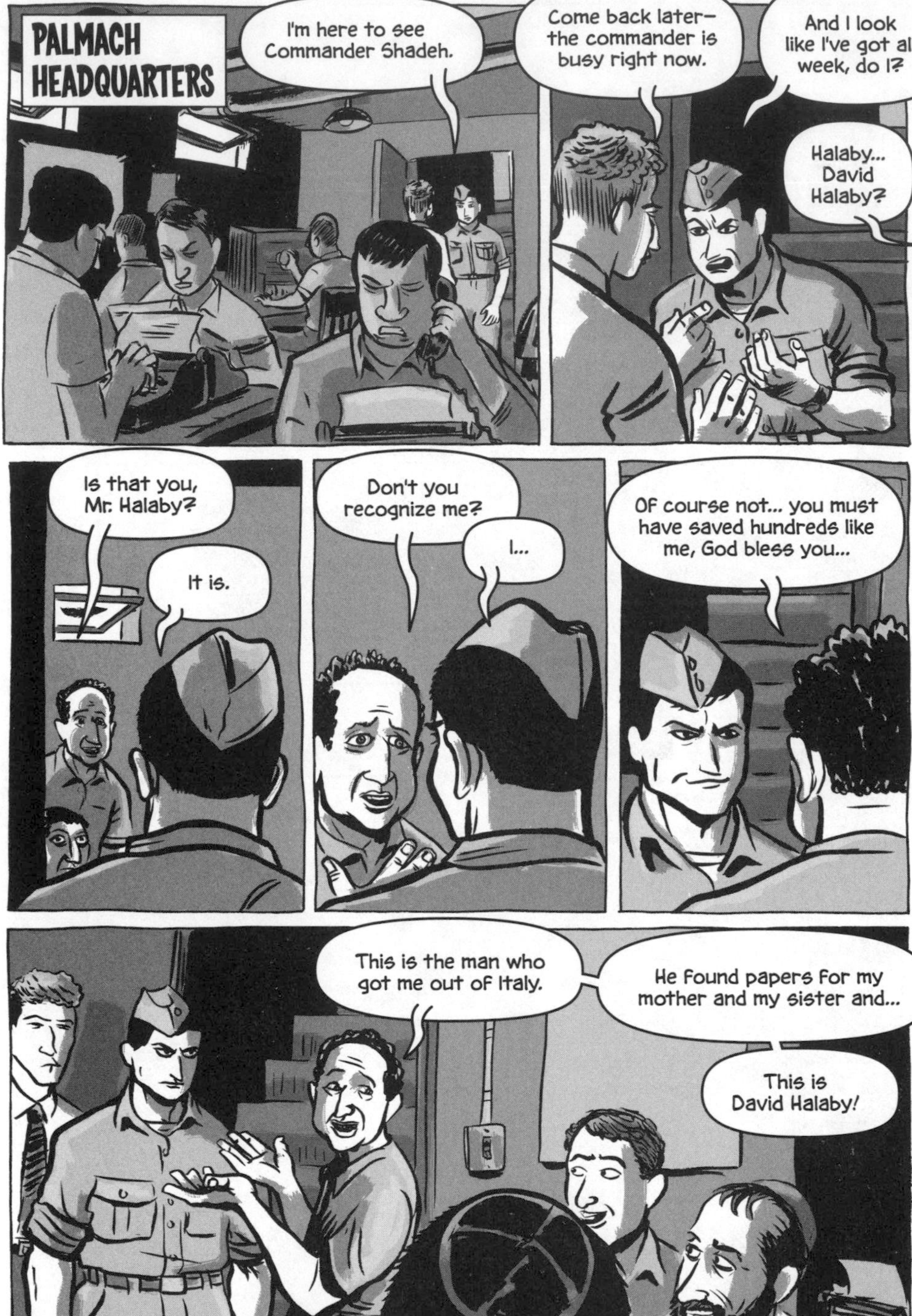
PALMACH HEADQUARTERS
I'm here to see Commander Shadeh.
Come back later— the commander is busy right now.
And I look like I've got all week, do I?
Halaby... David Halaby?
Is that you, Mr. Halaby?
It is.
Don't you recognize me?
I...
Of course not... you must have saved hundreds like me, God bless you...
This is the man who got me out of Italy.
He found papers for my mother and my sister and...
This is David Halaby!

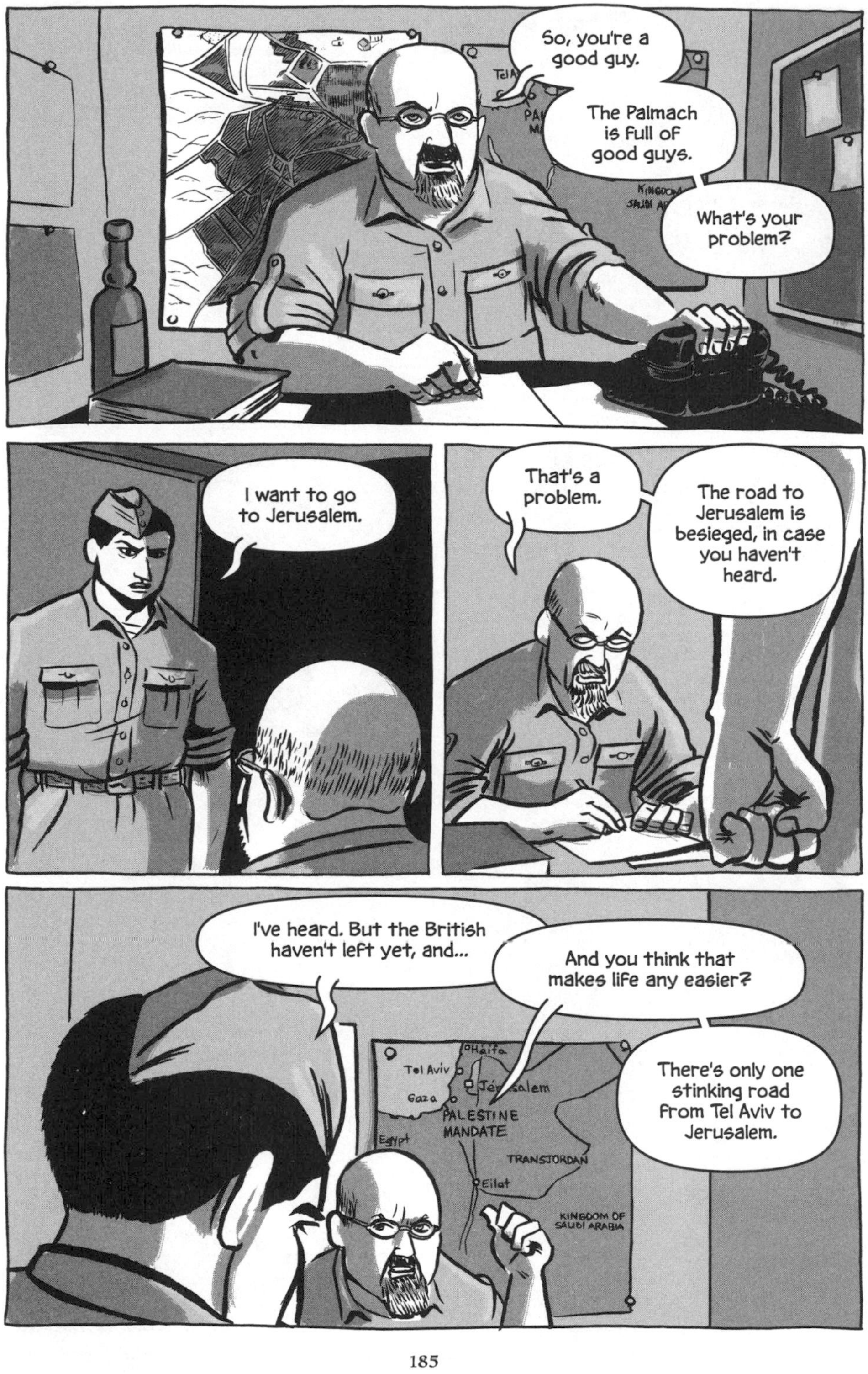
So, you're a good guy.
The Palmach is full of good guys.
What's your problem?
I want to go to Jerusalem.
That's a problem.
The road to Jerusalem is besieged, in case you haven't heard.
I've heard. But the British haven't left yet, and...
And you think that makes life any easier?
There's only one stinking road from Tel Aviv to Jerusalem.
Haifa
Tel Aviv
Jerusalem
Gaza
PALESTINE MANDATE
Egypt
TRANSJORDAN
Eilat
KINGDOM OF SAUDI ARABIA

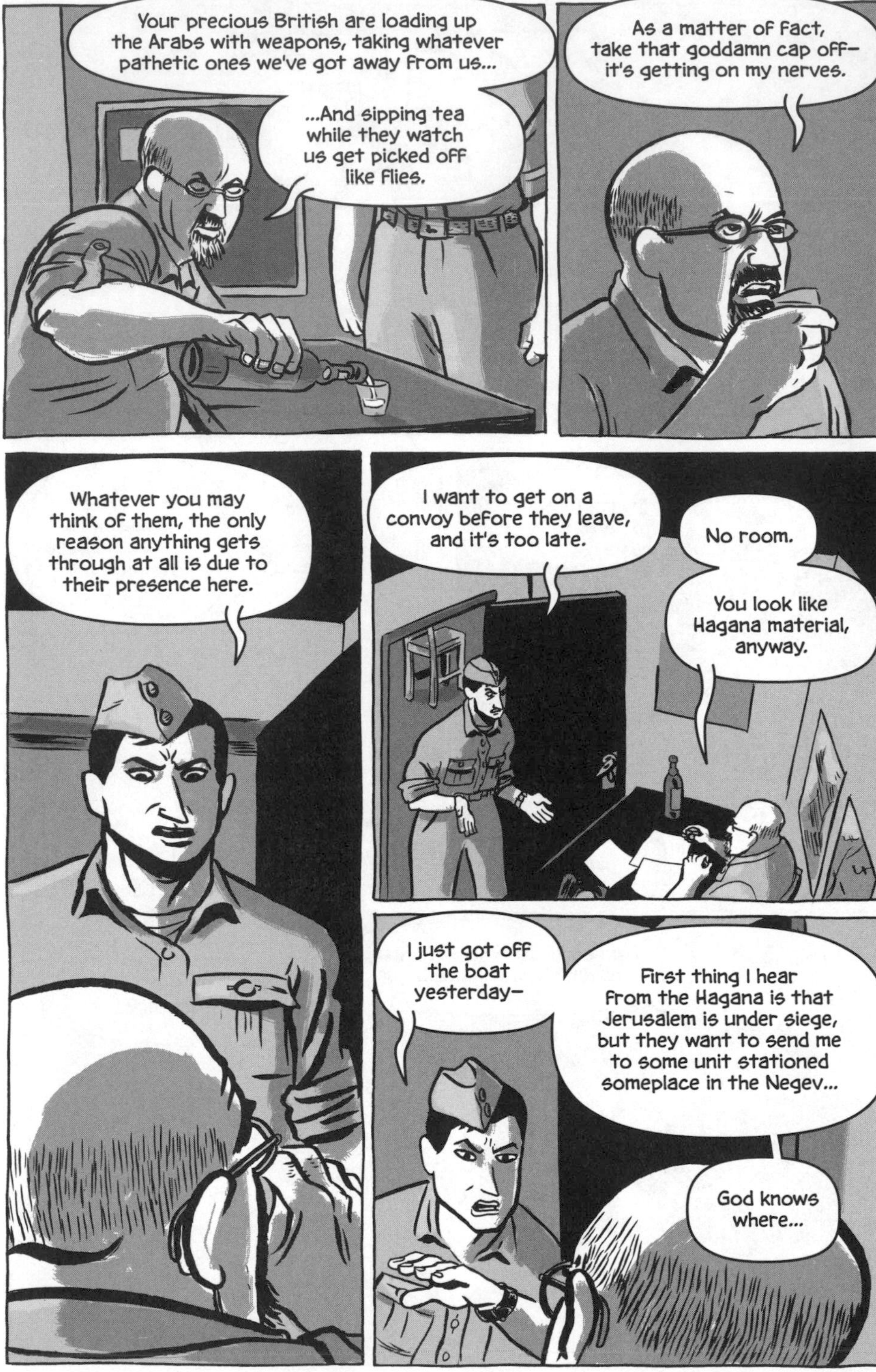
Your precious British are loading up the Arabs with weapons, taking whatever pathetic ones we've got away from us...
...And sipping tea while they watch us get picked off like flies.
As a matter of fact, take that goddamn cap off— it's getting on my nerves.
Whatever you may think of them, the only reason anything gets through at all is due to their presence here.
I want to get on a convoy before they leave, and it's too late.
No room.
You look like Hagana material, anyway.
I just got off the boat yesterday—
First thing I hear from the Hagana is that Jerusalem is under siege, but they want to send me to some unit stationed someplace in the Negev...
God knows where...

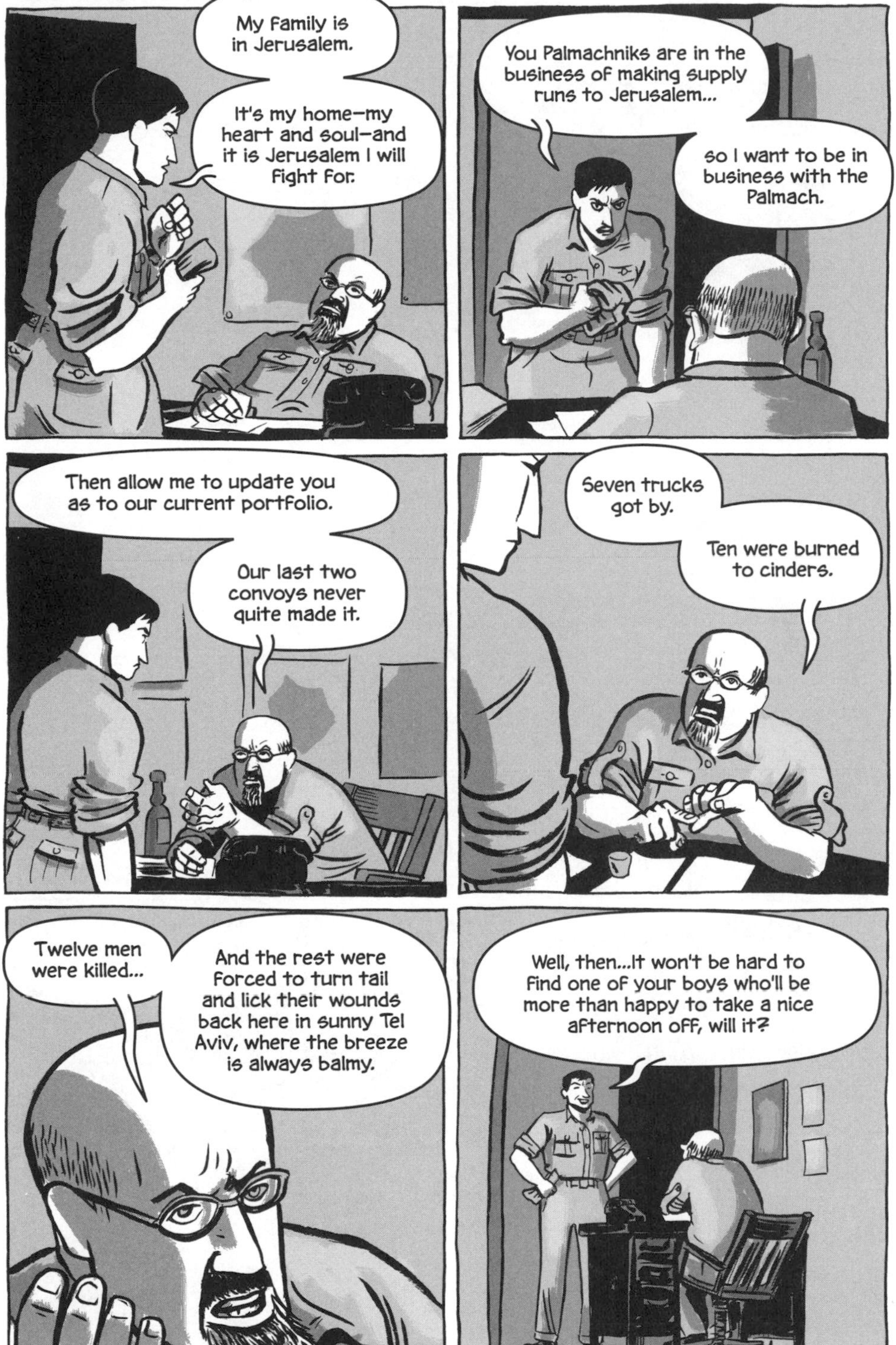
My family is in Jerusalem.
It's my home—my heart and soul—and it is Jerusalem I will fight for.
You Palmachniks are in the business of making supply runs to Jerusalem...
so I want to be in business with the Palmach.
Then allow me to update you as to our current portfolio.
Our last two convoys never quite made it.
Seven trucks got by.
Ten were burned to cinders.
Twelve men were killed...
And the rest were forced to turn tail and lick their wounds back here in sunny Tel Aviv, where the breeze is always balmy.
Well, then...It won't be hard to find one of your boys who'll be more than happy to take a nice afternoon off, will it?

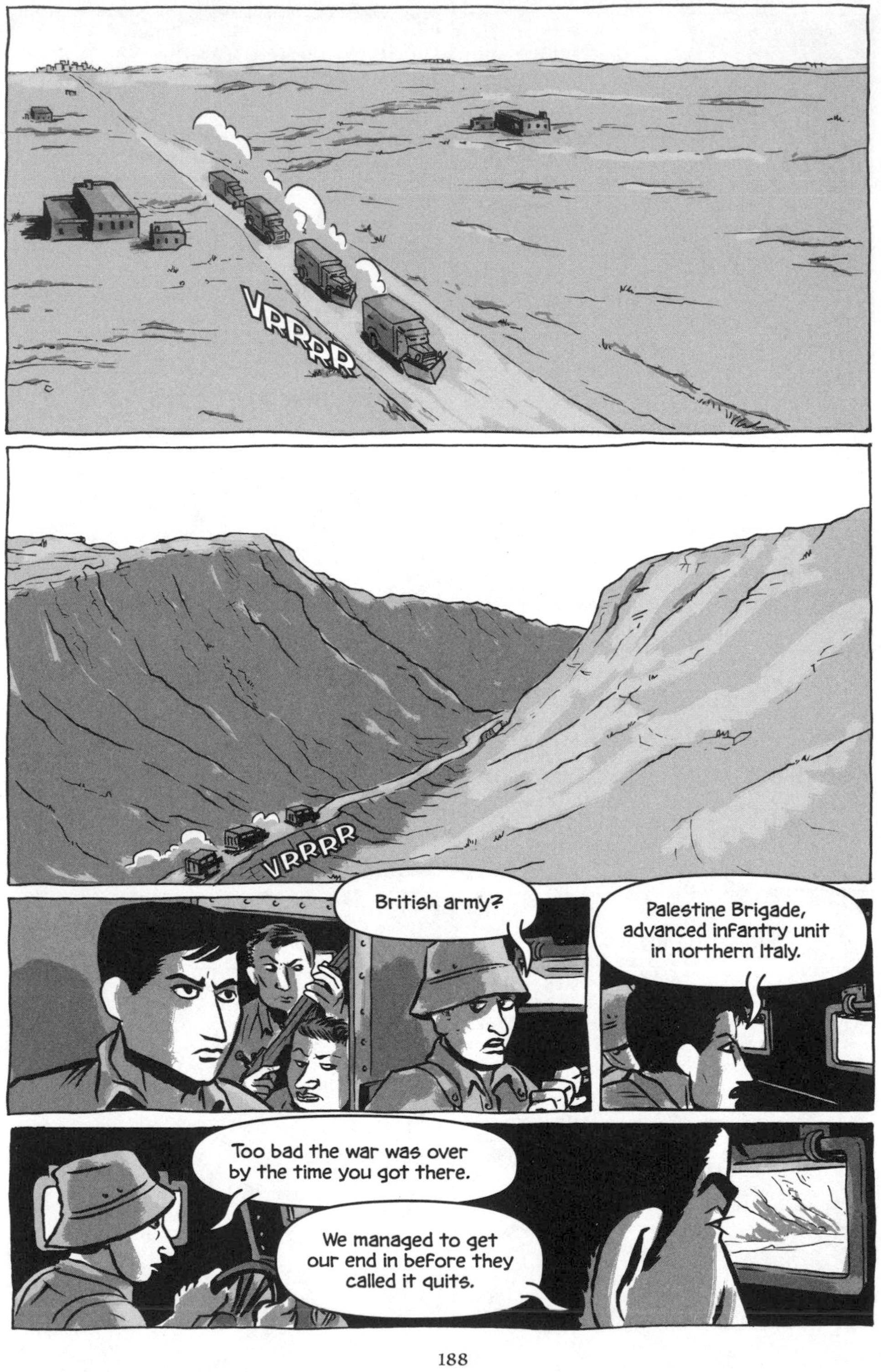
VRRRRR
VRRRR
British army?
Palestine Brigade, advanced infantry unit in northern Italy.
Too bad the war was over by the time you got there.
We managed to get our end in before they called it quits.

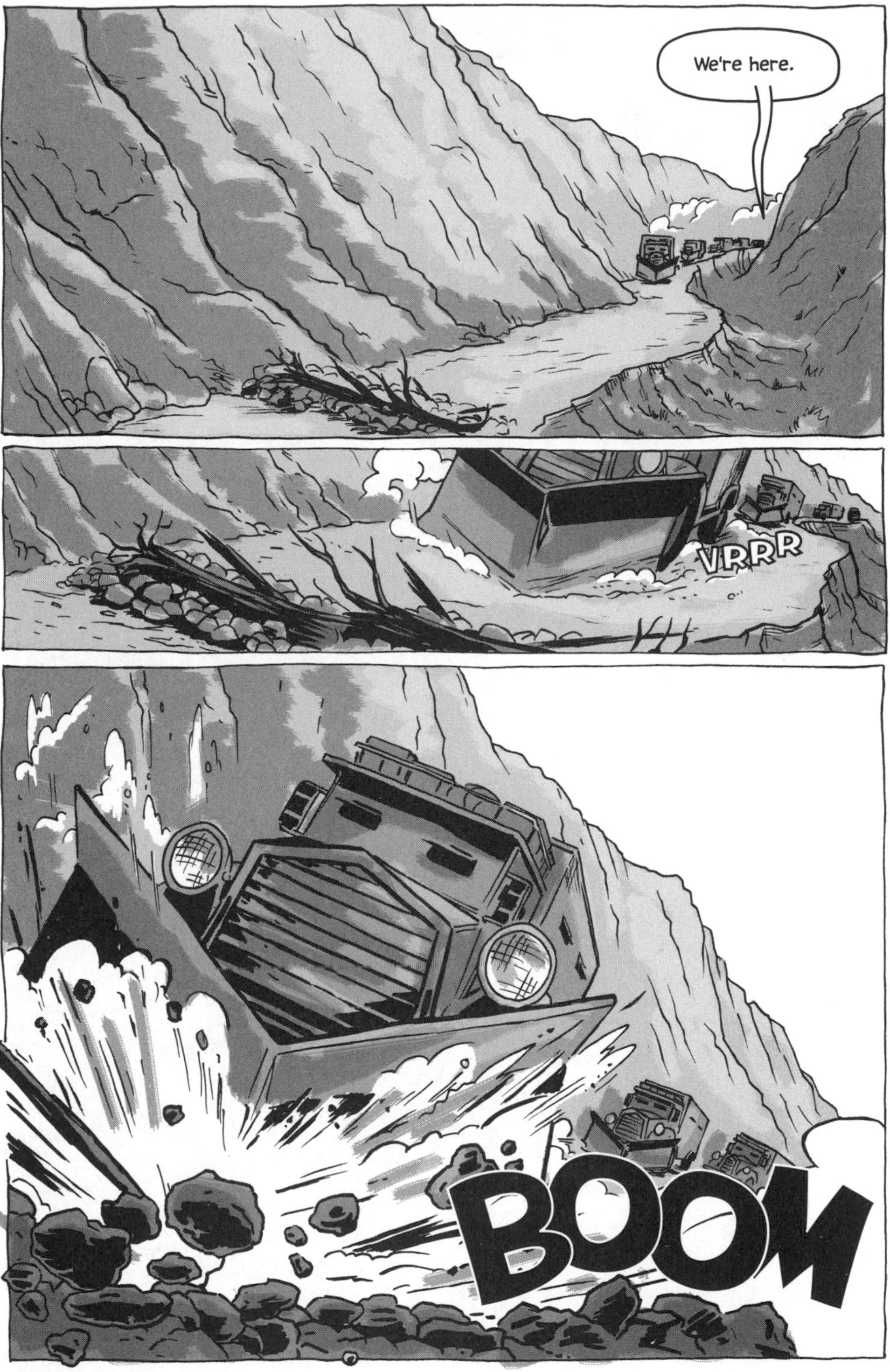
We're here.
VRRR
BOOM

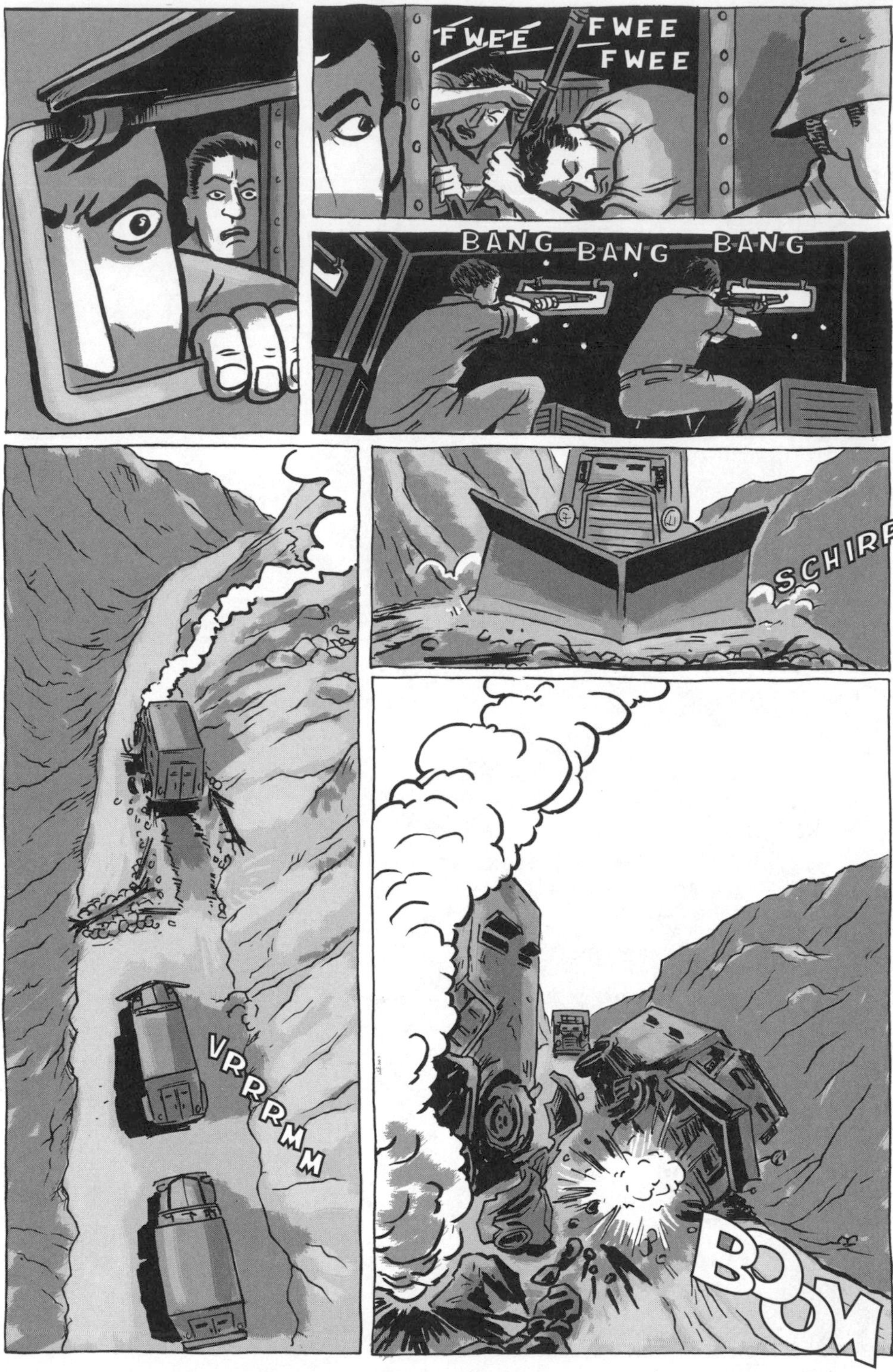
FWEE
FWEE
FWEE
BANG
BANG
BANG
SCHIRR
VRRRMM
BOOM

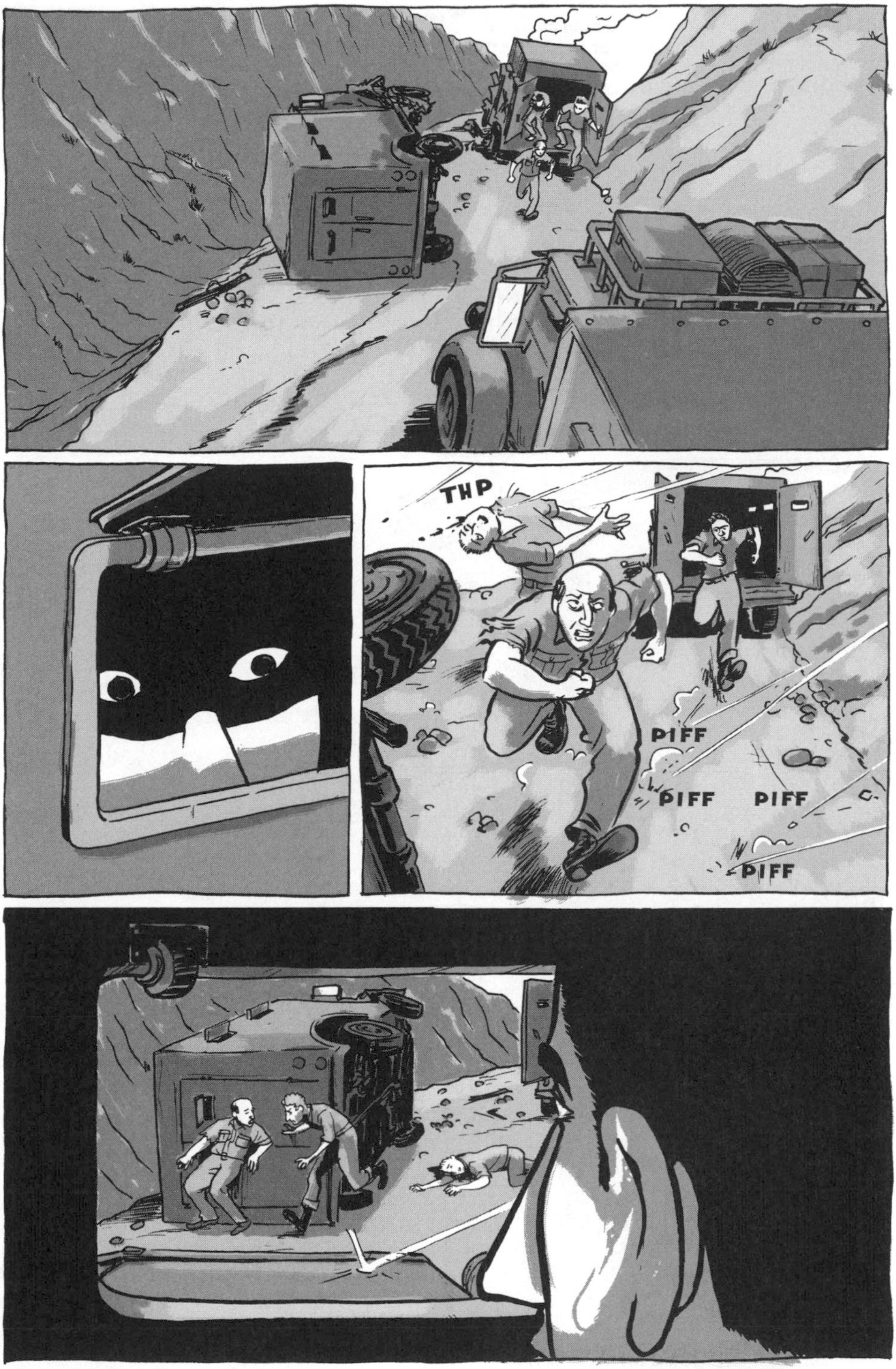
THP
PIFF
PIFF
PIFF
PIFF

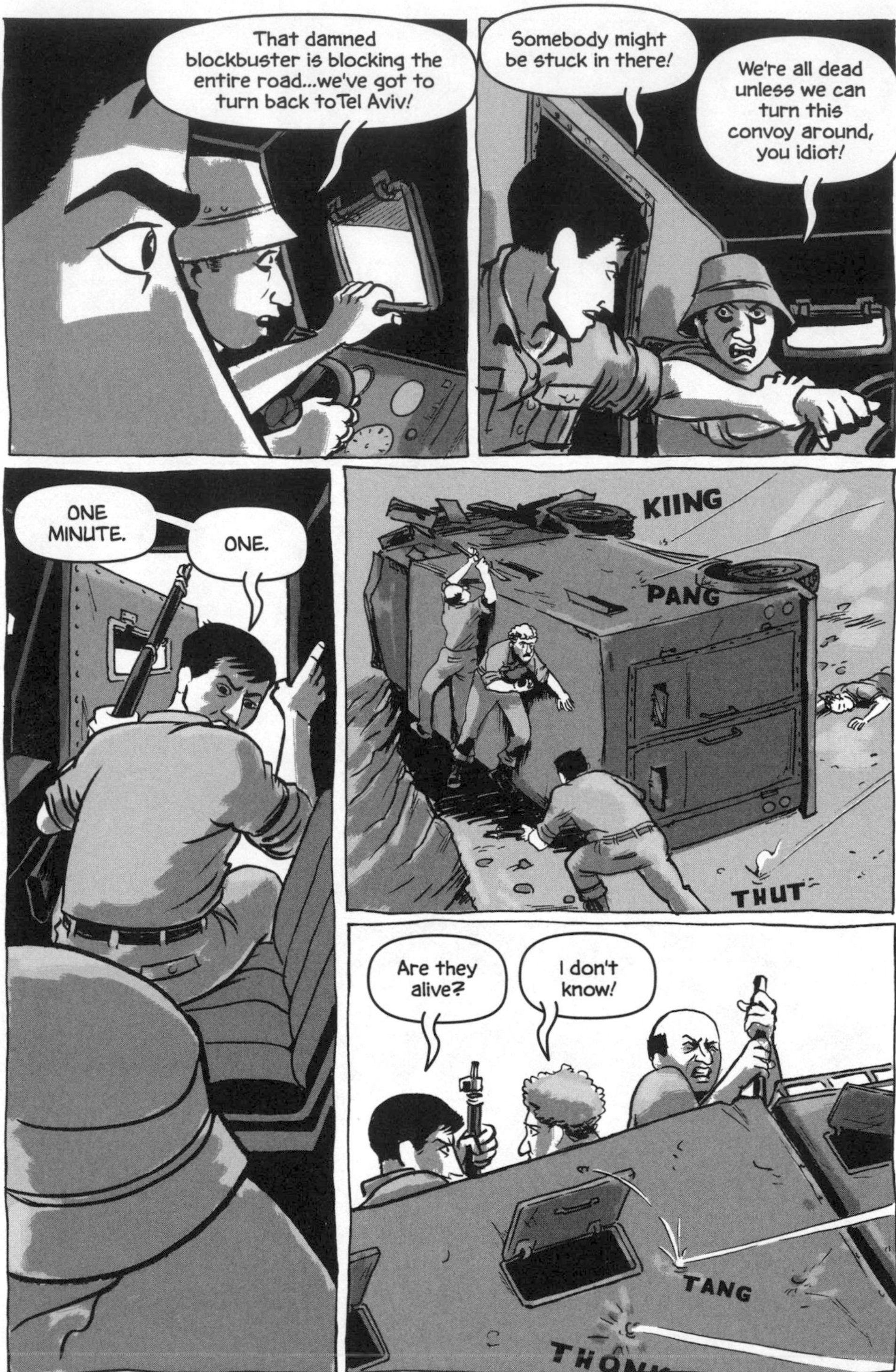
That damned blockbuster is blocking the entire road...we've got to turn back toTel Aviv!
Somebody might be stuck in there!
We're all dead unless we can turn this convoy around, you idiot!
ONE MINUTE.
ONE.
KIING
PANG
THUT
Are they alive?
I don't know!
TANG
THONK

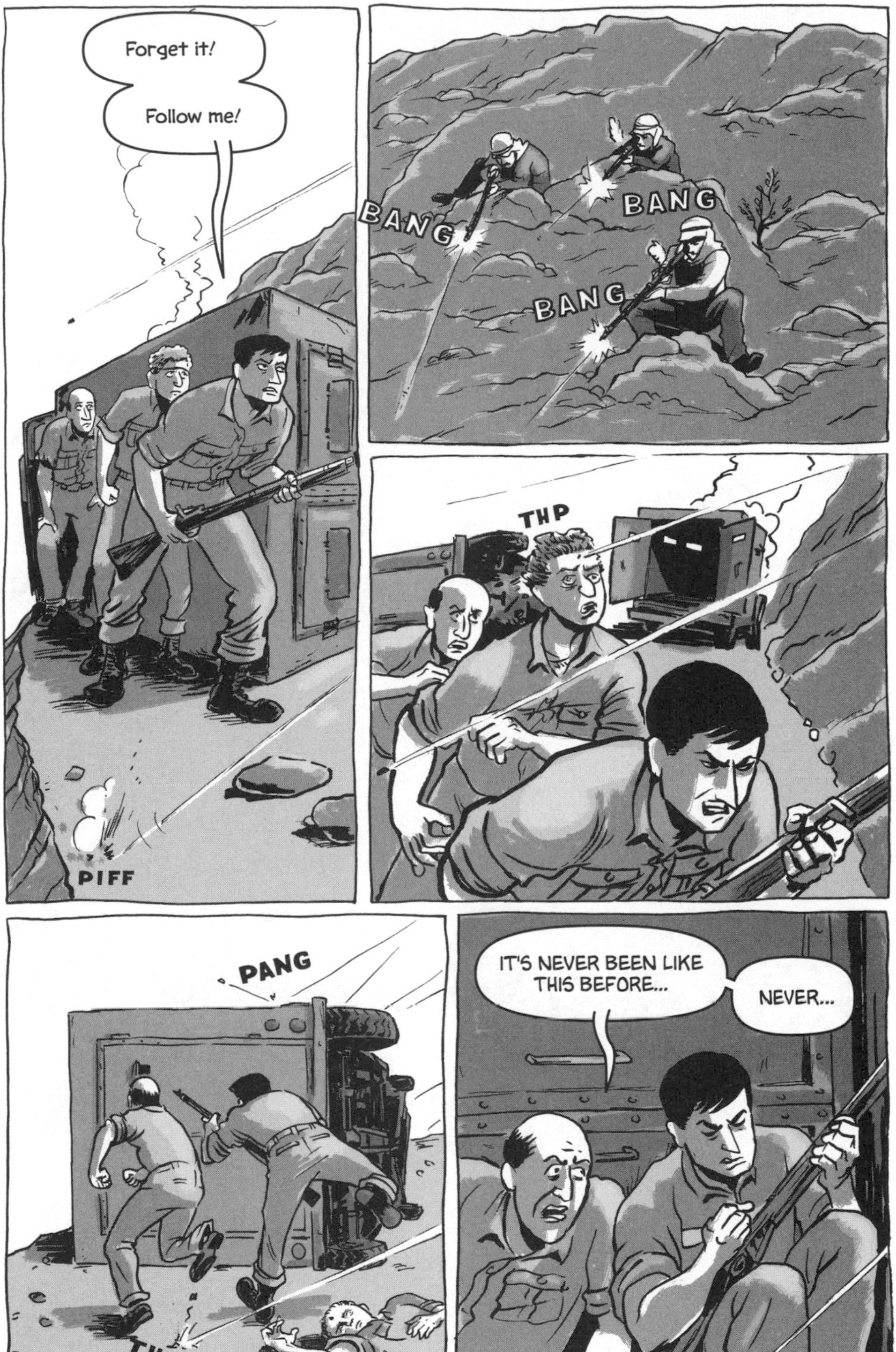
Forget it!
Follow me!
PIFF
BANG
BANG
BANG
THP
PANG
THUT
IT'S NEVER BEEN LIKE THIS BEFORE...
NEVER...

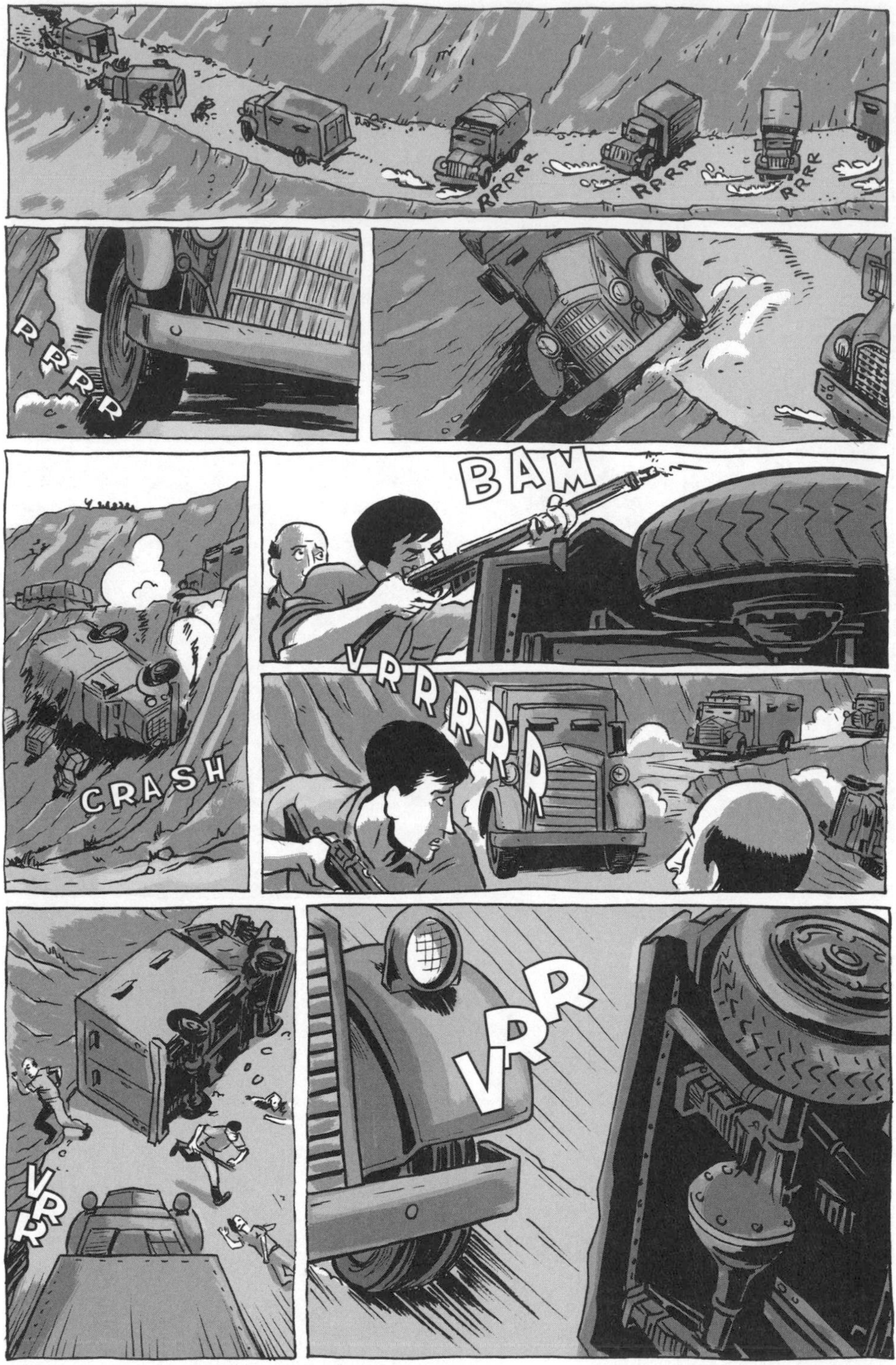
RRRRR
RRRR
RRRR
RRRRR
CRASH
BAM
VRRRRRRR
VRR
VRR

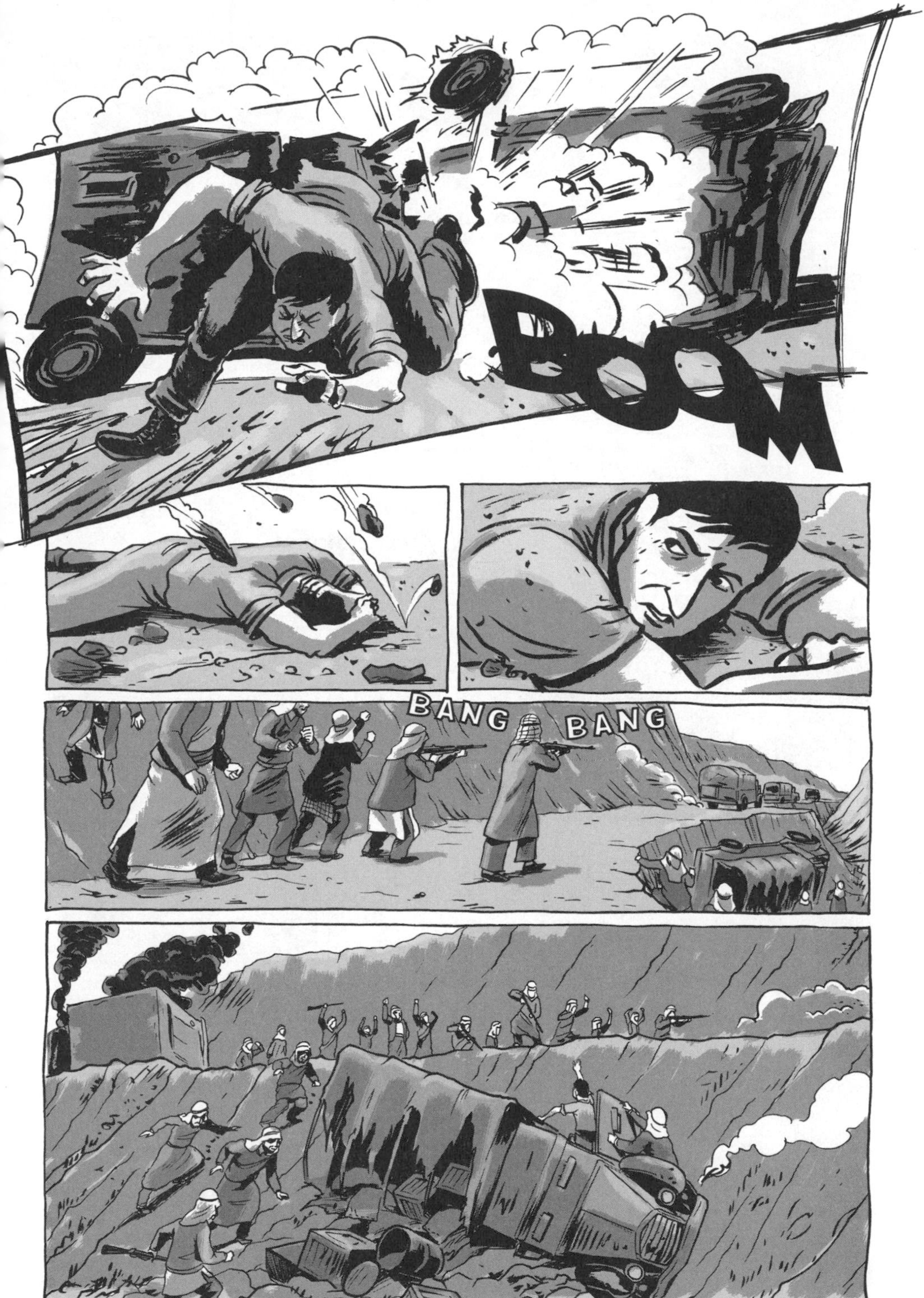
BOOM
BANG
BANG

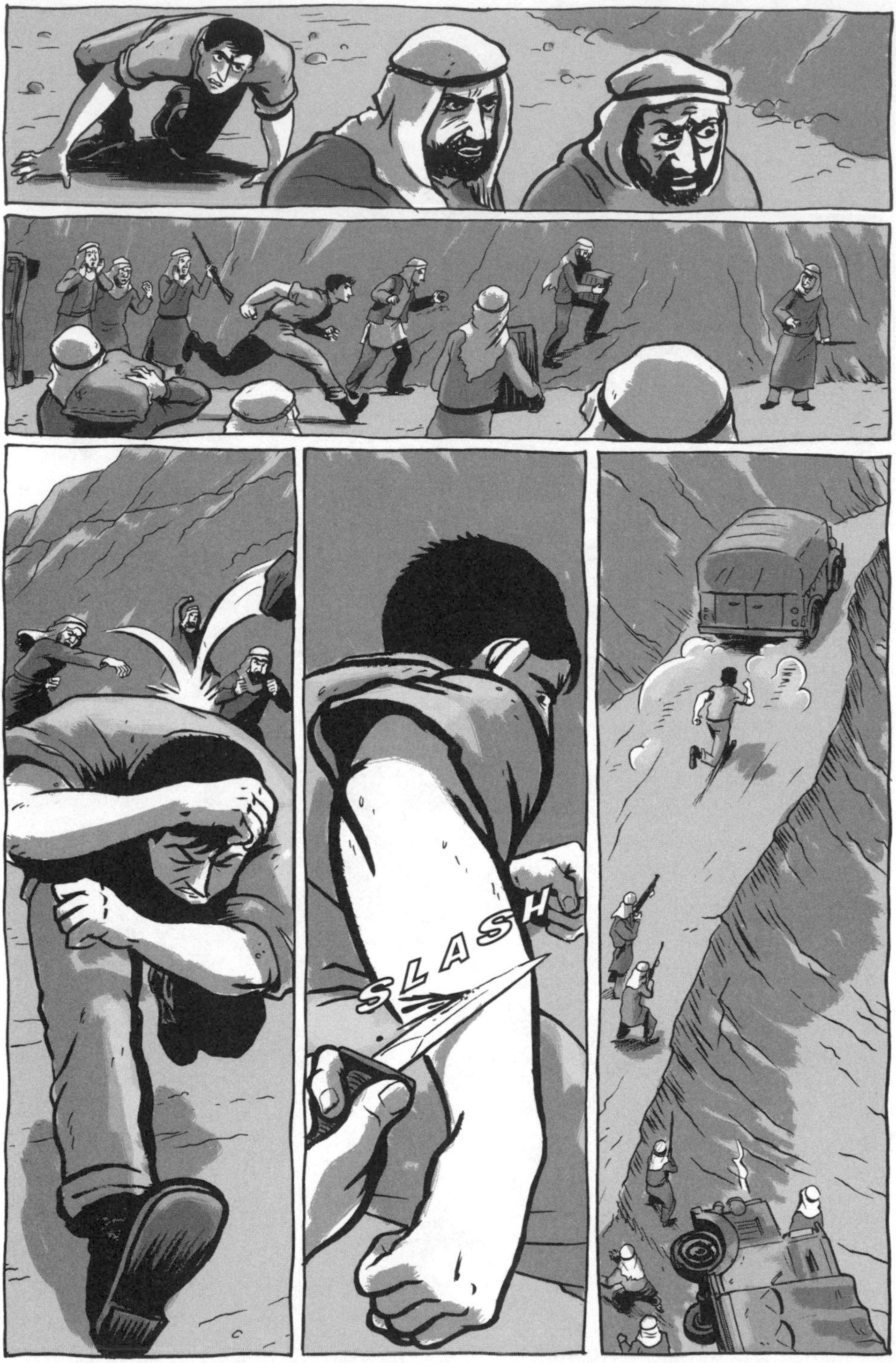
SLASH

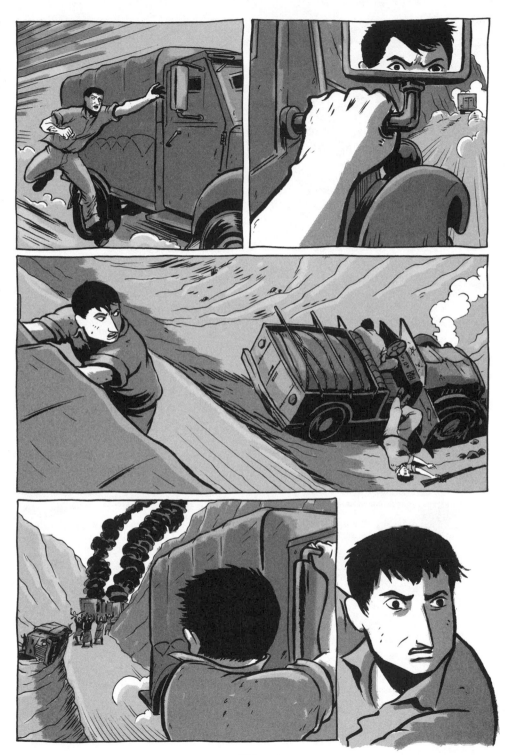

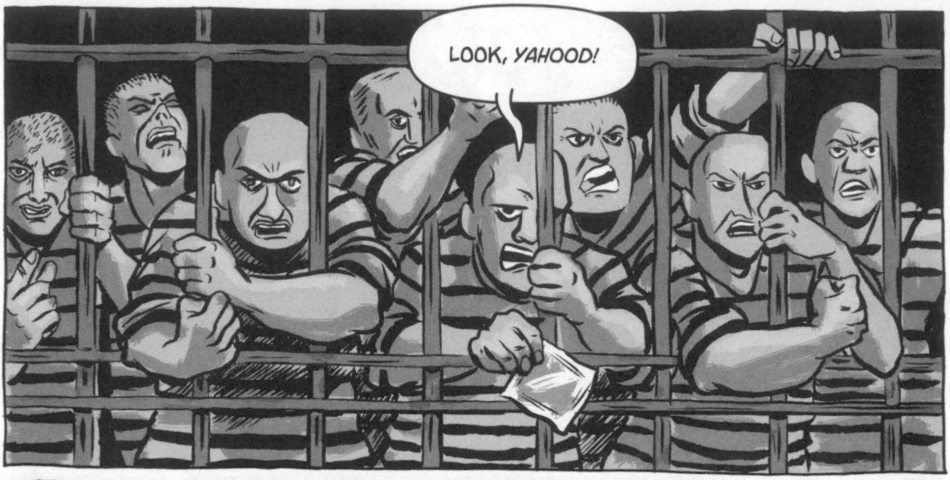
LOOK, *YAHOOD!*

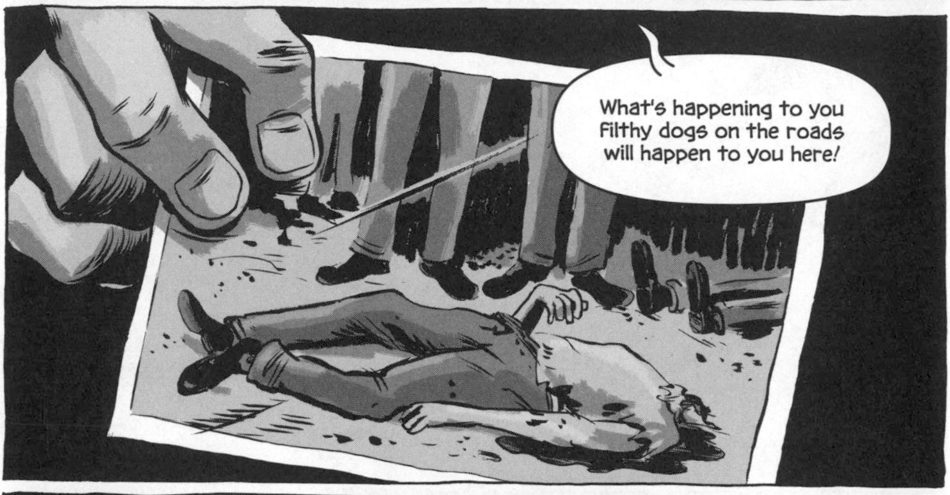
What's happening to you filthy dogs on the roads will happen to you here!

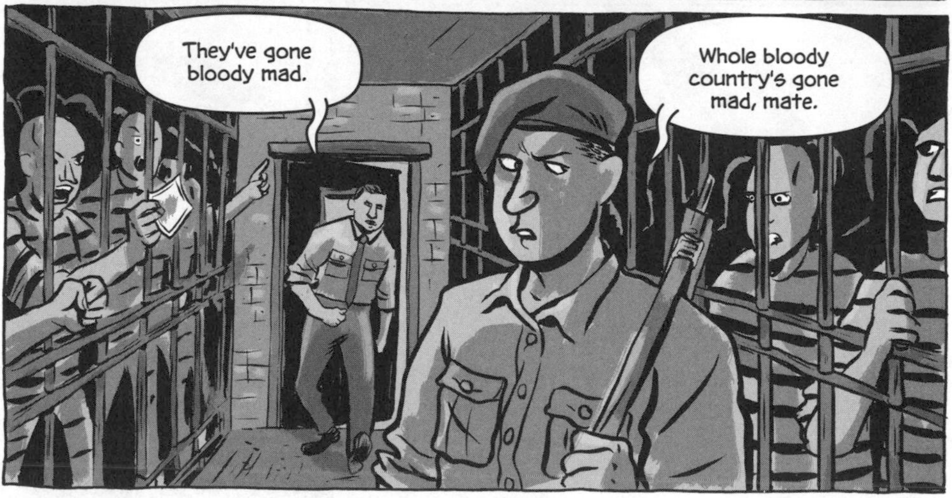
They've gone bloody mad.
Whole bloody country's gone mad, mate.

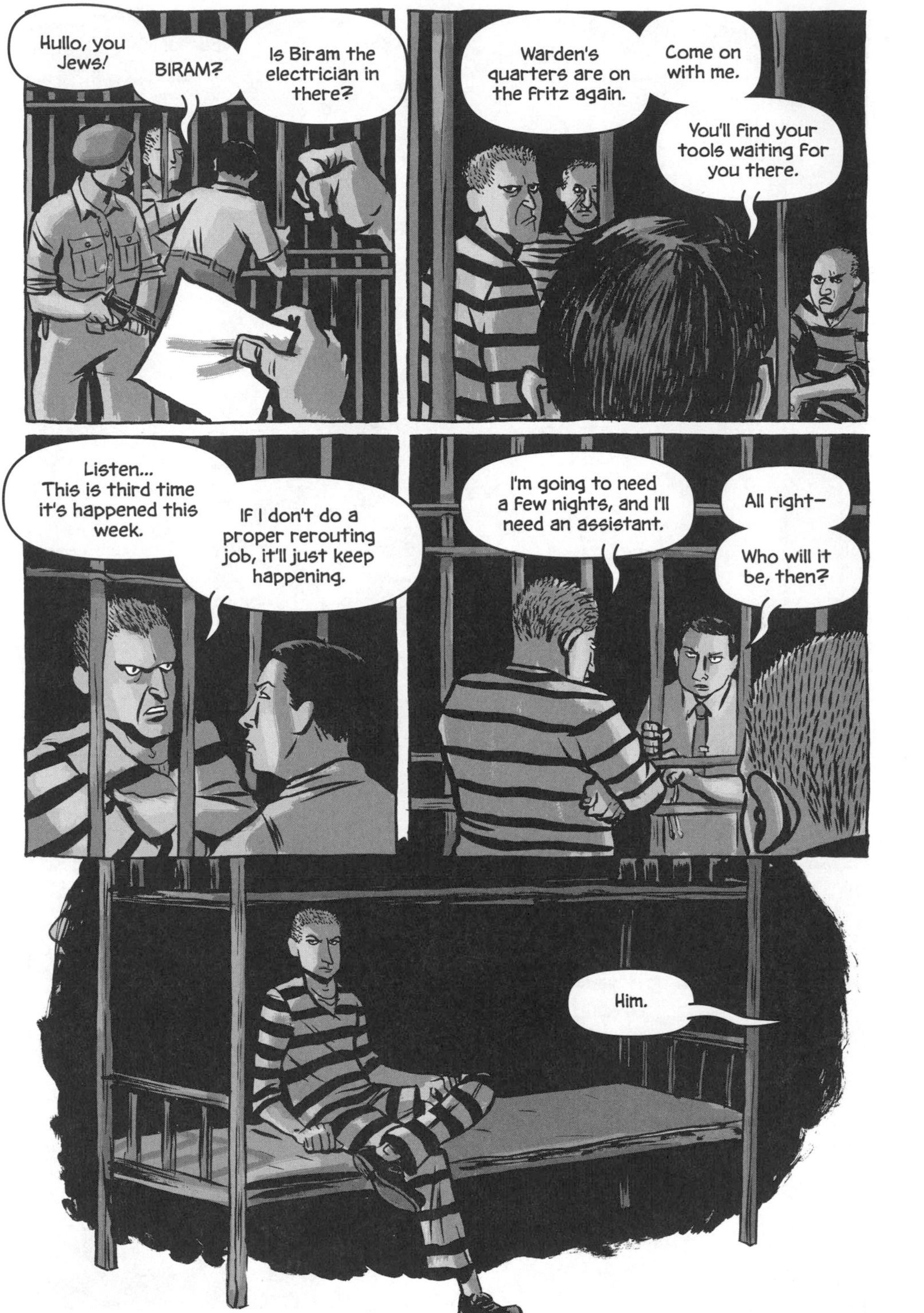
Hullo, you Jews!
BIRAM?
Is Biram the electrician in there?
Warden's quarters are on the fritz again.
Come on with me.
You'll find your tools waiting for you there.
Listen... This is third time it's happened this week.
If I don't do a proper rerouting job, it'll just keep happening.
I'm going to need a few nights, and I'll need an assistant.
All right—
Who will it be, then?
Him.

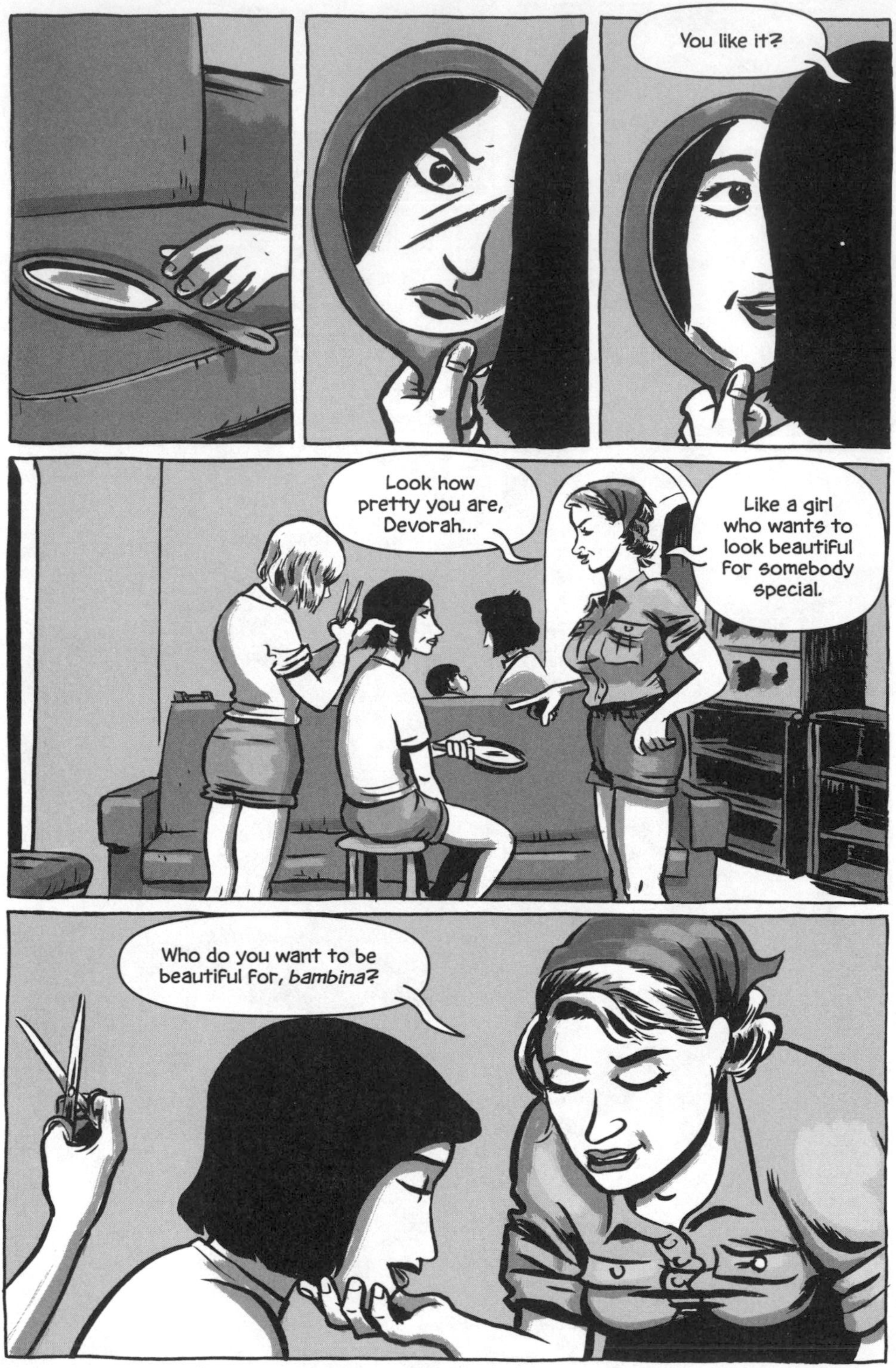
You like it?
Look how pretty you are, Devorah...
Like a girl who wants to look beautiful for somebody special.
Who do you want to be beautiful for, *bambina*?

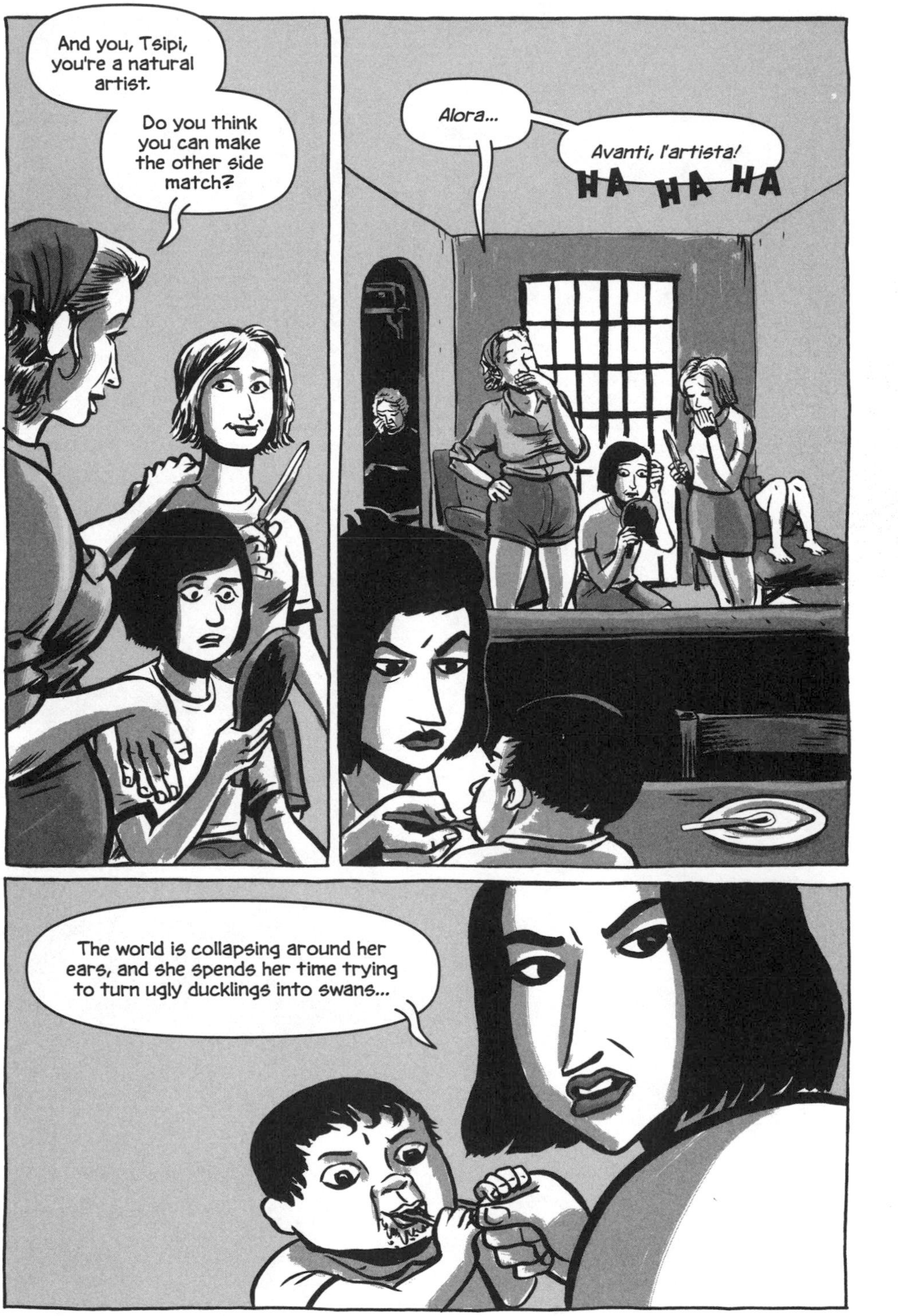
And you, Tsipi, you're a natural artist.
Do you think you can make the other side match?
Alora...
Avanti, l'artista!
HA HA HA HA
The world is collapsing around her ears, and she spends her time trying to turn ugly ducklings into swans...

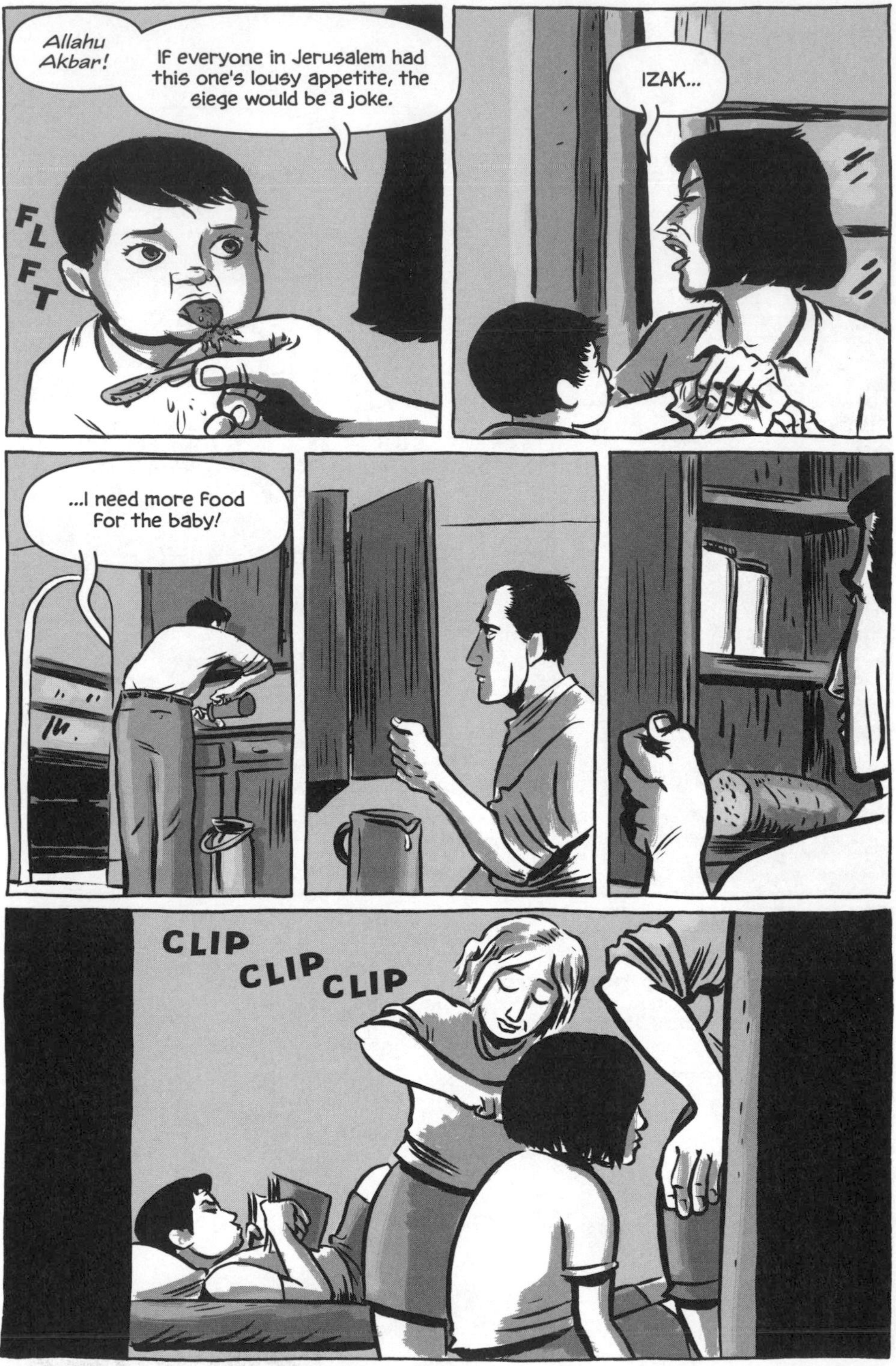
Allahu Akbar!
If everyone in Jerusalem had this one's lousy appetite, the siege would be a joke.
FLFFT
IZAK...
...I need more food for the baby!
CLIP CLIP CLIP

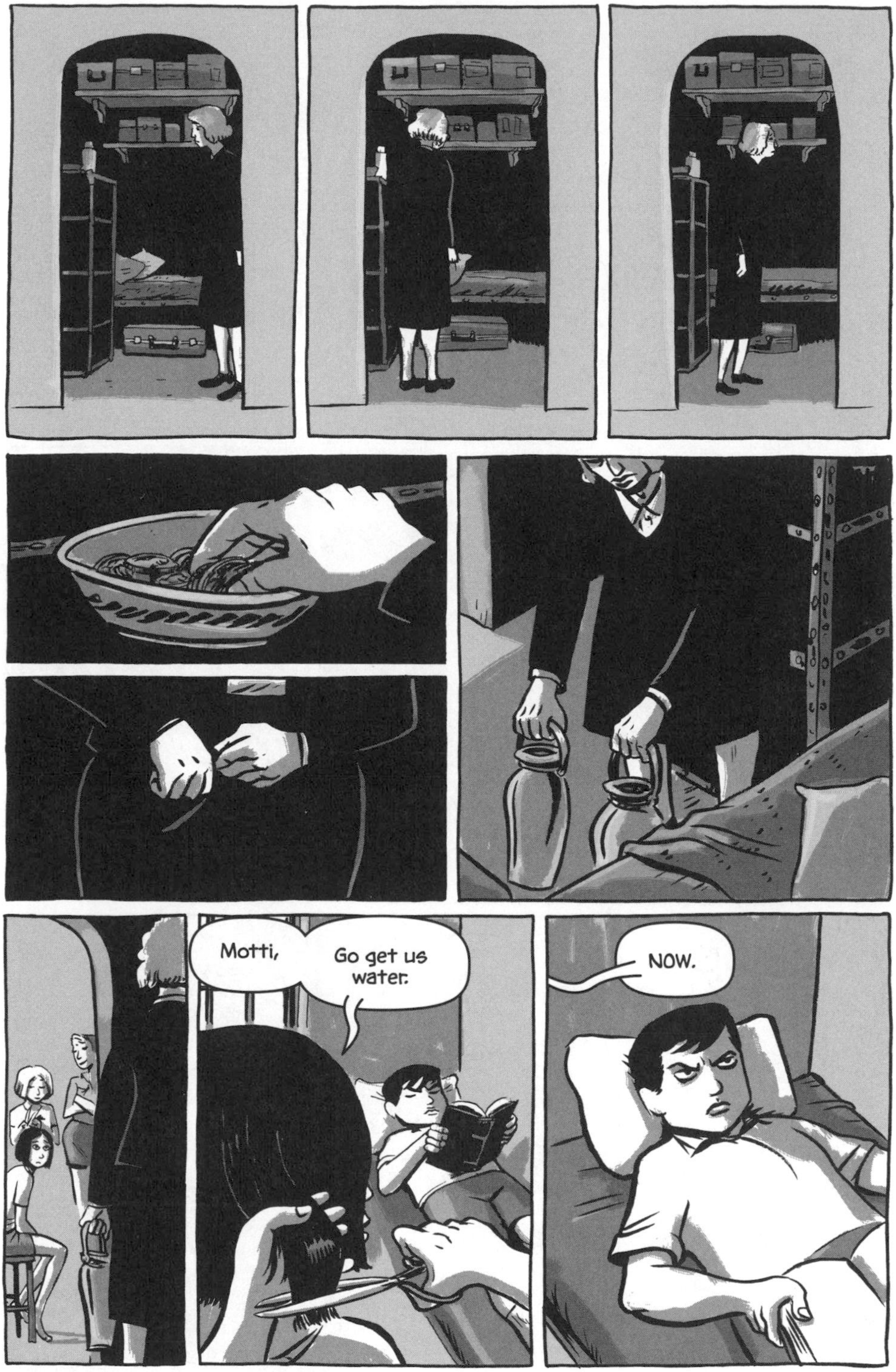
Motti,
Go get us water.
NOW.

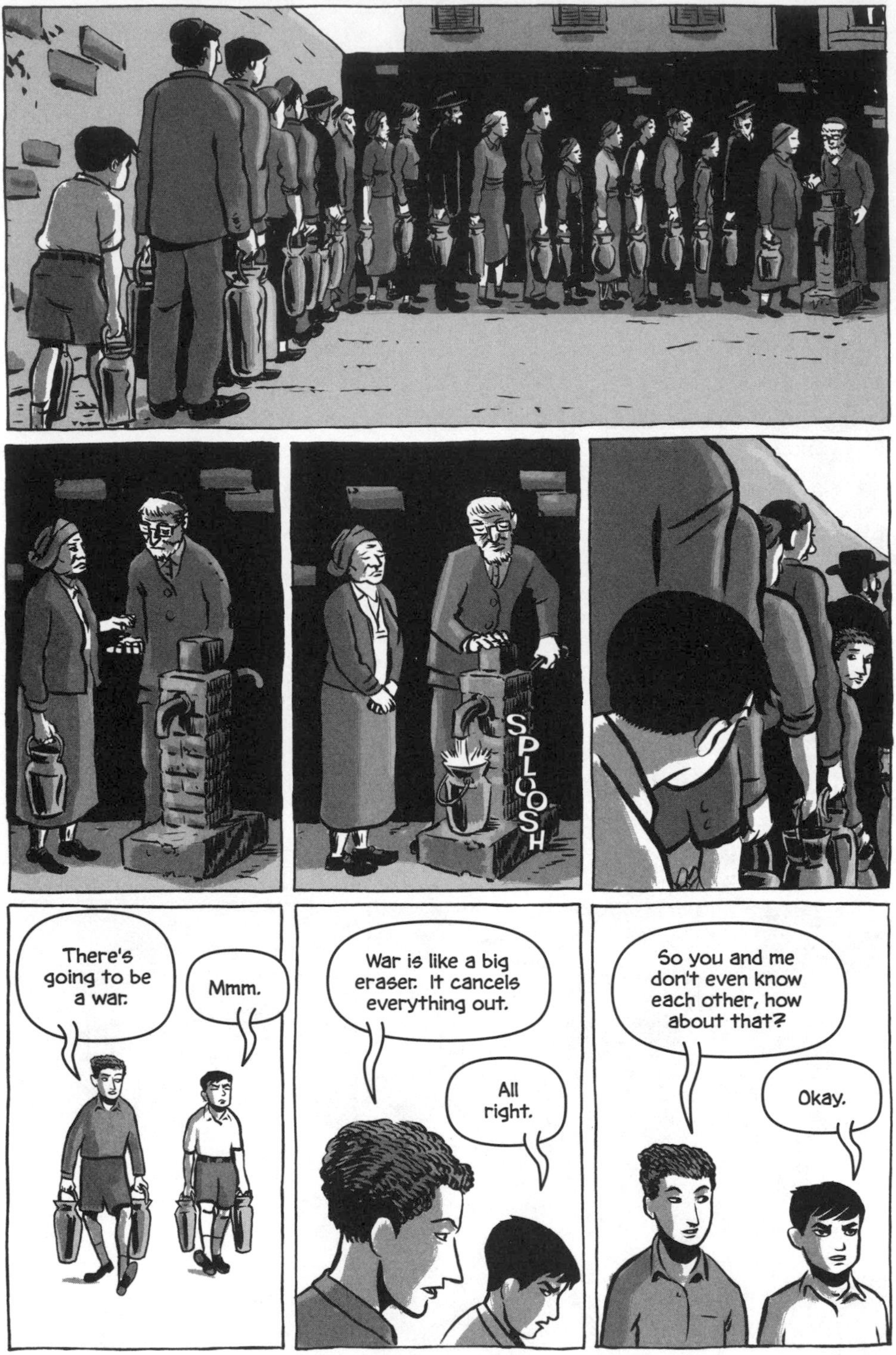
SPLOOSH
There's going to be a war.
Mmm.
War is like a big eraser. It cancels everything out.
All right.
So you and me don't even know each other, how about that?
Okay.

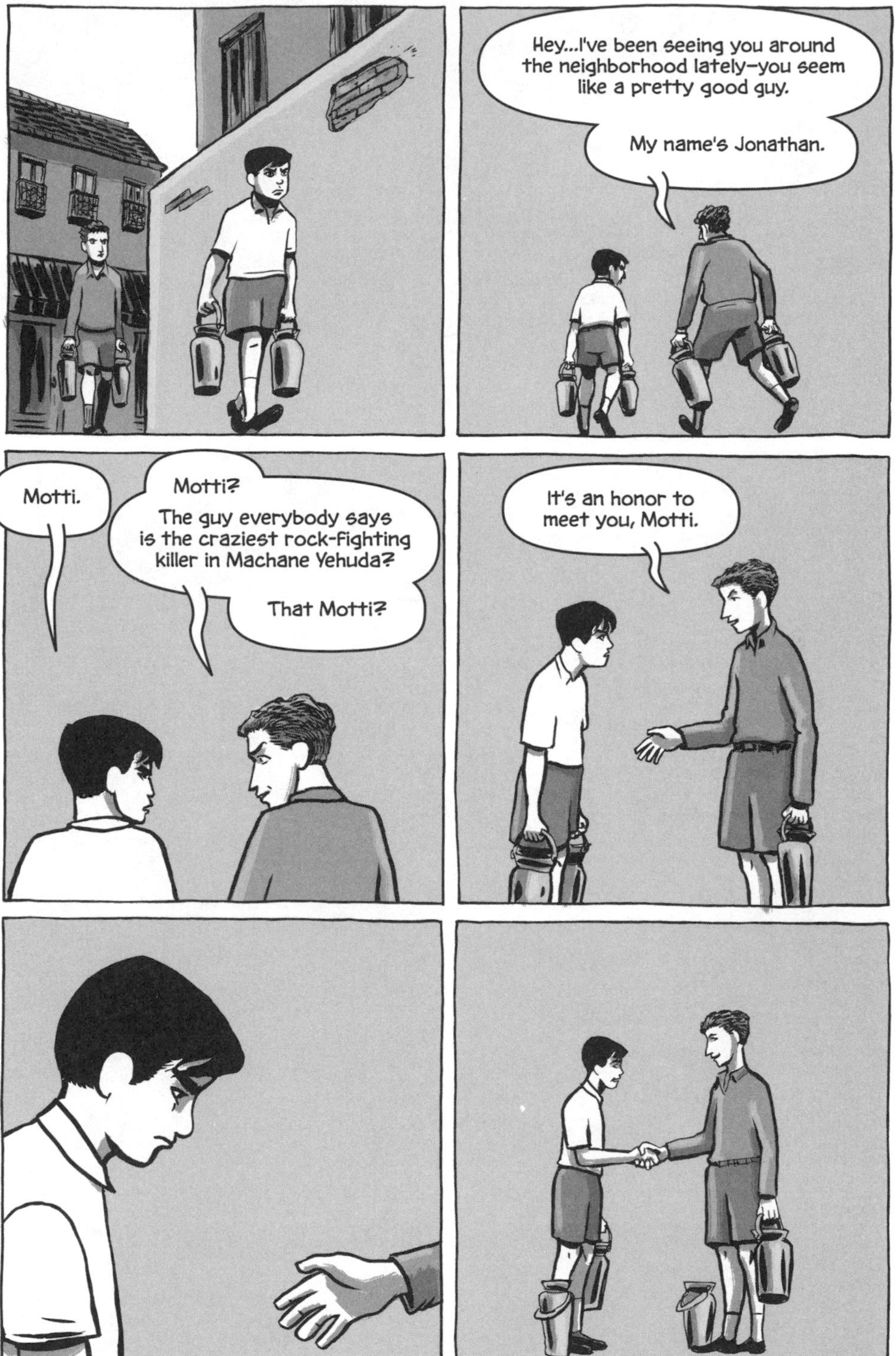
Hey...I've been seeing you around the neighborhood lately—you seem like a pretty good guy.
My name's Jonathan.
Motti.
Motti?
The guy everybody says is the craziest rock-fighting killer in Machane Yehuda?
That Motti?
It's an honor to meet you, Motti.

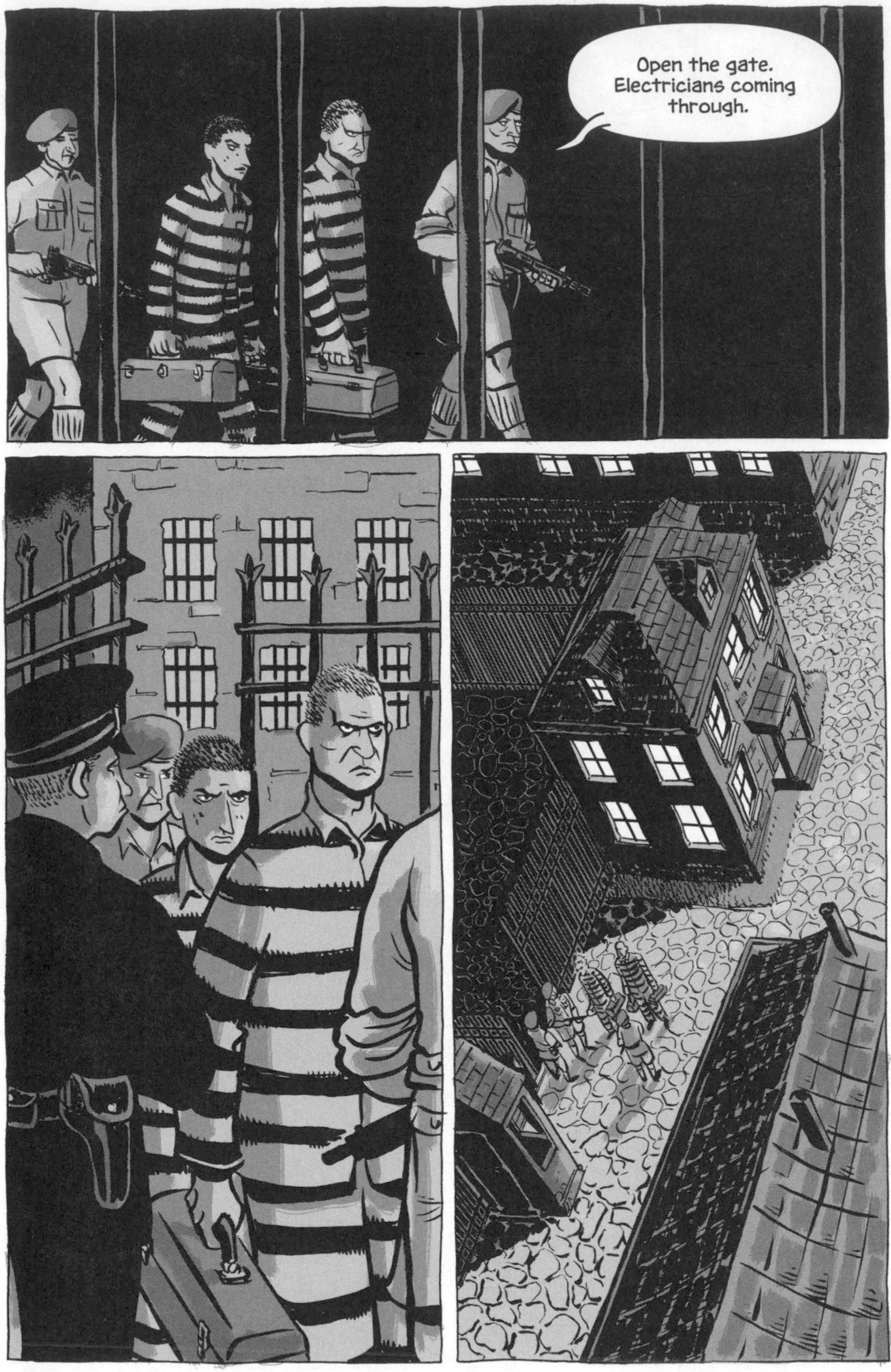
Open the gate. Electricians coming through.

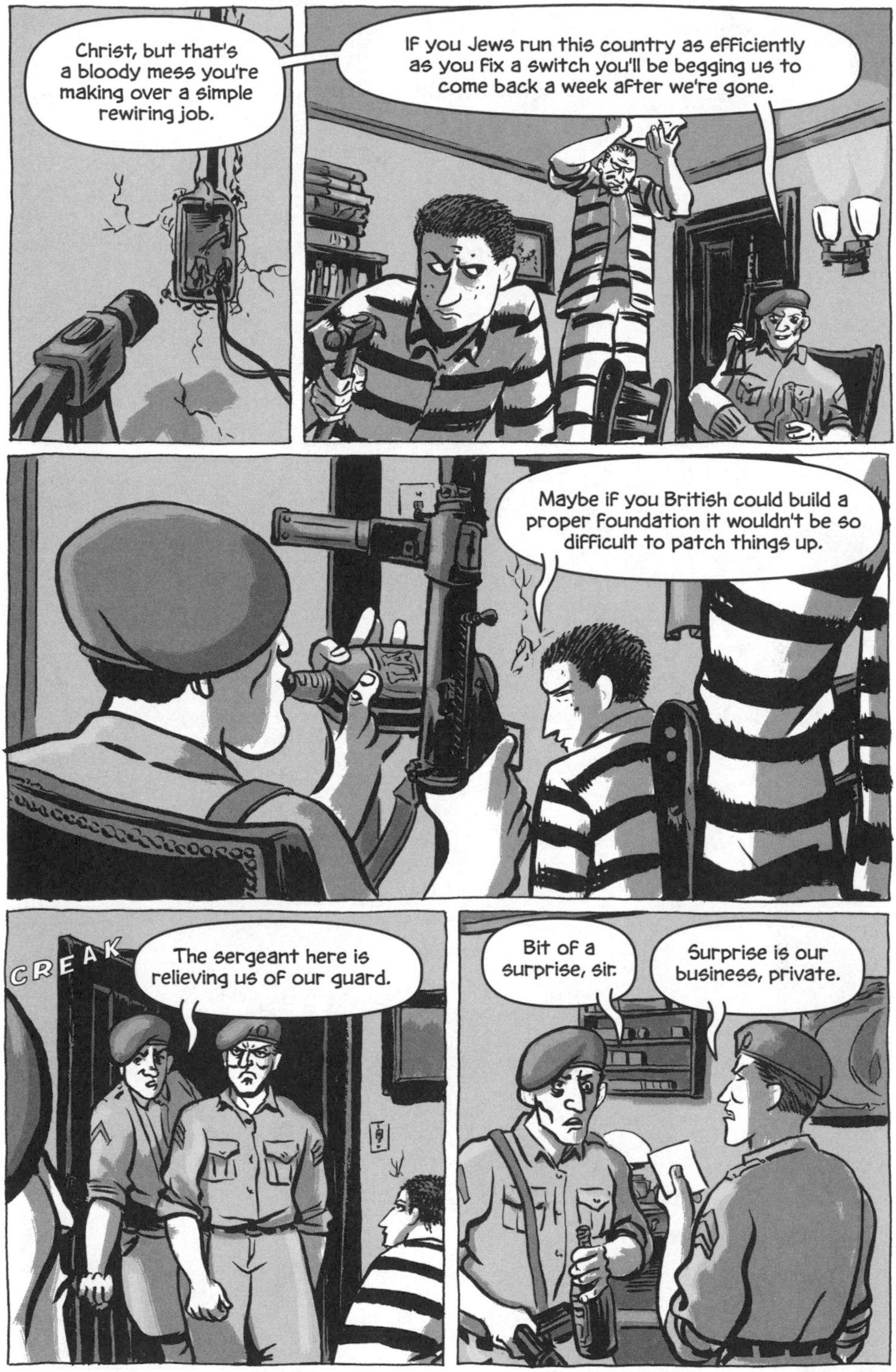

Christ, but that's a bloody mess you're making over a simple rewiring job.
If you Jews run this country as efficiently as you fix a switch you'll be begging us to come back a week after we're gone.
Maybe if you British could build a proper foundation it wouldn't be so difficult to patch things up.
CREAK
The sergeant here is relieving us of our guard.
Bit of a surprise, sir.
Surprise is our business, private.

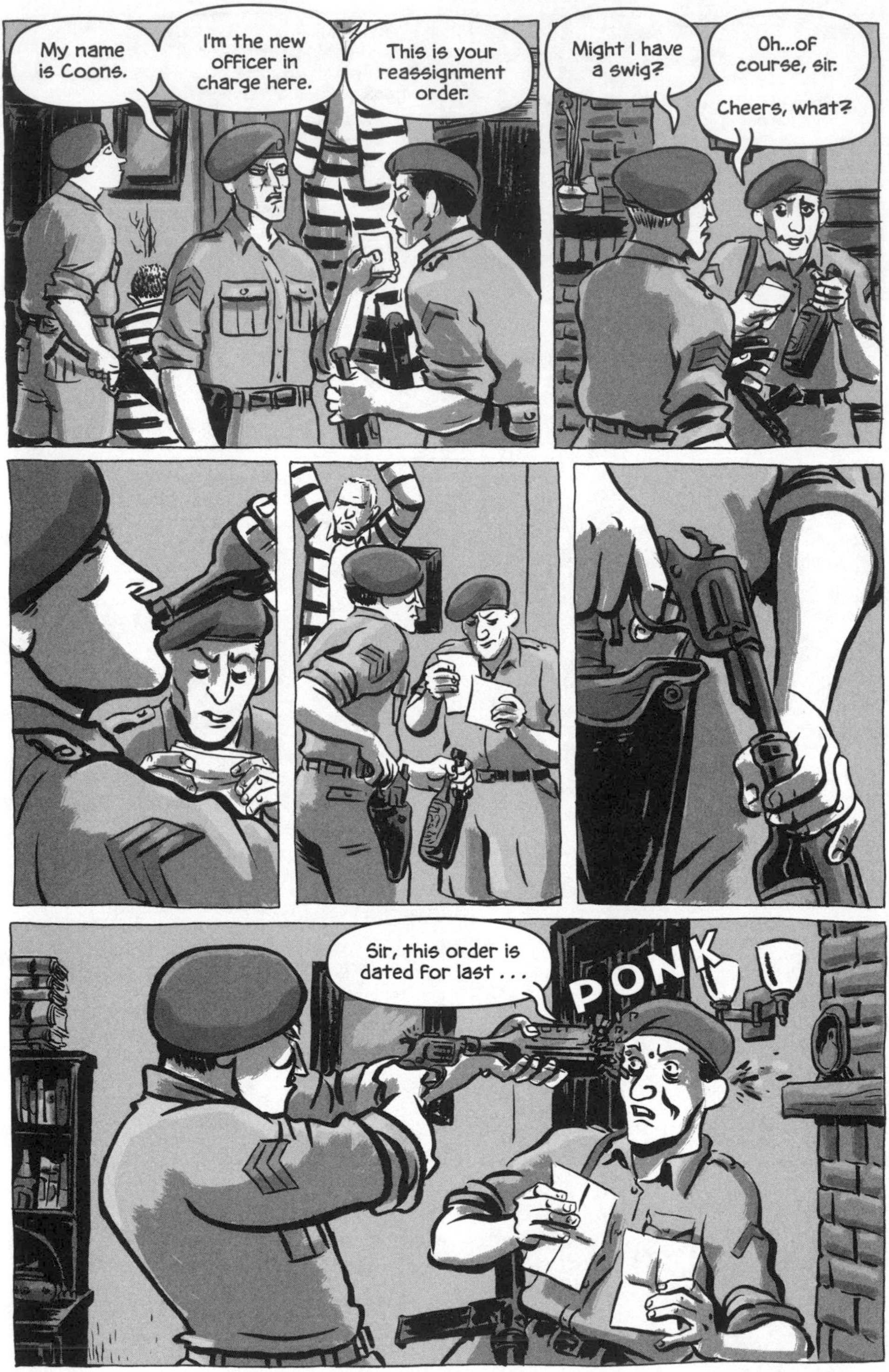
My name is Coons.
I'm the new officer in charge here.
This is your reassignment order.
Might I have a swig?
Oh...of course, sir.
Cheers, what?
Sir, this order is dated for last . . .
PONK

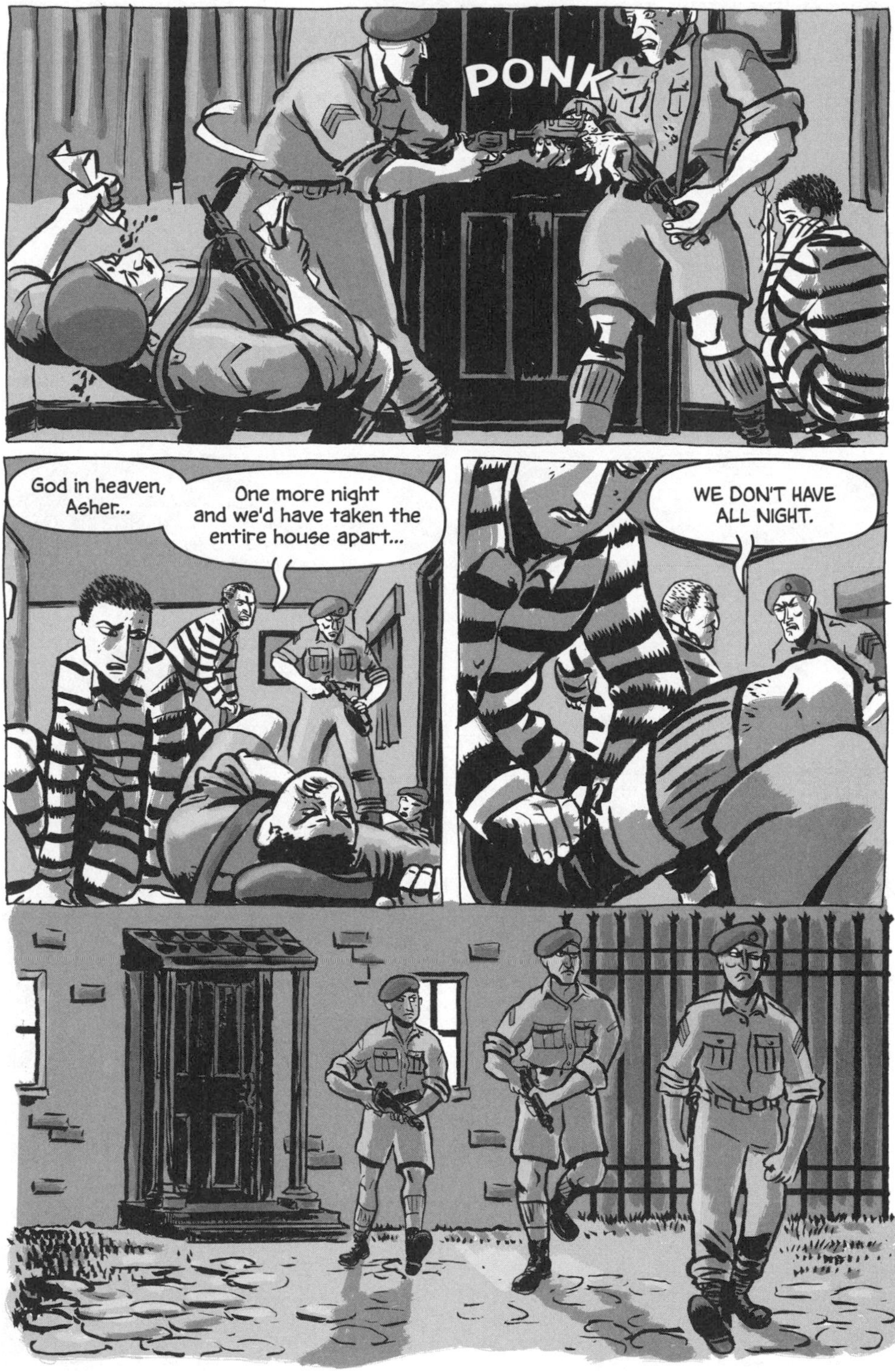
PONK
God in heaven, Asher...
One more night and we'd have taken the entire house apart...
WE DON'T HAVE ALL NIGHT.

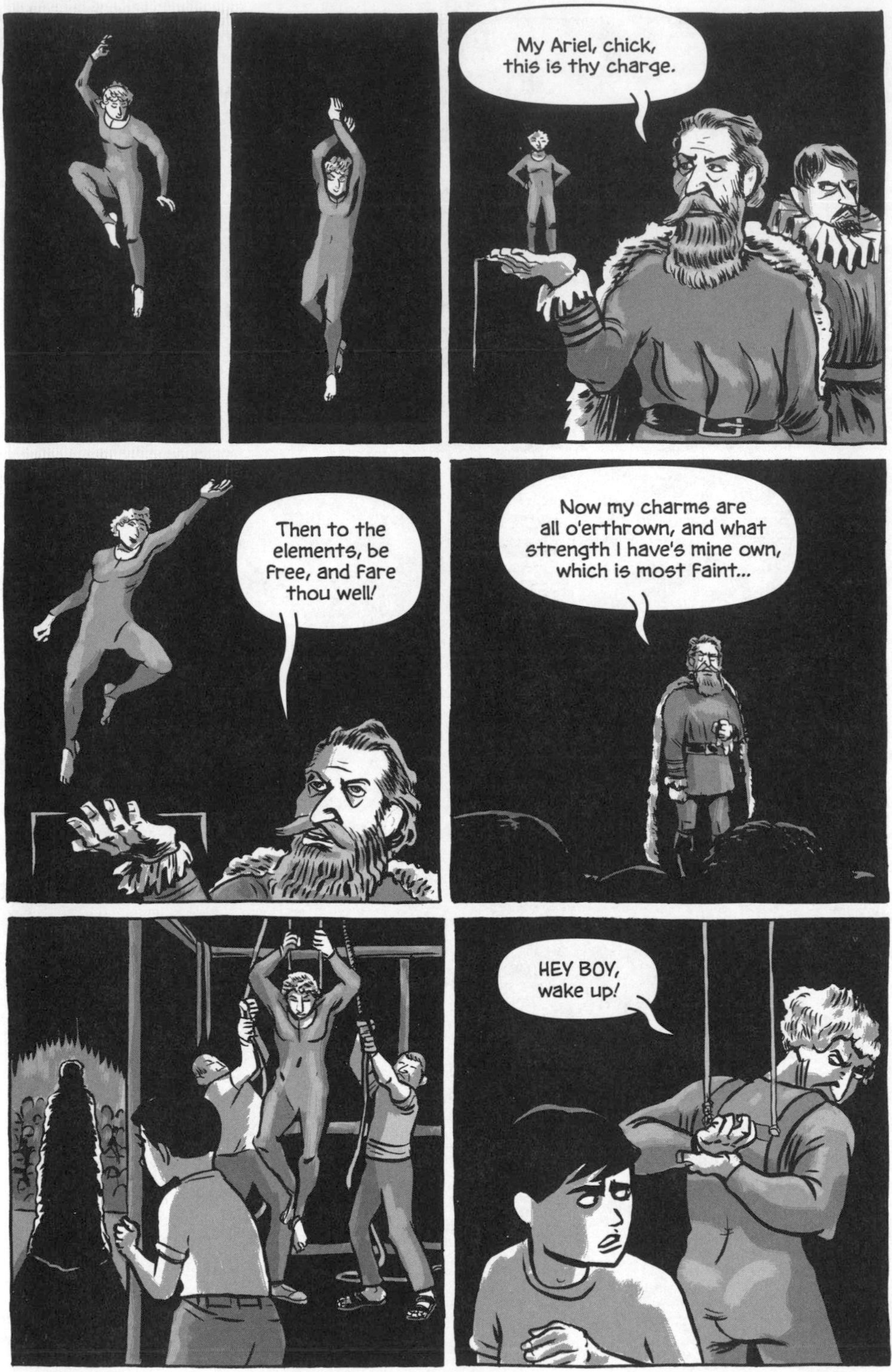
My Ariel, chick, this is thy charge.
Then to the elements, be free, and fare thou well!
Now my charms are all o'erthrown, and what strength I have's mine own, which is most faint...
HEY BOY, wake up!

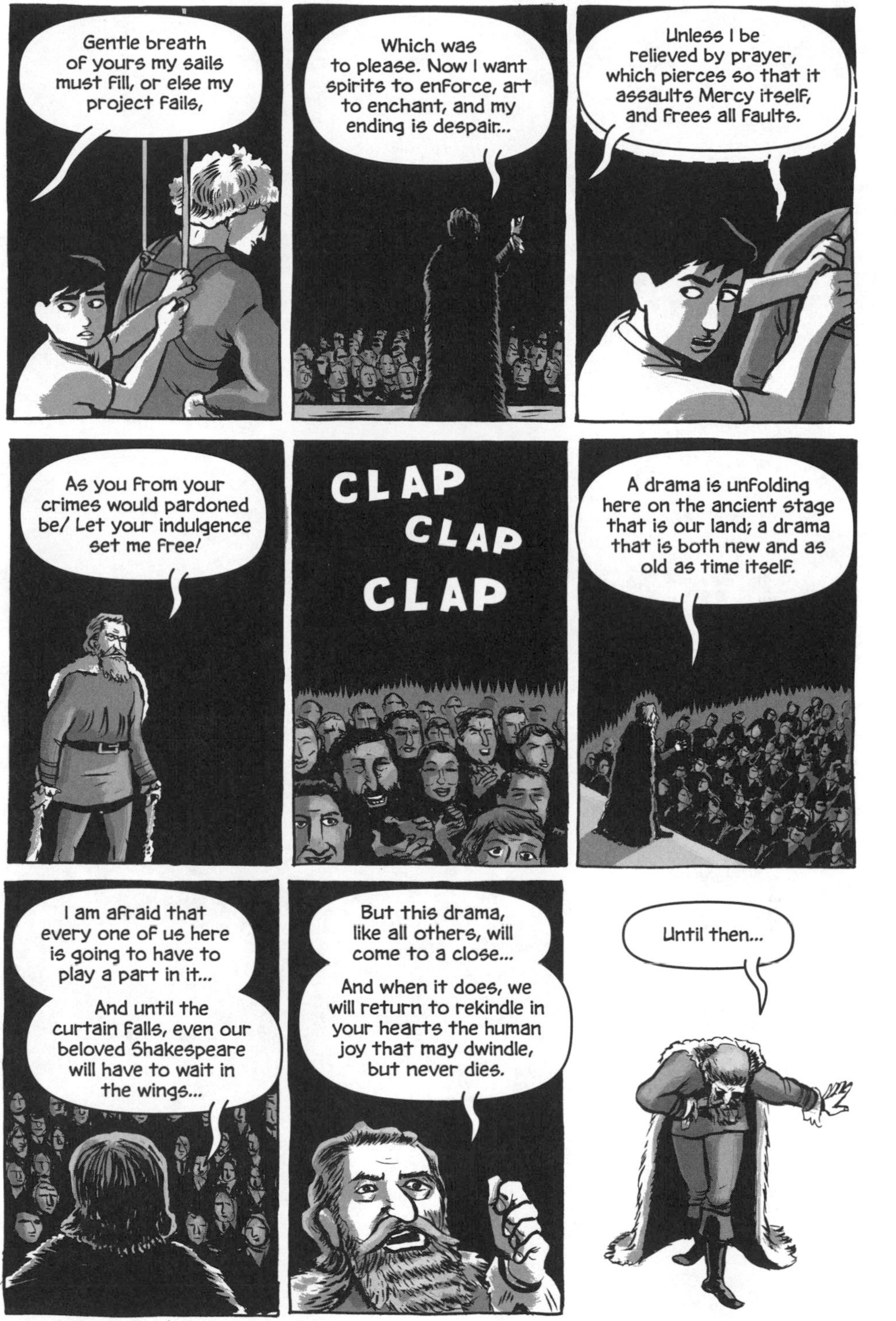
Gentle breath of yours my sails must fill, or else my project fails,
Which was to please. Now I want spirits to enforce, art to enchant, and my ending is despair...
Unless I be relieved by prayer, which pierces so that it assaults Mercy itself, and frees all faults.
As you from your crimes would pardoned be/ Let your indulgence set me free!
CLAP
CLAP
CLAP
A drama is unfolding here on the ancient stage that is our land; a drama that is both new and as old as time itself.
I am afraid that every one of us here is going to have to play a part in it...
And until the curtain falls, even our beloved Shakespeare will have to wait in the wings...
But this drama, like all others, will come to a close...
And when it does, we will return to rekindle in your hearts the human joy that may dwindle, but never dies.
Until then...

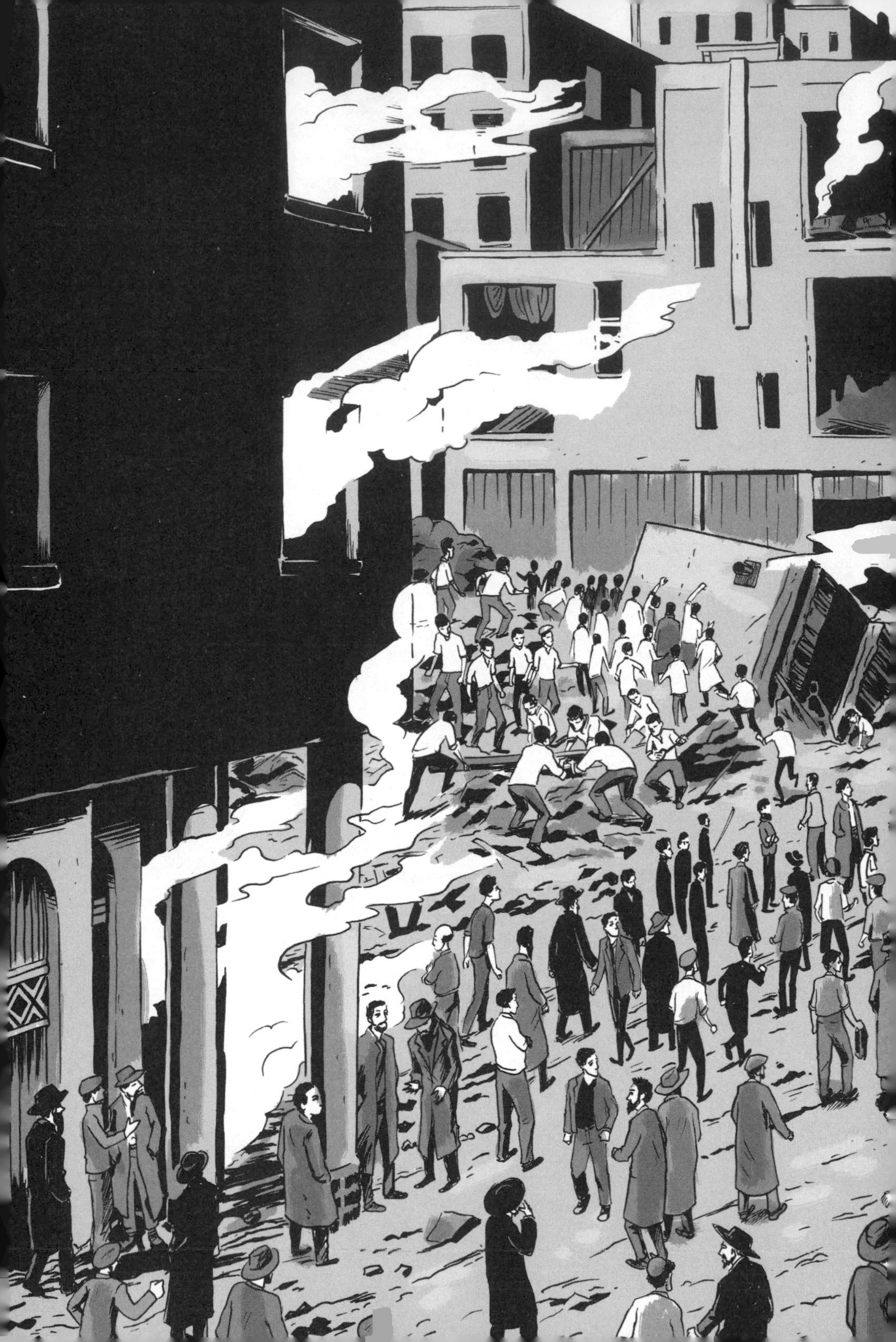

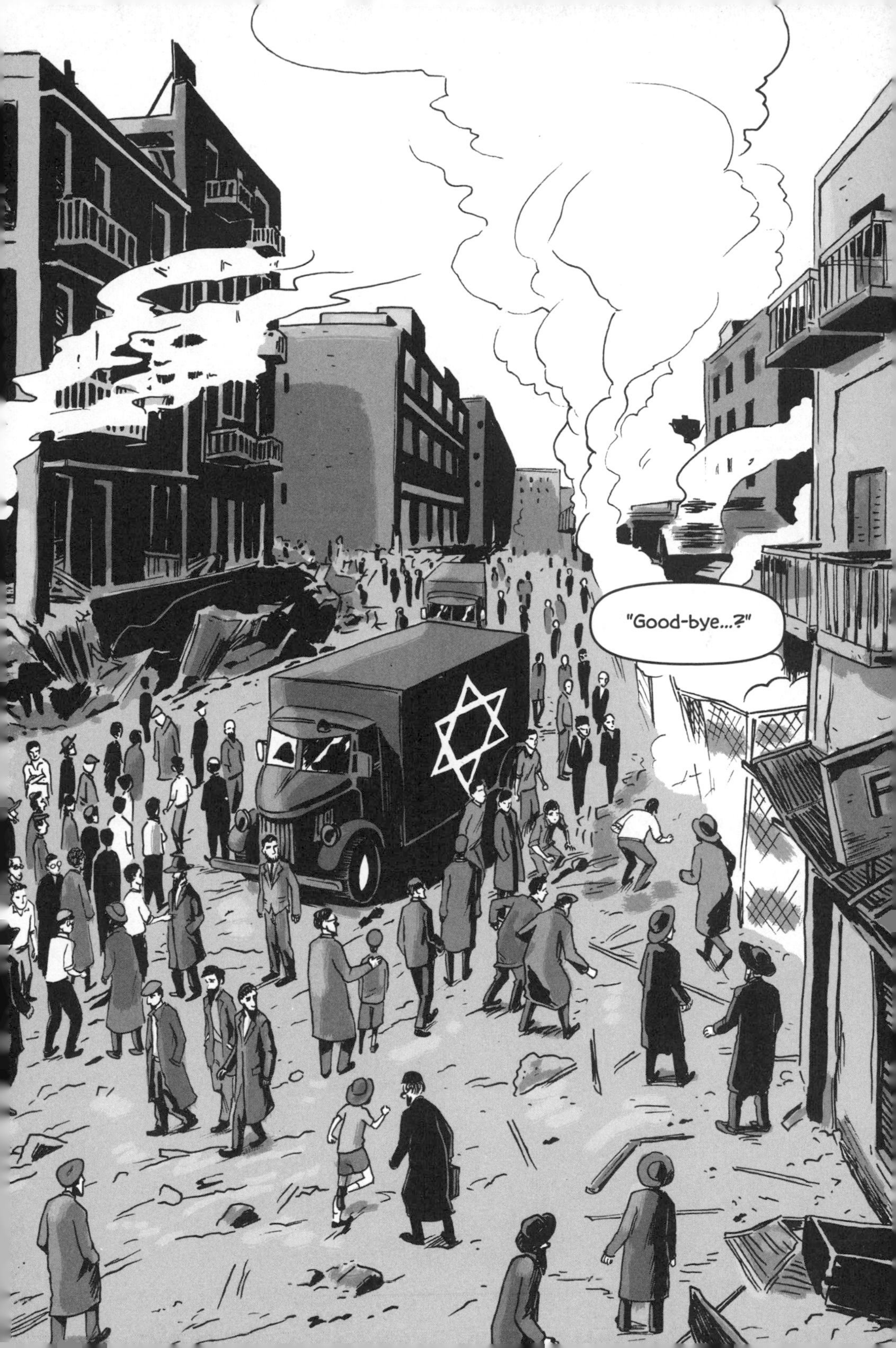
"Good-bye...?"

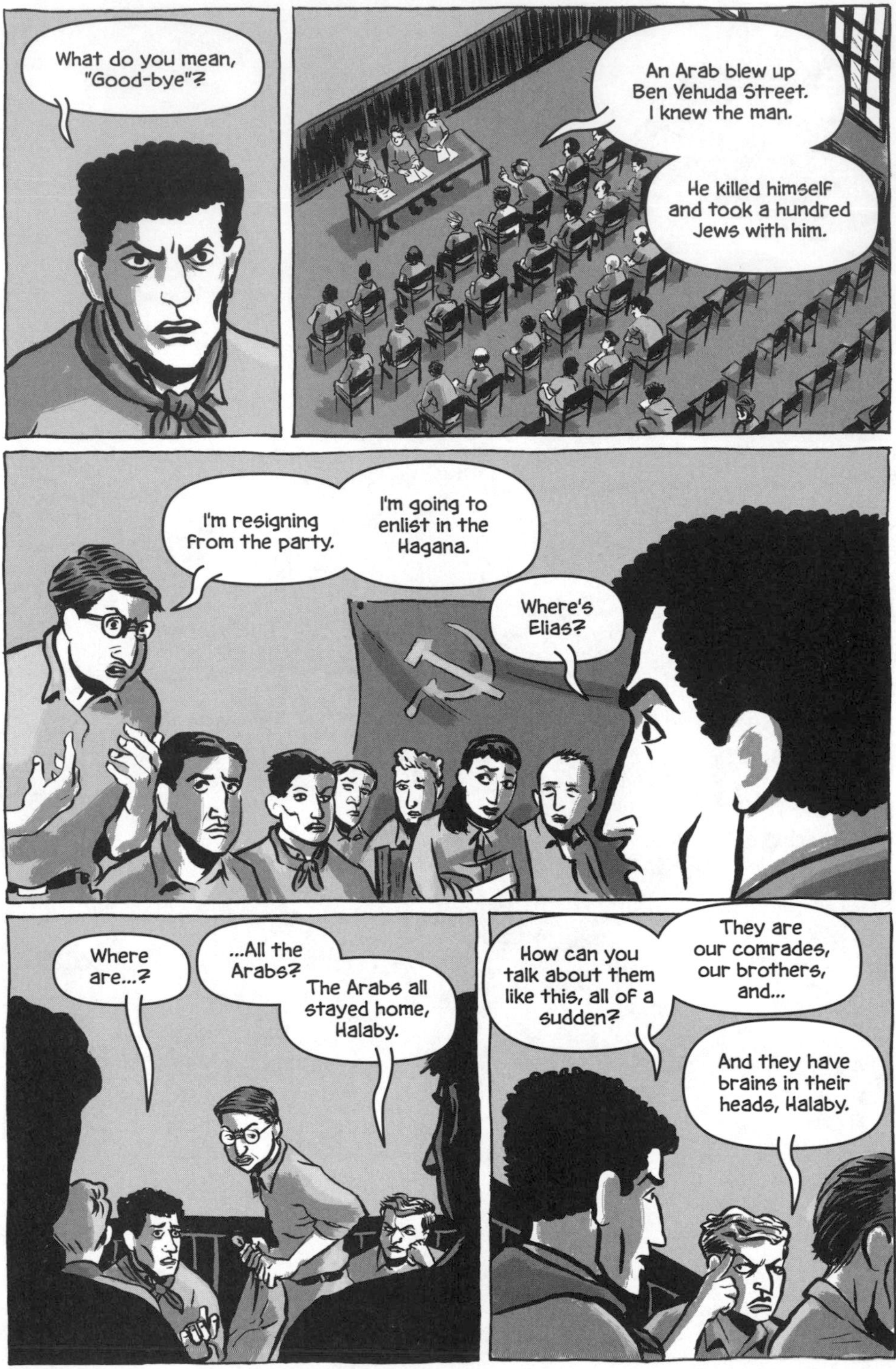
What do you mean, "Good-bye"?
An Arab blew up Ben Yehuda Street. I knew the man.
He killed himself and took a hundred Jews with him.
I'm resigning from the party.
I'm going to enlist in the Hagana.
Where's Elias?
Where are...?
...All the Arabs?
The Arabs all stayed home, Halaby.
How can you talk about them like this, all of a sudden?
They are our comrades, our brothers, and...
And they have brains in their heads, Halaby.

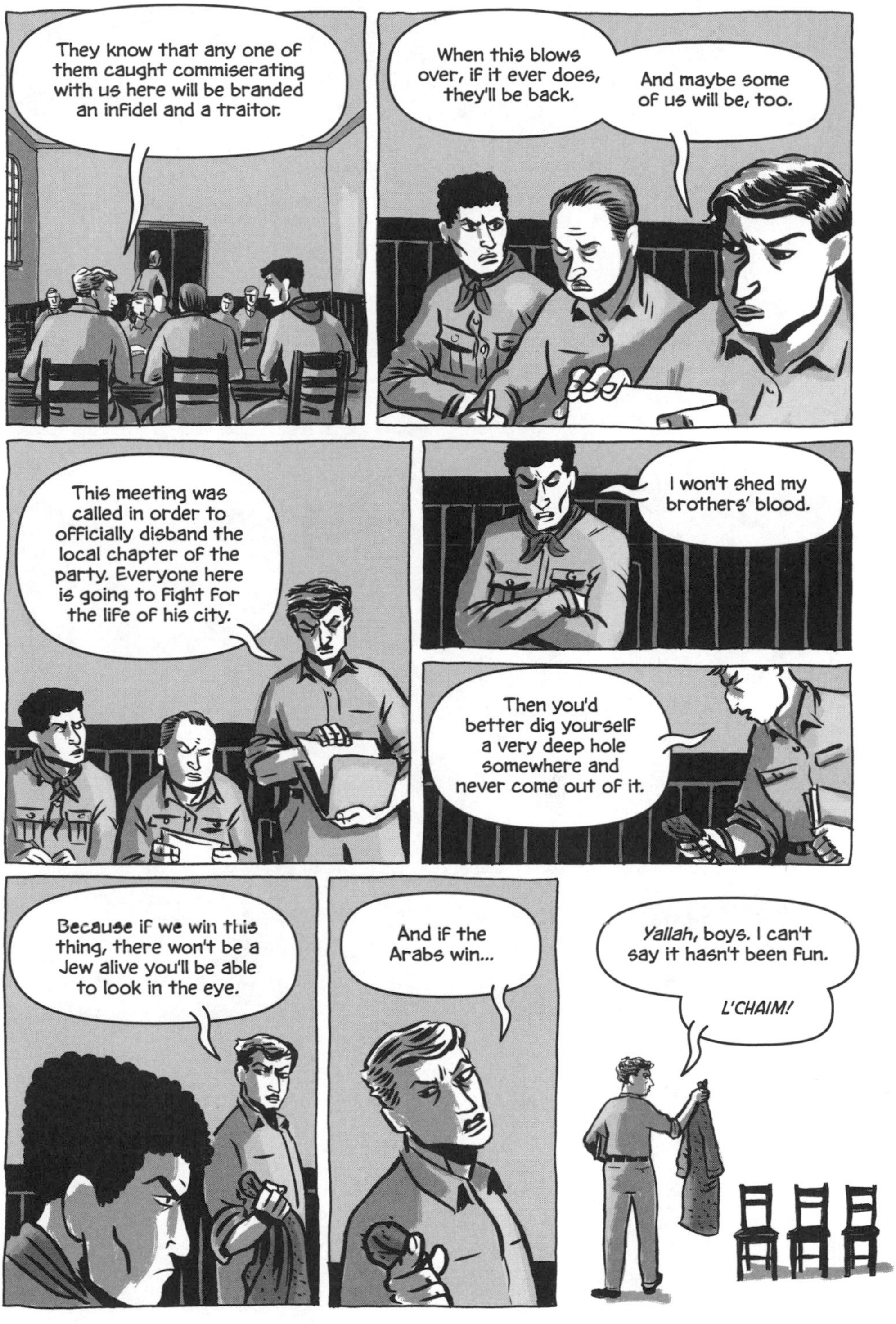
They know that any one of them caught commiserating with us here will be branded an infidel and a traitor.
When this blows over, if it ever does, they'll be back.
And maybe some of us will be, too.
This meeting was called in order to officially disband the local chapter of the party. Everyone here is going to fight for the life of his city.
I won't shed my brothers' blood.
Then you'd better dig yourself a very deep hole somewhere and never come out of it.
Because if we win this thing, there won't be a Jew alive you'll be able to look in the eye.
And if the Arabs win...
*Yallah*, boys. I can't say it hasn't been fun.
*L'CHAIM!*

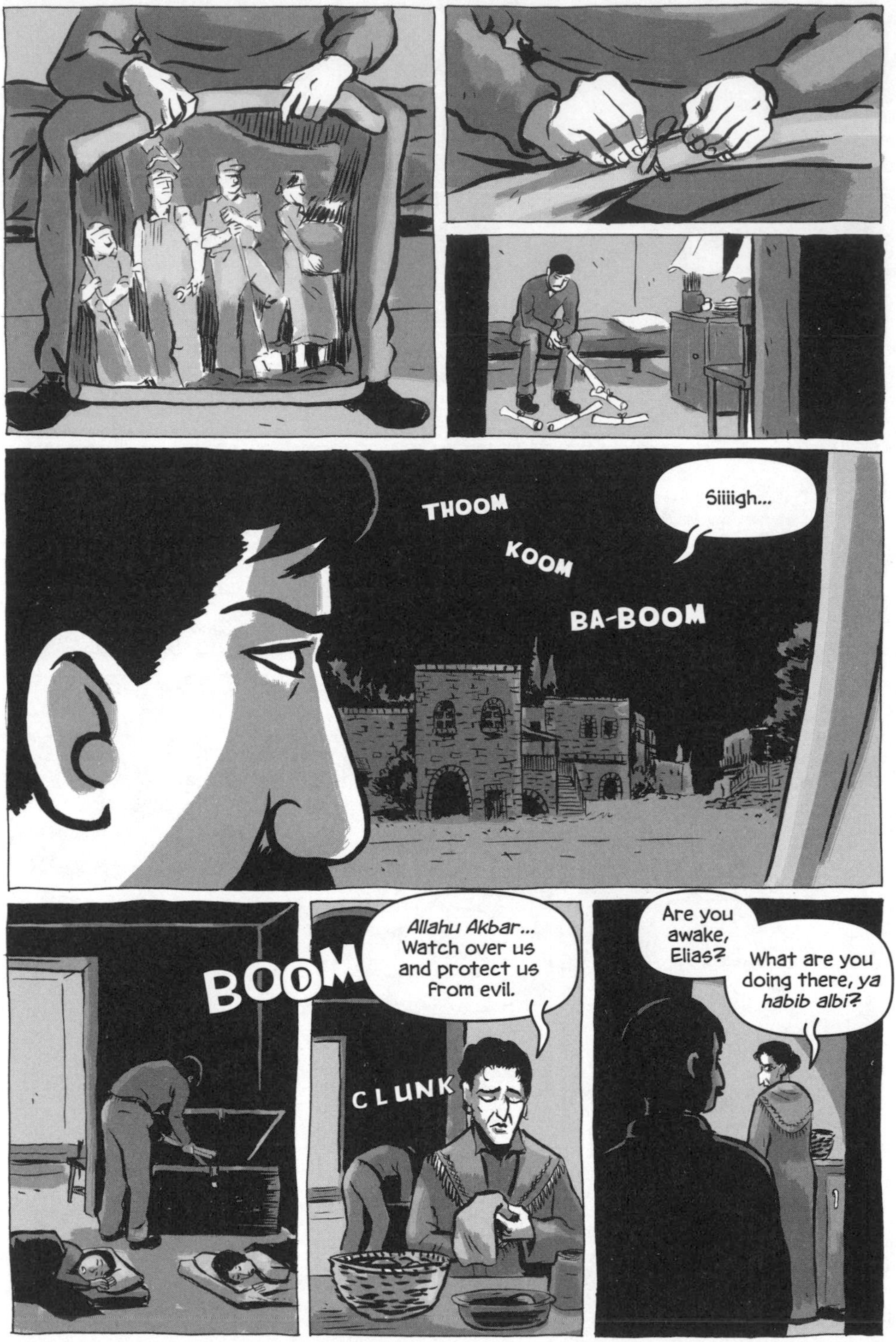
THOOM
KOOM
BA-BOOM
Siiiigh...
BOOM
Allahu Akbar... Watch over us and protect us from evil.
CLUNK
Are you awake, Elias?
What are you doing there, ya habib albi?

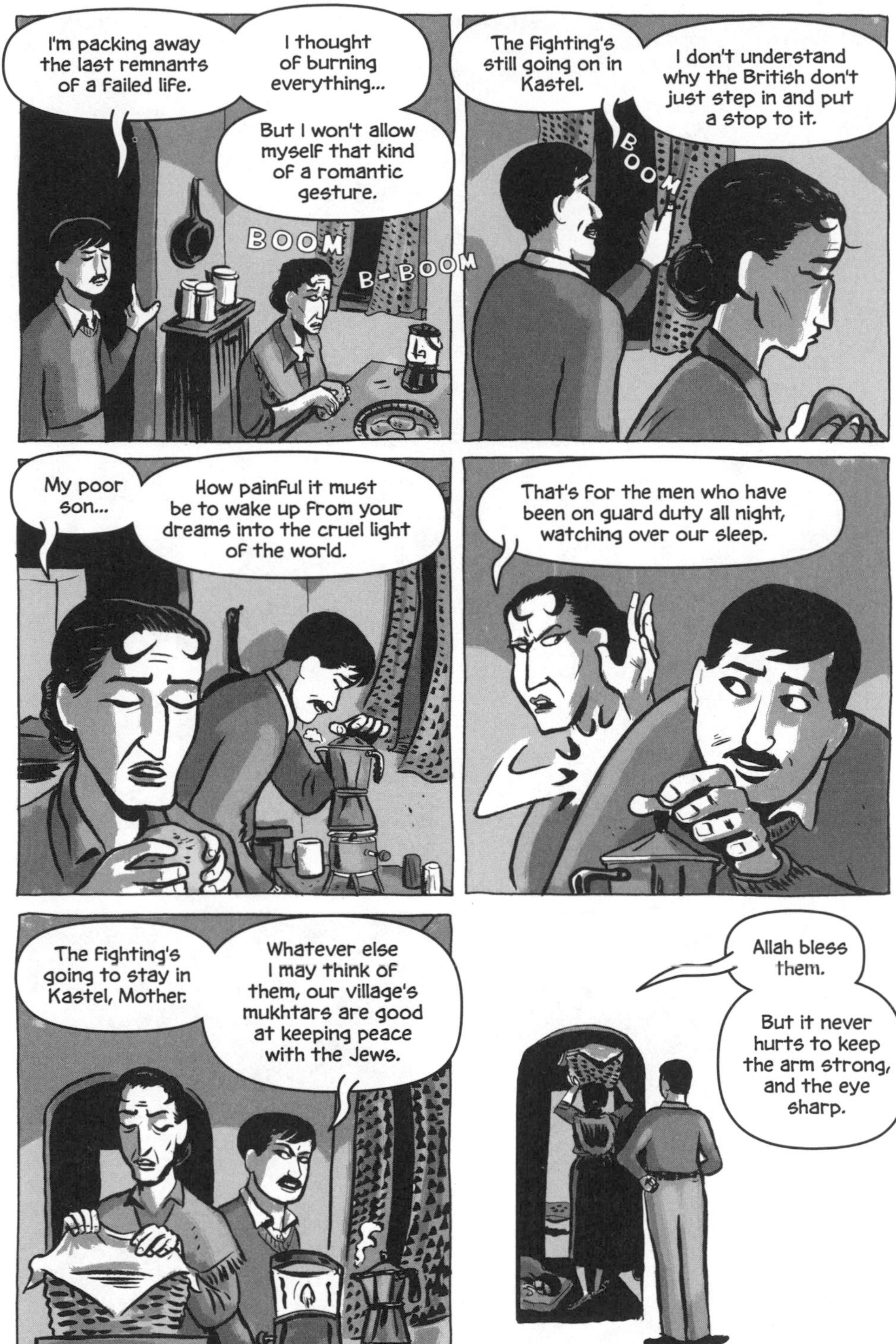
I'm packing away the last remnants of a failed life.
I thought of burning everything...
But I won't allow myself that kind of a romantic gesture.
BOOM
B-BOOM
The fighting's still going on in Kastel.
I don't understand why the British don't just step in and put a stop to it.
BOOM
My poor son...
How painful it must be to wake up from your dreams into the cruel light of the world.
That's for the men who have been on guard duty all night, watching over our sleep.
The fighting's going to stay in Kastel, Mother.
Whatever else I may think of them, our village's mukhtars are good at keeping peace with the Jews.
Allah bless them.
But it never hurts to keep the arm strong, and the eye sharp.

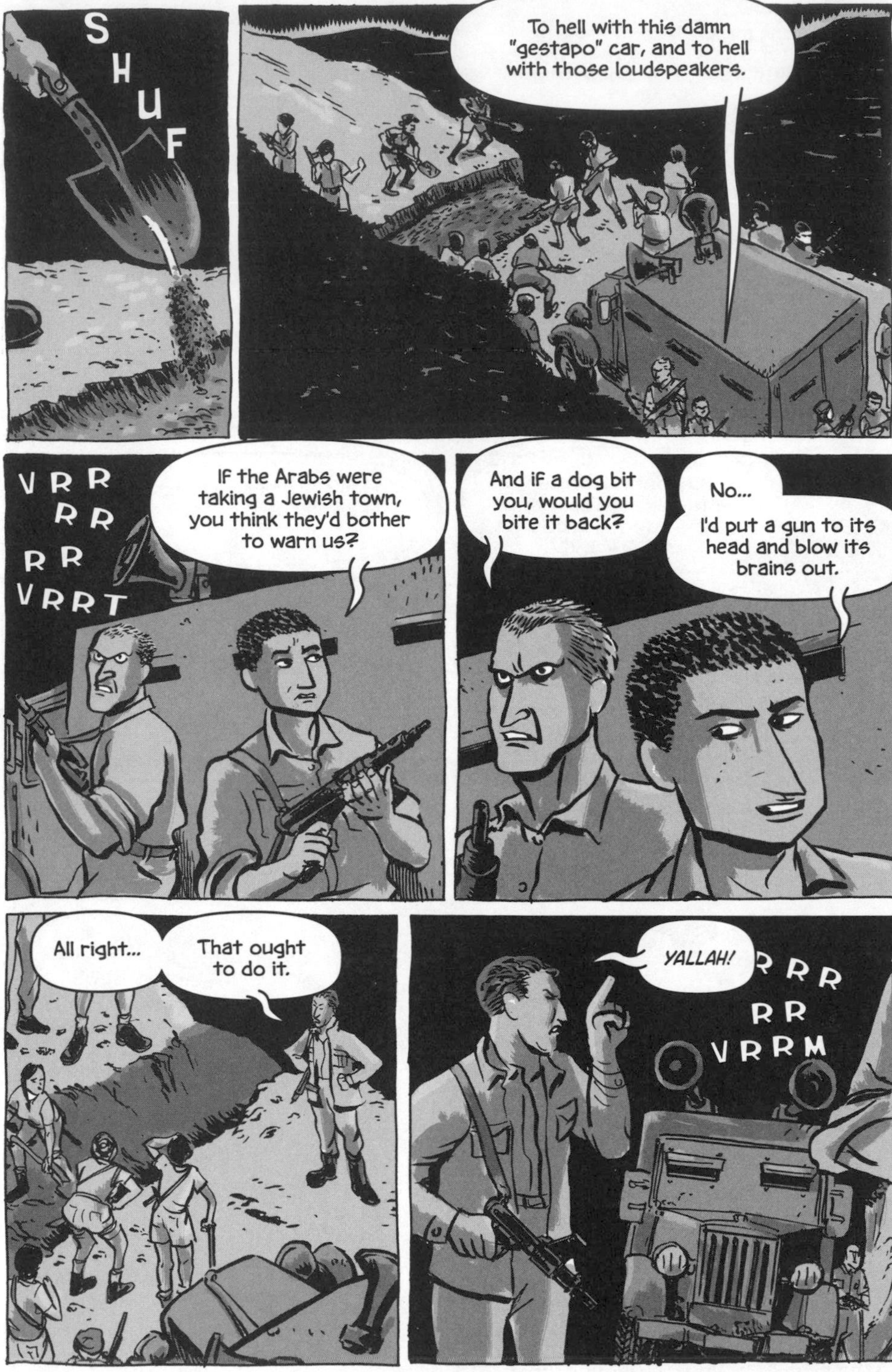
SHUF
To hell with this damn "gestapo" car, and to hell with those loudspeakers.
VRR RR RR VRRT
If the Arabs were taking a Jewish town, you think they'd bother to warn us?
And if a dog bit you, would you bite it back?
No...
I'd put a gun to its head and blow its brains out.
All right...
That ought to do it.
YALLAH!
RRR RR VRRM

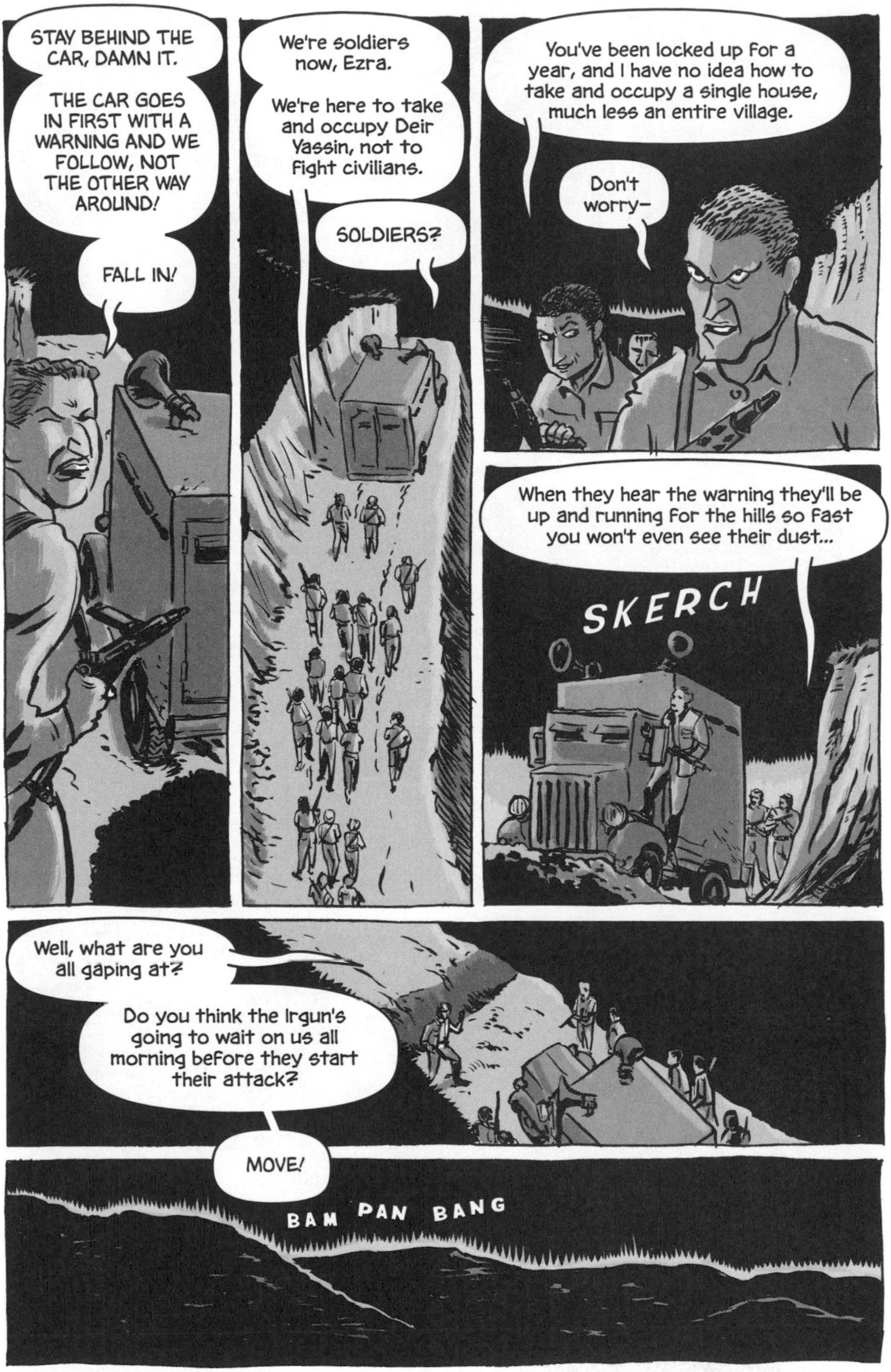
STAY BEHIND THE CAR, DAMN IT.
THE CAR GOES IN FIRST WITH A WARNING AND WE FOLLOW, NOT THE OTHER WAY AROUND!
FALL IN!
We're soldiers now, Ezra.
We're here to take and occupy Deir Yassin, not to fight civilians.
SOLDIERS?
You've been locked up for a year, and I have no idea how to take and occupy a single house, much less an entire village.
Don't worry–
When they hear the warning they'll be up and running for the hills so fast you won't even see their dust...
SKERCH
Well, what are you all gaping at?
Do you think the Irgun's going to wait on us all morning before they start their attack?
MOVE!
BAM PAN BANG

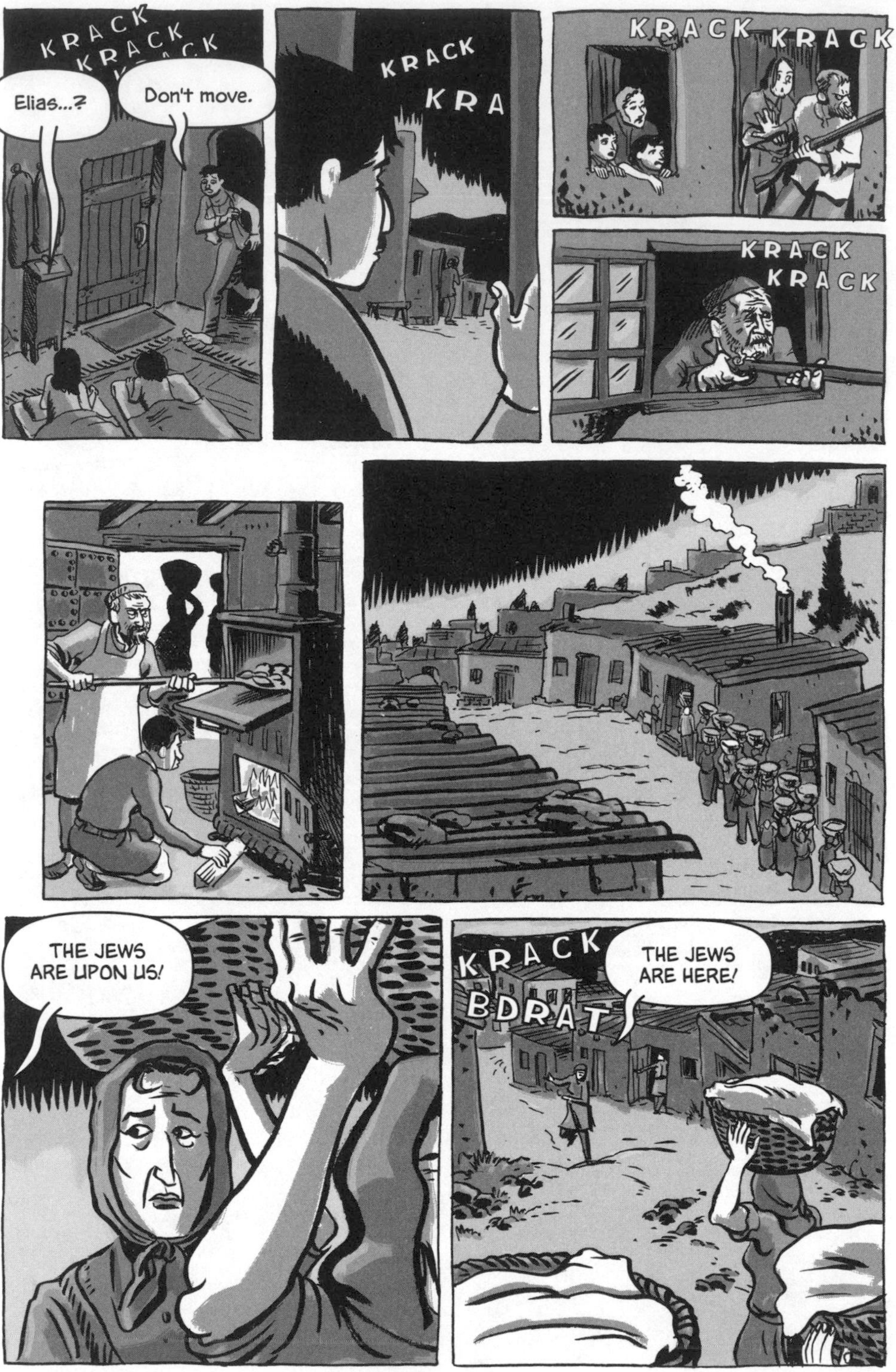
KRACK
KRACK
Elias...?
Don't move.
KRACK
KRA
KRACK KRACK
KRACK
KRACK
THE JEWS ARE UPON US!
KRACK
BDRAT
THE JEWS ARE HERE!

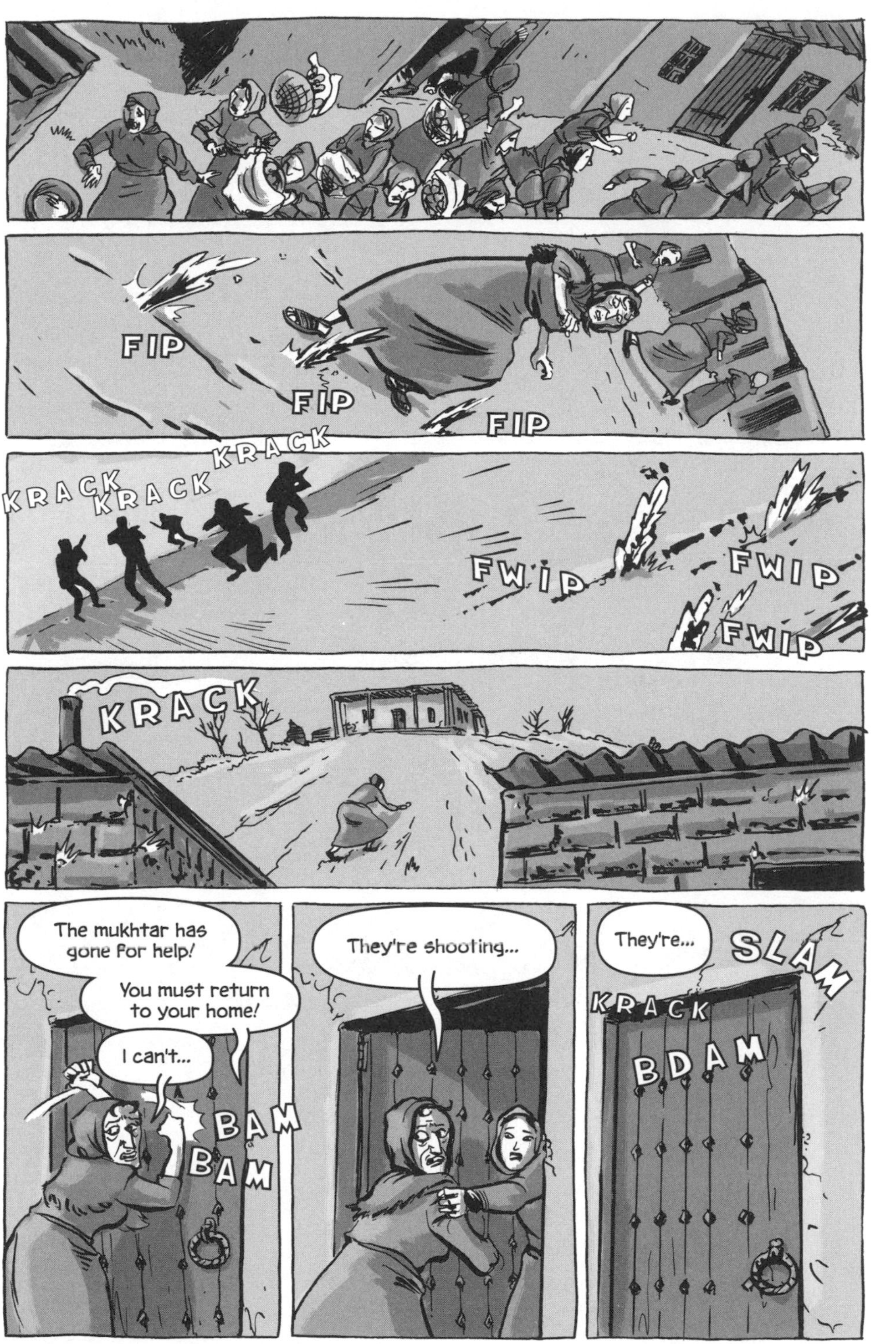
FIP
FIP
FIP
KRACK
KRACK
KRACK
FWIP
FWIP
FWIP
KRACK
The mukhtar has gone for help!
You must return to your home!
I can't...
BAM
BAM
They're shooting...
They're...
SLAM
KRACK
BDAM

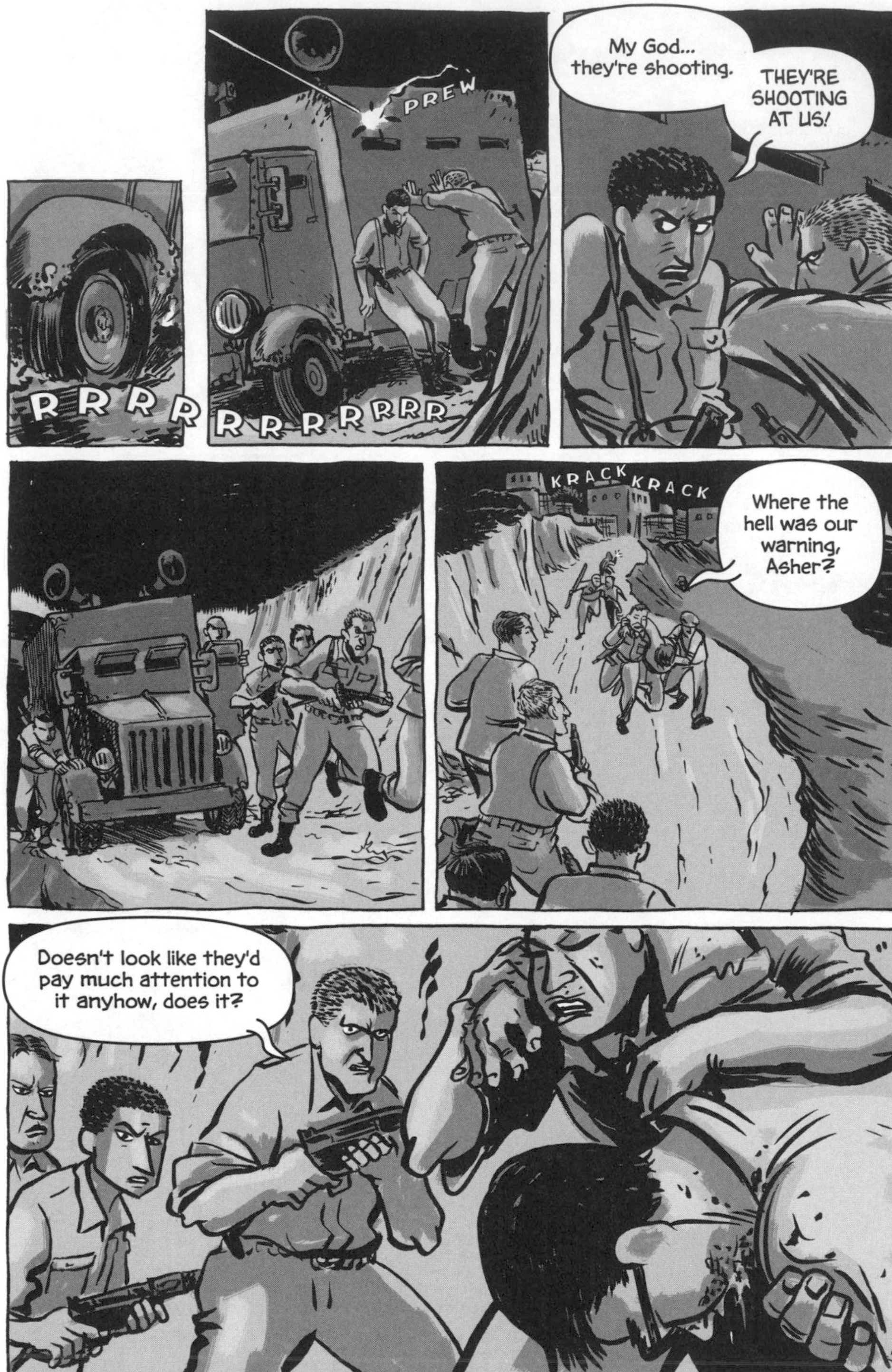
PREW
R R R R R R R R RRR
My God... they're shooting.
THEY'RE SHOOTING AT US!
KRACK KRACK
Where the hell was our warning, Asher?
Doesn't look like they'd pay much attention to it anyhow, does it?

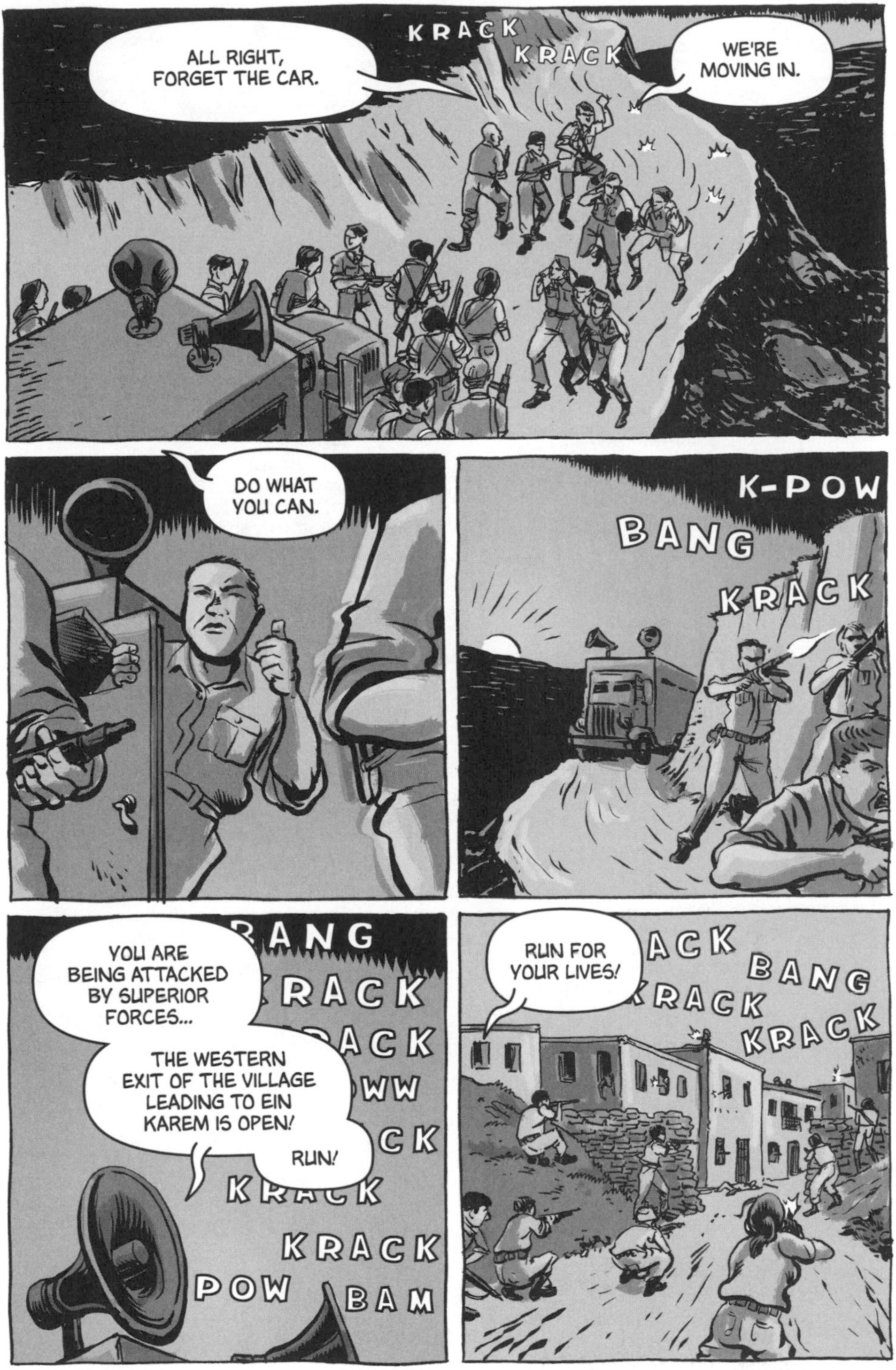
KRACK
KRACK
ALL RIGHT, FORGET THE CAR.
WE'RE MOVING IN.
DO WHAT YOU CAN.
K-POW
BANG
KRACK
BANG
YOU ARE BEING ATTACKED BY SUPERIOR FORCES...
THE WESTERN EXIT OF THE VILLAGE LEADING TO EIN KAREM IS OPEN!
RUN!
KRACK
KRACK
POW
BAM
RUN FOR YOUR LIVES!
ACK
BANG
KRACK
KRACK

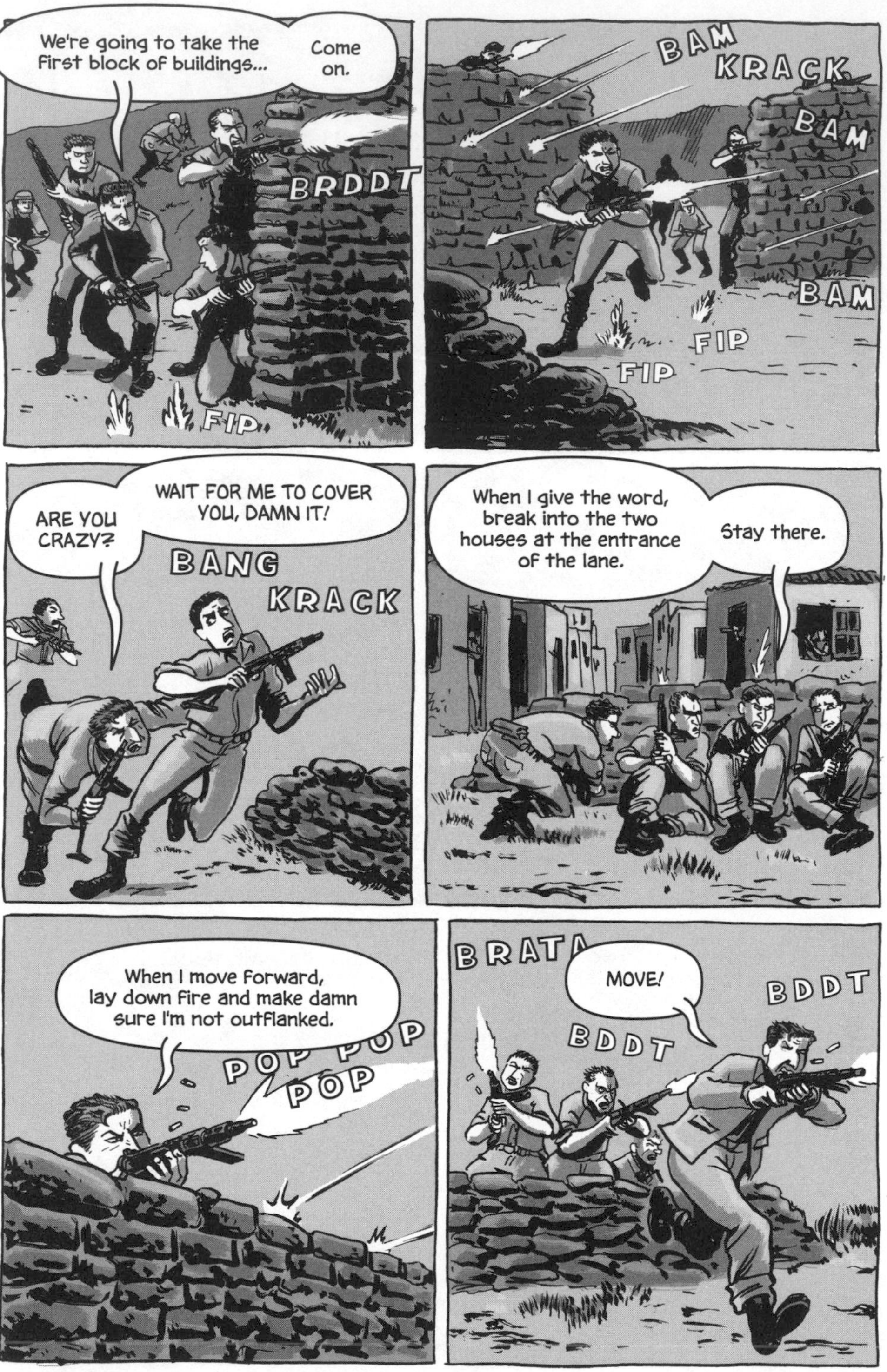
We're going to take the first block of buildings...
Come on.
BRDDT
FIP
BAM
KRACK
BAM
BAM
FIP
FIP
ARE YOU CRAZY?
WAIT FOR ME TO COVER YOU, DAMN IT!
BANG
KRACK
When I give the word, break into the two houses at the entrance of the lane.
Stay there.
When I move forward, lay down fire and make damn sure I'm not outflanked.
POP POP POP
POP
BRATA
MOVE!
BDDT
BDDT

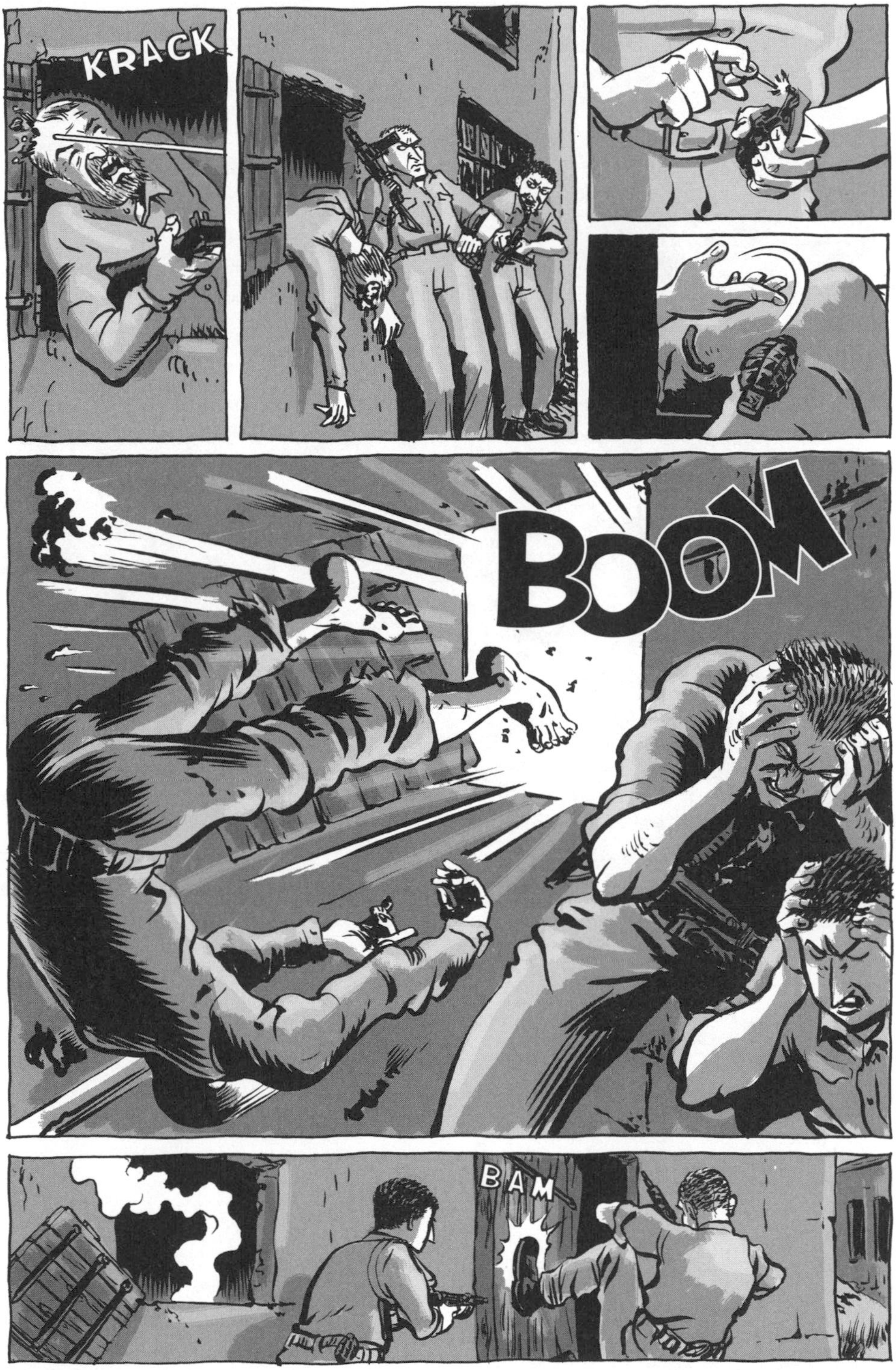
KRACK
BOOM
BAM

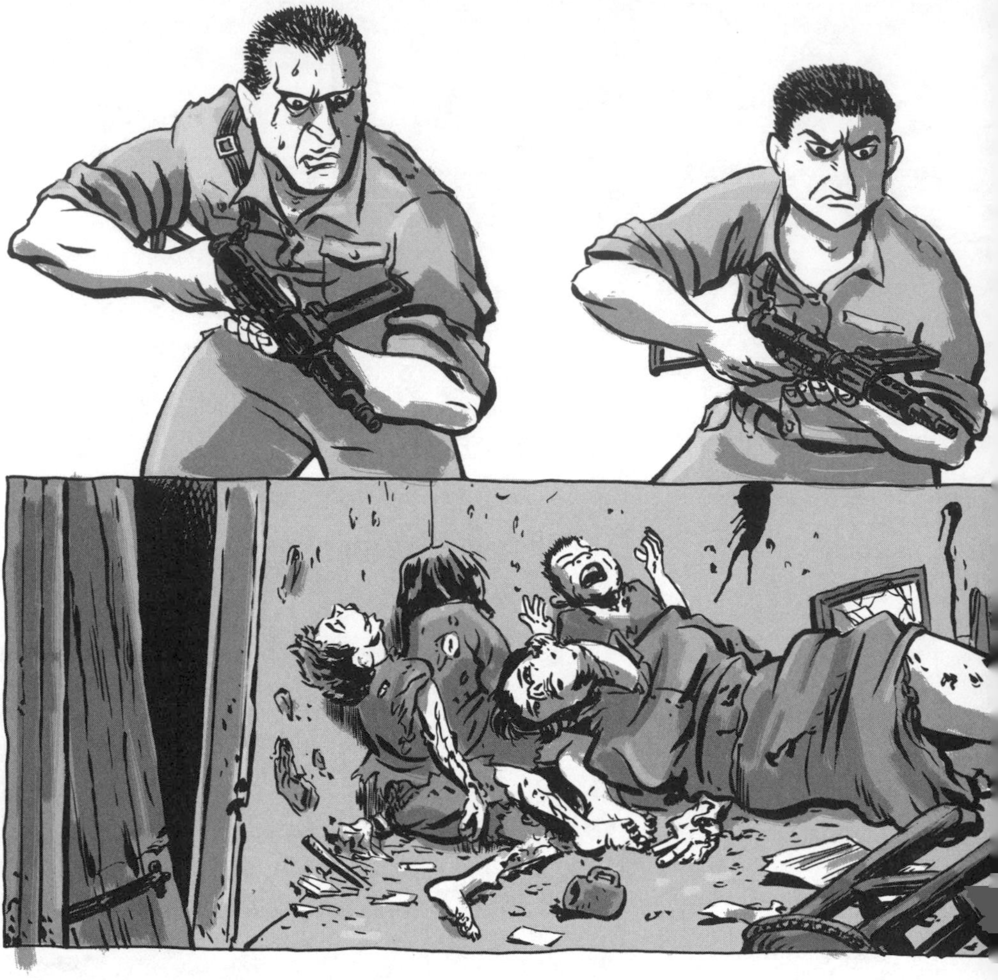

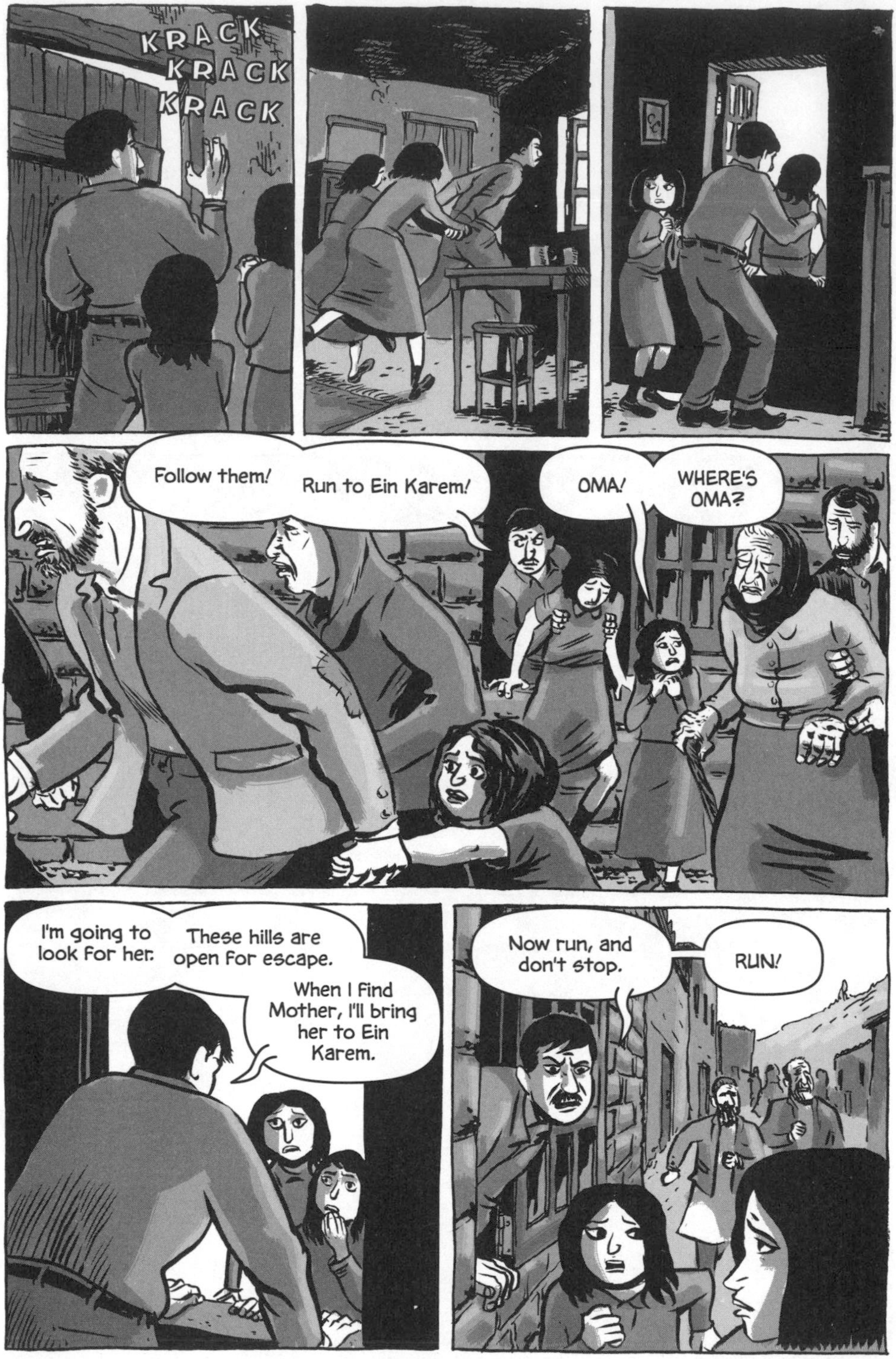
KRACK
KRACK
KRACK
Follow them!
Run to Ein Karem!
OMA!
WHERE'S OMA?
I'm going to look for her.
These hills are open for escape.
When I find Mother, I'll bring her to Ein Karem.
Now run, and don't stop.
RUN!

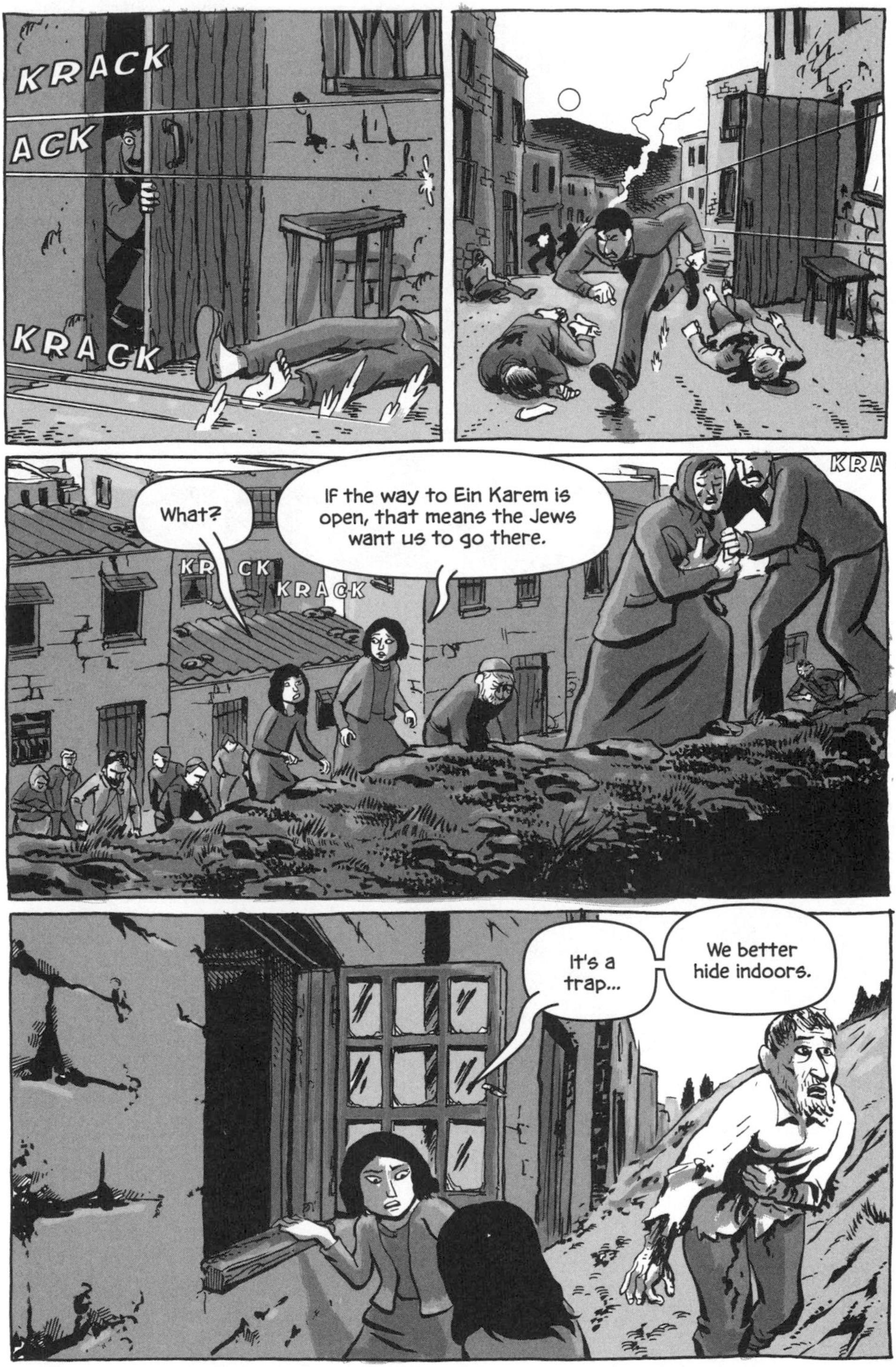
KRACK
ACK
KRACK
KRA
What?
KRACK
KRACK
If the way to Ein Karem is open, that means the Jews want us to go there.
It's a trap...
We better hide indoors.

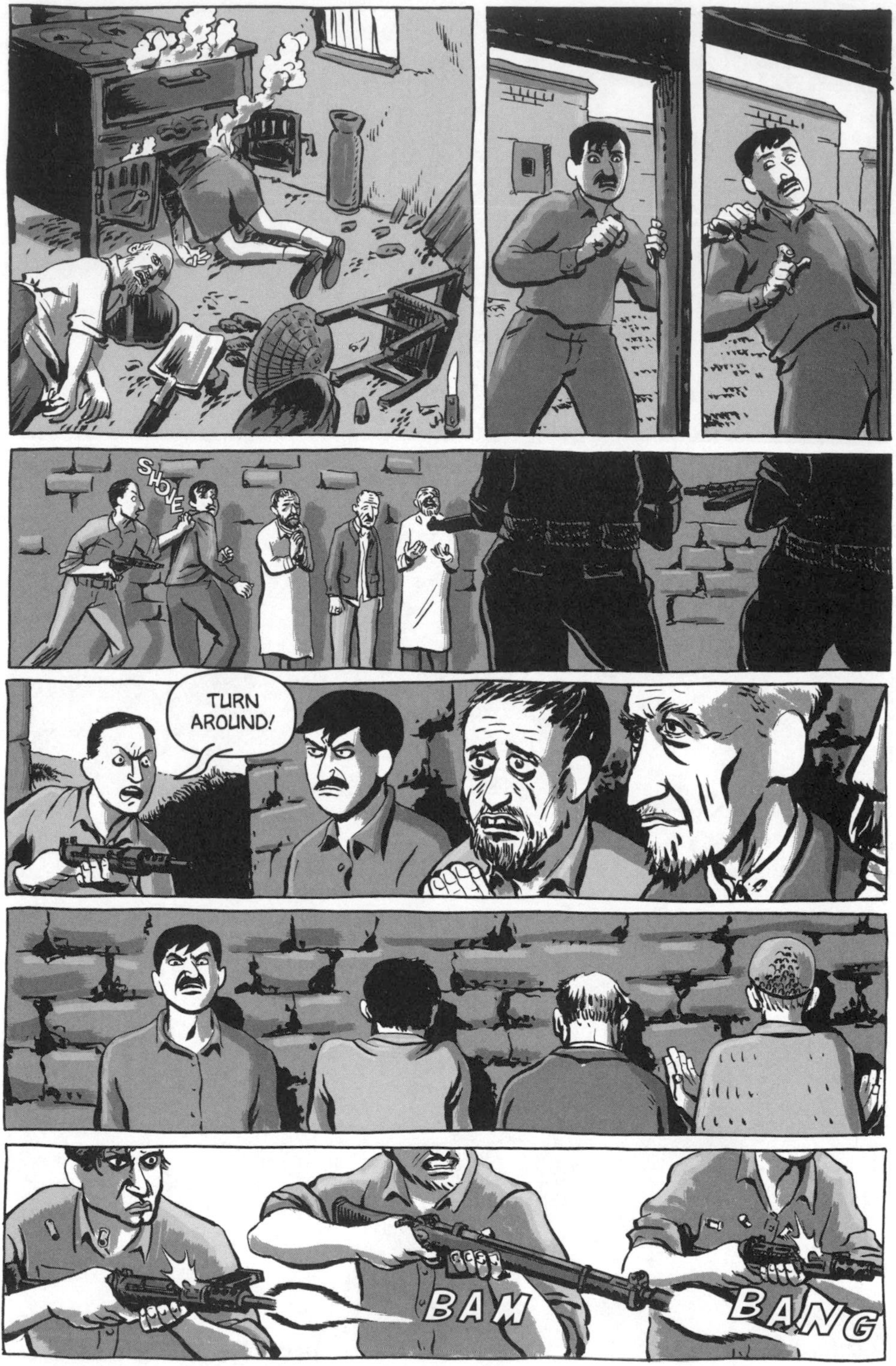
SHOVE
TURN AROUND!
BAM
BANG

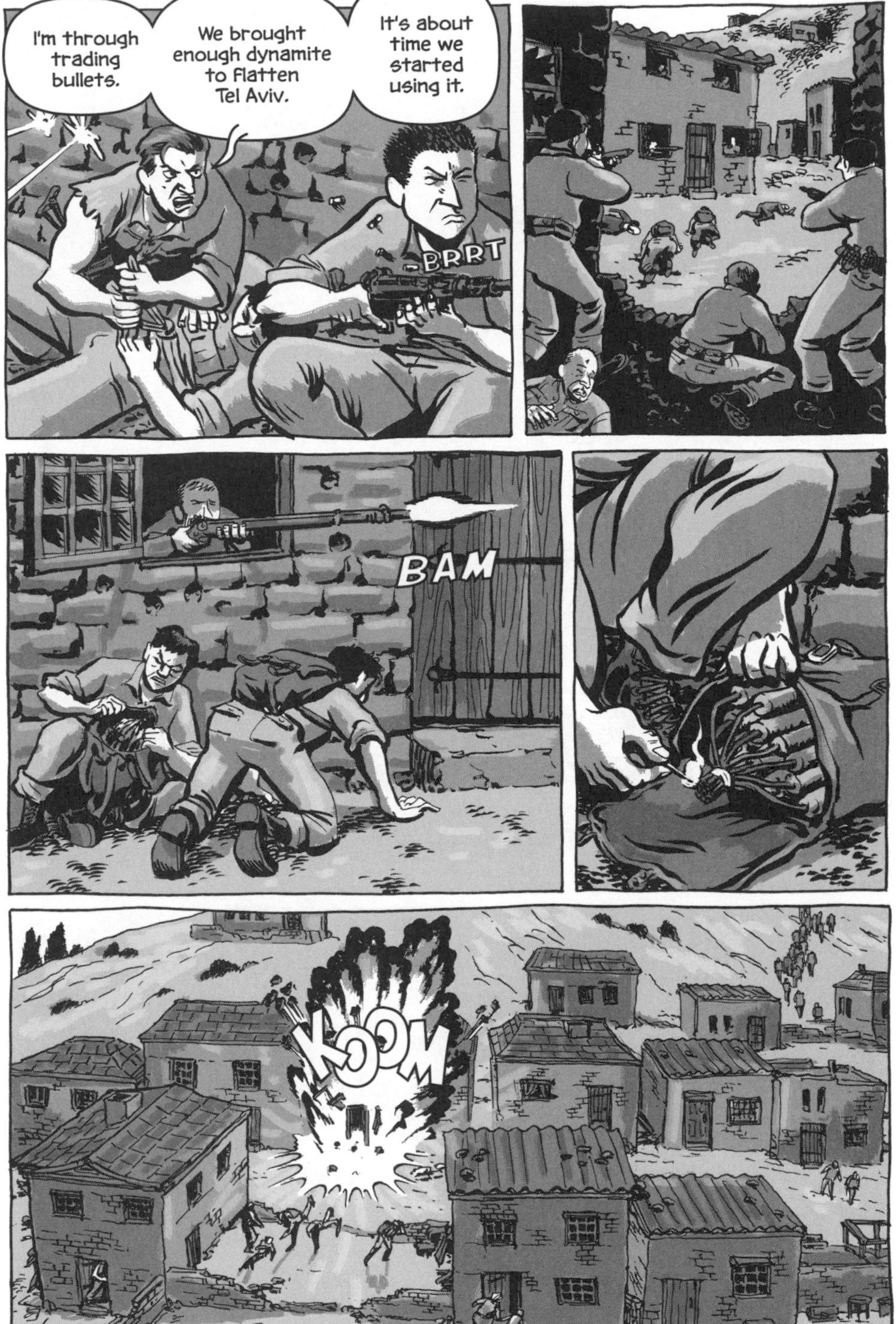
I'm through trading bullets.
We brought enough dynamite to flatten Tel Aviv.
It's about time we started using it.
BRRRT
BAM
KOOM

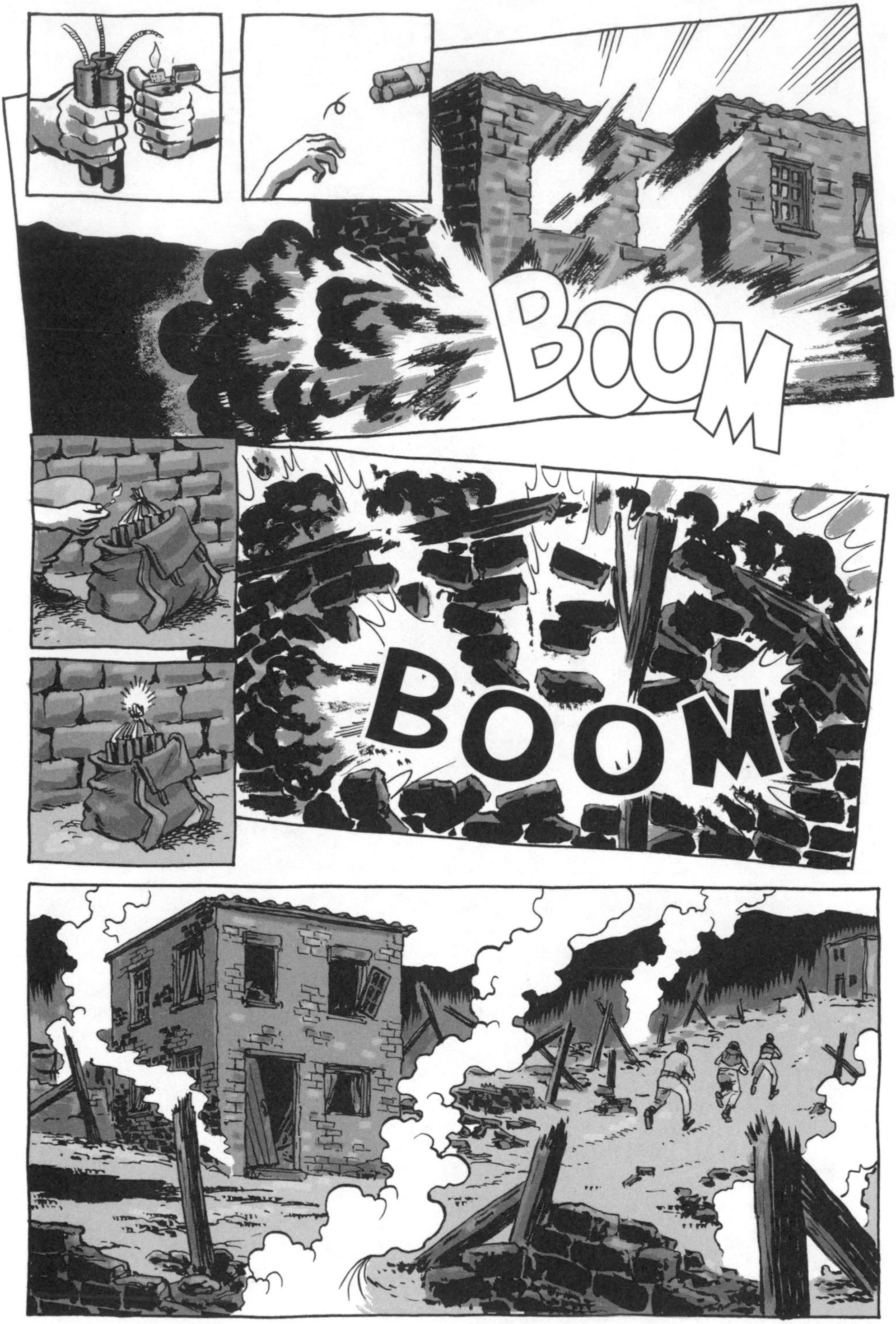

BOOM
BOOM

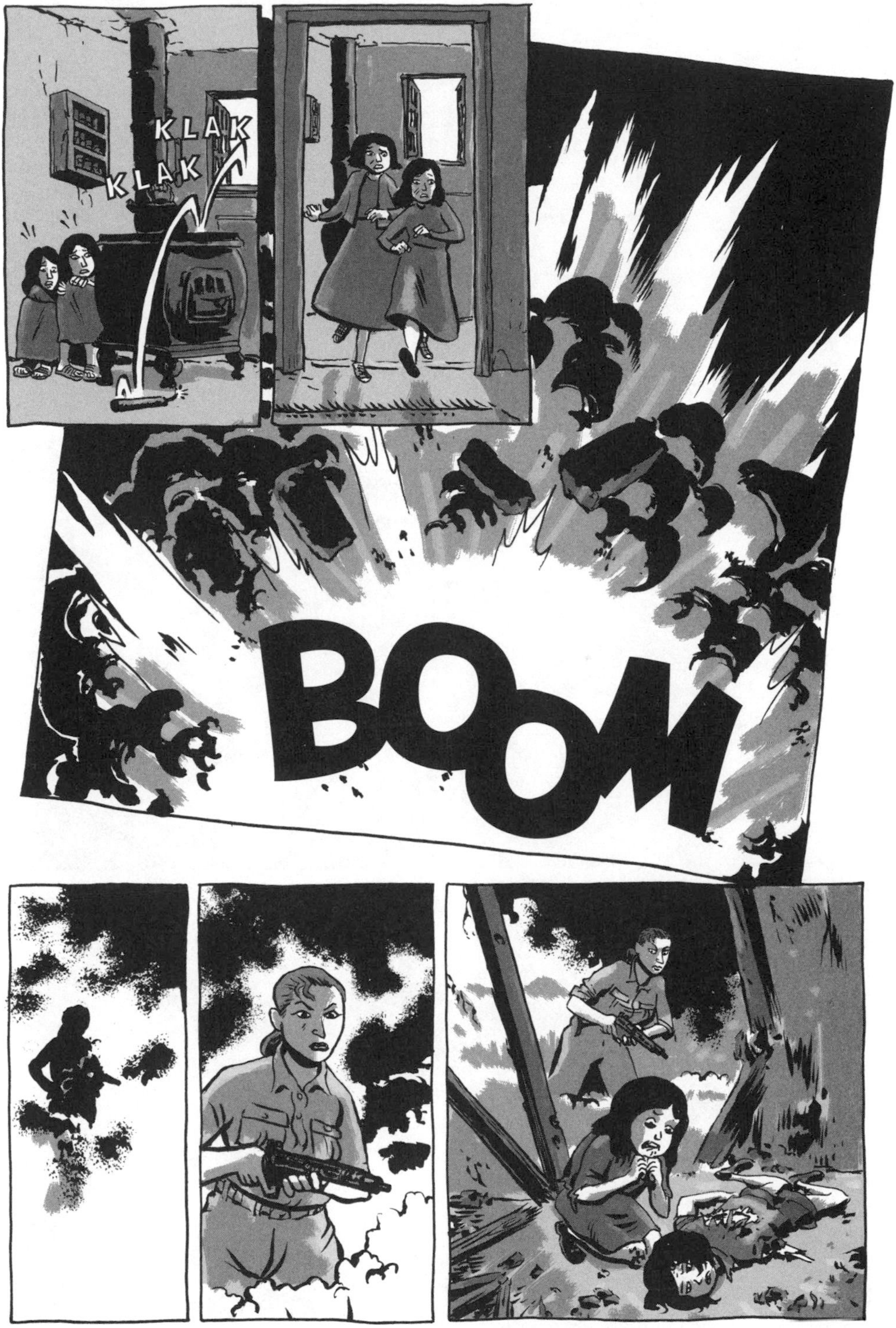
KLAK
KLAK
BOOM

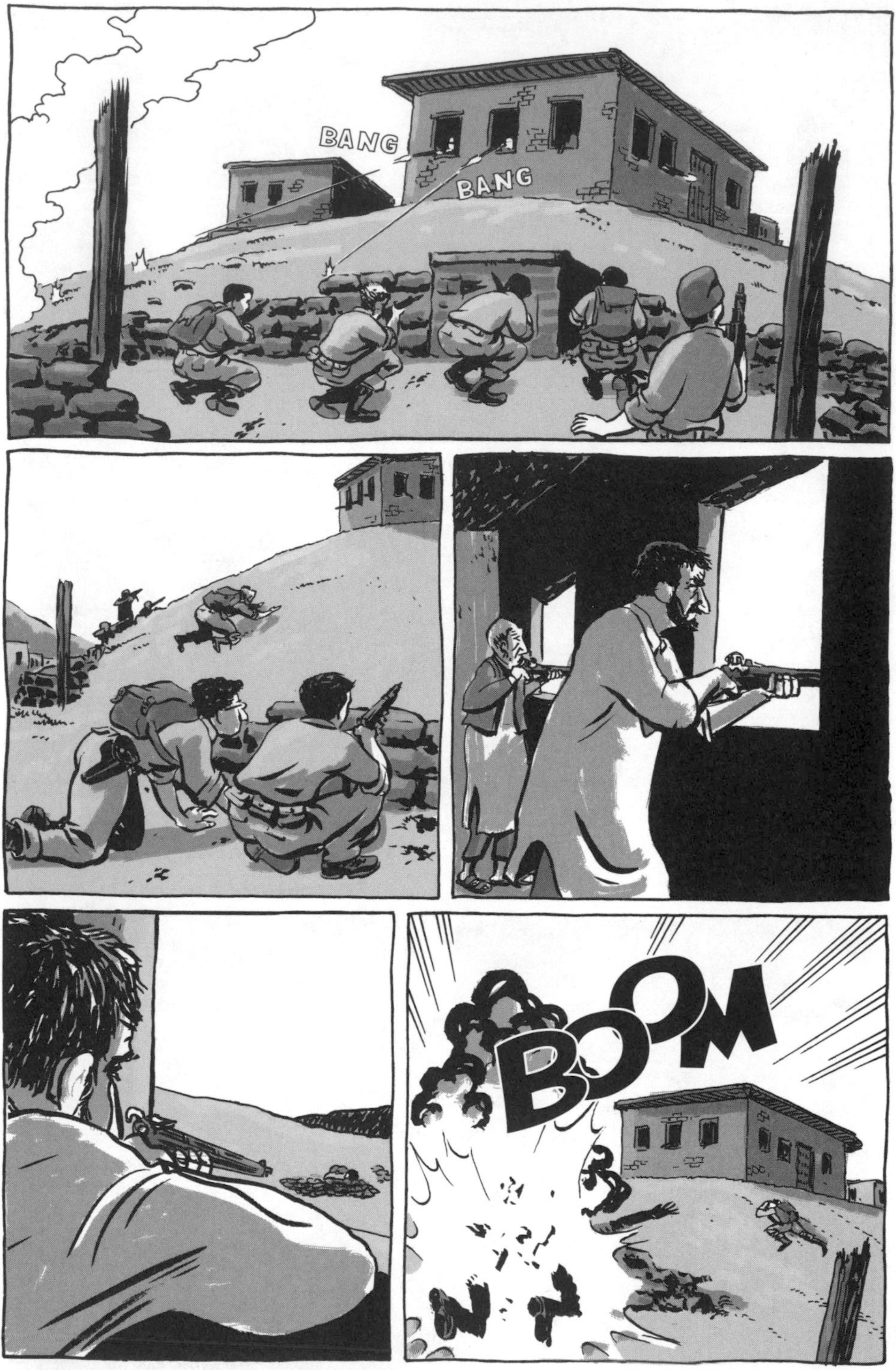
BANG
BANG
BOOM

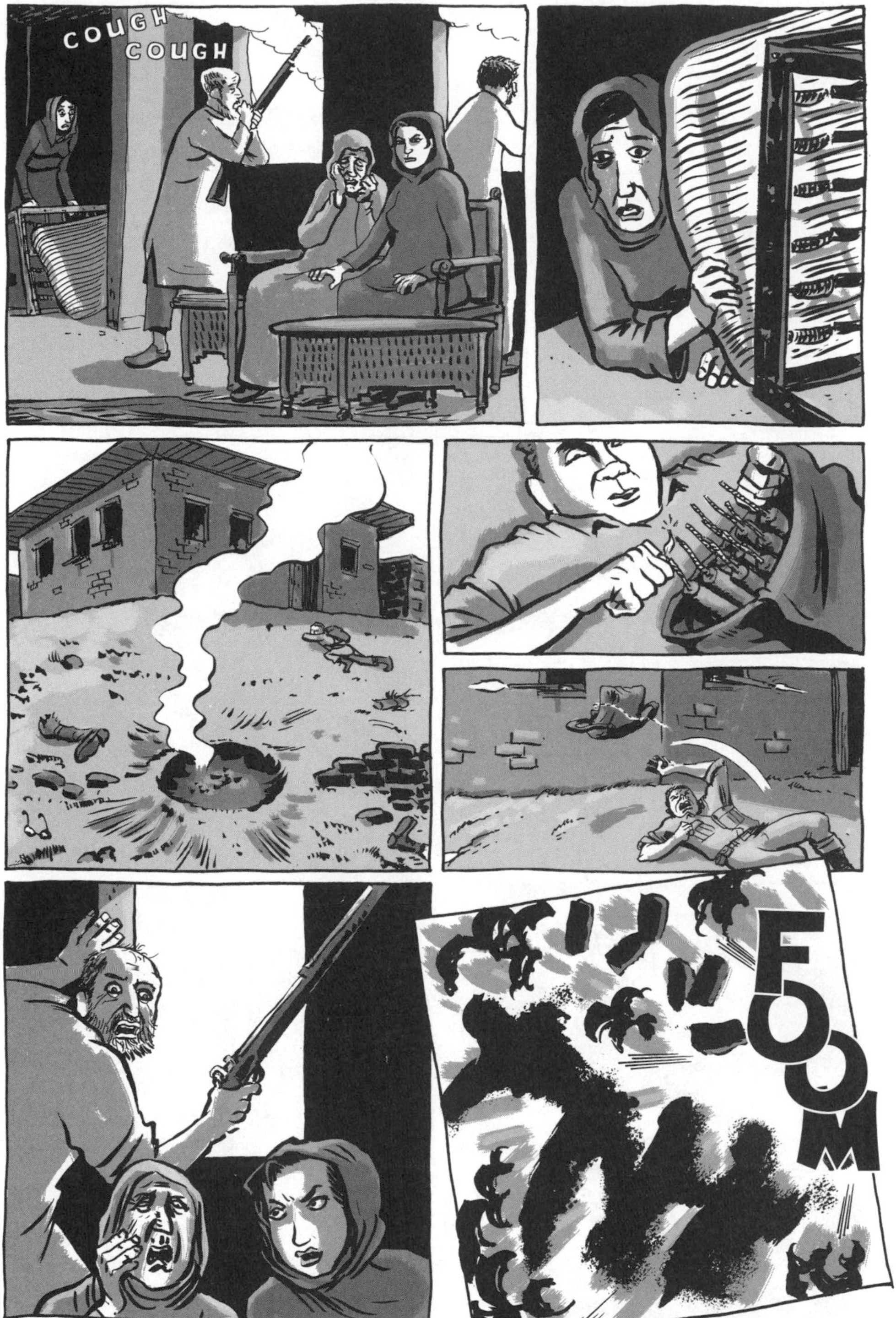
COUGH
COUGH
FOOM

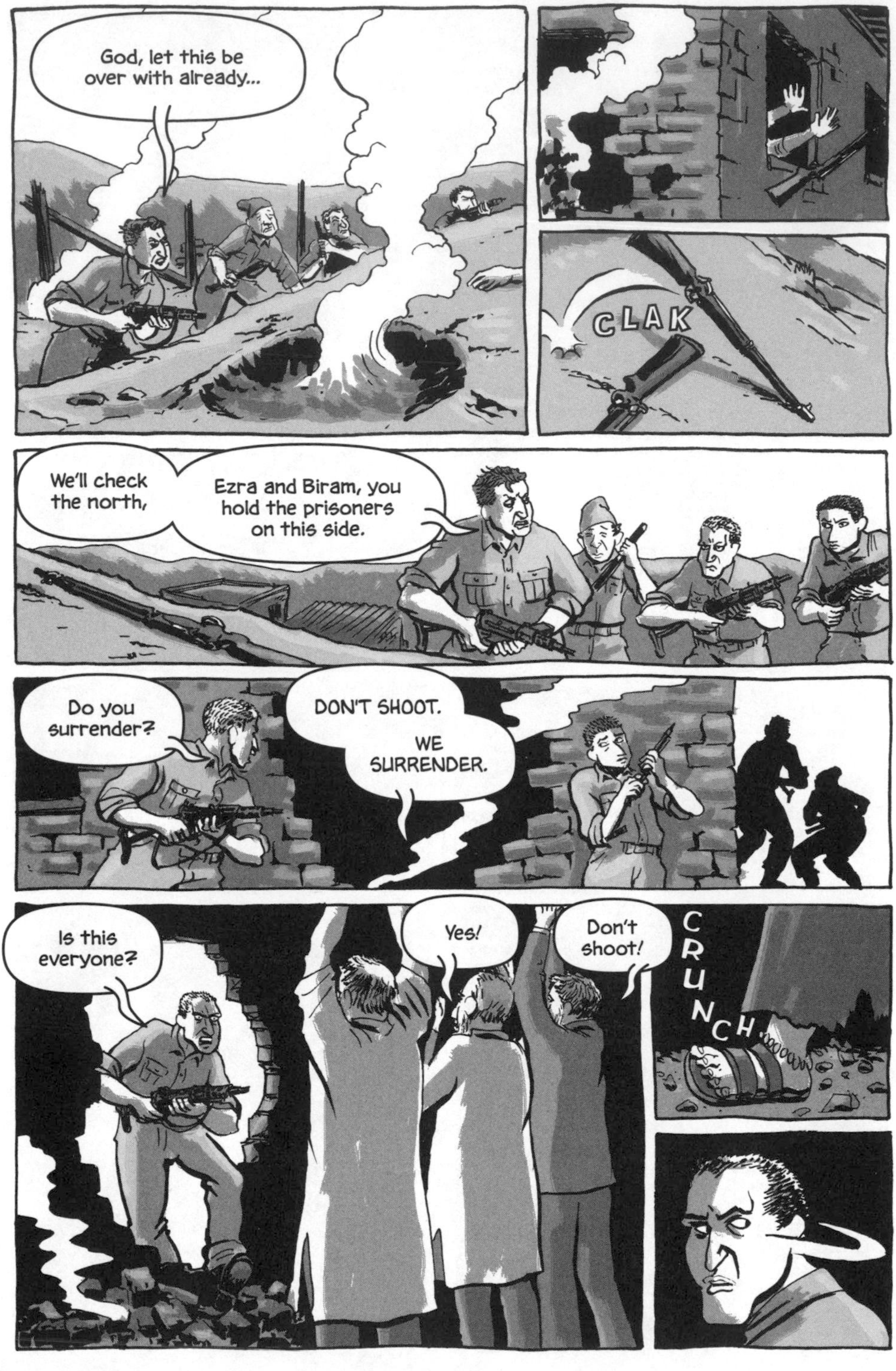
God, let this be over with already...
CLAK
We'll check the north,
Ezra and Biram, you hold the prisoners on this side.
Do you surrender?
DON'T SHOOT.
WE SURRENDER.
Is this everyone?
Yes!
Don't shoot!
CRUNCH

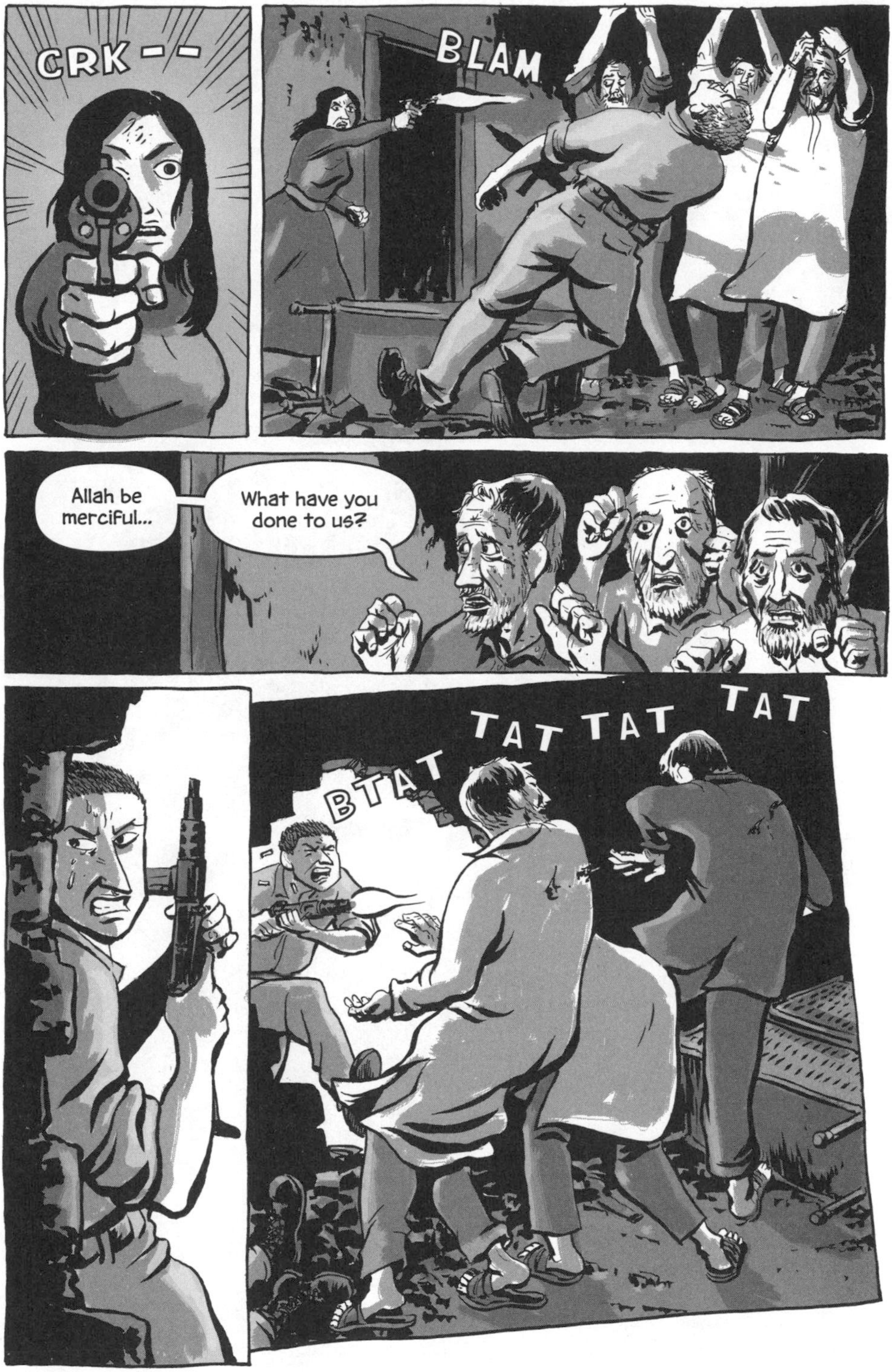
CRK--
BLAM
Allah be merciful...
What have you done to us?
BTAT TAT TAT TAT

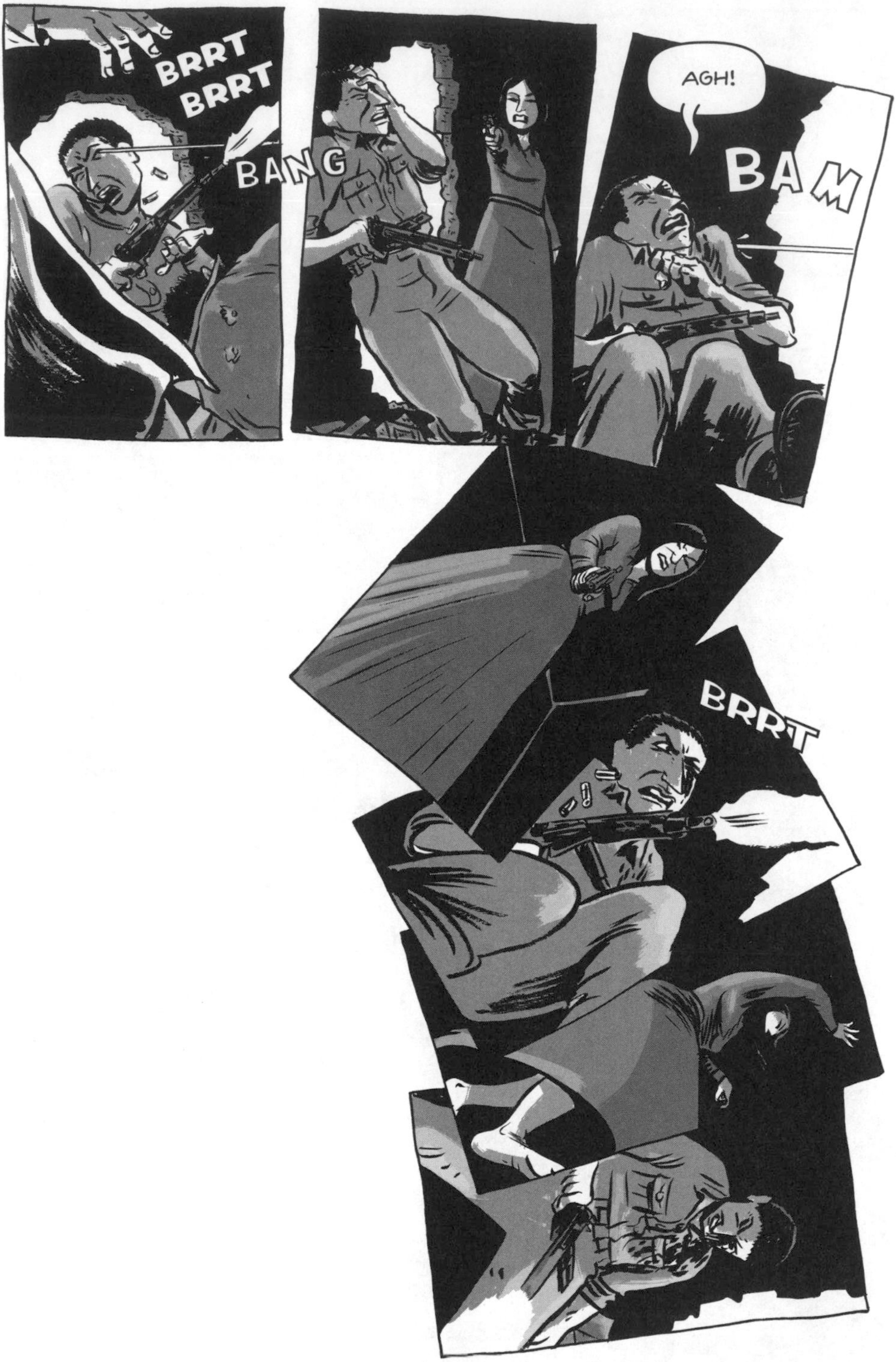
BRRT
BRRT
BANG
AGH!
BAM
BRRT

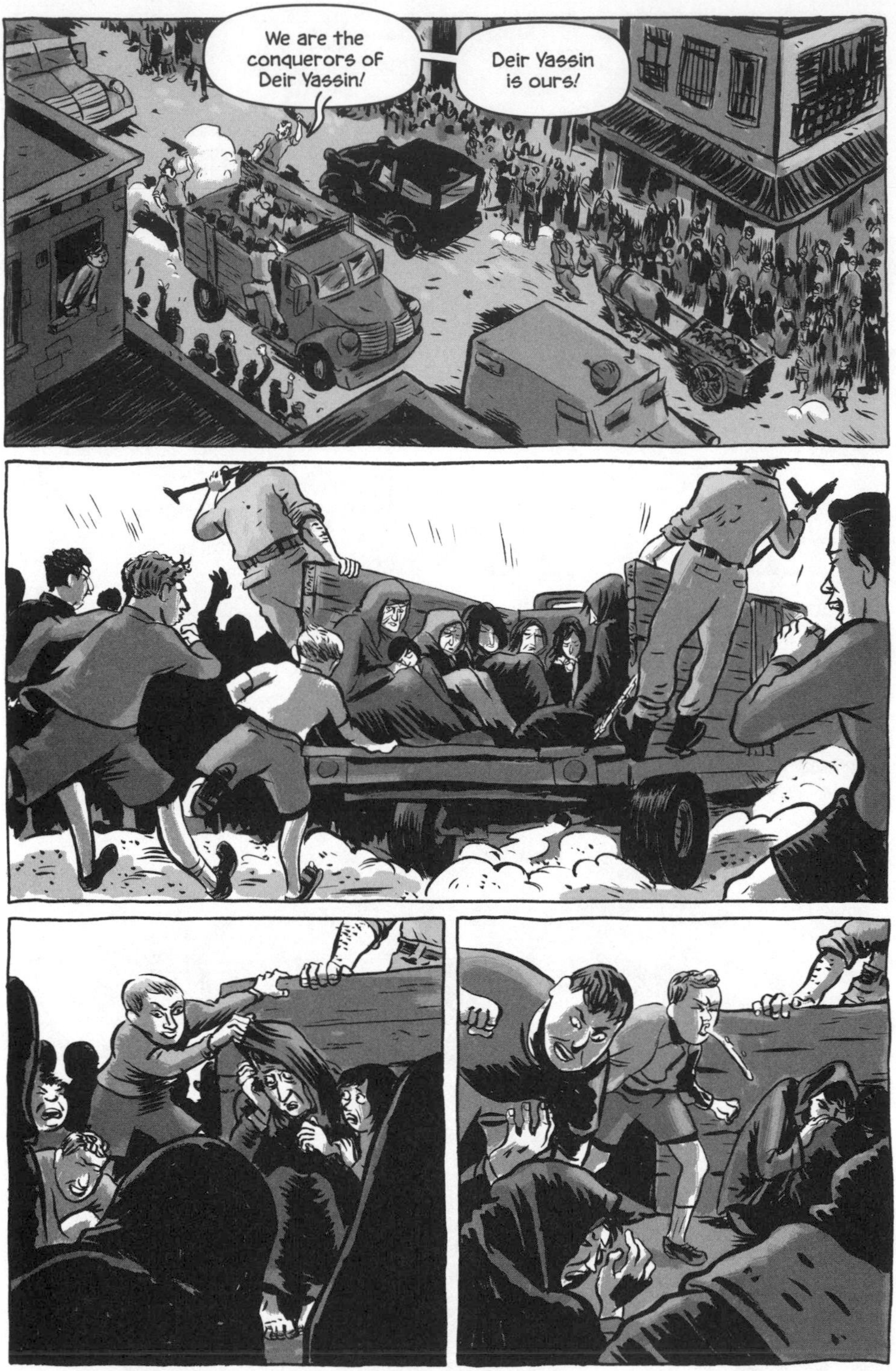
We are the conquerors of Deir Yassin!
Deir Yassin is ours!

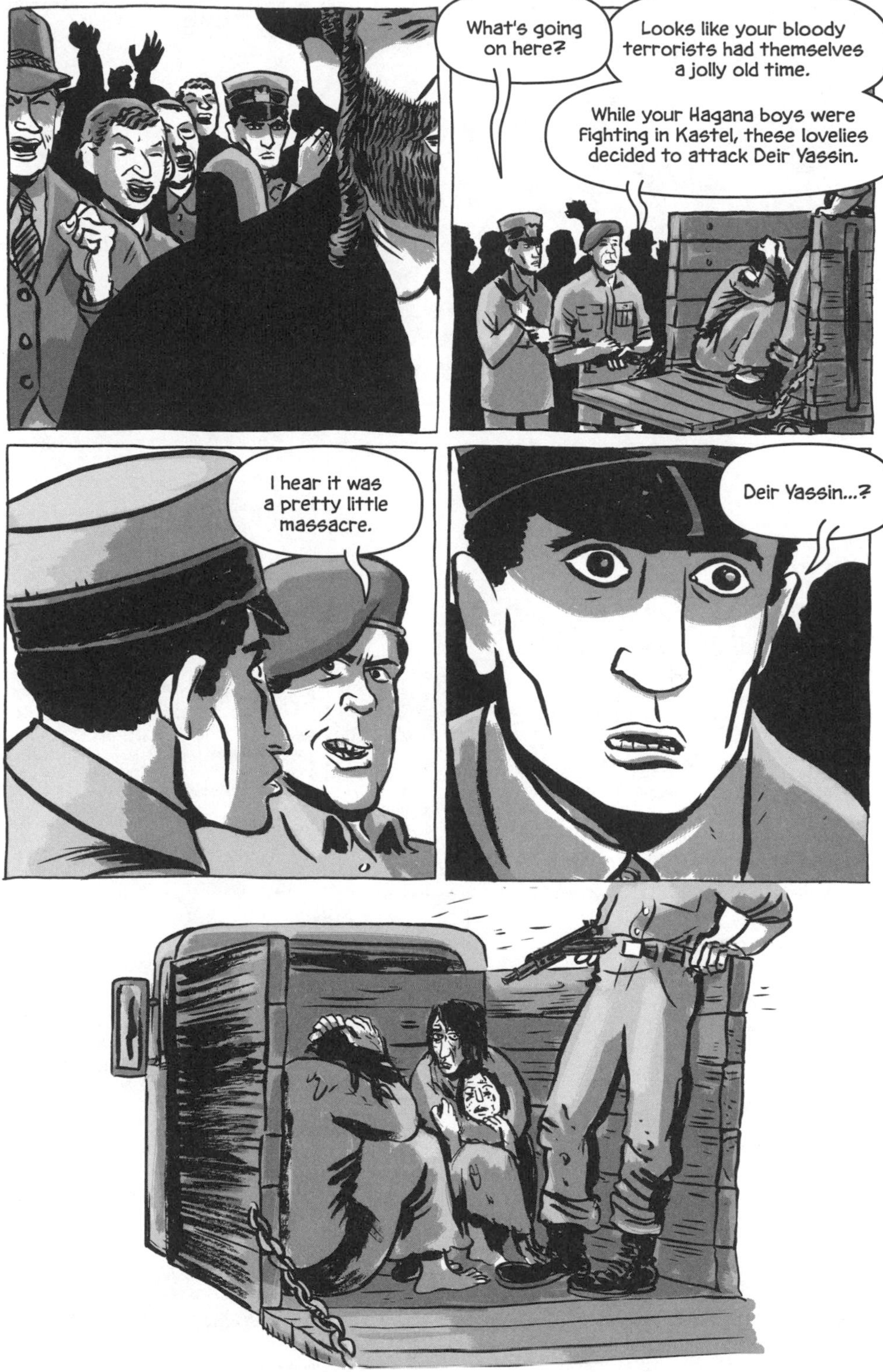
What's going on here?
Looks like your bloody terrorists had themselves a jolly old time.
While your Hagana boys were fighting in Kastel, these lovelies decided to attack Deir Yassin.
I hear it was a pretty little massacre.
Deir Yassin...?

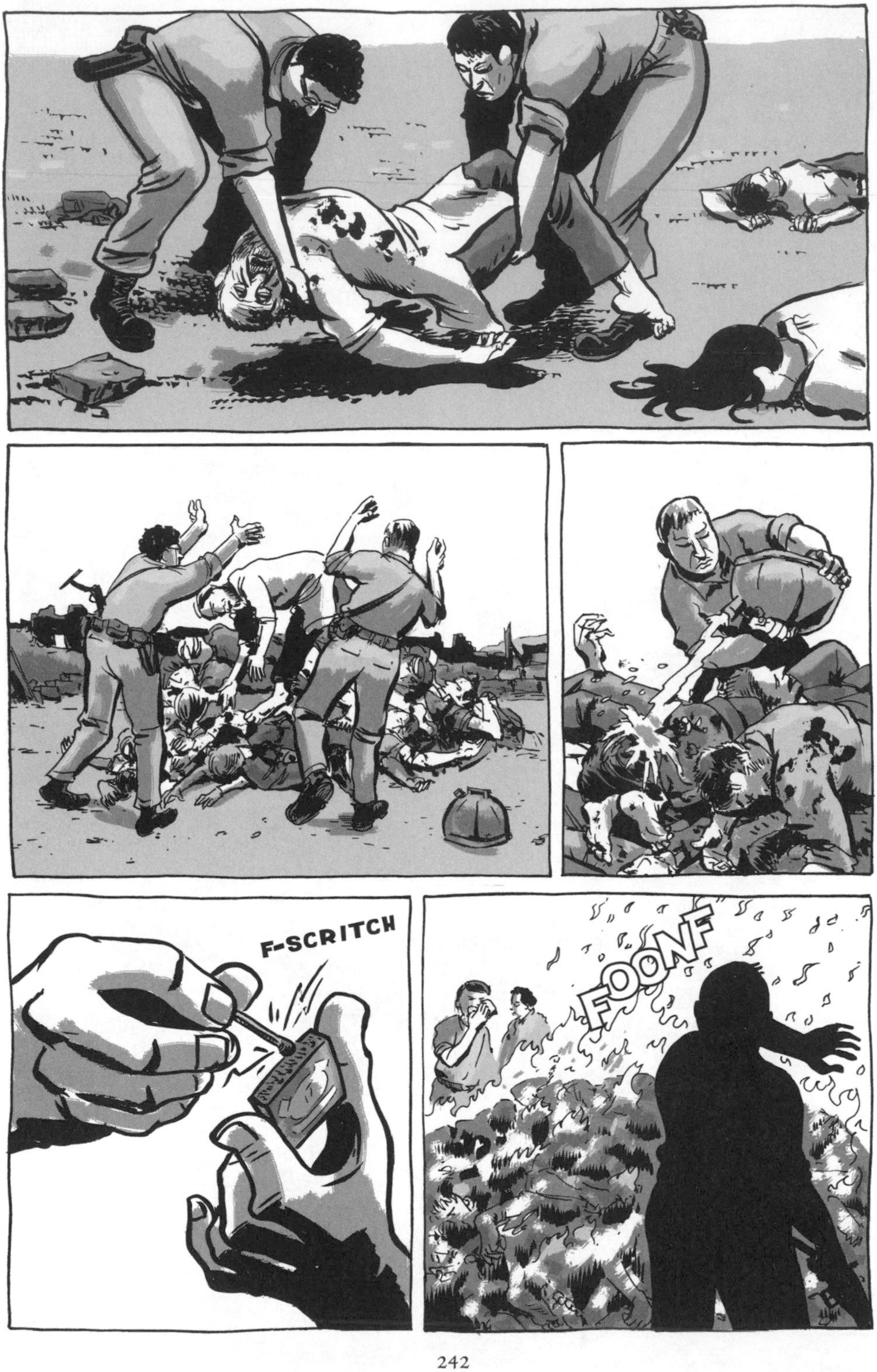
F-SCRITCH
FOONF

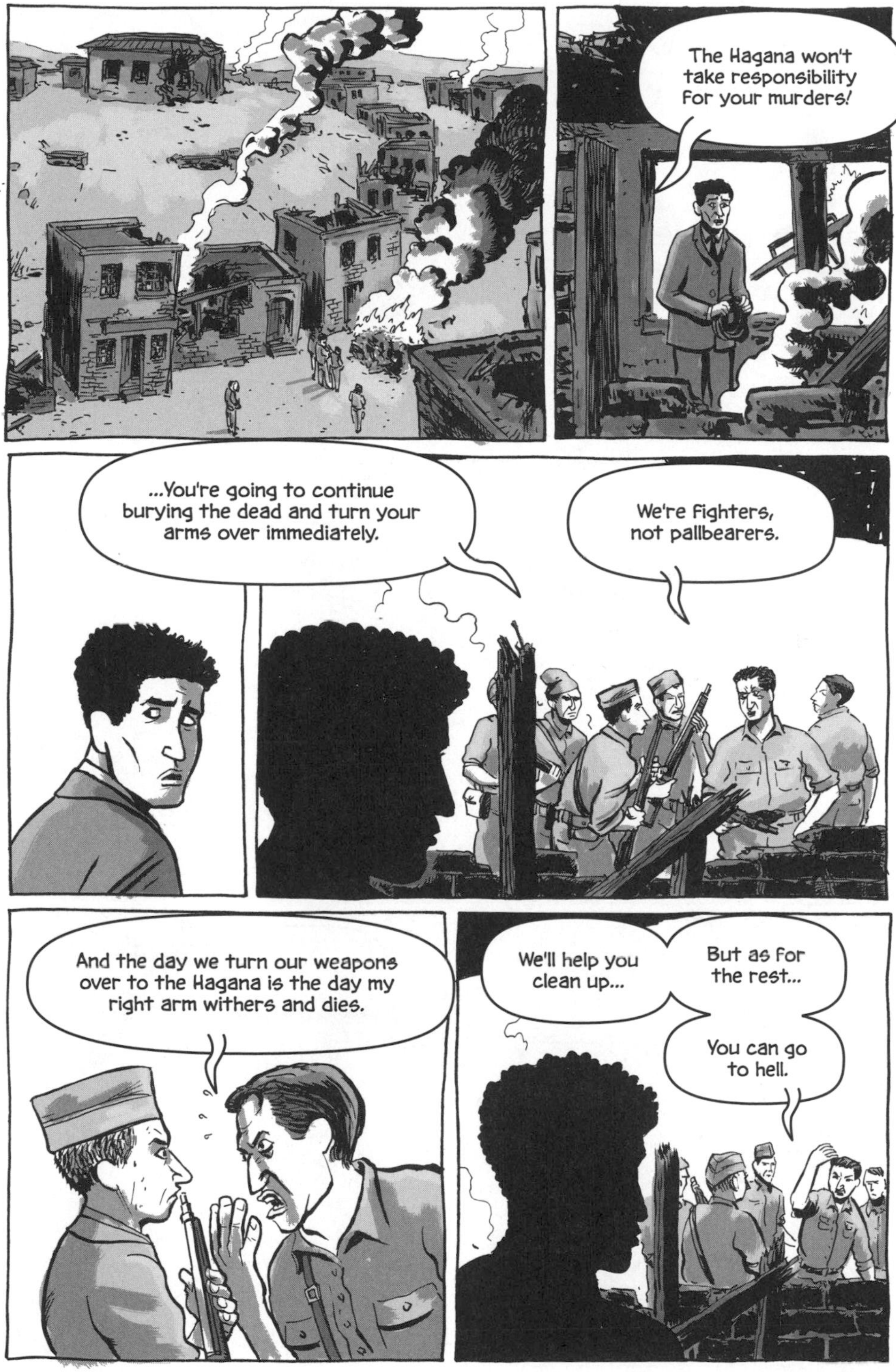
The Hagana won't take responsibility for your murders!
...You're going to continue burying the dead and turn your arms over immediately.
We're fighters, not pallbearers.
And the day we turn our weapons over to the Hagana is the day my right arm withers and dies.
We'll help you clean up...
But as for the rest...
You can go to hell.

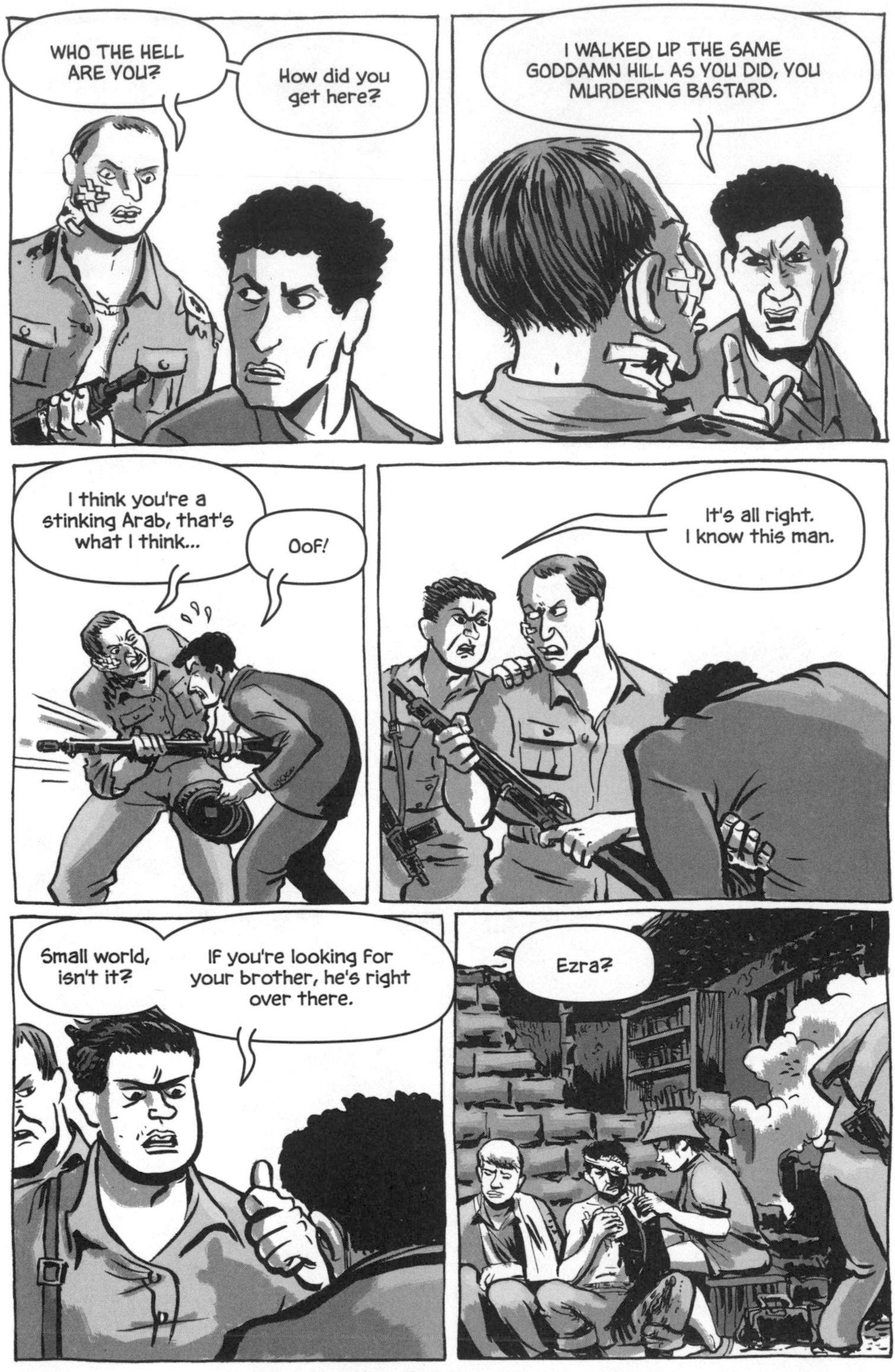
WHO THE HELL ARE YOU?
How did you get here?
I WALKED UP THE SAME GODDAMN HILL AS YOU DID, YOU MURDERING BASTARD.
I think you're a stinking Arab, that's what I think...
Oof!
It's all right. I know this man.
Small world, isn't it?
If you're looking for your brother, he's right over there.
Ezra?

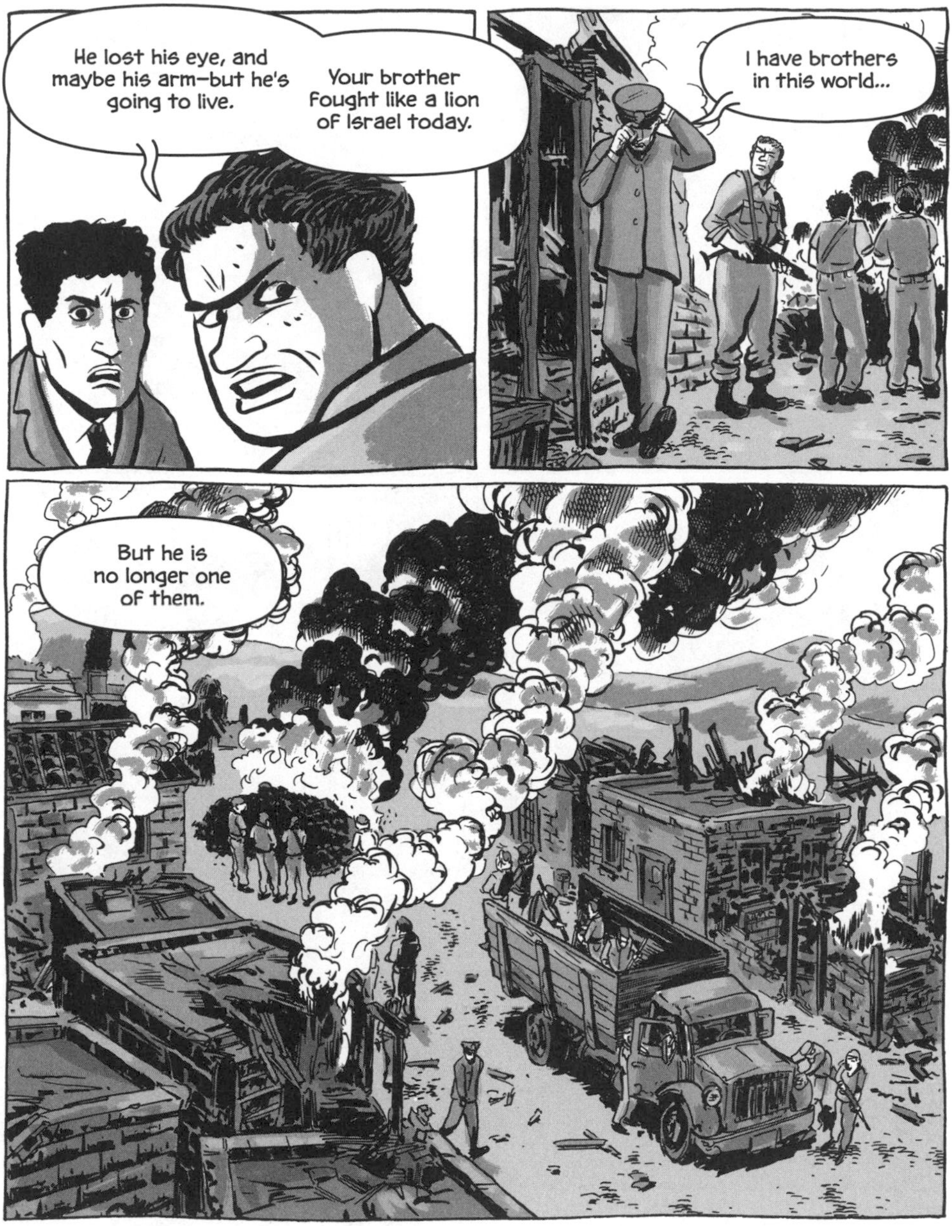
He lost his eye, and maybe his arm—but he's going to live.
Your brother fought like a lion of Israel today.
I have brothers in this world...
But he is no longer one of them.

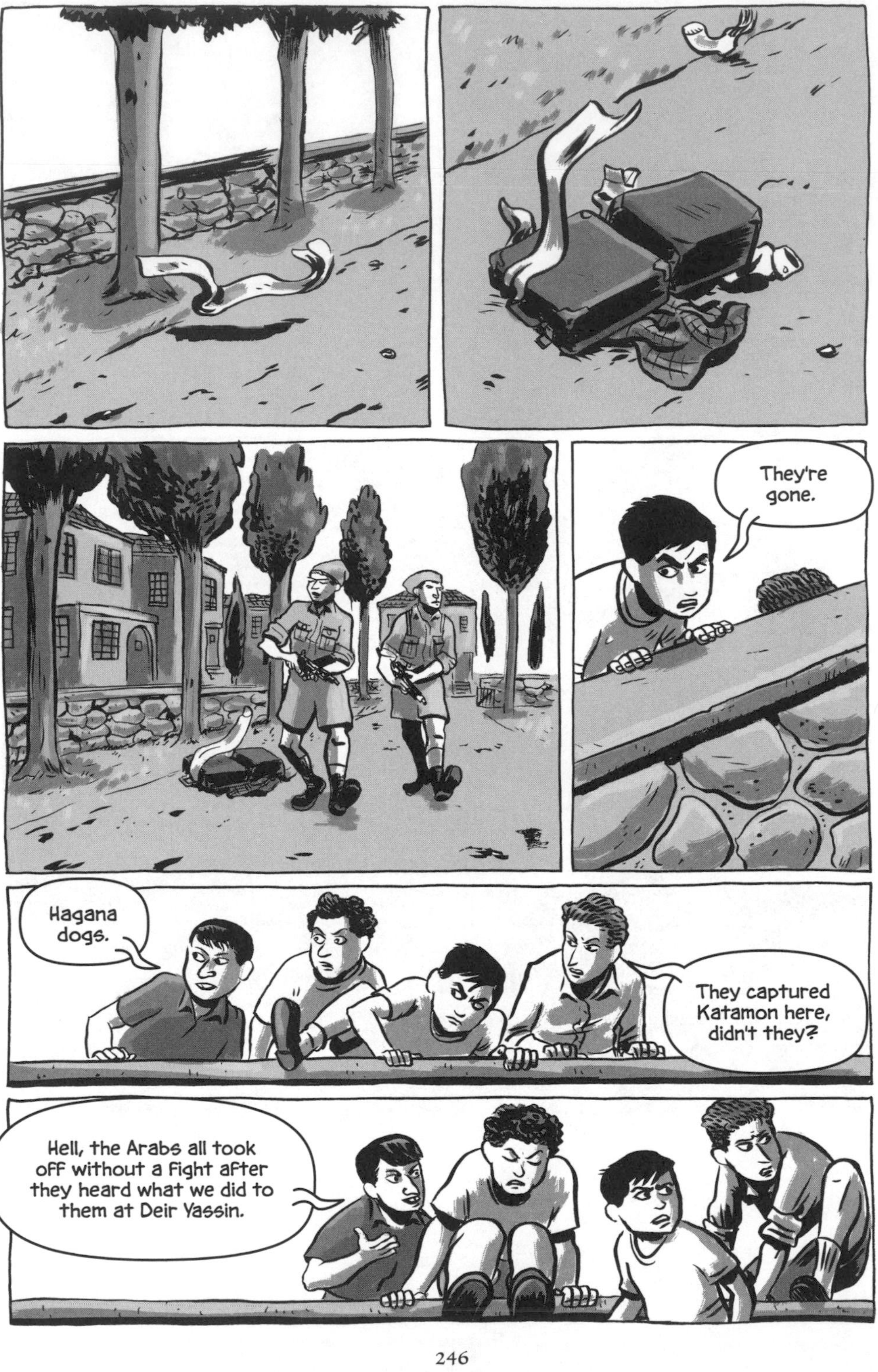

They're gone.
Hagana dogs.
They captured Katamon here, didn't they?
Hell, the Arabs all took off without a fight after they heard what we did to them at Deir Yassin.

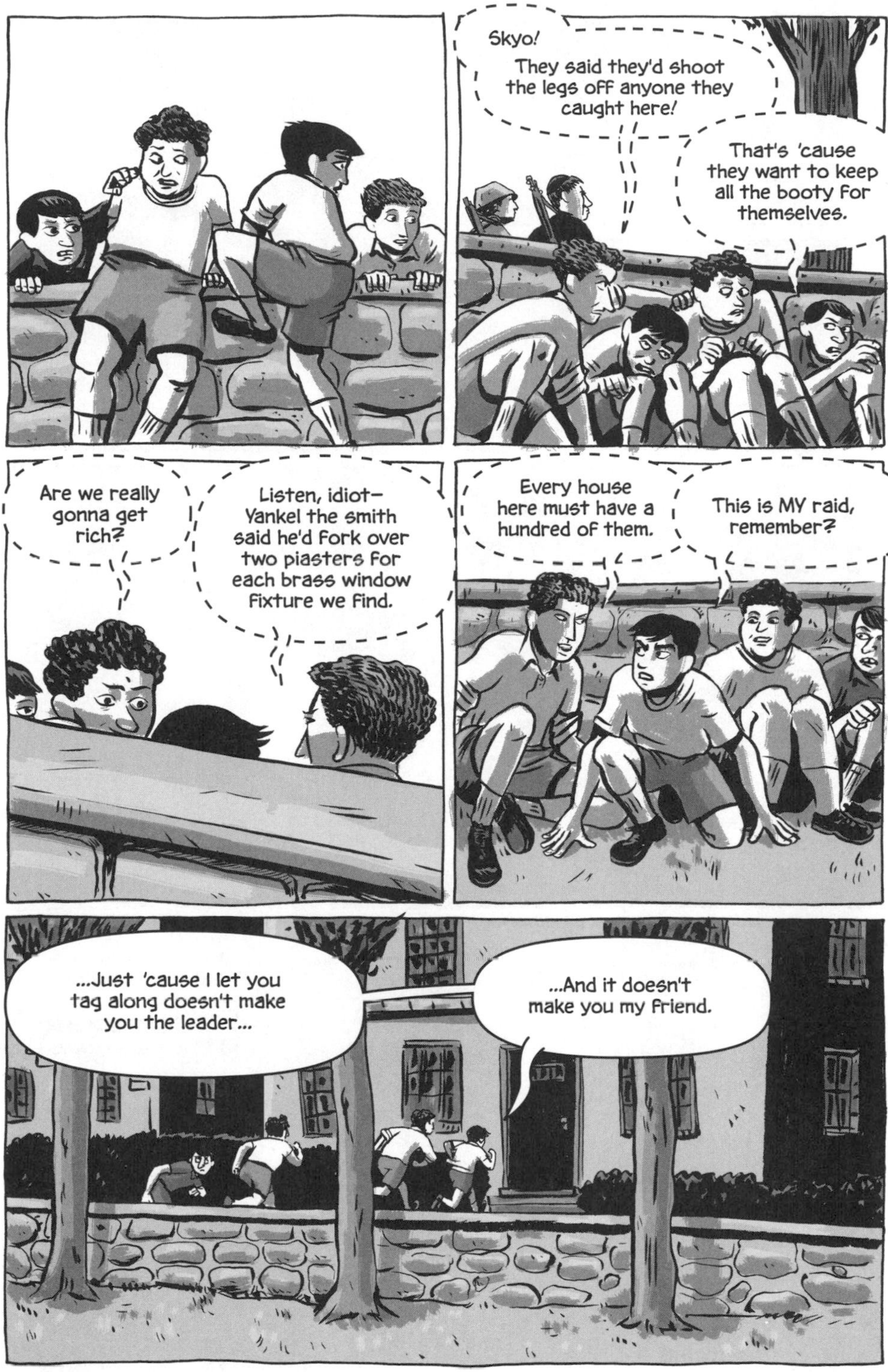
Skyo!
They said they'd shoot the legs off anyone they caught here!
That's 'cause they want to keep all the booty for themselves.
Are we really gonna get rich?
Listen, idiot— Yankel the smith said he'd fork over two piasters for each brass window fixture we find.
Every house here must have a hundred of them.
This is MY raid, remember?
...Just 'cause I let you tag along doesn't make you the leader...
...And it doesn't make you my friend.

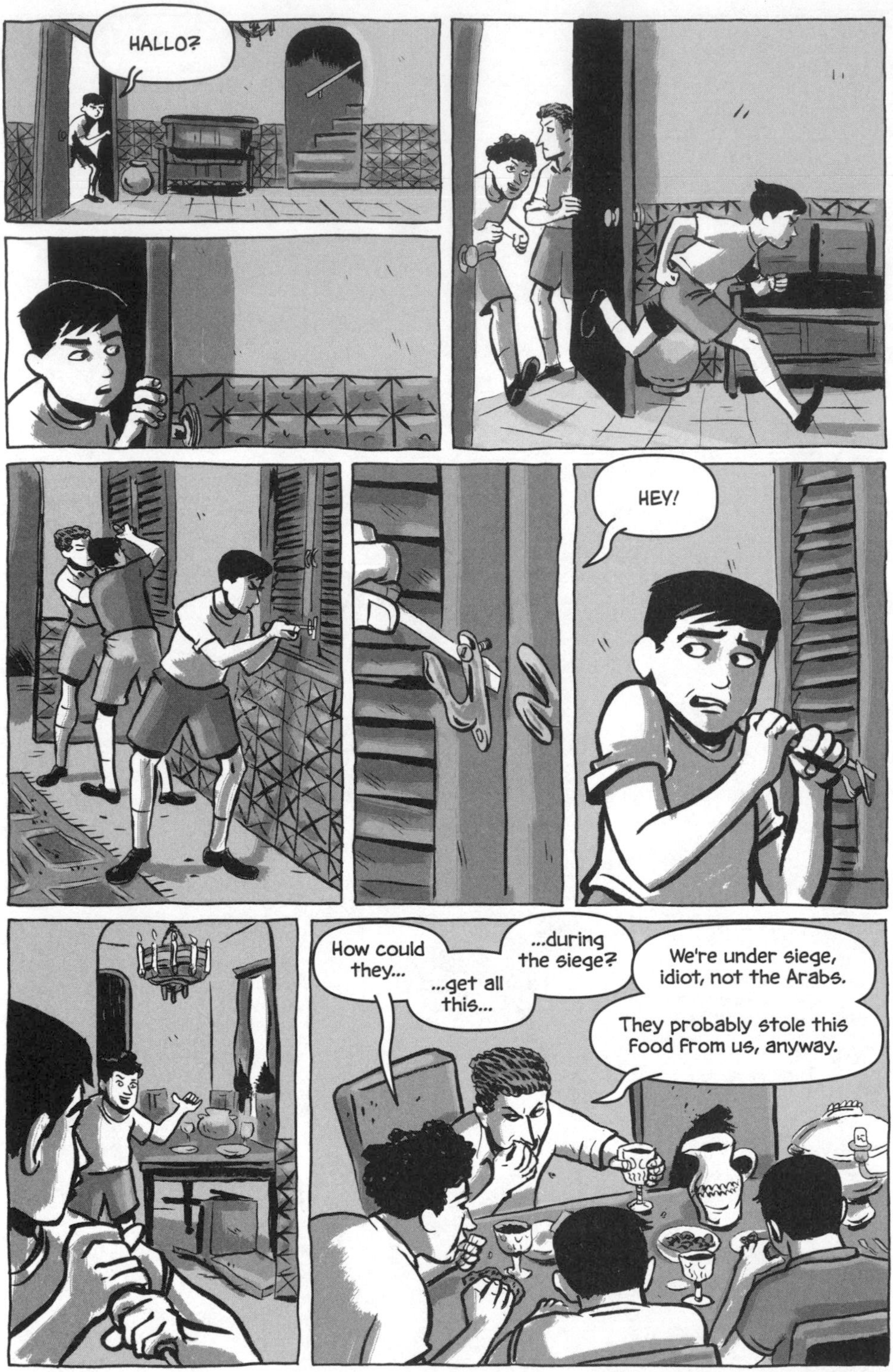

HALLO?
HEY!
How could they...
...get all this...
...during the siege?
We're under siege, idiot, not the Arabs.
They probably stole this food from us, anyway.

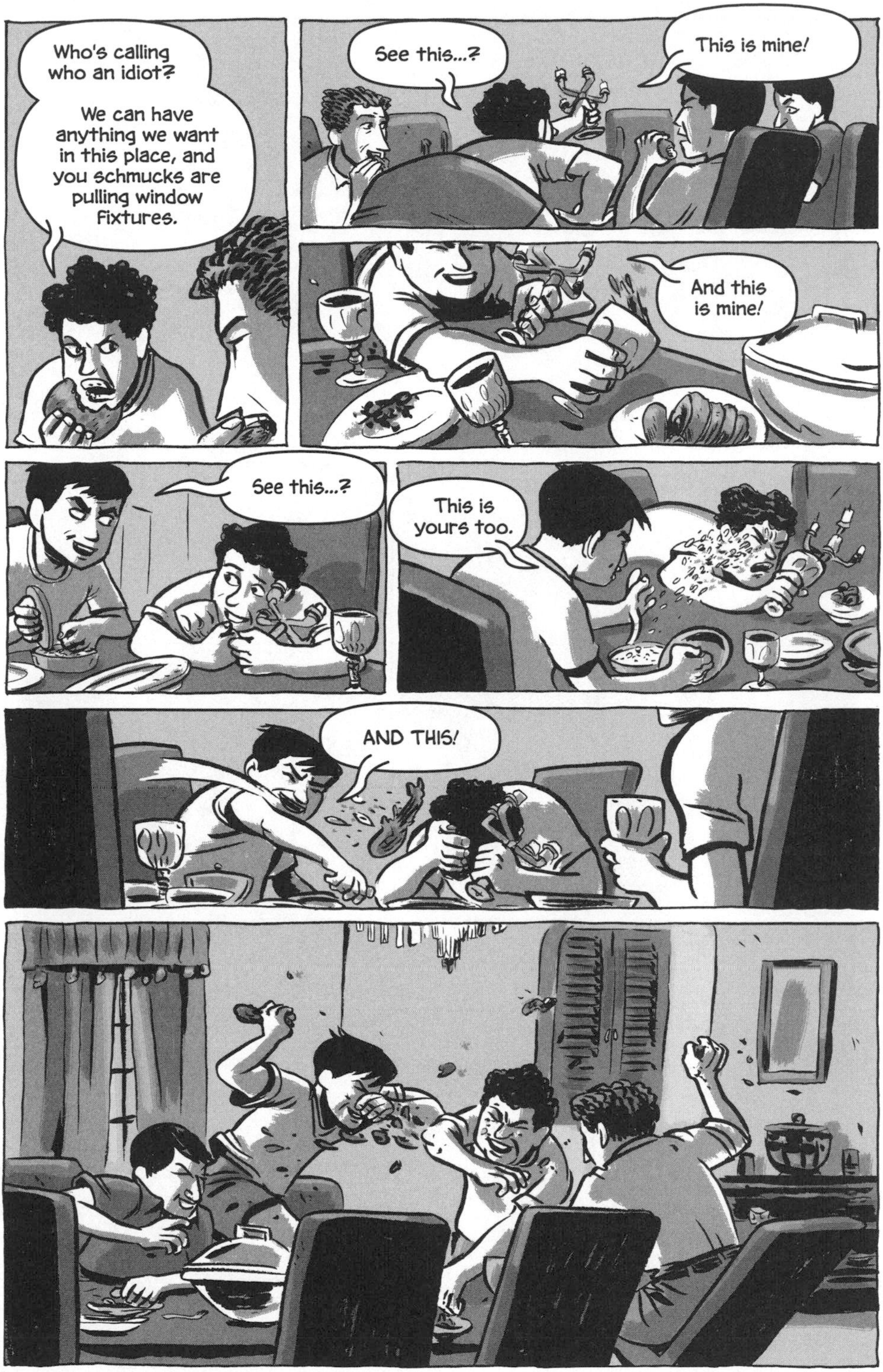
Who's calling who an idiot?
We can have anything we want in this place, and you schmucks are pulling window fixtures.
See this...?
This is mine!
And this is mine!
See this...?
This is yours too.
AND THIS!

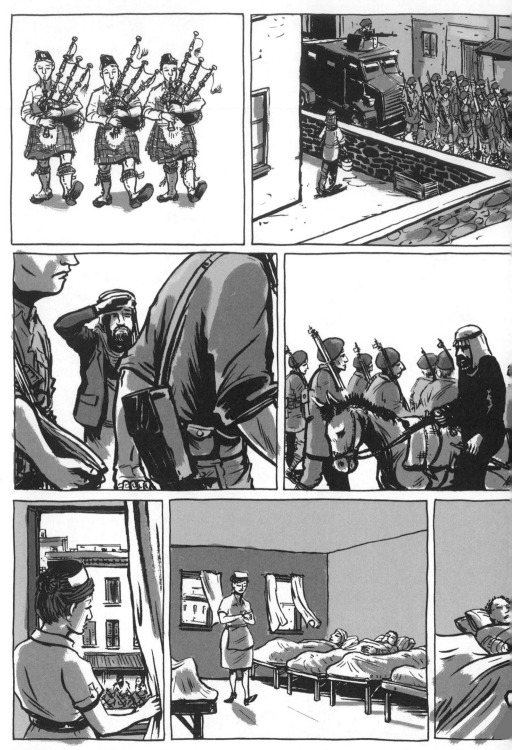

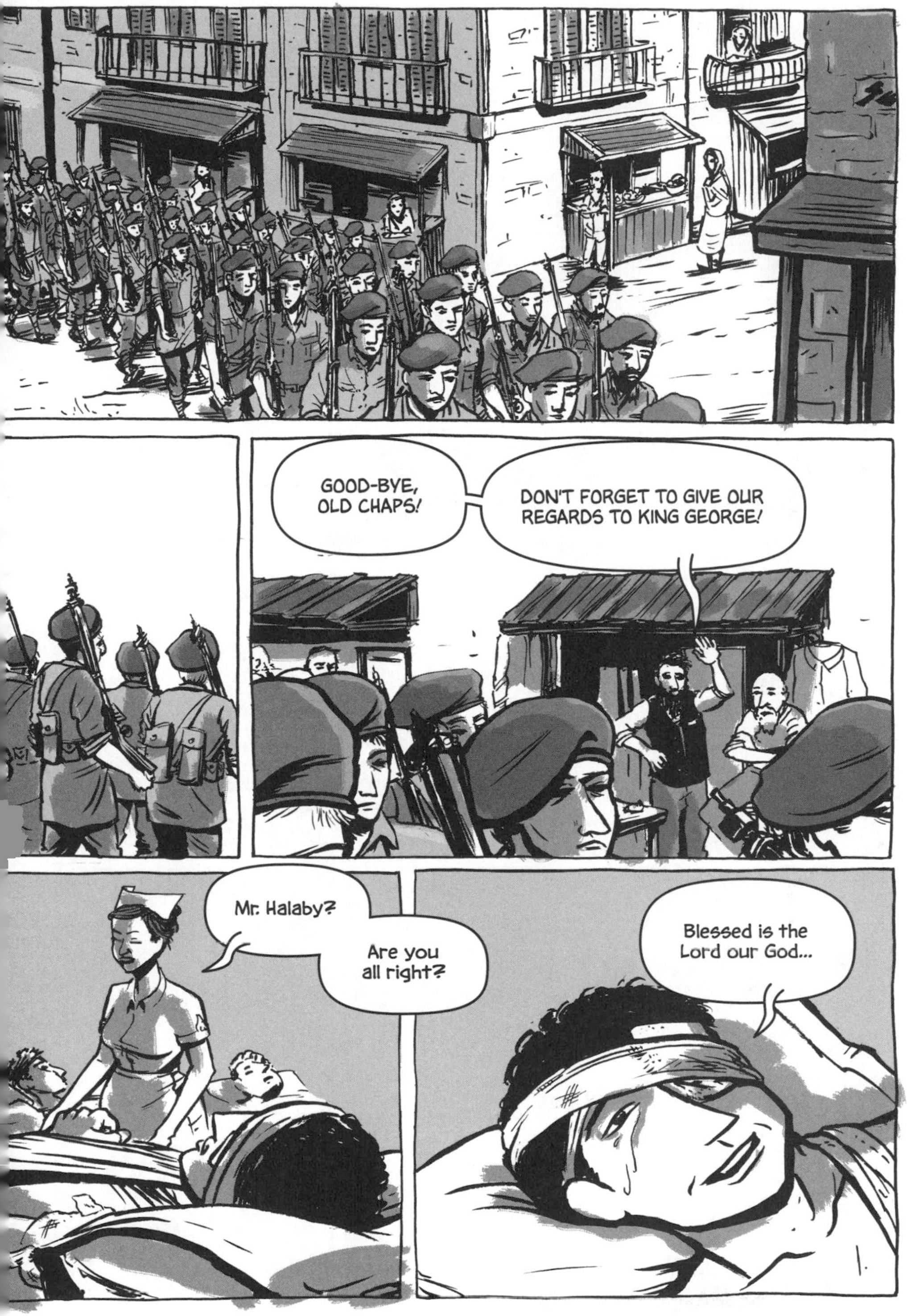
GOOD-BYE, OLD CHAPS!
DON'T FORGET TO GIVE OUR REGARDS TO KING GEORGE!
Mr. Halaby?
Are you all right?
Blessed is the Lord our God...

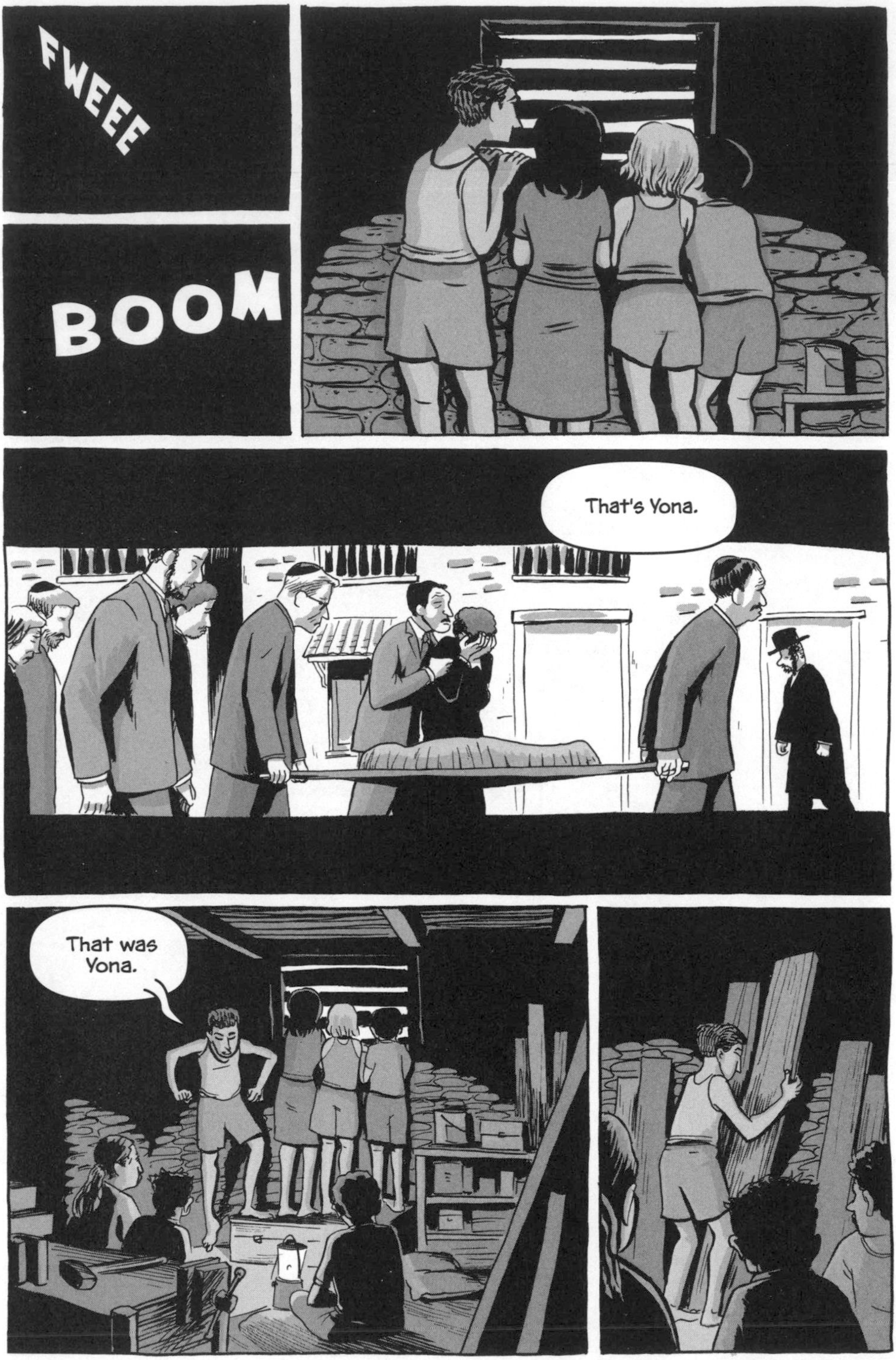
FWEEE
BOOM
That's Yona.
That was Yona.

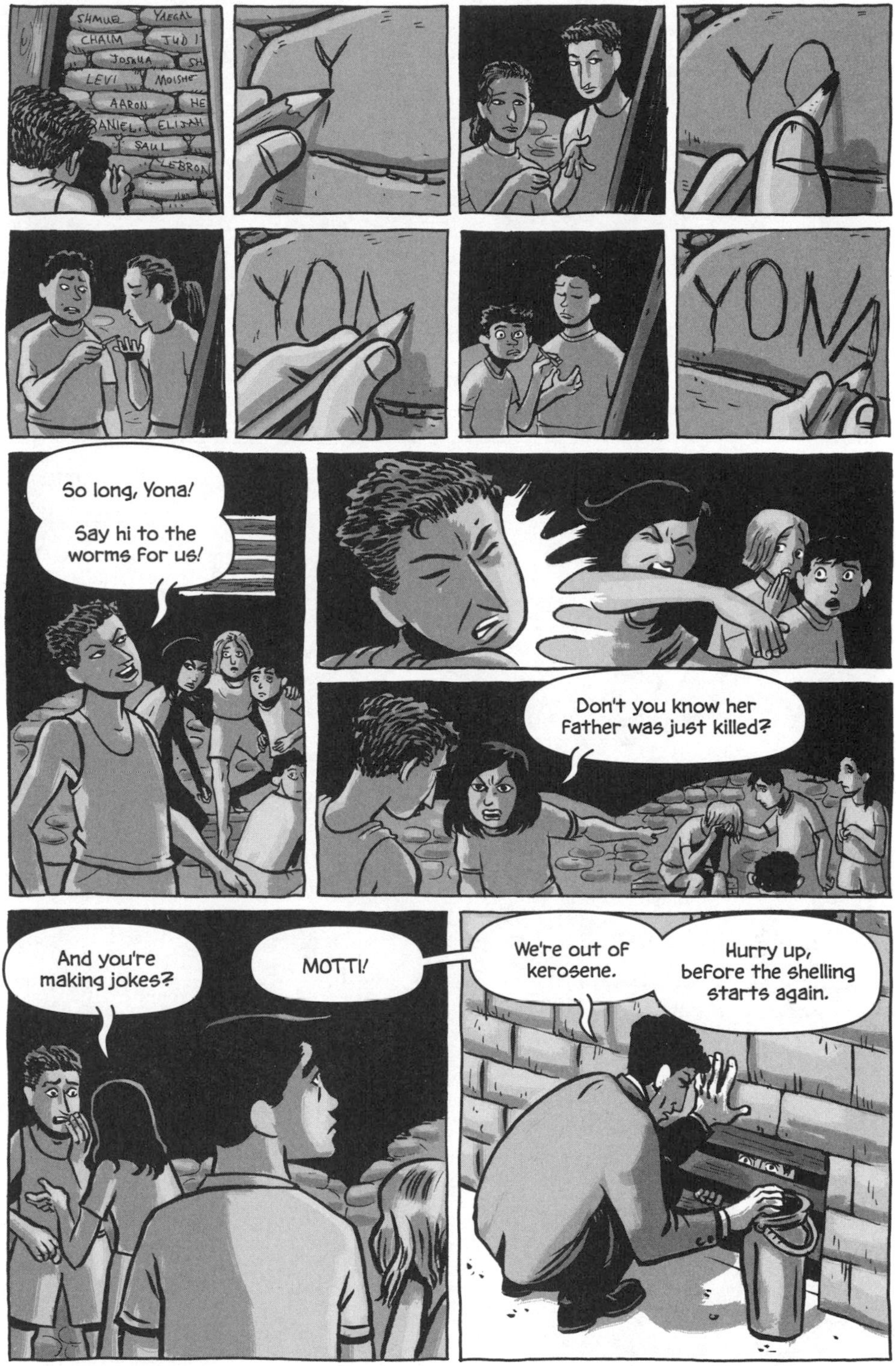
SHMUEL
YAEGAL
CHAIM
JOSHUA
LEVI
MOISHE
AARON
ELIJAH
SAUL
LEBRON
YONA
So long, Yona!
Say hi to the worms for us!
Don't you know her father was just killed?
And you're making jokes?
MOTTI!
We're out of kerosene.
Hurry up, before the shelling starts again.

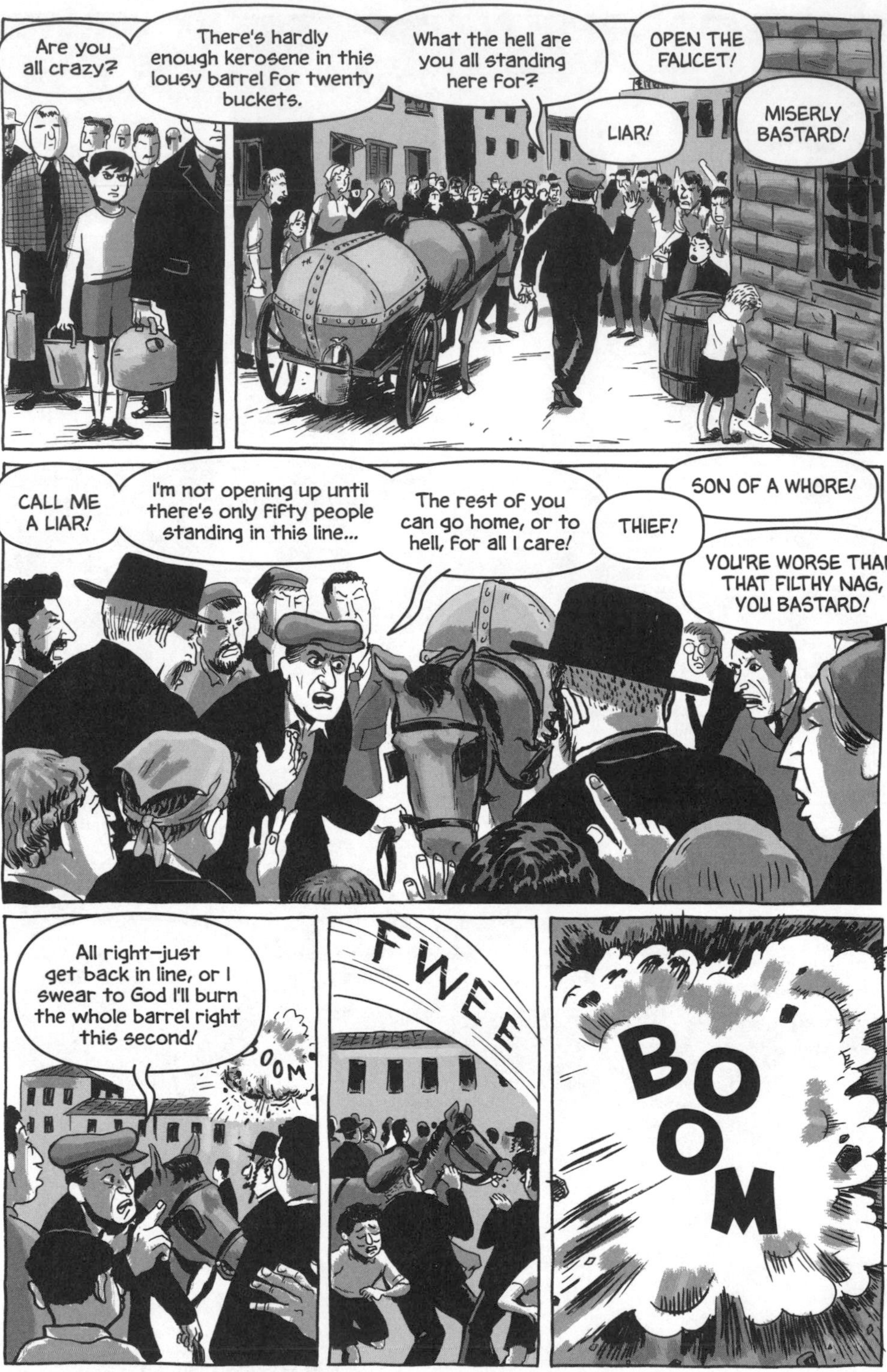
Are you all crazy?
There's hardly enough kerosene in this lousy barrel for twenty buckets.
What the hell are you all standing here for?
OPEN THE FAUCET!
LIAR!
MISERLY BASTARD!
CALL ME A LIAR!
I'm not opening up until there's only fifty people standing in this line...
The rest of you can go home, or to hell, for all I care!
SON OF A WHORE!
THIEF!
YOU'RE WORSE THAN THAT FILTHY NAG, YOU BASTARD!
All right—just get back in line, or I swear to God I'll burn the whole barrel right this second!
BOOM
FWEE
BOOM

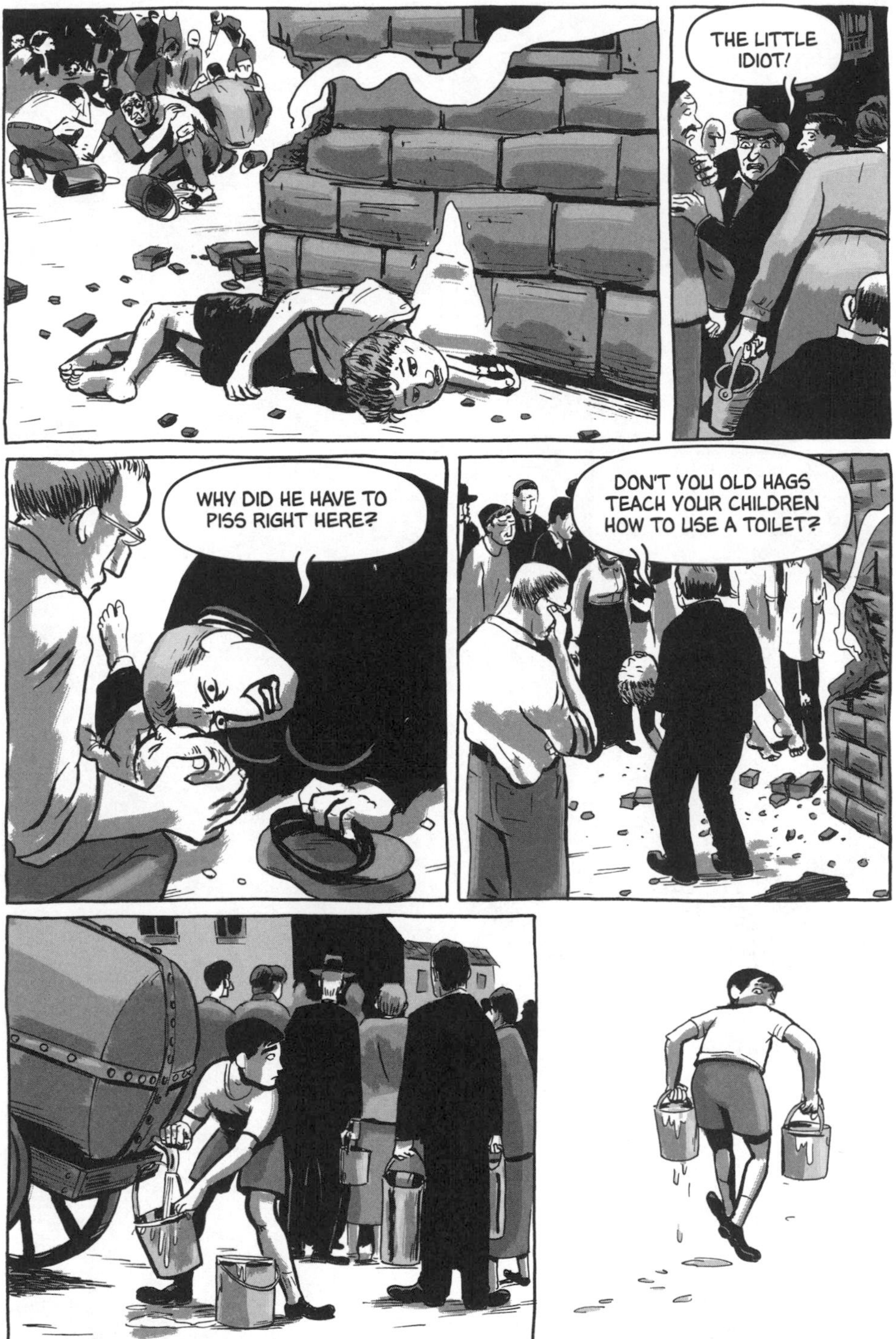
THE LITTLE IDIOT!
WHY DID HE HAVE TO PISS RIGHT HERE?
DON'T YOU OLD HAGS TEACH YOUR CHILDREN HOW TO USE A TOILET?

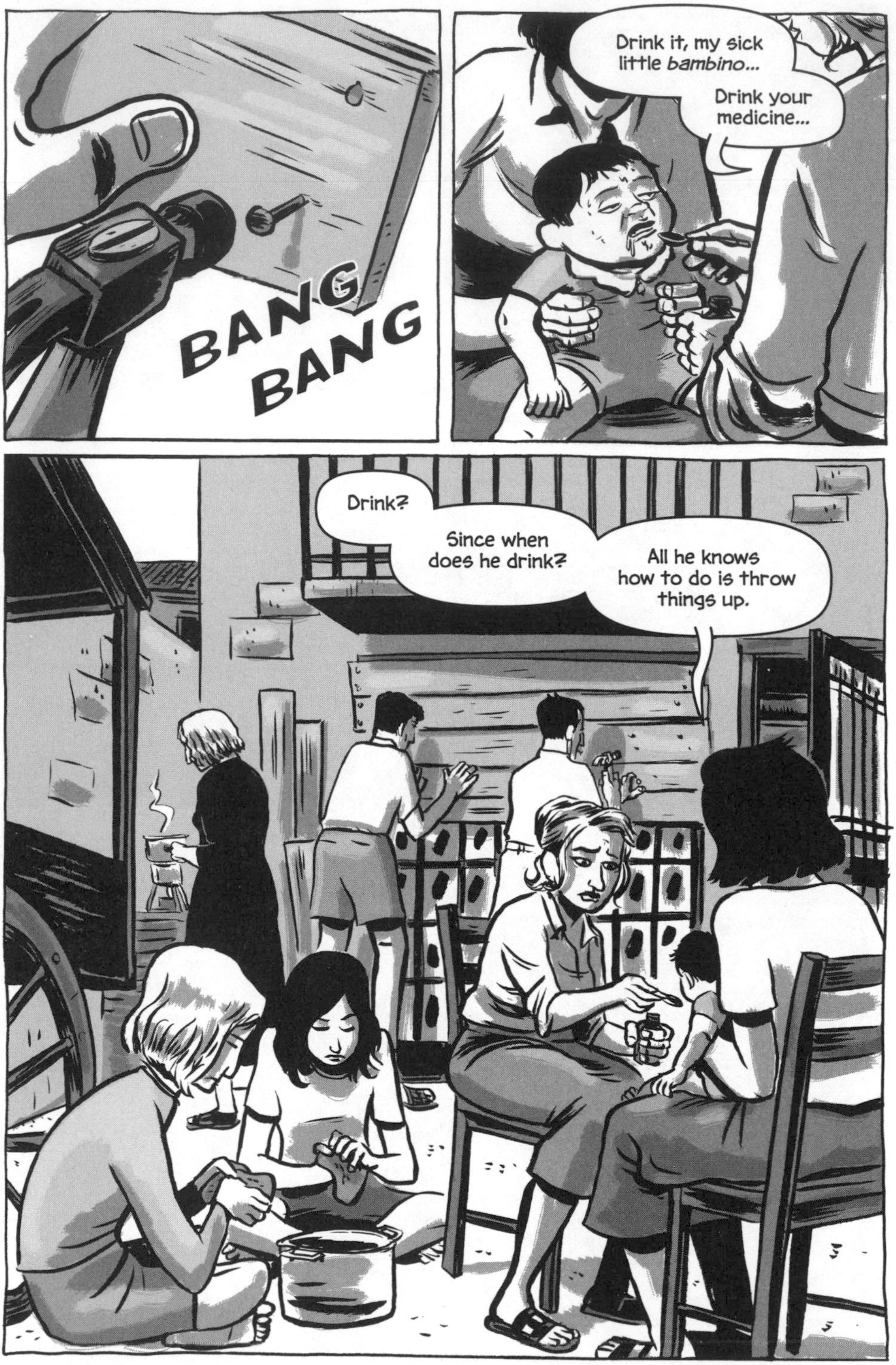
BANG
BANG
Drink it, my sick little *bambino*...
Drink your medicine...
Drink?
Since when does he drink?
All he knows how to do is throw things up.

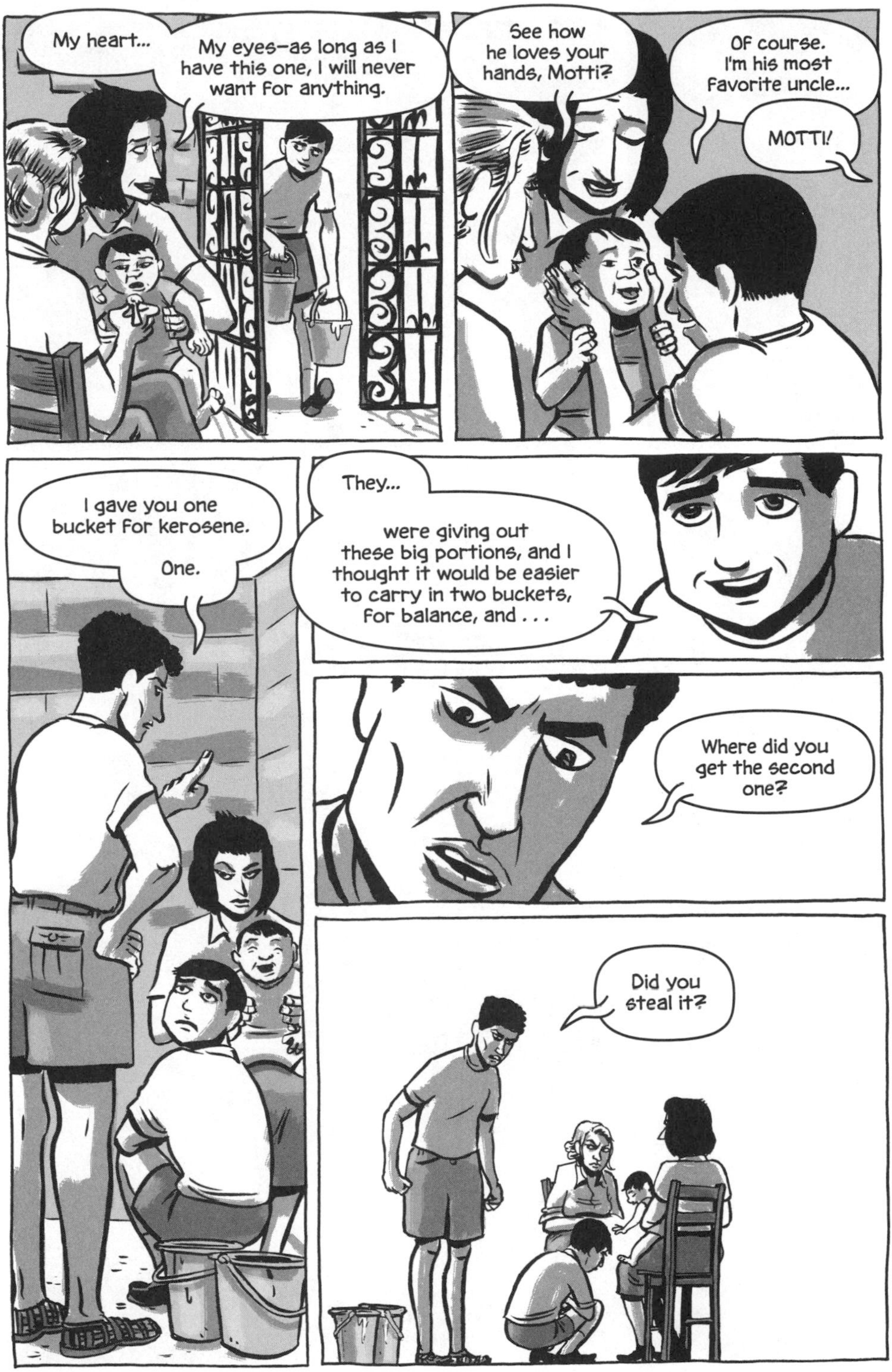
My heart...
My eyes—as long as I have this one, I will never want for anything.
See how he loves your hands, Motti?
Of course. I'm his most favorite uncle...
MOTTI!
I gave you one bucket for kerosene.
One.
They...
were giving out these big portions, and I thought it would be easier to carry in two buckets, for balance, and . . .
Where did you get the second one?
Did you steal it?

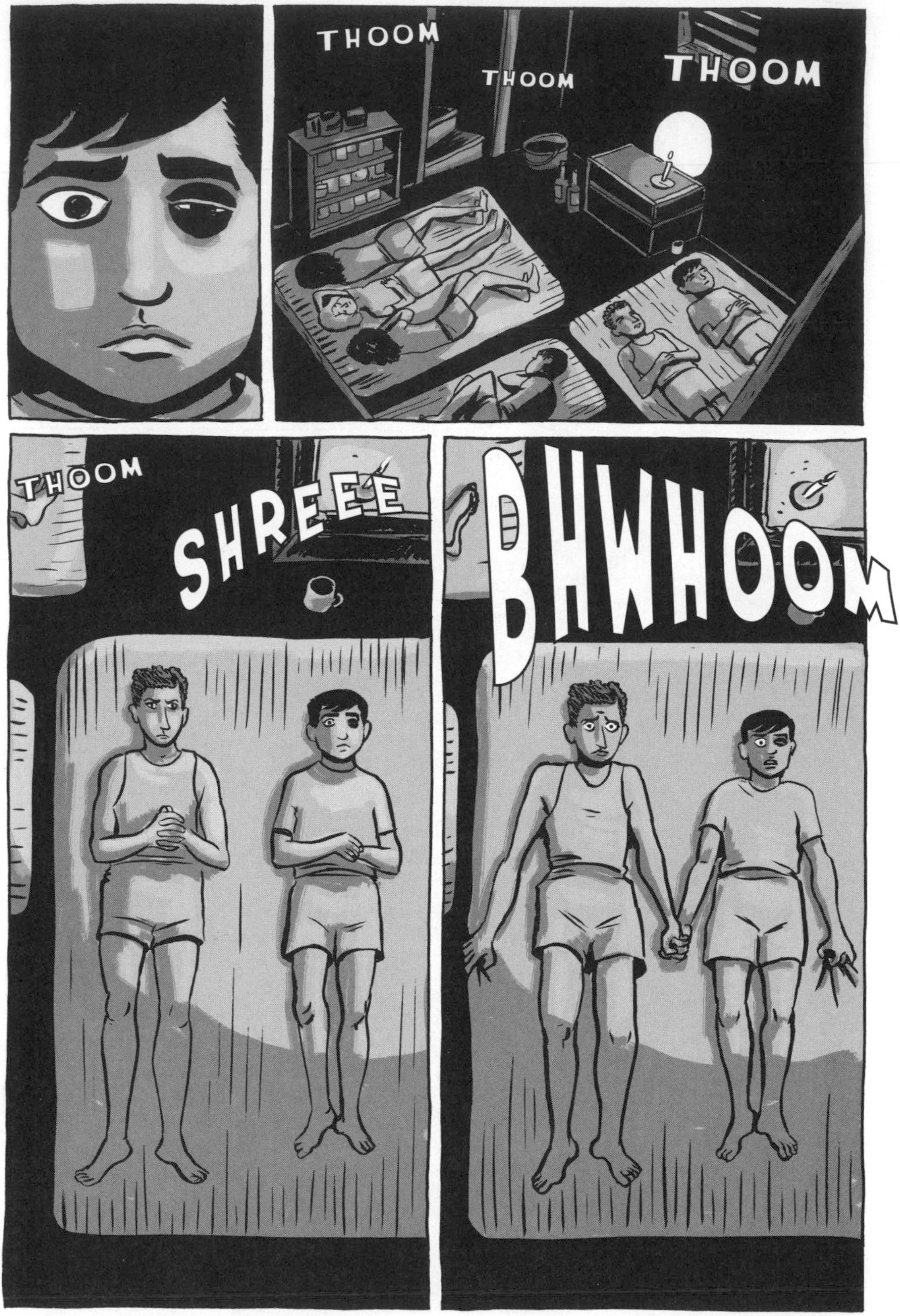
THOOM
THOOM
THOOM
THOOM
SHREEE
BHWHOOM

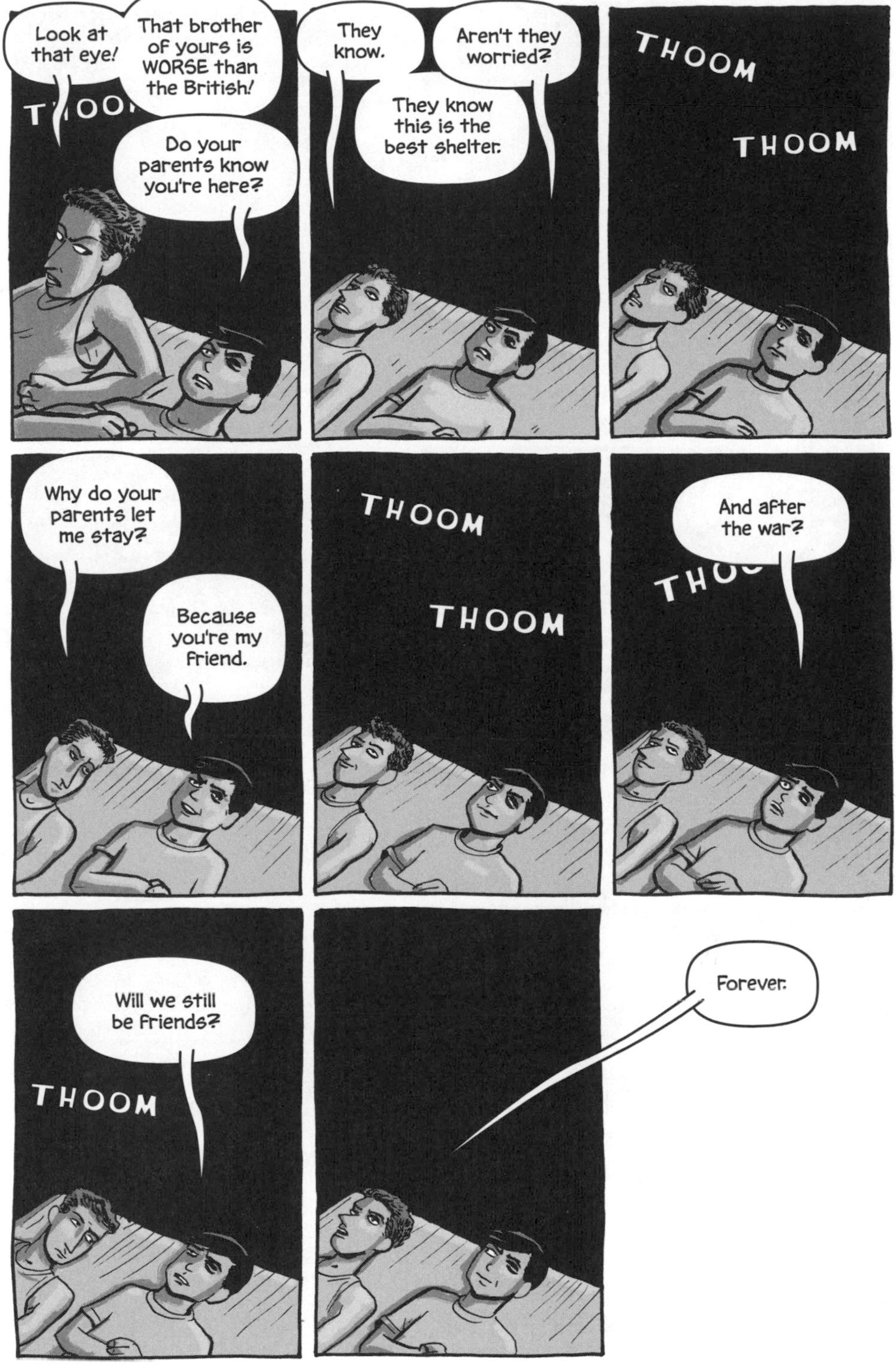
Look at that eye!
That brother of yours is WORSE than the British!
THOO
Do your parents know you're here?
They know.
Aren't they worried?
They know this is the best shelter.
THOOM
THOOM
Why do your parents let me stay?
Because you're my friend.
THOOM
THOOM
And after the war?
THO
Will we still be friends?
THOOM
Forever.

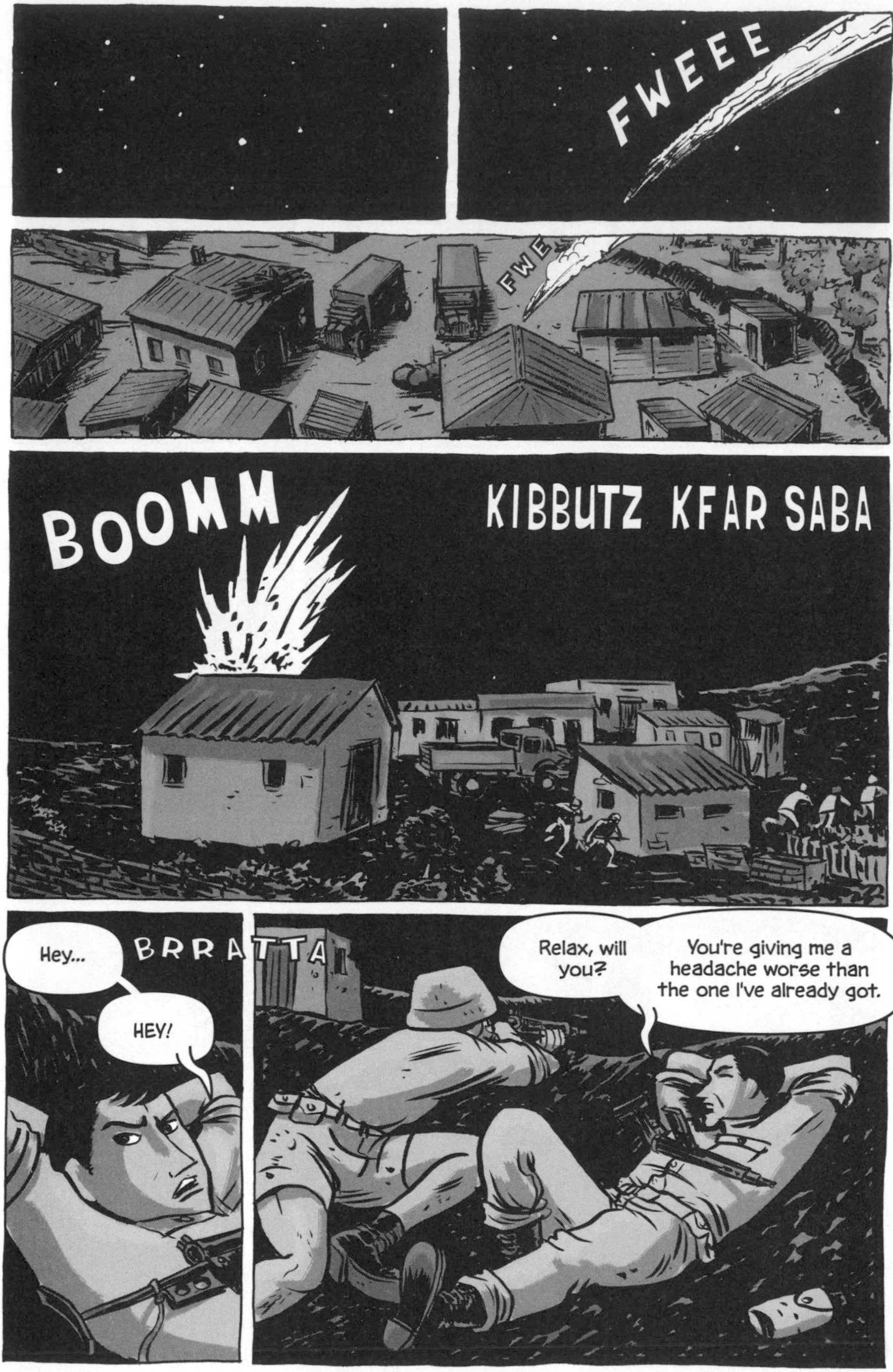
FWEEE
FWE
BOOMM
KIBBUTZ KFAR SABA
Hey...
BRRATTTA
HEY!
Relax, will you?
You're giving me a headache worse than the one I've already got.

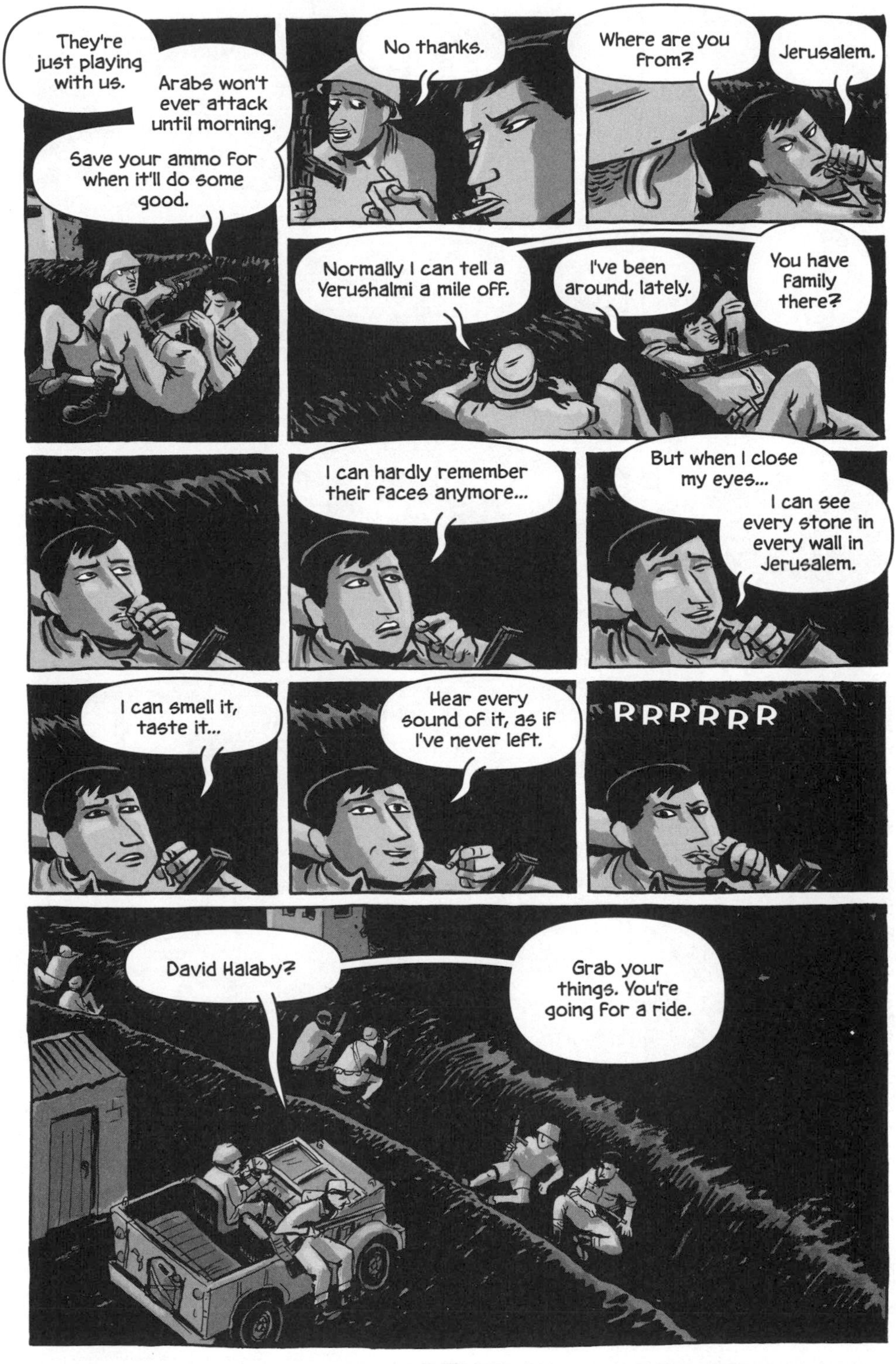
They're just playing with us.
Arabs won't ever attack until morning.
Save your ammo for when it'll do some good.
No thanks.
Where are you from?
Jerusalem.
Normally I can tell a Yerushalmi a mile off.
I've been around, lately.
You have family there?
I can hardly remember their faces anymore...
But when I close my eyes...
I can see every stone in every wall in Jerusalem.
I can smell it, taste it...
Hear every sound of it, as if I've never left.
RRRRRR
David Halaby?
Grab your things. You're going for a ride.

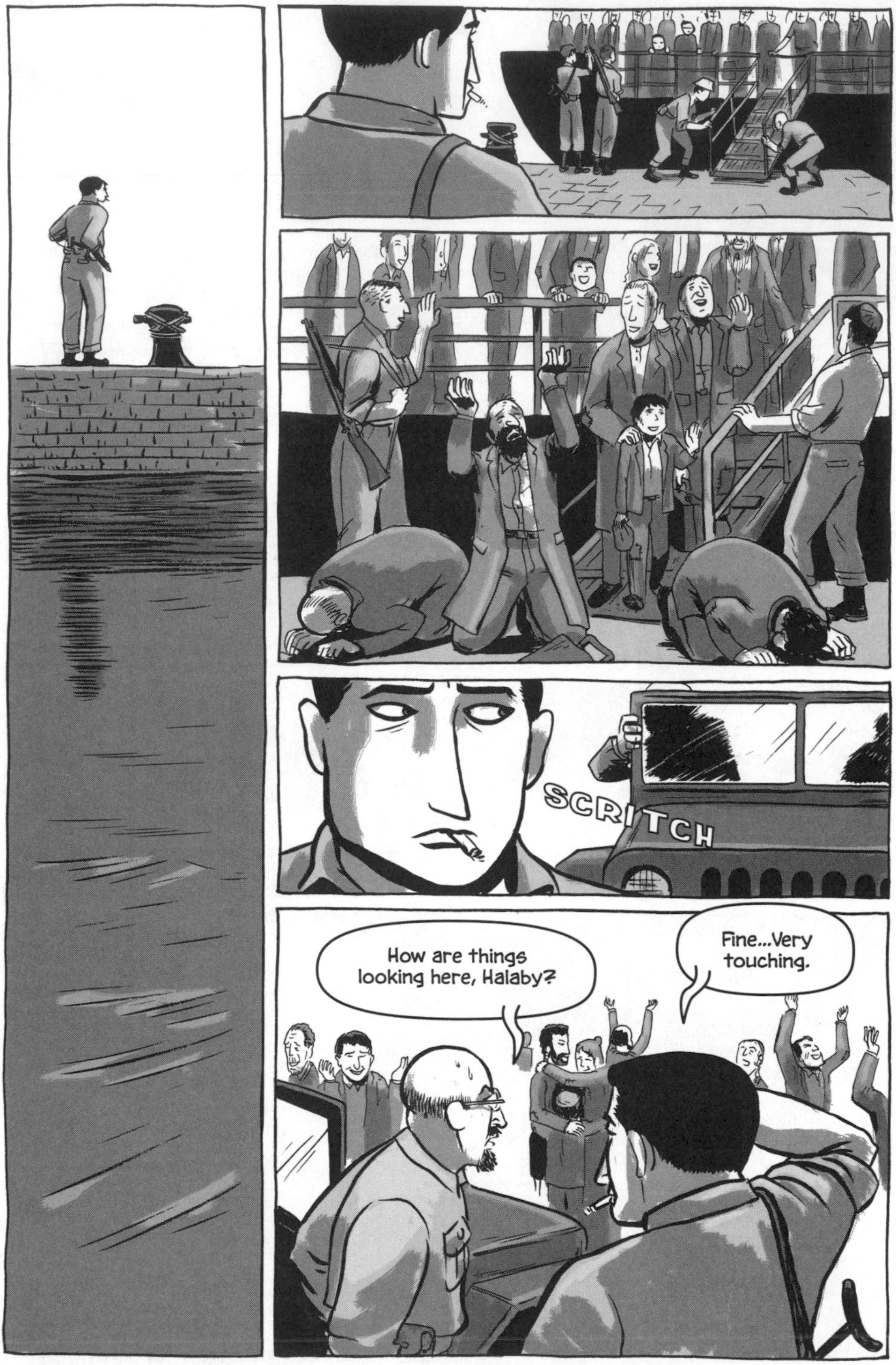
SCRITCH
How are things looking here, Halaby?
Fine...Very touching.

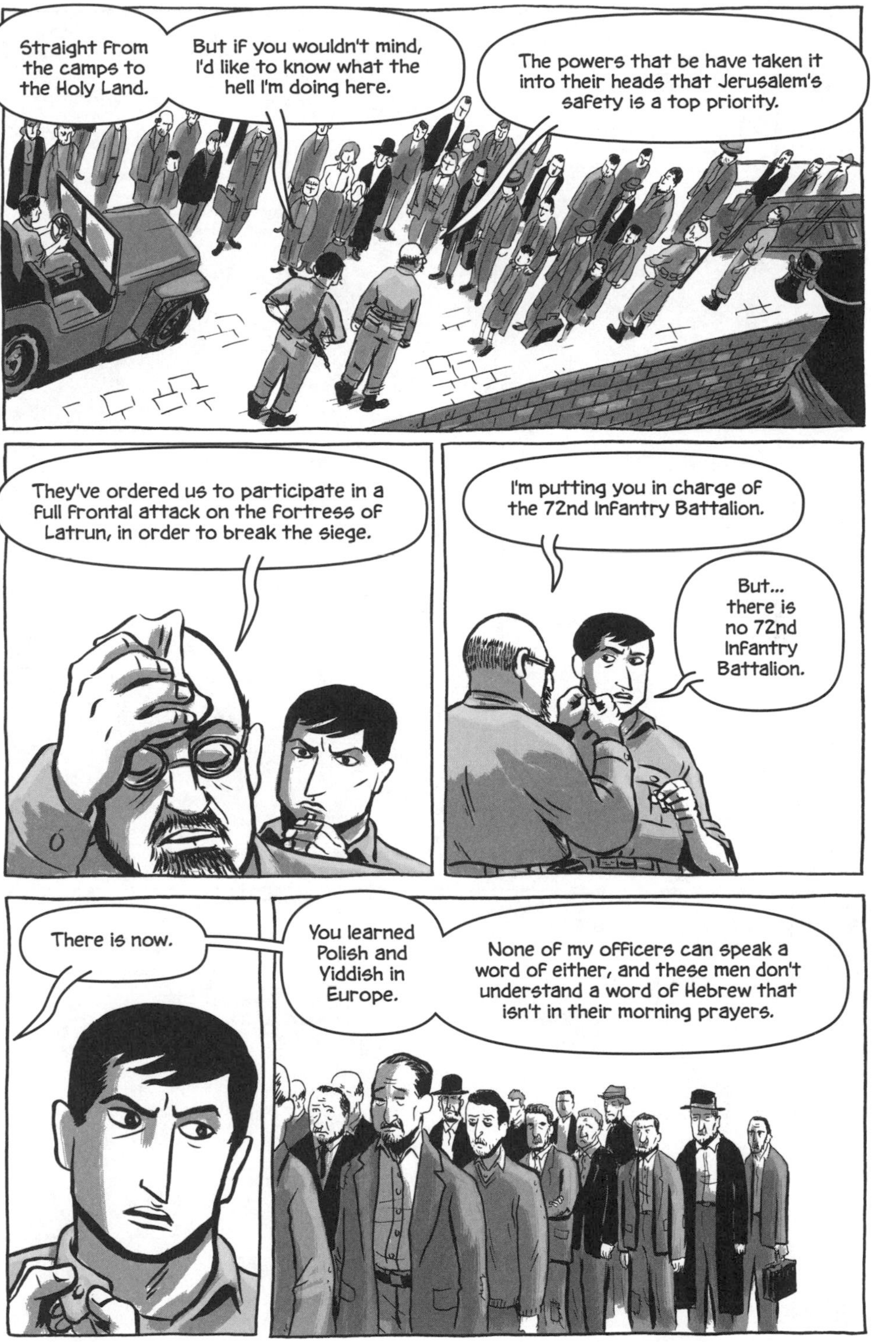
Straight from the camps to the Holy Land.
But if you wouldn't mind, I'd like to know what the hell I'm doing here.
The powers that be have taken it into their heads that Jerusalem's safety is a top priority.
They've ordered us to participate in a full frontal attack on the fortress of Latrun, in order to break the siege.
I'm putting you in charge of the 72nd Infantry Battalion.
But... there is no 72nd Infantry Battalion.
There is now.
You learned Polish and Yiddish in Europe.
None of my officers can speak a word of either, and these men don't understand a word of Hebrew that isn't in their morning prayers.

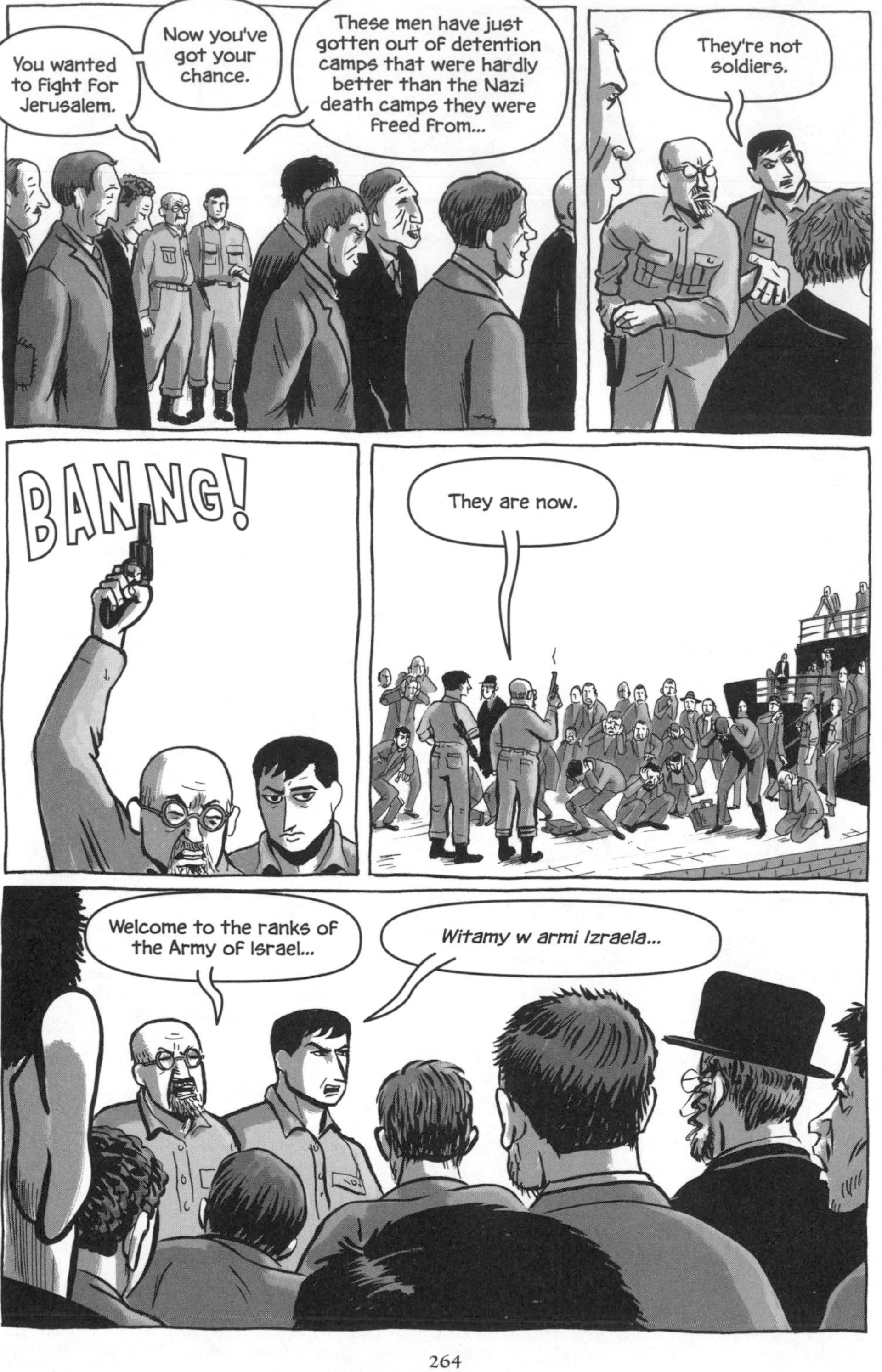
You wanted to fight for Jerusalem.
Now you've got your chance.
These men have just gotten out of detention camps that were hardly better than the Nazi death camps they were freed from...
They're not soldiers.
BANNG!
They are now.
Welcome to the ranks of the Army of Israel...
*Witamy w armi Izraela...*

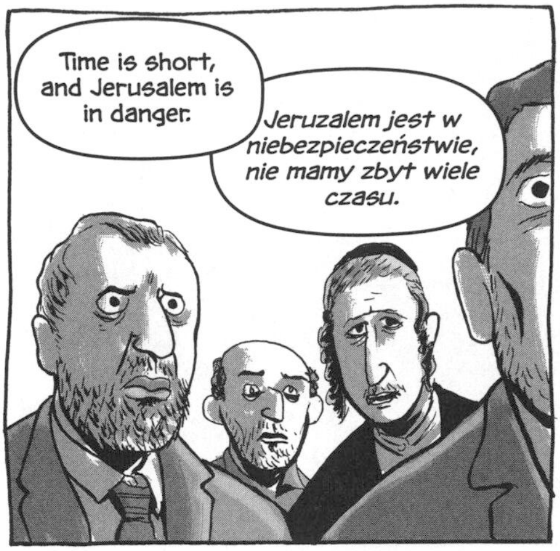
Time is short, and Jerusalem is in danger.
Jeruzalem jest w niebezpieczeństwie, nie mamy zbyt wiele czasu.

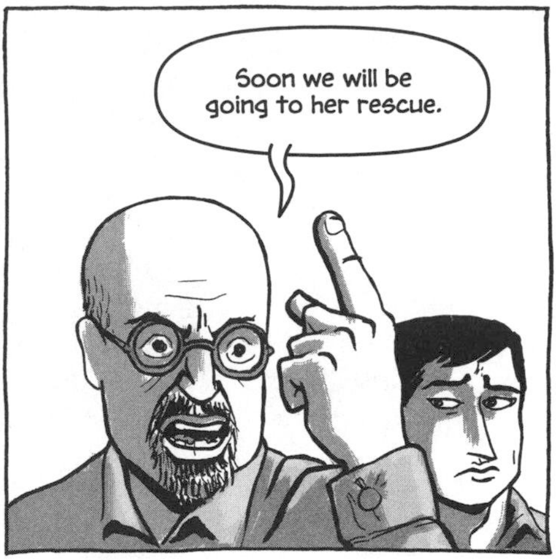
Soon we will be going to her rescue.

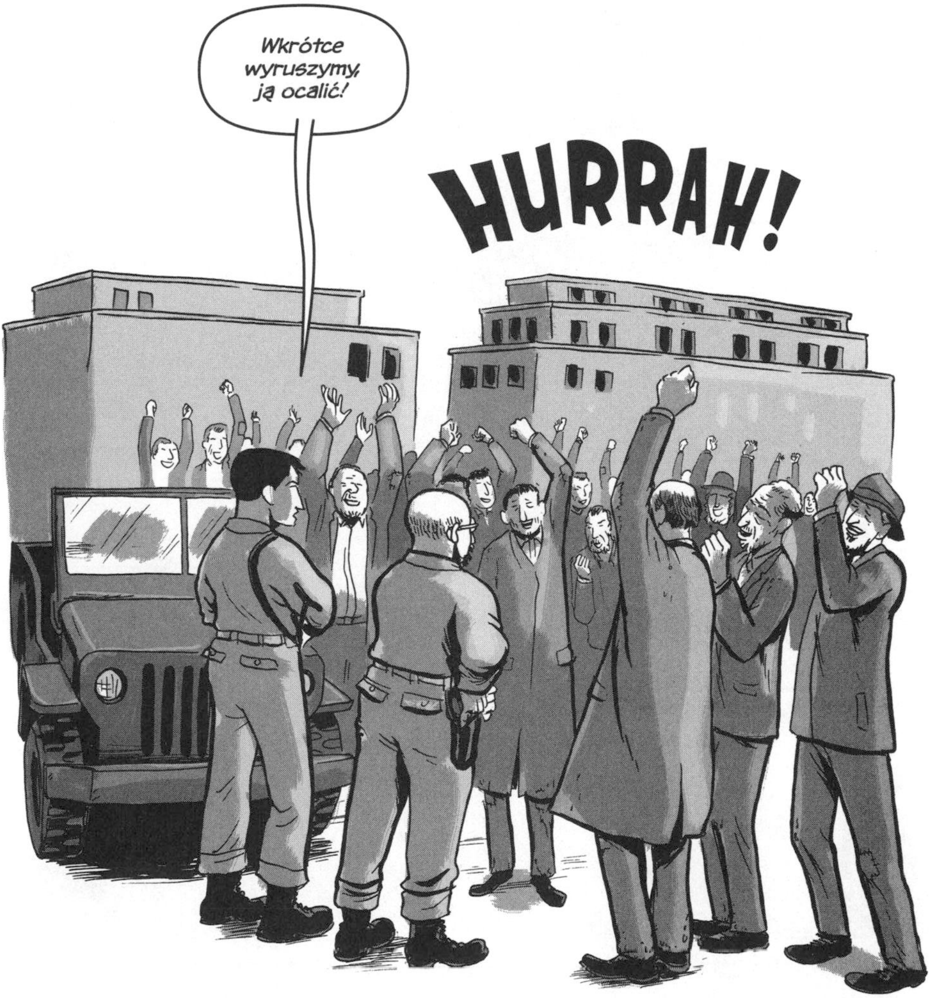
Wkrótce wyruszymy, ją ocalić!
HURRAH!

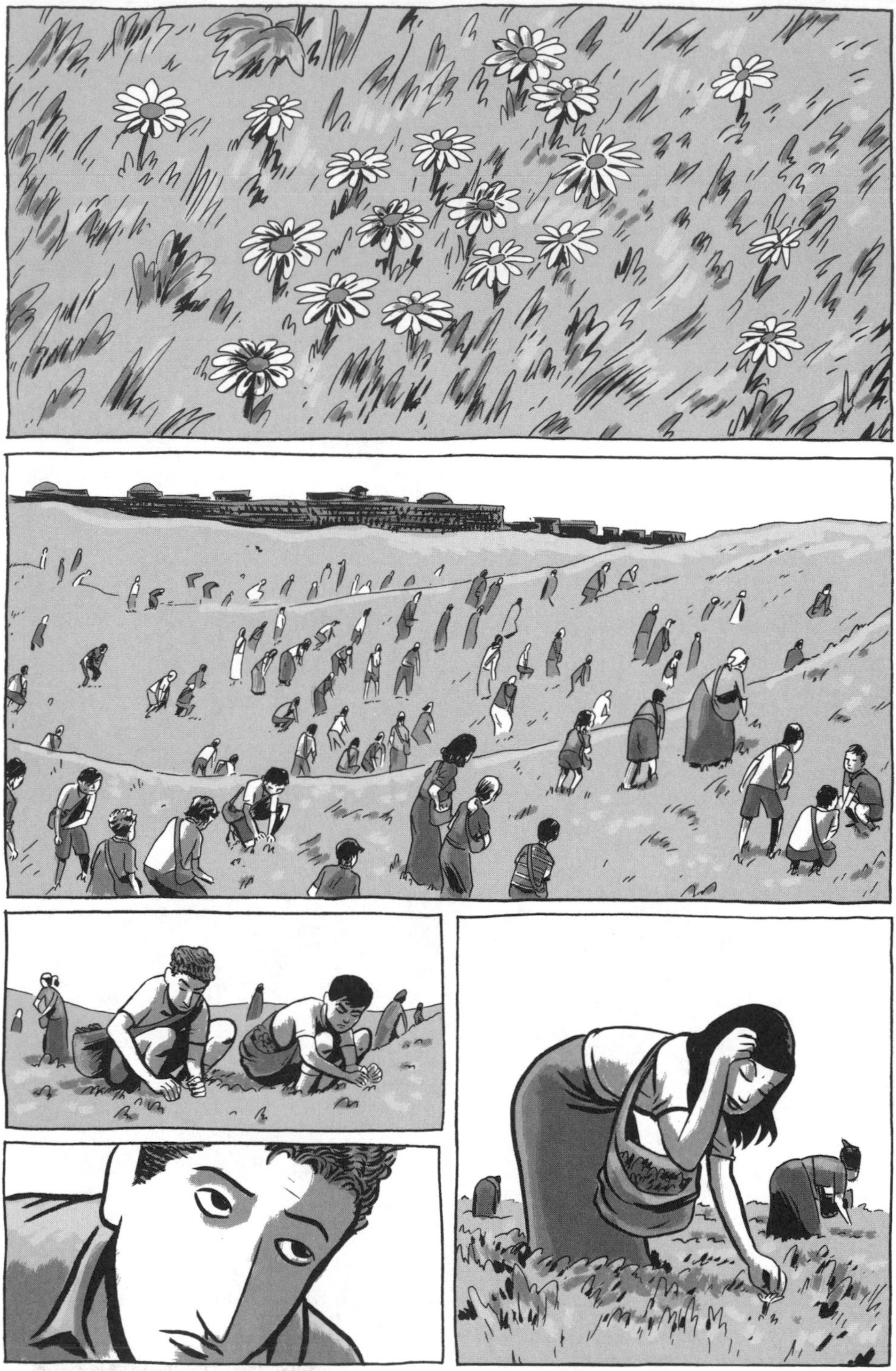

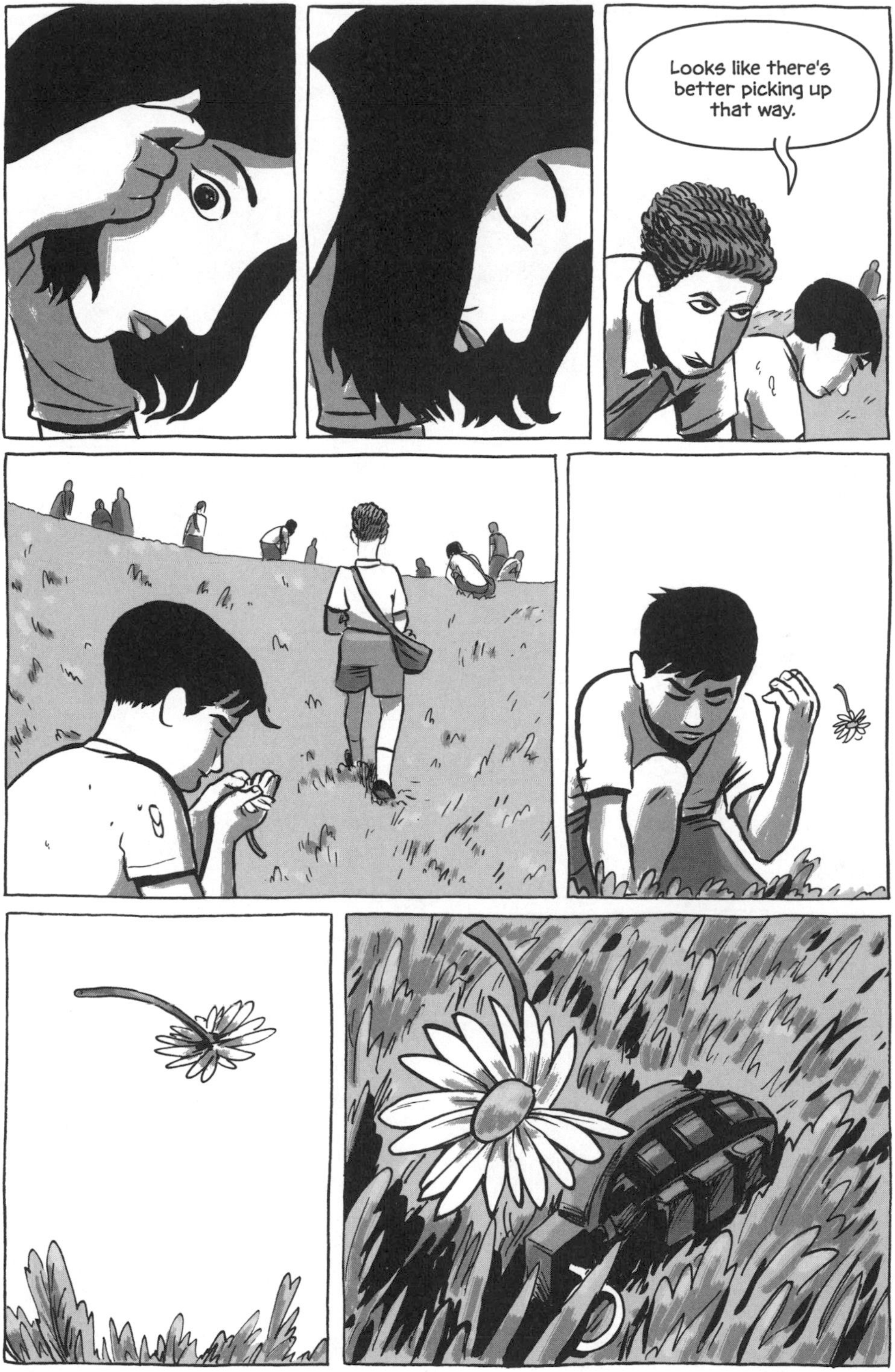
Looks like there's better picking up that way.

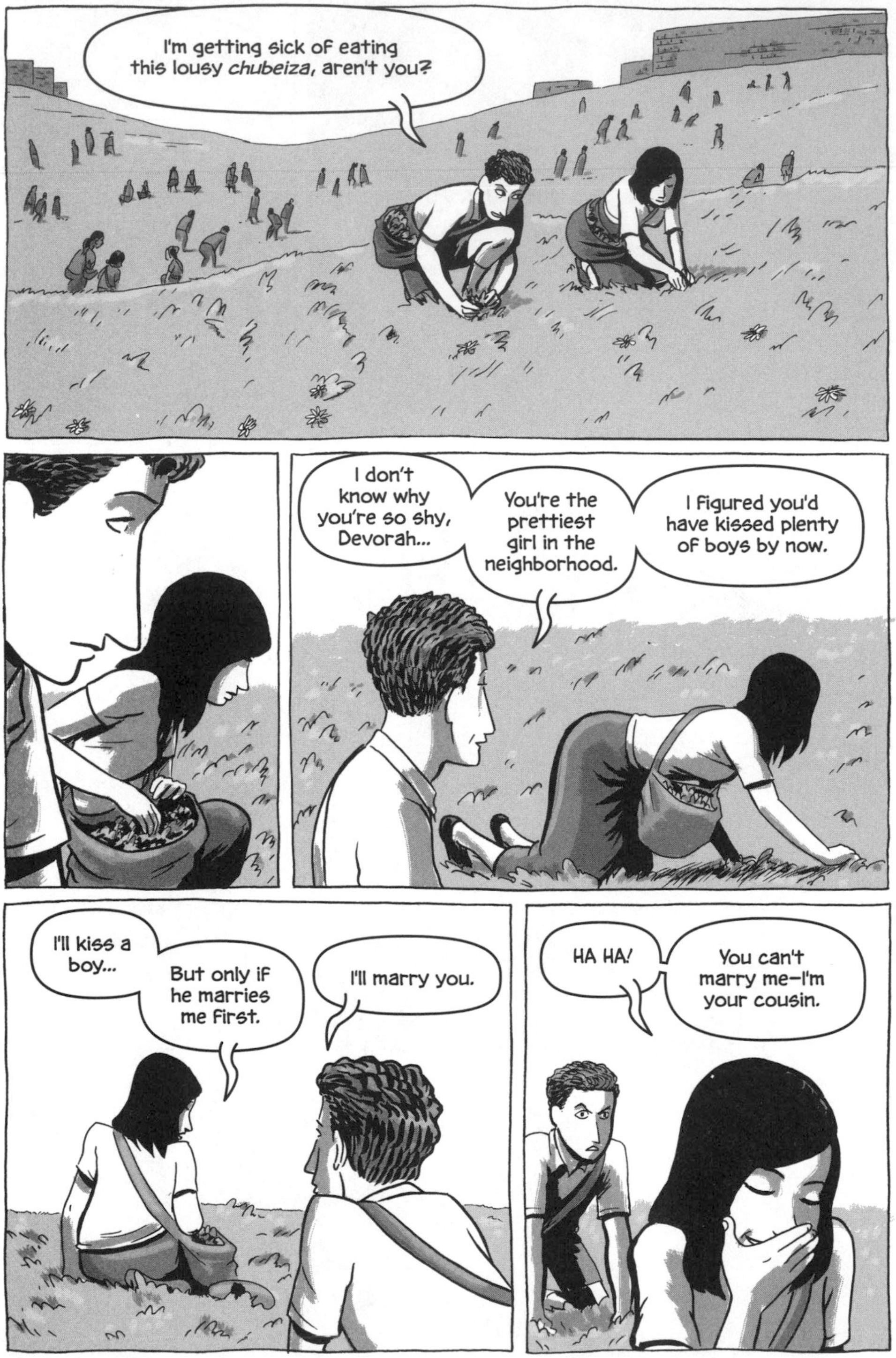
I'm getting sick of eating this lousy *chubeiza*, aren't you?
I don't know why you're so shy, Devorah...
You're the prettiest girl in the neighborhood.
I figured you'd have kissed plenty of boys by now.
I'll kiss a boy...
But only if he marries me first.
I'll marry you.
HA HA!
You can't marry me—I'm your cousin.

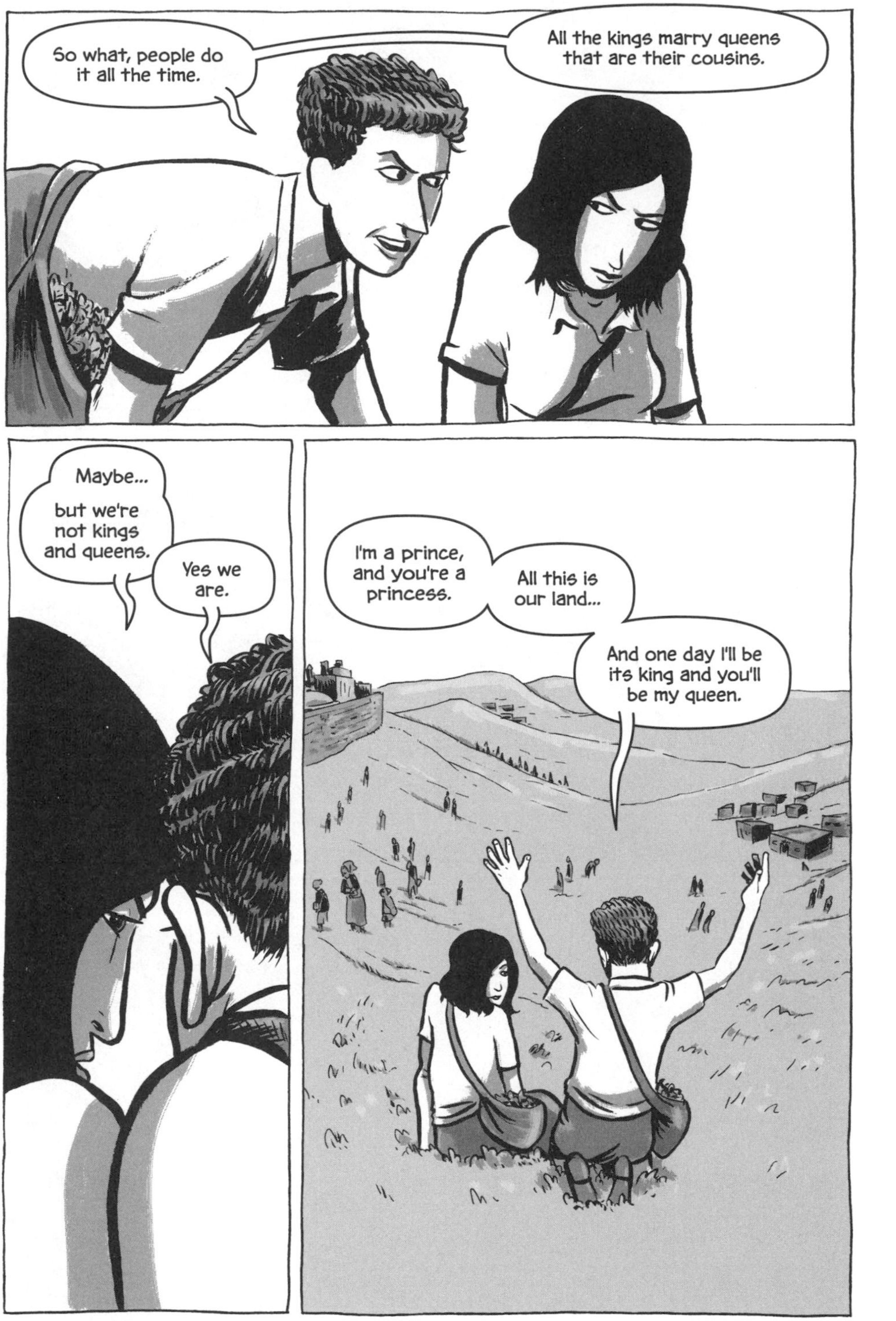
So what, people do it all the time.
All the kings marry queens that are their cousins.
Maybe...
but we're not kings and queens.
Yes we are.
I'm a prince, and you're a princess.
All this is our land...
And one day I'll be its king and you'll be my queen.

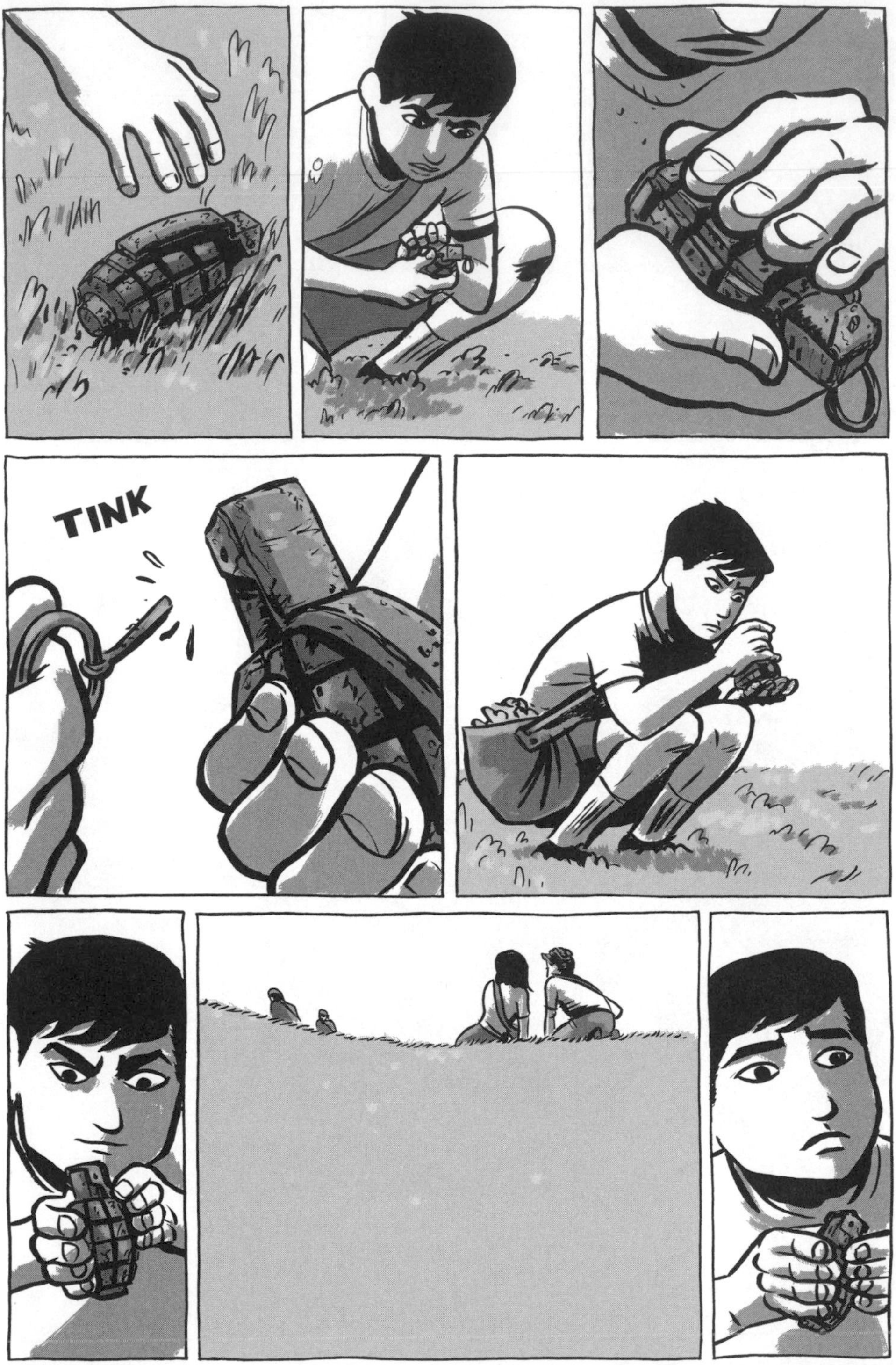
TINK

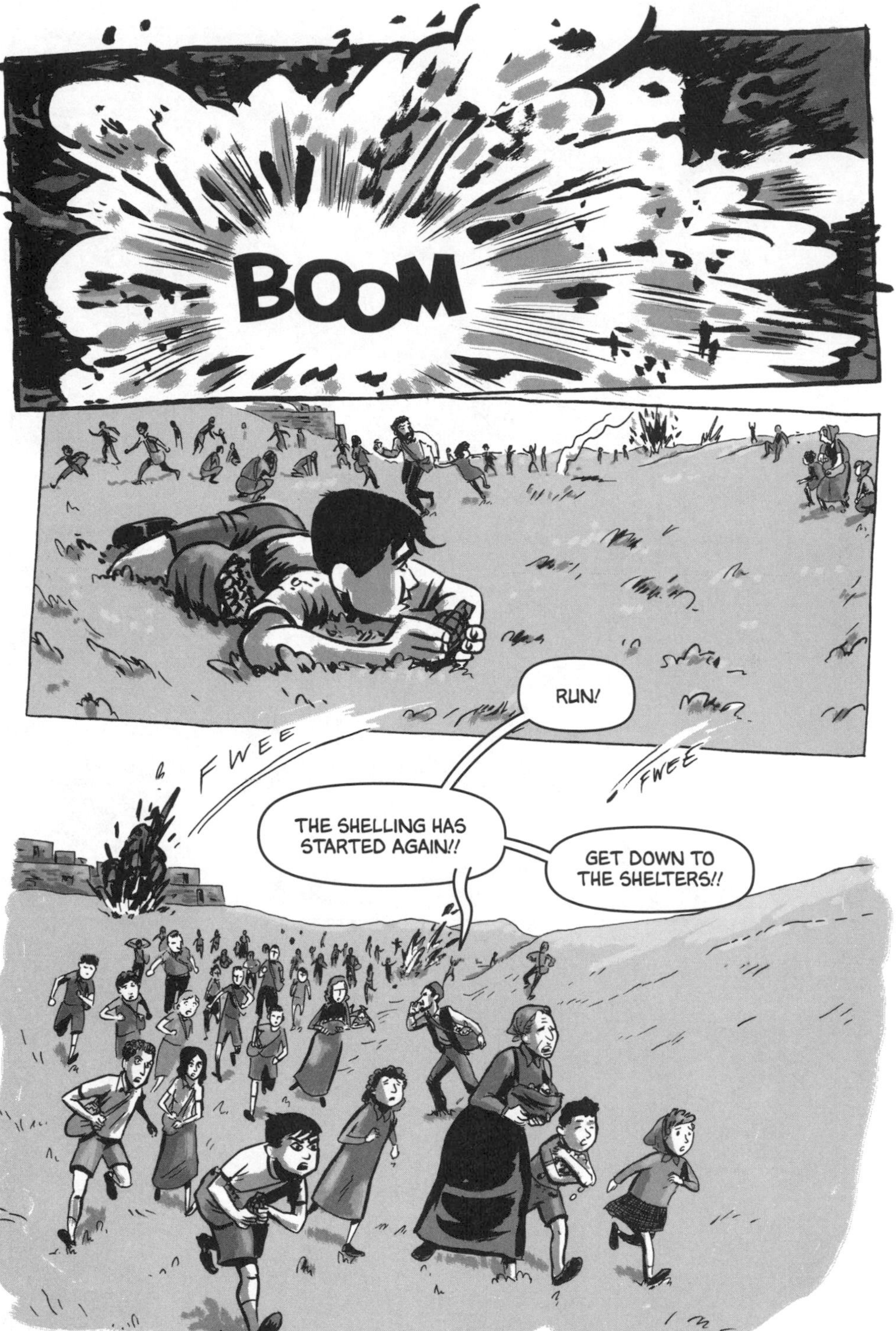
BOOM
RUN!
FWEE
FWEE
THE SHELLING HAS STARTED AGAIN!!
GET DOWN TO THE SHELTERS!!

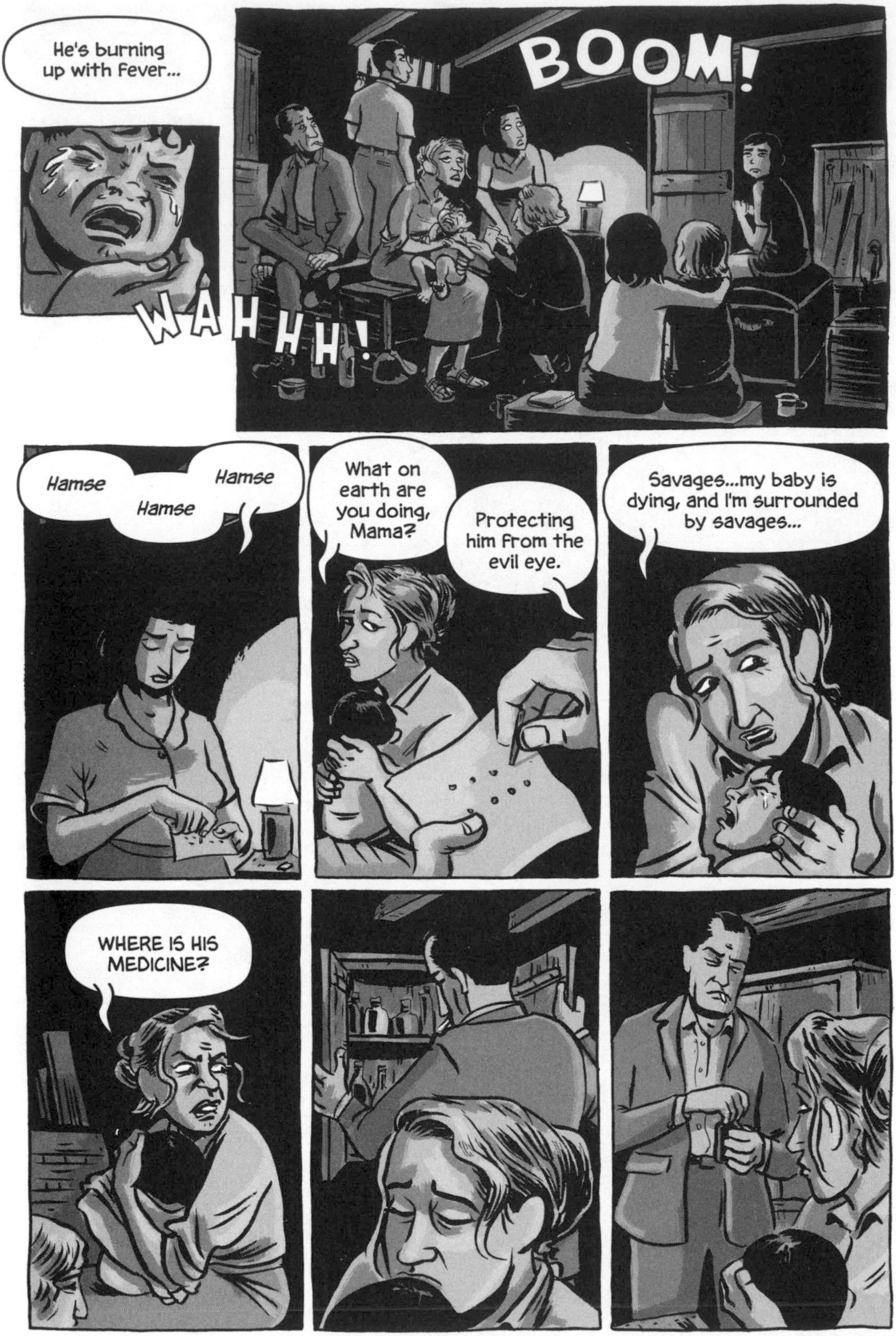
He's burning up with fever...
BOOM!
WAHHH!
Hamse
Hamse
Hamse
What on earth are you doing, Mama?
Protecting him from the evil eye.
Savages...my baby is dying, and I'm surrounded by savages...
WHERE IS HIS MEDICINE?

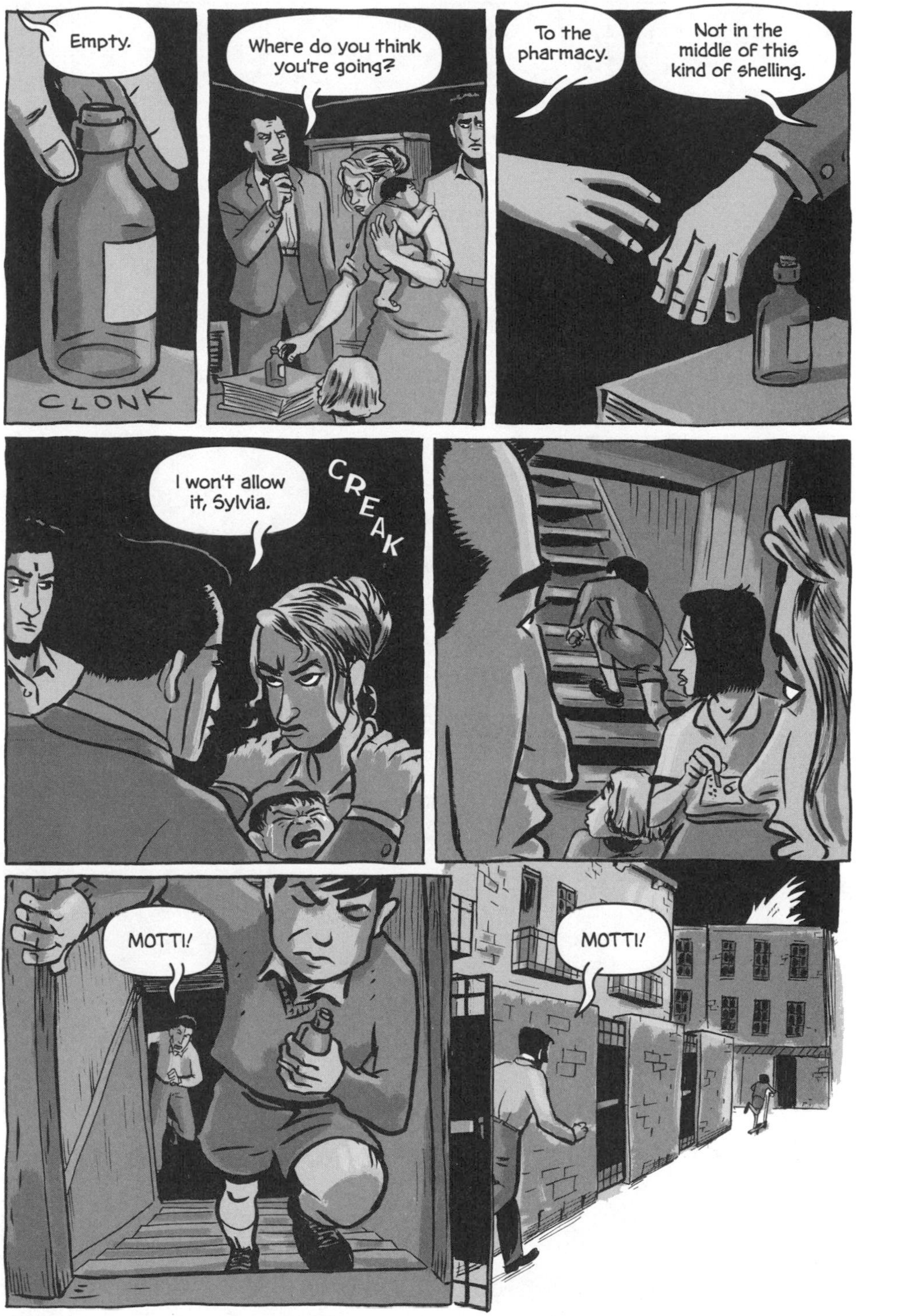
Empty.
CLONK
Where do you think you're going?
To the pharmacy.
Not in the middle of this kind of shelling.
I won't allow it, Sylvia.
CREAK
MOTTI!
MOTTI!

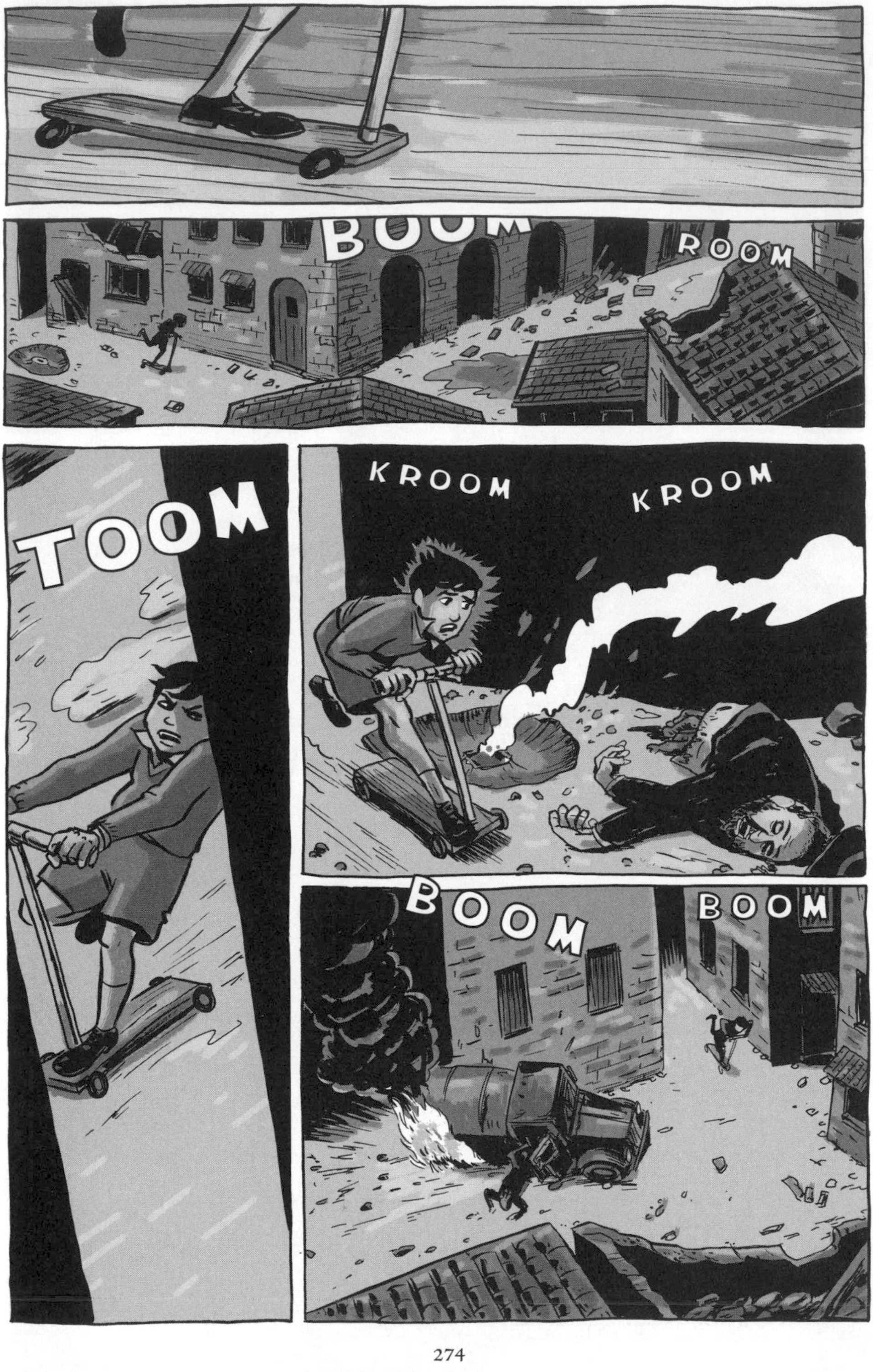
BOOM
ROOM
TOOM
KROOM
KROOM
BOOM
BOOM

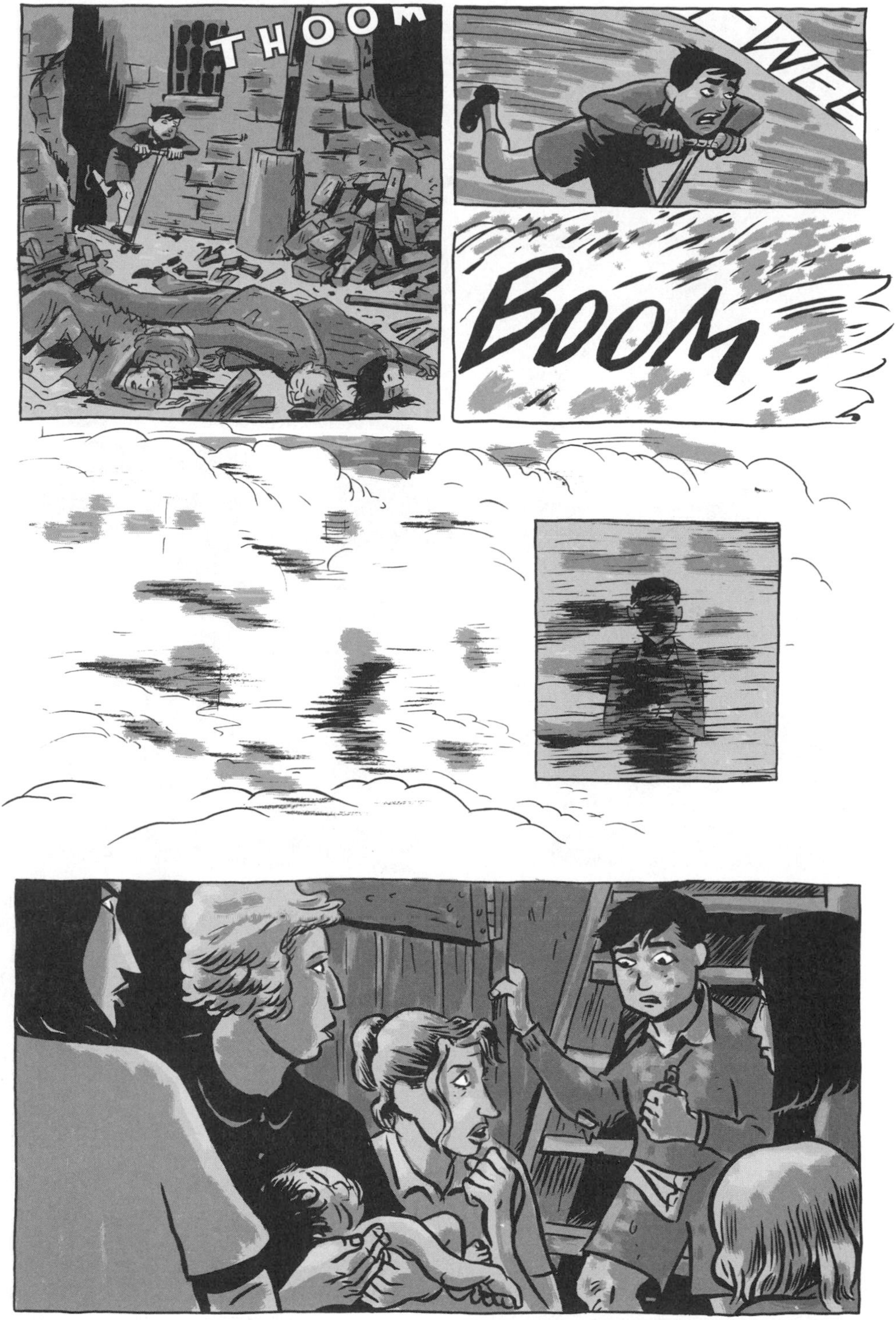
THOOM
WEE
BOOM

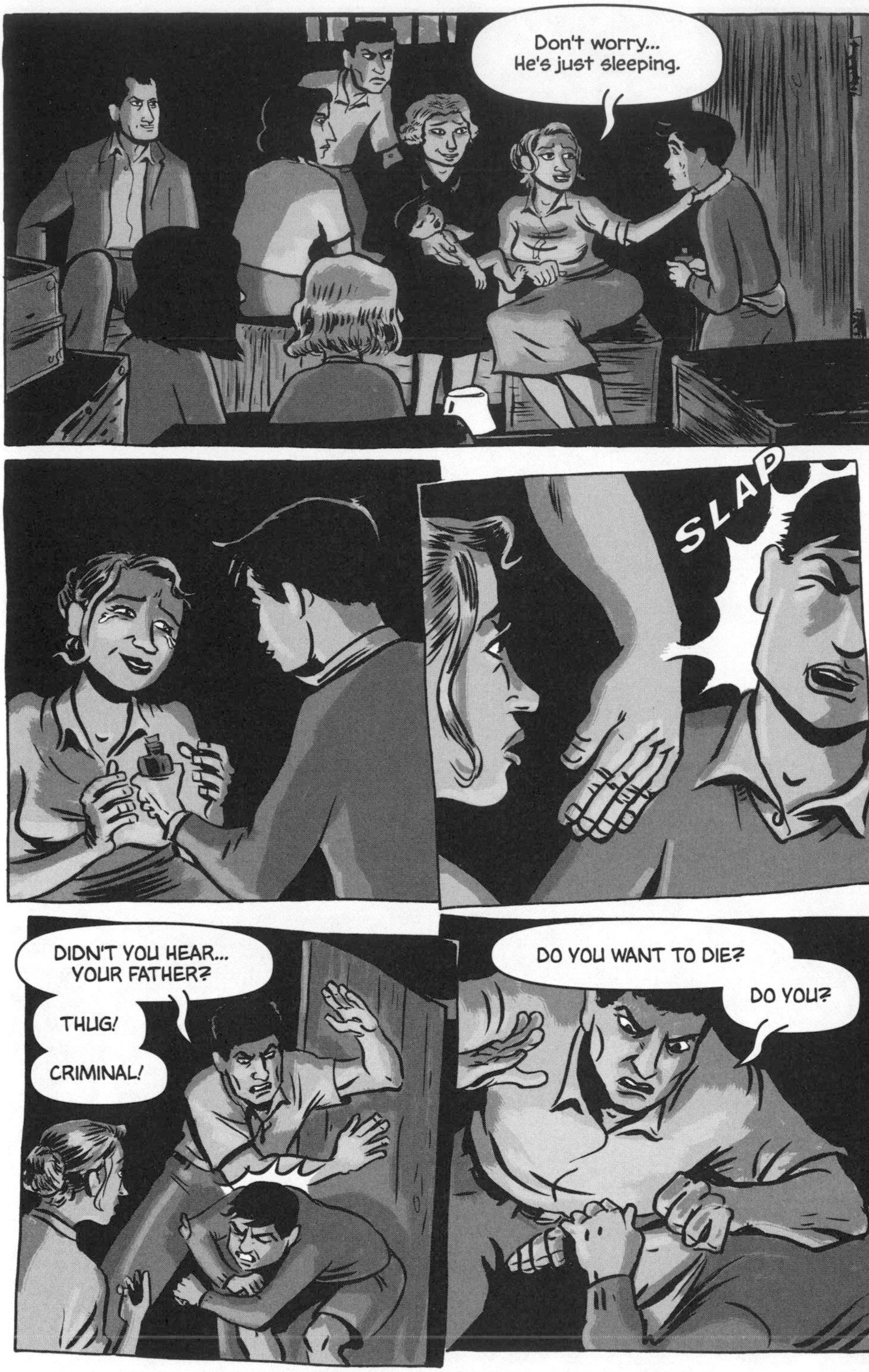
Don't worry... He's just sleeping.
SLAP
DIDN'T YOU HEAR... YOUR FATHER?
THUG!
CRIMINAL!
DO YOU WANT TO DIE?
DO YOU?

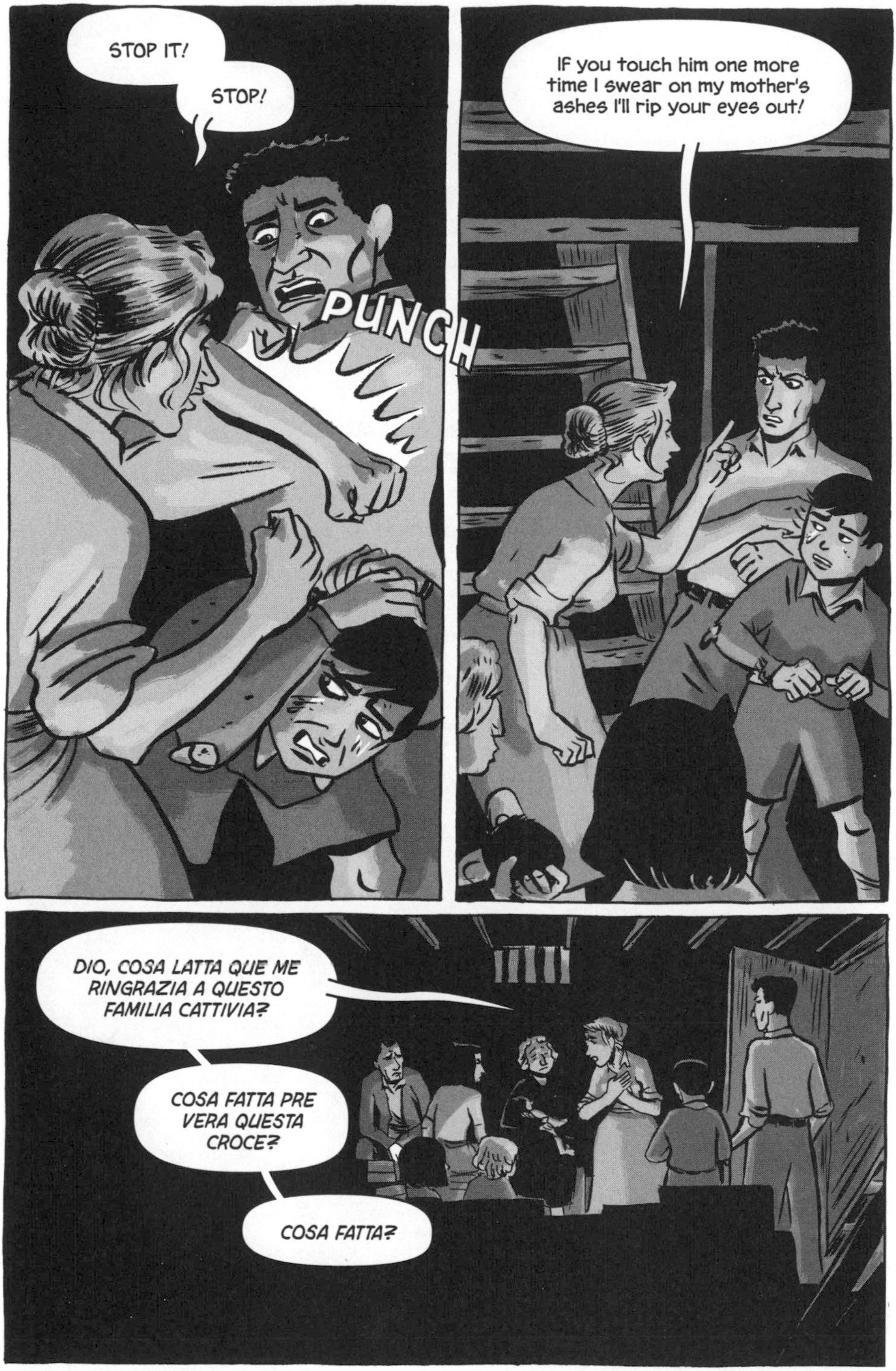
STOP IT!
STOP!
PUNCH
If you touch him one more time I swear on my mother's ashes I'll rip your eyes out!
DIO, COSA LATTA QUE ME RINGRAZIA A QUESTO FAMILIA CATTIVIA?
COSA FATTA PRE VERA QUESTA CROCE?
COSA FATTA?

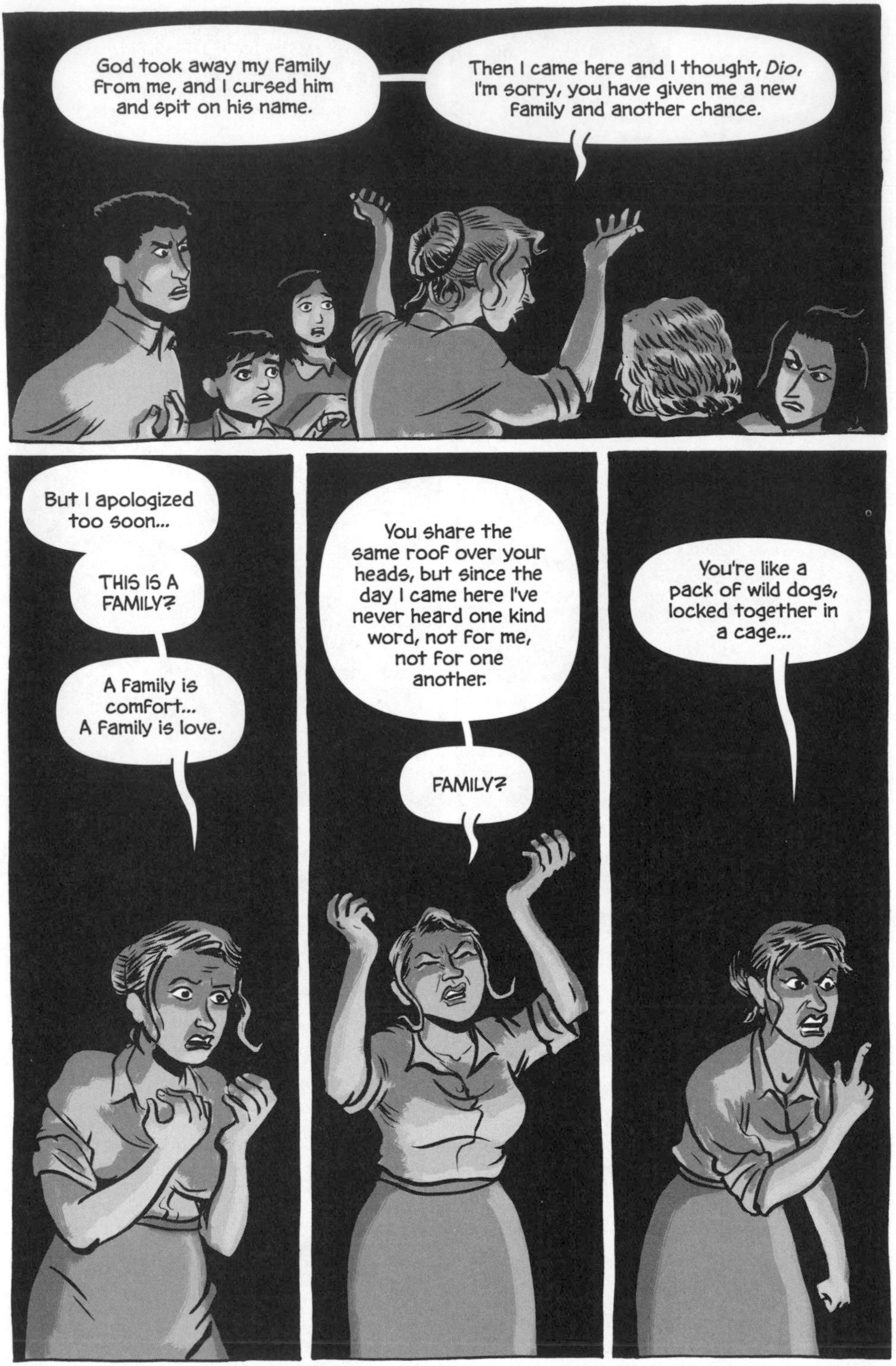
God took away my family from me, and I cursed him and spit on his name.
Then I came here and I thought, *Dio*, I'm sorry, you have given me a new family and another chance.
But I apologized too soon...
THIS IS A FAMILY?
A family is comfort... A family is love.
You share the same roof over your heads, but since the day I came here I've never heard one kind word, not for me, not for one another.
FAMILY?
You're like a pack of wild dogs, locked together in a cage...

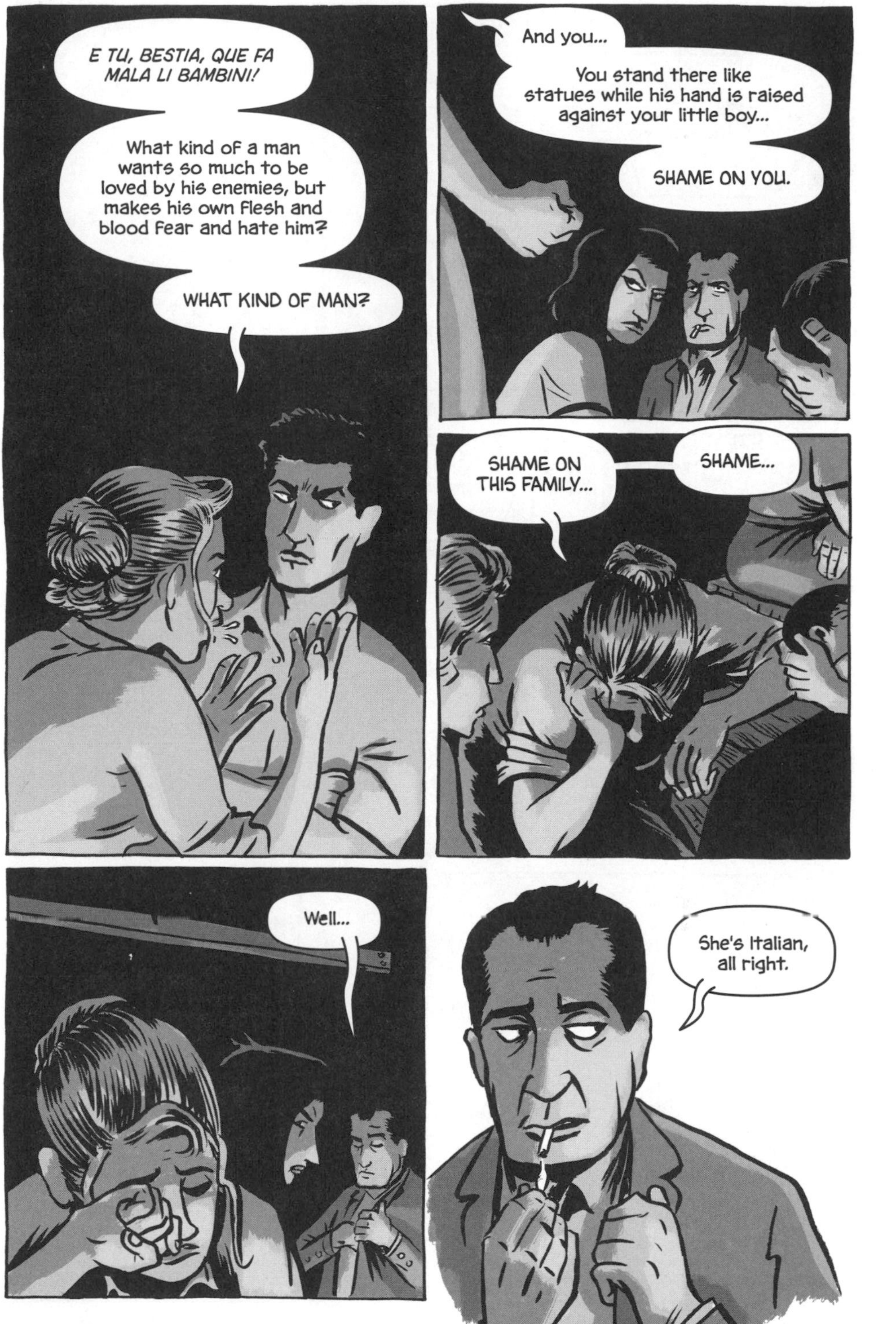
E TU, BESTIA, QUE FA MALA LI BAMBINI!
What kind of a man wants so much to be loved by his enemies, but makes his own flesh and blood fear and hate him?
WHAT KIND OF MAN?
And you...
You stand there like statues while his hand is raised against your little boy...
SHAME ON YOU.
SHAME ON THIS FAMILY...
SHAME...
Well...
She's Italian, all right.

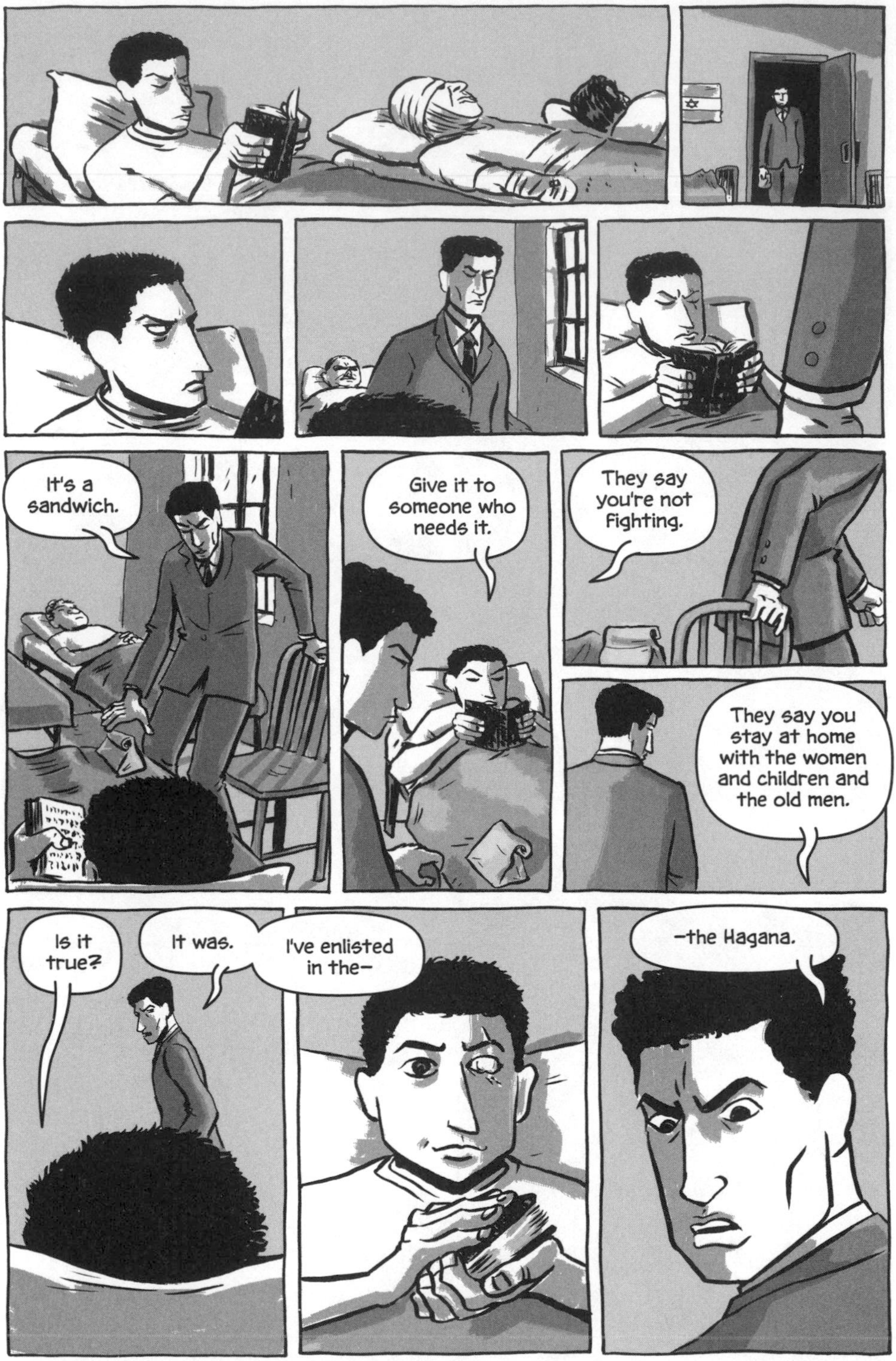

It's a sandwich.
Give it to someone who needs it.
They say you're not fighting.
They say you stay at home with the women and children and the old men.
Is it true?
It was.
I've enlisted in the–
–the Hagana.

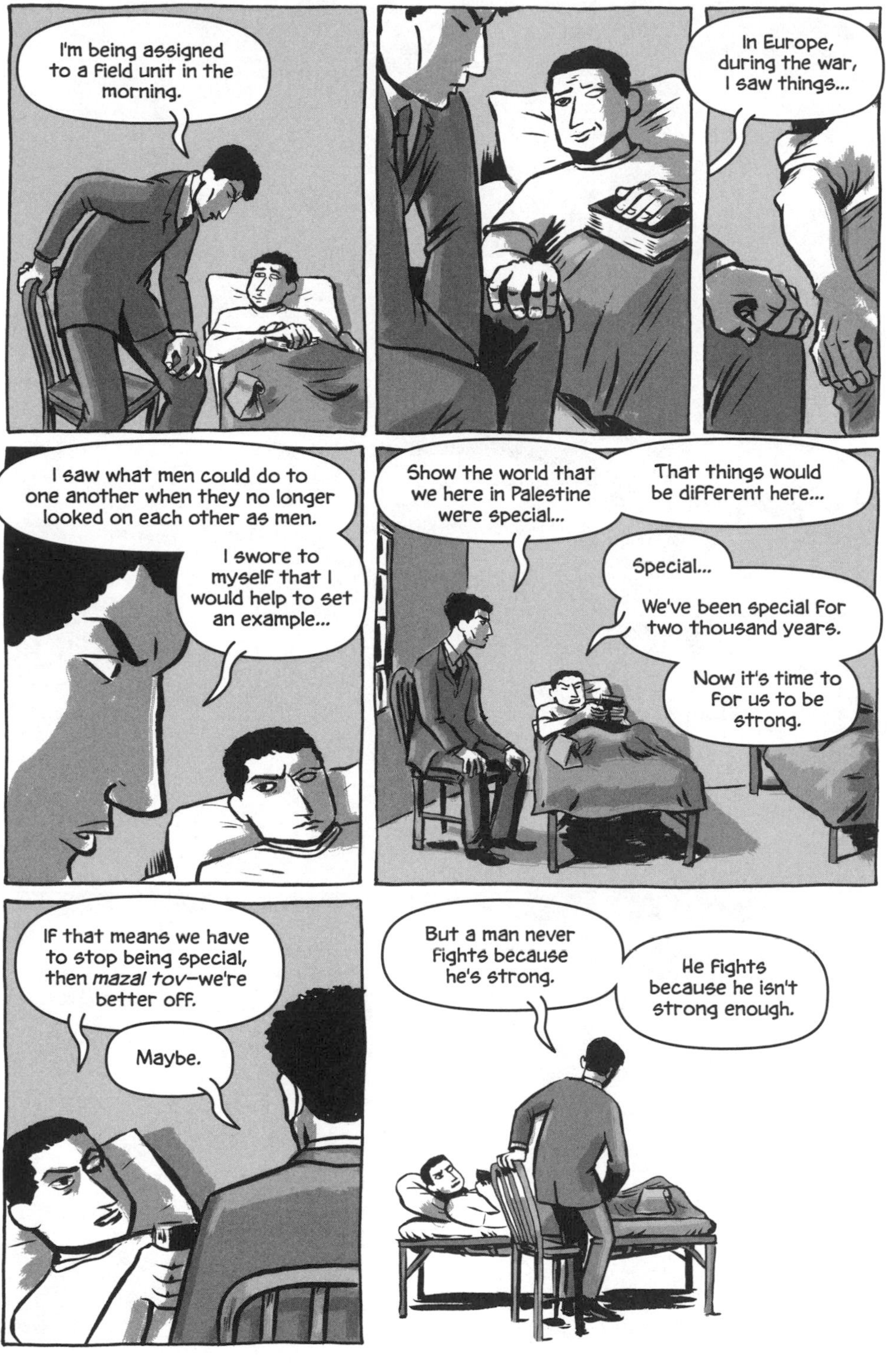
I'm being assigned to a field unit in the morning.
In Europe, during the war, I saw things...
I saw what men could do to one another when they no longer looked on each other as men.
I swore to myself that I would help to set an example...
Show the world that we here in Palestine were special...
That things would be different here...
Special...
We've been special for two thousand years.
Now it's time to for us to be strong.
If that means we have to stop being special, then *mazal tov*—we're better off.
Maybe.
But a man never fights because he's strong.
He fights because he isn't strong enough.

THOOM

KOOM

BOOM

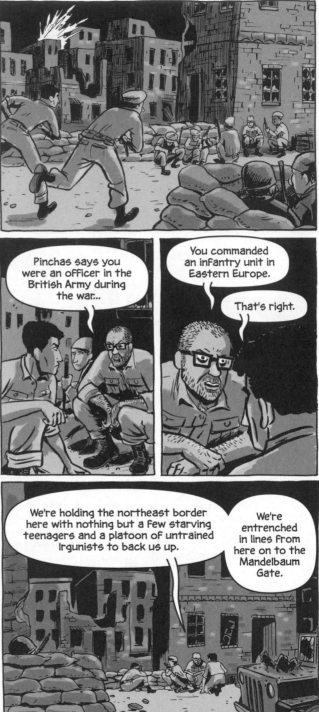

Pinchas says you were an officer in the British Army during the war...

You commanded an infantry unit in Eastern Europe.

That's right.

We're holding the northeast border here with nothing but a few starving teenagers and a platoon of untrained Irgunists to back us up.

We're entrenched in lines from here on to the Mandelbaum Gate.

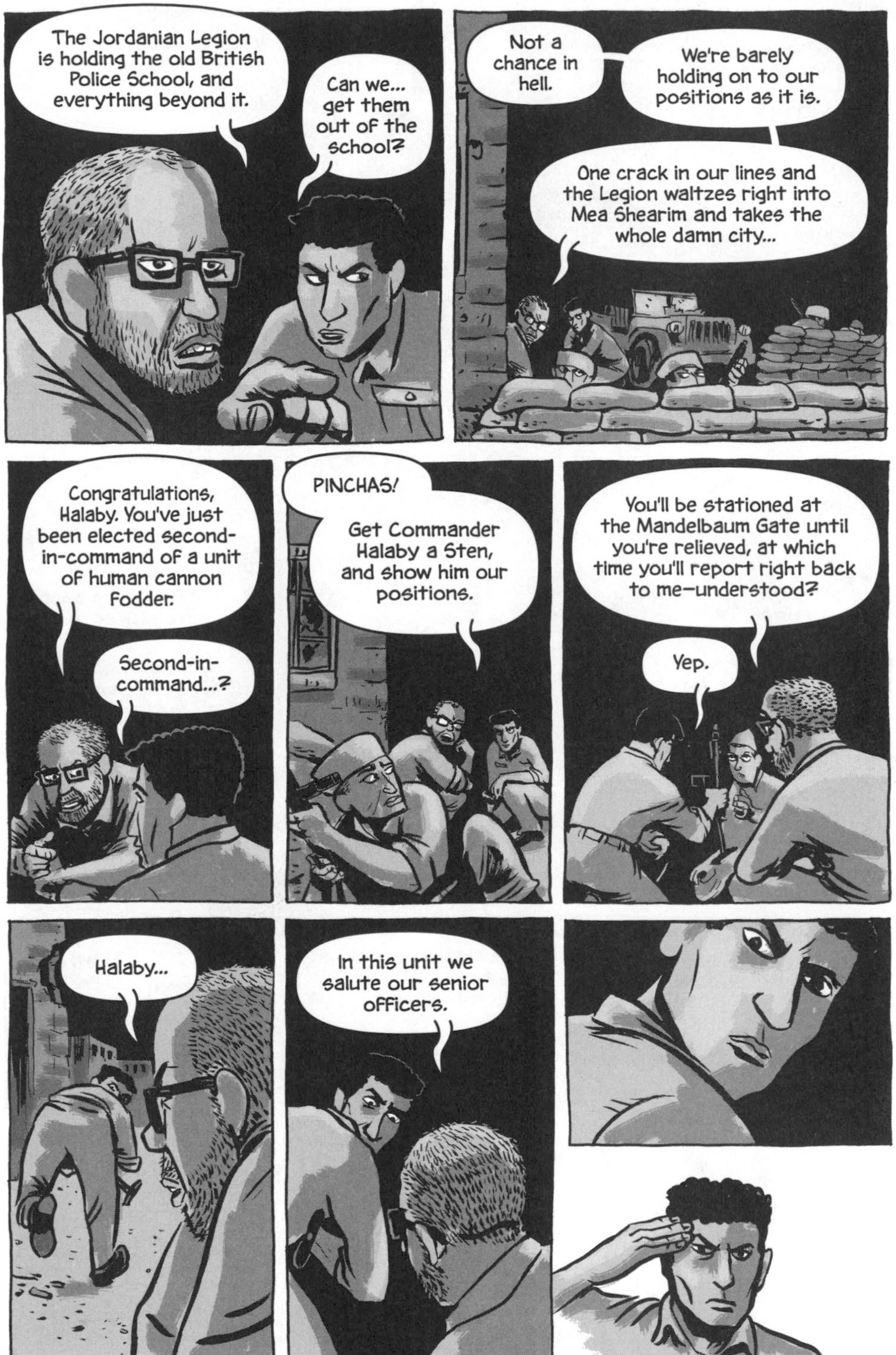
The Jordanian Legion is holding the old British Police School, and everything beyond it.
Can we... get them out of the school?
Not a chance in hell.
We're barely holding on to our positions as it is.
One crack in our lines and the Legion waltzes right into Mea Shearim and takes the whole damn city...
Congratulations, Halaby. You've just been elected second-in-command of a unit of human cannon fodder.
Second-in-command...?
PINCHAS!
Get Commander Halaby a Sten, and show him our positions.
You'll be stationed at the Mandelbaum Gate until you're relieved, at which time you'll report right back to me—understood?
Yep.
Halaby...
In this unit we salute our senior officers.

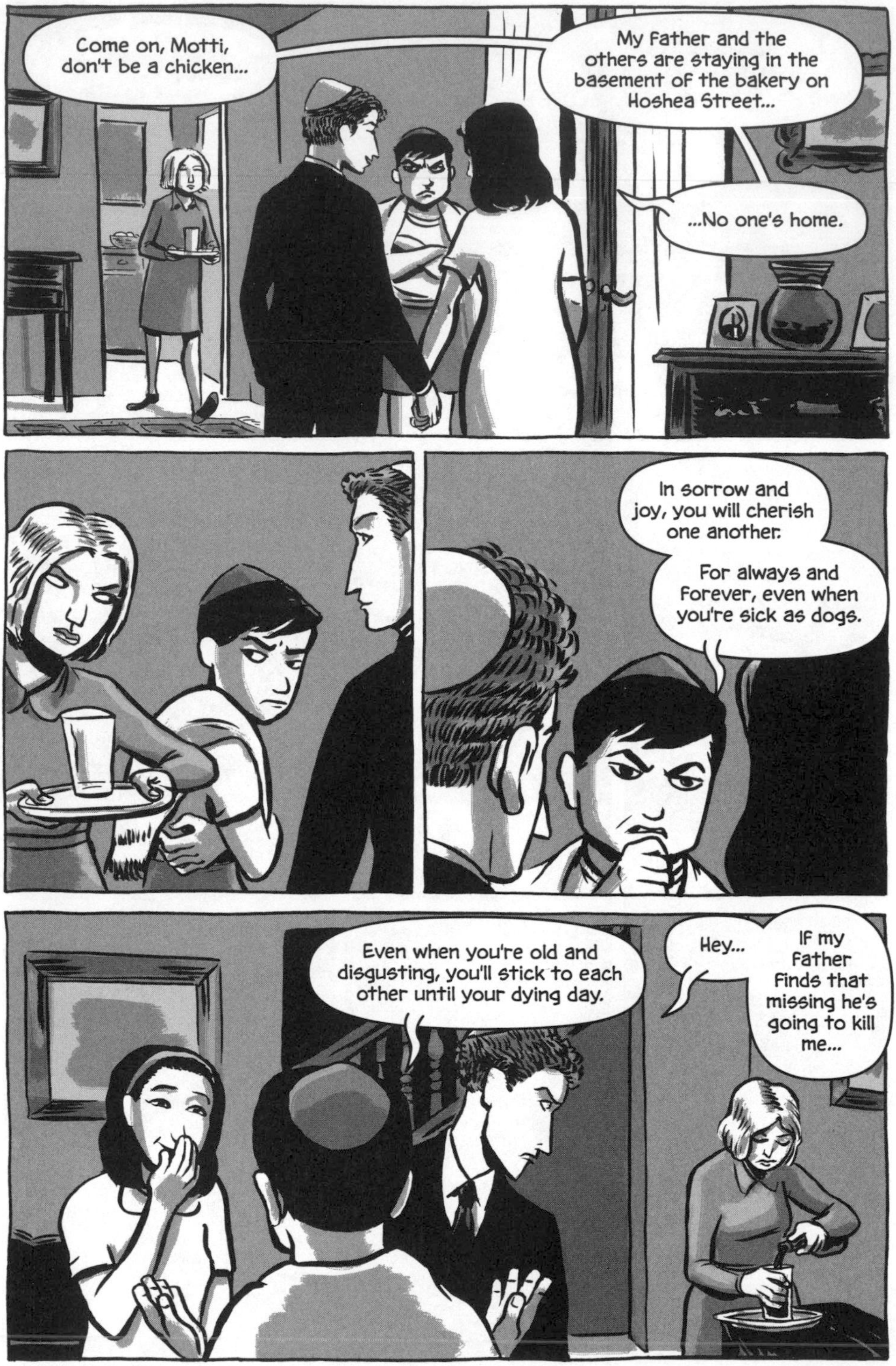
Come on, Motti, don't be a chicken...
My father and the others are staying in the basement of the bakery on Hoshea Street...
...No one's home.
In sorrow and joy, you will cherish one another.
For always and forever, even when you're sick as dogs.
Even when you're old and disgusting, you'll stick to each other until your dying day.
Hey...
If my father finds that missing he's going to kill me...

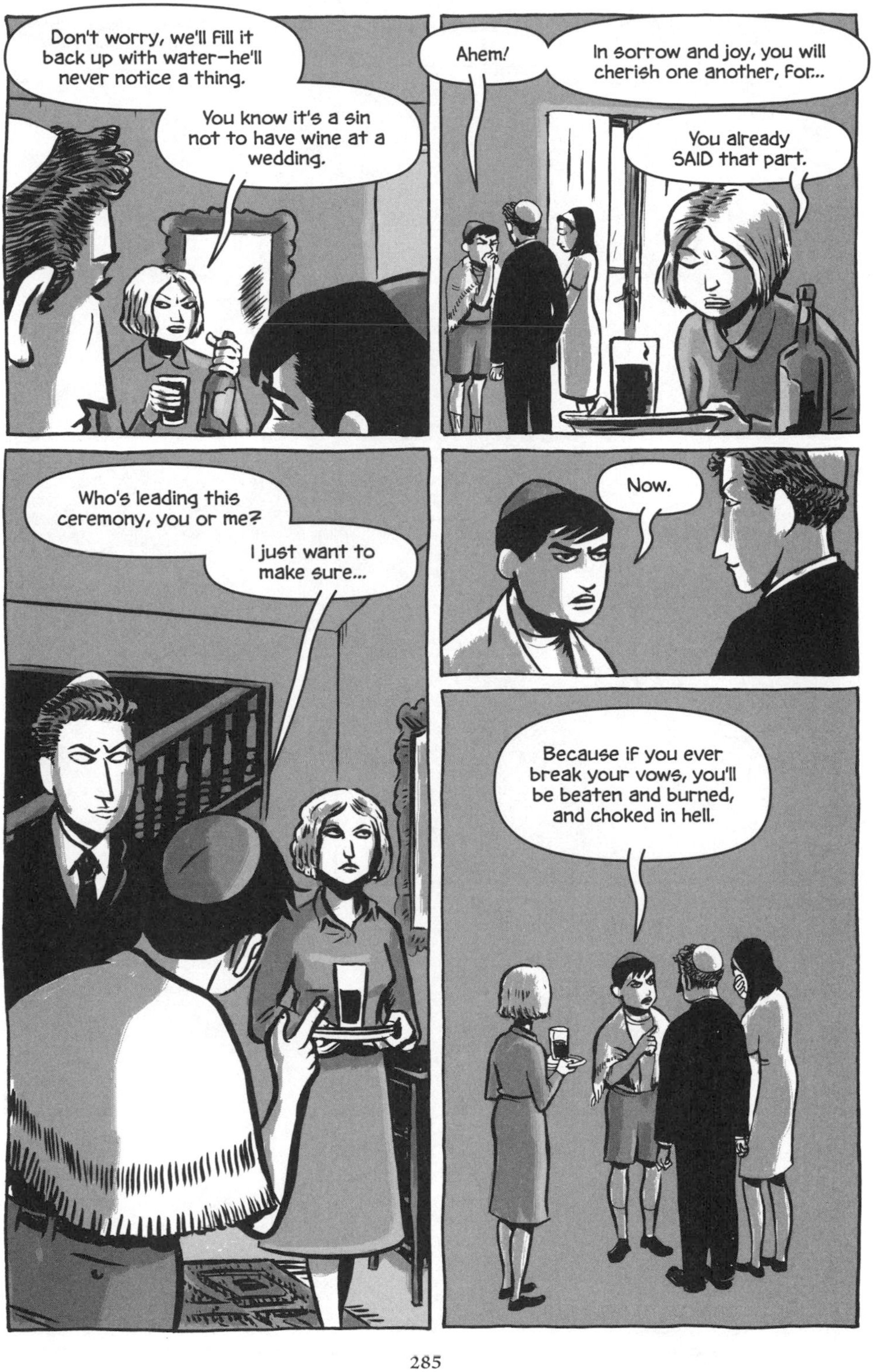
Don't worry, we'll fill it back up with water—he'll never notice a thing.
You know it's a sin not to have wine at a wedding.
Ahem!
In sorrow and joy, you will cherish one another, for...
You already SAID that part.
Who's leading this ceremony, you or me?
I just want to make sure...
Now.
Because if you ever break your vows, you'll be beaten and burned, and choked in hell.

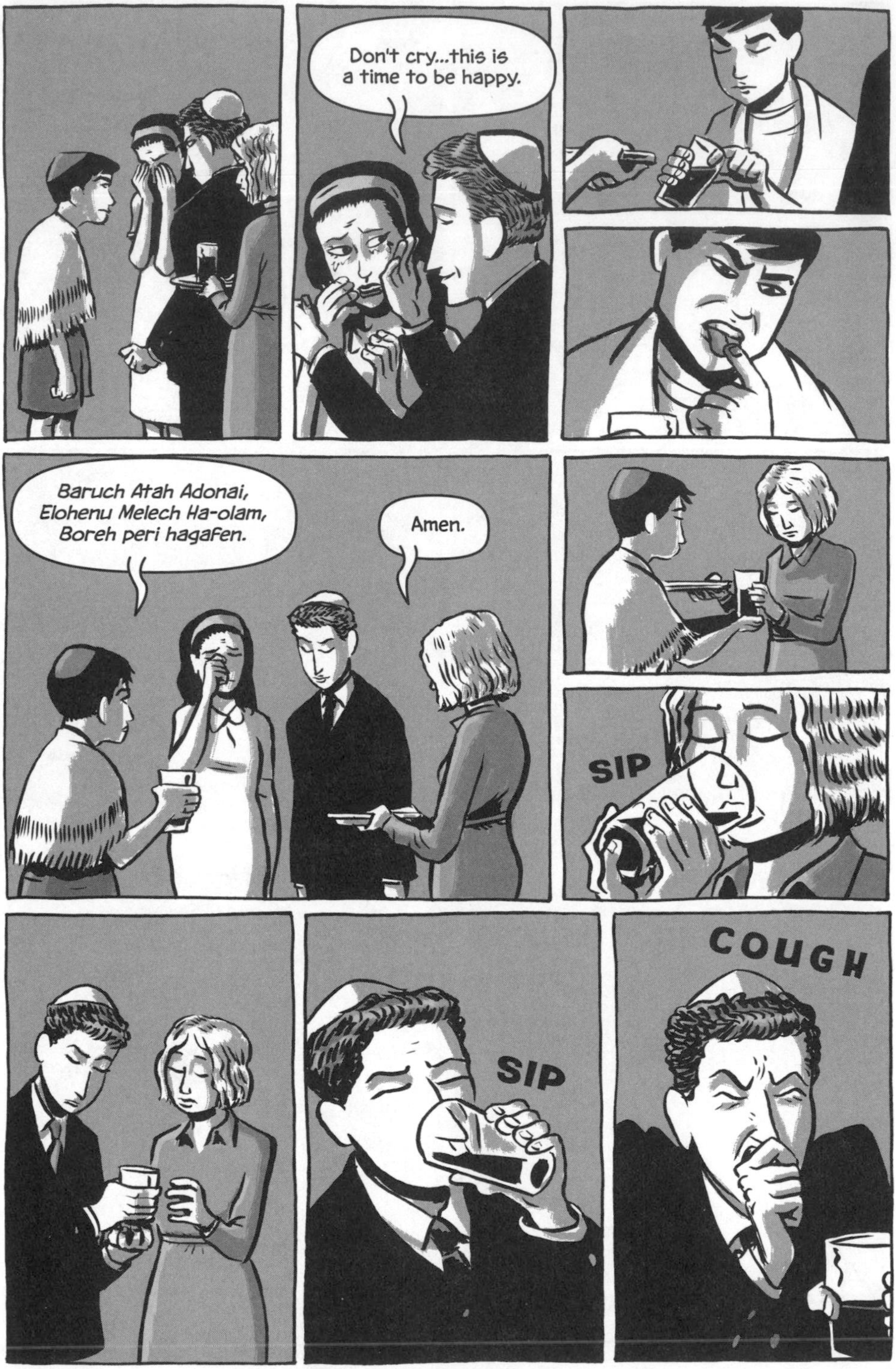
Don't cry...this is a time to be happy.
Baruch Atah Adonai, Elohenu Melech Ha-olam, Boreh peri hagafen.
Amen.
SIP
SIP
COUGH

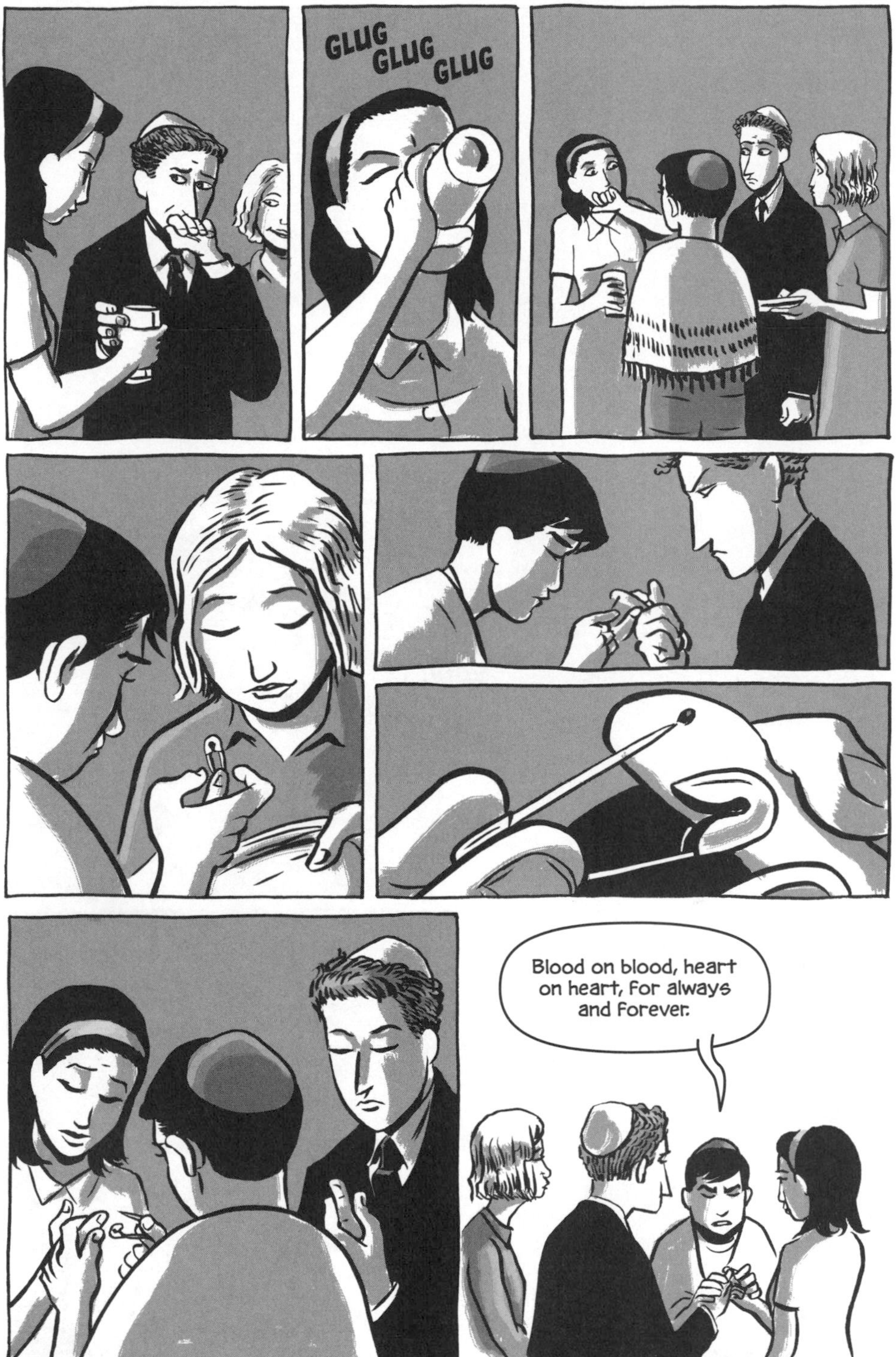
GLUG GLUG GLUG
Blood on blood, heart on heart, for always and forever.

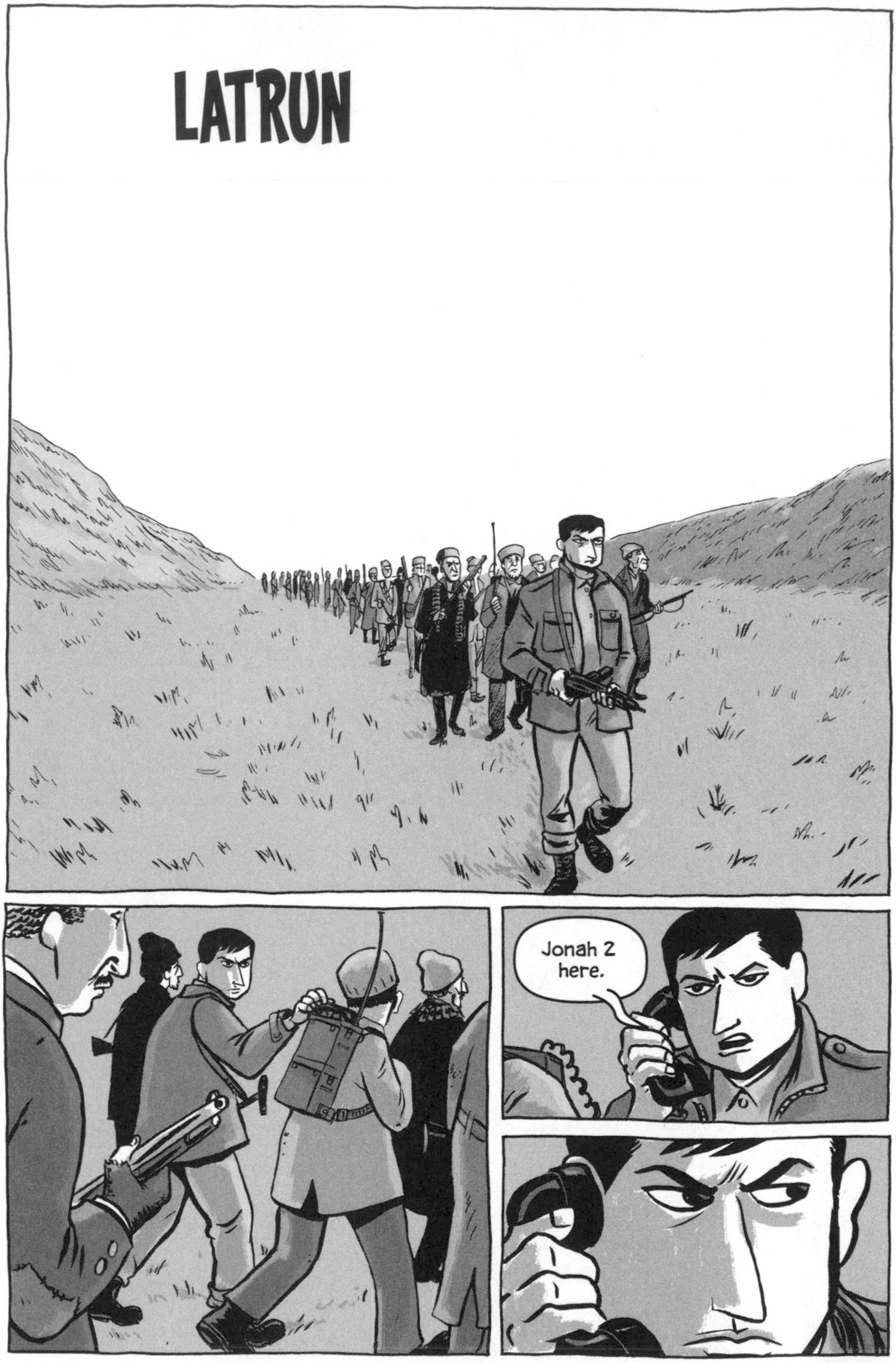
LATRUN
Jonah 2 here.

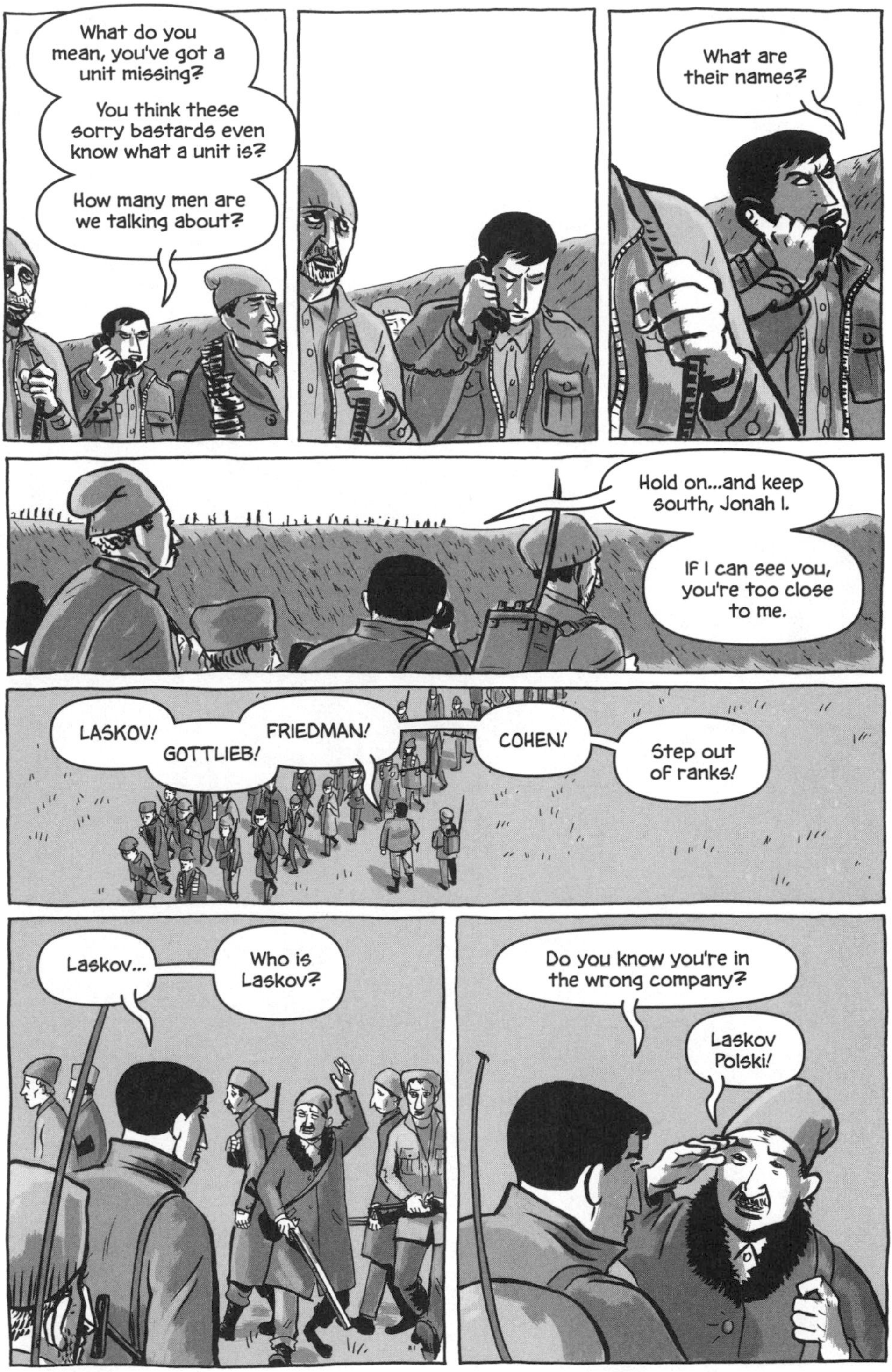
What do you mean, you've got a unit missing?
You think these sorry bastards even know what a unit is?
How many men are we talking about?
What are their names?
Hold on...and keep south, Jonah I.
If I can see you, you're too close to me.
LASKOV!
GOTTLIEB!
FRIEDMAN!
COHEN!
Step out of ranks!
Laskov...
Who is Laskov?
Do you know you're in the wrong company?
Laskov Polski!

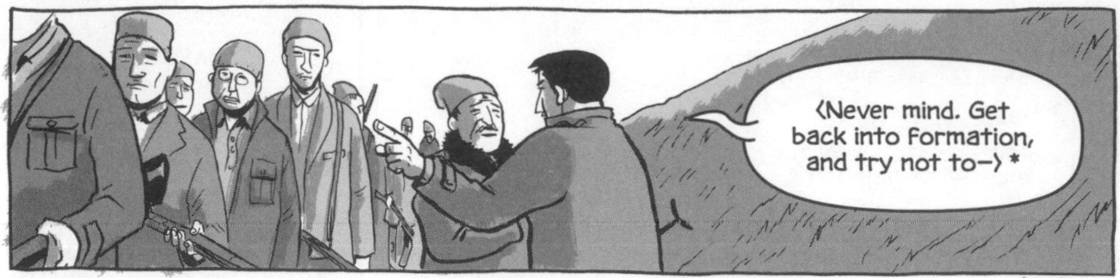
〈Never mind. Get back into formation, and try not to–〉 *

* In Polish

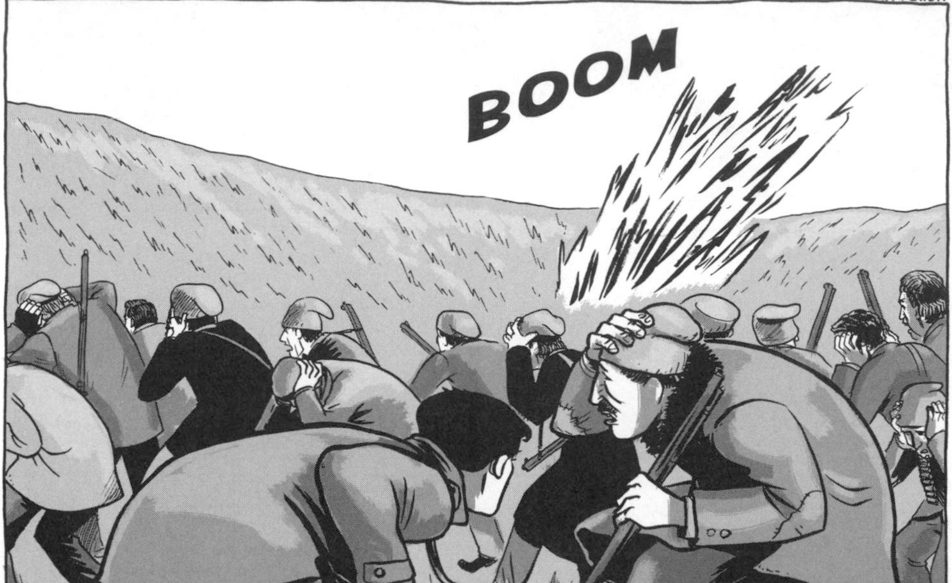
BOOM

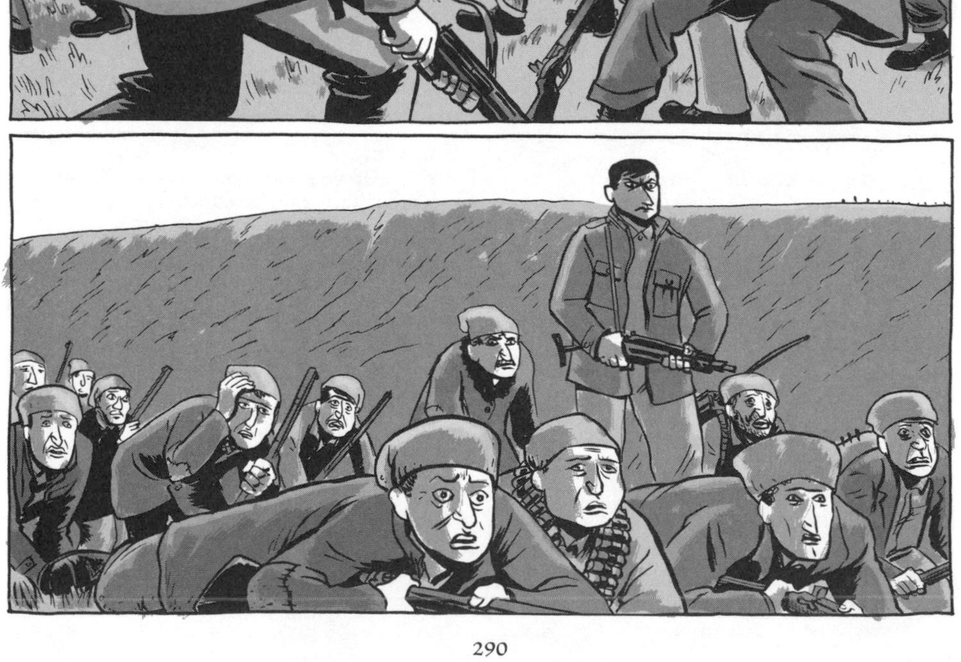

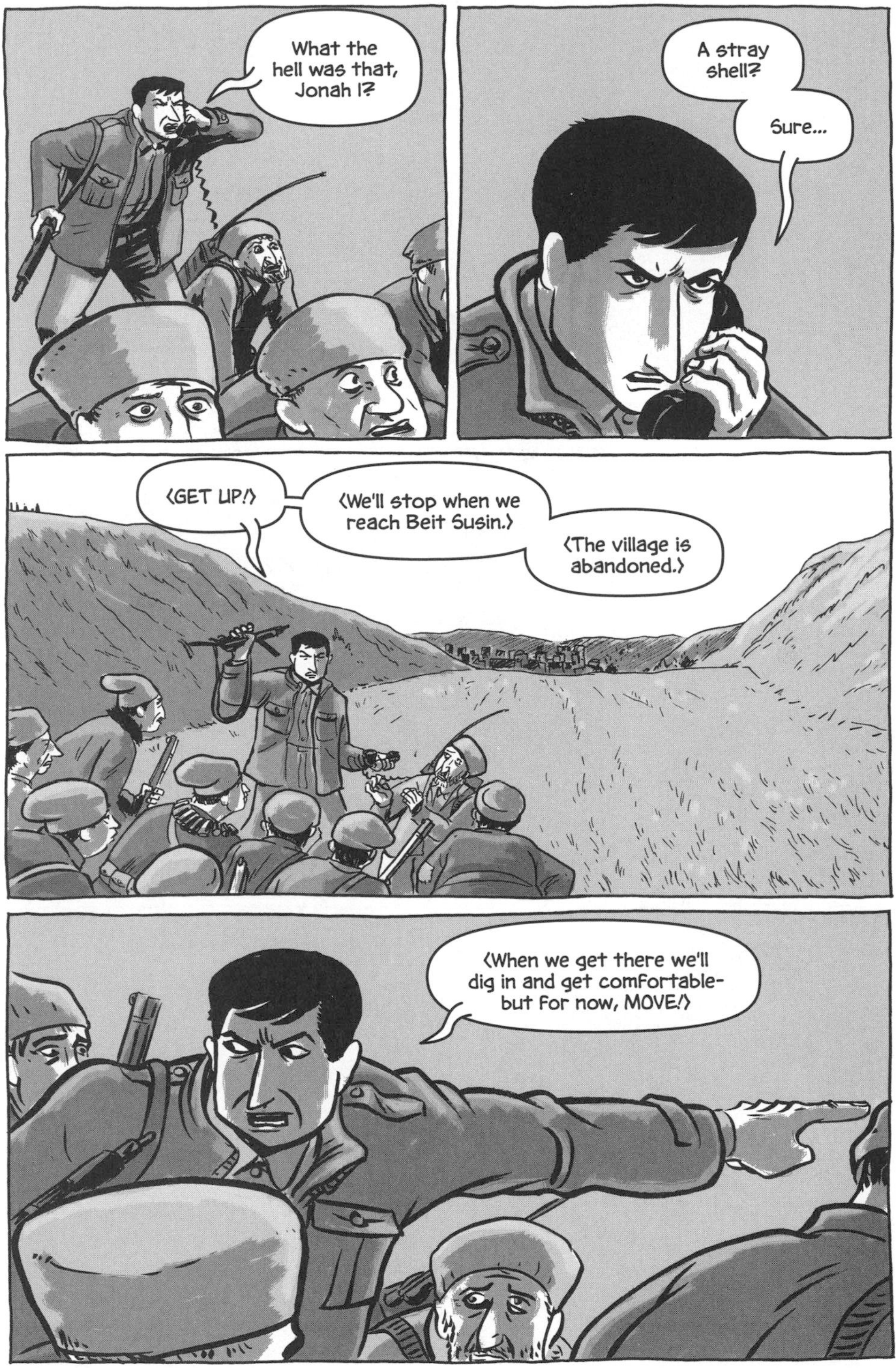
What the hell was that, Jonah !?
A stray shell?
Sure...
<GET UP!>
<We'll stop when we reach Beit Susin.>
<The village is abandoned.>
<When we get there we'll dig in and get comfortable- but for now, MOVE!>

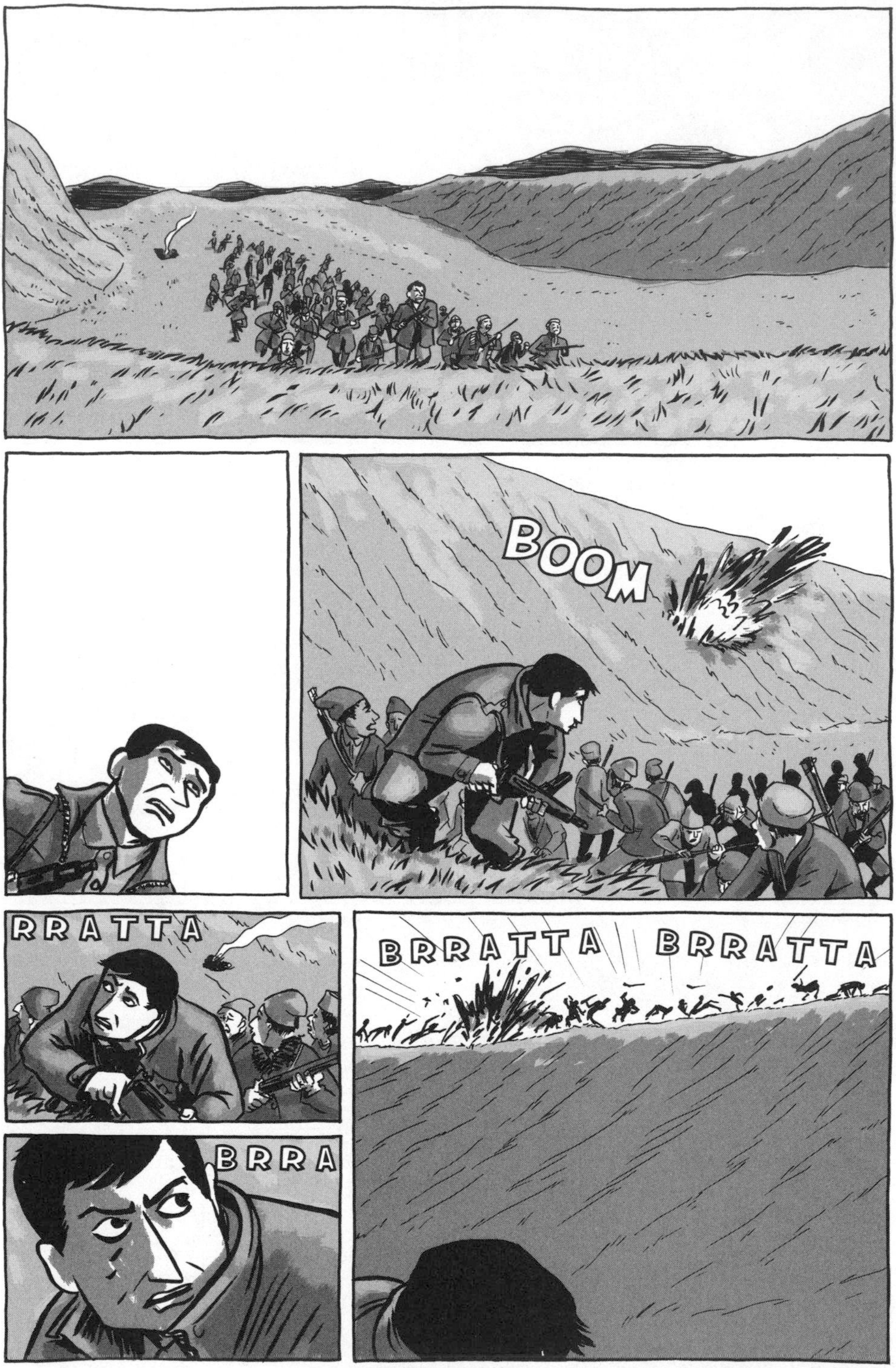
BOOM
RRATTA
BRRATTA BRRATTA
BRRA

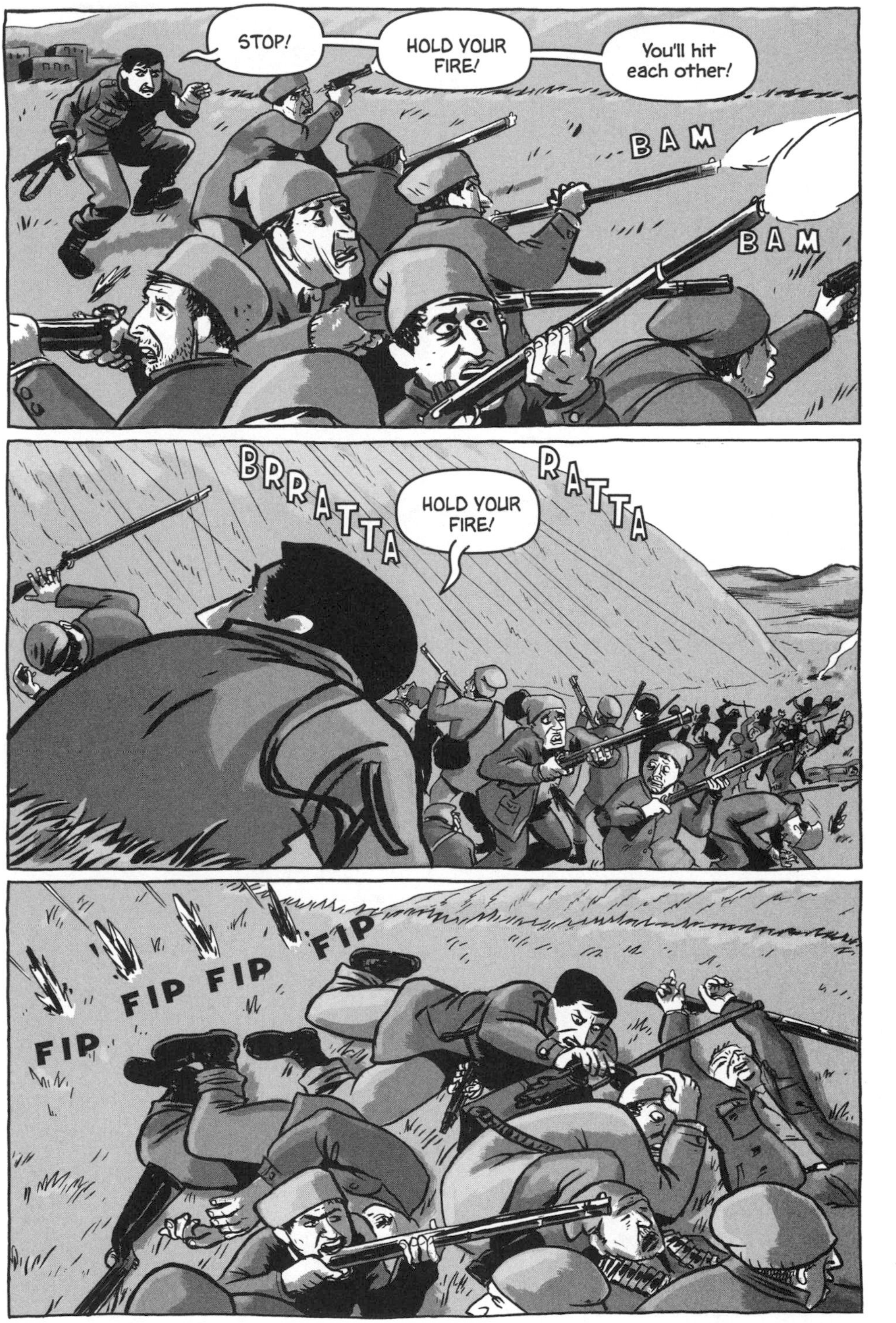
STOP!
HOLD YOUR FIRE!
You'll hit each other!
BAM
BAM
BRRRATTTA
RATTTA
HOLD YOUR FIRE!
FIP
FIP FIP
FIP

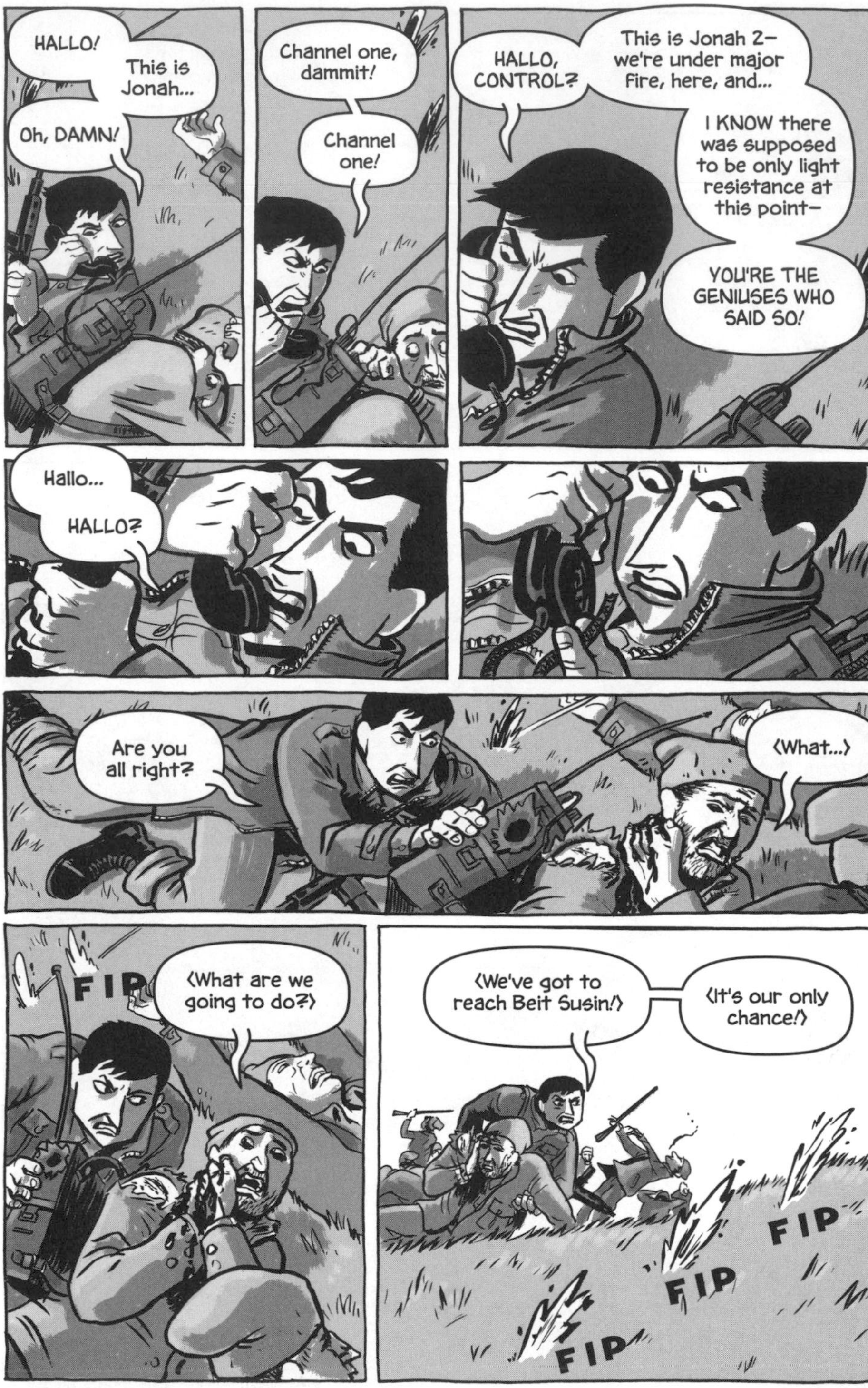
HALLO!
This is Jonah...
Oh, DAMN!
Channel one, dammit!
Channel one!
HALLO, CONTROL?
This is Jonah 2— we're under major fire, here, and...
I KNOW there was supposed to be only light resistance at this point—
YOU'RE THE GENIUSES WHO SAID SO!
Hallo...
HALLO?
Are you all right?
‹What...›
FIP
‹What are we going to do?›
‹We've got to reach Beit Susin!›
‹It's our only chance!›
FIP
FIP
FIP

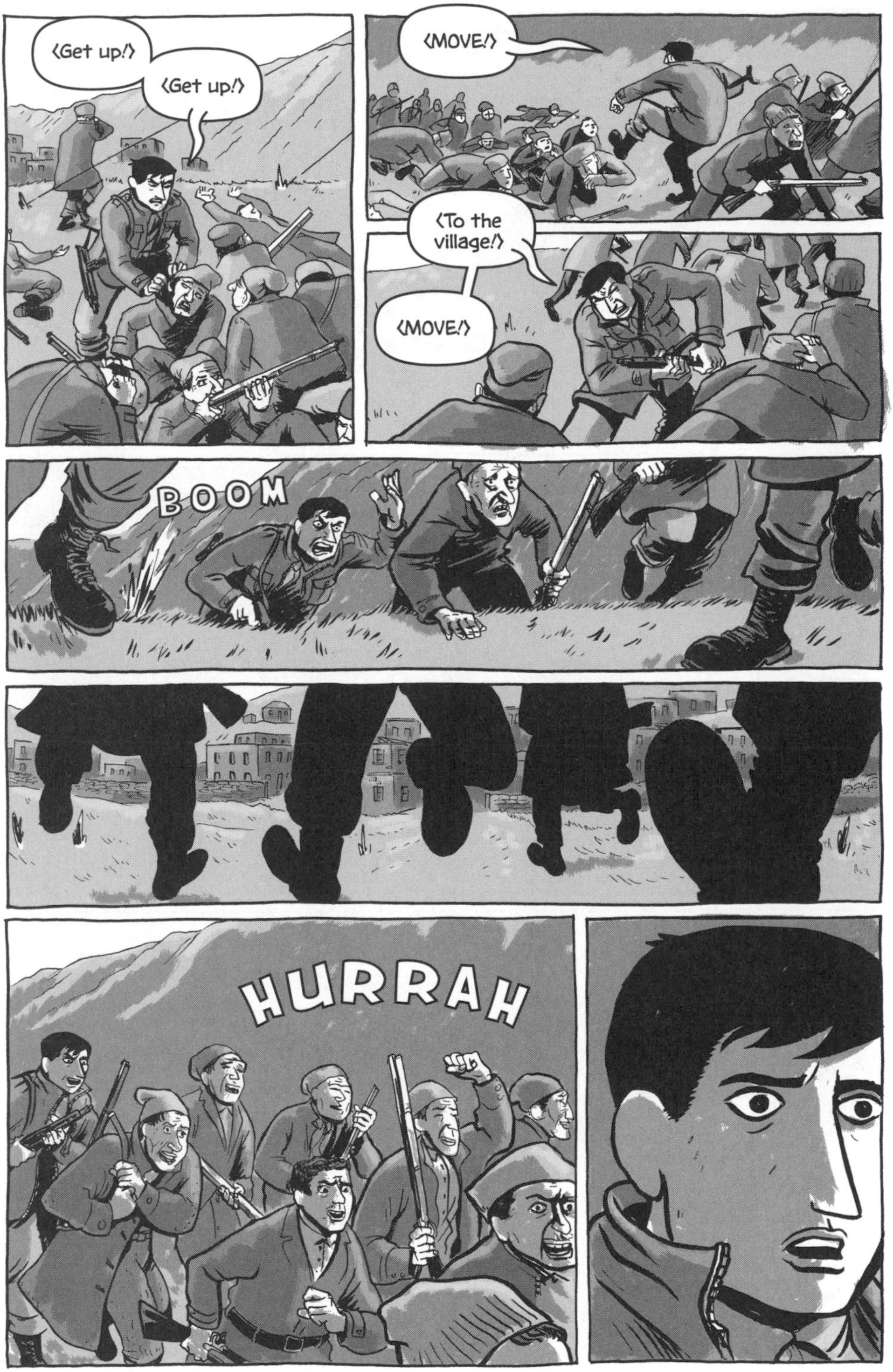

⟨Get up!⟩
⟨Get up!⟩
⟨MOVE!⟩
⟨To the village!⟩
⟨MOVE!⟩
BOOM
HURRAH

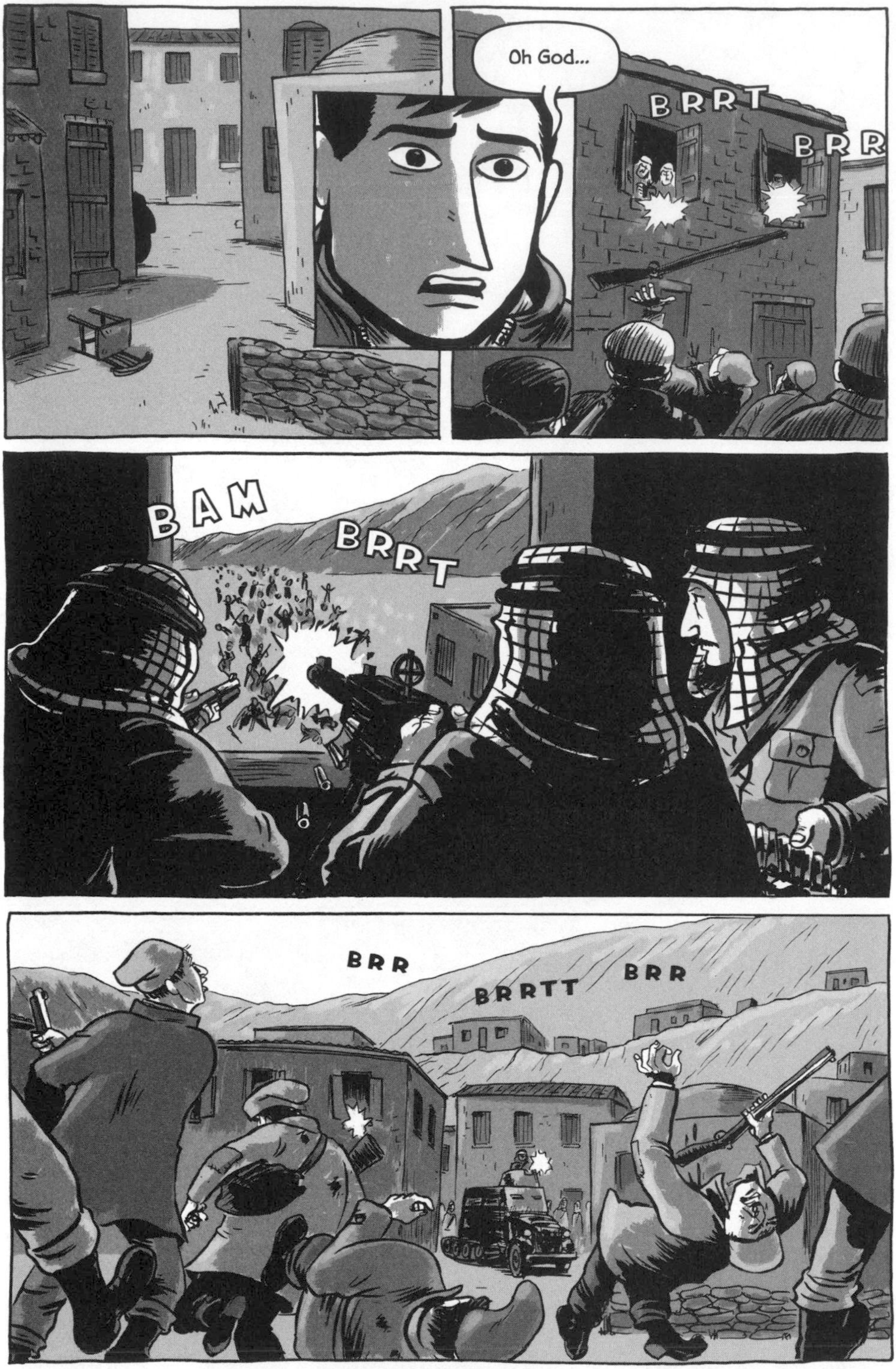
Oh God...
BRRT
BRR
BAM
BRRT
BRR
BRRTT
BRR

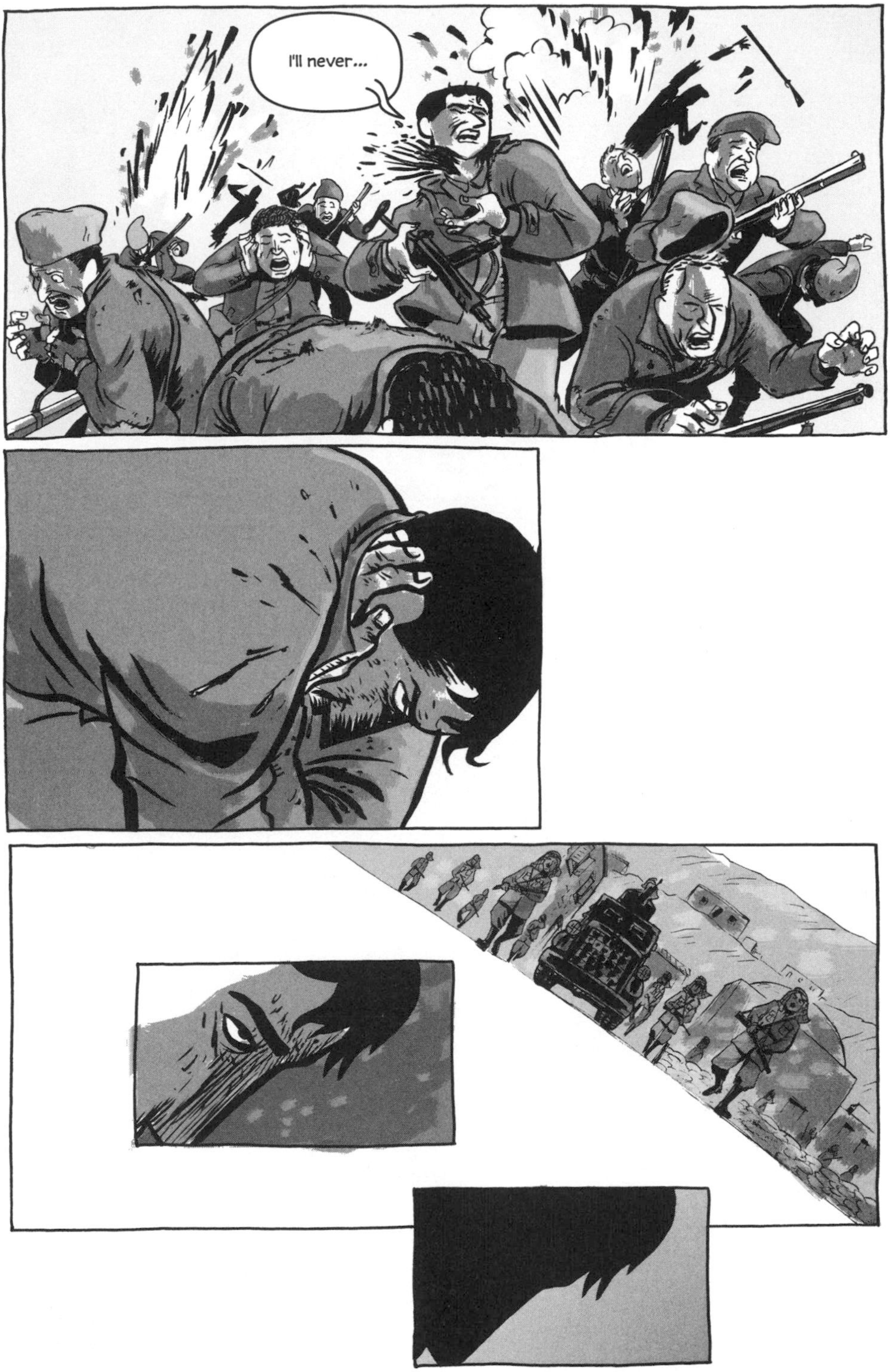
I'll never...

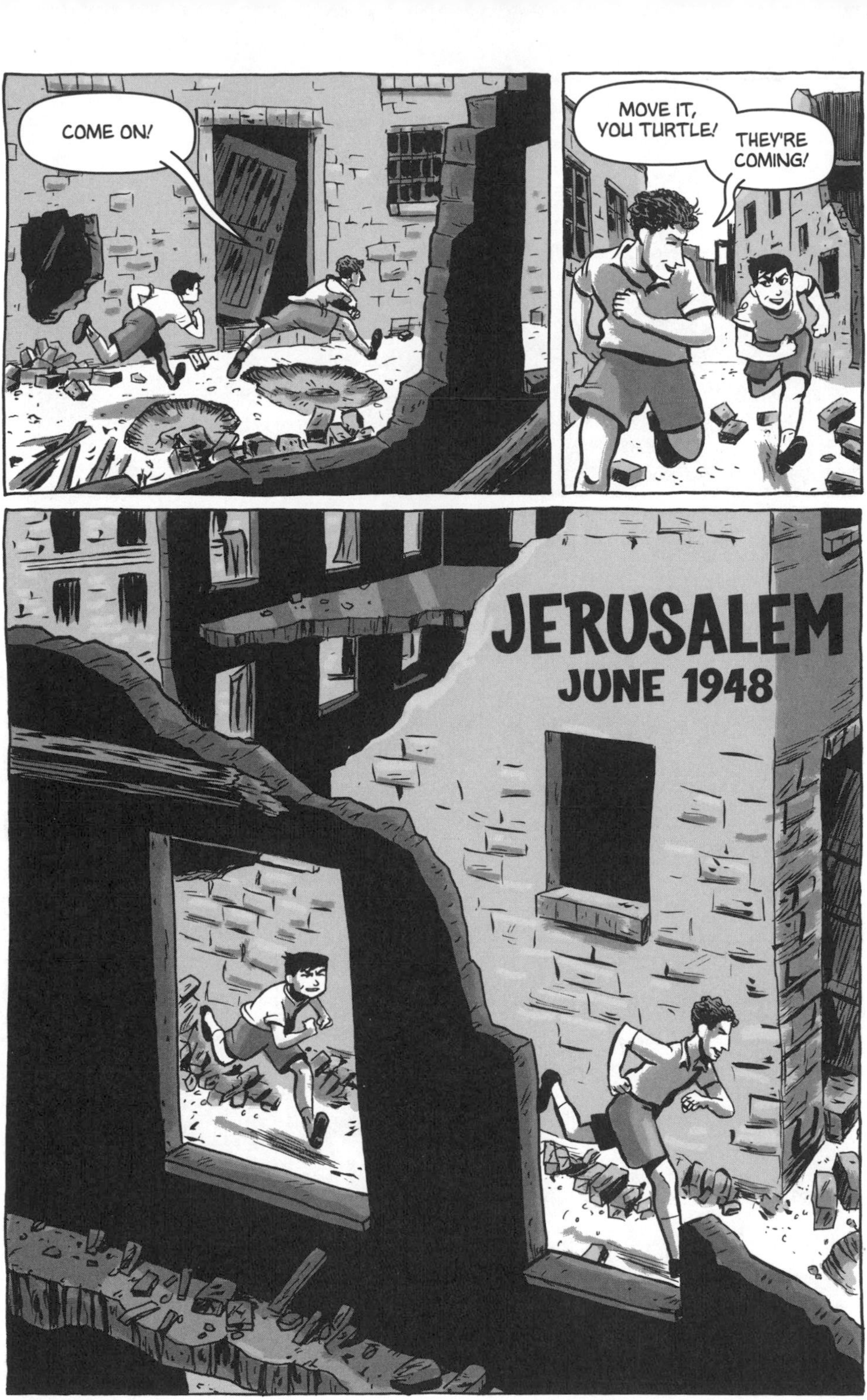
COME ON!
MOVE IT, YOU TURTLE!
THEY'RE COMING!
JERUSALEM
JUNE 1948

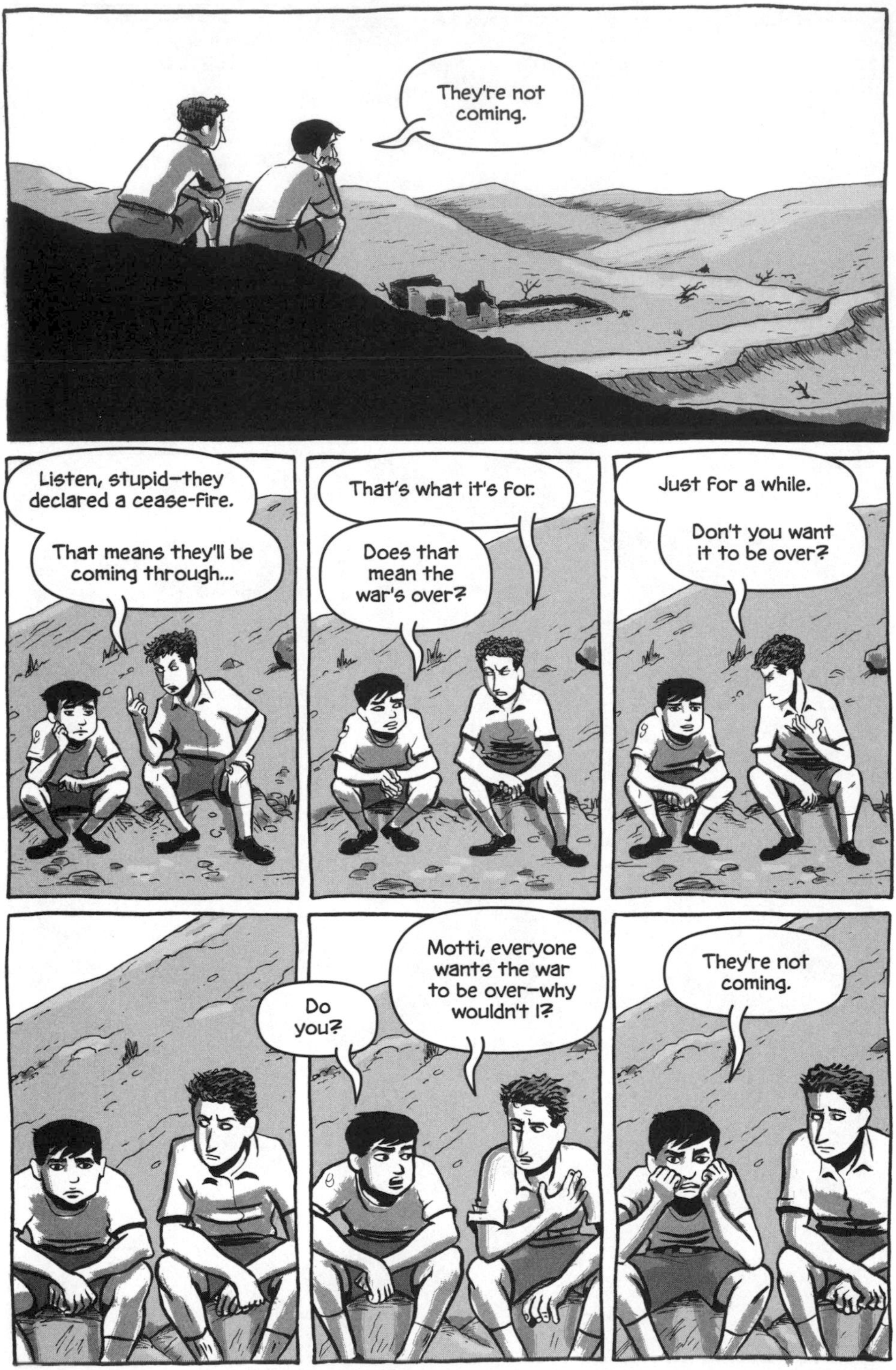
They're not coming.
Listen, stupid—they declared a cease-fire.
That means they'll be coming through...
That's what it's for.
Does that mean the war's over?
Just for a while.
Don't you want it to be over?
Do you?
Motti, everyone wants the war to be over—why wouldn't I?
They're not coming.

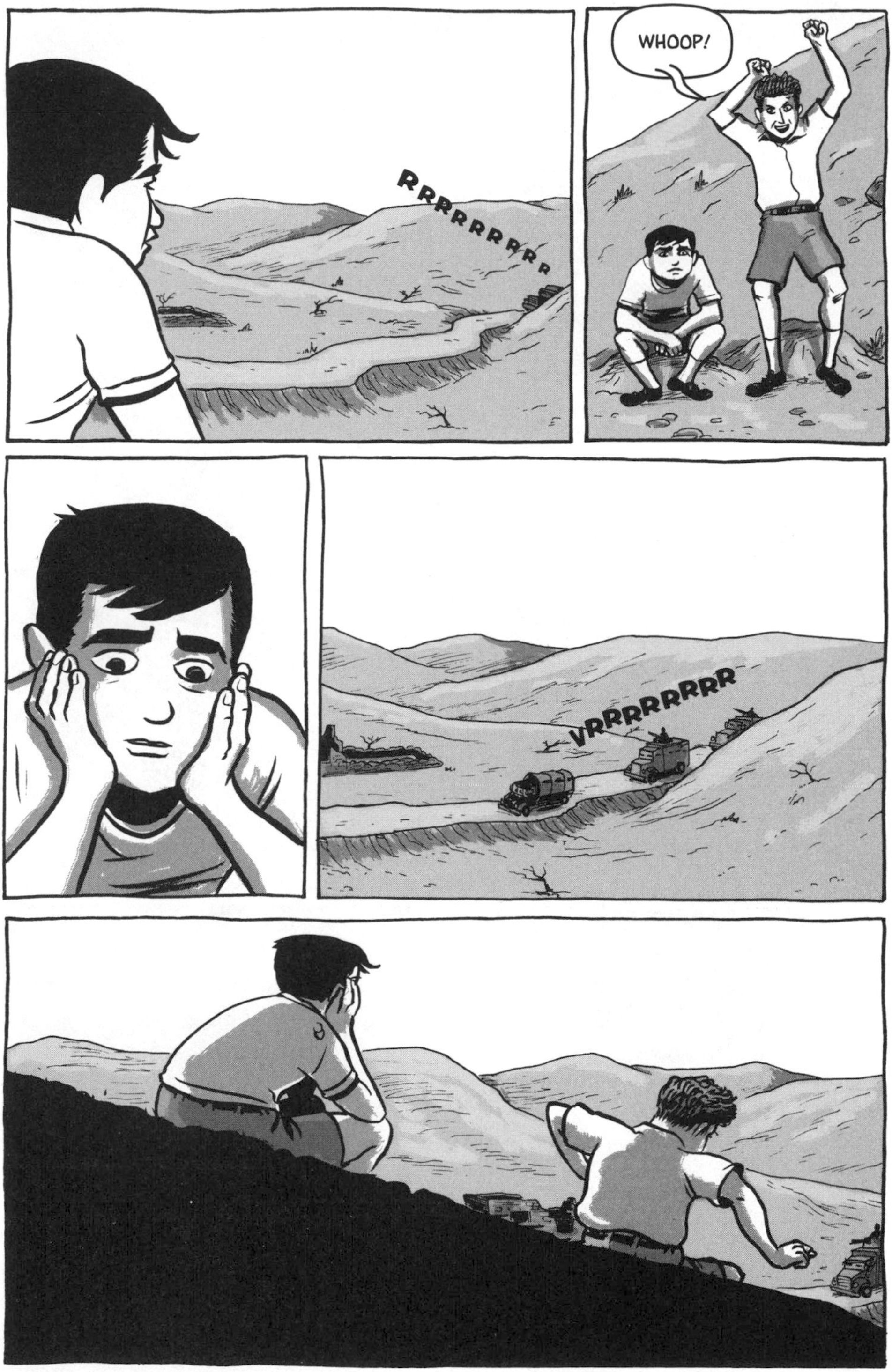
RRRRRRRRRR
WHOOP!
VRRRRRRRR

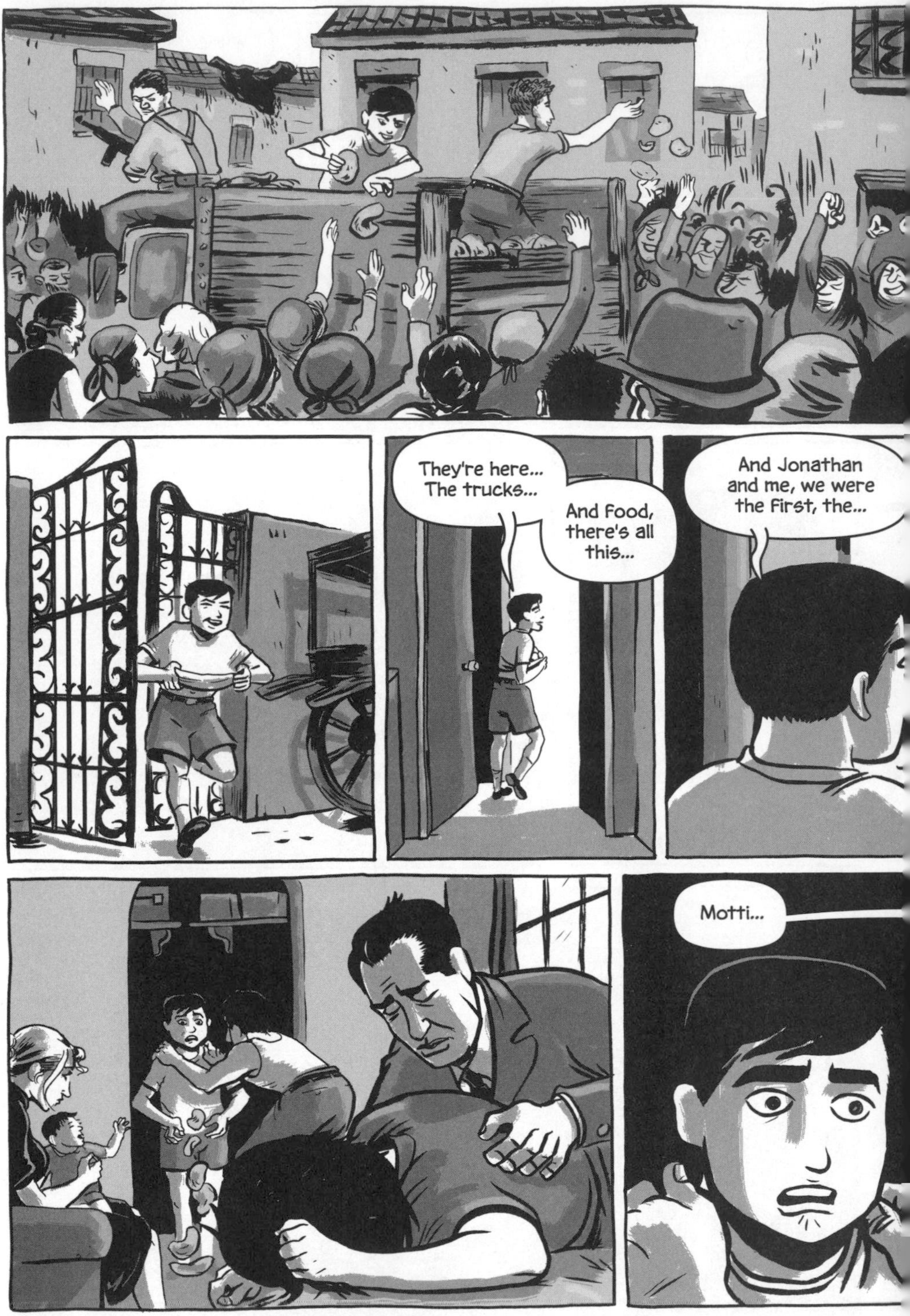
They're here... The trucks...
And food, there's all this...
And Jonathan and me, we were the first, the...
Motti...

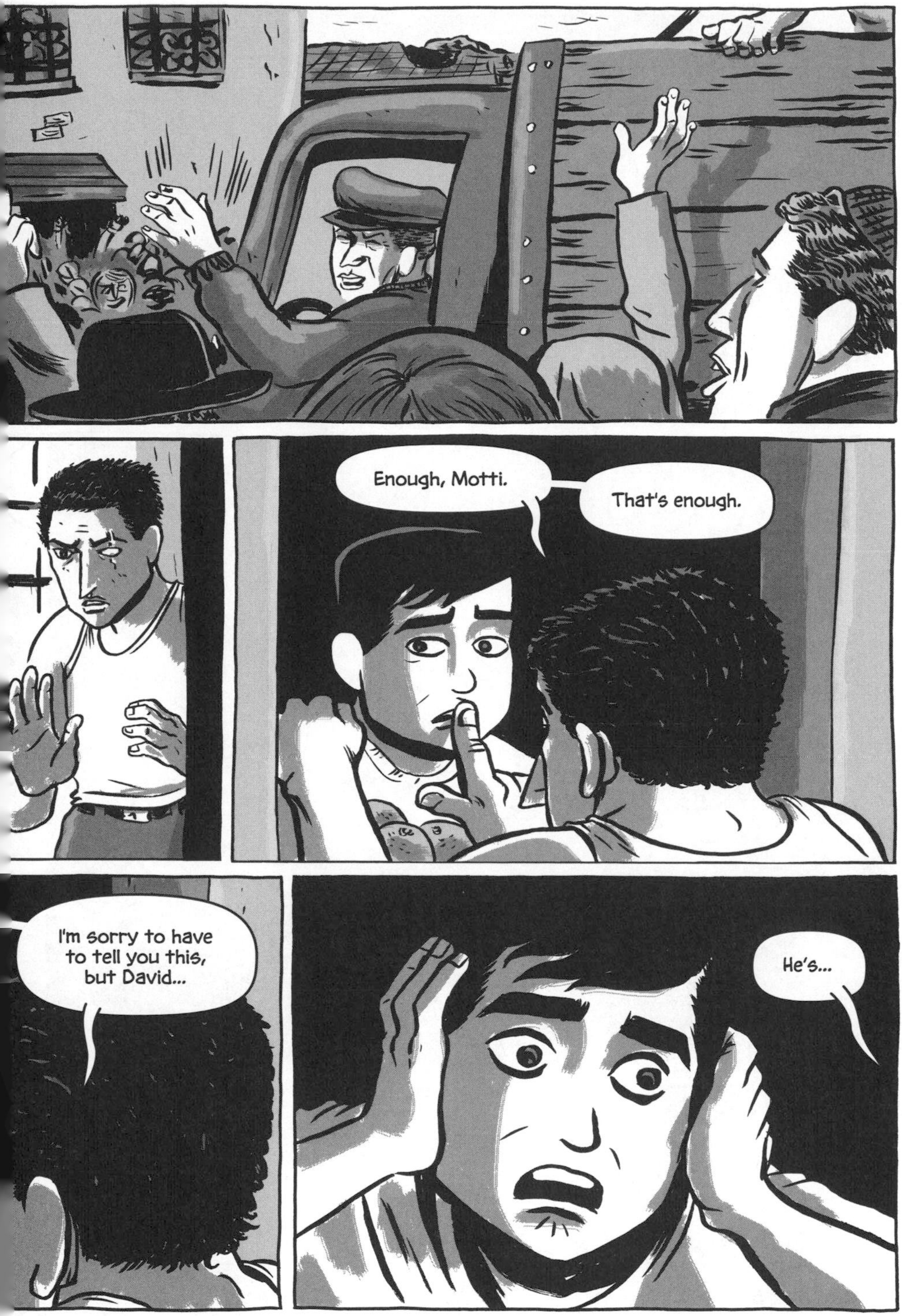
Enough, Motti.
That's enough.
I'm sorry to have to tell you this, but David...
He's...

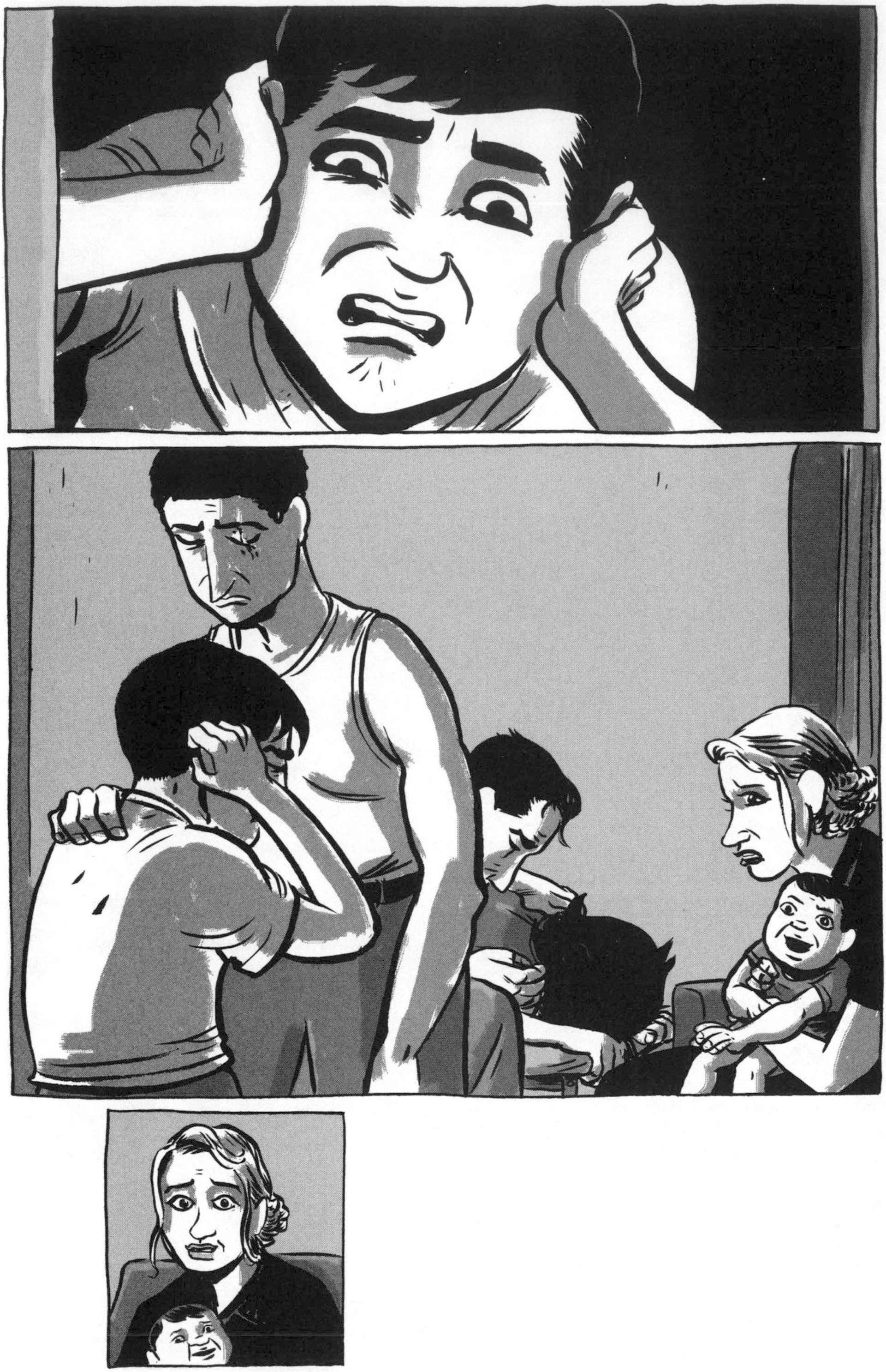

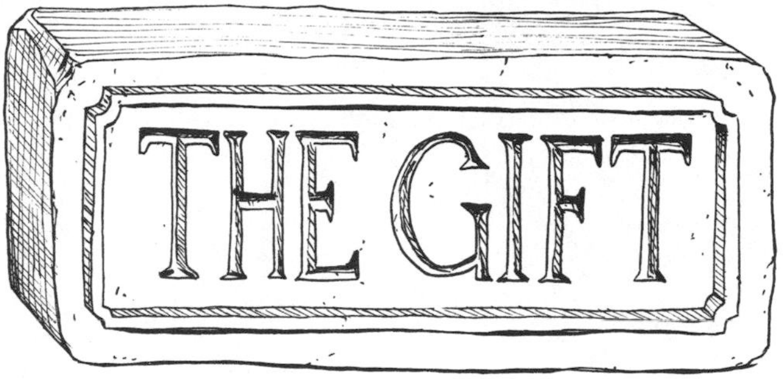
THE GIFT

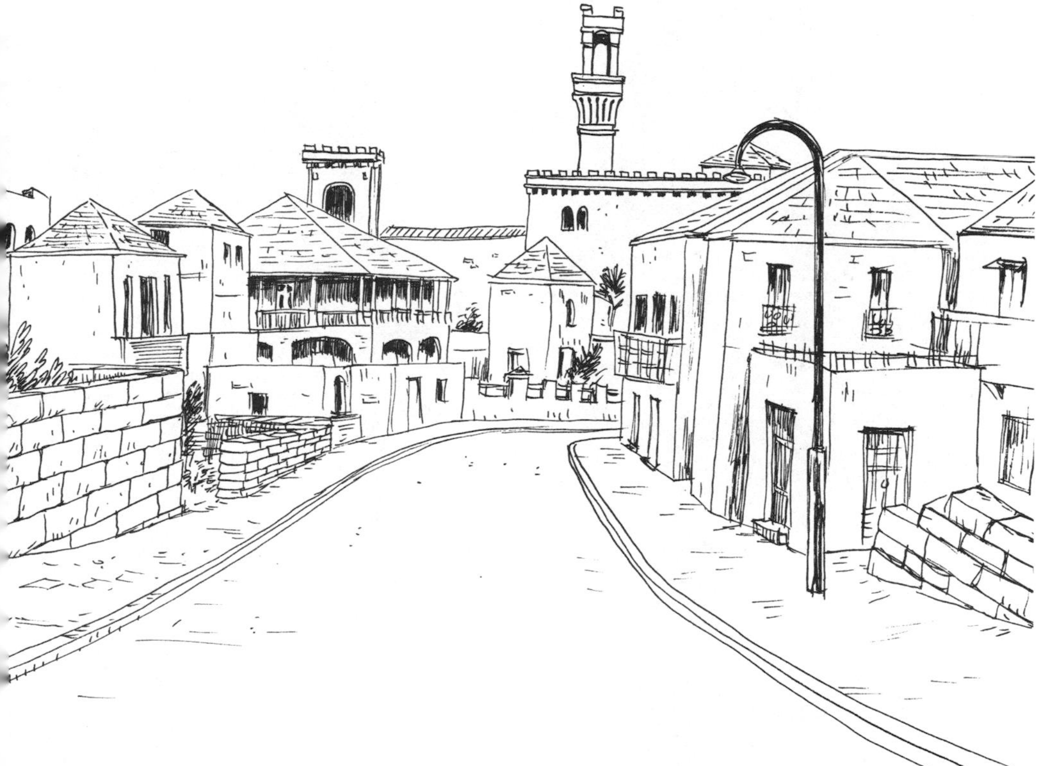

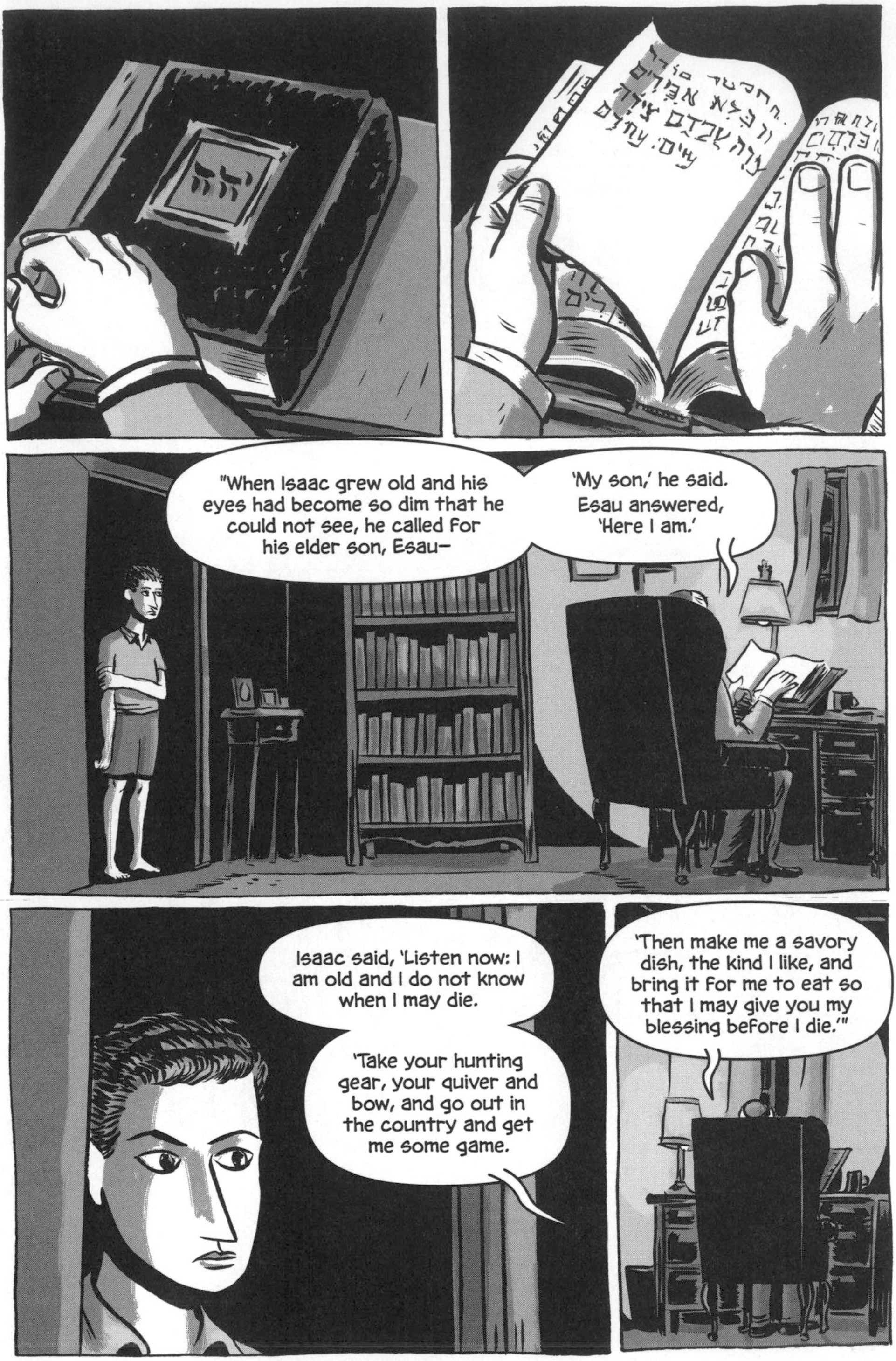
"When Isaac grew old and his eyes had become so dim that he could not see, he called for his elder son, Esau—
'My son,' he said. Esau answered, 'Here I am.'
Isaac said, 'Listen now: I am old and I do not know when I may die.
'Take your hunting gear, your quiver and bow, and go out in the country and get me some game.
'Then make me a savory dish, the kind I like, and bring it for me to eat so that I may give you my blessing before I die.'"

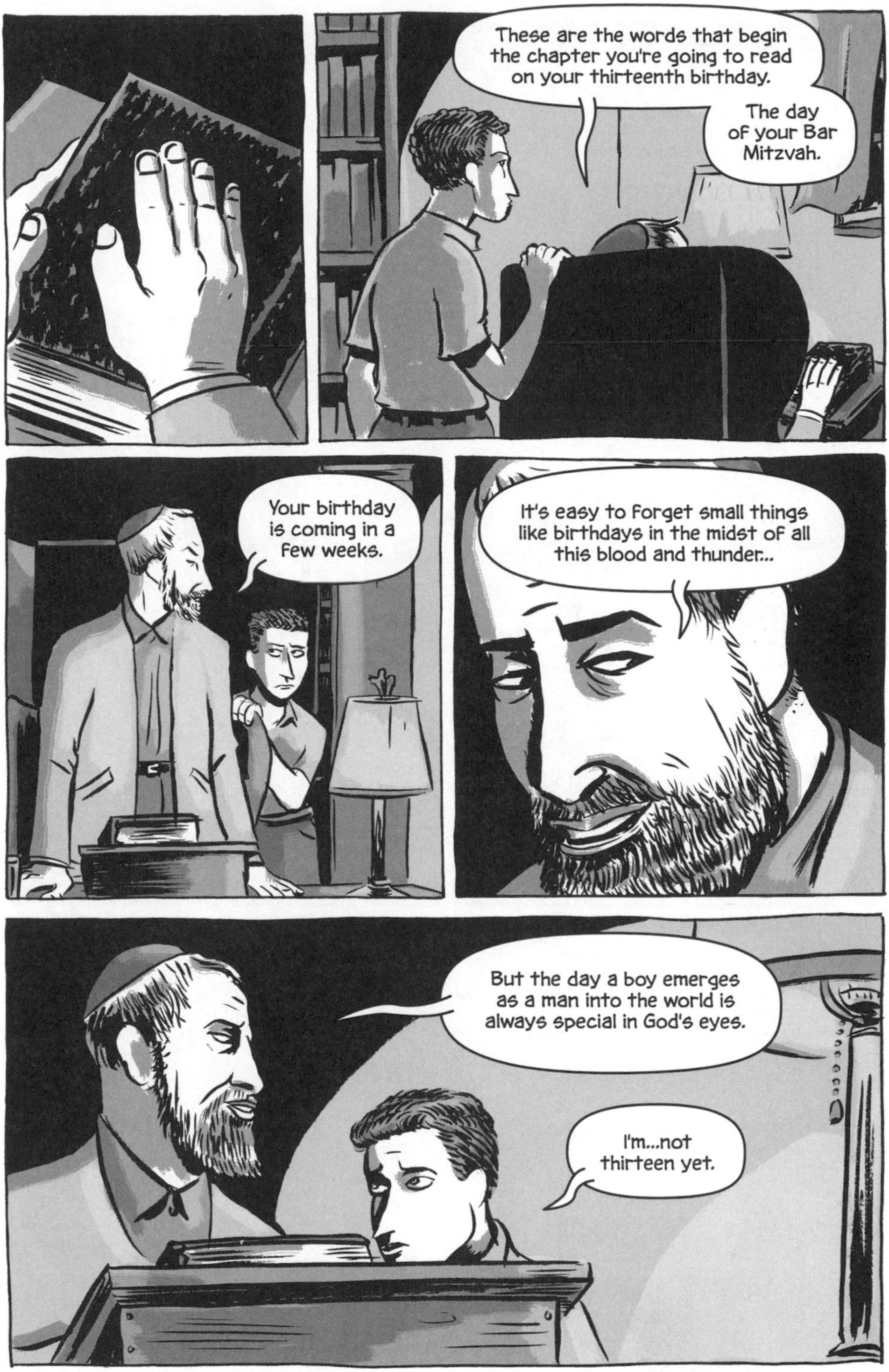
These are the words that begin the chapter you're going to read on your thirteenth birthday.
The day of your Bar Mitzvah.
Your birthday is coming in a few weeks.
It's easy to forget small things like birthdays in the midst of all this blood and thunder...
But the day a boy emerges as a man into the world is always special in God's eyes.
I'm...not thirteen yet.

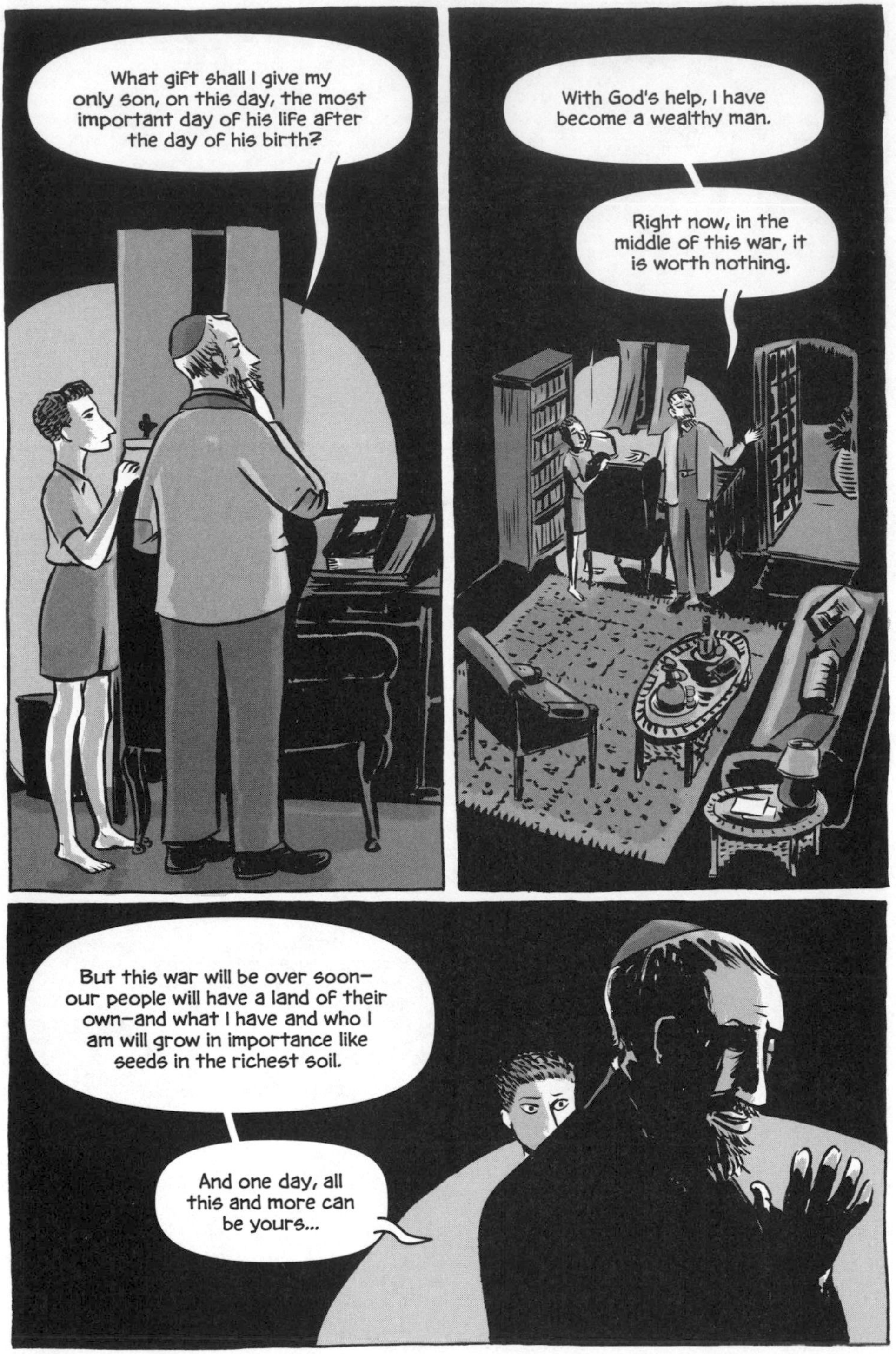
What gift shall I give my only son, on this day, the most important day of his life after the day of his birth?
With God's help, I have become a wealthy man.
Right now, in the middle of this war, it is worth nothing.
But this war will be over soon—our people will have a land of their own—and what I have and who I am will grow in importance like seeds in the richest soil.
And one day, all this and more can be yours...

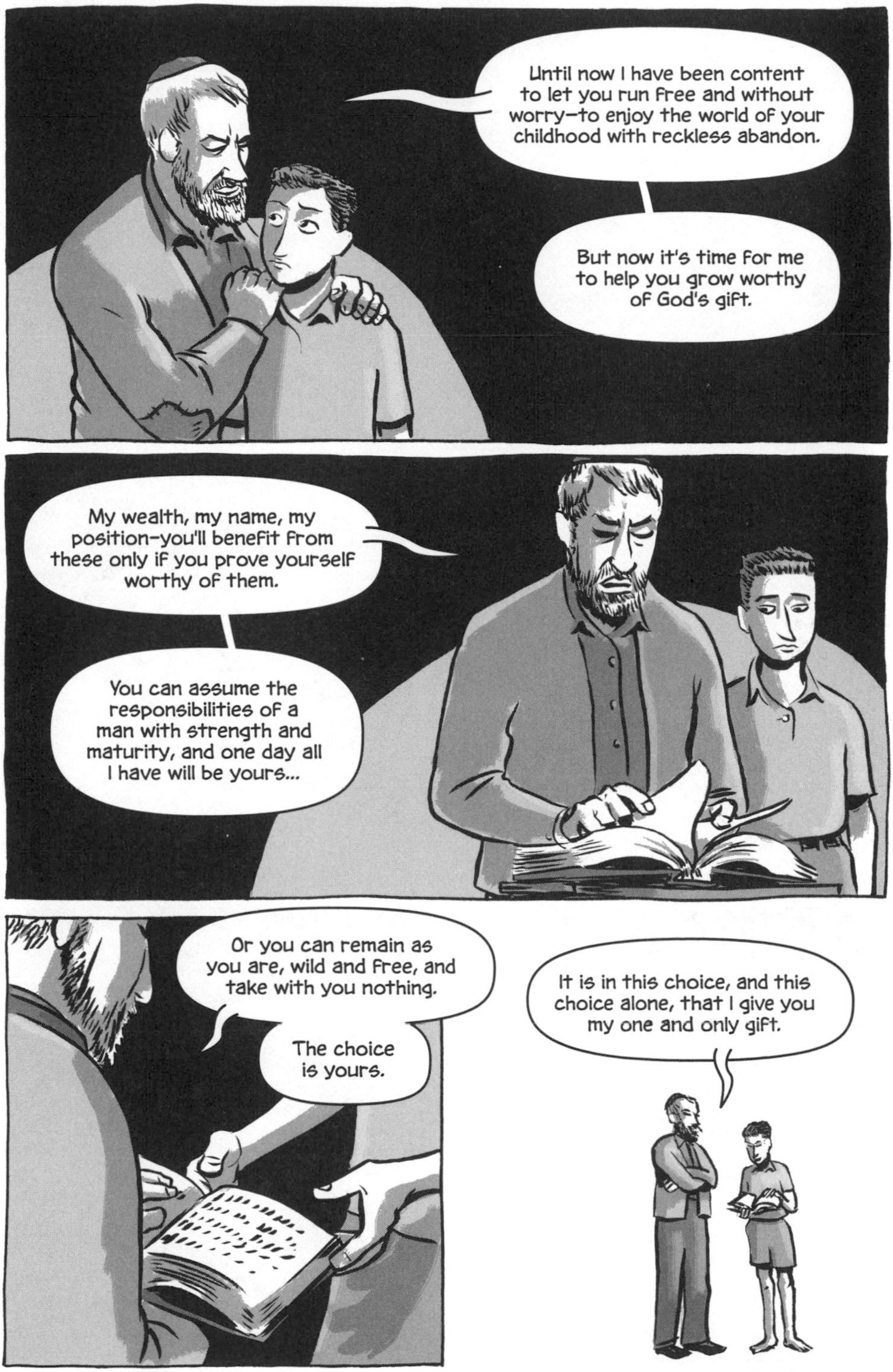
Until now I have been content to let you run free and without worry—to enjoy the world of your childhood with reckless abandon.
But now it's time for me to help you grow worthy of God's gift.
My wealth, my name, my position–you'll benefit from these only if you prove yourself worthy of them.
You can assume the responsibilities of a man with strength and maturity, and one day all I have will be yours...
Or you can remain as you are, wild and free, and take with you nothing.
The choice is yours.
It is in this choice, and this choice alone, that I give you my one and only gift.

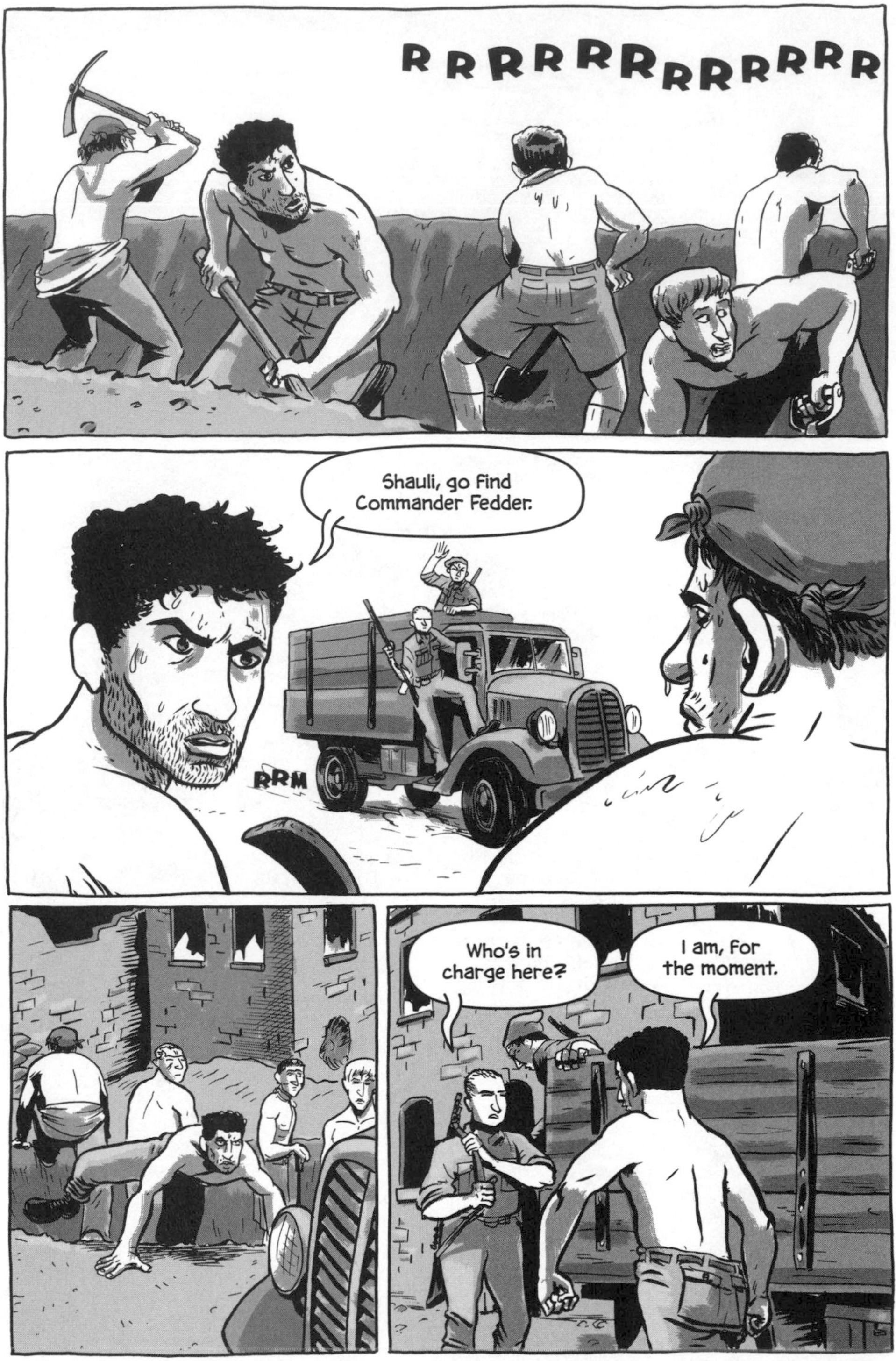
RRRRRRRRRRRR
Shauli, go find Commander Fedder.
RRM
Who's in charge here?
I am, for the moment.

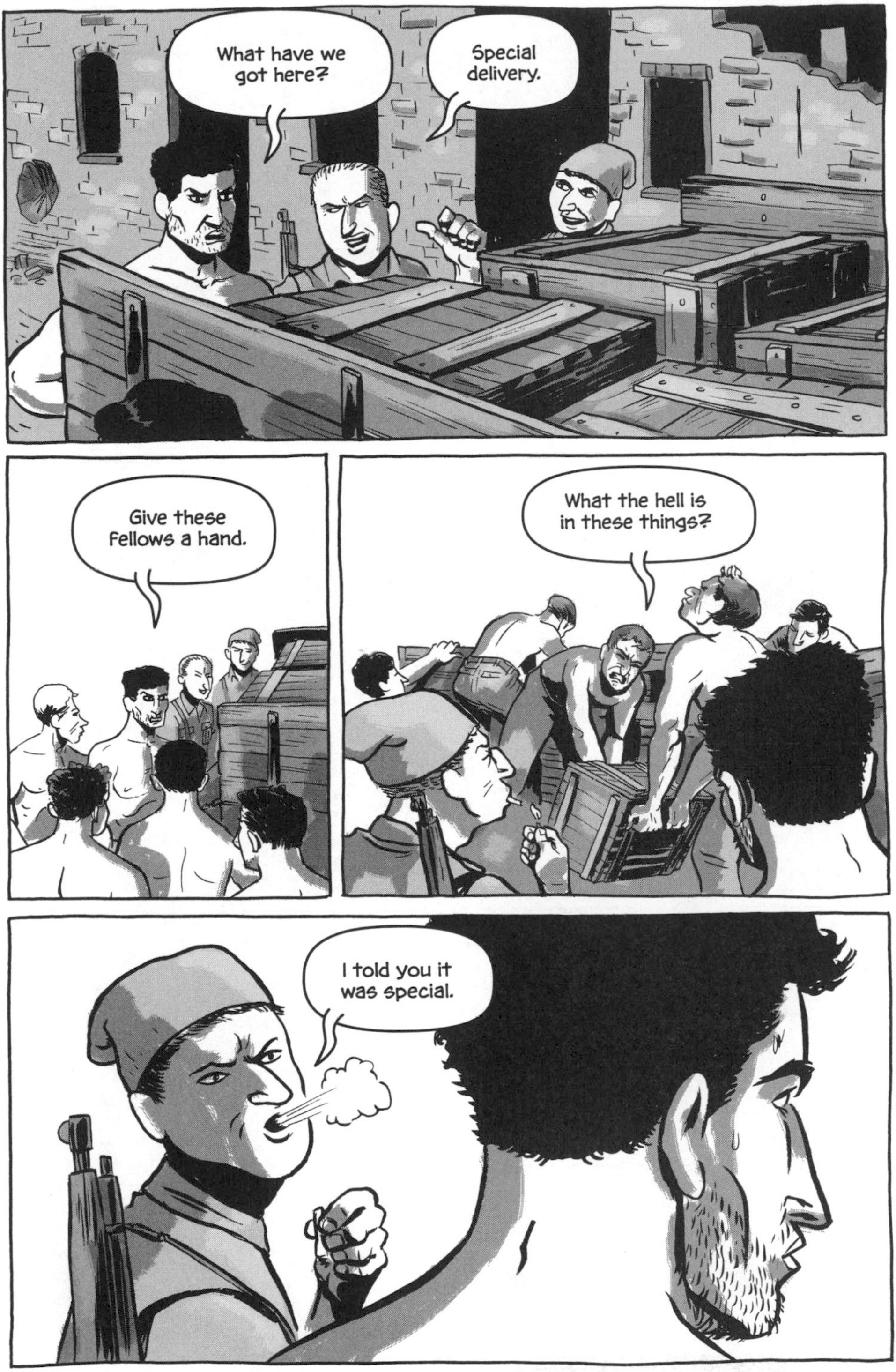
What have we got here?
Special delivery.
Give these fellows a hand.
What the hell is in these things?
I told you it was special.

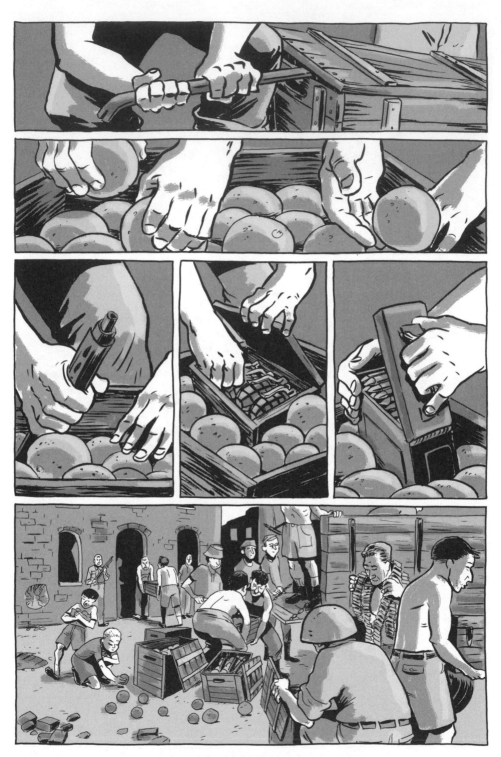

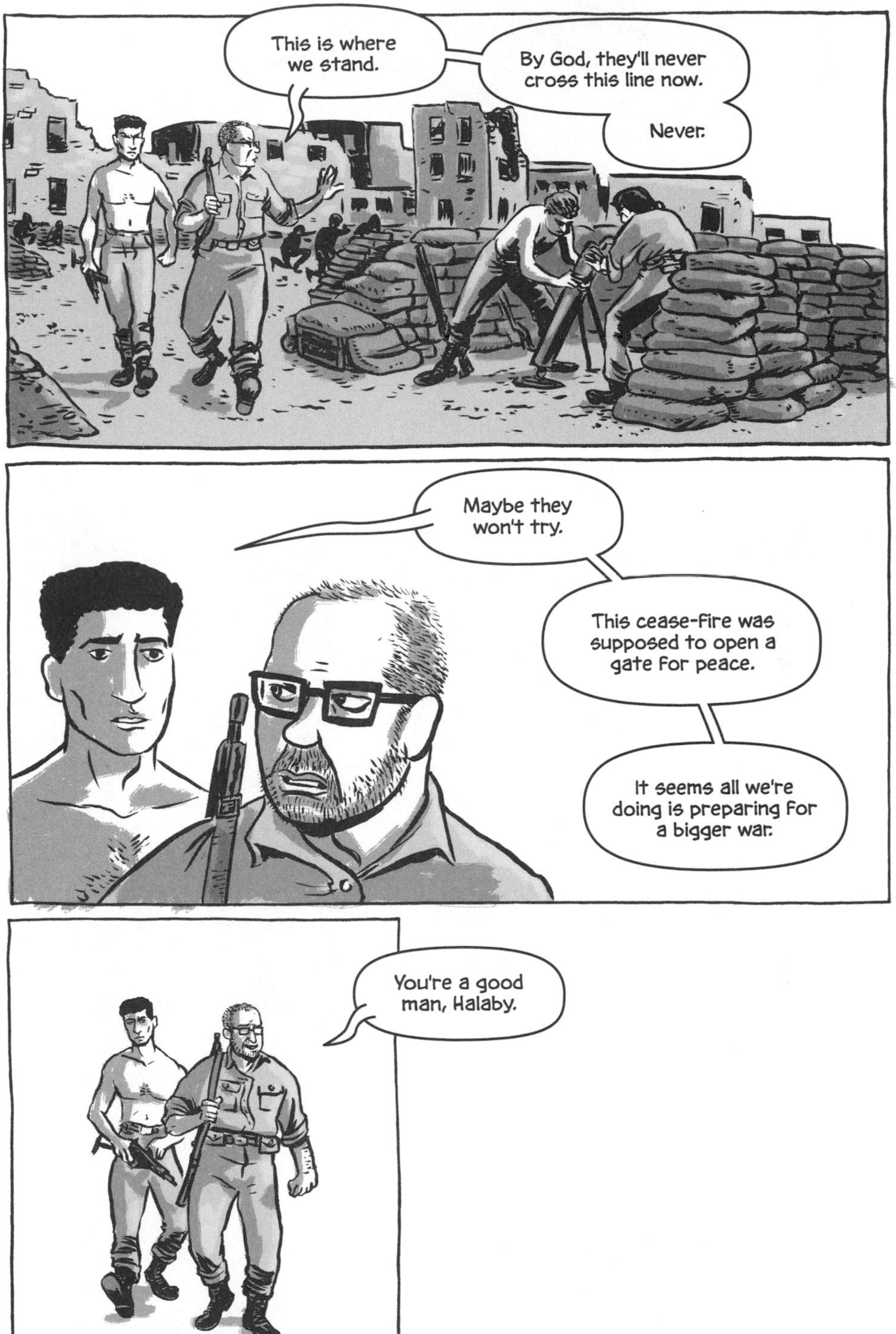
This is where we stand.
By God, they'll never cross this line now.
Never.
Maybe they won't try.
This cease-fire was supposed to open a gate for peace.
It seems all we're doing is preparing for a bigger war.
You're a good man, Halaby.

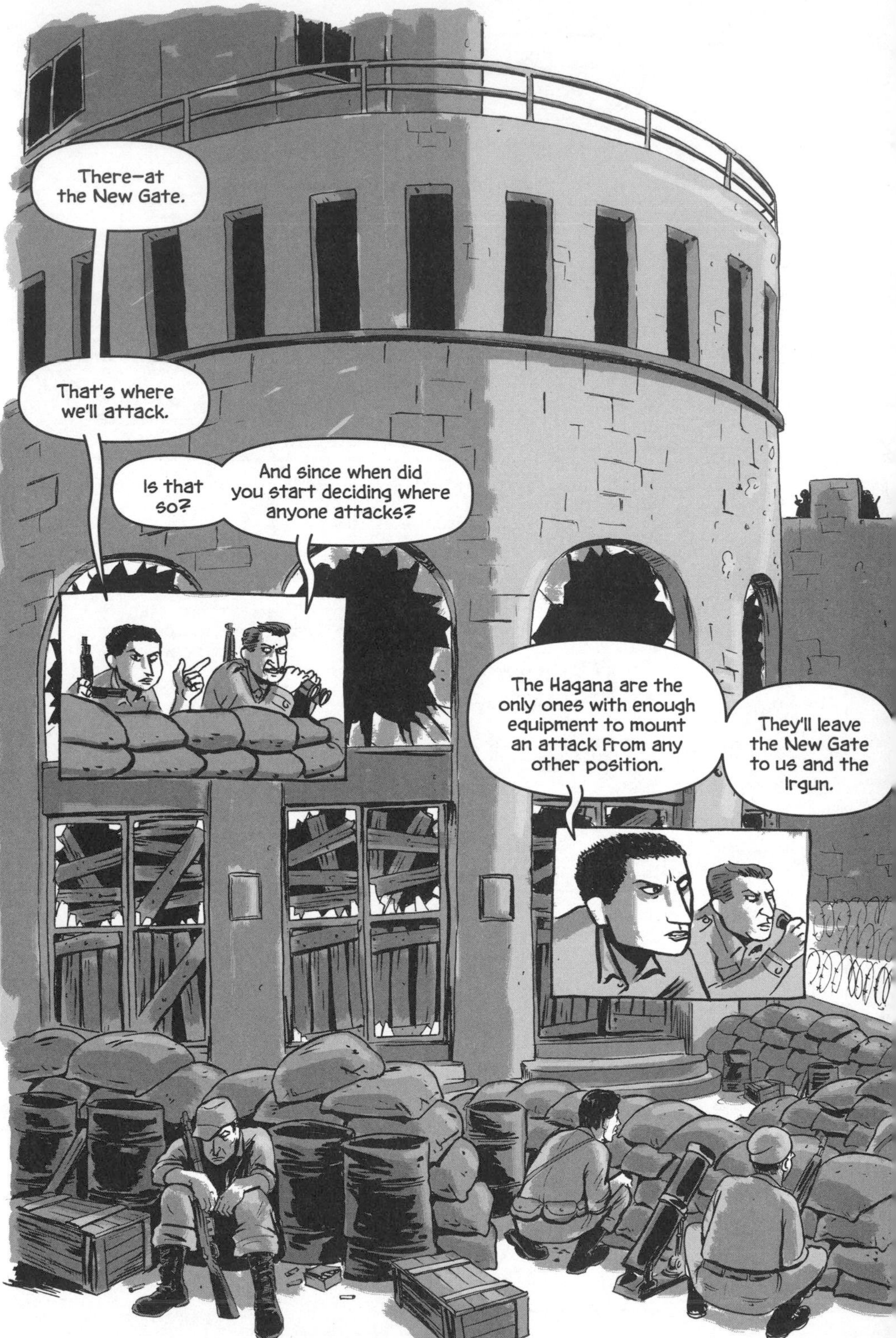
There—at the New Gate.
That's where we'll attack.
Is that so?
And since when did you start deciding where anyone attacks?
The Hagana are the only ones with enough equipment to mount an attack from any other position.
They'll leave the New Gate to us and the Irgun.

# THE OLD CITY

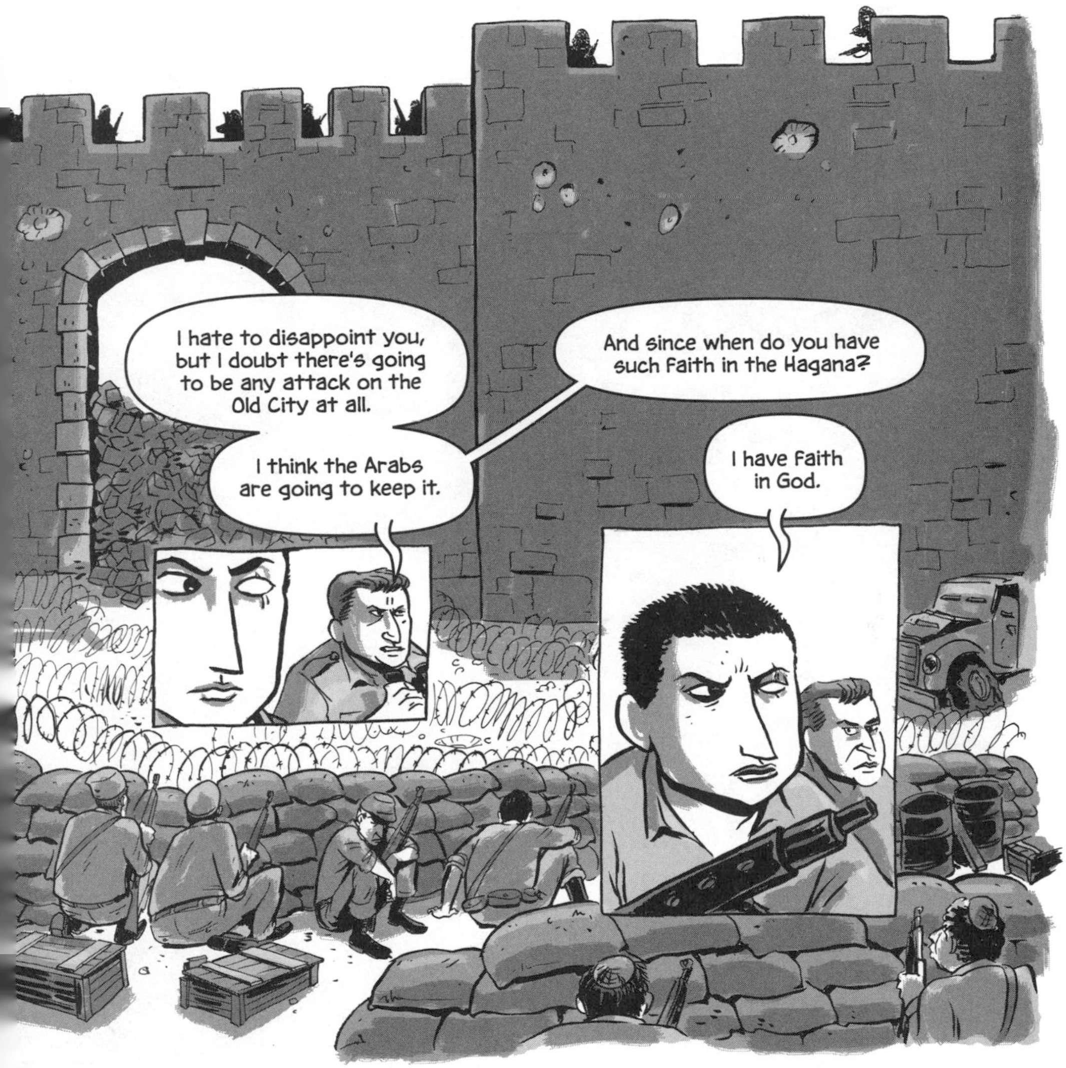
I hate to disappoint you, but I doubt there's going to be any attack on the Old City at all.
I think the Arabs are going to keep it.
And since when do you have such faith in the Hagana?
I have faith in God.

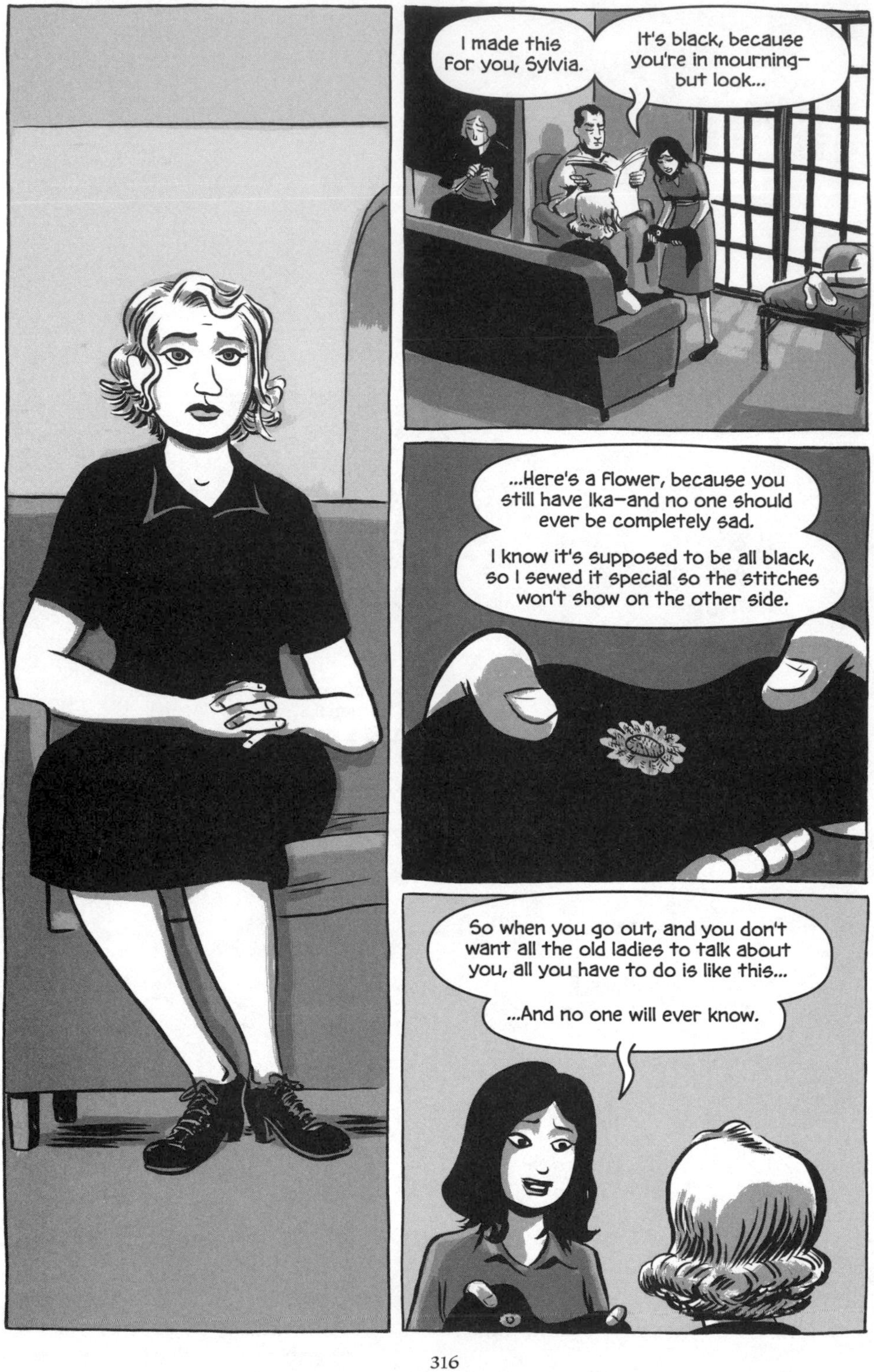
I made this for you, Sylvia.
It's black, because you're in mourning—but look...
...Here's a flower, because you still have Ika—and no one should ever be completely sad.
I know it's supposed to be all black, so I sewed it special so the stitches won't show on the other side.
So when you go out, and you don't want all the old ladies to talk about you, all you have to do is like this...
...And no one will ever know.

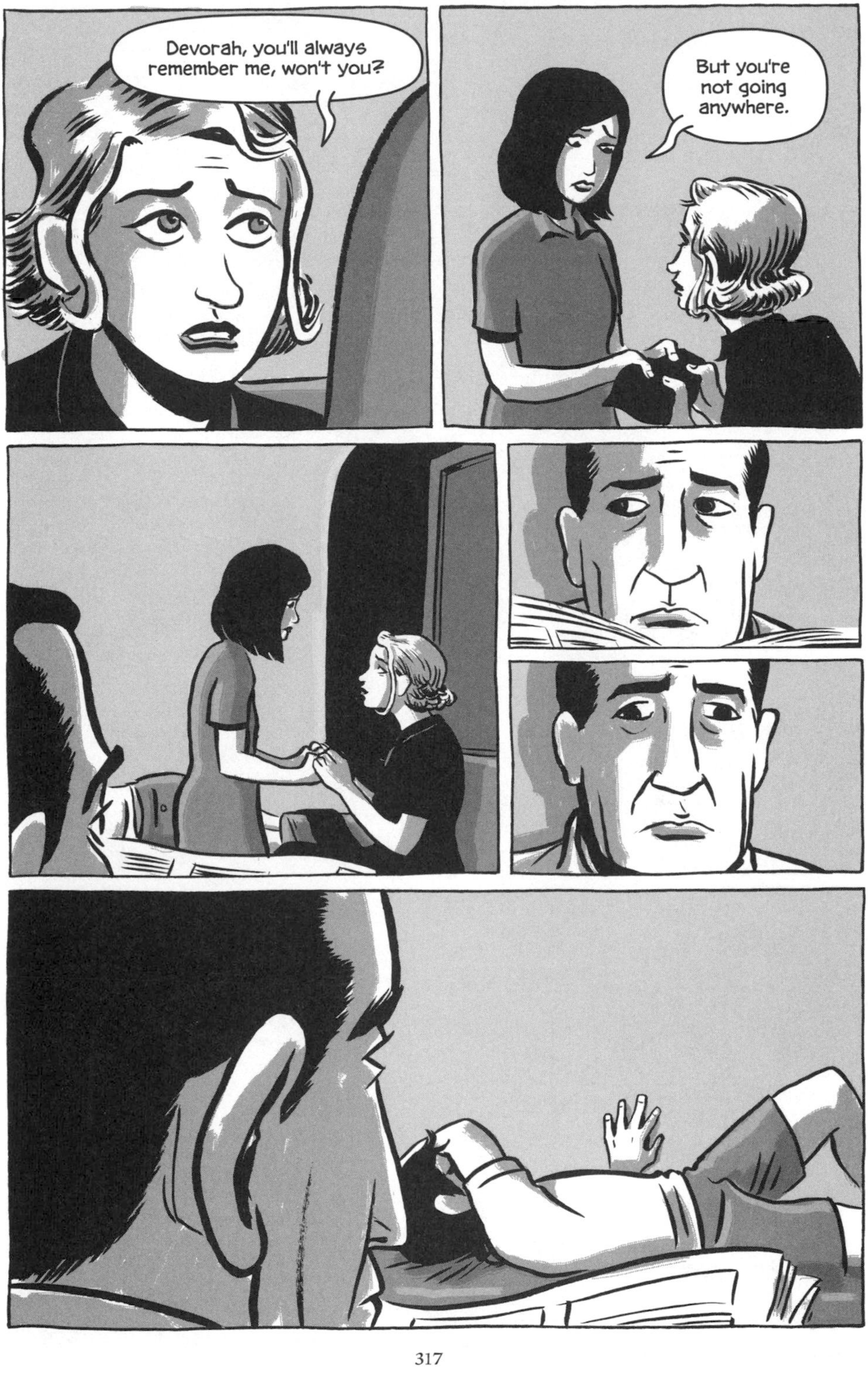
Devorah, you'll always remember me, won't you?
But you're not going anywhere.

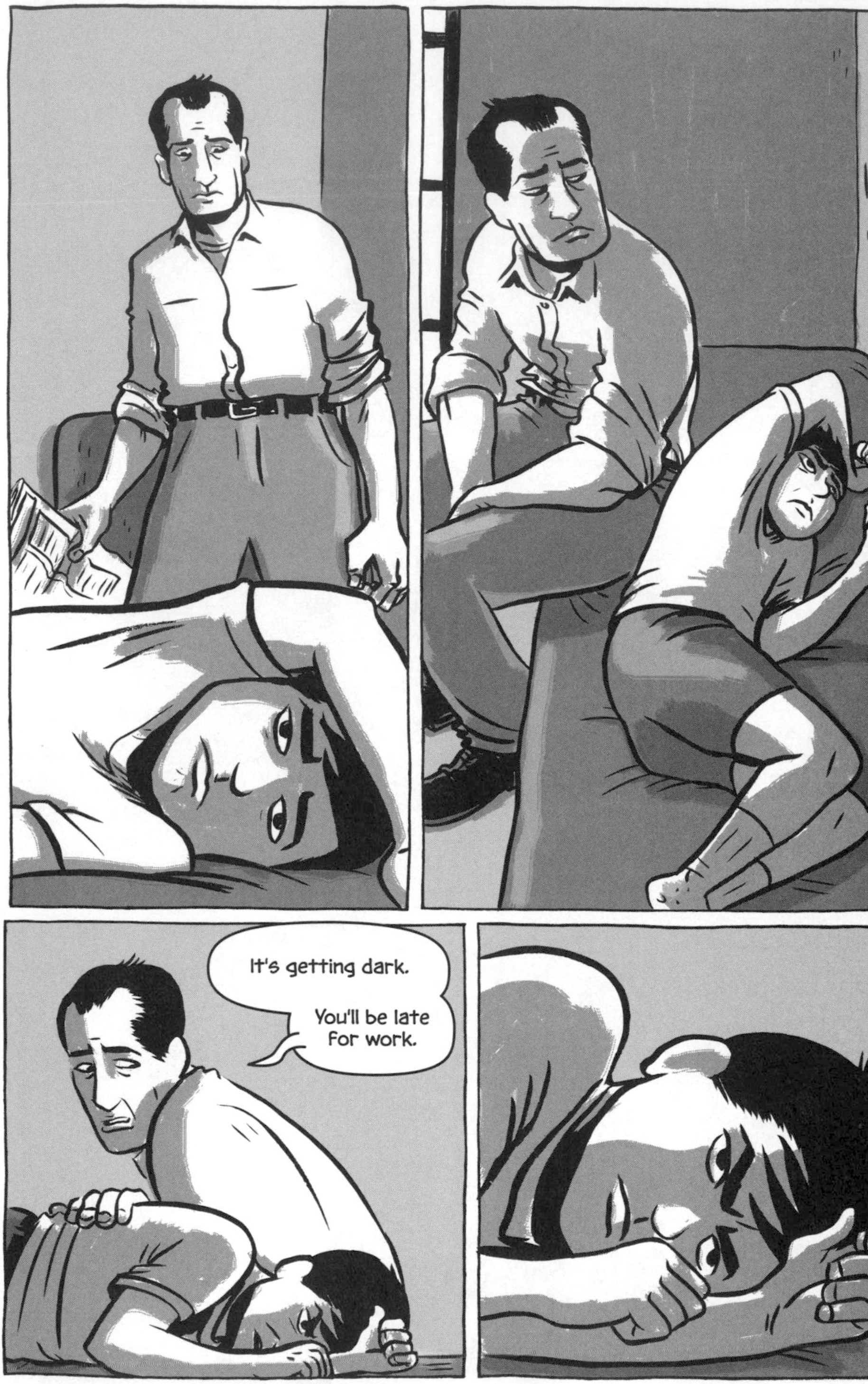
It's getting dark.
You'll be late for work.

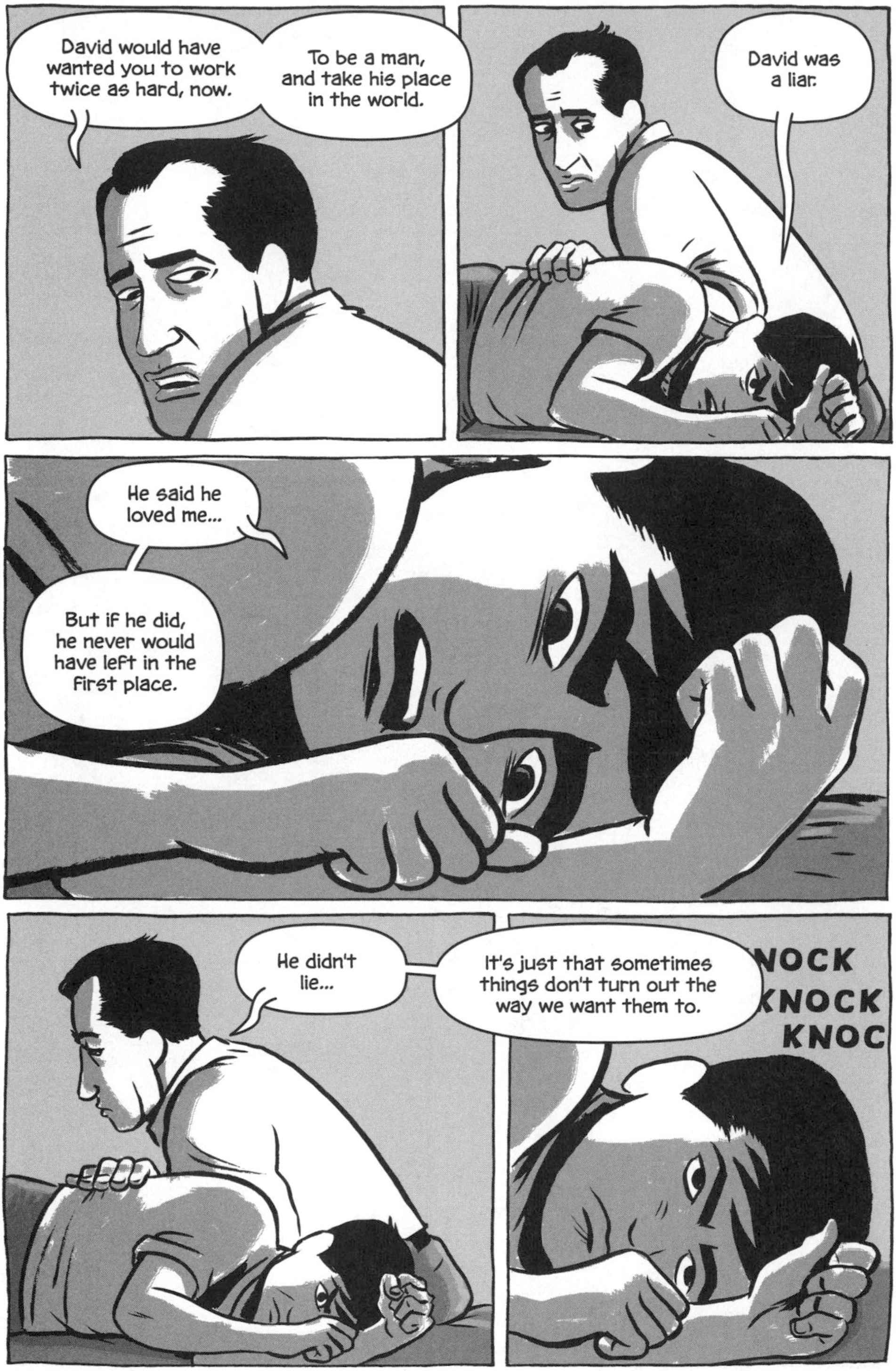
David would have wanted you to work twice as hard, now.
To be a man, and take his place in the world.
David was a liar.
He said he loved me...
But if he did, he never would have left in the first place.
He didn't lie...
It's just that sometimes things don't turn out the way we want them to.
NOCK
KNOCK
KNOC

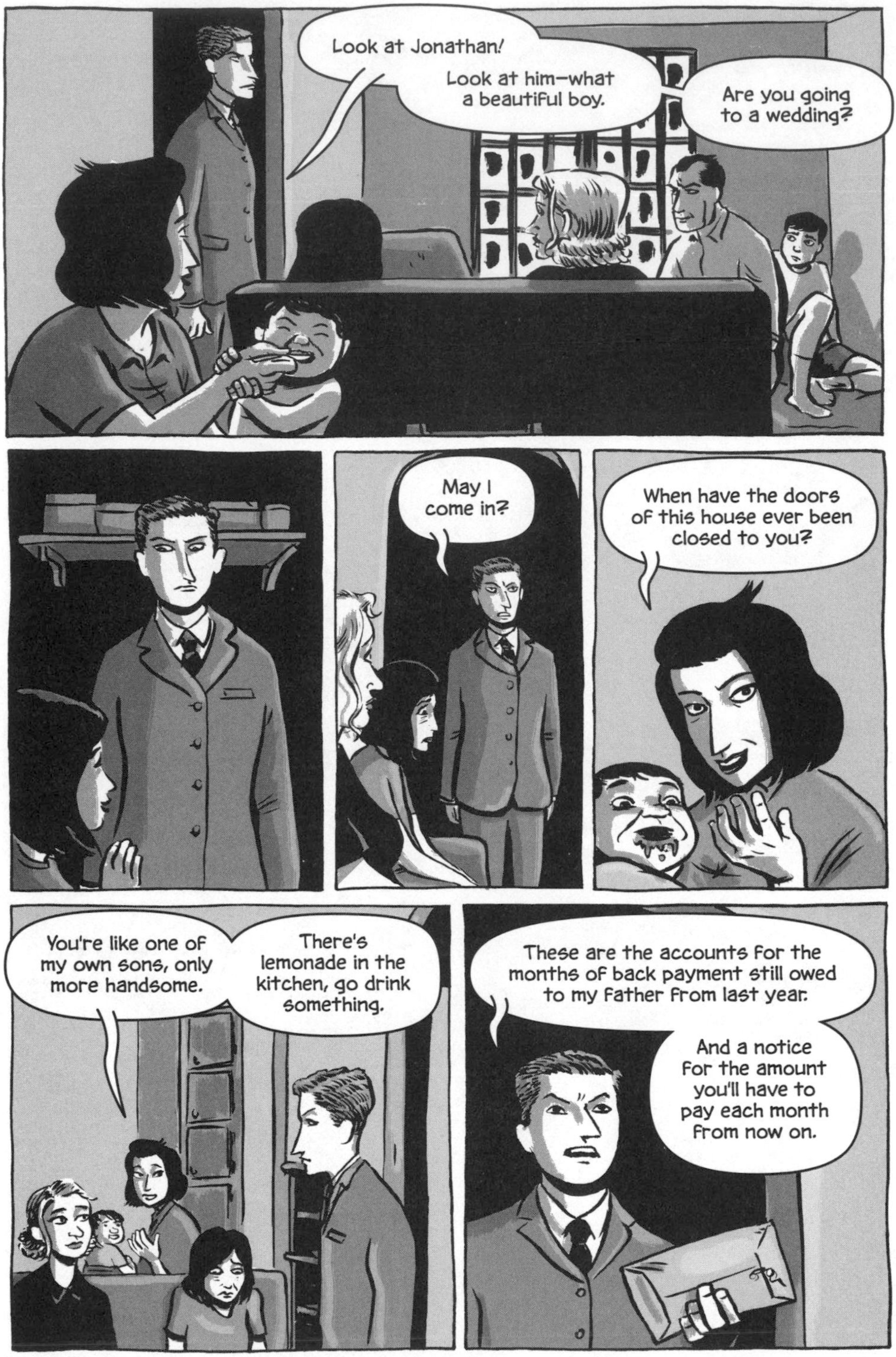
Look at Jonathan!
Look at him—what a beautiful boy.
Are you going to a wedding?
May I come in?
When have the doors of this house ever been closed to you?
You're like one of my own sons, only more handsome.
There's lemonade in the kitchen, go drink something.
These are the accounts for the months of back payment still owed to my father from last year.
And a notice for the amount you'll have to pay each month from now on.

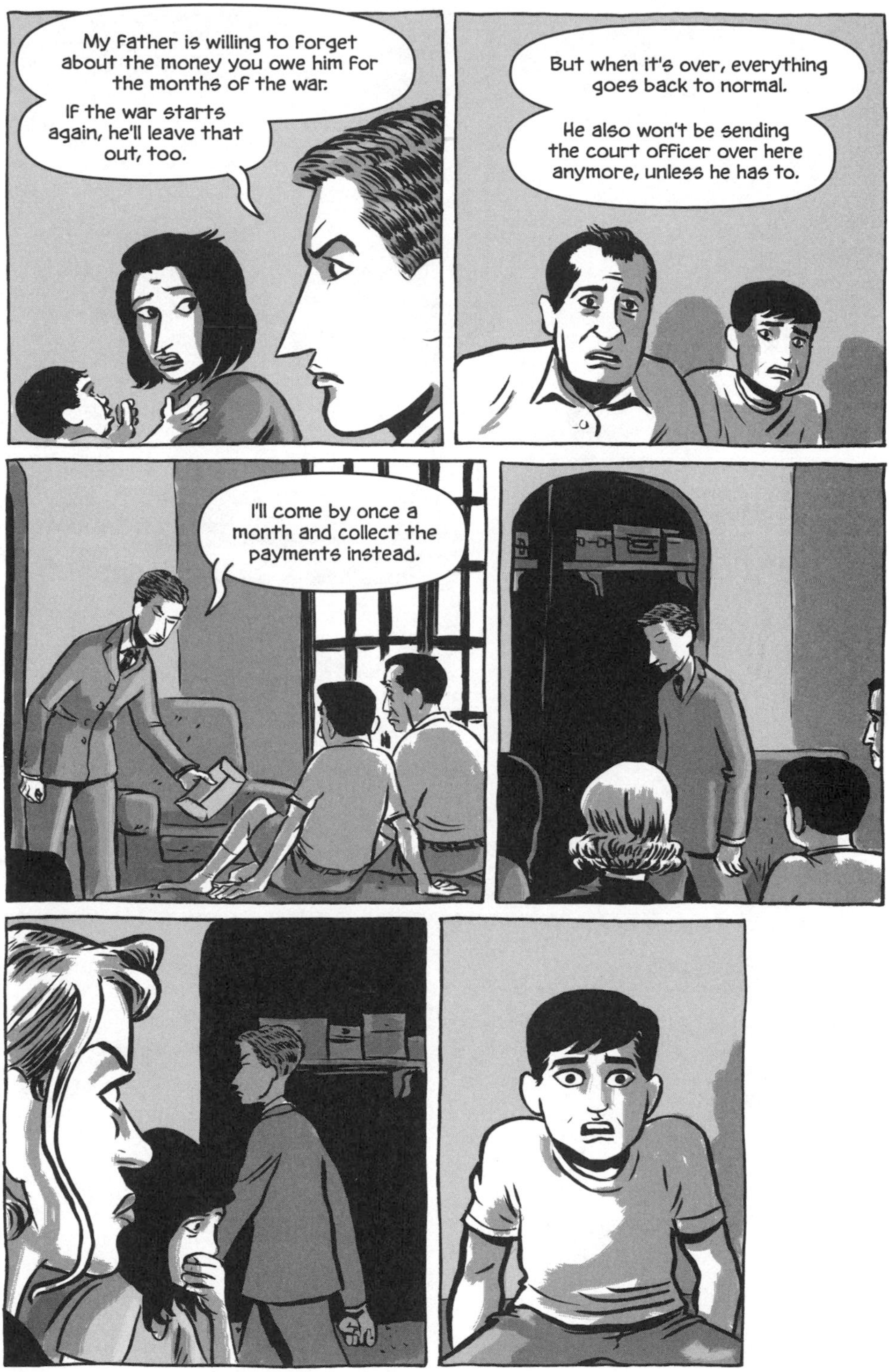
My father is willing to forget about the money you owe him for the months of the war.
If the war starts again, he'll leave that out, too.
But when it's over, everything goes back to normal.
He also won't be sending the court officer over here anymore, unless he has to.
I'll come by once a month and collect the payments instead.

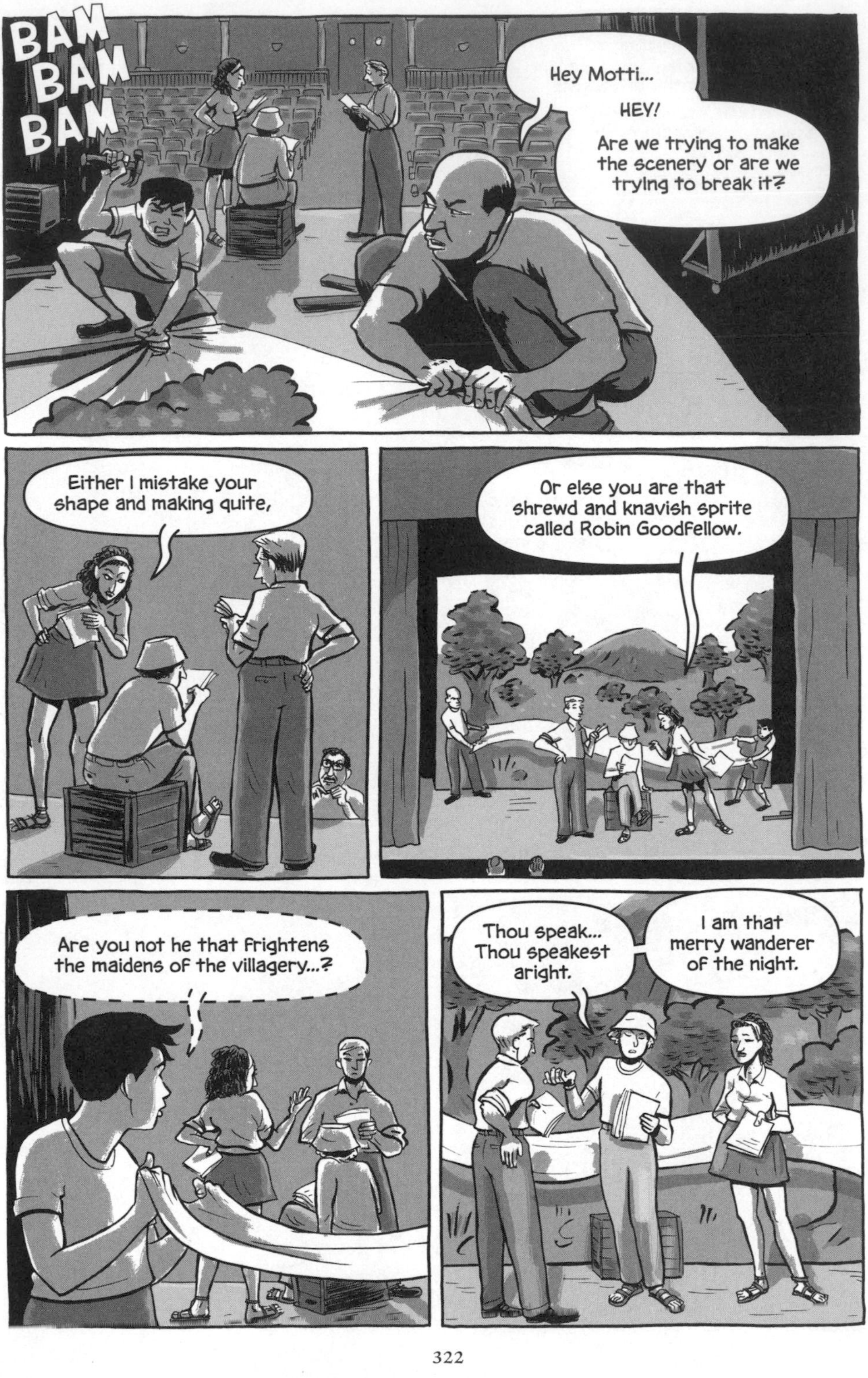
BAM
BAM
BAM
Hey Motti...
HEY!
Are we trying to make the scenery or are we trying to break it?
Either I mistake your shape and making quite,
Or else you are that shrewd and knavish sprite called Robin Goodfellow.
Are you not he that frightens the maidens of the villagery...?
Thou speak... Thou speakest aright.
I am that merry wanderer of the night.

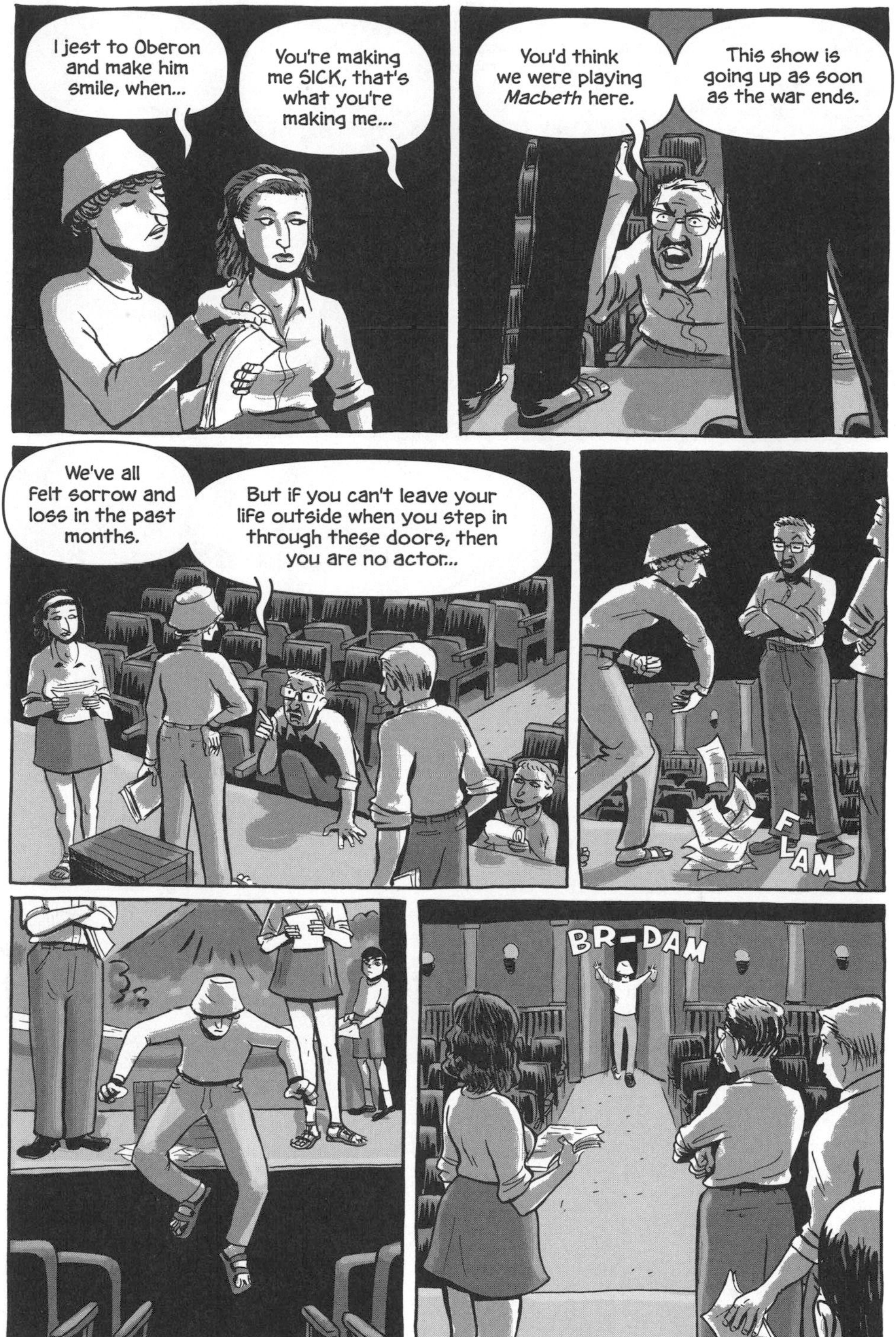
I jest to Oberon and make him smile, when...
You're making me SICK, that's what you're making me...
You'd think we were playing *Macbeth* here.
This show is going up as soon as the war ends.
We've all felt sorrow and loss in the past months.
But if you can't leave your life outside when you step in through these doors, then you are no actor...
FLAM
BR-DAM

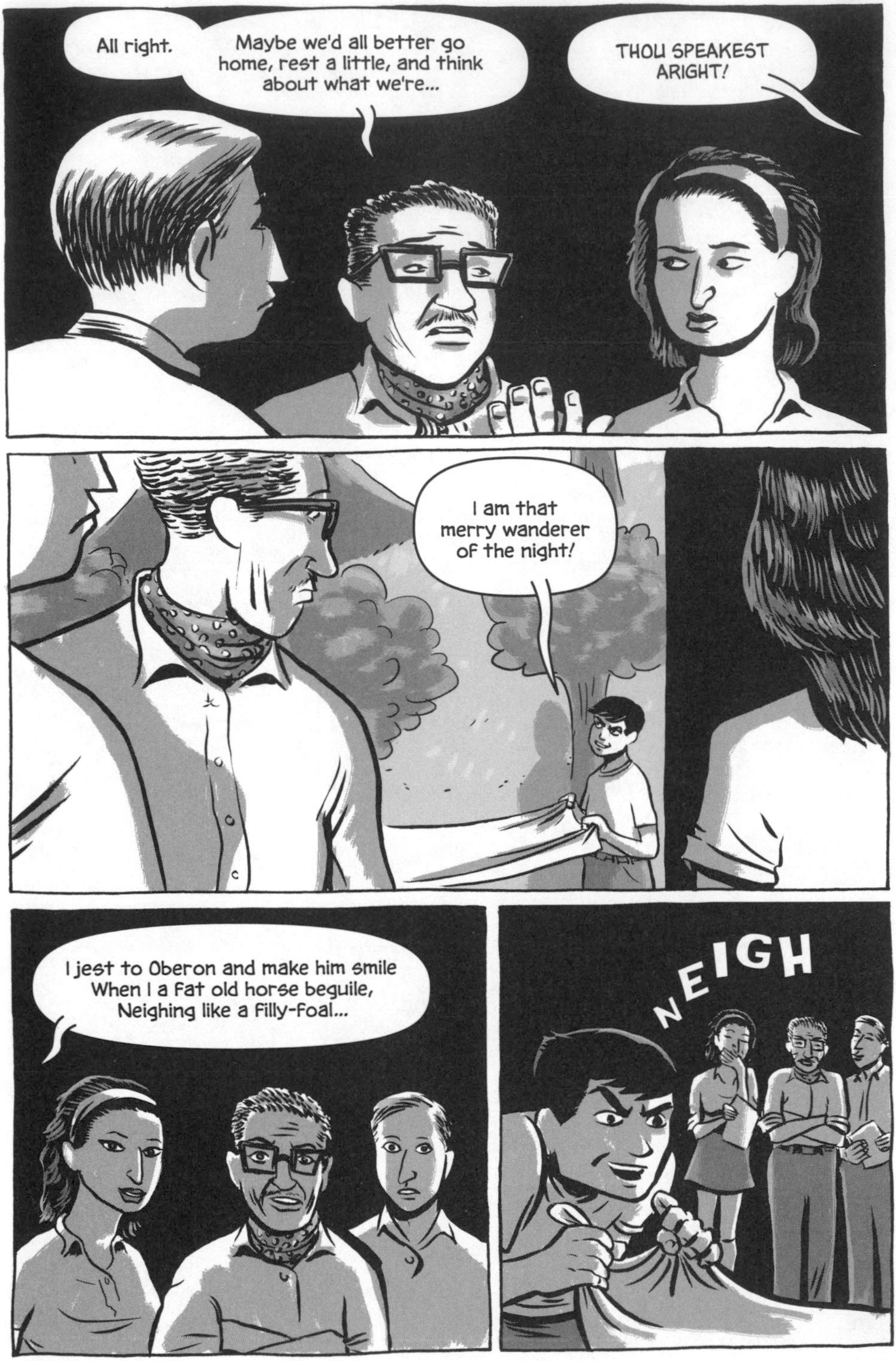
All right.
Maybe we'd all better go home, rest a little, and think about what we're...
THOU SPEAKEST ARIGHT!
I am that merry wanderer of the night!
I jest to Oberon and make him smile When I a fat old horse beguile, Neighing like a filly-foal...
NEIGH

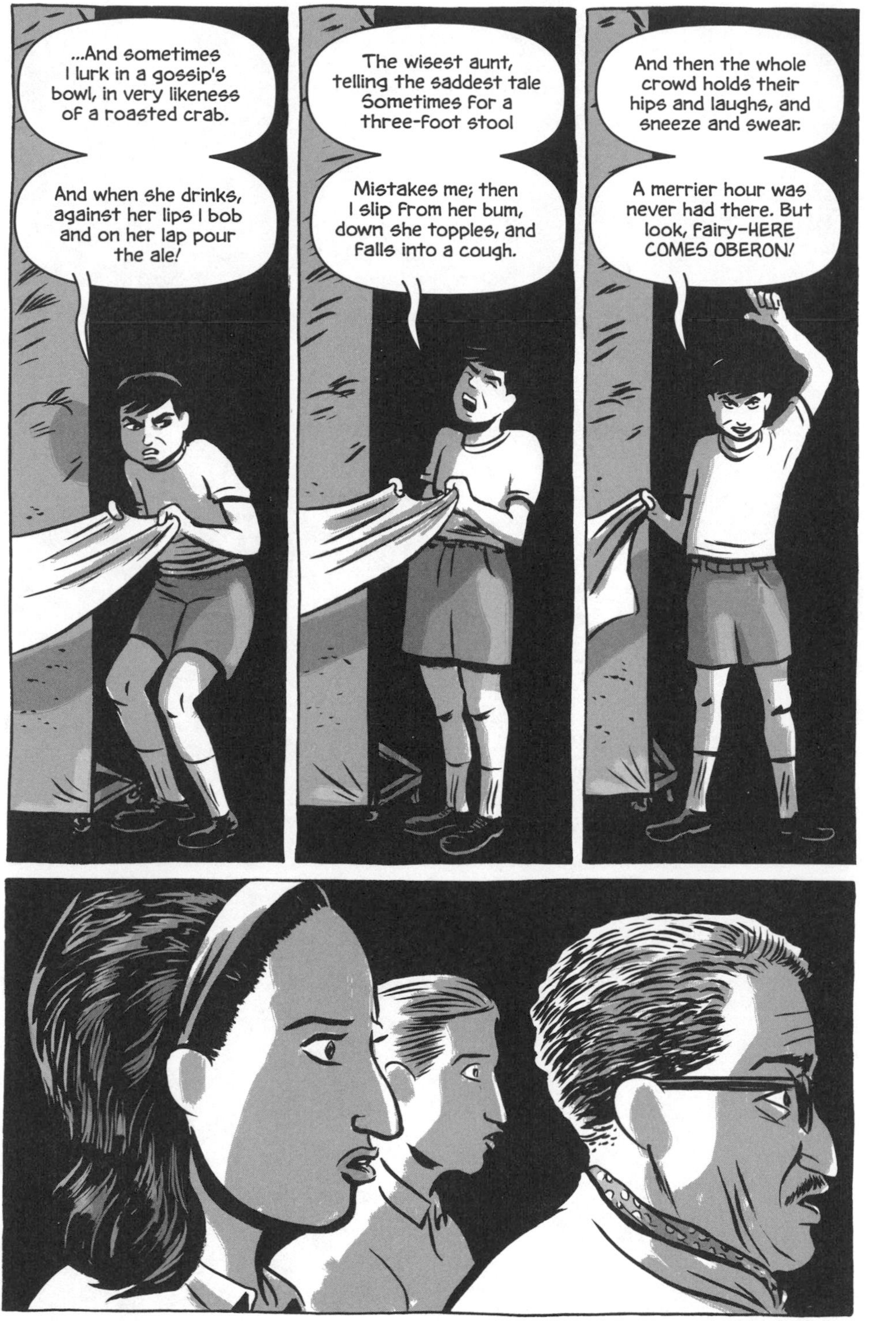
...And sometimes I lurk in a gossip's bowl, in very likeness of a roasted crab.
And when she drinks, against her lips I bob and on her lap pour the ale!
The wisest aunt, telling the saddest tale Sometimes for a three-foot stool
Mistakes me; then I slip from her bum, down she topples, and falls into a cough.
And then the whole crowd holds their hips and laughs, and sneeze and swear.
A merrier hour was never had there. But look, Fairy–HERE COMES OBERON!

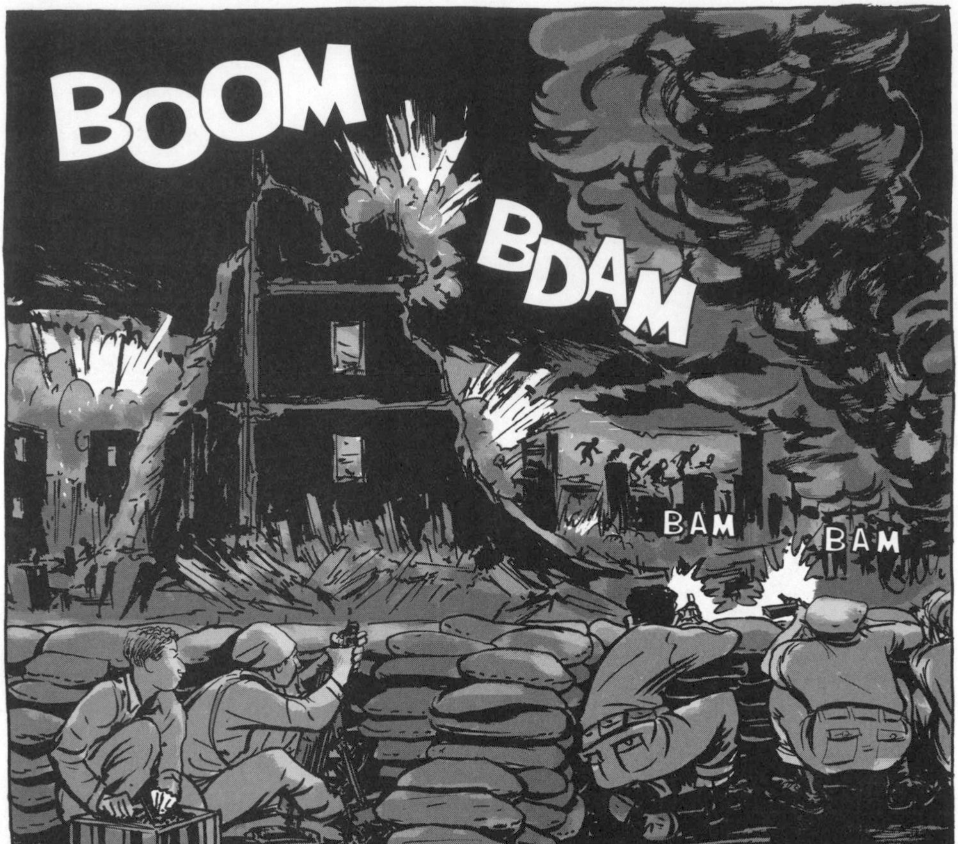
BOOM
BDAM
BAM
BAM

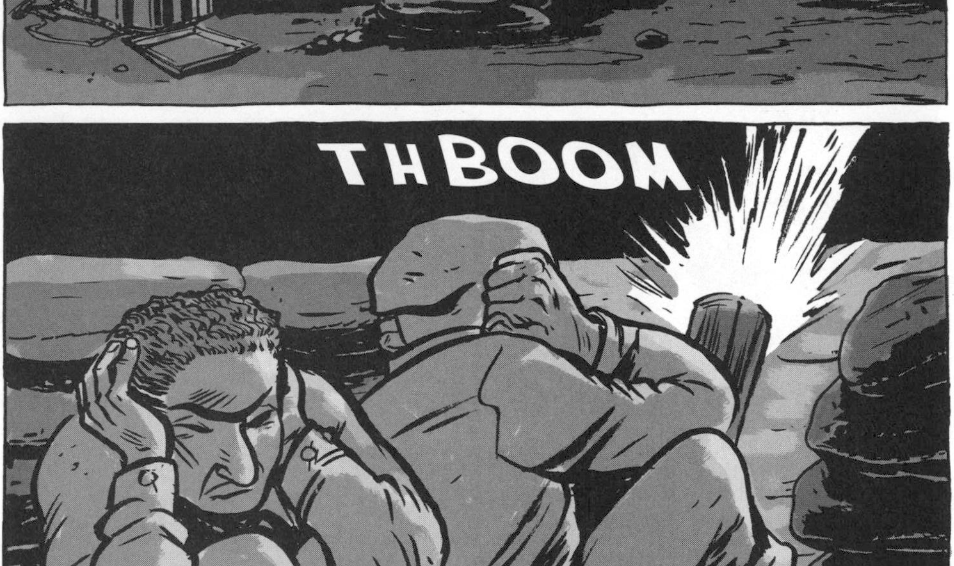
THBOOM

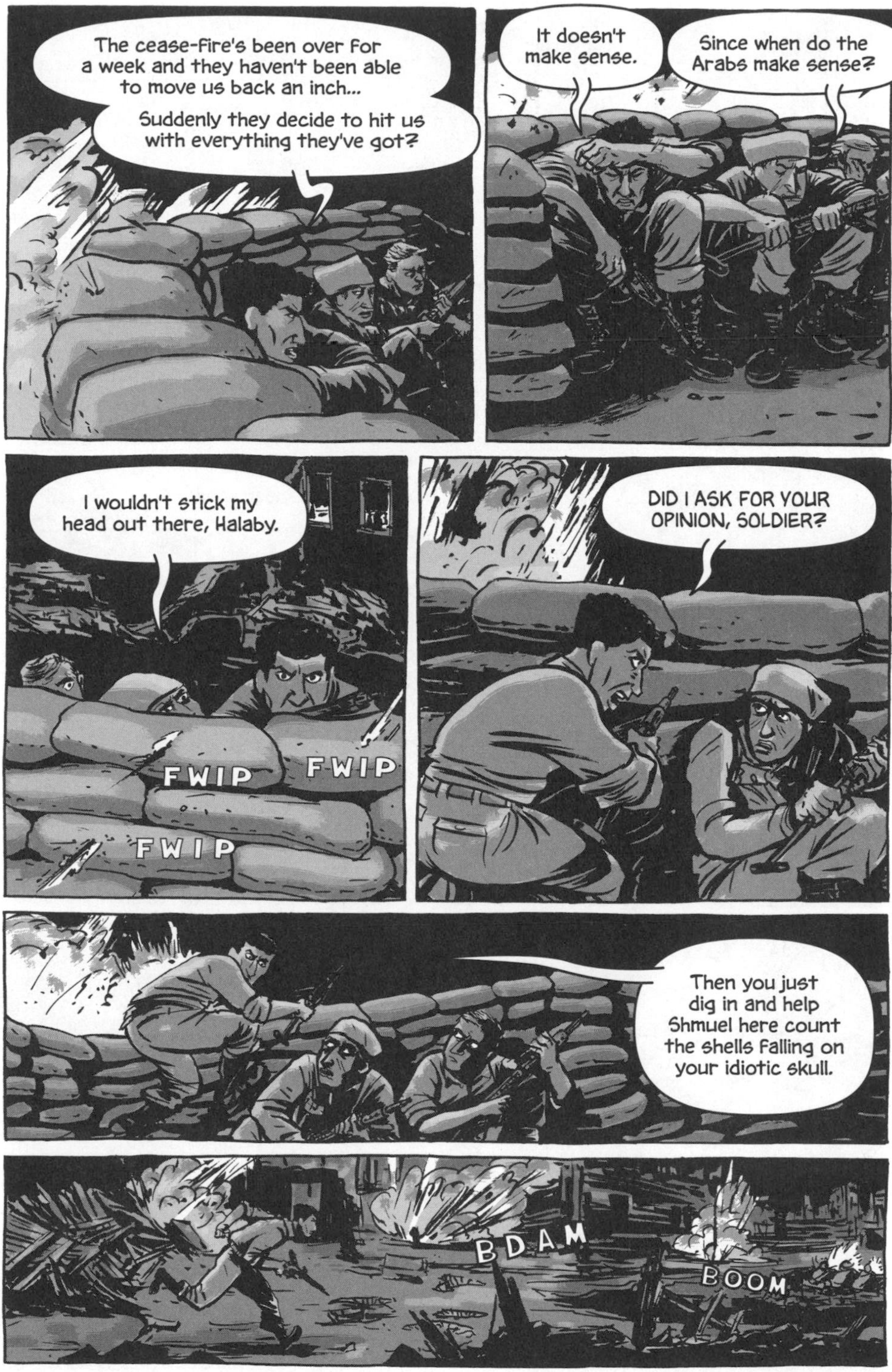
The cease-fire's been over for a week and they haven't been able to move us back an inch...
Suddenly they decide to hit us with everything they've got?
It doesn't make sense.
Since when do the Arabs make sense?
I wouldn't stick my head out there, Halaby.
FWIP
FWIP
FWIP
DID I ASK FOR YOUR OPINION, SOLDIER?
Then you just dig in and help Shmuel here count the shells falling on your idiotic skull.
BDAM
BOOM

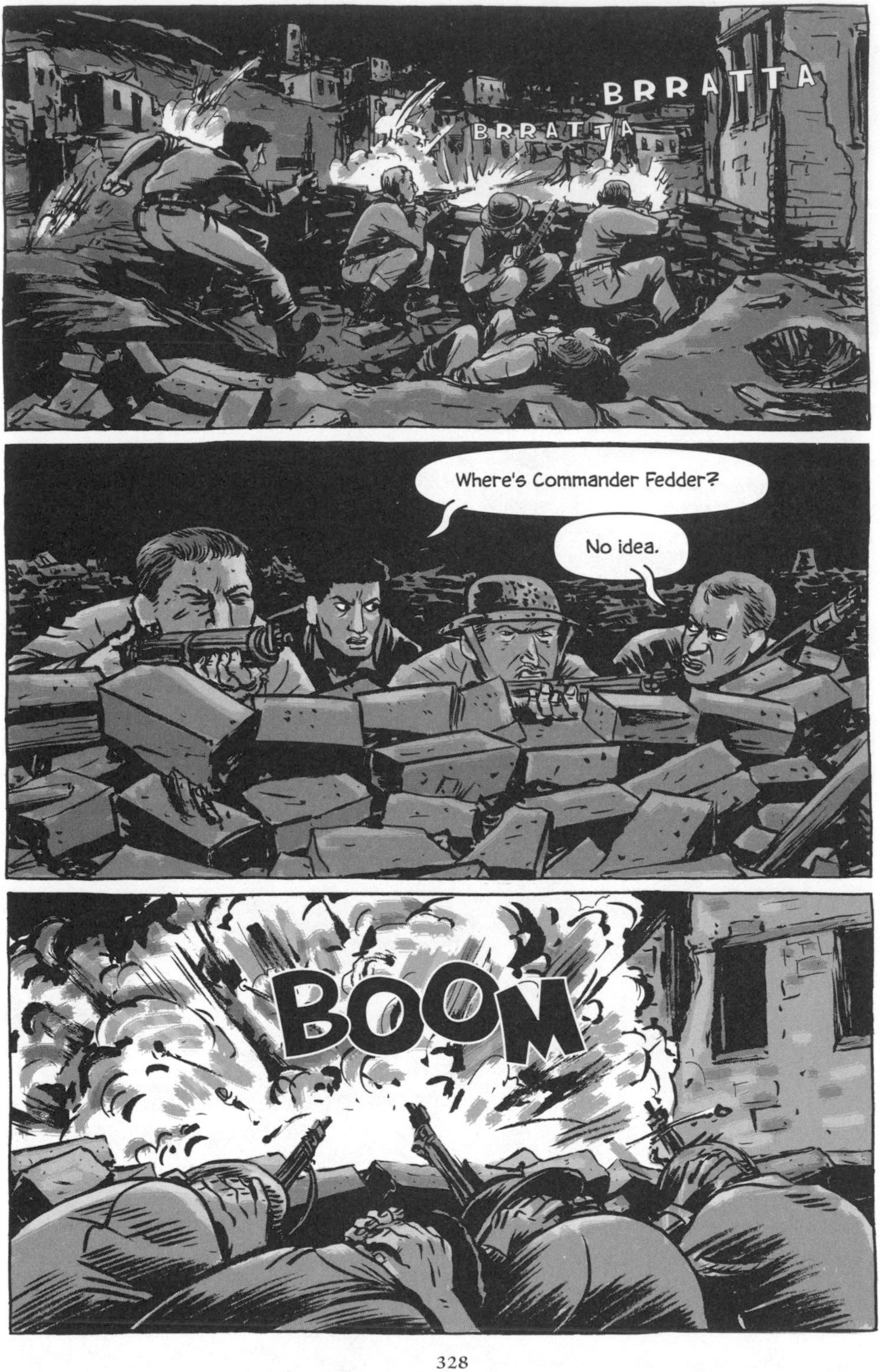
BRRATTA
BRRATTA
Where's Commander Fedder?
No idea.
BOOM

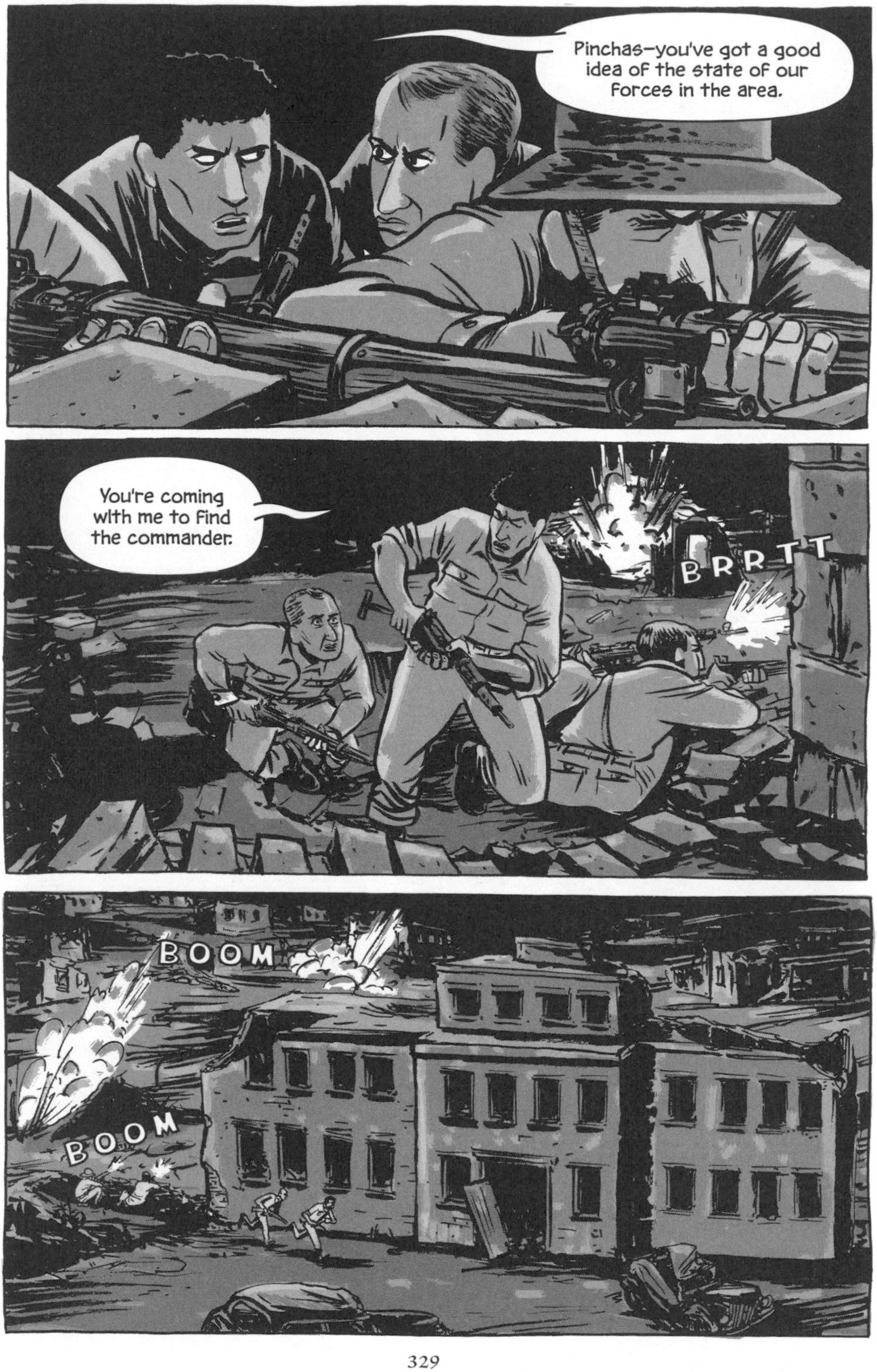
Pinchas—you've got a good idea of the state of our forces in the area.
You're coming with me to find the commander.
BRRTT
BOOM
BOOM

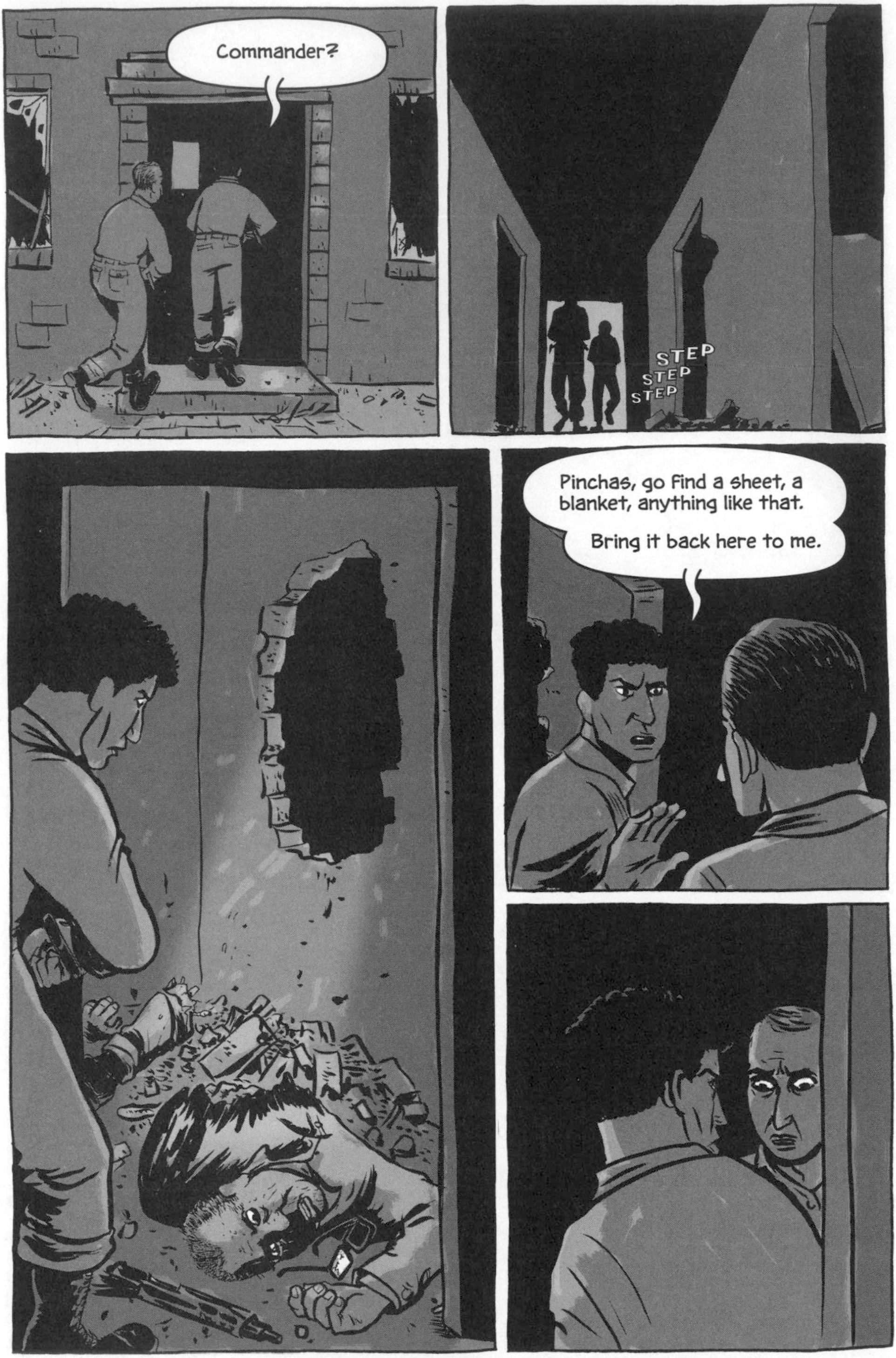
Commander?
STEP
STEP
STEP
Pinchas, go find a sheet, a blanket, anything like that.
Bring it back here to me.

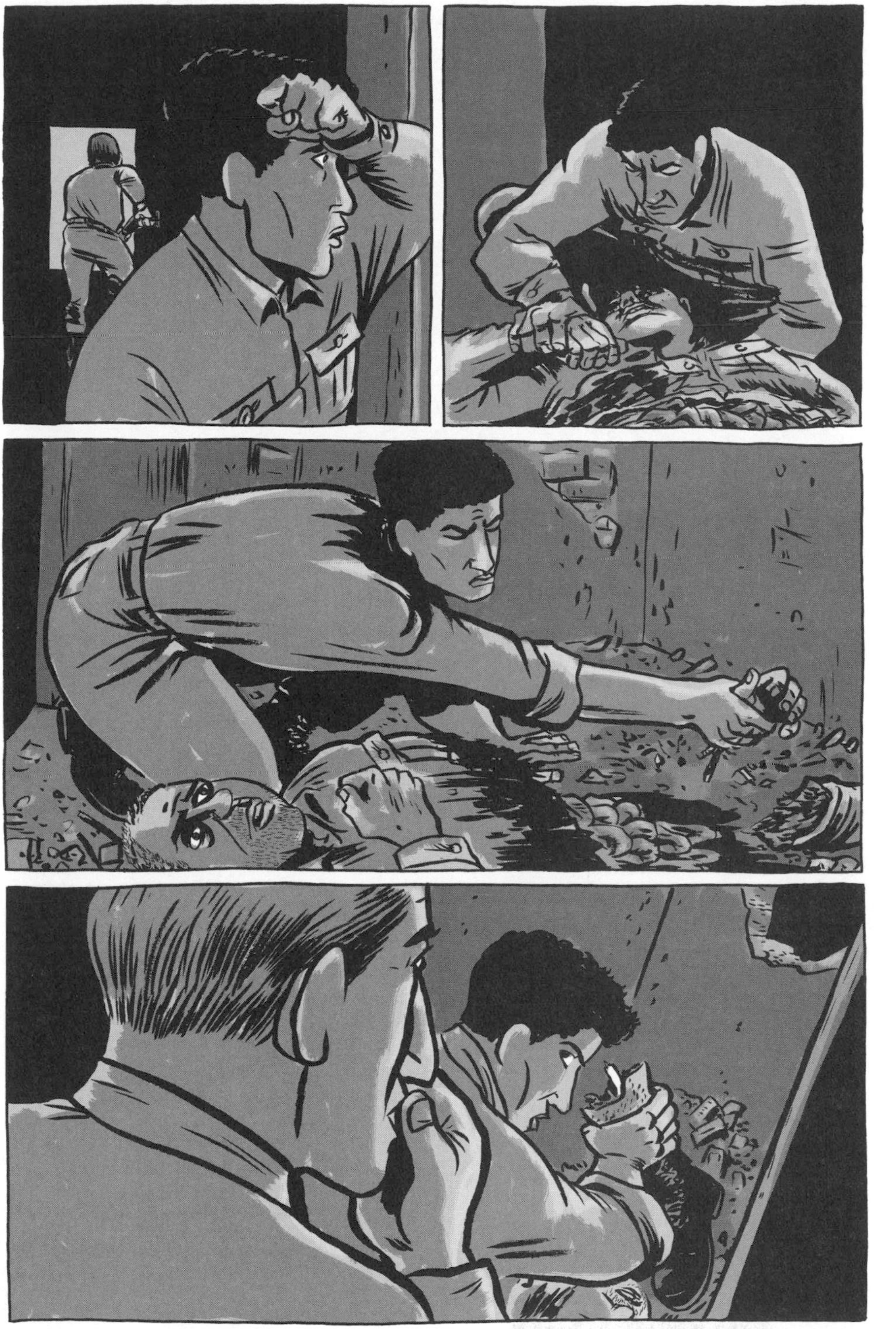

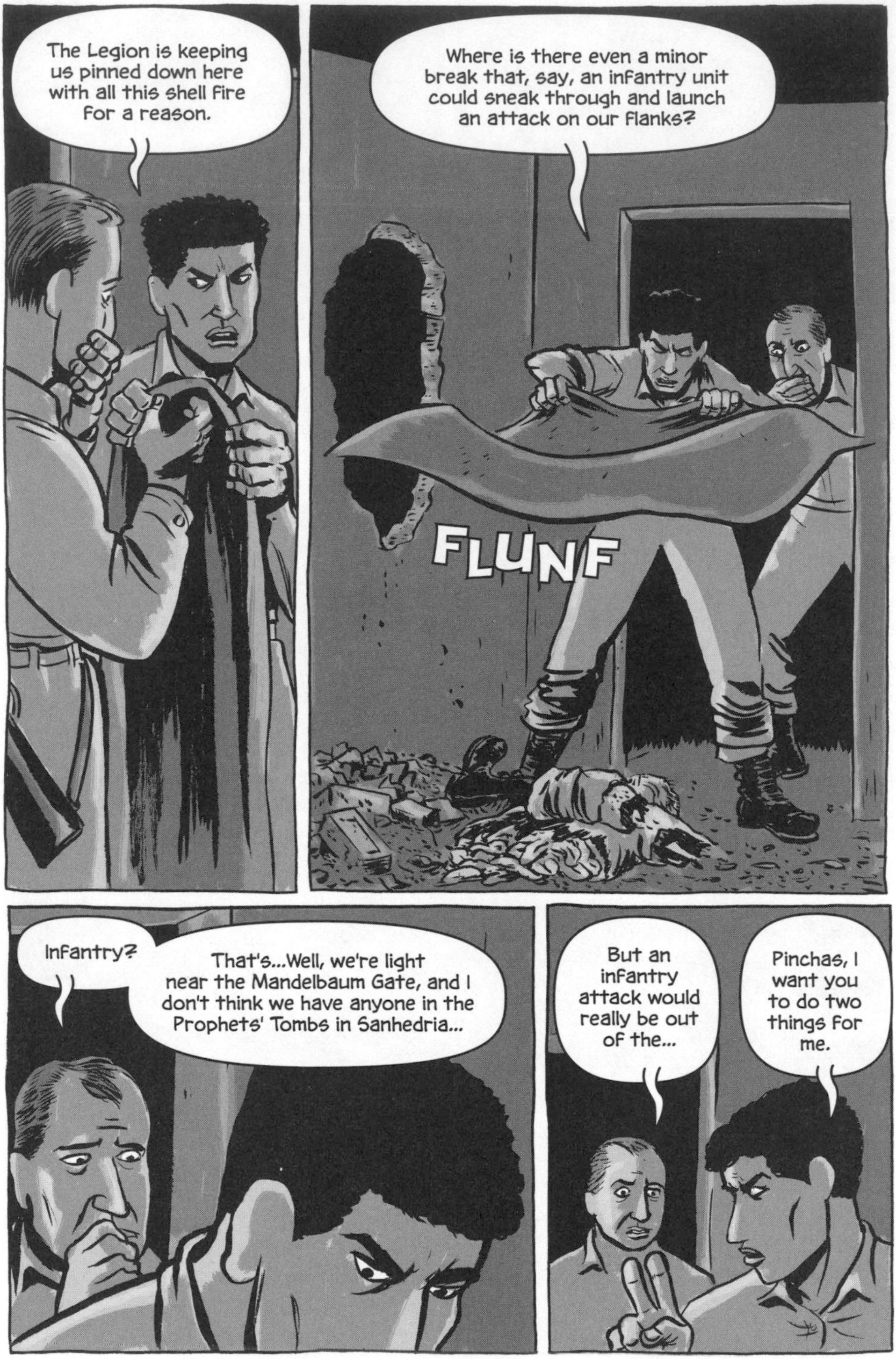
The Legion is keeping us pinned down here with all this shell fire for a reason.
Where is there even a minor break that, say, an infantry unit could sneak through and launch an attack on our flanks?
FLUNF
Infantry?
That's...Well, we're light near the Mandelbaum Gate, and I don't think we have anyone in the Prophets' Tombs in Sanhedria...
But an infantry attack would really be out of the...
Pinchas, I want you to do two things for me.

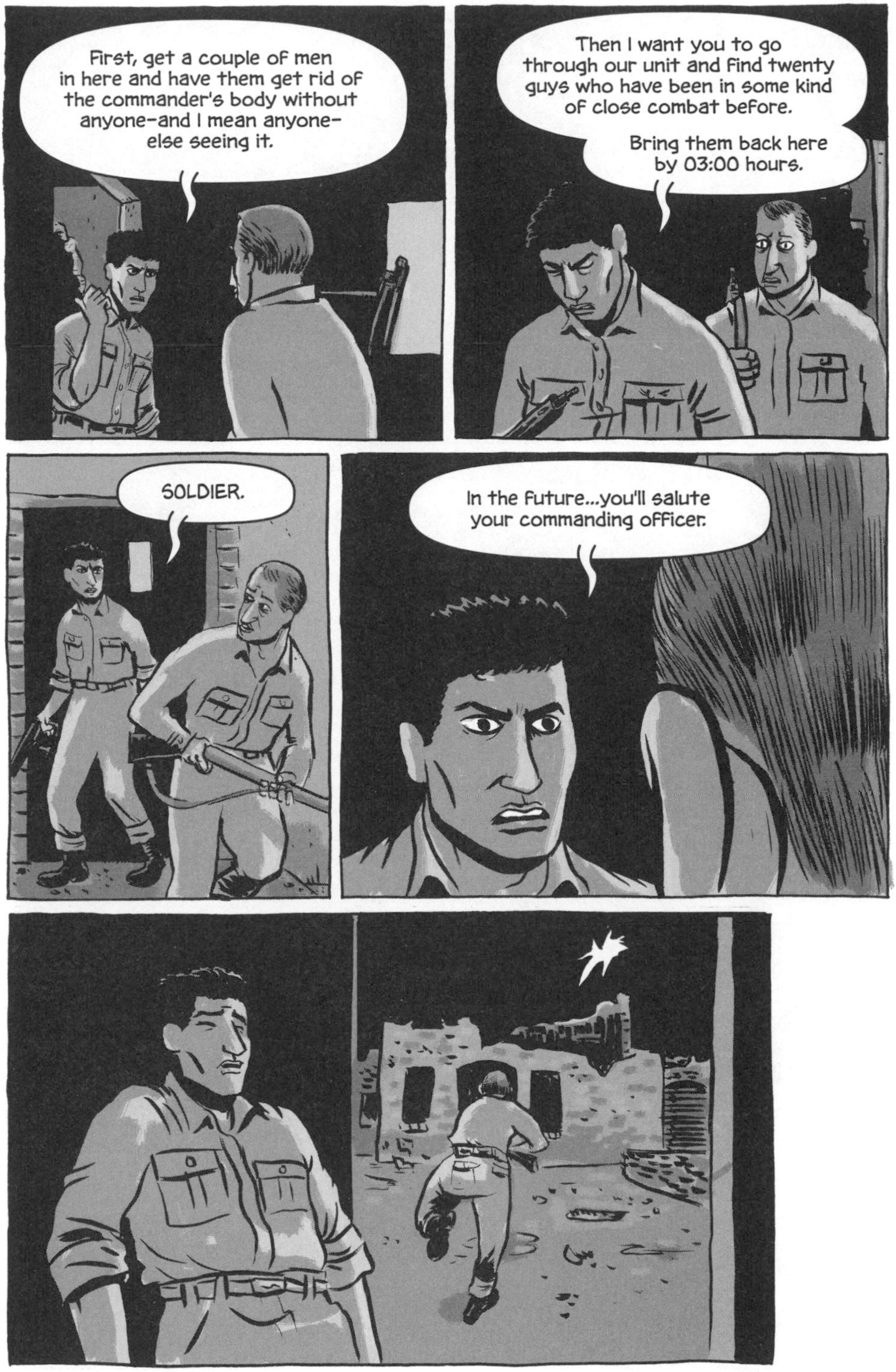
First, get a couple of men in here and have them get rid of the commander's body without anyone—and I mean anyone—else seeing it.
Then I want you to go through our unit and find twenty guys who have been in some kind of close combat before.
Bring them back here by 03:00 hours.
SOLDIER.
In the future...you'll salute your commanding officer.

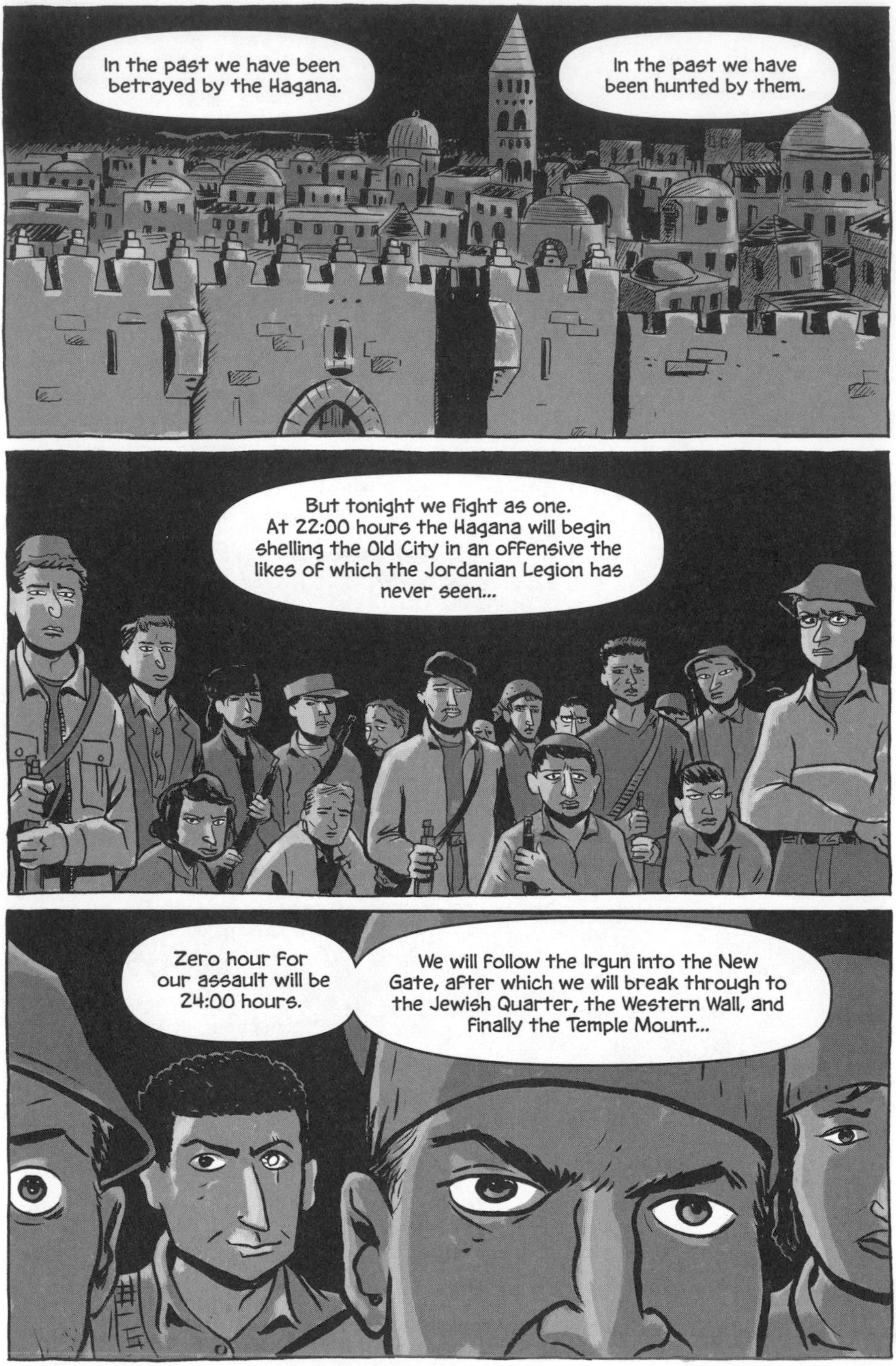
In the past we have been betrayed by the Hagana.
In the past we have been hunted by them.
But tonight we fight as one. At 22:00 hours the Hagana will begin shelling the Old City in an offensive the likes of which the Jordanian Legion has never seen...
Zero hour for our assault will be 24:00 hours.
We will follow the Irgun into the New Gate, after which we will break through to the Jewish Quarter, the Western Wall, and finally the Temple Mount...

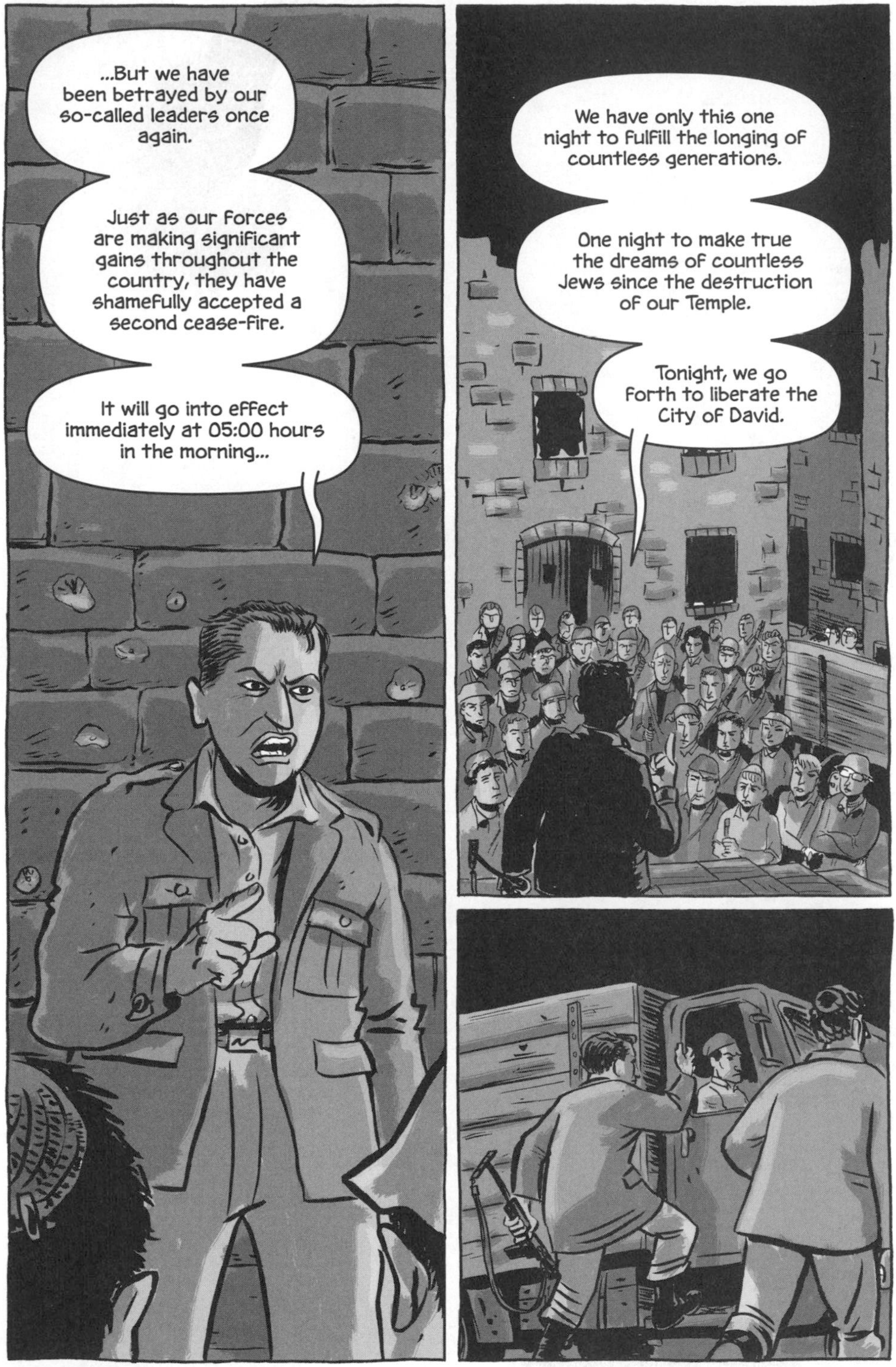
...But we have been betrayed by our so-called leaders once again.
Just as our forces are making significant gains throughout the country, they have shamefully accepted a second cease-fire.
It will go into effect immediately at 05:00 hours in the morning...
We have only this one night to fulfill the longing of countless generations.
One night to make true the dreams of countless Jews since the destruction of our Temple.
Tonight, we go forth to liberate the City of David.

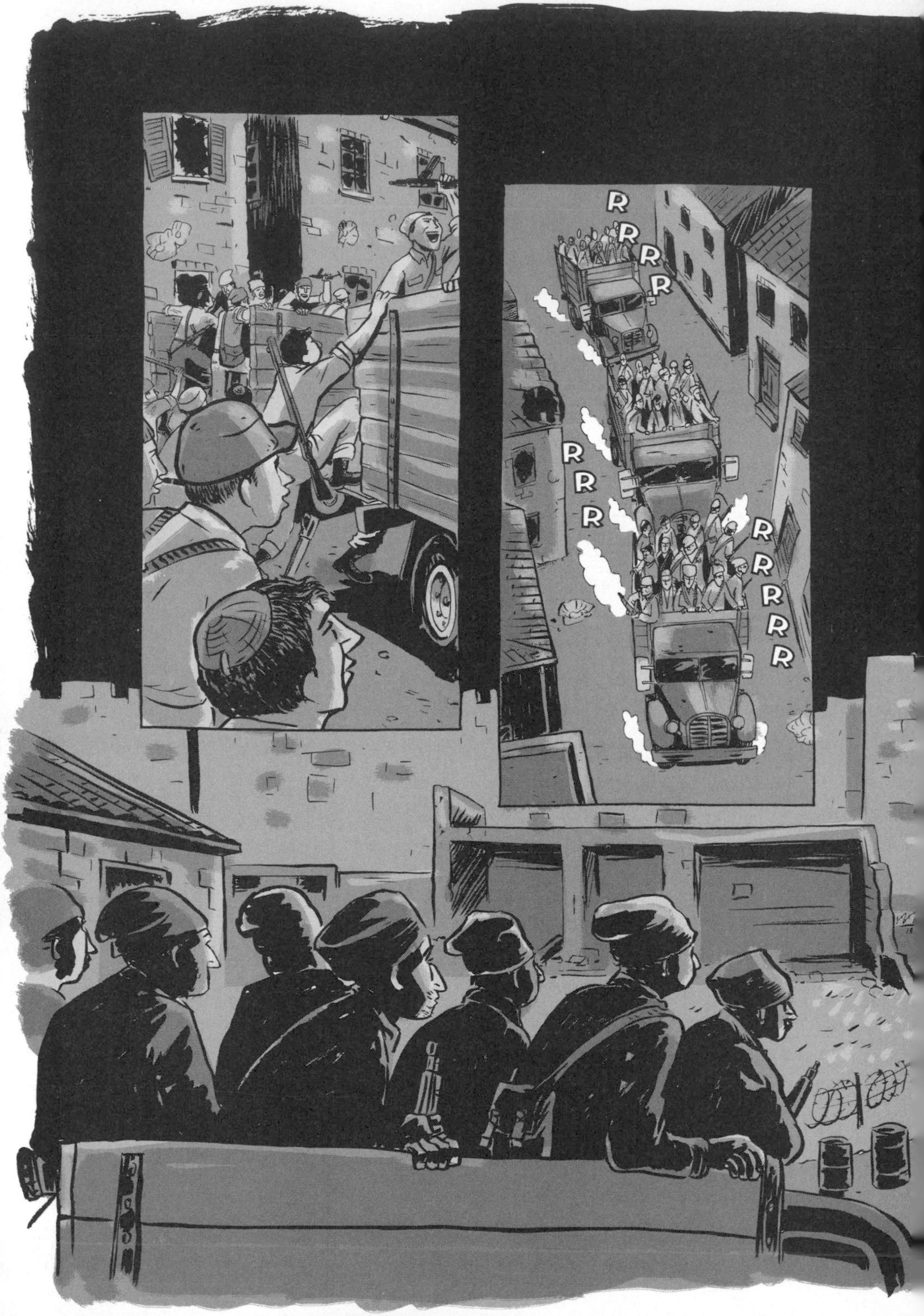

RRRRR
RRR
RRRRR

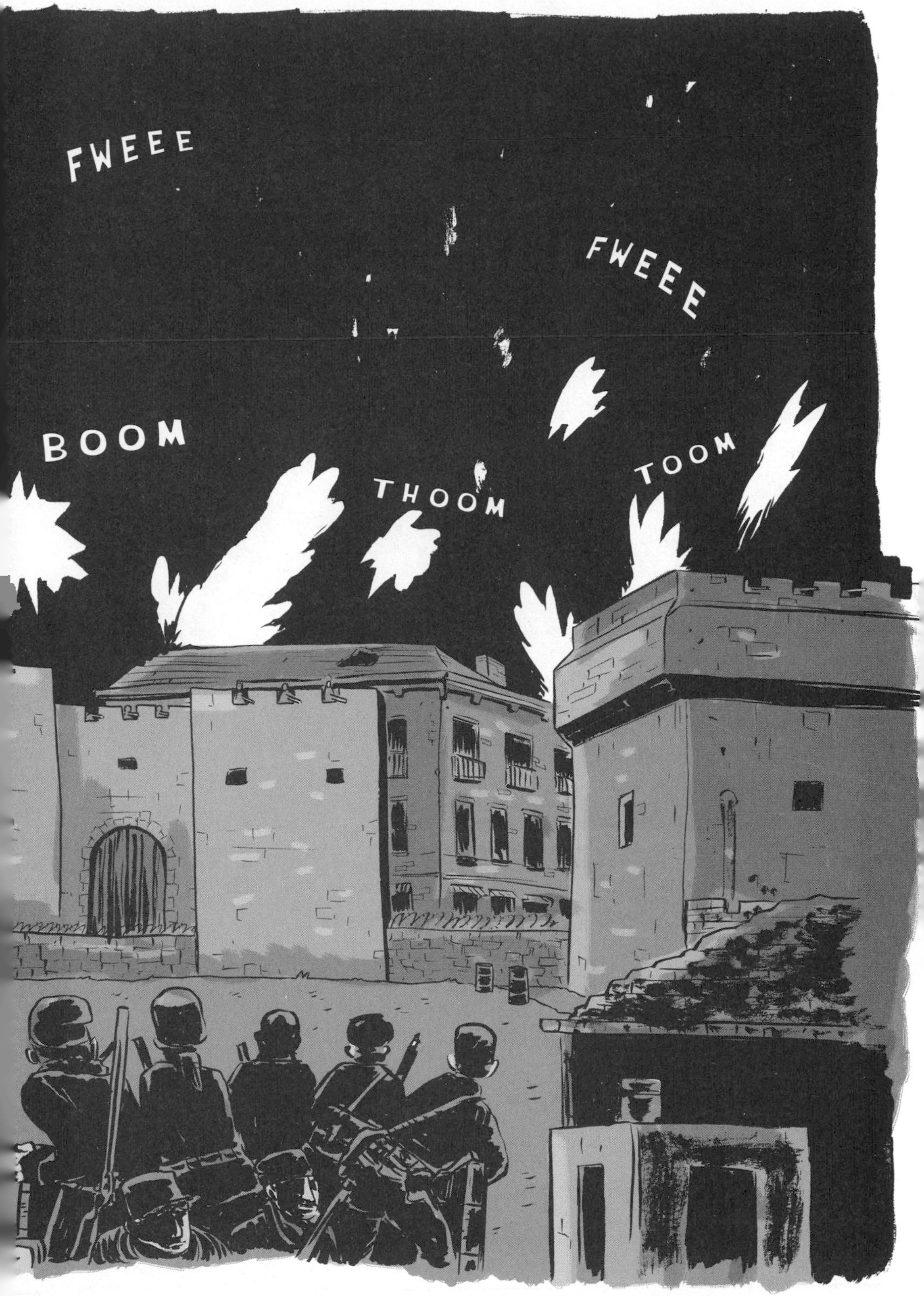
FWEEE
FWEEE
BOOM
THOOM
TOOM

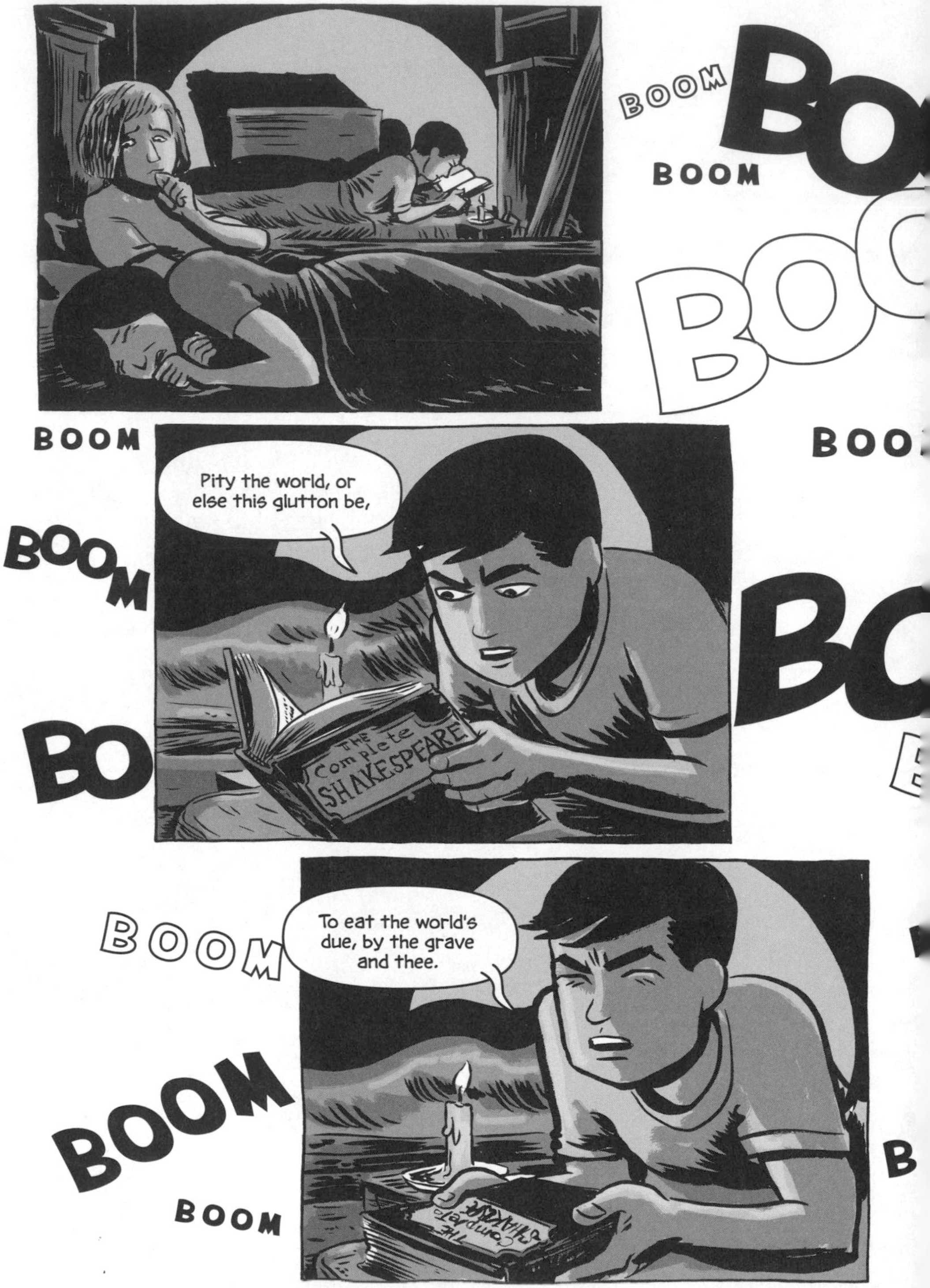
BOOM
BOOM
BOOM
BOOM
Pity the world, or else this glutton be,
THE Complete SHAKESPEARE
BOOM
To eat the world's due, by the grave and thee.
BOOM
BOOM

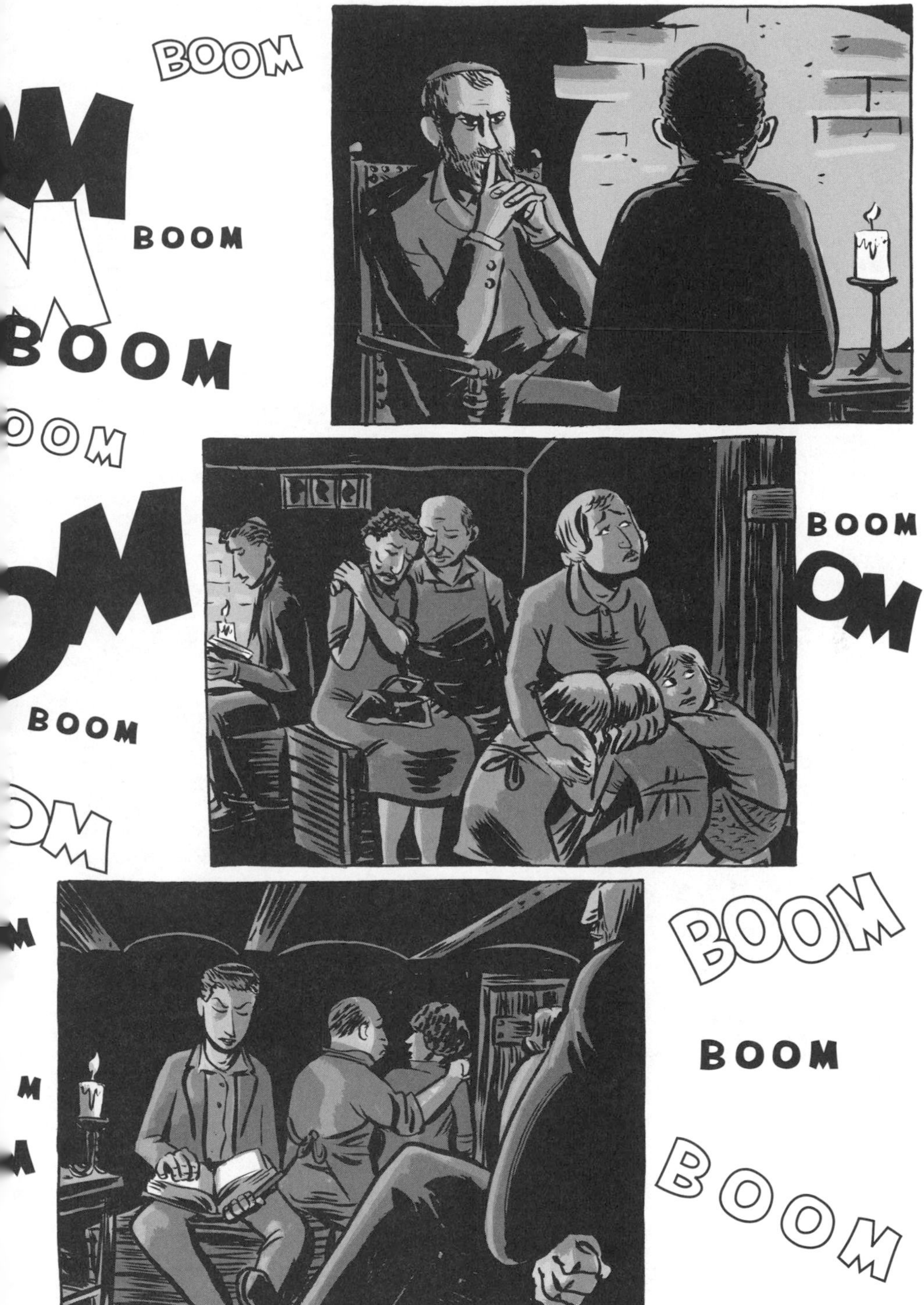
BOOM
BOOM
BOOM
BOOM
BOOM
BOOM
BOOM
BOOM

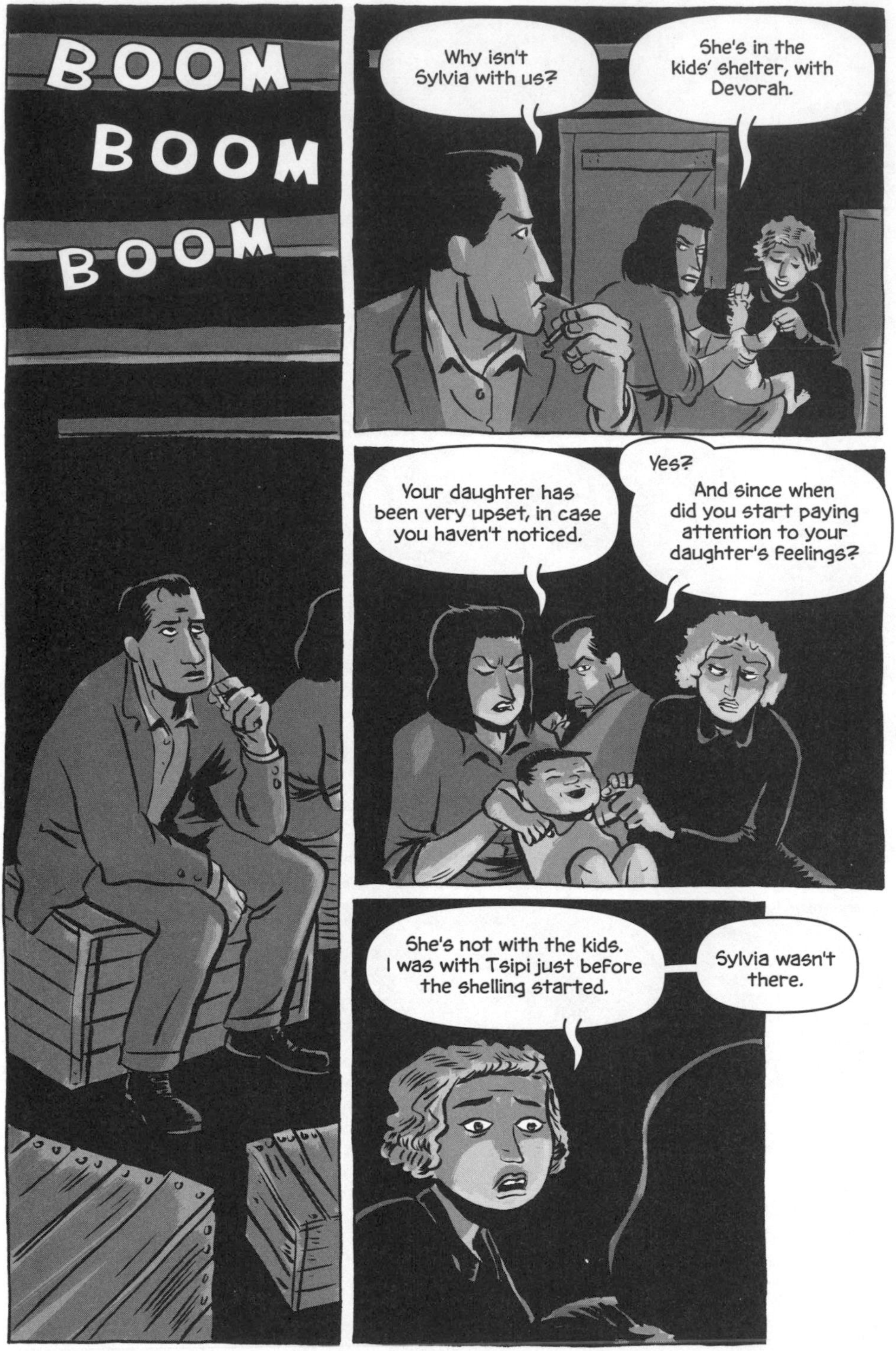
BOOM
BOOM
BOOM
Why isn't Sylvia with us?
She's in the kids' shelter, with Devorah.
Your daughter has been very upset, in case you haven't noticed.
Yes?
And since when did you start paying attention to your daughter's feelings?
She's not with the kids. I was with Tsipi just before the shelling started.
Sylvia wasn't there.

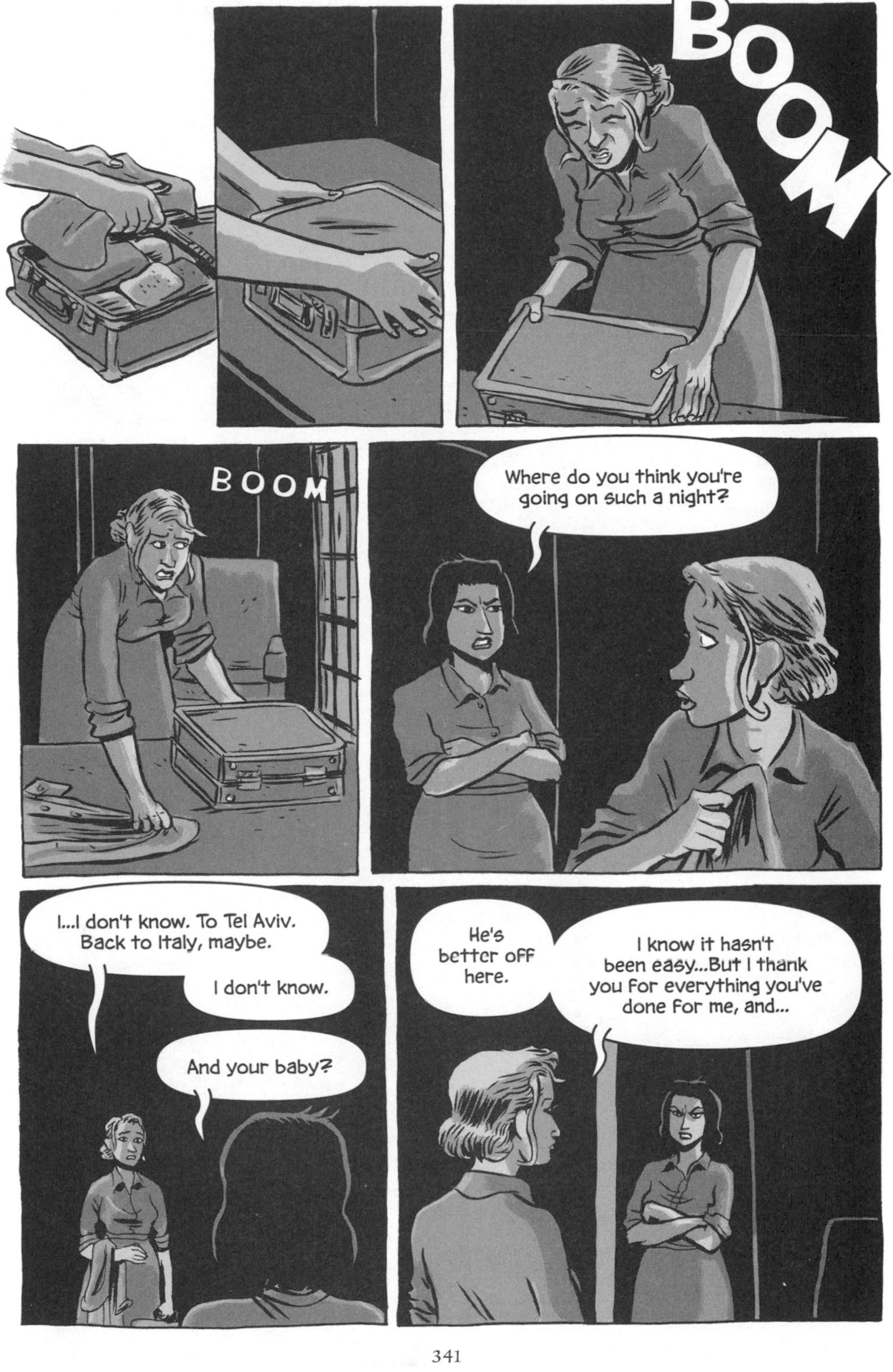
BOOM
BOOM
Where do you think you're going on such a night?
I...I don't know. To Tel Aviv. Back to Italy, maybe.
I don't know.
And your baby?
He's better off here.
I know it hasn't been easy...But I thank you for everything you've done for me, and...

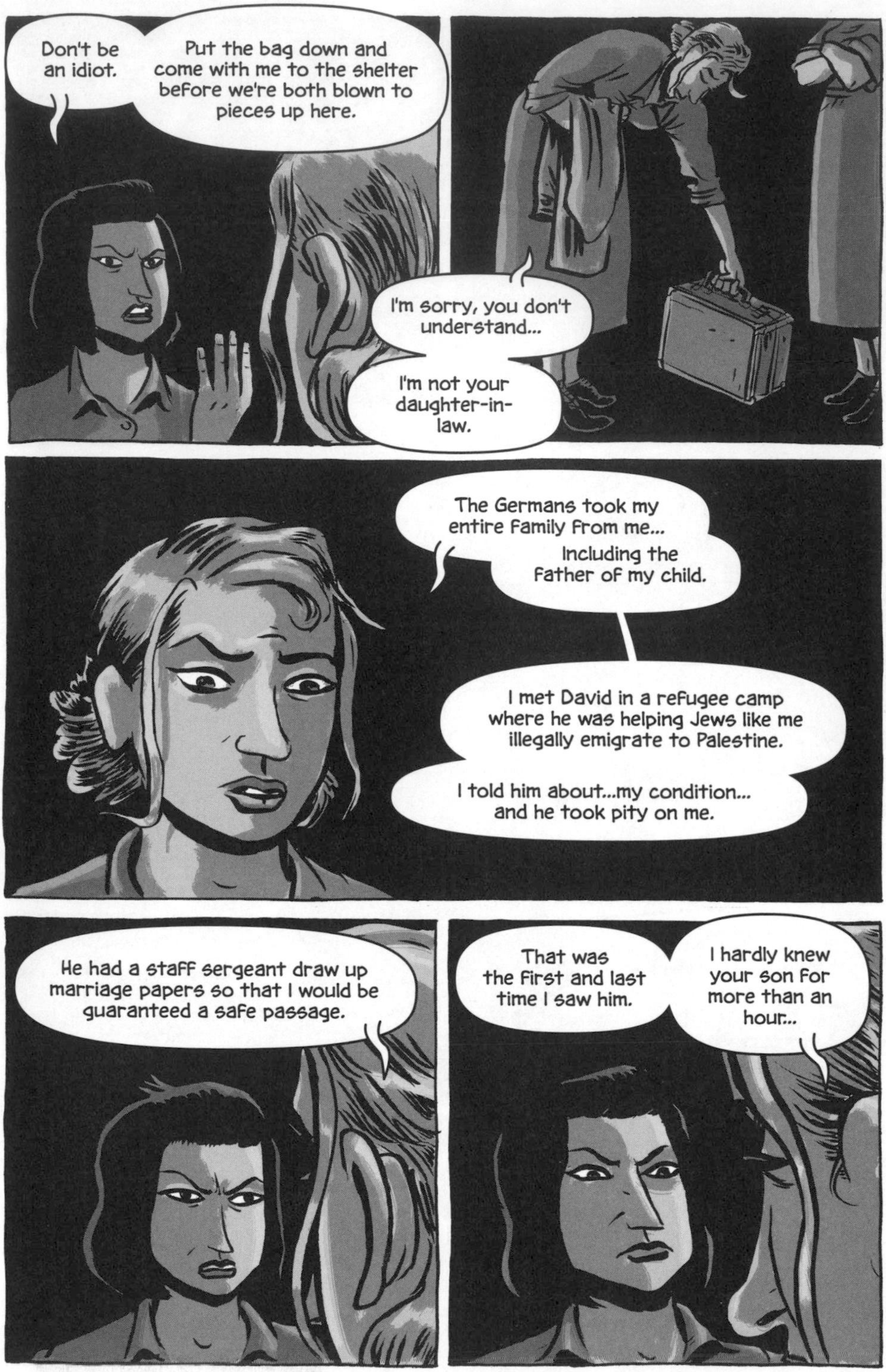
Don't be an idiot.
Put the bag down and come with me to the shelter before we're both blown to pieces up here.
I'm sorry, you don't understand...
I'm not your daughter-in-law.
The Germans took my entire family from me...
Including the father of my child.
I met David in a refugee camp where he was helping Jews like me illegally emigrate to Palestine.
I told him about...my condition... and he took pity on me.
He had a staff sergeant draw up marriage papers so that I would be guaranteed a safe passage.
That was the first and last time I saw him.
I hardly knew your son for more than an hour...

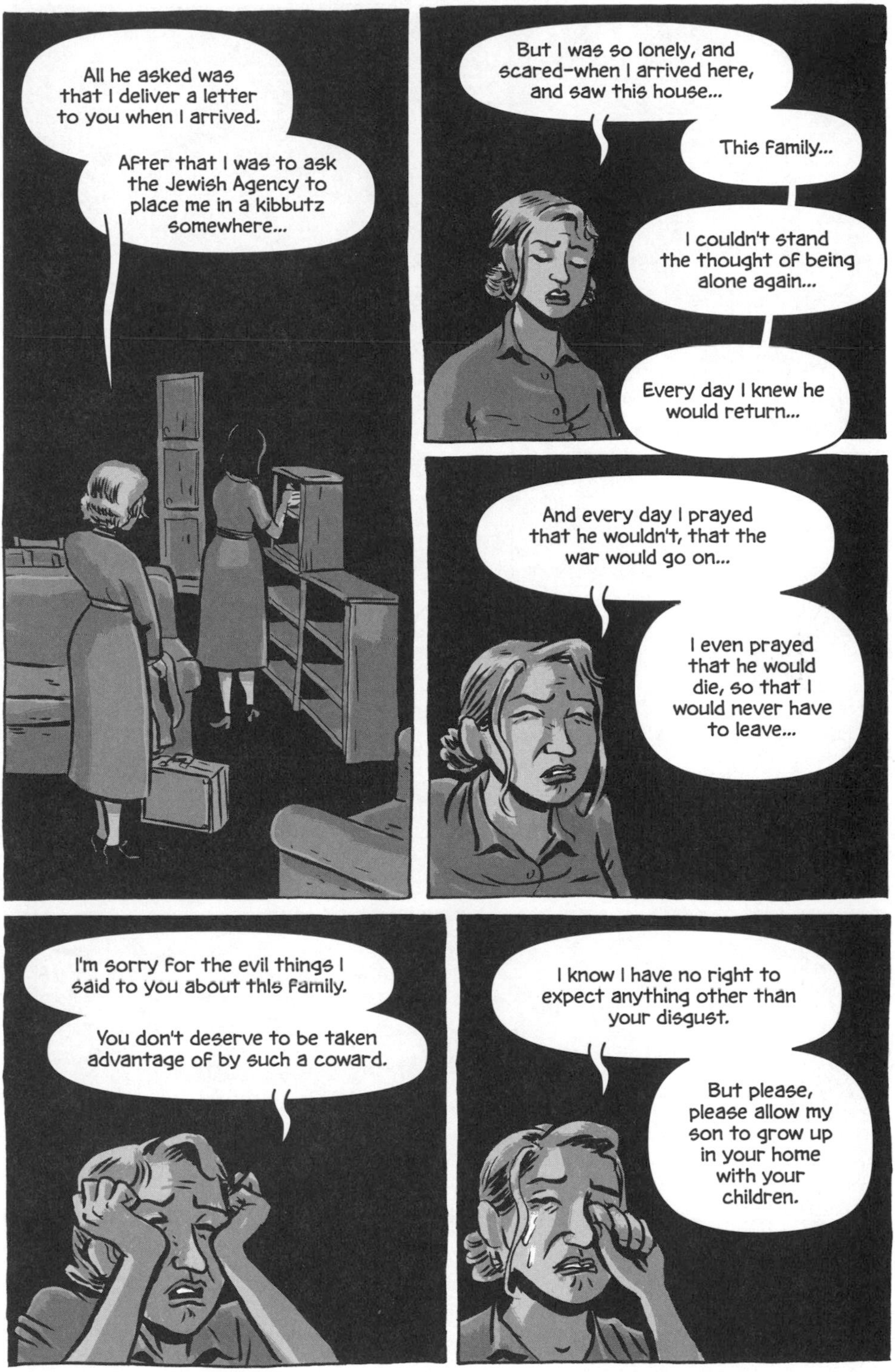
All he asked was that I deliver a letter to you when I arrived.
After that I was to ask the Jewish Agency to place me in a kibbutz somewhere...
But I was so lonely, and scared—when I arrived here, and saw this house...
This family...
I couldn't stand the thought of being alone again...
Every day I knew he would return...
And every day I prayed that he wouldn't, that the war would go on...
I even prayed that he would die, so that I would never have to leave...
I'm sorry for the evil things I said to you about this family.
You don't deserve to be taken advantage of by such a coward.
I know I have no right to expect anything other than your disgust.
But please, please allow my son to grow up in your home with your children.

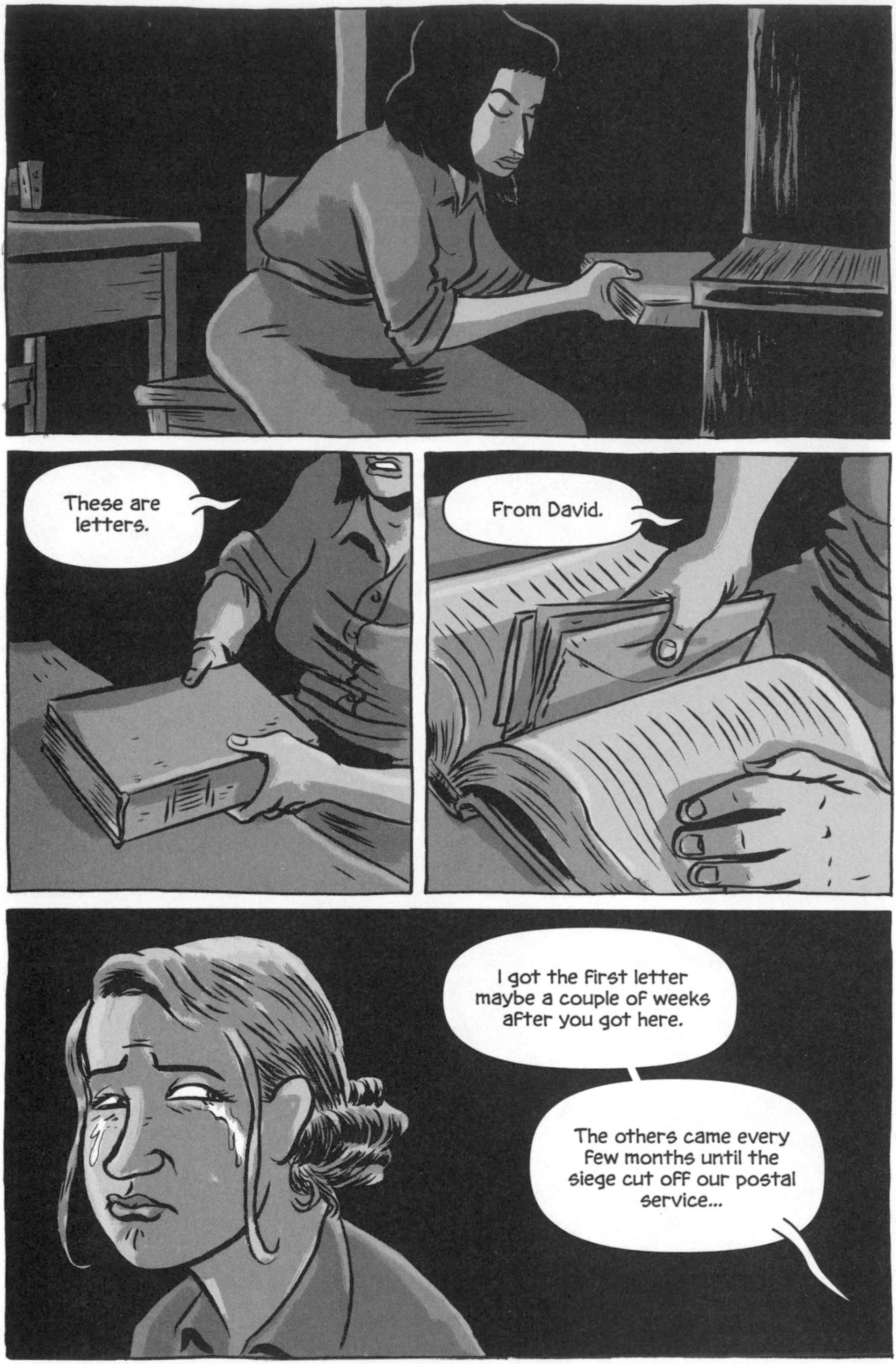

These are letters.
From David.
I got the first letter maybe a couple of weeks after you got here.
The others came every few months until the siege cut off our postal service...

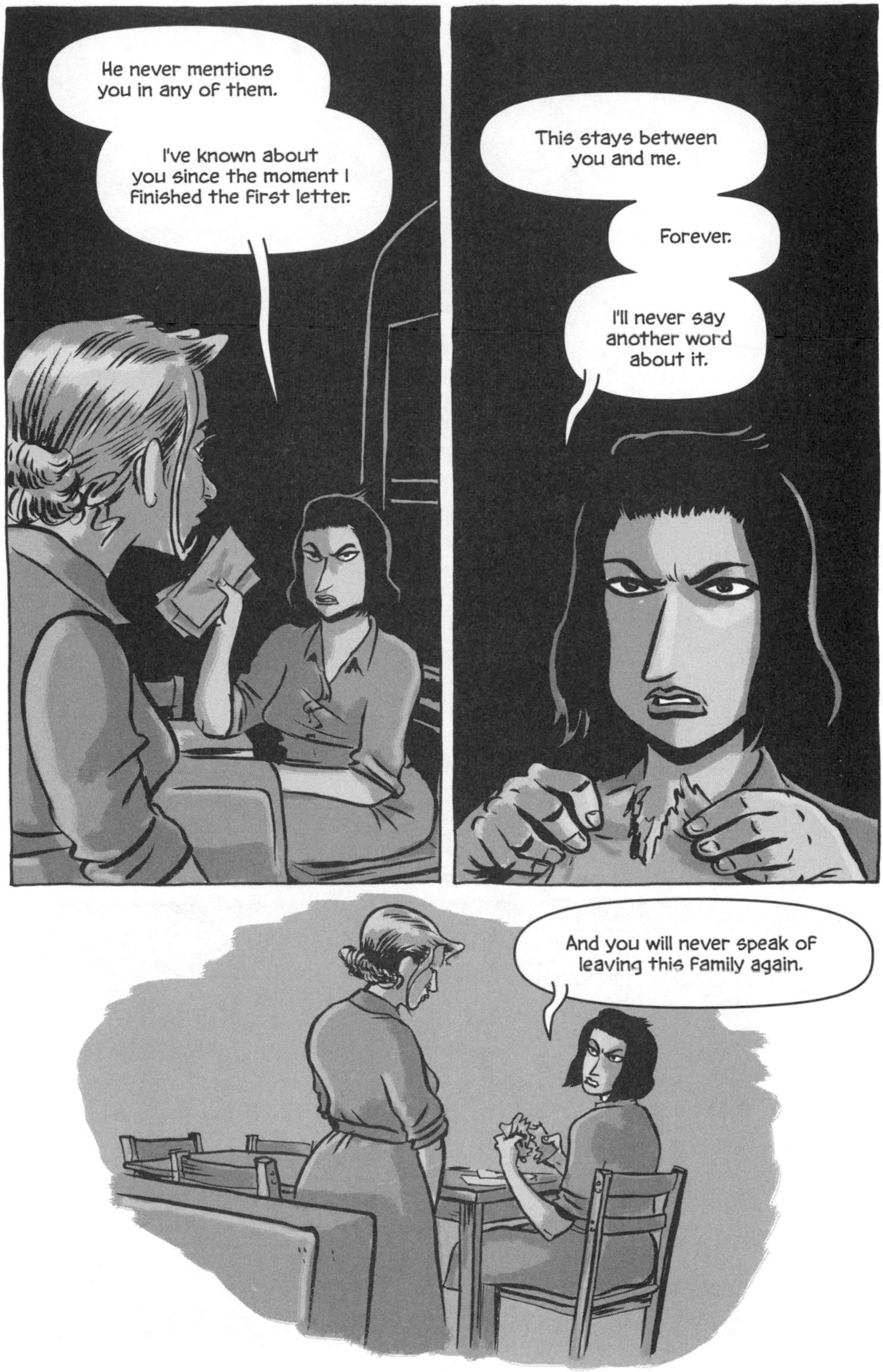
He never mentions you in any of them.
I've known about you since the moment I finished the first letter.
This stays between you and me.
Forever.
I'll never say another word about it.
And you will never speak of leaving this family again.

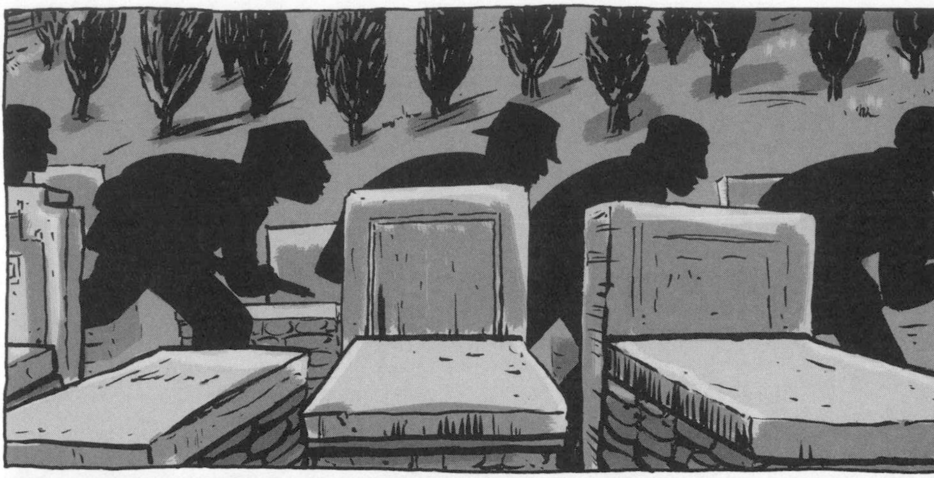

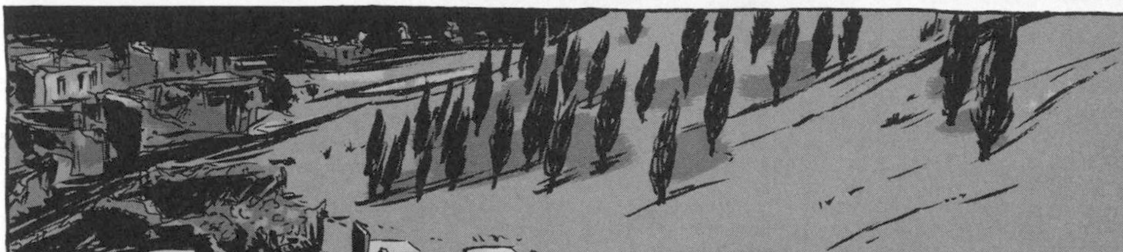

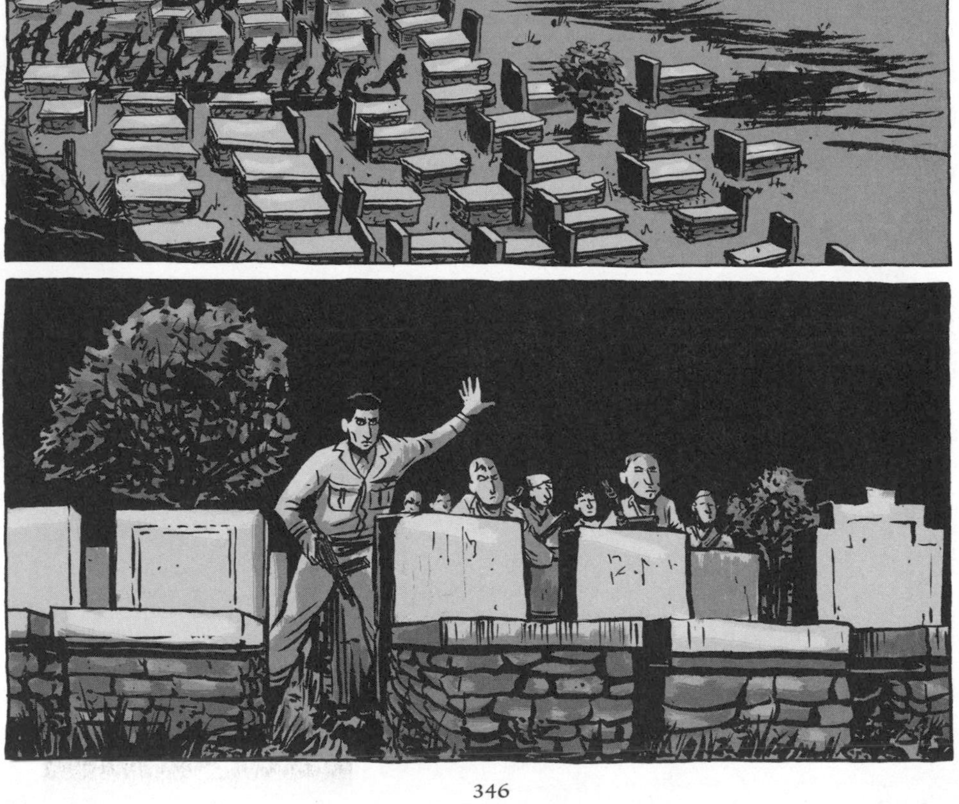

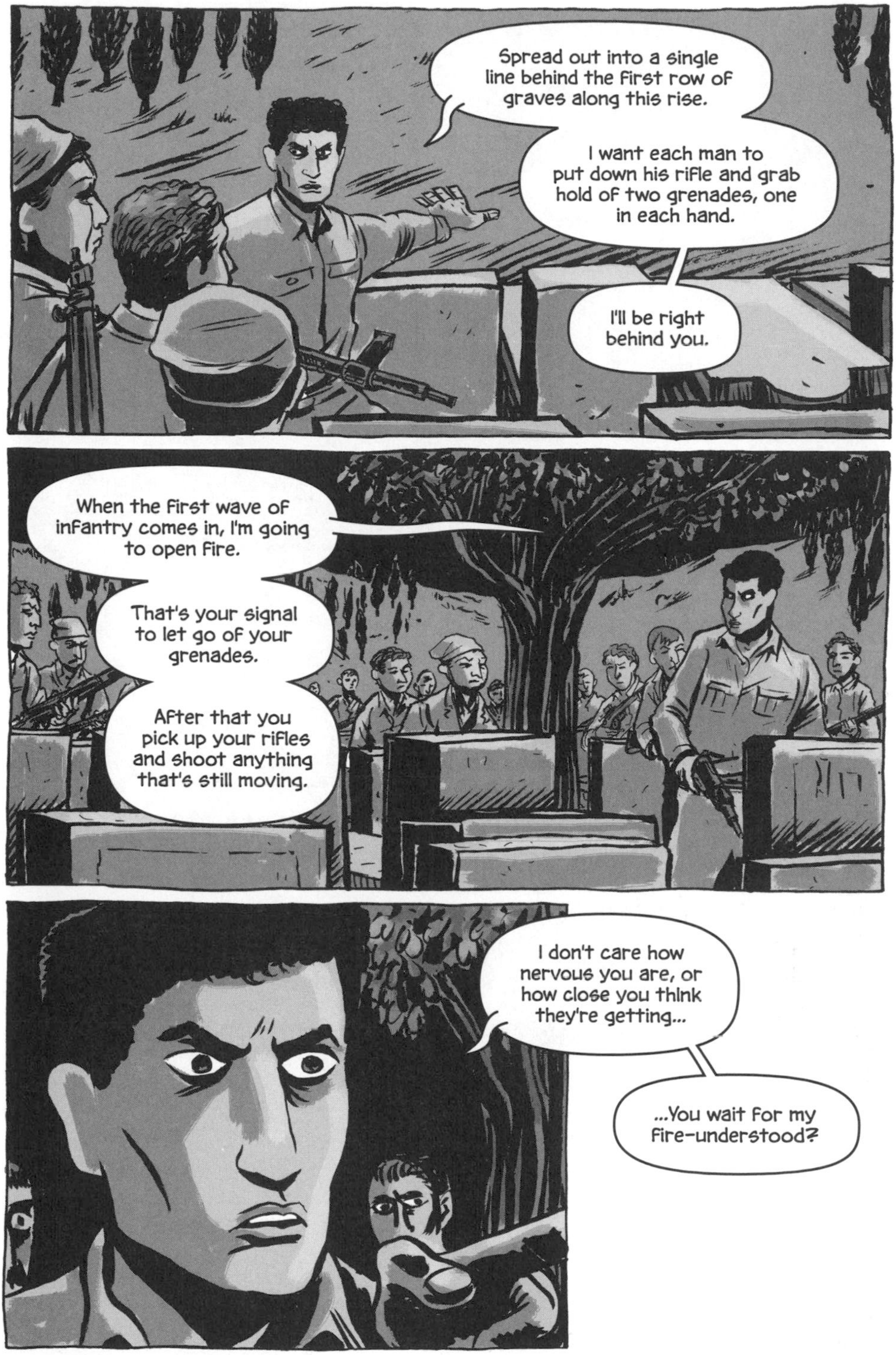

Spread out into a single line behind the first row of graves along this rise.
I want each man to put down his rifle and grab hold of two grenades, one in each hand.
I'll be right behind you.
When the first wave of infantry comes in, I'm going to open fire.
That's your signal to let go of your grenades.
After that you pick up your rifles and shoot anything that's still moving.
I don't care how nervous you are, or how close you think they're getting...
...You wait for my fire—understood?

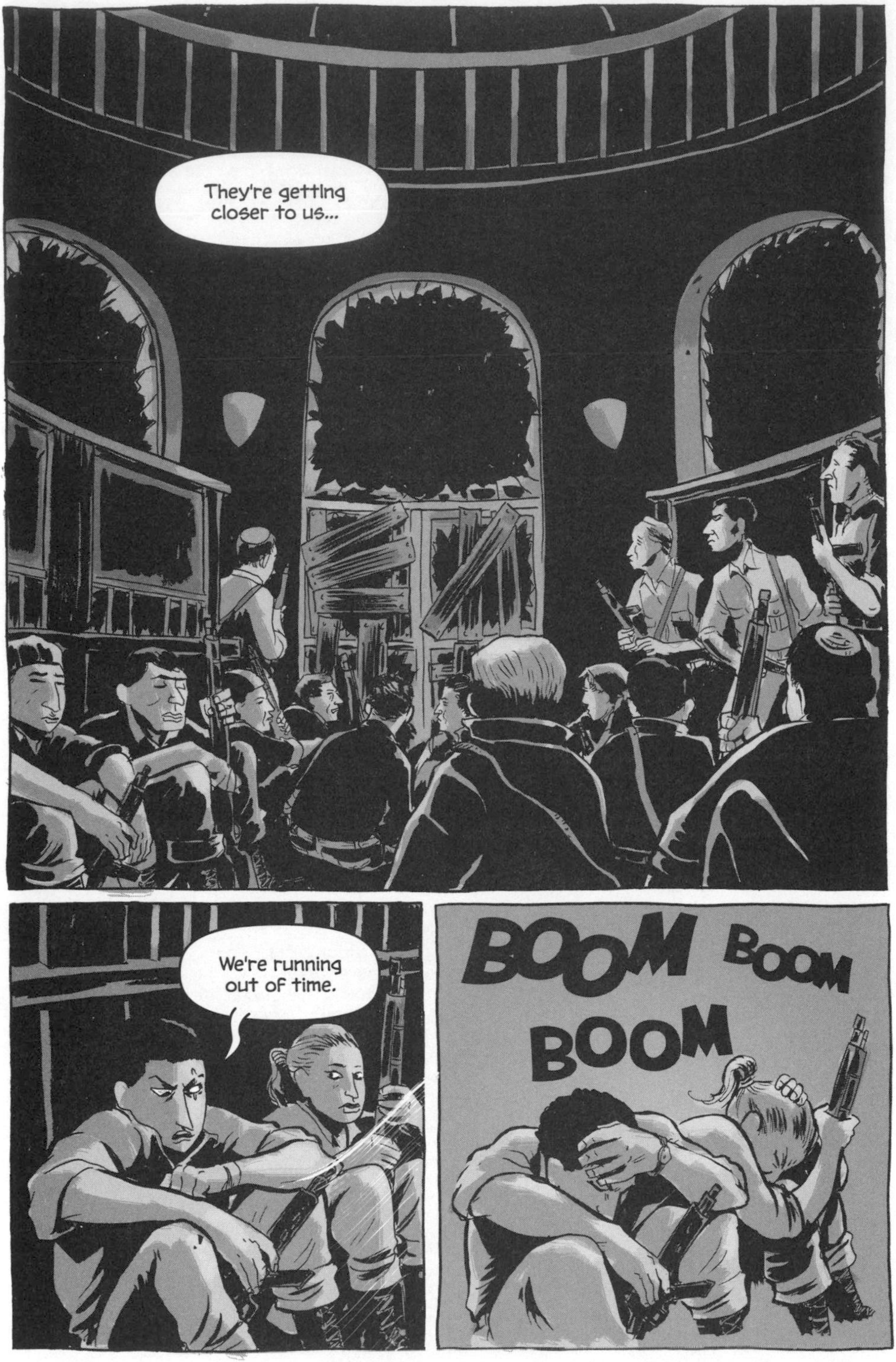
They're getting closer to us...
We're running out of time.
BOOM BOOM
BOOM

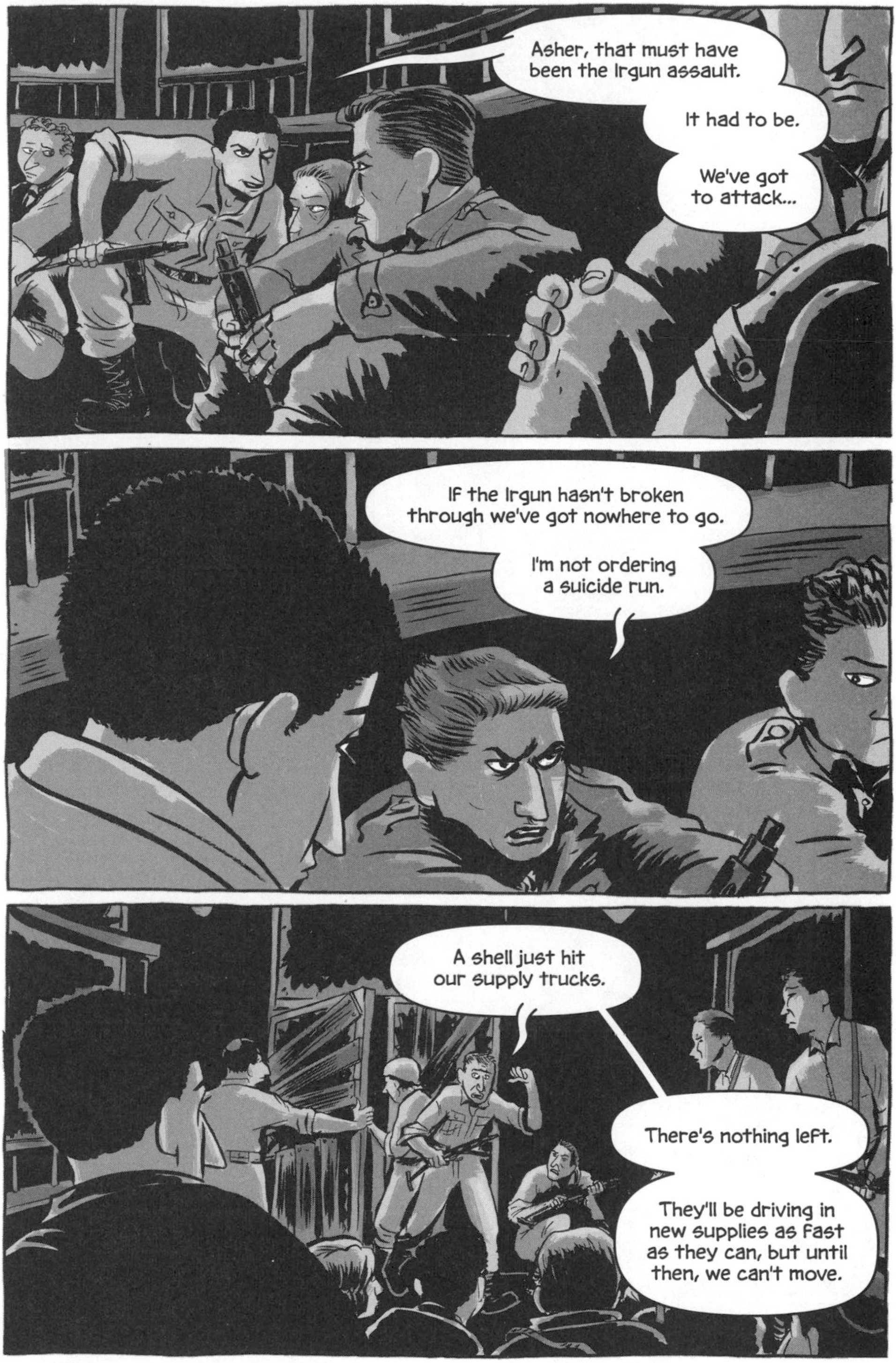
Asher, that must have been the Irgun assault.
It had to be.
We've got to attack...
If the Irgun hasn't broken through we've got nowhere to go.
I'm not ordering a suicide run.
A shell just hit our supply trucks.
There's nothing left.
They'll be driving in new supplies as fast as they can, but until then, we can't move.

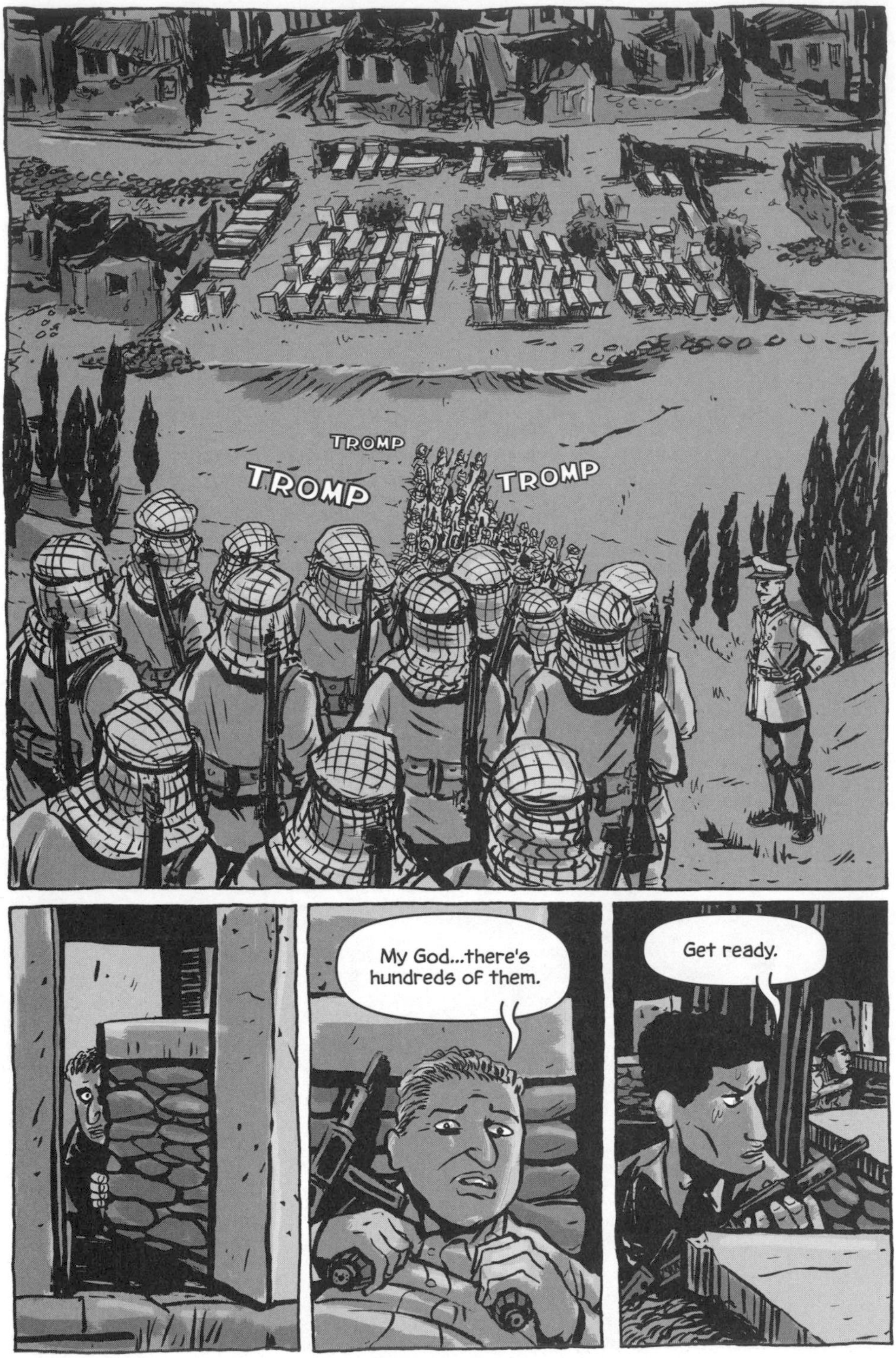
TROMP
TROMP
TROMP
My God...there's hundreds of them.
Get ready.

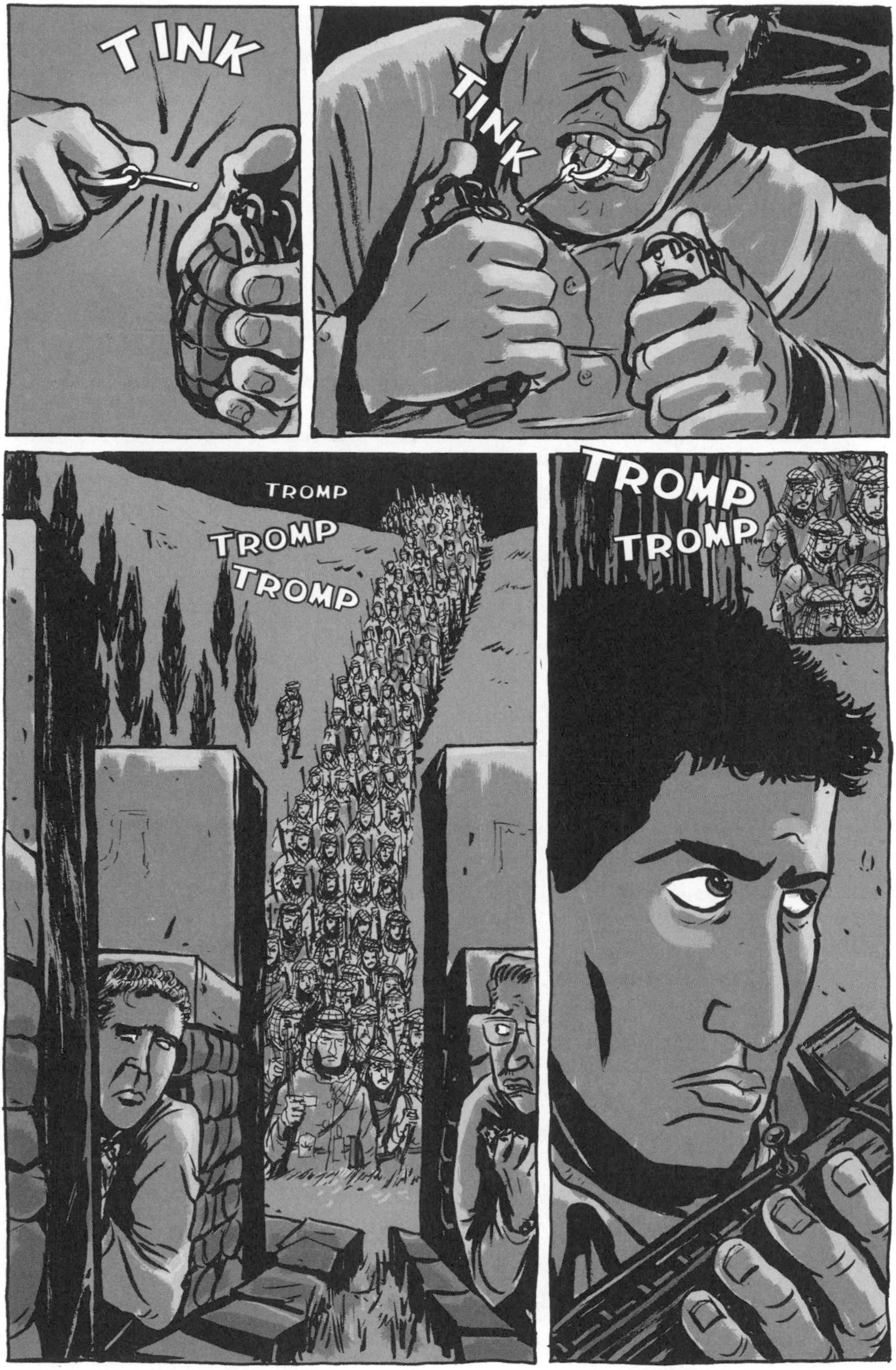
TINK
TINK
TROMP
TROMP
TROMP
TROMP
TROMP

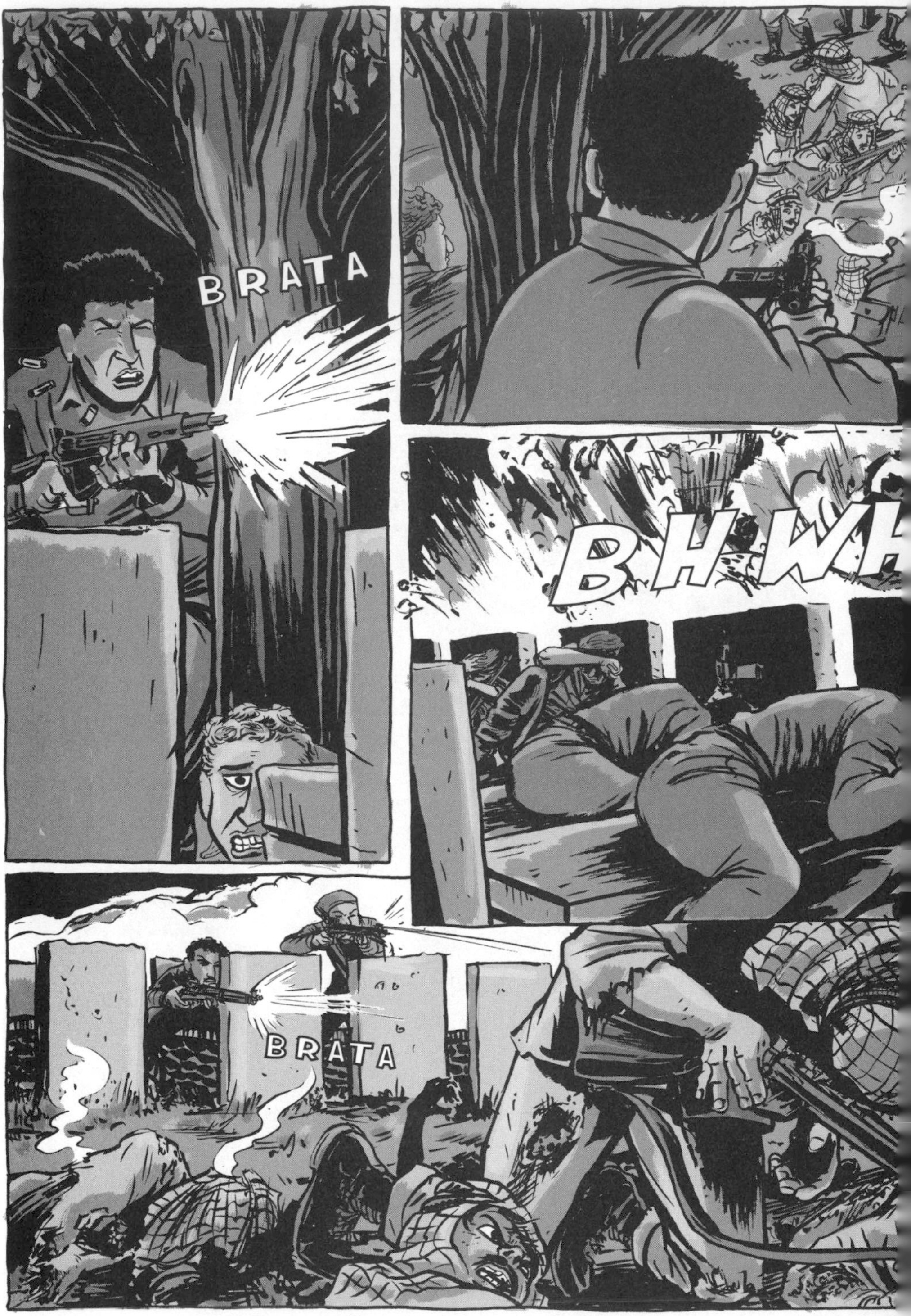
BRATA
BHW
BRATA

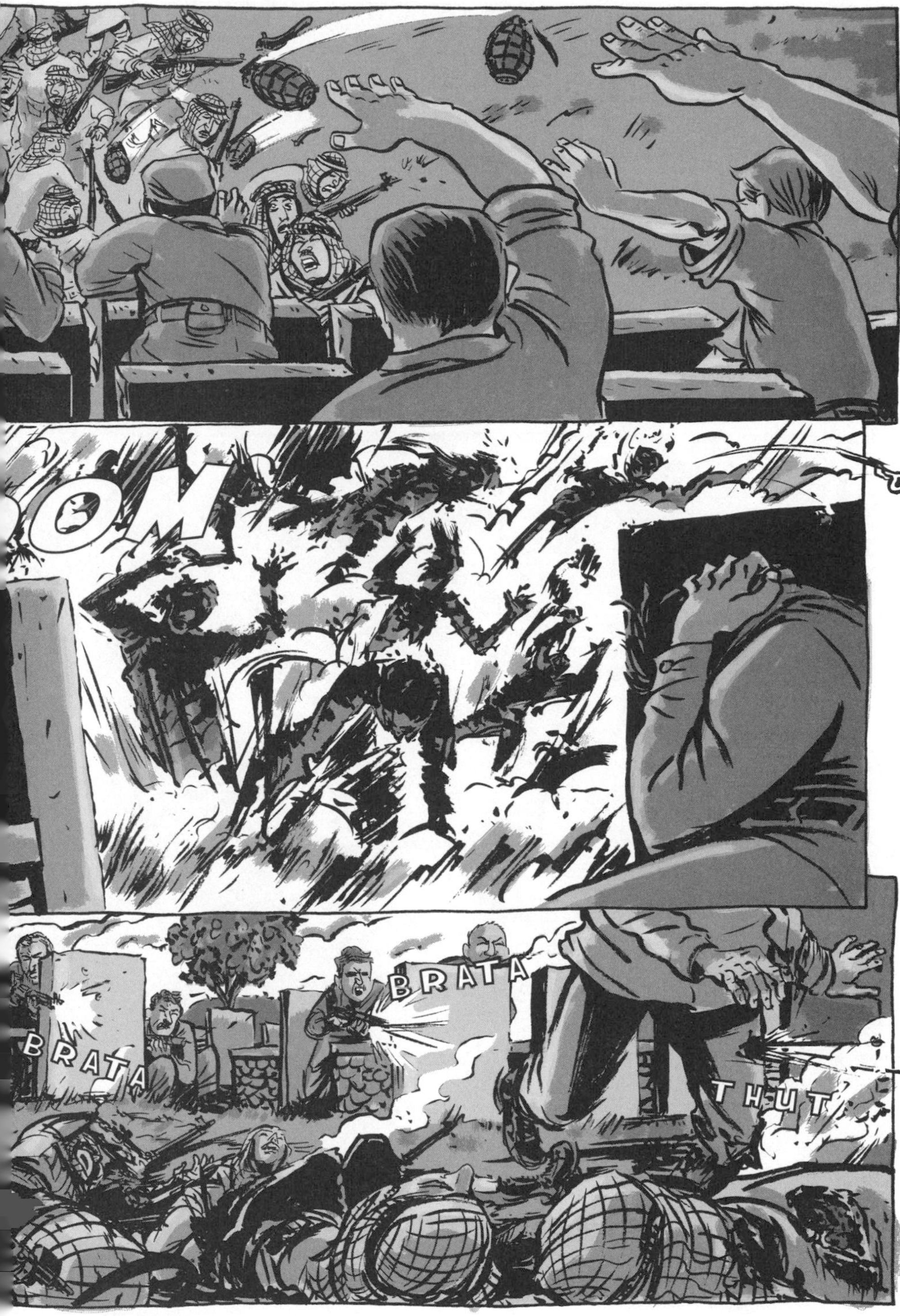
BRATA
BRATA
THUT

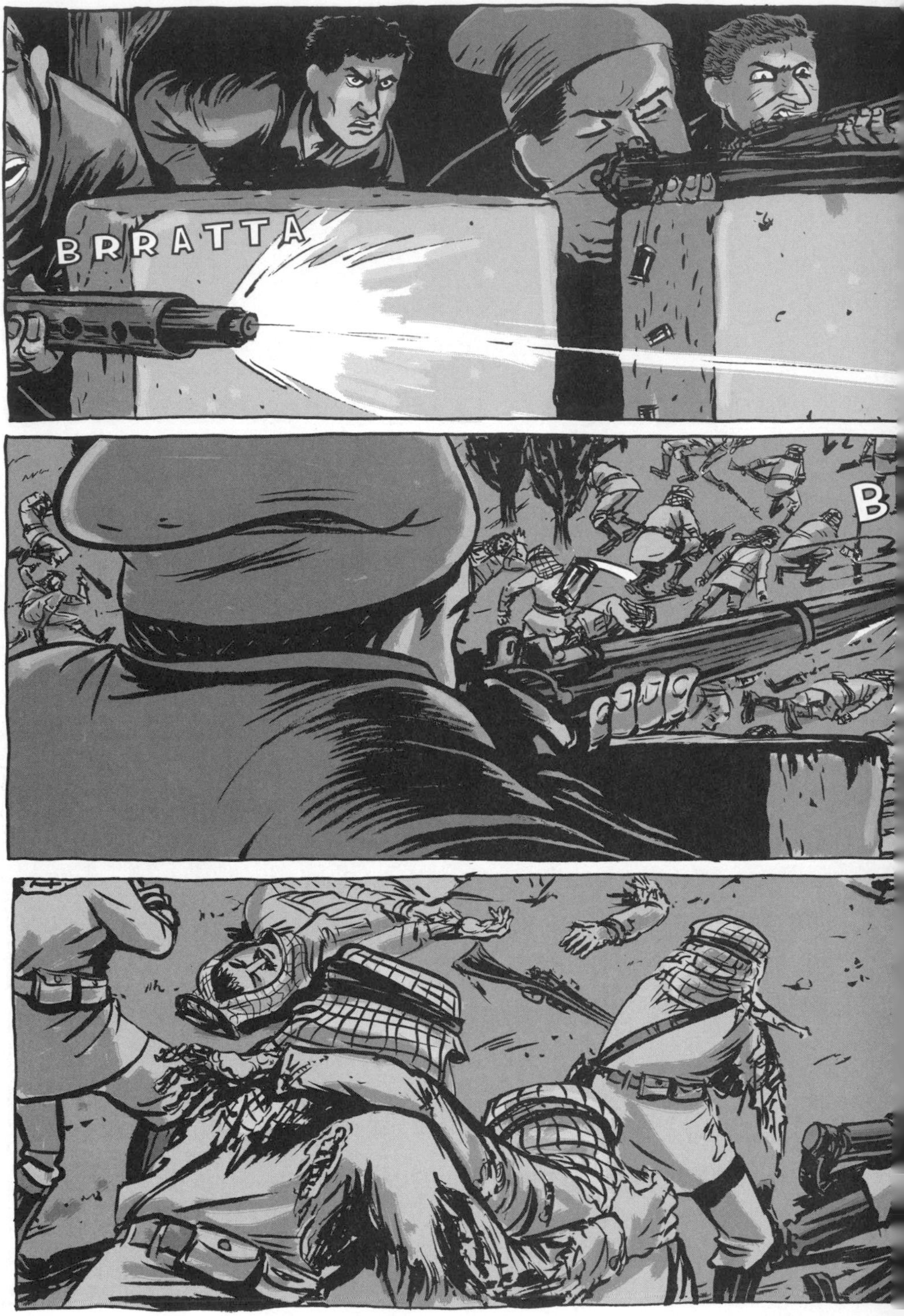
BRRATTA
B

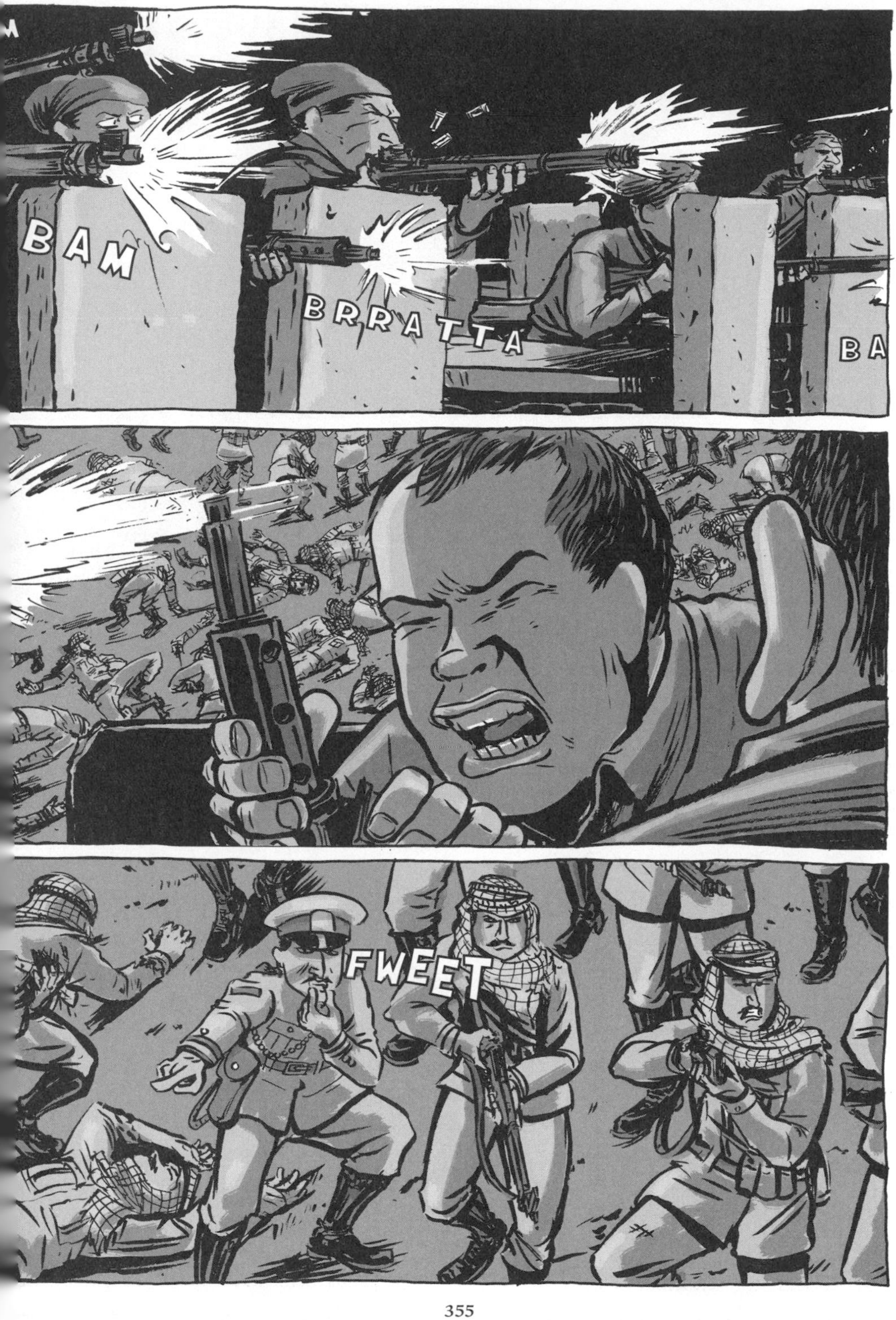
BAM
BRRATTA
BA
FWEET

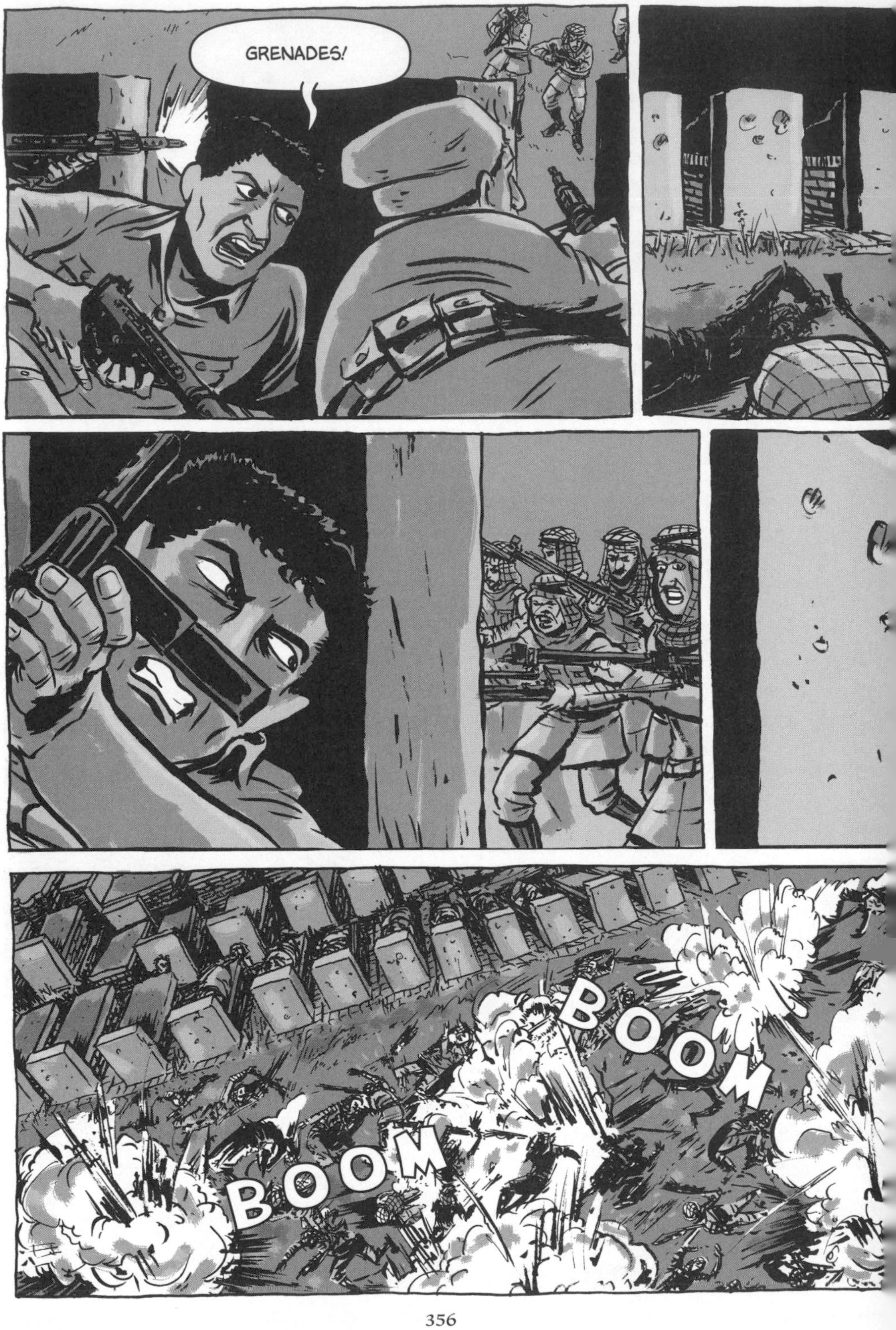
GRENADES!
BOOM
BOOM

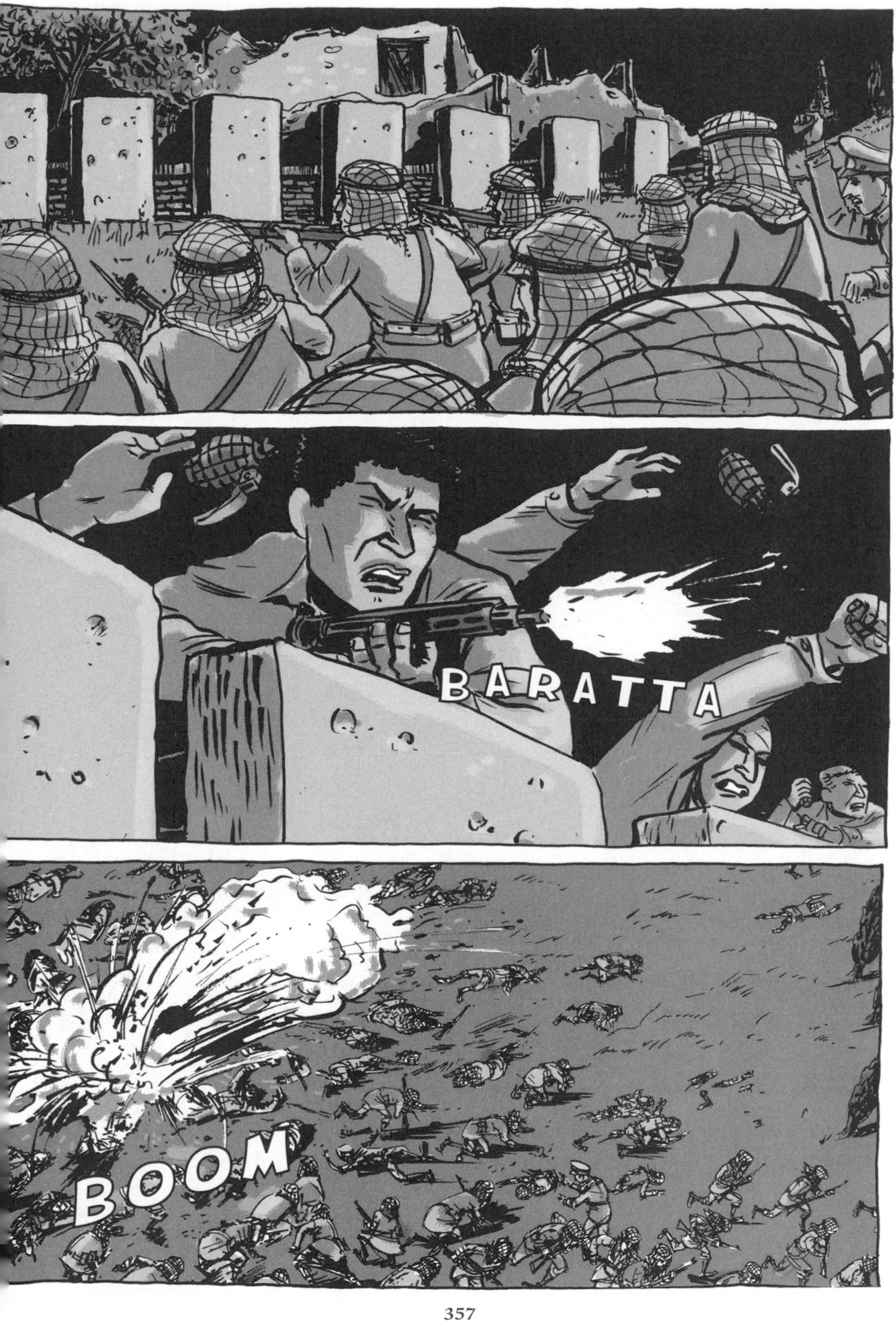
BARATTA
BOOM

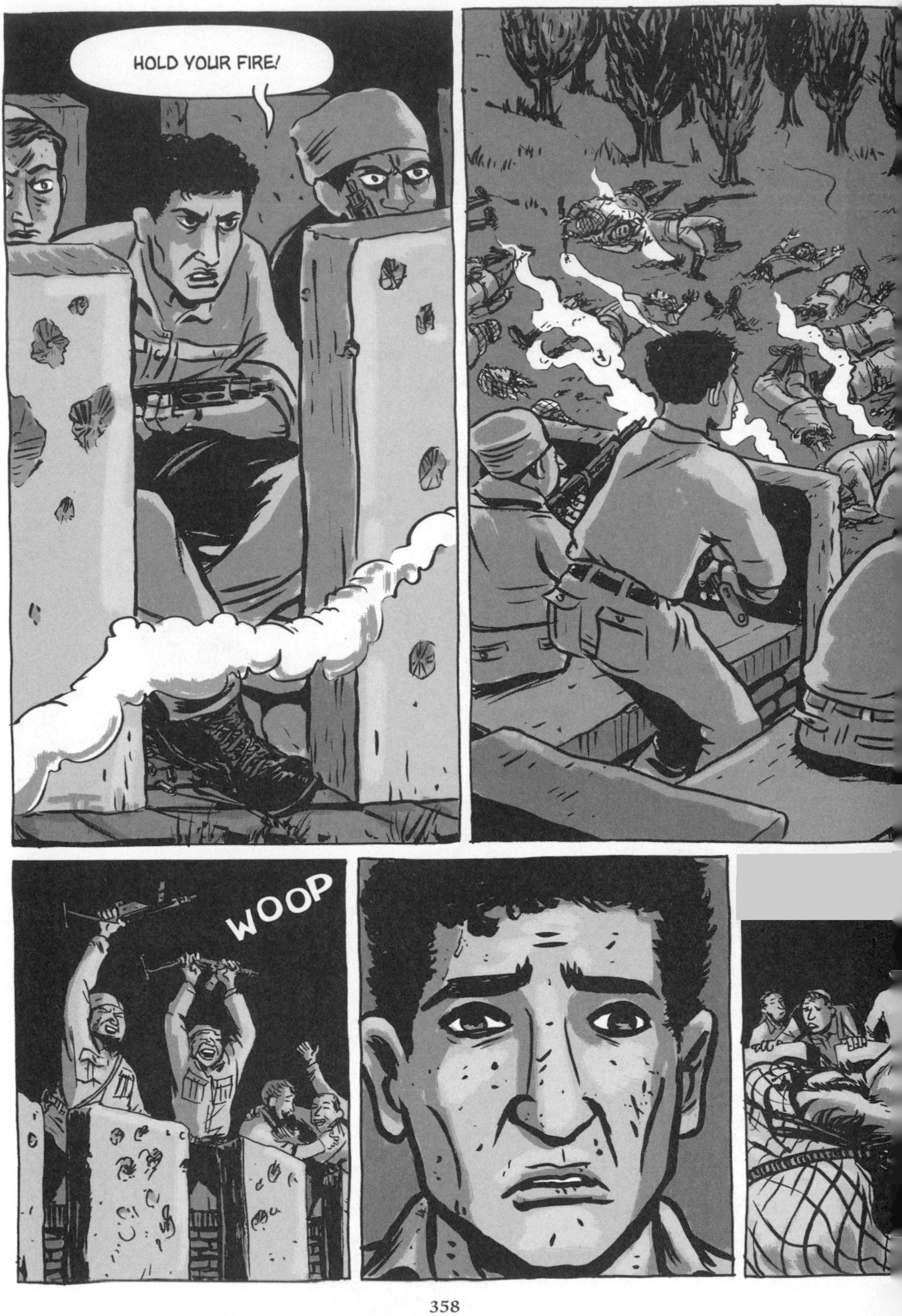
HOLD YOUR FIRE!
WOOP

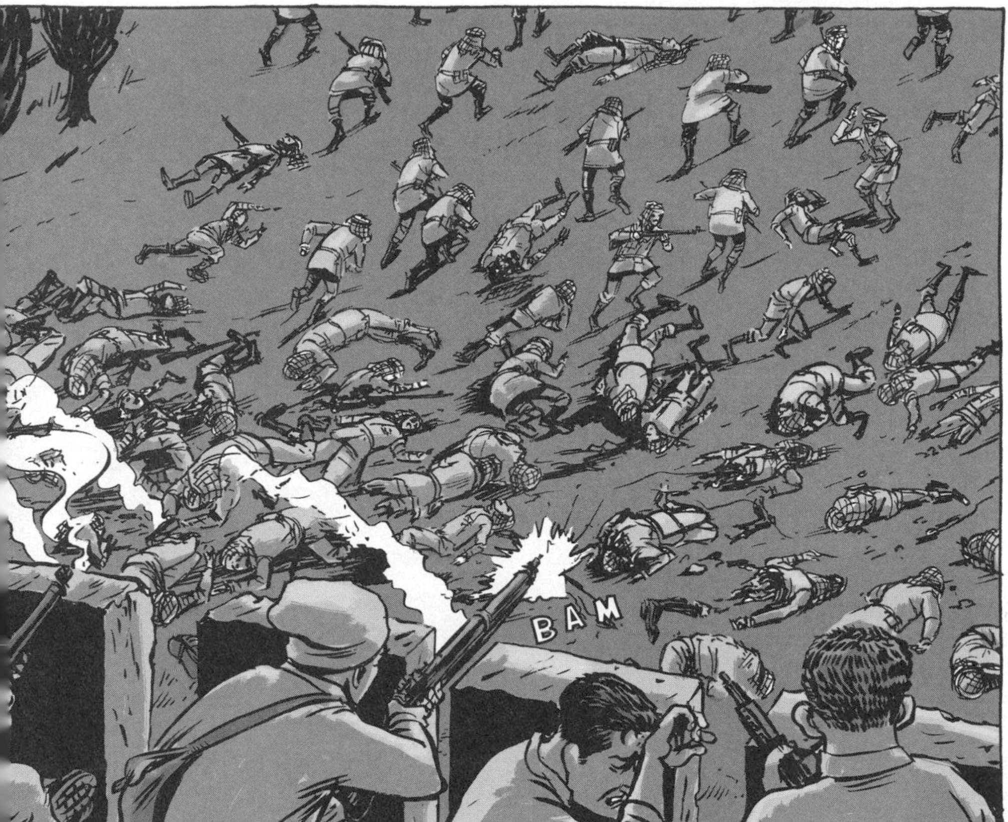
BAM

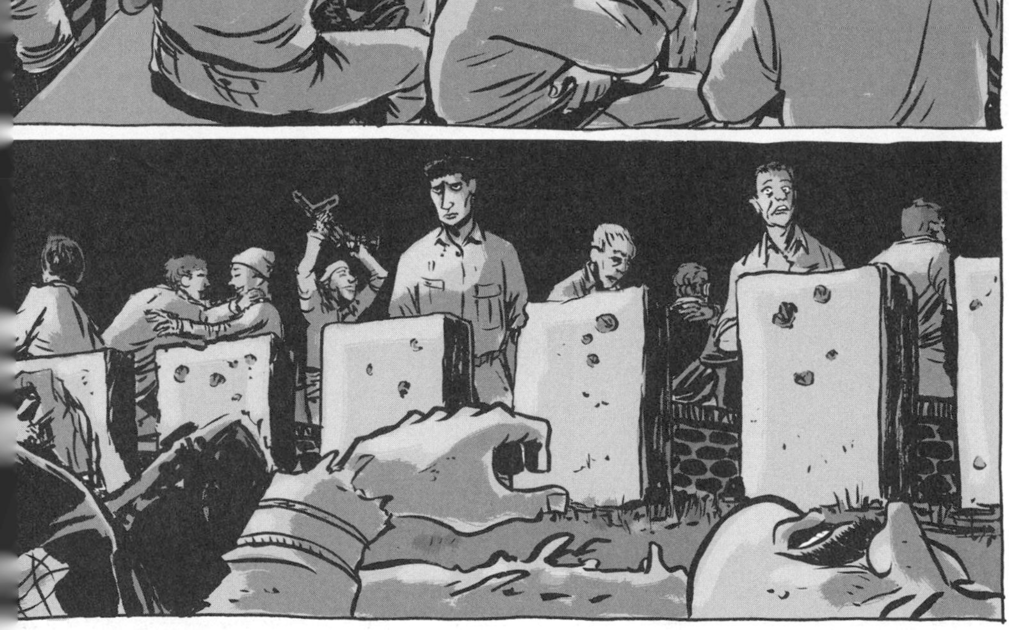

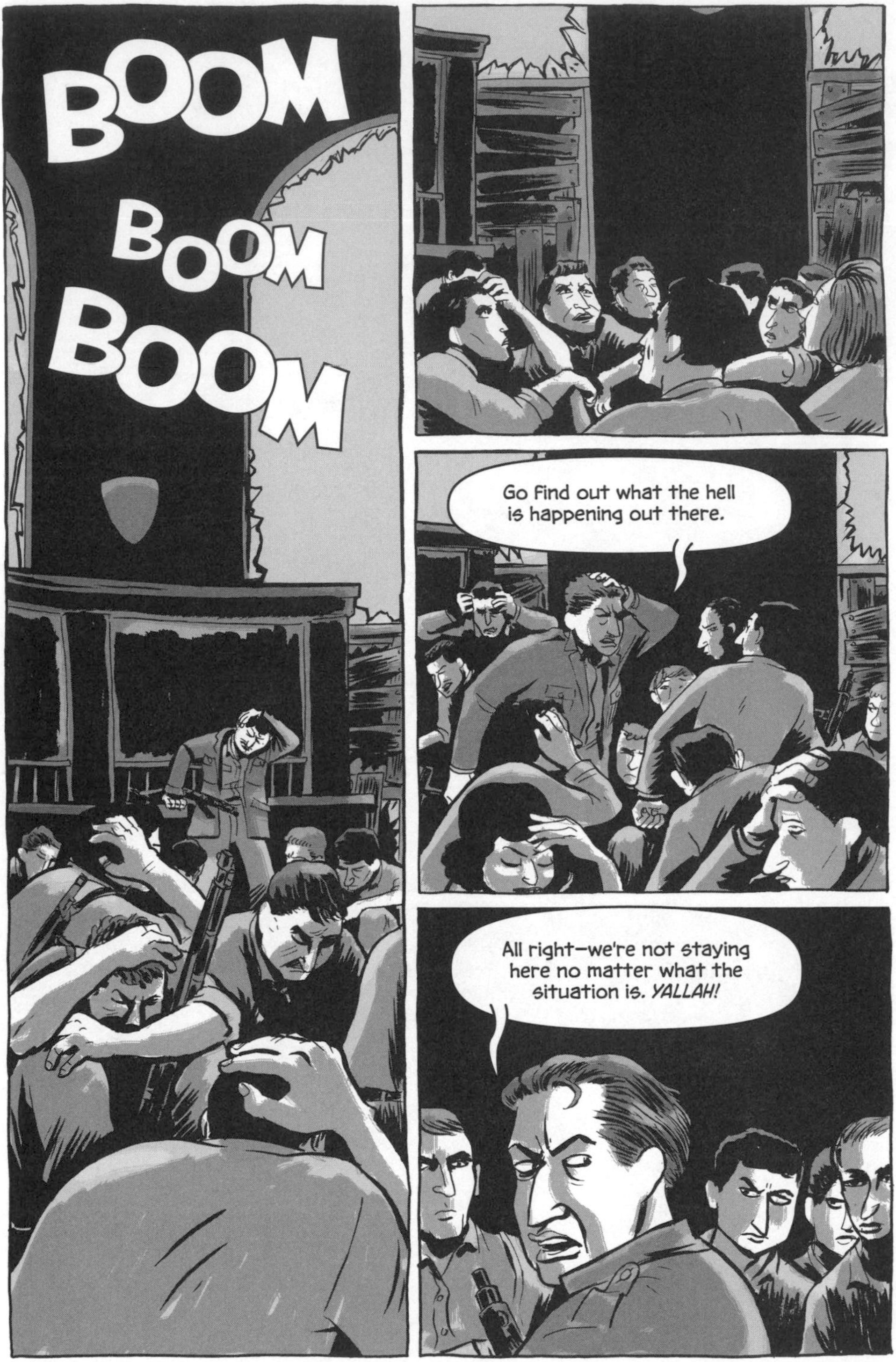

BOOM
BOOM
BOOM
Go find out what the hell is happening out there.
All right—we're not staying here no matter what the situation is. *YALLAH!*

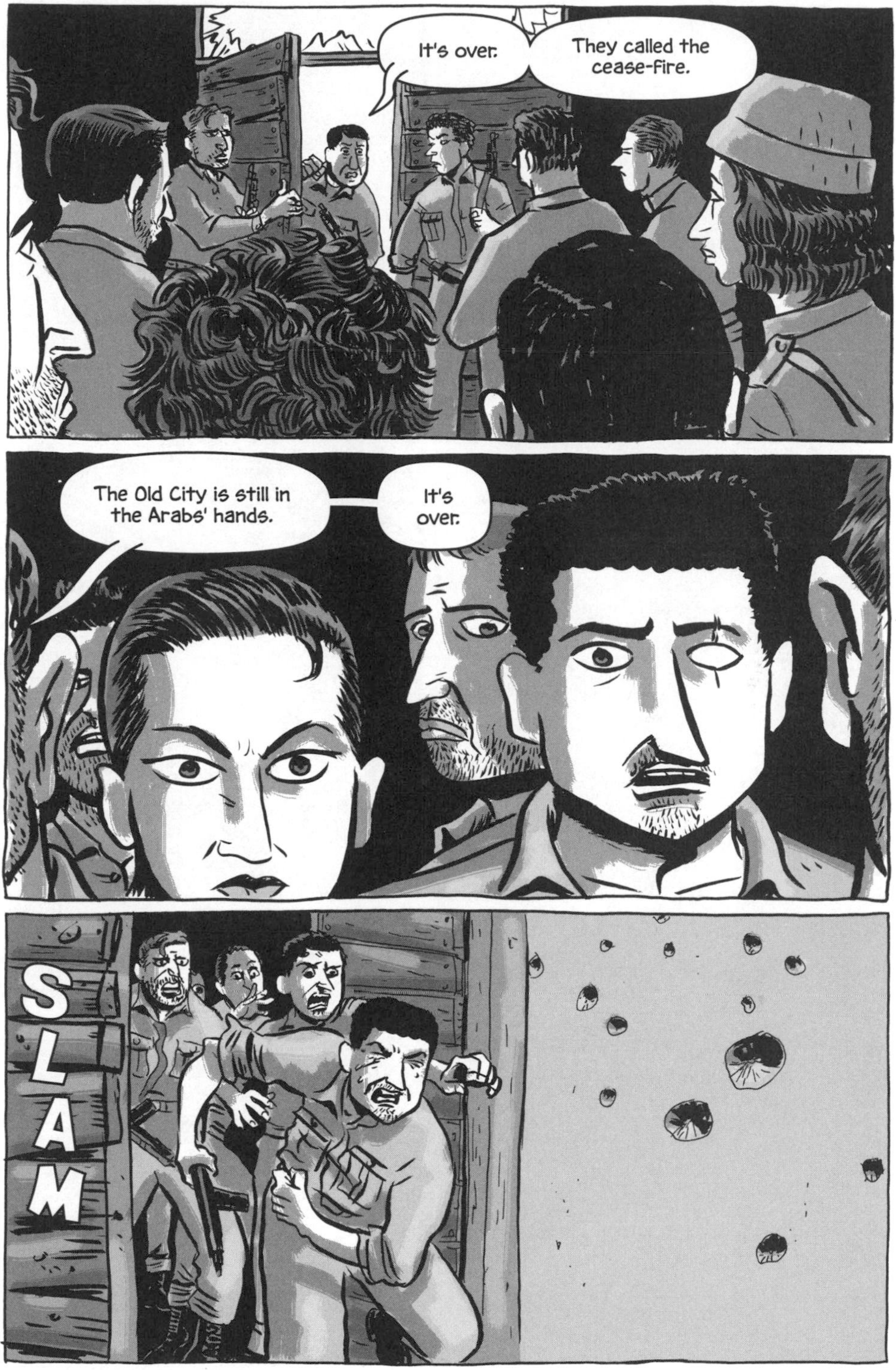
It's over.
They called the cease-fire.
The Old City is still in the Arabs' hands.
It's over.
SLAM

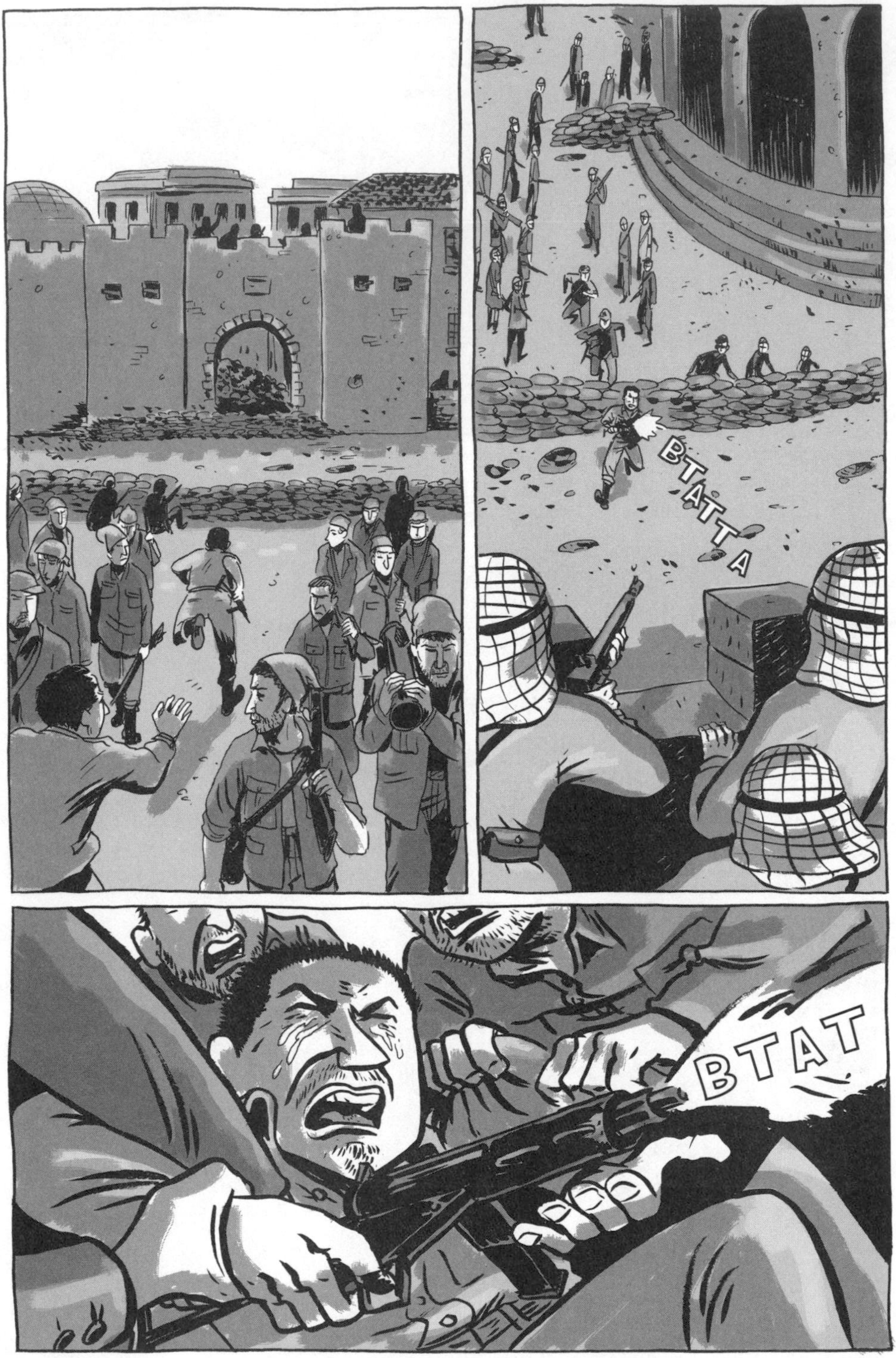
BTATTA
BTAT

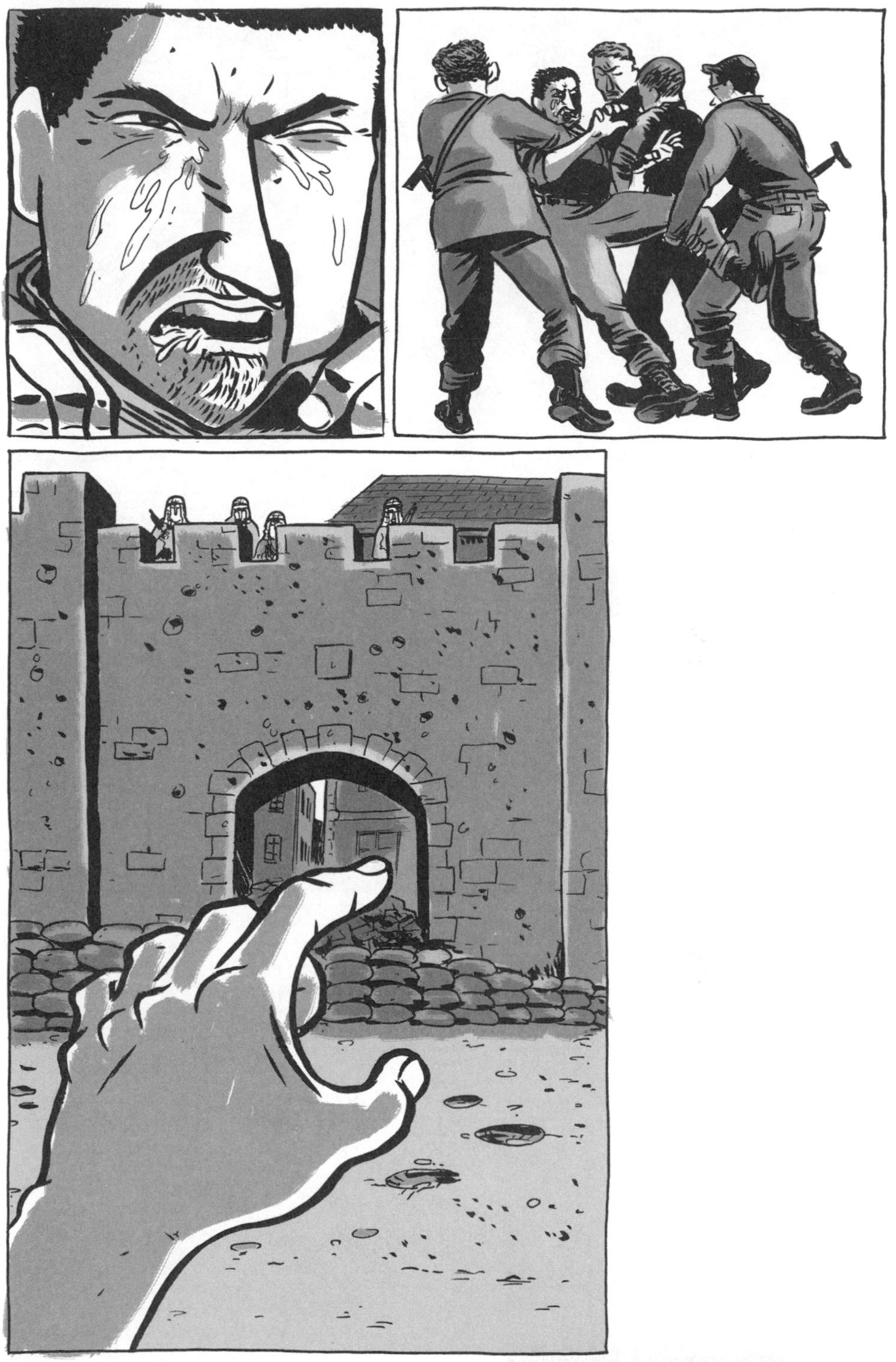

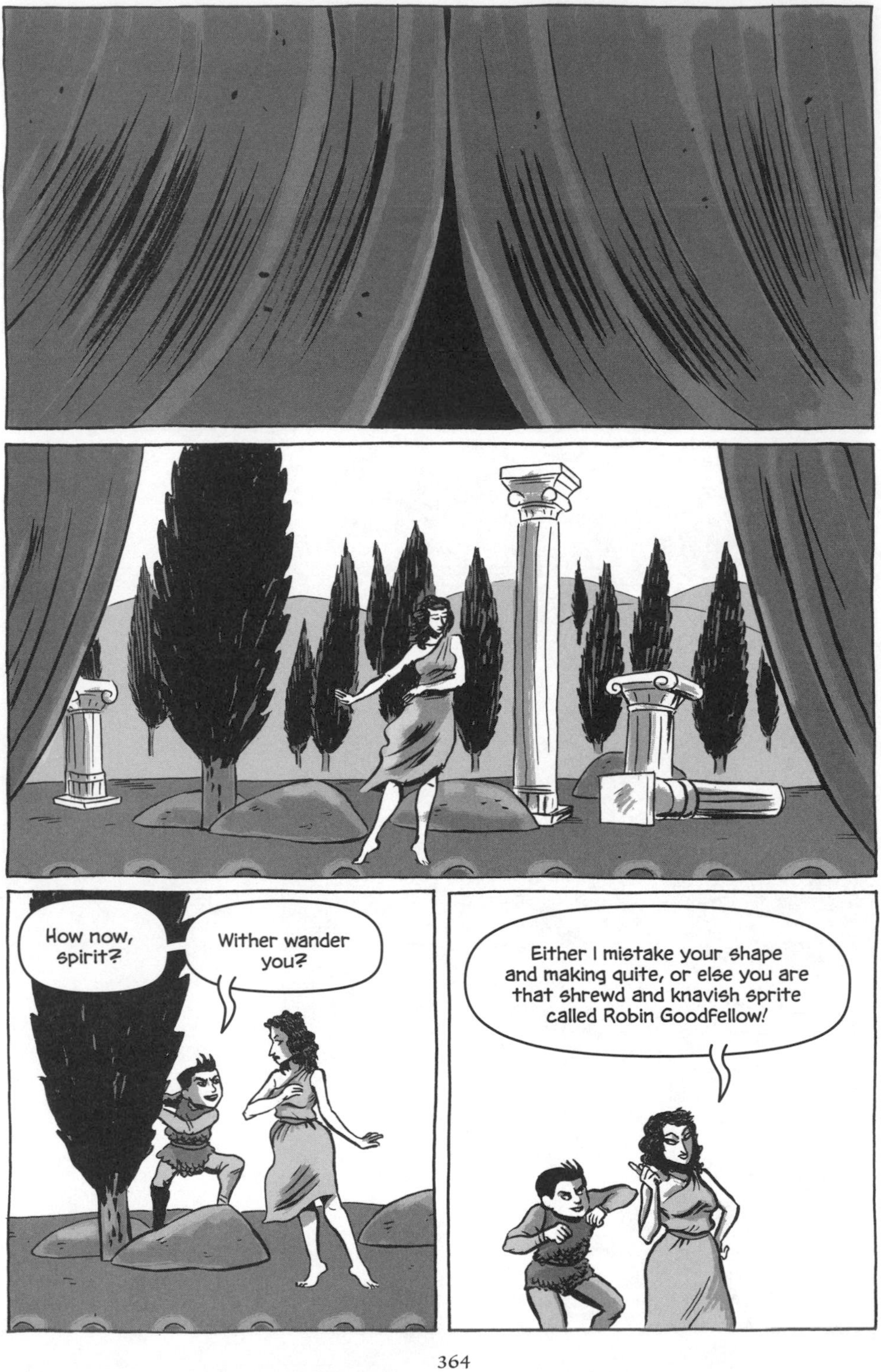
How now, spirit?
Wither wander you?
Either I mistake your shape and making quite, or else you are that shrewd and knavish sprite called Robin Goodfellow!

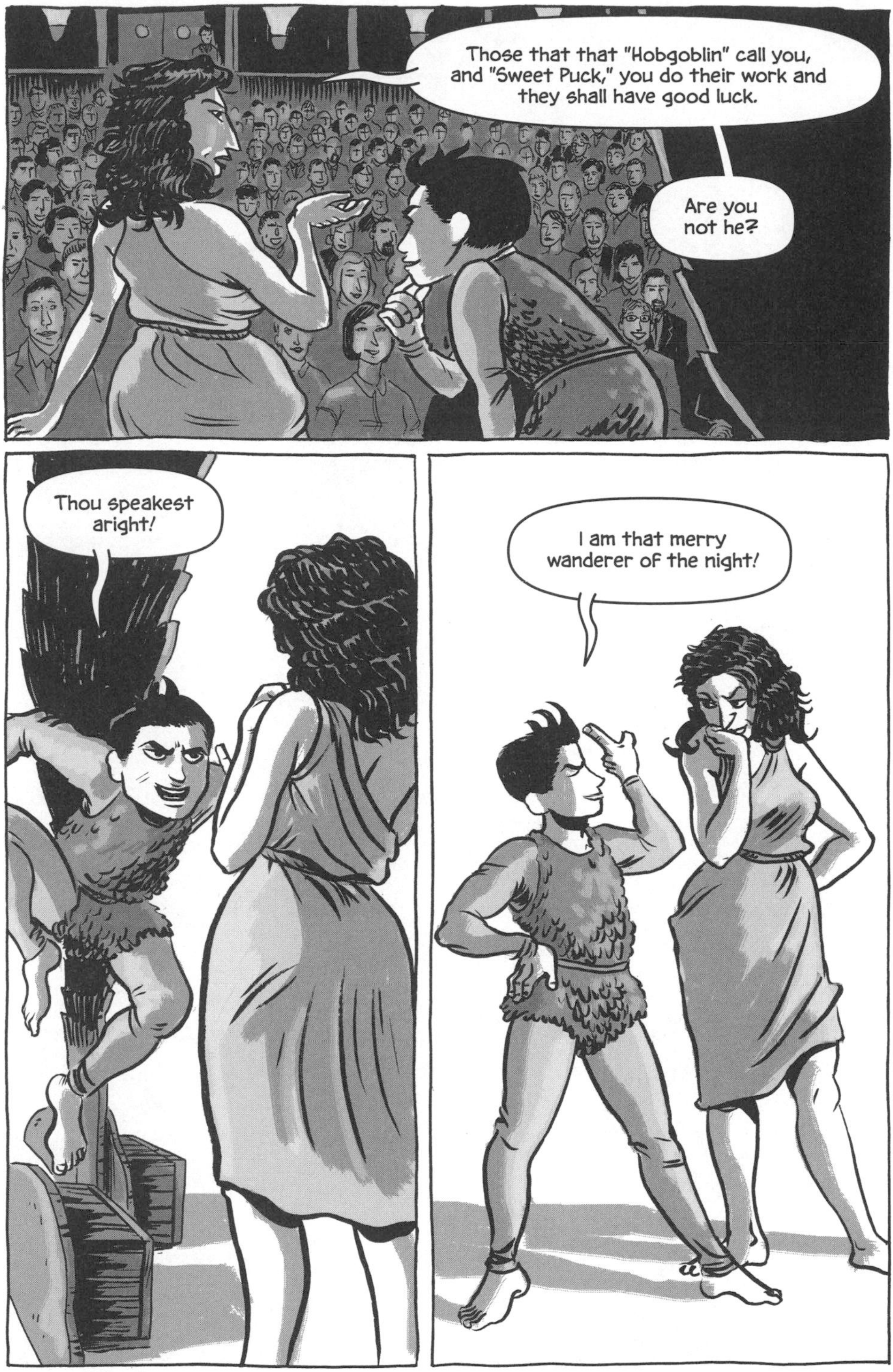
Those that that "Hobgoblin" call you, and "Sweet Puck," you do their work and they shall have good luck.
Are you not he?
Thou speakest aright!
I am that merry wanderer of the night!

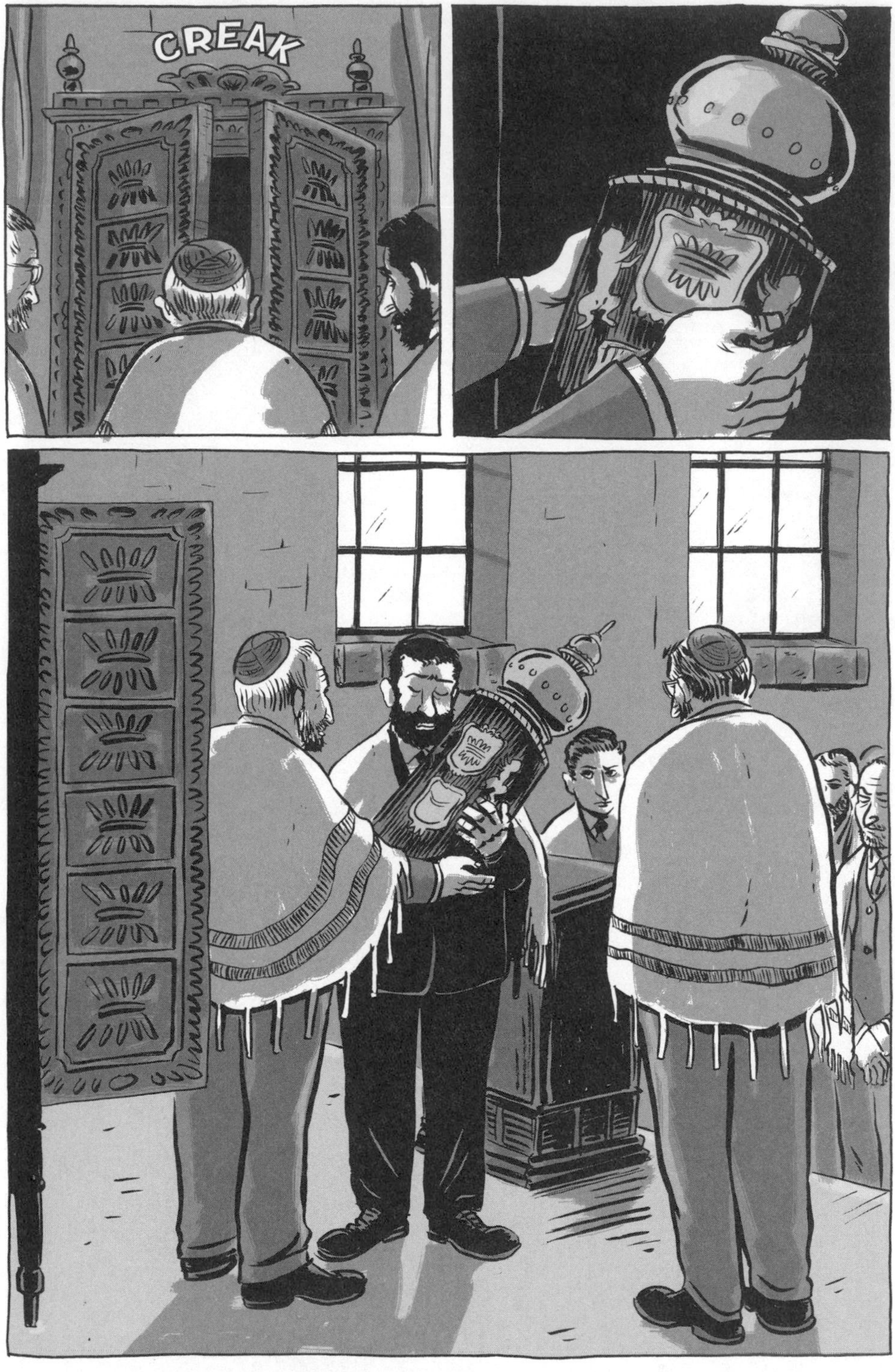
CREAK

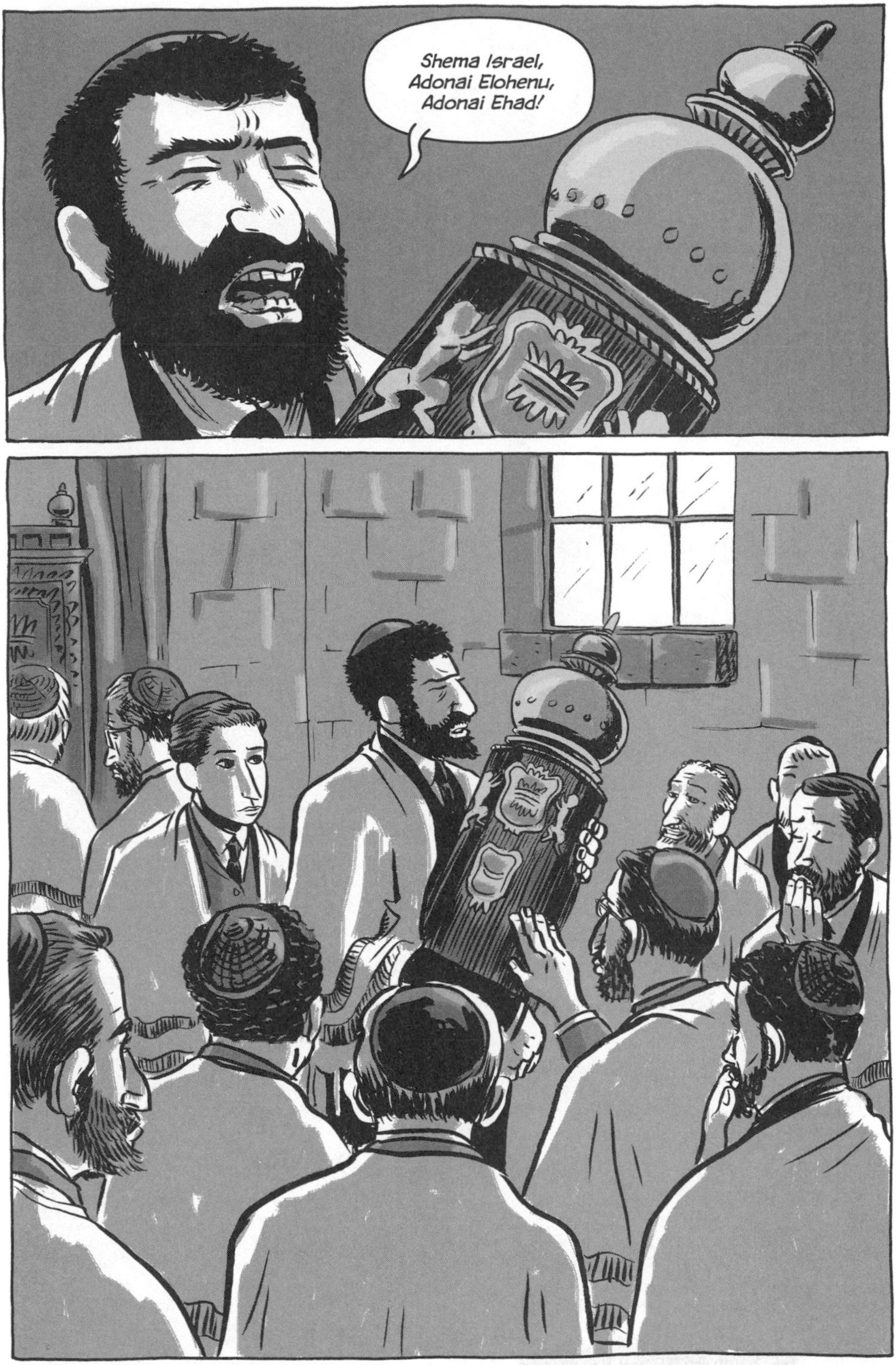
Shema Israel, Adonai Elohenu, Adonai Ehad!

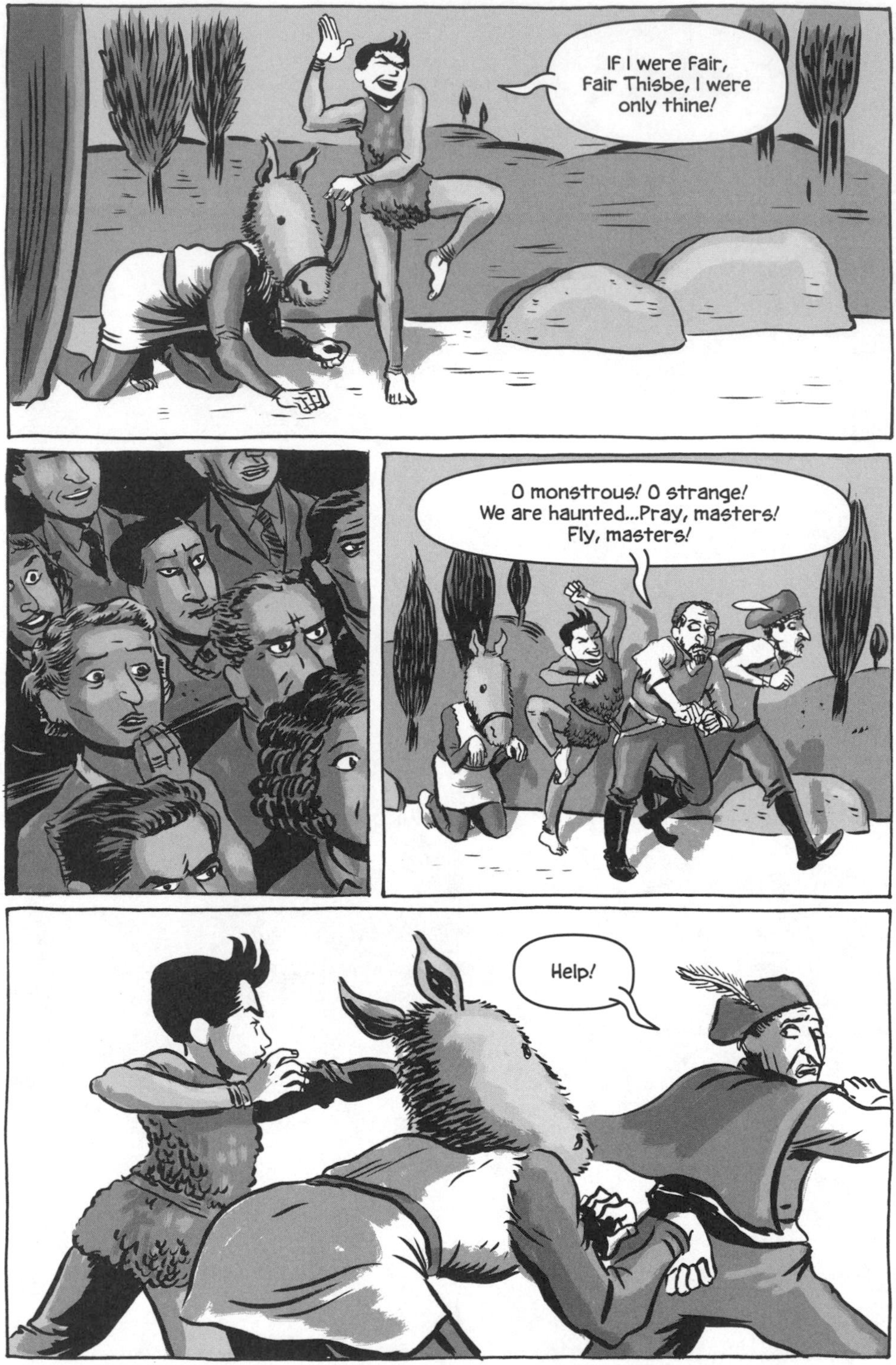
If I were fair, fair Thisbe, I were only thine!
O monstrous! O strange! We are haunted...Pray, masters! Fly, masters!
Help!

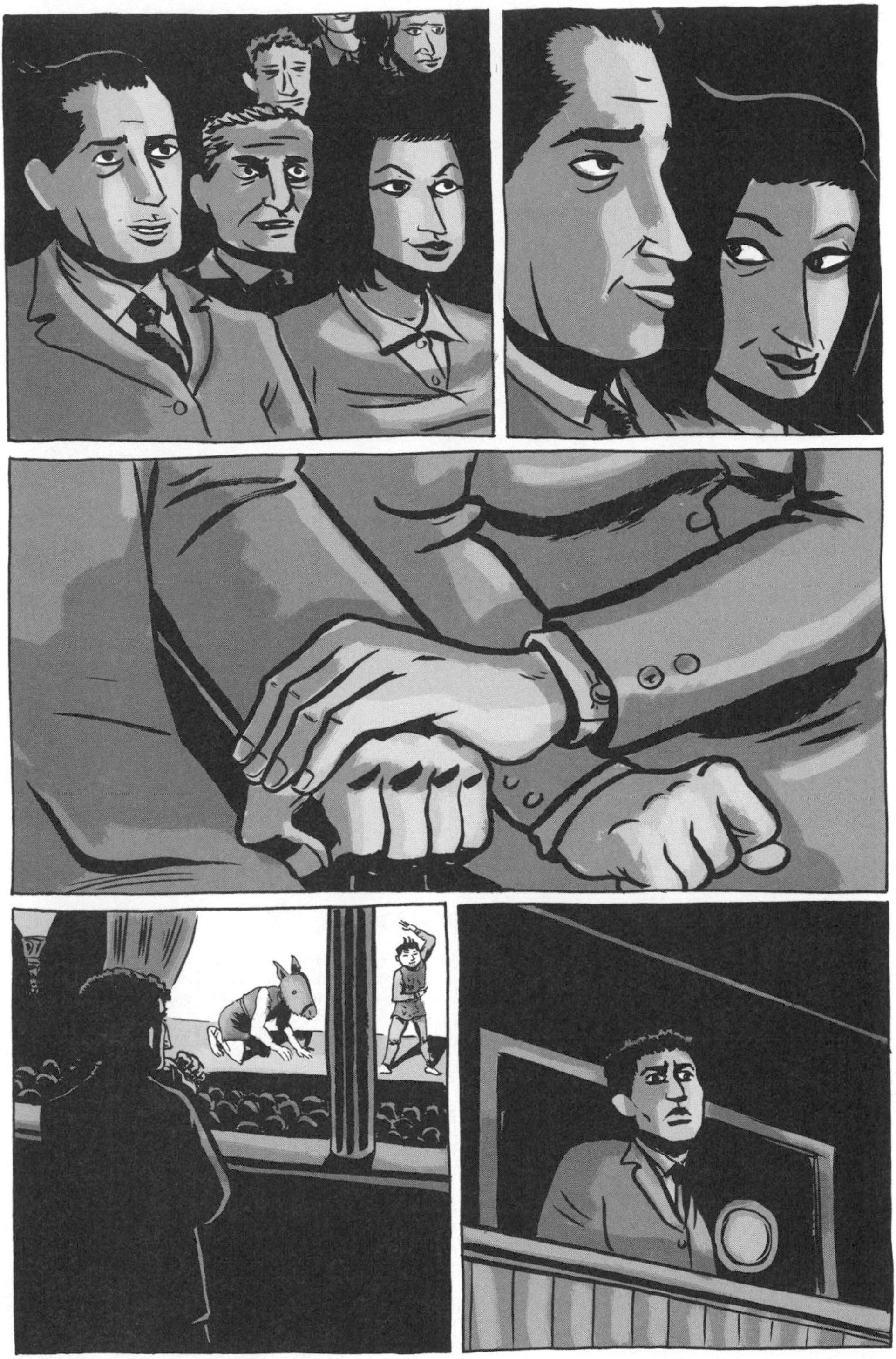

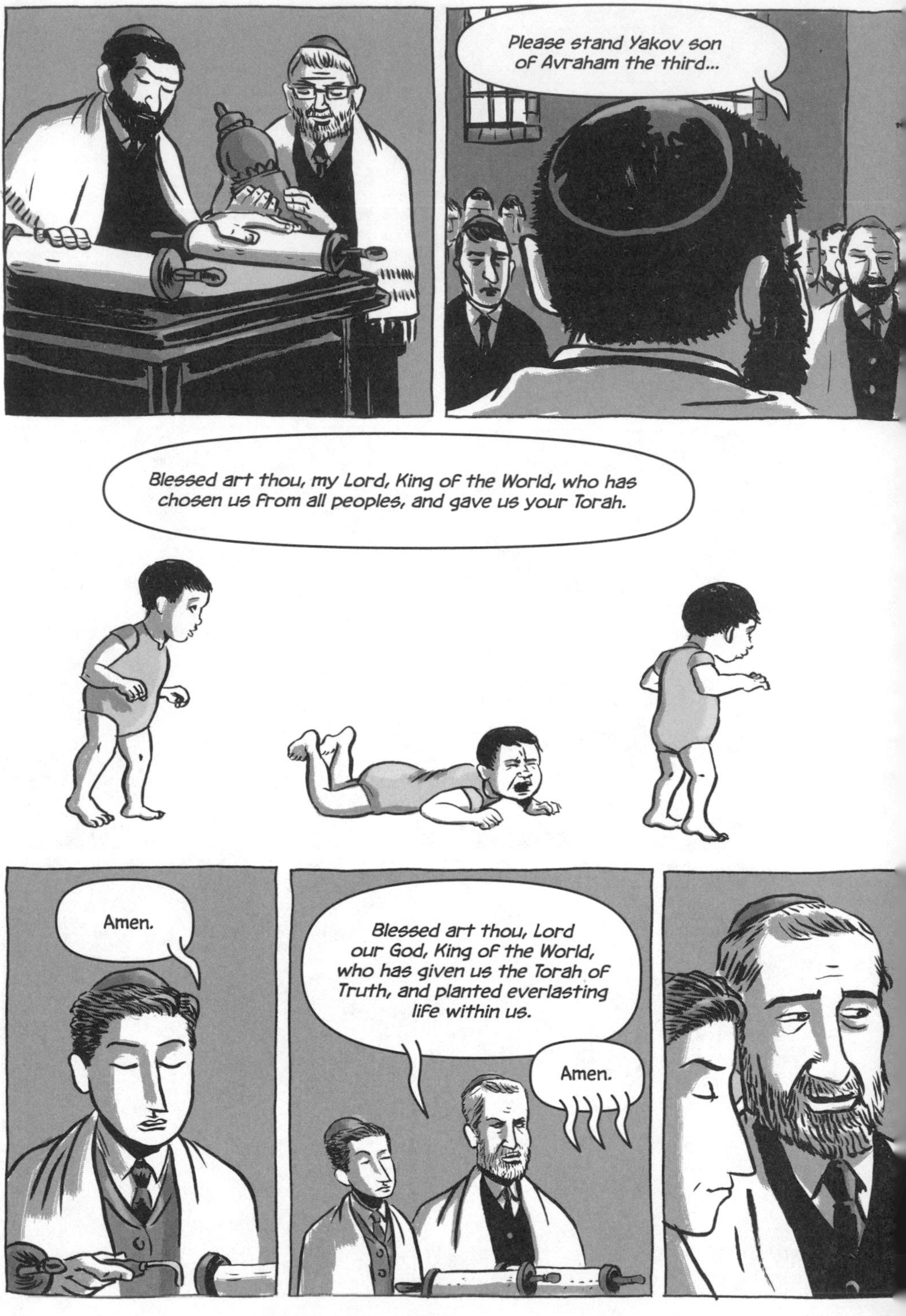
Please stand Yakov son of Avraham the third...
Blessed art thou, my Lord, King of the World, who has chosen us from all peoples, and gave us your Torah.
Amen.
Blessed art thou, Lord our God, King of the World, who has given us the Torah of Truth, and planted everlasting life within us.
Amen.

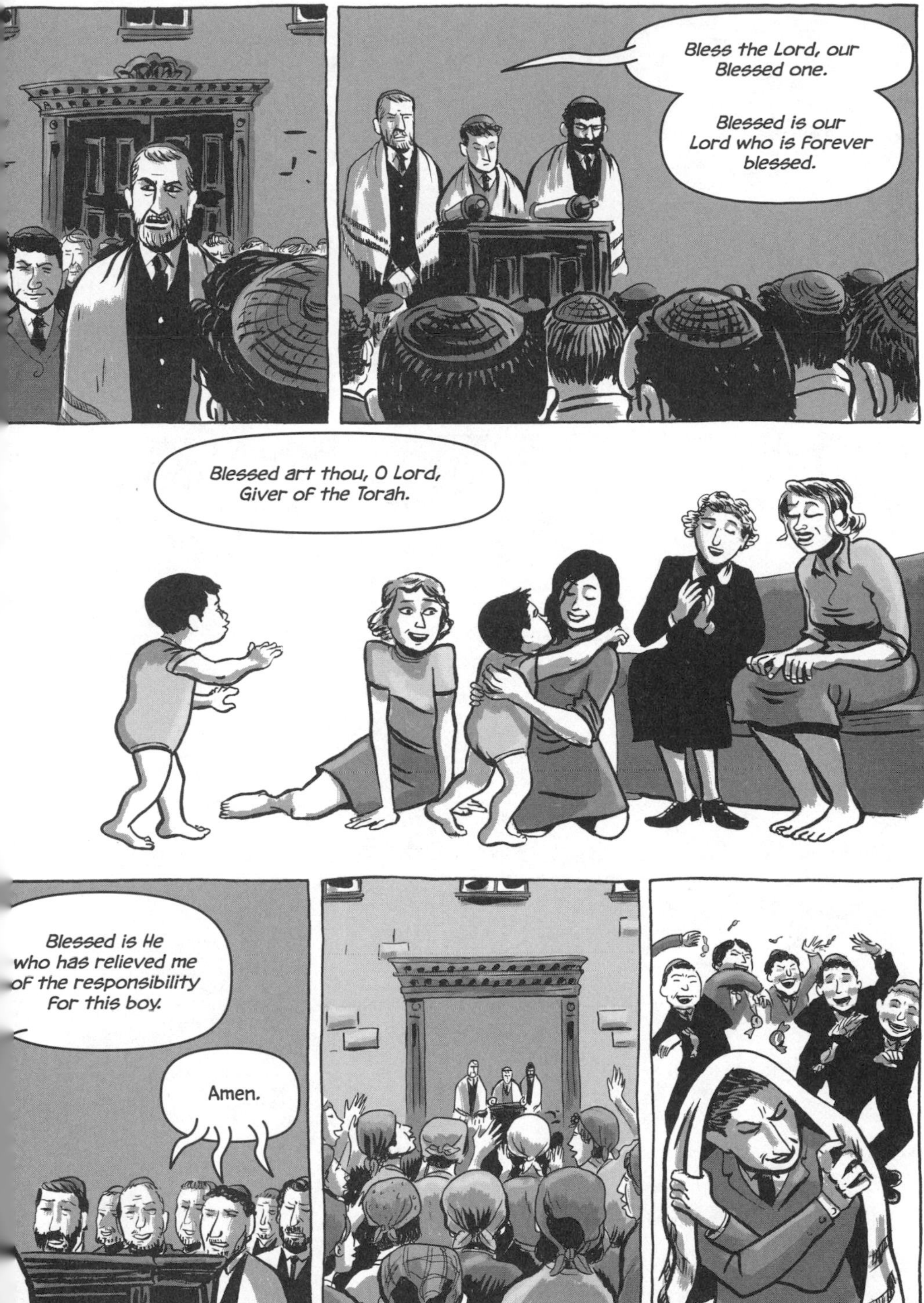
Bless the Lord, our Blessed one.
Blessed is our Lord who is forever blessed.
Blessed art thou, O Lord, Giver of the Torah.
Blessed is He who has relieved me of the responsibility for this boy.
Amen.

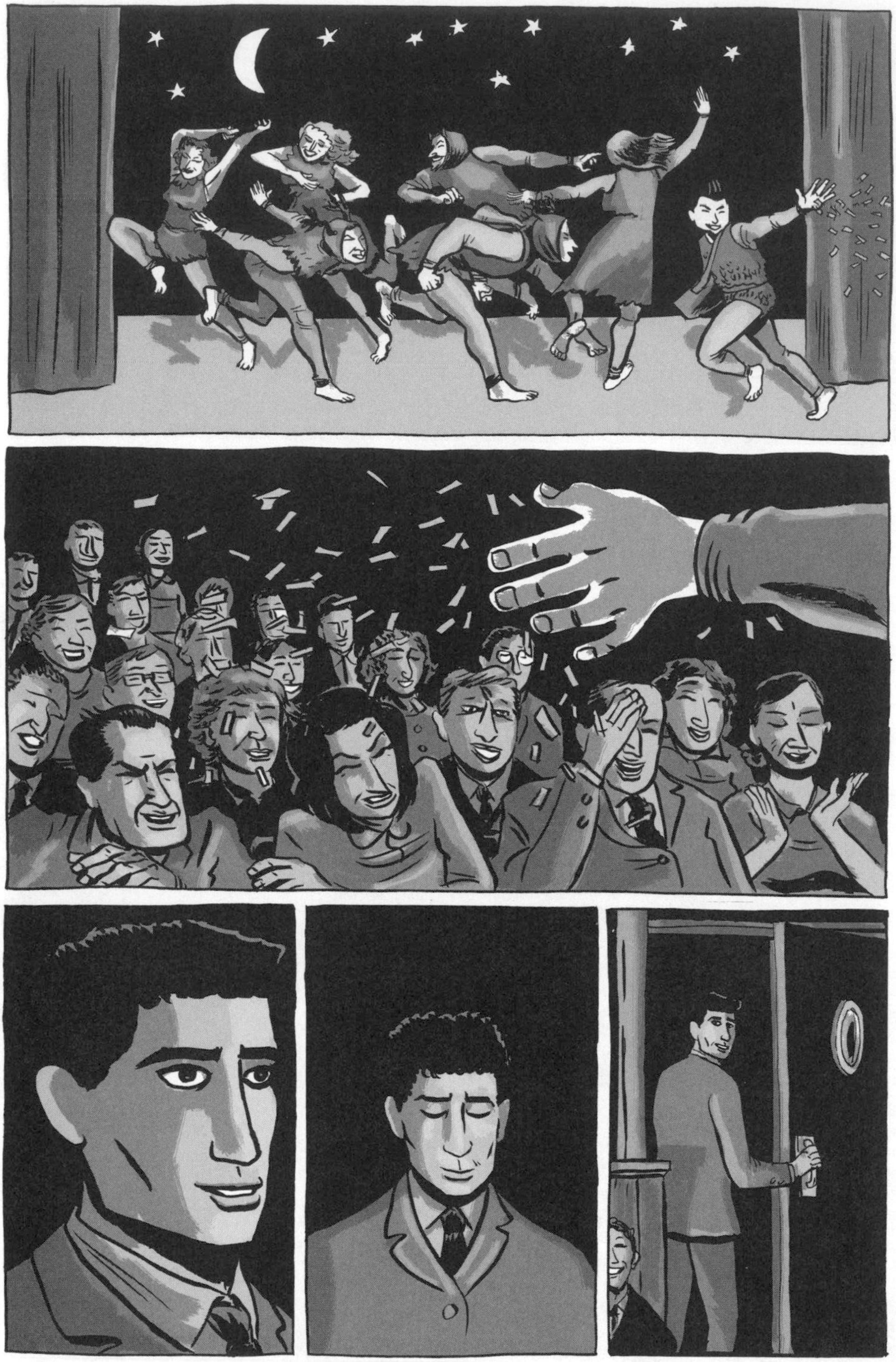

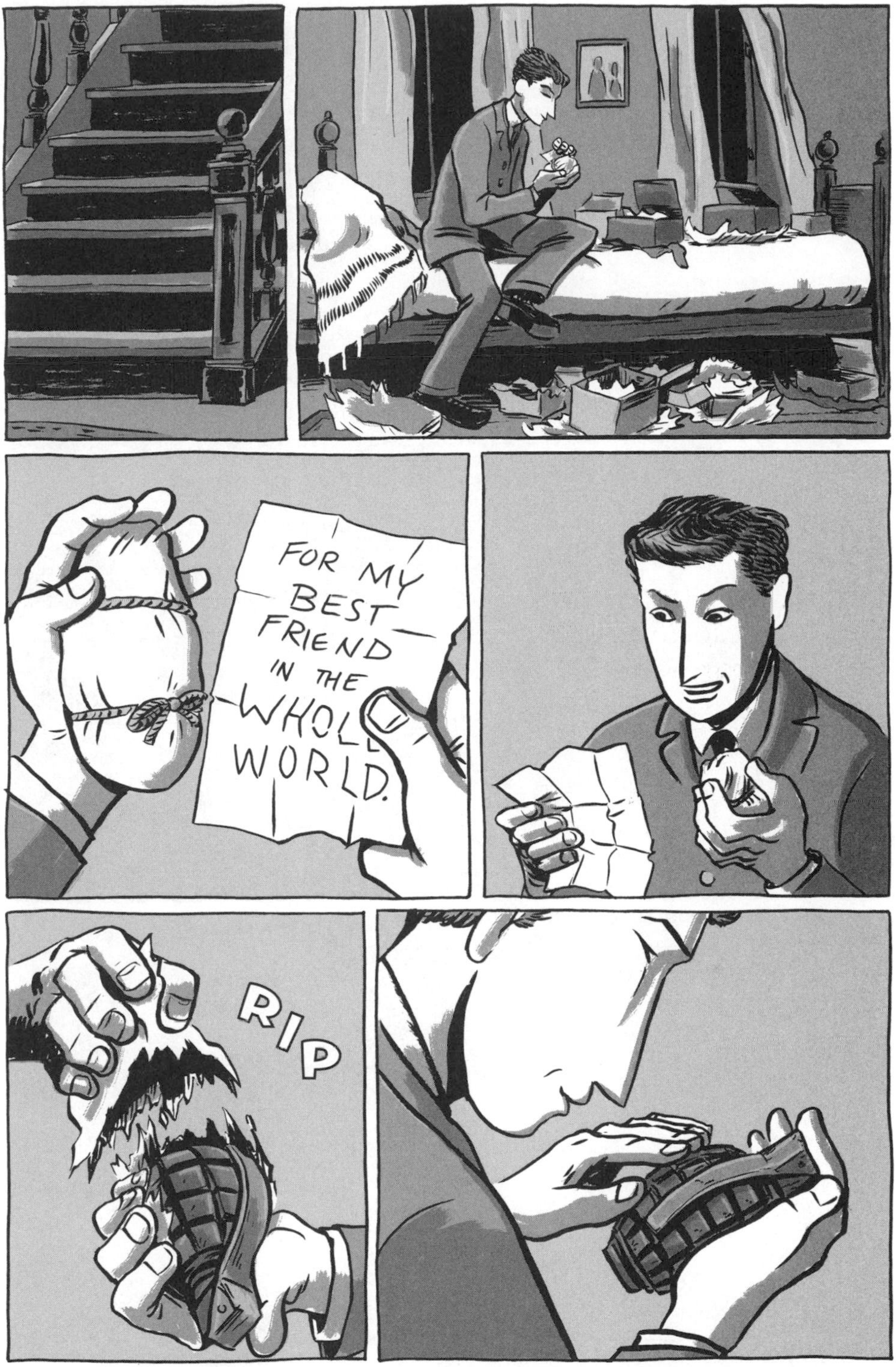
FOR MY BEST FRIEND IN THE WHOLE WORLD.
RIP

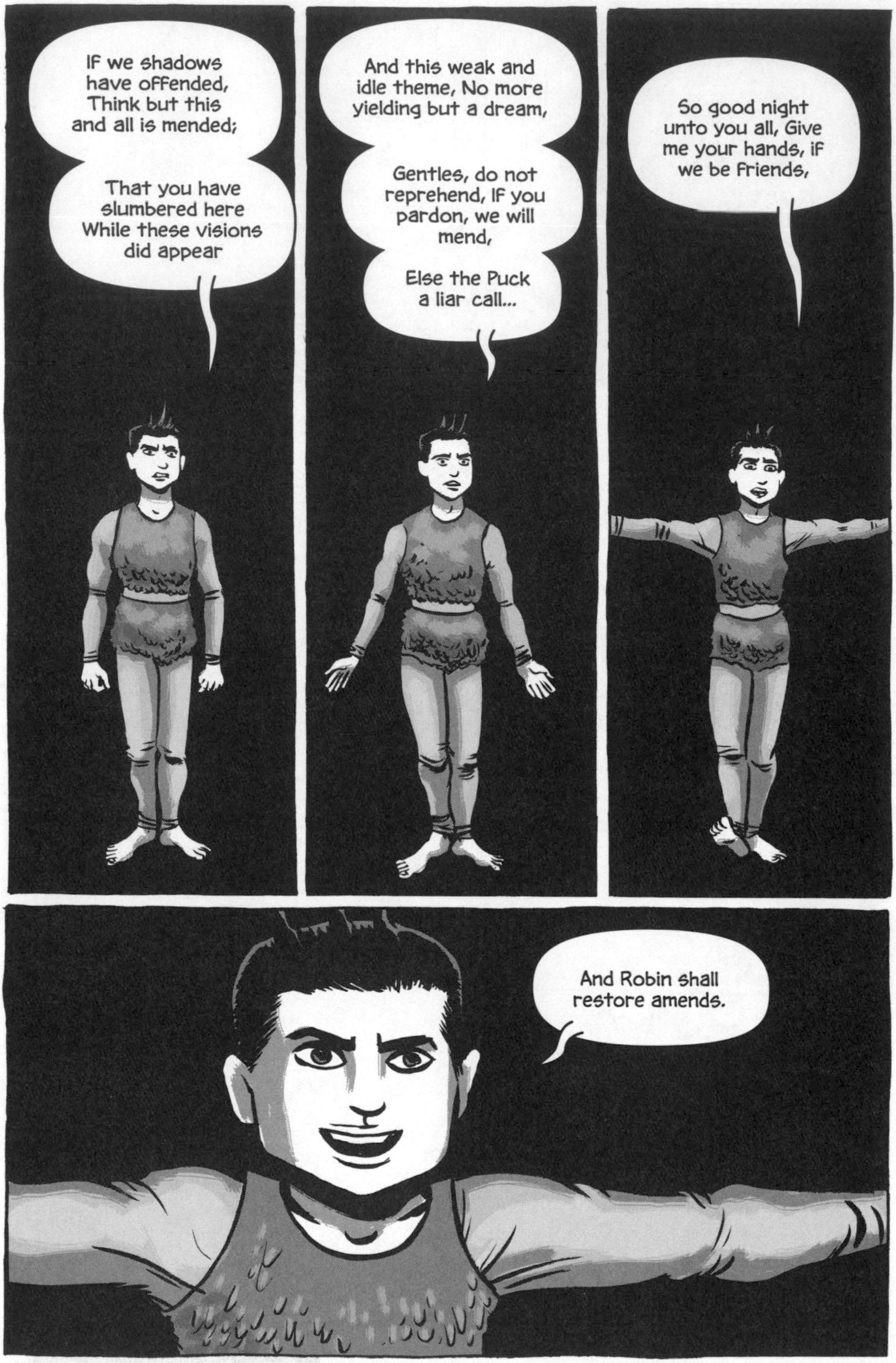

If we shadows have offended, Think but this and all is mended;
That you have slumbered here While these visions did appear
And this weak and idle theme, No more yielding but a dream,
Gentles, do not reprehend, If you pardon, we will mend,
Else the Puck a liar call...
So good night unto you all, Give me your hands, if we be friends,
And Robin shall restore amends.

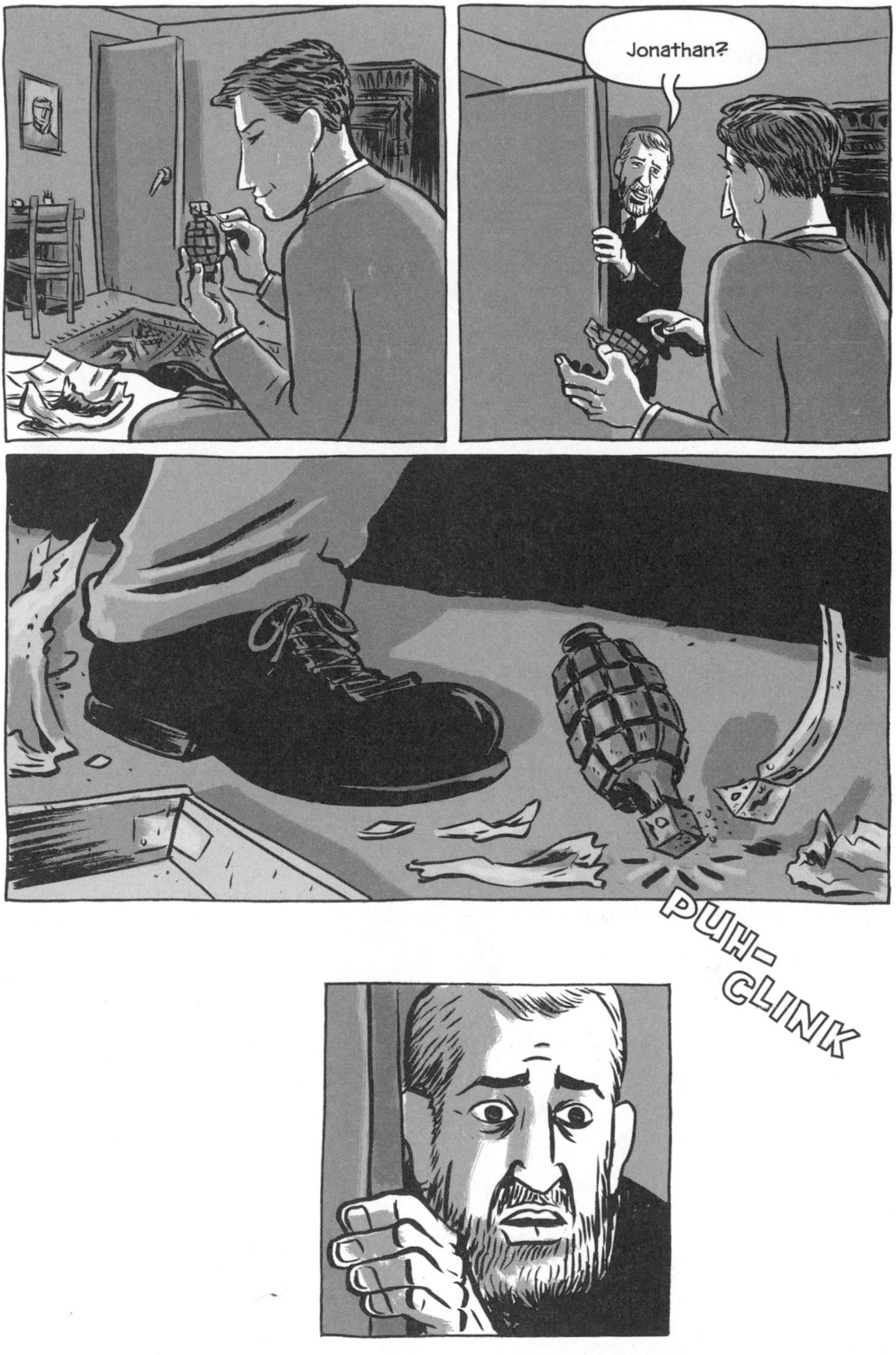
Jonathan?
PUH-
CLINK

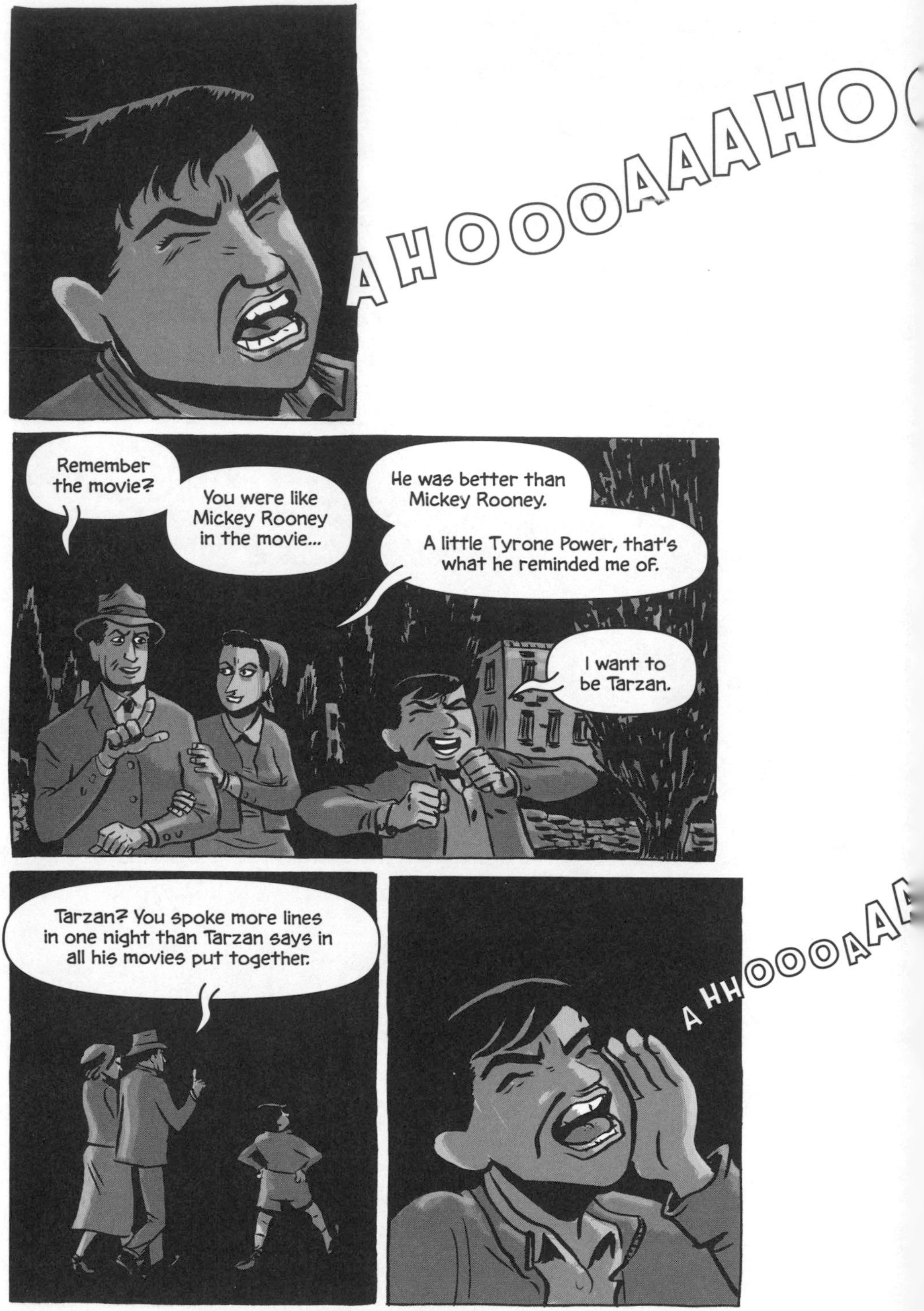
AHOOOAAAHO
Remember the movie?
You were like Mickey Rooney in the movie...
He was better than Mickey Rooney.
A little Tyrone Power, that's what he reminded me of.
I want to be Tarzan.
Tarzan? You spoke more lines in one night than Tarzan says in all his movies put together.
AHHOOOAA

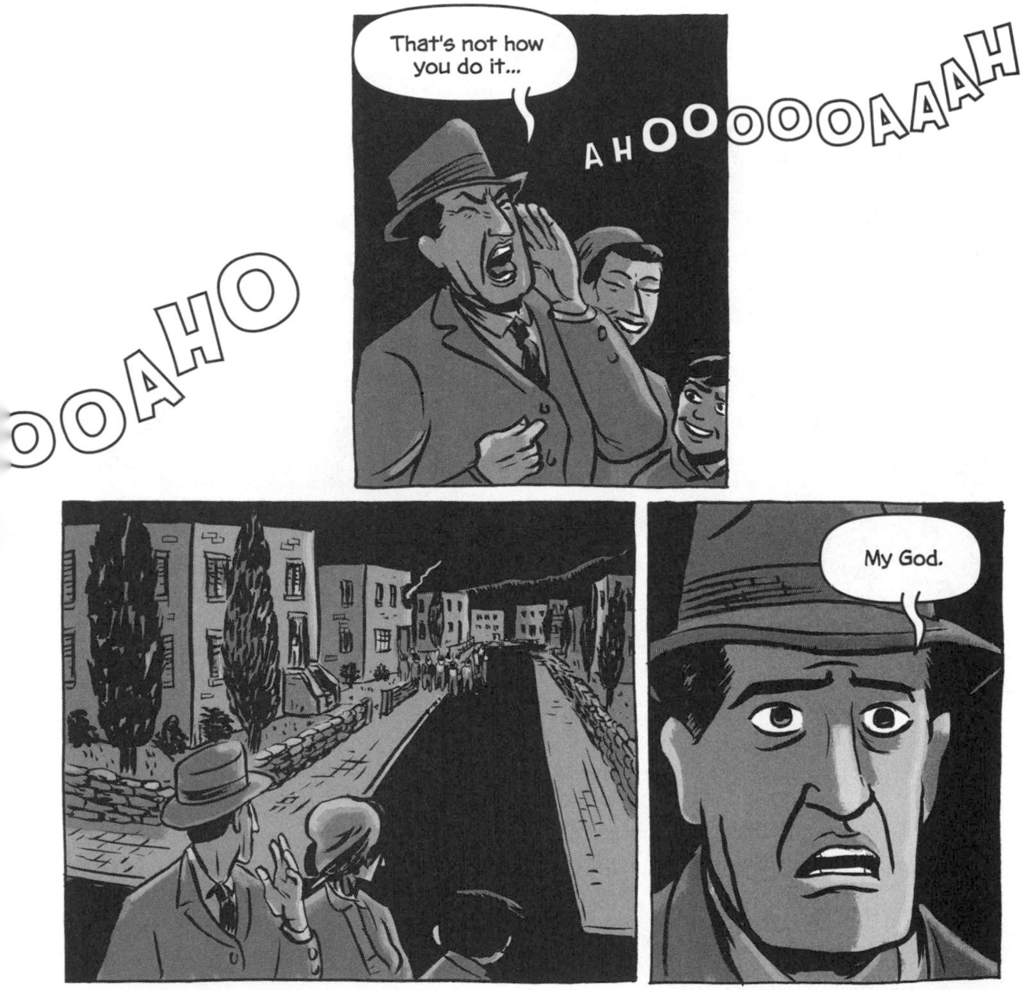
That's not how you do it...
AHOOOOOOAAAH
OOAHO
My God.

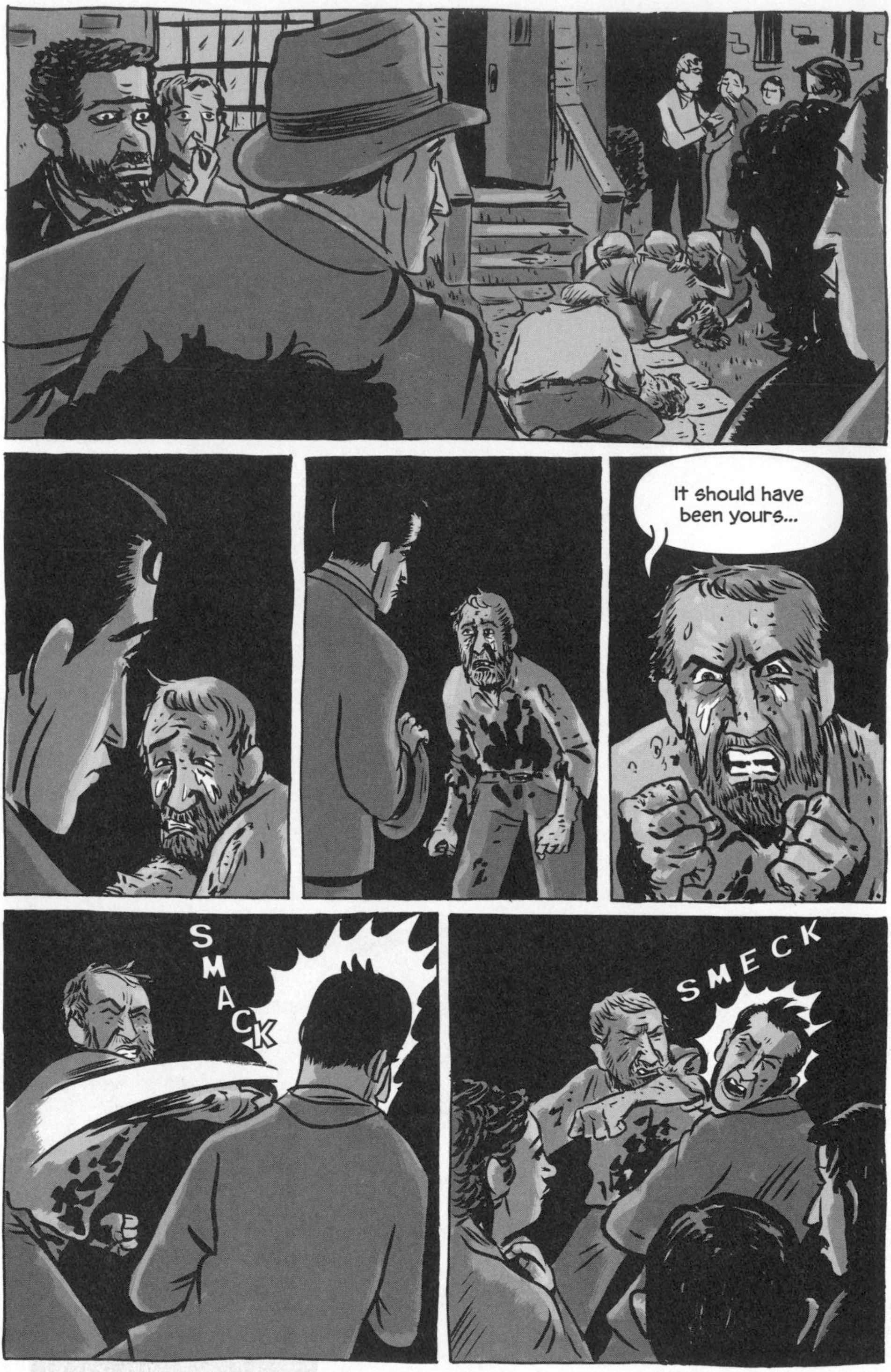
It should have been yours...
SMACK
SMECK

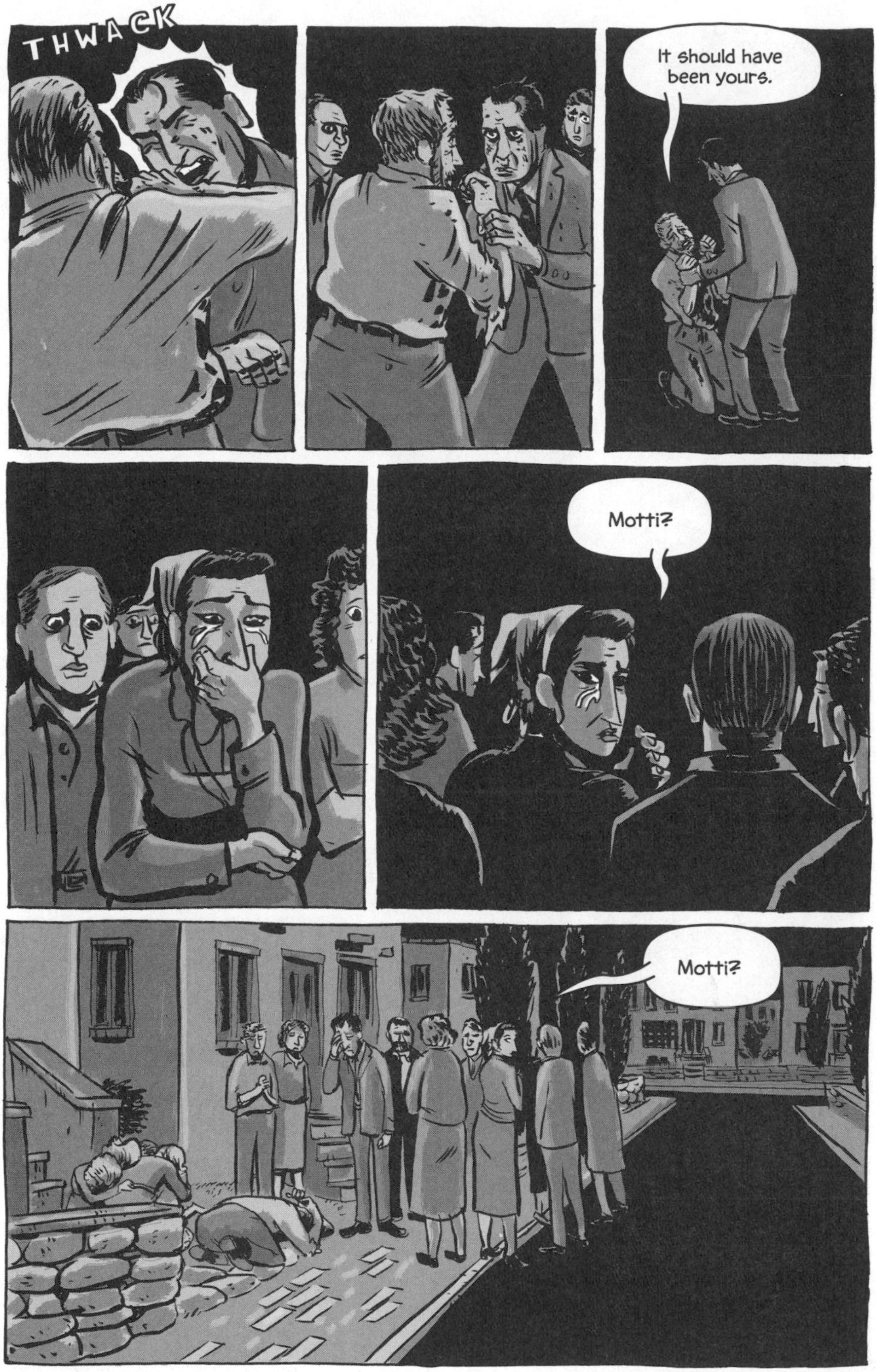
THWACK
It should have been yours.
Motti?
Motti?

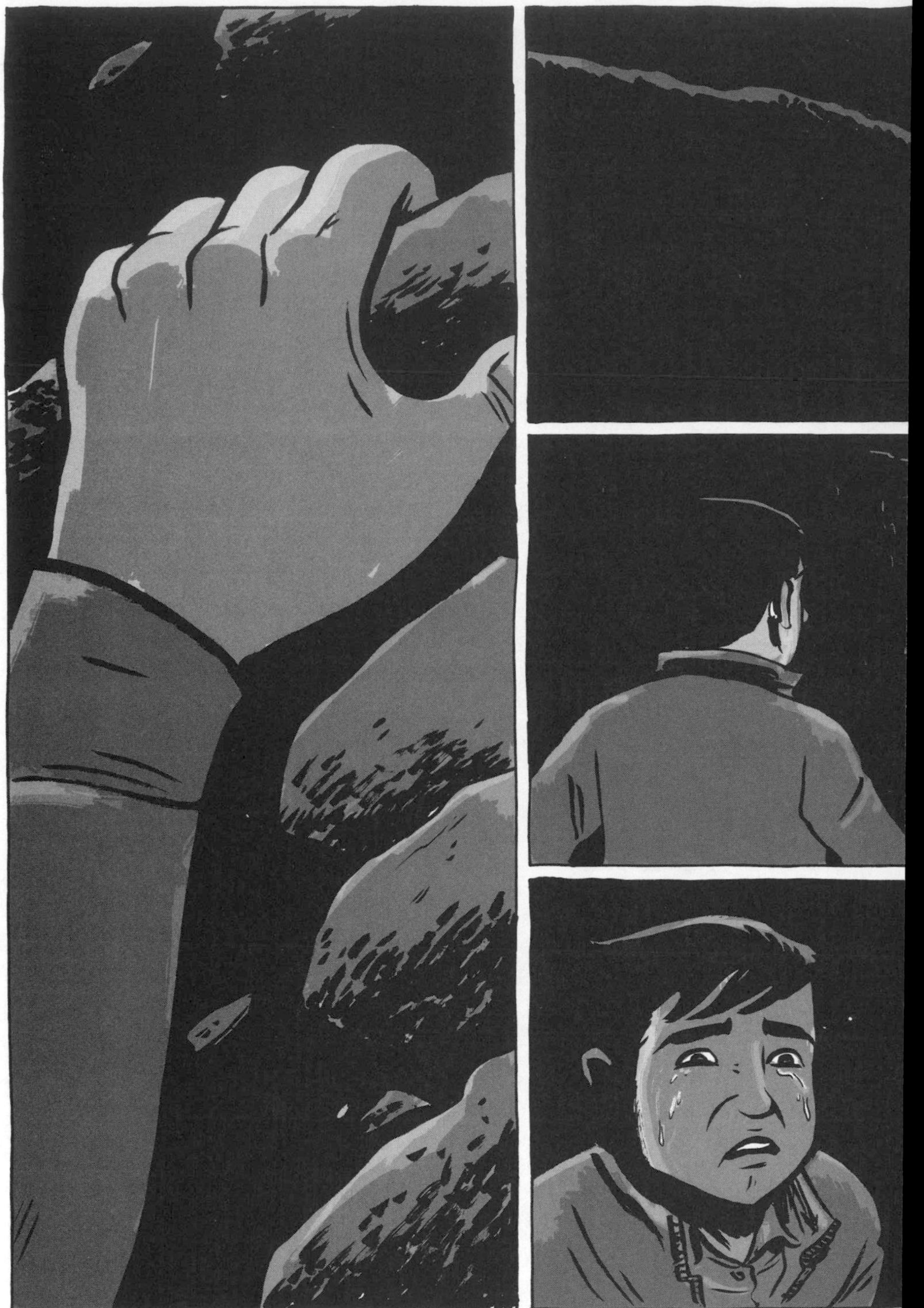

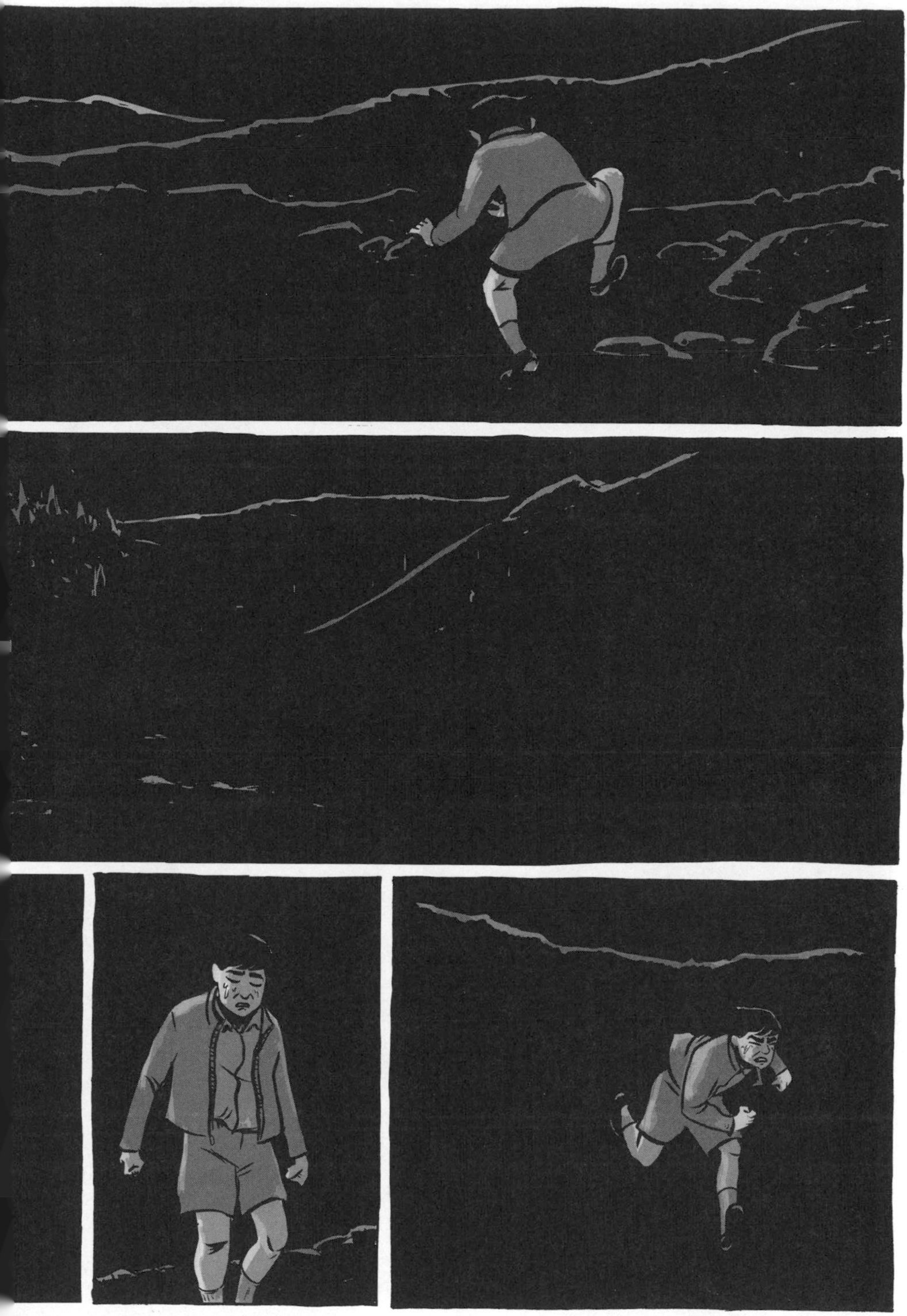

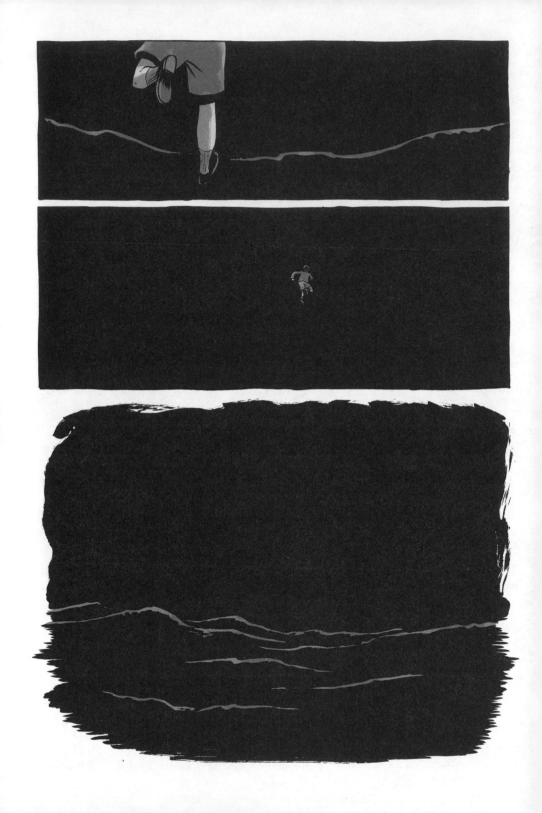

The help I received researching this project involved too many people over too many years for me to remember or mention them all; but I am grateful to each and every one and I hope the results of their support do them justice.

I would like to thank: Jordan Mechner, Mark Siegel, and Nick Bertozzi for making this book a reality. Mina Yakin and Erez Yakin for their unwavering support.

I would especially like to thank: Berto Yakin, Dudu Yakin, Zuri Yakin, Sylvana Yakin, and though they were no longer with us when I was writing this story, Emily Yakin, Izhak Yakin, and Salvo Yakin.

Most of all, I'd like to thank my father, Moni Yakin, without whose stories, guidance, and generosity of spirit this book would never have been.

—Boaz Yakin

Thank you to Kim, friends and family, Boaz, Chris, and the artists who helped me finish this book.

—Nick Bertozzi

**First Second**
NEW YORK

Text copyright © 2013 by Boaz Yakin
Illustrations copyright © 2013 by Nick Bertozzi

Chris Sinderson, Art Director
Book design by Rob Steen

Additional penciling and inking:

Shamus Beyale
Nic Breutzman
Scott Cohn
Nate Doyle
Isaac Goodhart
Conor Hughes
Dennis Pacheco
Tom Pitilli
Kevin Raganit
Lydia Roberts
Steve Shih
Nick Sumida

Additional art assists and toning by:

Genesis Crespo
Sarah Crowe
Kate Drwecka
Eitan Harcsztark
Kevin Hsi
Alexa James
Li Reina
Lindsey Richter
Dion Sandy
Wellington Sun

Published by First Second
First Second is an imprint of Roaring Brook Press,
a division of Holtzbrinck Publishing Holdings Limited Partnership
175 Fifth Avenue, New York, New York 10010

Cataloging-in-Publication Data is on file at the Library of Congress.

ISBN: 978-1-59643-575-9

First Second books are available for special promotions and premiums.
For details, contact: Director of Special Markets, Holtzbrinck Publishers.

First edition 2013

Printed in the United States of America

1 3 5 7 9 10 8 6 4 2